Africa Yearbook

Africa Yearbook

Politics, Economy and Society South of the Sahara in 2014

VOLUME 11

Edited by

Sebastian Elischer
Rolf Hofmeier
Andreas Mehler
Henning Melber

BRILL

LEIDEN | BOSTON

This publication has been typeset in the multilingual 'Brill' typeface. With over 5,100 characters covering Latin, IPA, Greek, and Cyrillic, this typeface is especially suitable for use in the humanities. For more information, please see www.brill.com/brill-typeface.

ISSN 1871-2525
ISBN 978-90-04-29153-9 (hardback)
ISBN 978-90-04-30505-2 (e-book)

This book is printed on acid-free paper.

Contents

Preface

In May 2003, the Africa-Europe Group of Interdisciplinary Studies (AEGIS) encouraged some of its member institutions to publish an *Africa Yearbook* with a wider international appeal. The African Studies Centre in Leiden (ASC), the Institute of African Affairs in Hamburg (IAA) and the Nordic Africa Institute in Uppsala (NAI) – all very active AEGIS centres with similar profiles – accepted this challenge and their joint efforts first bore fruit in the initial volume of the series in 2004. In 2007, the Dag Hammarskjöld Foundation in Uppsala (DHF) joined this international project, while the NAI ended its involvement with the fifth volume, published in 2009. As from 2014, the DHF ended its collaboration, and for the present volume the NAI rejoined the collaborating institutions, ensuring the *Yearbook*'s continued publication. This current volume therefore reflects some shifts and changes in terms of both ownership and content. We also have a new group of editors, reflecting the institutional arrangements. We take this opportunity to offer our profound thanks to Klaas van Walraven for his dedicated service as one of the co-editors over the ten first years. He has set a lasting example for those who follow him.

As in previous volumes, the country-specific articles cover domestic politics, foreign affairs and socioeconomic developments in the states of sub-Saharan Africa during the calendar year under review. While we recognise the impossibility of finding fully objective indicators for the relative importance of each of the states covered by the *Yearbook*, the length of the country-specific articles aims to reflect the approximate weight of each country. The four sub-regions are also introduced by means of an overview article. Further overviews summarise general continental developments and European-African relations, while we have reverted to including a summary of African relations with the UN in the general overview chapter rather than in a separate section.

The *Yearbook* is based on scholarly work, but is oriented towards a wider target readership, including students, politicians, diplomats, administrators, journalists, teachers, practitioners in the sphere of development cooperation and business people. Without forcing the individual contributions too much into a straitjacket, the volume is primarily concerned with providing factual (though not necessarily neutral) information. Each issue, in focusing almost exclusively on developments during a particular calendar year, provides a completely fresh annual overview of events and thereby adds to the cumulative record of ongoing developments

In November 2012, the *Yearbook* received the prestigious biennial Conover-Porter Award for outstanding Africa-related reference works from the African Studies Association and the Africana Librarians Council in the USA. This was an encouraging sign that the *Yearbook* has become a permanent and appreciated feature in Africanist publishing. The same year, thanks to a generous arrangement by Brill, the

Africa Institute of South Africa joined as an African co-publisher, thereby greatly enhancing local distribution on the continent.

This is the eleventh *Yearbook*, and we are proud now to have covered a full decade of African affairs in what we believe is a solid scholarly contribution towards a better understanding of and more knowledge about SSA countries. Brill has now taken the initiative to compile a country-focused chronology of these first ten years (2004 to 2013), with a separate small book on Mozambique. More may follow, hopefully showing the value of information steadily accumulated over time and enhancing accessibility to readers with a main interest in one specific country.

Once again we wish to express our gratitude to all the contributors for their collaboration in this endeavour; to the partner institutions in AEGIS for encouraging us to embark on this ambitious project; to Carol Rowe for her meticulous language editing; to Bas van der Mije for his unfailing coordinating assistance; and to Brill Publishers for their continued commitment. And last but not least, we would once again like to thank our participating institutions for their ongoing support.

The Editors
(Hamburg and Uppsala, June 2015)

List of Abbreviations

ABN	Autorité du Bassin du Niger (Niamey)
ACP	African, Caribbean, and Pacific Group of Countries (Lomé/Cotonou Agreement)
ADF	African Development Fund (Abidjan)
AfDB	African Development Bank (Abidjan)
AFD	Agence Française de Développement (Paris)
AGOA	African Growth and Opportunity Act
AI	Amnesty International
APR	African Peer Review
APRM	African Peer Review Mechanism
AU	African Union (Addis Ababa)
BCEAO	Banque Centrale des Etats de l'Afrique de l'Ouest (Dakar)
BEAC	Banque des Etats de l'Afrique Centrale (Yaoundé)
CAR	Central African Republic
CBLT	Commission du Bassin du Lac Tchad (N'Djaména)
CEEAC	Communauté Economique des Etats de l'Afrique Centrale (Libreville) = ECCAS
CEMAC	Communauté Economique et Monétaire de l'Afrique Centrale
CEN-SAD	Community of Sahel-Saharan States (Tripoli)
CEPGL	Communauté Economique des Pays des Grands Lacs (Gisenyi/Rwanda)
CFAfr	Franc de la Communauté Financière Africaine (BCEAO; BEAC)
COMESA	Common Market for Eastern and Southern Africa (Lusaka)
CPLP	Comunidade dos Países de Língua Portuguesa
DAC	Development Assistance Committee (Paris)
DDR	Disarmament, Demobilisation and Reintegration
DFID	Department for International Development (London)
DRC	Democratic Republic of the Congo
EAC	East African Community
ECA	Economic Commission for Africa (United Nations; Addis Ababa)
ECCAS	Economic Community of Central African States (Libreville)
ECF	Extended Credit Facility (IMF)
ECOWAS	Economic Community of West African States (Abuja)
EDF	European Development Fund (Brussels)
EIB	European Investment Bank (Luxemburg)
EPA	Economic Partnership Agreement
ESAF	Enhanced Structural Adjustment Facility (IMF)
EU	European Union (Brussels)
FAO	Food and Agricultural Organisation (Rome)

FDI	Foreign Direct Investment
FTA	Free Trade Area
GDP	Gross Domestic Product
HDI	Human Development Index (UNDP)
HIPC	Heavily Indebted Poor Countries
HRW	Human Rights Watch
ICC	International Criminal Court
ICG	International Crisis Group
ICGLR	International Conference on the Great Lakes Region
IDA	International Development Association (Washington)
IDP	Internally Displaced Person
IFAD	International Fund for Agricultural Development (Rome)
IFC	International Finance Corporation (Washington)
IGAD	Intergovernmental Authority on Development (Djibouti)
ILO	International Labour Organisation (Geneva)
IMF	International Monetary Fund (Washington)
IOC	Indian Ocean Commission (Ebène/Mauritius)
IORA	Indian Ocean Rim Association (Ebène/Mauritius)
MDGS	Millennium Development Goals
MDRI	Multilateral Debt Relief Initiative
MRU	Mano River Union (Freetown)
NEPAD	New Partnership for Africa's Development
NGO	Non-Governmental Organisation
OAU	Organization of African Unity
ODA	Official Development Assistance
OECD	Organisation for Economic Cooperation and Development (Paris)
OIC	Organisation of the Islamic Conference (Jeddah)
OIF	Organisation Internationale de la Francophonie (Paris)
OPEC	Organisation of Petroleum Exporting Countries (Vienna)
PALOP	Países Africanos de Lingua Oficial Portugesa
PPP	Purchasing Power Parity
PRGF	Poverty Reduction and Growth Facility
PRSC	Poverty Reduction Support Credit
PRSP	Poverty Reduction Strategy Paper
SACU	Southern African Customs Union (Pretoria)
SADC	Southern African Development Community (Gaborone)
SAF	Structural Adjustment Facility (IMF)
SDR	Special Drawing Right (IMF)
SSA	Sub-Saharan Africa
TI	Transparency International
UAE	United Arab Emirates
UEMOA	Union Économique et Monétaire Ouest-Africaine (Ouagadougou)

UMA	Union du Maghreb Arabe
UN	United Nations (New York)
UNCTAD	United Nations Conference on Trade and Development (Geneva)
UNDP	United Nations Development Programme (New York)
UNEP	United Nations Environment Programme (Nairobi)
UNECA	United Nations Economic Commission for Africa (Addis Ababa)
UNESCO	United Nations Educational, Scientific and Cultural Organisation (Paris)
UNHCR	United Nations High Commissioner for Refugees (Geneva)
UNICEF	United Nations Children's Fund (New York)
UNSC	United Nations Security Council
USAID	United States Agency for International Development (Washington)
WFP	World Food Programme (Rome)
WHO	World Health Organisation (Geneva)
WTO	World Trade Organisation (Geneva)

Factual Overview (as of 31 December 2014)

West Africa

Country	Area (in sq km)	Population (in m)[1]	Currency	HDI (2014)	Head of State	Prime Minister
Benin	112,622	10,3	CFA Franc	0.476	Boni Yayi	
Burkina Faso	274,122	17.9	CFA Franc	0.388	Michel Kafando (interim)	Isaac Zida (interim)
Cape Verde	4,033	0.5	Cape Verdean Escudo	0.636	Jorge Carlos Fonseca	José Maria Pereira Neves
Côte d'Ivoire	322,462	20.8	CFA Franc	0.452	Alassane Ouattara	Daniel Kablan Duncan
Gambia	11,295	1.9	Dalasi	0.441	Yahya Jammeh	
Ghana	238,500	27.0	Cedi	0.573	John Dramani Mahama	
Guinea	245,857	11.6	Guinean Franc	0.392	Alpha Condé	Mohamed Said Fofana
Guinea-Bissau	36,125	1.7	CFA Franc	0.396	José Mário Vaz	Domingos Simões Pereira
Liberia	111,370	4.4	Liberian Dollar	0.412	Ellen Johnson- Sirleaf	
Mali	1,240,000	15.9	CFA Franc	0.407	Ibrahim Boubacar Keïta	Moussa Mara
Mauritania	1,030,700	4.0	Ouguiya	0.487	Mohamed Ould Abdel Aziz	Yahya Ould Hademine
Niger	1,267,000	18.2	CFA Franc	0.337	Mahamadou Issoufou	Brigi Rafini
Nigeria	923,768	177,5	Naira	0.504	Goodluck Jonathan	
Senegal	197,162	13.9	CFA Franc	0.485	Macky Sall	Mohammed Dionne
Sierra Leone	71,740	6.3	Leone	0.374	Ernest Bai Koroma	
Togo	56,785	7.0	CFA Franc	0.473	Faure Gnassingbé	Kwesi Ahoomey-Zunu

Central Africa

Country	Area (in sq km)	Population (in m)	Currency	HDI	Head of State	Prime Minister
Cameroon	475,442	22.8	CFA Franc BEAC	0.504	Paul Biya	Philémon Yang
Central African Republic	622,984	4.8	CFA Franc BEAC	0.341	Catherine Samba-Panza (interim)	Mahamat Kamoun (interim)
Chad	1,284,000	13.3	CFA Franc BEAC	0.372	Idriss Déby	Kalzeube Pahimi Deubet
Congo	342,000	4.6	CFA Franc BEAC	0.564	Denis Sassou-Nguesso	
DR Congo	2,344,855	71.2	Congolese Franc	0.338	Joseph Kabila	Augustin Matata Ponyo Mapon
Equatorial Guinea	28,051	0.8	CFA Franc BEAC	0.556	Teodoro Obiang Nguema Mbasogo	Vicente Ehate Tomi
Gabon	267,667	1.7	CFA Franc BEAC	0.674	Ali Bongo Ondimba	Daniel Ona Ondo
São Tomé and Príncipe	1,001	0.2	Dobra	0.558	Manuel Pinto da Costa	Patrice Trovoada

Eastern Africa

Country	Area (in sq km)	Population (in m)	Currency	HDI	Head of State	Prime Minister
Burundi	26,338	10.5	Burundi Franc	0.389	Pierre Nkurunziza	
Comoros	1.862	0.7	Comoran Franc	0.488	Ikililou Dhoinine	
Djibouti	23,200	0.9	Djiboutian Franc	0.467	Ismail Omar Guelleh	Abdoulkader Mohamed Kamil
Eritrea	124,320	6.5	Nakfa	0.381	Isaias Afewerki	
Ethiopia	1,121,900	95.9	Birr	0.435	Mulatu Teshome	Hailemariam Desalegn
Kenya	569,259	43.2	Kenya Shilling	0.535	Uhuru Kenyatta	
Rwanda	26,338	11.1	Rwanda Franc	0.506	Paul Kagame	Anastase Murekezi
Seychelles	455	0.1	Seychelles Rupee	0.756	James Michel	
Somalia	637,600	10.8	Somali Shilling	n.a.	Hassan Sheikh Mohamud	Omar Abdirashid Ali Sharmarke
(Somaliland)	137,600	3.5	Somaliland Shilling	n.a.	Ahmed Mohamed Mahamoud 'Silanyo'	
Sudan	2,505,805	38.3	Sudanese Pound	0.473	Omar Hassan Ahmad al-Bashir	
South Sudan	619,745	11,7	South Sudanese Pound	n.a.	Salva Kiir Mayardit	
Tanzania	945,087	50.8	Tanzania Shilling	0.488	Jakaya Kikwete	Mizengo Pinda
Uganda	197,000	38.8	Uganda Shilling	0.484	Yoweri Kaguta Museveni	Ruhakana Rugunda

Southern Africa

Country	Area (in sq km)	Population (in m)	Currency	HDI	Head of State	Prime Minister
Angola	1,246,700	22.4	Kwanza	0.526	José Eduardo dos Santos	
Botswana	581,730	12.0	Pula	0.683	Seretse Khama Ian Khama	
Lesotho	30,344	1,9	Lesotho Loti	0.486	King Letsie III	Thomas Motsoahae Thabane
Madagascar	592,000	22.4	Malagasy Ariary	0.498	Hery Rajaonarimampianina	Kolo Roger
Malawi	118,484	16.8	Malawian Kwacha	0.414	Peter Mutharika	
Mauritius	2,040	1.3	Mauritian Rupee	0.771	Rajkeswur Kailash Purryag	Navinchandra Ramgoolam
Mozambique	799,380	25.1	Mozam-biquen Métical	0.393	Filipe Nyussi	Carlos Agostinho do Rosário
Namibia	824,269	2.3	Namibian Dollar	0.624	Hifikepunye Lucas Pohamba	Hage Geingob
South Africa	1,219,090	53.7	Rand	0.658	Jacob Zuma	
Swaziland	17,364	1.3	Swazi Lilangeni	0.53	King Mswati III	Sibusiso Dlamini
Zambia	752,614	15.1	Zambian Kwacha	0.561	Guy Scott (interim)	
Zimbabwe	390,580	14.7	Zimbabwean Dollar	0.492–	Robert Gabriel Mugabe	

(Population figures are for mid-2014 according to Stiftung Weltbevölkerung, www.weltbevölkerung.de)

List of Authors

Kwesi Aning
Director, Faculty of Academic Affairs and Research (FAAR), Kofi Annan International Peacekeeping Training Centre, Accra, Ghana, Kwesi.Aning@kaiptc.org

Nancy Annan
Researcher, Faculty of Academic Affairs and Research (FAAR), Kofi Annan International Peacekeeping Training Centre, Ghana, Nancy.Annan@kaiptc.org

Alfred Babo
Scholar in Residence at the Lewis Global Studies Center, Professor of African Studies and Anthropology, Smith College, Northampton, USA, ababo@smith.edu

Jean-Nicolas Bach
Associate Researcher in the research institute Les Afriques dans le Monde, Bordeaux, where he leads a programme on contemporary politics and security issues in the Horn of Africa, jeannicolas.bach@scpobx.fr

Alice Bellagamba
Associate Professor, Cultural and Social Anthropology, Department of Human Sciences for Education "Riccardo Massa", University of Milan-Bicocca, alice.bella gamba@unimib.it

Heinrich Bergstresser
Media Consultant, Freelance Research Associate of the Institute of African Affairs in Hamburg and Freelance Tutor of Deutsche Gesellschaft für Internationale Zusammenarbeit GIZ, Germany, heinrich.bergstresser@web.de

Keratilwe Bodilenyane
Lecturer, Department of Political & Administrative Studies, University of Botswana, Keratilwe.Bodilenyane@mopipi.ub.bw

Emmanuelle Bouilly
PhD student, CESSP, Department of Political Science, Université Paris 1 Panthéon Sorbonne, Paris, France, emmanuelle.bouilly@yahoo.fr

Marie Brossier
Assistant Professor of Political Science, Departement of Political science, Université Laval, Québec, Canada, marie.brossier@pol.ulaval.ca

Sheila Bunwaree
Professor of Development Studies, Department of Sociology, University of Mauritius, sheila_bun@yahoo.co.uk

Brett Logan Carter
PhD, Fellow, Center for Democracy, Development, and the Rule of Law, and the Hoover Institution, Stanford University, blcarter@post.harvard.edu

Tiyesere Mercy Chikapa-Jamali
Lecturer at the Department of Political and Administrative Studies, University of Malawi, tiyeserec@yahoo.com

Lewis B. Dzimbiri
Professor of Public Administration, Chancellor College, University of Malawi, proflewisdzimbiri@gmail.com

Daniel Eizenga
Doctoral Candidate, Department of Political Science, University of Florida, USA, deizenga@ufl.edu

Sebastian Elischer
PhD (2010) in Comparative Politics, Jacobs University Bremen is assistant professor of comparative politics at the Leuphana University Lüneburg and the German Institute of Global and Area Studies Hamburg, selischer@ufl.edu

Lansana Gberie
Academic and Writer, Ottawa, Canada, lagberie@yahoo.com

Christine Hackenesch
Researcher, German Development Institute / Deutsches Institut für Entwicklungspolitik (DIE), Bonn, Germany, christine.hackenesch@die-gdi.de

Joseph Hanlon
Visiting Senior Fellow, Department of International Development, London School of Economics, UK and Visiting Senior Research Fellow at the Development Policy and Practice Centre of the Open University, UK, j.hanlon@open.ac.uk

Stig Jarle Hansen
is mainly focusing on the wider Red Sea region, Yemen, Somalia, Eritrea, Ethiopia, and Kenya. His latest book is "Al Shabaab in Somalia". He is currently leading Norway's only master program in International relations at the NMBU, stig.hansen@nmbu.no

Ketil Fred Hansen
Associate Professor in Modern African History, University of Stavanger, Norway. ketil.f.hansen@uis.no

Kurt Hirschler
Freelance Political Scientist, Hamburg, Germany, kurt_hirschler@web.de

Nicole Hirt
Freelance Research Associate, Institute of African Affairs, GIGA German Institute of Global and Area Studies, Hamburg, Germany, e-mail: nicole.hirt@giga-hamburg.de

Rolf Hofmeier
Former Director, Institute of African Affairs, GIGA German Institute of Global and Area Studies, Hamburg, Germany, hofmeier@giga-hamburg.de

Amin Y. Kamete
Senior Lecturer, University of Glasgow, Scotland, UK, amini.kamete@glasgow.ac.uk

Niels Keijzer
Researcher, German Development Institute/Deutsches Institut für Entwicklungs politik (DIE), Bonn, Germany, niels.keijzer@die-gdi.de

Christoph Kohl
Researcher, Peace Research Institute Frankfurt, Frankfurt am Main, Germany, kohl@hsfk.de

Dirk Kohnert
Retired Deputy Director, Institute of African Affairs, GIGA German Institute of Global and Area Studies, Hamburg, Germany, Kohnert@giga-hamburg.de

Gabrielle Lynch
Associate Professor of Comparative Politics at the University of Warwick, UK, g.lynch@warwick.ac.uk

Joseph N. Mangarella
Lecturer at the Université de Panthéon-Assas (Paris 2), Adjunct Professor at the Université Paris 1 Panthéon-Sorbonne and INSEEC, joseph.mangarella@gmail.com

Richard R. Marcus
Professor and Director, The Global Studies Institute and the International Studies Program, California State University, Long Beach, USA, richard.marcus@csulb.edu

Andreas Mehler
Director, Institute of African Affairs, GIGA German Institute of Global and Area Studies, Hamburg, Germany, mehler@giga-hamburg.de

Henning Melber
Senior Adviser/Director emeritus, Dag Hammarskjöld Foundation, Uppsala, Sweden, henning.melber@dhf.uu.se

Sanusha Naidu
Research Associate, Department of Political Science, University of Pretoria, South Africa, sanushanaidu72@gmail.com

Senzwesihle Ngubane
General Manager Operations at the African Centre for the Constructive Resolution of Disputes (ACCORD), Durban, South Africa, senzo@accord.org.za

Claes Olsson
Political Scientist and Editor at Global Publications Foundation, Uppsala, Sweden, claesolsson@globalpublications.org

Helena Olsson
Political Scientist and Staff Member at the Department of Sociology, Uppsala University, Sweden, helena.olsson@soc.uu.se

Krijn Peters
Associate Professor in Armed Conflict & Post-war Reconstruction, Department of Political & Cultural Studies, Swansea University, UK, k.peters@swansea.ac.uk

Fanny Pigeaud
Journalist, France, Fanny.pigeaud@gmail.com

Marisha Ramdeen
Senior Programme Officer at the African Centre for the Constructive Resolution of Disputes (ACCORD) in Durban, South Africa. Marisha@accord.org.za

Edalina Rodrigues Sanches
Postdoctoral Research Fellow at the Institute of Social Sciences-University of Lisbon, the Portuguese Institute of International Relations-New University of Lisbon and the Centre for Social Science Research-University of Cape Town, ersanches@ics.ul.pt

Anita Schroven
Researcher at the Max Planck Institute for Social Anthropology, Halle/Saale, Germany, schroven@eth.mpg.de

Jon Schubert
Postdoctoral Research Fellow, Centre for Area Studies, University of Leipzig, jon.schubert@uni-leipzig.de

David Sebudubudu
Professor of Political Studies and Head of the Department of Political and Administrative Studies, University of Botswana, Sebudubu@mopipi.ub.bw

Gerhard Seibert
Associate professor at the Universidade da Integração Internacional da Lusofonia Afro-Brasileira (UNILAB), São Francisco do Conde, Bahia, Brazil, mailseibert@yahoo.com

Claudia Simons
Researcher at German Institute for International and Security Affairs, Berlin, Germany, Claudia.Simons@swp-berlin.org

Roger Southall
Professor Emeritus, Department of Sociology, University of the Witwatersrand, South Africa, Roger.Southall@wits.ac.za

Alexander Stroh
Assistant Professor of African Politics and Development Policy, University of Bayreuth, Germany, alexander.stroh@uni-bayreuth.de

Susan Thomson
Assistant Professor of Peace and Conflict Studies, Colgate University, Hamilton, USA, sthomson@colgate.edu

Stef Vandeginste
Lecturer, Institute of Development Policy and Management, University of Antwerp, Belgium, stef.vandeginste@uantwerpen.be

Klaas van Walraven
Researcher, African Studies Centre, Leiden, The Netherlands, walraven@ascleiden.nl

Volker Weyel
Consultant, Former Editor-in-chief 'Vereinte Nationen' (1977–2004), Bonn, Germany, weyel@o2online.de

Bruce Whitehouse
Director, Global Studies Program, Associate Professor of Anthropology, Lehigh University, USA, bruce.whitehouse@lehigh.edu

Peter Woodward
Emeritus professor, School of Politics and International Relation, University of Reading, UK, p.r.woodward@reading.ac.uk

Douglas A. Yates
Professor of Political Science at the American Graduate School in Paris, France, douglas.yates@ags.edu

PART 1

Sub-Saharan Africa

Andreas Mehler, Henning Melber and Klaas van Walraven

The continent made international headlines during the year with the outbreak of the Ebola virus epidemic and its devastating consequences for some West African countries, as well as the international implications of its potential wider spread and the consequent precautionary measures. The epidemic was brought under control towards the end of the year. Boko Haram added to the negative publicity about the region, with the spectacular abduction of 276 schoolgirls in mid-April, most of whom remained captive for the rest of the year. In terms of political stability, no decisive shifts took place despite peaceful changes of government in a few cases and efforts to seize power through violence in some other states. Eleven countries held national elections with the usually mixed bag of either more or less legitimate results. The AU maintained its critical stance vis-à-vis the ICC and also increased its flexibility towards heads of state with dubious claims to hold office. Extending presidential mandates remained a temptation for sitting presidents. Economic performance was on average slightly below the levels forecast and, despite frequent reference to a growing middle class, poverty remained a major socioeconomic challenge. Sustained interest in the continent's resources meant that foreign economic actors continued to increase their presence. China, India and Japan were among the countries seeking to further expand economic relations on the continent. While acts of piracy almost ceased along the Indian Ocean coast, a growing number of ships were hijacked in the Gulf of Guinea and along the west coast further south, with the pirates displaying an unexpected degree of sophistication in looting the cargos.

Africa in the Global Economy

The IMF predicted in the third quarter an average *growth* of 5.1%, which was lower than the 6% forecast in January, while the World Bank forecast even lower overall African growth of 4.6%. The decline in commodity prices (if not yet that of oil) played its part, as did expectations of the strengthening of the US dollar. Specific negative factors were conflicts in countries such as the CAR, South Sudan and the wider Sahelian region, while the Ebola epidemic in West Africa impacted on growth rates in the countries affected. In the third quarter, the IMF's estimate, usually higher than the World Bank's, was nevertheless comparable to that of the previous year and predicted 4.3% growth for oil-importing states and an average of 6% for oil-exporting countries.

 | DOI 10.1163/9789004305052_002

The World Economic Forum (WEF), held in Abuja (Nigeria) on 7–9 May, discussed growth issues under the theme 'Forging Inclusive Growth, Creating Jobs', which alluded to the problems underlying overall growth figures. While the *poverty* level had fallen between 1990 and 2010 from 56.5% to 48.5%, in practice this meant that 300 m Africans were still living on less than $ 1 a day. More than 600 m people were still without electricity but, while 80% of Africa's poor continued to be active in agriculture, real growth was taking place in other sectors.

A more buoyant note was struck by an AfDB survey of 37 African countries that reported a rise in Africa's *middle class* (defined as those with a purchasing power of between $ 2.2 and $ 20 a day). Much of this was attributed to the growth rates of previous years, although there were considerable sub-regional variations. Moreover, some middle classes, such as in Central Africa, were deemed vulnerable to setbacks. A report by South Africa's Standard Bank largely confirmed the phenomenon, reporting that 11 of SSA's most important economies counted a total of some 15 m households as middle-class. This constituted an increase of 230% over 14 years, and the IMF estimated that Africa's middle classes now totalled 150 m people.

Though a significant long-term development, this said little about the majority of Africans living in the rural areas. The WEF in Abuja therefore paid much attention to *agriculture*. Commitments on agriculture and food security doubled. Still, the 4th African Green Revolution Forum, held early September in Addis Ababa (Ethiopia), was again confronted with the problem of food imports, as many countries continued to be major food importers. Inevitably, *food security* remained a headache, not just in the Sahel zone but also in the Ebola-hit countries to the south. Against this, the FAO Food Price Index continued its slide downwards. If positive for urban communities, this had the potential to hit agricultural producers. FAO therefore organised a meeting to discuss reforms in international agricultural commodity markets. The problem of food security remained acute in the broader Sahelian region as a result of drought and armed conflict. The UN reported that the number of people who were food insecure, estimated at some 25 m, was now double that in 2013. Acute malnutrition, including among children under five, increased, and it was estimated that some $ 1.9 bn was needed to cope with the Sahel's humanitarian needs.

Working abroad remained an alternative strategy for numerous Africans. *Remittances* were expected to reach $ 67 bn, with most of the money (80%) going to North and West Africa. Of this, 40% originated from Europe, 28% from the US, 13% from other African countries and some 9% from the Middle East. This growth went hand in hand, however, with *illegal migration*. Morocco reported that about 30,000 migrants, principally sub-Saharan Africans, were waiting on its territory to make the dangerous journey across the Mediterranean; on 28 February, some 200 Africans assaulted the fence separating Morocco from the Spanish enclave of Melilla. At about the same time, the Tunisian navy rescued sub-Saharan migrants off the island of Djerba, while early in March it was reported that dozens of migrants, including women and children, had drowned off the coast of Yemen. It was estimated that in the previous five years at least half a million Somalis, Ethiopians and Eritreans had crossed the Gulf of Aden, despite continued maltreatment by smugglers. In the Mediterranean, the number of people rescued by the Italians in the first half of the year reached 50,000 (including Syrians and others, as well as Africans). Many had tried to reach Europe from unstable Libya. The International Organisation for Migration reported in late September that the death toll had reached 3,000 (three times the 2013 estimate), making 2014 a particularly deadly year. Networks of smugglers taking people to Europe and North America were thought to generate a total of $ 7 bn a year.

Foreign economic interest in Africa, by contrast, followed mostly above-ground, legal routes. *China* announced an investment plan that would lead to a doubling of trade to $ 400 bn by 2020. The China-Africa Development Fund was boosted to a total of $ 5 bn and, perhaps more importantly, it was announced that Chinese manufacturing companies intended to relocate to Africa. *India*, too, planned to increase its trade from the current $ 70 bn to a projected $ 100 bn in 2015. Africa now accounted for 9% of India's imports (mainly hydrocarbon resources) and India was now Africa's fourth-largest trading partner. It was especially China's activity, however, that pushed *Japan* to try to boost its economic profile. Prime Minister Abe made his first tour of the continent in January, pledging $ 32 bn in funds till 2018. Around 60% of Japanese companies were reported as wanting to expand in African markets, including in telecommunications, manufacturing and agriculture. At a ministerial meeting of the Tokyo International Conference on African Development in Cameroon on 4 May, agricultural cooperation was discussed further. *Singapore* held the third Africa-Singapore Business Forum on 27–28 August, bringing together around 1,000 business leaders from 30 countries. Singapore's trade with Africa had increased to well over $ 11 bn in 2013.

Against this background, the *US* felt an increased need to reinforce its economic commitments. On 4–6 August, it held the first US-African Leaders Summit in Washington, DC, and in the run-up to the conference US Energy Secretary Ernest Moniz met with African energy ministers in Addis Ababa on 3–4 June to discuss cooperation in the sector. At the Washington summit, President Obama declared that the US would shift its support to Africa from aid to more equal economic cooperation, although the US also announced $ 33 bn in new investment and loans, targeting especially Africa's power sector.

Taken together, this meant that *FDI* was boosted significantly. Net inflows in 2013 had seen an increase of 9%, to $ 57 bn, much of this going to the mining sector. However, a survey by Ernst & Young reported that many companies were now trying to invest in other sectors such as telecommunications, retail and consumer products, and financial services, partly in an effort to benefit from the growth of the middle classes. A worrying trend concerned the huge growth in the transfer of state bonds to private lenders, whose failure to impose conditions in the field of governance had to be set against the high rates of interest charged (up to 10%, sometimes even 17%). These expensive loans had grown from $ 200 m in 2009 to $ 7.6 bn in 2014.

At the 'Africa Rising' conference in Mozambique on 29–30 May, leaders discussed the problem of *infrastructure*. According to IMF director Christine Lagarde, Africa would need $ 90 bn to make substantial improvements in this field; it was estimated that only 16% of Africa's roads were paved, compared with 85% in South Asia. The World Bank announced a new Global Infrastructure Facility to help funding, partly because private investment in infrastructure in emerging markets had fallen from $ 186 bn in 2012 to $ 150 bn in 2013.

The *IMF* and *World Bank* annual meetings took place in Washington on 9–11 October. Infrastructure and the economic impact of Ebola were discussed. The *AfDB* began its golden jubilee at a meeting in Tunis on 22 April.

The African Union and the APRM

After the AU's disastrous inability to make a decisive impact on the crisis in Mali in 2013, its first *biannual summit* of 2014, held in Addis Ababa on 24–31 January, was marked by cautious optimism. The AU Commission's department for peace and security boasted that the AU-led 'Mission Internationale de Soutien à la Centrafrique sous Conduite Africaine' (MISCA) had quickly restored some order to the CAR's capital (with French help), while two member states suspended for unconstitutional takeovers (Mali and Madagascar) were readmitted. The summit took place under the theme of food security and agriculture. Leaders committed themselves to end hunger in Africa by 2025. The 'Agenda 2063', a characteristically grand attempt pushed by Commission President Dlamini-Zuma to revive the debate on continental integration, made headlines too. Its extended time horizon did not, however, divert attention from more mundane matters. Mauritania's President Abdel Aziz took over as chair of the AU's Assembly of Heads of State and Government (hereafter 'the Assembly'). and ten new members were appointed to the Peace and Security Council (PSC).

Although the newly elected presidents of Madagascar and Mali made their appearance at the summit, this could not hide the fact that some member states were still barred from participation, not least Egypt, which had been suspended in July 2013 after the overthrow of President Mohamed Morsi by the army. On 17 June, however, doubtless having in mind Egypt's 12.5% contribution to the AU budget, the PSC decided to reinstate that country, after Abdel al-Fattah al-Sisi's May victory in presidential elections (boycotted by Morsi's followers). Such pragmatism even extended to the CAR. Its transitional leader, Catherine Samba-Panza, was invited by Equatorial Guinea to the second biannual summit held in Malabo on 26–27 June, although the CAR was still under the AU's *rules of suspension*. Guinea-Bissau was readmitted officially, and on 17 November the AU welcomed the appointment of a new interim president in Burkina Faso after a popular revolt had forced long-standing Blaise Compaoré to finally abandon office. (Former OAU secretary-general Edem Kodjo had already been appointed AU special envoy there.)

The Assembly adopted the *AU budget* for 2015 to the tune of $ 522,121,602, of which at least $ 379 m was earmarked for programmes, leaving the rest for operational expenses. It decided that the next ordinary summit would take place in Addis Ababa on the theme of women's empowerment, while member states committed themselves to spending a minimum of 10% of national budgets to double agricultural productivity.

Armed conflict, particularly *Islamist violence*, was uppermost in the minds of Assembly delegates. The kidnapping of Nigerian school girls in April had sent shockwaves throughout the world, and both Commission President Dlamini-Zuma and the new Assembly chair went on record appealing for an end to all armed conflict by 2020 and for Africa to take its security into its own hands. The Assembly called for firm action against a threat that by now extended from Mali in the west to Kenya in the east, and Dlamini-Zuma asked the PSC to study new ways of countering this particular menace. More concretely, the AU gathered African intelligence chiefs in Nairobi (Kenya) in late August to discuss a more robust response, ahead of a heads of state conference to be presided over by the chairman of the PSC, although it seems that the meetings went no further than simply calling for practical steps.

More conventional efforts to help in the management of *conflicts* also continued. The Addis Ababa summit was followed by a donor conference to raise money for the CAR, which would be used to boost the supplying of MISCA with more non-lethal equipment; some $ 314 m was pledged. The Malabo summit also discussed the conflict in South Sudan. AMISOM (AU Mission to Somalia) was reinforced with troops from Ethiopia, with total personnel projected to rise to more than 22,000.

Debate on collective forms of security also continued. Following the formal adoption of the formation of the African Capacity for Immediate Response to Crises (ACIRC) as part of the long-awaited *African Standby Force* (ASF), the heads of state proceeded to negotiate its details. Despite concern about the conflicts in the CAR, South Sudan and the countries facing jihadists, the legal ramifications of final agreement on ACIRC were still somewhat unclear. Moreover, only 12 countries agreed to provide troops, as several were concerned about the potential abuse of such a force. Notably, Nigeria changed its position and called for controls on ACIRC. However, at the Malabo summit, Egypt and Burkina Faso joined the countries pledging troops to ACIRC. East African countries agreed to establish the Eastern African Standby Force as part of the ASF and the AU's peace and security architecture.

The AU's Panel of the Wise, another component of its security arrangements, got a new chairman, former Mozambiquan prime minister Luisa Diogo. Curiously, the Panel singled out election disputes as the gravest threat to the continent's political stability. Even less helpful, in its continued war against the ICC and its perceived anti-African bias, the AU approved a protocol on the Court of Justice and Human and Peoples Rights containing an amendment that provided *immunity from prosecution* to incumbent "senior state officals". Moreover, the Court, to be based in Arusha (Tanzania), was still not operational, with only 26 states having ratified its constitutive document. Only six states had so far allowed their citizens the legal option to bring matters before the Pan-African court, once it began work.

With regard to *external affairs*, the AU tried to reinforce a common stance on a permanent African seat on the UNSC. The Addis Ababa summit requested its Committee of Ten, established for this purpose, to organise a retreat to study UNSC reform; Turkey attended the summit as an observer, trying to plead its candidature for a non-permanent seat on the UNSC in 2015–16. *Economic issues* that made it onto AU agendas included the so-called Common African Position on the Post 2015 Development Agenda (adopted by the Assembly at the Addis summit); the continent's tottering infrastructure, discussed at an AU-NEPAD conference in Dakar (Senegal) on 14–15 June (the AU was now even considering high-speed rail links); and industrialisation, discussed at an Abuja conference on 27 March. More tangible steps towards further integration included the approval at Malabo of an African Monetary Fund to be provided with an initial capital of $ 22.6 bn, which could help correct payment imbalances. It would be based in Yaoundé (Cameroon). The AU belatedly organised a donor conference in Addis Ababa on 8 November for the Ebola-affected countries; $ 28 m was pledged. The Pan-African body had been criticised for its slow response to the crisis.

The originally much applauded *APRM* continued during its 11th year of existence on its downward spiral, with fewer heads of state showing support by attending its meetings. The APR Forum, established by the AU in 2003, held its 20th summit on 29 January in Addis Ababa. By then, 34 countries had acceded to the APRM, of which 17 had completed their self-assessment and been peer-reviewed by the Forum of Heads of State and Government. Slow progress and internal conflicts on the APR Panel of Eminent Persons were contributing factors to a gradual erosion of the APR's image and credibility. The 20th summit appointed a new leadership of the APR Panel. On 6 September, a strategic session was held in Johannesburg (South Africa) between the APR Focal Points and the Panel of Eminent Persons "to re-galvanize the momentum for the effective promotion of the Mechanism", according to a press release. As observed in an analysis of the APRM programme carried out by the South African Institute of International Affairs, enthusiasm in the APRM had markedly declined among African states, with fewer countries joining the voluntary process and fewer reviews undertaken: "What started out as an initiative that could transform Africa became an overly complex and technical academic review, with member states seemingly lacking the political will to implement proposed changes."

The United Nations and Africa

A UN ECA conference on Land Policy in Africa was held in Addis Ababa on 1–14 November. It focused on some main concerns arising during recent years over large-scale land acquisitions: "ensuring agricultural development and inclusive growth". The conference was the first of a series and it was agreed that it be held on a biannual basis. The 2014 African Economic Conference was also held in the Ethiopian capital (1–3 November) and focused on "Knowledge and Innovation for Africa's Transformation", thus covering mostly technology issues. The 69th Session of the UN General Assembly (starting on 16 September) had on its agenda several issues that directly related to SSA, such as taking stock of one decade of rolling back malaria (particularly in Africa). The Ebola epidemic received major attention, arguably second only to the various crises in the Middle East (Syria, Islamic State, Palestine). Though initially not on the agenda, the Assembly asked the Secretary-General on 19 September to take steps to promptly establish a UN Mission for Ebola Emergency Response (UNMEER).

The causes of armed conflict in Africa were also a main topic and touched on one of the UN's prime activities on the continent: peacekeeping. In fact, the UNSC also focused strongly on Africa, as was clear from the high number of 28 resolutions on African countries or situations passed during the year, of which 18 were renewals (or adaptations) of mandates of existing peacekeeping missions. The UN continued to maintain seven established peacekeeping missions and the UNSC authorised an eighth with the UN Multidimensional Integrated Stabilization Mission in the Central African Republic (known by its French acronym MINUSCA) in the CAR on 10 April. The UN Stabilization Mission in the Democratic Republic of the Congo (known by its French acronym MINUSCO) remained the largest, with nearly 25,000 mandated personnel, followed by the AU–UN Hybrid Operation in Darfur (UNAMID) with nearly 21,000. All in all, the personnel involved in such missions totalled roughly 105,000 (mandated), attesting to the importance of this form of engagement. However, the UNSC also dealt with the Ebola crisis, the maintenance of an arms embargo on Somalia, and reconciliation (in Côte d'Ivoire). Of specific importance were two UNSC resolutions on the winding down of the International Criminal Tribunal for Rwanda (ICTR; in Arusha). Twenty years after its creation, only one case (comprising six separate appeals) was still pending before the ICTR Appeals Chamber in October. The UNSC called on the ICTR to finish its work by 31 December and to prepare for its closure (in resolution 2194 of 18 December).

Democracy and Elections

For a ninth consecutive year, the US-based NGO Freedom House noted an overall decrease in global *freedom*. The general impression may have been driven by events in Syria, Russia and Egypt, but SSA did not contradict the global negative trend. In fact, many East African countries fared worse than previously, including Burundi, Rwanda, South Sudan and Uganda. Although not having direct impacts on ratings, some problematic trends were detected in other countries. For example, in West Africa, Gambia confirmed its increasing pariah status with new legislation against LGBT (lesbian, gay, bisexual and transgender) people. Improvements were noted mostly in Madagascar and Guinea-Bissau as an expression of normalisation after earlier turmoil and coups. Overall, the picture painted by applying the 'free', 'partly free' and 'not free' categories only deteriorated slightly, with 21 countries now listed as 'not free', up from 20 in 2013, and 18 listed as 'partly free', down from 19 (plus ten 'free' countries, unchanged). Burundi and Uganda dropped to the 'not free' category and Guinea-Bissau rose to the 'partly free'.

In the name of national security or the fight against terrorism, many governments embarked on a course to restrict *civil liberties*. The government of Kenya, for example, pushed for new security laws, which Parliament passed in December. They were meant, *inter alia*, to foster state control over the media and limit individual rights in cases of suspected terrorism. According to Reporters Without Borders (RSF, to use the French acronym), violations of press freedom were rising steadily on the continent, though, again, not at the same pace as, for example, in Eastern Europe, Central Asia or the Arab World. RSF singled out Congo and South Sudan as countries in rapid decline, while both Côte d'Ivoire and Madagascar were presented as countries with strong gains. It goes without saying that citizens of countries involved in armed conflict were not experiencing democracy; this certainly applied to the majority of citizens in South Sudan and the CAR plus a good part of the DRC. But there were also a few signs of softening positions in the more repressive countries – arguably somewhat in Zimbabwe – and problematic trends of curtailing freedom in hitherto relatively open 'hybrid' regimes, such as Tanzania.

In Botswana, Mauritius, Namibia, São Tomé and Príncipe, and South Africa – making half of the ten countries classified as 'free' by Freedom House – *national elections* were held and were to a large extent up to standard. However, the results were dissimilar and could be variously interpreted. The former liberation movements in power in both Namibia and South Africa managed to retain their dominance, though *Namibia*'s South West African People's Organisation (SWAPO), with sweeping victories in both parliamentary and presidential elections, appeared more successful than *South Africa*'s African National Congress (ANC), which had to compete harder with newly emerging parties, faced aggressive criticism and found it hard to mobilise first-time voters. The dominant party in *Botswana*, which had not experienced the same level of armed resistance, had little trouble maintaining its leading position, though it held only a relative majority nation-wide. This picture of continuity contrasted with Mauritius, where another election-led change of government attested to the vitality of democracy. Veteran politician (and former president) Anerood Jugnauth became prime minister for the third time. The ever-changing majorities in elections on the other democratic island archipelago, *São Tomé and Príncipe*, brought back – also for a third time – Patrice Trovoada as the new prime minister.

Arguably more was at stake in elections in Guinea-Bissau, Malawi and Mozambique. *Guinea-Bissau* held presidential and parliamentary elections in two rounds. José Mario Vaz, and his 'Partido Africano da Independência da Guiné e Cabo Verde' (PAIGC) managed to win both, making the PAIGC again the main player in a complex and challenging post-conflict environment. In *Malawi*, incumbent president Joyce Banda came only third in the presidential race, which was won by Arthur Peter Mutharika (brother of former president Bingu wa Mutharika); Banda initially claimed that the elections were rigged. The elections were clearly highly contested and four parties managed to win a substantial number of seats in the parallel legislative elections, which could be seen as a sign of a vital democracy. However, the prospect of a violent confrontation was only narrowly avoided when Banda gave in to pressure and accepted the election results. In *Mozambique*, the essential element for the authenticity of the elections was the participation of the main opposition party, Renamo (Resistência Nacional Moçambicana), which had threatened for a while to leave the playing field and return to waging a bush war. Results confirmed the lead of the governing party, Frelimo, but also showed the strength of its major opponent: Renamo won majorities in three out of ten provincial assemblies, which were reconstituted in parallel elections.

In authoritarian *Mauritania*, President Abdel Aziz was easily re-elected with about 82% of the votes, roughly 30% more than in the 2009 elections. The main opposition parties boycotted the elections as they had the legislative elections held in 2013 – making them virtually meaningless. The official participation rate of 56% was no sign of complete success for either the opposition or the presidential camp. All the signs indicated a further shrinking of political rights and civil liberties.

Half of *Liberia*'s senate was renewed in elections that saw campaigning severely restricted due to the Ebola outbreak. Referring to the epidemic, President Sirleaf Johnson not only postponed the election date, but also banned political rallies, which could have facilitated the spread of infection. Seven parties and three independents shared the 15 contested seats, indicating the growing fragmentation of the political landscape. Senatorial elections were also held in Congo.

Parliamentary (and communal) elections in the *Comoros*, originally scheduled for November/December were postponed to early 2015.

Unconstitutional Rule, Coups and Armed Conflicts

African heads of states usually enjoy considerable constitutional power but one of the strong remaining constraints is frequently a *presidential term limit*. A change of constitution to allow for a third term in office or unlimited renewal had become over time one of the core subjects of political debate and some, mostly autocratic, rulers had already succeeded in removing such barriers to unlimited rule. This was the case with the current presidents in Cameroon, Chad and Uganda. Others, who had died in office (Ali Bongo in Gabon, Gnassingbé Eyadéma in Togo), had been removed by force (Tandja in Niger) or had stepped down after an extra term (Sam Nujoma in Namibia), had also previously successfully extended their stay in office, while the Angolan president dos Santos and Zimbabwe's Mugabe had remained in office since 1979 and 1980 respectively.

During the year, the efforts of *Burkina Faso*'s President Blaise Compaoré to change the constitution strongly polarised society and motivated many defections from the regime by members of the political elite. After weeks of street demonstrations against him, the army staged a coup on 31 October. The junta quickly announced that it would only serve as a caretaker government until fresh elections could be held. This kind of 'pro-democracy coup' had a certain tradition in West Africa, with the 1992 coup in Mali and the two coups in Niger (in 1999 and 2010) serving as precedents, and the message was clearly not lost on other presidents planning similar constitutional changes. With the end of their terms approaching (in 2015 or 2016), the presidents of both Congos (Kabila and Sassou Nguesso) and Burundi's Pierre Nkurunziza were preparing for moves to change or interpret their countries' constitutions in a way that would allow them a further term. In all three countries, some nervousness set in. Further down the road, similar situations awaited Liberia, Rwanda and Sierra Leone, while both Tanzania and Benin were believed to be largely (but not completely) immune to the threat of an uprising; their heads of state (Jacaya Kikwete and Yayi Boni) clearly showed a tendency to reduce the quality of democracy in their countries.

In *Lesotho*, Prime Minister Tom Thabane narrowly escaped removal by force when parts of the army attempted a coup on 30 August. Their efforts failed not least because Thabane was able to secure crucial support from the South African government and SADC. Earlier, on 19 June, Thabane had already invoked a coup plot to suspend parliament, using possibly extra-constitutional manoeuvres to avoid a vote of no-confidence. The management of the crisis involved South African and SADC-based diplomatic actions. Thabane was finally escorted back from his South African exile to Maseru. Negotiations resulted in an agreement to hold early elections (in February 2015).

A return to constitutional rule in the *CAR* was postponed multiple times in the face of on-going turmoil and little progress in preparations for elections. While the interim authorities were suspected of profiting from such delays, it was also true that the country was not prepared for this exercise. The increasing deployment of peacekeepers (French, European and African missions, the last turning into a UN operation) had pacifying effects particularly in the capital, Bangui, but they were not able to prevent revenge attacks by the so-called Anti-Balaka militias on the Muslim minority, blindly assumed to be sympathisers of the Séléka rebellion. In the countryside, it was mostly the Mbororo nomads who both came under attack and were actively engaged in combat. Both parties to the conflict were highly fragmented and the ceasefire signed on 23 July was immediately contested by some of the main players. Although the peacekeepers were unable to stop a substantial exodus of the Muslim minority, the prospects for a degree of stabilisation were clearly better at the end of the year than at its start.

A particularly bloody civil war, begun in December 2013, continued in *South Sudan*. The personal confrontation between the top politicians Salva Kiir (president) and Riek Machar (formerly vice-president) had escalated into a full war with ethnic connotations. Machar's troops managed to make some territorial gains in January before being driven back by regime loyalists. Both parties agreed to a ceasefire on 23 January, but this had little meaning on the ground. The same was true of a further agreement on 9 May. Endless mediation efforts by IGAD brought little progress over the year. Rebels conquering Bentiu were accused of killing over 200 persons on 16 April in one of the worst massacres of the war. The lack of credible sources meant that casualty figures were to some extent guesswork but, in November, the ICG advanced a very rough estimate of between 50,000 and 100,000 deaths. In the shadow of this crisis, Sudan's various conflict arenas were not at peace either, with the government and its allies stepping up attacks in Darfur. Some 3,300 villages were reportedly destroyed over the year, accompanied by killings and rape.

On the face of it, the government of *Somalia* made substantial military progress helped by the AU-led military mission and bilateral support, not least from the US, which employed drones. In August, the government launched a further offensive to remove the last pockets of resistance. On 1 September, al-Shabaab leader Mokthar Ali Zubeir was killed by a US drone, upon which some observers predicted a fragmentation or even complete disintegration of the movement. However, groups claiming to be al-Shabaab continued to operate here and there, and the government never managed to clear even Mogadishu of terrorists – several attacks occurred after Zubeir's death. Al-Shabaab also claimed responsibility for several terrorist attacks in Kenya and allegedly had a support network in Tanzania and Uganda.

Compared with previous years, less military activity was recorded in the *DRC*, but in the aftermath of the victory against the M-23 rebels (in 2013) government troops and the two international military missions, failed to be similarly effective against the main Hutu militia operating in eastern DRC (but ultimately aiming at an overthrow of the Rwandan government). This was strongly resented in Kigali and once more resulted in tensions between the two countries. The government had to deal with other hot spots, including the south, where the Kata Katanga movement was involved in several violent incidents.

Despite the 2013 peace agreement, *Mali* was not yet fully at peace. In May, Tuareg rebels managed to retake the northern city of Kidal from government forces, killing some soldiers and resulting in substantial international concern. A fresh round of negotiations started in Algiers in July and dragged on for the rest of the year. Further jihadi attacks were recorded against foreign troops in Mali, who had a stabilisation mandate. Negotiations between the government and Tuareg representatives continued in difficult circumstances, with the issue of rebel disarmament hampering progress. France remained the country most actively involved in security issues, shifting the main base of its anti-terror engagement from Mali to Chad (Operation Bherkane replacing Operation Serval), while the US government remained active in fighting the Lord's Resistance Army (LRA) operating mainly in Sudan (where the government in Khartoum was suspected of sheltering the LRA), South Sudan, the CAR and the DRC.

Whether terrorism was the right description for *Boko Haram* activities was at times debatable, but many actions were definitely meant to cause shock in Nigerian society, more particularly in the north-east of the country. About 2,000 civilians were killed by Boko Haram in numerous attacks and suicide bombings throughout the year. Abductions were also meant to shock. The singular most prominent incident was the abduction of 276 school girls on the night of 14–15 April from a government secondary school in the town of Chibok. Boko Haram leader Shekau threatened to sell the girls. The ensuing campaign, 'Bring Back Our Girls', raised international support, but had little effect on the ground. After a month of negotiations facilitated by Chad's President Idriss Déby (in Saudi Arabia), a truce was announced between Boko Haram and the Nigerian army. It was hoped that this would bring the release of hostages, but soon afterwards new confrontations erupted. Boko Haram, like Islamic State, now clearly aimed at controlling territory. Neighbouring states, particularly *Cameroon*, were increasingly targeted. By the end of the year, Nigeria and its neighbours had begun to better coordinate their counter-strategies.

The opaque context of politics in *Gambia* did not allow a proper assessment of the substance of coup plot allegations by President Jammeh against the former commander of the State Guards, Lamin Sanneh. Two mutinies by former rebels in the pro-Ouattara camp were recorded in *Côte d'Ivoire* in November and December, with the fighters demanding payment of promised bonuses. In all these instances, further escalation was avoided.

The encouraging downward trend of *piracy* activities in the *Gulf of Aden* and the Indian Ocean continued until the phenomenon, which was making headlines only a few years previously, virtually disappeared. The EU naval force mission Atalanta nevertheless continued to function, as did the two Combined Task Forces (CTF 150 and 151) responsible for maritime security and fighting piracy, which were sponsored by 30 nations from across the globe. In November, the EU Council extended the Atalanta mission by two years until December 2016. Atalanta reported only five suspicious events and two attacks during the whole year. The same could not be said for the *Gulf of Guinea*, where intense pirate activities centring around Nigeria expanded quite far south, even reaching Angola, where a crude oil tanker was reported missing from the Luanda anchorage on 18 January; pirates took a large part of the cargo before releasing the crew. According to the International Maritime Bureau, the cargo was transferred in a ship-to-ship operation all along the coast towards Nigeria. The logistical capacities and efficiency of the pirates were clearly above expectations. Similarly, a product tanker was hijacked at sea south of Accra (Ghana) on 5 June. The cargo and crew's belongings were stolen before the vessel and personnel were released a week later. By coincidence, on the same day, pirates hijacked a large fishing vessel in Ghanaian waters and forced the captain to sail towards Nigeria, obviously planning to hijack other vessels. Other instances of such hijackings of potential mother vessels were also reported. All in all, 41 piracy events were recorded for West Africa, mostly aiming at stealing oil, and many occurring in harbours and anchorages, which made international protective efforts at sea difficult. Crew members of hijacked vessels were frequently manhandled.

Epidemics and Disasters

The first cases of a new outbreak of the *Ebola* virus disease were reported in March. It rapidly spread to become the deadliest occurrence since the discovery of the virus in 1976 and had devastating effects on the people, mainly in Liberia, Sierra Leone and Guinea. By the end of the year, it had claimed an estimated 10,000 deaths, but the lack of reliable data led to fears being articulated that this number was a vast under-estimate. The highest number of casualties was recorded in Liberia, followed by Sierra Leone and then Guinea. In an initial response, on 25 March ECOWAS declared Ebola a serious threat to regional security. On 12 June, the government of Sierra Leone announced a state of emergency in the Kailahun district. WHO convened an emergency ministerial meeting on Ebola in Accra on 2–3 July. On 10 July, the ECOWAS summit adopted a sub-regional approach to containment and management of the outbreak. On 8 August, WHO finally declared the epidemic an international public health emergency. Precautionary measures were taken by governments and border control agencies around the world to avoid the spread of the disease by travellers. Isolated cases in other countries (USA, Spain, Mali and Nigeria) made international news. The epidemic peaked in August and September and, according to a statement by 'Médecins Sans Frontières' in mid-September, the disease was "totally out of control". On 3 December, a first batch of 150 volunteer health workers trained on behalf of the AU and ECOWAS were deployed to the most affected areas. By then the epidemic was on the decline. The IMF and the World Bank estimated that the short-term fiscal impacts on the three countries mainly affected were \$ 113 m (5.1% of GDP) for Liberia, \$ 95 m (2.1% of GDP) for Sierra Leone and \$ 120 m (1.8% of GDP) for Guinea.

An outbreak of *measles* was recorded in Guinea and Somalia. *Cholera* took lives in northern Namibia early in the year, by mid-year in South Sudan and Ghana, during August in Cameroon's northern region, in September/October in southern Niger and at the end of the year in Mozambique. Initial cases of *plague* were recorded in Madagascar from November.

Floods were registered in late January in Tanzania's Morogoro region, in early February in parts of Burundi, and in early March in South Africa's Mpumalanga region. Parts of Sudan and South Sudan were flooded during July and August, parts of Niger in August and of Somalia and Ethiopia in October. *Drought* affected parts of Kenya throughout the year and the combination of conflict and lack of rain escalated problems in the region. By mid-year some 14.4 m people were estimated as food insecure in nine countries, with Sudan, South Sudan, Ethiopia, Somalia and Kenya the most affected. Parts of Southern Africa were drought prone, too, and rainfall deficits during the first half of the year also negatively affected the regions of West Africa.

Food security remained at risk for considerable parts of the continent's people. The Global Food Security Index (GFSI) presented by the Economist Intelligence Unit for 2014 ranked SSA the lowest of all regions on all scores (availability, affordability, and quality and safety), with an overall score of just two-thirds of that of Asia and the Pacific. Climate, poverty and civil strife remained the most contributory factors to the precarious situation, though the GFSI recorded an overall tendency towards a gradual improvement of the general supply as a result of several fast-growing economies. According to the report, apart from Europe, SSA had seen the greatest increase in food affordability as a result of economic growth rates leading to higher household incomes. A policy brief by the AfDB published mid-year warned of the devastating effects of global warming on food production and prices and more generally the critical threat it posed to social, economic and demographic life.

PART 2

African-European Relations

Christine Hackenesch and Niels Keijzer

A key highlight of the year was the third Africa-EU Summit, which was held in Brussels. The summit was considered a step forward in relations but left many controversial areas untouched. The year also saw the beginning of the end of a major headache in Africa-EU relations through the completion of EPAs, which had dragged on for an additional seven years after the passing of the initial negotiations deadline in December 2007. The Ebola crisis presented formidable challenges to Africa that went far beyond the states and people directly affected by the outbreak. Migration continued to be high on the agenda of EU-Africa relations.

Beyond these 'continental' trends, African crises at the national level once again drew a lot of attention in European media and political circles, with regard to both the Mali crisis and its aftermath and the disappointing lack of progress in the CAR and South Sudan. While not witnessing any diplomatic disasters, the year fell short on major breakthroughs in the relationship between the two continents. Yet there was more than enough going on. The EU observed a number of elections; the year in fact brought several critical elections, notably the twentieth anniversary of multiparty democracy in both South Africa and Malawi. With a new European Commission entering office in October and a new Pan-African Instrument financed from the EU budget, and no longer from the intergovernmental EDF, careful optimism could be expressed as regards the chances for a further strengthening of Africa-EU relations.

Responses to the Ebola Crisis

After the reporting of the outbreak in March 2014, the Ebola crisis in Guinea, Liberia and Sierra Leone took a high place on the EU's agenda. In contrast to their regional neighbours, Senegal and Nigeria, which were both declared Ebola-free by WHO in the course of 2014, the three governments failed to control the outbreak from their own resources. The epidemic therefore accentuated existing differences between African states, as shown by those states that did and did not independently manage to contain Ebola. The EU and member states together raised about € 1.2 bn to respond to the crisis, of which the European Commission provided about € 400 m. These *funds* were used for the most urgent needs (i.e. support for hospitals and clinics, awareness raising, etc.) and were mostly *channelled through international NGOs*. EU funds were also used to support government capacities to improve health care, food security and water and sanitation, as well as to maintain macroeconomic

 | DOI 10.1163/9789004305052_003

stability. Finally, beyond the use of its ODA budget, the EU made available over € 138 m for more than a dozen projects developing clinical trials for new vaccines, rapid diagnostic tests and treatments under Horizon 2020 and the Innovative Medicines Initiative. It also called on European pharmaceutical industries to do the same.

After the new European Commissioners had taken office in November, the European Council tasked the new Commissioner for Humanitarian Aid and Crisis Management, Christos Stylianides, with coordinating the EU's response to the Ebola crisis. The EU also set up a task force that brought together the European Commission, the External Action Service, member states, representatives of the UN and NGOs in order to better coordinate the assistance provided. Moreover, the EU agreed to organise a meeting of the EU and West African leaders scheduled for March 2015, a year after the start of the outbreak, to discuss the next steps and how to sustain the improvements achieved.

African Migration to Europe

As in 2013, thousands of migrants died when trying to cross the Mediterranean. More than 200,000 people – most of them Syrians, but also many Eritreans – set out for Europe; more than 3,000 lost their lives. The growing numbers of migrants and asylum seekers kept the topic high on the agenda in both Europe and Africa. During the EU-Africa summit in Brussels in April, European and African political leaders signed a joint declaration on 'Migration and Mobility'. The declaration, timid in tone, stressed both sides' commitment to improve policies for legal migration and address illegal migration, while respecting migrants' fundamental human rights. Changes in the EU's migration policy raised international criticism. According to AI, Italy's 'Mare Nostrum' operation on the Mediterranean had saved over 140,000 human lives. But, during its presidency of the EU in the second half of 2014, Italy decided to stop the operation. The successor to 'Mare Nostrum', the EU's 'Operation Triton', was substantially reduced in terms of funding and its mandate to search and rescue refugees trying to cross the Mediterranean. Moreover, EU member states discussed reforming the burden-sharing scheme for receiving migrants, but could not reach an agreement. On 12 December, the EU Foreign Affairs (Development) Council called on the European Commission to develop new guidelines for migration policy and the European Commission was planning to issue a new communication in 2015. The topic clearly received strong public attention and undermined Europe's reputation in Africa. In his speech at the European Parliament on 25 November, Pope Francis vehemently criticised the EU's policy, saying, "There needs to be a united response to the question of migration. We cannot allow the Mediterranean to become a vast cemetery."

Economic Partnership Agreements

In the second half of the year, important progress towards the conclusion of EPAS with regional organisations in West, Eastern and Southern Africa was finally made. The EPA negotiations had become an increasing *diplomatic headache* for the EU. Above all, the EPAS did not promise to bring substantial economic gains for all partners. The trade deals to be ratified and consolidated in 2015 were meant to stabilise trade relations between Europe and Africa by providing incentives for trade and business. They would replace a system of asymmetrical trade preferences that expired in June 2008 with a symmetrical and WTO-compatible scheme of trade liberalisation, entailing the elimination of "cross-border policy barriers" between countries, such as tariffs, quotas and other restrictions on trade. Now that the EPAS were 'initialled', the EU assured the negotiation partners that the current market access rules would be continued until the agreements came into force. Compared with the Caribbean EPA concluded in 2007, the African EPAS concluded seven years later were less comprehensive in scope, with the Caribbean agreement covering trade in services, for instance, while the African EPAS were limited to trade in goods. A gradual process of trade liberalisation for a fixed percentage of the total trade volume between the EU and each EPA grouping was foreseen, with West Africa having the lowest target (of 75%). Import tariffs and quotas would be gradually abolished with the exception of some particularly sensitive products. Given that customs duties had represented an important source of fiscal revenue for African states, it was expected that the EPAS would represent a major challenge, but also an incentive for further reform.

The EPA negotiations were particularly criticised for disrupting the *regional integration* processes that they were supposed to promote. The presence of 14 intergovernmental organisations nominally advancing regional cooperation in Africa was sufficient to temper expectations regarding the positive effect of the EPAS for regional integration. However, prospects were further obscured by African countries' choosing negotiation groups that did not match with existing Regional Economic Communities, with the exception of Eastern Africa. Among other effects, the negotiations posed challenges for those African countries who were members of more than one Regional Economic Community. More specifically, the negotiations put SACU under severe stress. One further problem was that the EU's unilateral 'Everything But Arms' scheme actually provided disincentives to active negotiations by least developed countries (*LDCs*) (e.g. 87% of the West African group consisted of LDCs) and forced other countries to enter into bilateral interim EPAS. As if dealing with the resulting consequences was not enough, Africa also saw itself suddenly confronted with the implications of a possible EU-US Transatlantic Trade and Investment Partnership, as well as other large trade agreements, which would certainly impact Africa's trade possibilities by setting the rules of the game.

Relations with Countries and Regions

Throughout the year, the High Representative and European Commission Vice President Catherine Ashton, and from November her successor Federica Mogherini, closely monitored and regularly commented on the deteriorating security situation in *Libya*. In a wide-ranging speech on EU foreign and security policy to the European Parliament on 3 April, Libya was the only African country to make a major appearance. Ashton recognised the 'knock-on' effects of the civil war in Libya on the crisis in Mali and announced the appointment of a personal special envoy to engage with the Libyan authorities to strengthen EU support to Libya. On 8 May she appointed to this role Bernardino Léon, an experienced Spanish diplomat who had previously worked as the EU special representative for the Mediterranean Region.

In July, fighting – including air strikes – intensified in Libya. According to the ICG, more than 1,000 Libyans died and the number of internally displaced persons grew fourfold to 400,000 in the course of the year. In response to the deteriorating security situation, the EU decided to temporarily relocate its staff from the EU delegation and from the EU Border Assistance Mission (EUBAM) to Brussels and Tunis. EUBAM was a civilian mission, launched in 2013 for a period of two years with an annual budget of € 26 m. Its objective was to strengthen Libya's border management and border security. The mission organised a number of training exercises, including one for Libya's naval coast guards in April. In May, a large number of migrants died off the Libyan coast while trying to reach Europe. This tragic event showed even more clearly the need to provide support for Libyan naval coast guards' search and rescue operations. On 3 December, the foreign affairs ministers of France, Germany, Italy, Spain and the UK, as well as the US Secretary of State, the UN Under-Secretary-General and the EU's High Representative, issued a joint statement to express their concern regarding the rapidly deteriorating security situation, particularly the air strikes, in Libya. They called on all key stakeholders to respect the peace process led by the UN and highlighted their willingness to adopt additional measures, if necessary, to strengthen stability, guarantee Libya's unity and prevent terrorism from expanding further in the region.

In response to the increase in piracy, illegal fishing, people and drug trafficking, oil theft and other forms of maritime insecurity and organised crime, the Council of the EU adopted a new strategy on the *Gulf of Guinea* on 17 March. The strategy highlighted that, as a first step, the EU and its member states should invest in developing a common understanding about the security challenges in the Gulf of Guinea, including better data collection and information sharing on maritime incidents. The EU placed particular emphasis on supporting regional governments and organisations such as ECOWAS, ECCAS and the Gulf of Guinea Commission in their own efforts at improving maritime security. The EU particularly supported the "Code of Conduct concerning the repression of piracy, armed robbery against ships and illicit activity in West and Central Africa" that the member states of the three regional organisations had signed in Yaoundé (Cameroon) in June 2013. Support for economic development in the region was seen as an important measure to prevent a further escalation of the maritime security situation. Moreover, the EU offered to provide more support to strengthen African governments' capacities to guarantee maritime security and rule of law.

In February, EU Council President van Rompuy met the Malian president during the latter's visit to Brussels, and later that same month gave a speech to the Malian National Assembly. The speech went far beyond addressing the current situation and analysed evolutions in Africa, the EU and intercontinental relations. Earlier in the year, van Rompuy gave a similar address to the national assembly of *Tunisia*, following the adoption of the new constitution. In April, the Council decided to send a civilian mission to support *Mali*'s internal security forces. The EU Capacity Building Mission in Mali (EUCAP Sahel Mali) was not officially launched until the end of the year. The objective of the mission was, however, already set: to support the Malian government to ensure stability and maintain the state's monopoly on power throughout the country. The mission would furthermore provide advice and training for the police (Gendarmerie and Garde Nationale) and seek to closely coordinate and work with other international partners.

During the fifth EU-*Nigeria* Ministerial Dialogue Meeting held in Abuja in November in the context of the EU-Nigeria 'Joint Way Forward', both sides stressed the urgency of fighting against increasing violence committed by Boko Haram in the north of Nigeria. Almost 300 school girls were kidnapped in April in Borno state. The UN put Boko Haram on the list of terrorist groups and the UNSC approved sanctions. The state of emergency continued in the states of Borno, Yobe and Adamawa. The numbers of IDPs and refugees increased considerably throughout the year; according to estimates, almost half a million people had been displaced due to the conflict. Moreover, violence continued to spread and destabilise neighbouring countries such as the north of Cameroon, Chad and Niger. About 150,000 refugees were registered in neighbouring countries. The EU welcomed the closer regional cooperation between Nigeria, Cameroon, Chad and Niger, agreed within the framework of the Lake Chad Basin Commission. While Nigeria remained reluctant to accept more international support to deal with the terrorist group, some neighbouring countries were more vocal in asking for assistance from the EU, its member states (particularly France) and other external partners. EU-Nigeria negotiations on a Common Agenda on Migration and Mobility started, but were not concluded by year's end.

The year also witnessed ongoing crisis in the *CAR*. The Séléka takeover in March 2013 had led to the total collapse of the state, including fundamental institutions such as the justice system, law enforcement apparatus, public administration and social services. While international engagement visibly increased, the situation in rural areas worsened during the year, and inter-communal clashes between pastoralists and farmers surged as a consequence of the conflict between ex-Séléka and anti-Balaka militia men. French and regional forces had been on the ground since the start of the crisis in December 2012, while the UN was monitoring developments through its Integrated Peace-building Office in the CAR. On 1 April, the EU agreed to launch an EU military operation, backed by a new UNSC resolution (2134 of 2014). The EU force would be around 1,000 troops strong and operate under French command (about 700 were later deployed). The decision also meant that Angela Merkel's remarks at the December 2013 Council that the EU would not provide funding for French military missions in Africa were of no consequence. The EU condemned the renewed spread of violence in its Council Conclusions on 20 October. In November, the EU operation was extended by the Council from the initial end date of December to 15 March 2015.

On 14 July, the EU, Germany, France and the Netherlands created a Trust Fund named 'Bekou' ('hope' in Sango) to support the transition from a crisis and emergency situation to stability and development. The trust fund sought to facilitate cooperation and joint activities of humanitarian and development actors in order to improve conditions for long-term development in the country, while reducing the administrative burden on local government. The trust fund was open to other EU and non-EU donors, with the founding members putting together an initial amount of € 64 m, which came in addition to the € 84.5 m of humanitarian assistance provided by the European Commission since December 2012. The possibility of designing and operating Union Trust Funds had been laid down in October 2012 under the financial rules applicable to the general budget of the Union.

December marked the first anniversary of the armed conflict in *South Sudan*, with little reason for optimism. Notwithstanding a full year of negotiations under the aegis of IGAD, the two parties failed to conclude any meaningful political agreement. Worryingly, insiders' accounts described a situation in which the main participants in the negotiations had little incentive to reach an agreement, which would in any case only result at best in restoring the status quo before the country's destabilisation, i.e. it would leave major potential for conflict still in place. Meanwhile, the South Sudanese delegations at the EU-funded talks held in hotels in Addis Ababa (Ethiopia) had already cost at least € 20 m.

While the negotiators appeared to some to have little interest in the plight of the people they claimed to represent, international assistance helped to avoid a famine among the most vulnerable population. Guided by its Strategy for the Horn of Africa and facilitated by the EU Special Representative appointed for this region, the Union had since its independence in 2011 sought to help stabilise the new state. The EU's main objectives remained avoiding the involvement of neighbouring countries in the conflict and supporting the initiation of a political transition. In Council Conclusions adopted by the EU's foreign ministers on 15 December, the EU expressed its dismay that all the efforts made so far, including its own, had been unsuccessful in resolving the stalemate. The ministers thus called for "tougher action by the international community as a whole to press all sides in the conflict to pursue the path of peaceful negotiation in the primary interest of the South Sudanese population".

In a rather unexpected turn of events, at the end of October *Burkina Faso*'s president Blaise Compaoré was ousted after 27 years in power. What was more surprising was that this happened as a result of a popular uprising, which also put the AU on the spot: its Constitutive Act allows for the condemnation of unconstitutional changes of government, but makes no mention of popular uprisings. With the country going through three leaders in less than 24 hours, the EU could not do much more than the issuance of a one-paragraph statement by the European External Action Services' spokesperson on 30 October, calling on "all parties to refrain from the use of violence and engage rapidly in a constructive dialogue", with the offer of EU support if so desired. The AU eventually overcame its own unease with the situation and adopted a communiqué in its Peace and Security Council that condemned the military takeover and legitimised the Burkinabe people's actions. It gave the military rulers a two-week deadline to hand over power to a civilian ruler, which the military respected. On 17 November, the former foreign minister, Michel Kafando, became interim leader. The EU's statements after 30 October did little more than express support for African diplomatic moves, including visits by the presidents of Nigeria, Senegal and Ghana. These proved instrumental in building an AU consensus and providing real leverage through an ECOWAS statement that unconstitutional access to power would not be tolerated. Although on the surface the EU refrained from direct involvement and instead supported continental and regional actors, the regional counterterrorism activities of the French special forces stationed in Burkina Faso meant that Europe was in fact more strongly involved, including by providing assistance to the ousted former leader Compaoré, with President Hollande commenting that his responsible behaviour had helped avert a blood bath.

On 19 February, the EU concluded its review of relations with *Zimbabwe*. It decided to lift most of the remaining sanctions with the exception of the arms embargo and those directly targeting President Mugabe, his wife and Zimbabwe Defence Industries. The EU did agree to give Mugabe a visa to attend the EU-Africa Summit in Brussels in April, but he refused because his wife was denied a visa. In October, the EU subsequently decided to lift trade sanctions and the use of Article 96 of the Cotonou Partnership Agreement, which suspended development cooperation with the Zimbabwean government (but allowed for humanitarian assistance channelled through NGOs and the UN). While the travel ban on the president and his wife remained in place, the EU head of delegation presented the decisions as an important step in the process of normalising the EU's relations with Zimbabwe.

EU Election Observation

2014 was a rich year on the electoral front, with 11 African states organising *national elections*. These ranged from economic heavyweight South Africa to Malawi, which in 2014 had the lowest GDP per capita in the world. Both countries celebrated 20 years of multiparty democratic elections in May. The CAR postponed elections to 2015 for security reasons.

Out of eight *EU election observation missions* during the year, five were conducted in African countries (including three in SSA: Guinea Bissau, Malawi and Mozambique). Election observation was one of the EU's key activities to support democracy, human rights and the rule of law. Election observation missions were (as usual) led by a member of the European Parliament. Elections in *Mozambique* in October were considered generally free. The election campaign remained peaceful and saw few acts of violence. The EU welcomed the new electoral legislation, which strengthened the inclusiveness of the electoral process. However, the EU criticised the uneven playing field that resulted from the ruling party's use of state human and material resources and also noted a number of irregularities on election day. Presidential and parliamentary elections in *Guinea Bissau* did not turn violent as on previous occasions and were considered relatively free and fair by the observers, although the EU noted a number of cases of intimidation, beatings and irregularities in the election process. The EU considered the presidential, parliamentary and local government councillor elections in May in *Malawi* relatively free and fair and noted that the fifth general elections since 1994 were very competitive with no political party seen as favourite. At the same time, they were also more tense than previous polls. At least partly due to a major public-sector corruption scandal, the incumbent Joyce Banda lost the presidency to Peter Mutharika.

Bilateral Relations

On 1 August, *French* President François Hollande launched 'Operation Barkhane' in the Sahel region, which highlighted France's continued interest in remaining politically and militarily engaged in African countries. 'Operation Barkhane' was the continuation of 'Operation Serval', launched in 2013 in Mali. 'Operation Serval' was limited to Mali and aimed at stopping the terrorist offensive, ensuring security in Bamako to protect French nationals and guaranteeing territorial integrity. By contrast, 'Operation Barkhane' took a more regional approach and aimed at fighting terrorist groups in the Sahel countries of Mauritania, Niger, Chad and Burkina Faso, as well as Mali. Led by the French army, the operation cooperated closely with the military forces in the countries involved. Critics pointed to the considerable challenges it faced: most of these countries' armies had at some point in the past rebelled against their governments and committed crimes against local populations. Collaborating closely with these armies could endanger the legitimacy of the new operation in the eyes of local people. On the other hand, if France had moved alone and unilaterally, without close cooperation with local military forces, its engagement would probably have faced even stronger criticism and lack of legitimacy.

The *UK* continued to send mixed signals to the African continent, with altruistic political discourse on the one hand alternating with the coalition government's clear emphasis on trade and economic relations with Africa on the other. In June, MPs gathered for an historic debate on the UK's relationship with Africa, which brought contributions from across the political spectrum. Three key themes emerged from the discussion – trade, aid and security – highlighting the breadth of views within Britain's political class. In response to a question from the House of Lords, the UK government announced on 15 October that it would not support any future search and rescue operations to prevent migrants and refugees drowning in the Mediterranean, claiming that this would simply encourage more people to attempt the crossing. On 5 December, the House of Commons voted by 146 votes to 5 to establish a legal basis for the government's commitment to provide 0.7% of its gross national income as ODA.

In May, the German Foreign Office published *new guidelines* defining the priorities, principles and context conditions for *Germany's Africa policy*. They aimed at strengthening cooperation and coordination between various ministries in their relations with African countries. The priorities listed included supporting regional integration, peace and security (in particular the African Peace and Security Architecture), reducing fragility and conflict and supporting human rights, fighting against poverty and hunger, supporting the rule of law, good governance and the fight against corruption, supporting education, and strengthening cooperation in global governance with particular regard to climate change and biodiversity. However, and in contrast to France, Germany remained reluctant to engage strongly in military operations in Africa.

In March, Foreign Minister Frank-Walter Steinmeier travelled to Ethiopia, Tanzania and Angola. In Ethiopia, he discussed Germany's contribution to the African Peace and Security Architecture. Germany funded a new building for the AU's Peace and Security Department. In Tanzania, Steinmeier celebrated the 50th anniversary of German-Tanzanian relations and discussed German development cooperation with Tanzania with his counterpart and the Tanzanian President Jakaya Kikwete. During his visit to Angola, the promotion of German business interests took centre-stage.

In December, Steinmeier announced a reform of the guidelines for the so-called Hermes export credit guarantees. German companies seeking to deliver goods and services to public customers in Ethiopia, Ghana, Mozambique, Nigeria and Tanzania were now entitled to apply for export credit guarantees, opening investment opportunities particularly for German small and medium enterprises. Previously, the German government had only provided coverage for contracts with private purchasers. Coverage for business with the public sector was restricted after debt relief had been granted to several African countries in the mid-1990s.

While most European countries sought to reduce the number of African migrants in Europe, the number of *Portuguese* migrating to Angola in search of better jobs continued to increase; about 100,000 Portuguese were living in Angola. On the other hand, rich Angolans (and Chinese) were the main beneficiaries of the so-called 'golden visa' that the Portuguese government offered to anyone investing more than € 500,000 in Portugal.

Meanwhile, the *Nordic states* agreed to continue their support for the East Africa Standby Force (EASF) and for capacity development in the area of security. EASF was expected to become operational in 2015 and was regarded by the Nordics as an important facilitator for the AU's ambition to promote security and stability in Africa.

The four Visegrad countries – *Poland, the Czech Republic, Slovakia and Hungary* – strengthened their ties to Africa. Under their former Communist regimes, they had welcomed thousands of African students and maintained strong bilateral relations. Since the end of the Cold War, relations with African countries were primarily driven by business interests and the Visegrad countries' desire to diversify their economies. While some EU member states were reducing their diplomatic presence in Africa, with the Netherlands having closed its embassies in Burkina Faso and Zambia in late 2013, the Visegrad countries had steadily increased their diplomatic network. They did so with a focus on similar, mostly Anglophone countries: Poland maintained five African embassies (Angola, Ethiopia, Kenya, Nigeria, and South Africa), the Czech Republic had now six (Ethiopia, Ghana, Senegal, Nigeria, South Africa, Zimbabwe), Slovakia maintained four (Ethiopia, Kenya, Nigeria, and South Africa), and Hungary now had three embassies (Kenya, South Africa, and Nigeria). Hungary also raised its profile at the UN-based negotiations on the post-2015 development agenda by co-chairing the Open Working Group on the Sustainable Development Goals together with the Kenyan government.

Summits, Partnerships and the Post-2015 Development Agenda

The fourth *EU-Africa Summit* took place in Brussels on 2–3 April, following earlier summits in Cairo (2000), Lisbon (2007) and Tripoli (2010). In his speech, EU Council President Herman van Rompuy noted that, with over 60 African heads of state and government in attendance, this was the first time that European institutions had hosted a conference of such magnitude.

In the run-up to the summit, the same sensitive matters as in previous summits came to the fore, including the EPAs, the ICC, and the participation of certain

African heads of state (Robert Mugabe). In addition, support for lesbian, gay, bisexual and transgender (LGBT) rights was seen by African policy-makers as Europe imposing its values, which was also among the reasons why a third revision of the Cotonou Partnership Agreement was not launched in the same year. Following what may be described as a more pragmatic approach when compared with the previous two summits, constructive deliberations were held on climate, the post-2015 development agenda, peace and security, and migration. In accordance with the deliberate decision to relegate 'elephants in the room' to other fora, contentious issues such as human rights, conditionality, EPAs and the ICC, were not part of the official discussions.

Another important step taken by the EU in the run-up to the summit was the agreement on a Pan-African Programme as part of its Development Cooperation Instrument, which in the period 2014–20 would dedicate € 845 m to funding cooperation activities at the inter-regional and continental level. Beyond financial inputs, the Juncker Commission as a whole also seemed ready to invest in the relationship, with four different Commissioners and the High Representative tasked to engage in various aspects of the African partnership.

A key result of the summit was a rethink of the main modus operandi relating to the *Joint Africa-EU Strategy* (*JAES*). Since its adoption in 2007, it had been criticised for being over-bureaucratic and having the appearance of a stand-alone framework while being mostly reliant on funding from the EDF. Moreover, political dialogue mainly took place in other intergovernmental frameworks and not in the context of the JAES. Finally, limited engagement by member states on both sides led to the JAES being perceived as a 'Commission to Commission strategy'. Beyond the attempt to revitalise the JAES, the summit also adopted an EU-Africa Declaration on Migration and Mobility, which commentators judged as a strongly EU-driven declaration with reference to 'illegal migration'. Partly because of the energy that went into discussing and agreeing on this declaration, other planned joint-declarations on the post-2015 development agenda, climate change, trade and food security were not adopted.

The EU and African countries made some progress in defining their positions regarding the *post-2015 development agenda negotiations*. The European Commission outlined its position in June in its communication, "A Decent Life for All: From Vision to Collective Action", highlighting the integrated nature of the three dimensions of sustainable development (environmental, social and economic development). On 16 December, the European Foreign Affairs Council confirmed the key principles and priority areas of this document as the basis for the EU's engagement in the negotiations. African heads of state and government had already adopted a common position at an Ordinary Session of the Assembly of the Union on 14 January. The African position focused on poverty eradication and human development as the two main goals, which were to be achieved through six pillars, including trade, peace and security. The African and European positions both outlined a broad framework for coordinating their respective positions in the negotiations. European-African cooperation during the negotiations remained limited. The EU-Africa summit in April failed to develop a joint position on the post-2015 agenda negotiations. It was rather the Joint Council of Minister of the EU and African, Caribbean and Pacific (ACP) countries, sitting on 16–18 June, that developed a joint declaration on the post-2015 agenda, highlighting the importance of a universal framework that would be developed on the basis of a single set of goals and targets but take into account the national contexts in different countries.

Development Cooperation

On 19–20 June, on the occasion of the Joint Council of Ministers of the ACP countries and the EU in Nairobi (Kenya), Commissioner Piebalgs and ministers from 16 ACP countries co-signed the first National Indicative Programmes under the 11th EDF for the period 2014–20. These programmes initiated concrete cooperation activities under the 11th EDF, amounting to € 29.1 bn during the indicated period.

The intergovernmental nature of the EDF, which was funded by the EU's member states through a distribution key different from that used for the EU budget, meant that only slow progress was made towards preparing the next phase of ACP-EU development cooperation. The EDF required individual ratification by all 28 EU member states. Given potential delays in this process, the EU made preparations for a bridging facility between the 10th EDF (2007–13) and its successor. It was expected that the debate on whether to integrate the EDF into the EU's budget would intensify halfway through the new budget execution period. It should be noted that this discussion was closely linked to the long-standing debate on whether to consolidate the 'special relationship' or to normalise the EU's relations with the ACP Group.

On the side of the *ACP Group*, in December, former Nigerian president Olusegun Obasanjo reported the interim findings of the Eminent Persons Group (EPG) that was mandated in 2012 to independently review the 79-member ACP Group as an international organisation. Building on two initial consultative roundtables held in 2013 in the Caribbean and Pacific regions, the EPG convened four roundtables in each of the four principal African regions. A key input to the EPG's final report was provided by Brussels-based ACP ambassadors, who formed a working group to draft an advisory report on the same topic. Well ahead of the EU in its own post-Cotonou preparations, which European Commission President Jean-Claude Juncker identified as a key priority for the EU Development Commissioner Neven Mimica, the ACP Group was expected to adopt the report at a Council meeting towards the summer of 2015.

PART 3

West Africa

Sebastian Elischer

Several political and economic upheavals shaped the trajectory of the continent's largest and politically most diverse region. Nigeria, the region's economic powerhouse and previous guarantor of regional stability, suffered some of the worst terrorist attacks by Boko Haram, which undermined the political credibility of the Jonathan administration and posed serious questions about the capacity of the Nigerian army to establish a modicum of order on its own territory. Mali was still coming to terms with the long-term consequences of the Tuareg rebellion and the jihadi occupation of the north of the country, which had shaken it in 2012. Like Mali, Côte d'Ivoire tried to come to terms with its immediate past, but its post-war reconciliation process produced mixed results. The Ebola virus epidemic brought public and political life in Sierra Leone, Liberia and Guinea to a virtual standstill and eradicated much of the economic progress of the last decade. Gambia, Mauritania and Togo remained firmly in the hands of autocratic regimes. Cabo Verde, Benin, Ghana, Senegal and Niger continued to be the region's democratic hopefuls, although political debate in several of these countries rarely if ever addressed the interests of their population. After months of opposition and civil society protest, Blaise Compaoré was forced to resign after 27 years as president of Burkina Faso.

Regime Dynamics and Human Rights

Cabo Verde, Benin, Ghana, Senegal and Niger remained *functioning democracies* and enjoyed the protection of human rights and civil liberties. These five countries clearly stood out as positive examples in an otherwise unstable and often autocratically governed region, though the political discourse in all countries left much to be desired. In Benin, Ghana, Senegal and Niger, recent aspects of political contestation raised doubts about the willingness of political elites to address the interests of their populations. Instead of making proposals or discussing the needs of the electorate, governments and oppositions more often than not engaged in *lengthy legalistic debates*, corruption charges (many of which rested on weak foundations) and allegations about the intentions of those in power.

In Benin, President Yayi failed to convince the parliamentary opposition and civil society that he would not seek an unconstitutional *third term* in the 2016 presidential elections. Senegal saw the return home of former President Wade and the trial of his son and former minister, Karim Wade. The trial reignited old political controversies and dominated much of the political scene. In Ghana, President John Mahama was unable to account for the country's irregular *electricity supply*, which

 | DOI 10.1163/9789004305052_004

worsened considerably as the year unfolded. Both Ghana's governing National Democratic Congress and the main opposition party, the New Patriotic Party, began to nominate candidates for the 2016 presidential and parliamentary elections. The process proved divisive for both parties. Niger's opposition leader and president of the National Assembly, Hama Amadou, fled the country after he and his wife were accused of involvement in a *baby trafficking scandal*. Amadou's sudden departure from Niger's political scene ensured a new level of political stability but raised serious questions about the conduct of Niger's political class as a whole.

Two other electoral democracies, Nigeria and Mali, had to confront serious security challenges. *Jihadi Salafi groups* brought death and destruction to both nations. In Nigeria, the group known as *Boko Haram* (which changed its full name to 'community of the people of the Sunna who fight for the cause of Islam according to the method of the Salaf') continued to terrorise large parts of northern Nigeria, while the north-east was affected by a number of particularly brutal suicide attacks, which left thousands of innocent people dead or wounded. One of the cruellest incidents was the abduction from Chibok of more than 270 female students. While a few of them managed to escape, most were said to have been married to Boko Haram fighters. The Jonathan administration ignored the abduction for almost two weeks. This led to the formation of the 'Bring Back Our Girls', initiative in which prominent individuals (including Michelle Obama) from across the world called on the Nigerian government to rescue the students. However, not only did the Nigerian military fail to free them, but it also failed to make serious headway against Boko Haram. On several occasions, Nigerian soldiers refused to go to the front line and fight the insurgents, raising serious questions about the capacity and willingness of the Nigerian military command to establish security within Nigeria's territory. It also undermined the legitimacy of the Jonathan administration, which often appeared to ignore the crisis and its consequences.

In Mali, the security situation in the north of the country remained tense and uncertain. After the election of a new government under Ibrahim Keita at the beginning of the year, two militant Islamist groups, the *Movement for Oneness and Jihad in West Africa* (MUJAO) and *al-Qaida in the Islamic Maghreb* (AQIM) stepped up their terrorist activities. Both groups had been involved in the occupation of the north of Mali by Tuareg rebels during the first six months of 2012. The jihadi attacks targeted UN, French and Malian troops. In addition, the relationship between the Malian government and the northern separatist Tuareg groups deteriorated over the question of rebel disarmament and the future institutional relationship between the central government and the northern regions. As a result, both sides agreed to work out a roadmap to peace in Algiers, a process in which the Algerian government acted as mediator. The most controversial question remained that of how much autonomy the northern regions would have vis-à-vis the government in Bamako. At the end of the year, the outcome of the Algiers negotiations remained uncertain.

While governments in Nigeria and Mali tried to avoid the disintegration of their territories, the regime in Côte d'Ivoire continued its attempts to consolidate stability in its post-conflict situation. The *reconciliation process* produced mixed results. Talks between the government and the opposition broke down several times, but each time the opposition agreed to return to the negotiating table. Local observers accused the Ivorian justice system of being politically biased as it had indicted only individuals who had sided with former president Gbagbo, while supporters of President Ouattara walked free. The national reconciliation commission ('Commission Dialogue Vérité et Reconciliation') ran into budget issues. It submitted its final report to the president, but the Ivorian public had no access to the Commission's findings. Military reforms led to two mutinies by former members of the 'Forces Nouvelles'. The rioting units claimed that the government had not complied with its earlier promise to integrate former rebels into the national army. Two major political parties, the 'Parti Démocratique de Côte d'Ivoire – Rassemblement Dèmocratique Africain' and the 'Front Populaire Ivorien', remained divided internally.

In Guinea, Liberia and Sierra Leone, both civil society and the fragile political systems were shaken by an *Ebola* virus epidemic. Efforts to contain the virus brought public life to a virtual standstill and overshadowed other pressing political issues. In Liberia, the outbreak distracted attention from serious allegations that the Sirleaf government had been unable to contain corruption at all levels of the state and it was also in Liberia that the Ebola outbreak posed a serious security risk in the capital after several demonstrations turned violent. In late July, Sirleaf declared a state of emergency and deployed troops across the country in order to quarantine the areas where the virus was spreading. The Ebola outbreak demonstrated the dependency of all three countries on the willingness of the international community to come to their rescue. Unfortunately, *international help* came late and only after it had become clear that the outbreak had the potential to turn into a pandemic.

Brutal autocratic rule continued in Togo, Mauritania and the Gambia. In Togo, the upcoming presidential elections set for 2015 dominated the debate between government and opposition. In contradiction to its earlier commitments, the Togolese government failed to pass electoral reforms such as a two-term limit and a return to a two-round majority system. Although Togolese civil society and the international donor community stood united in favour of electoral reform, the government managed to postpone such reforms until after the 2015 elections.

In Mauritania, President Aziz was re-elected in June with 81.9% of the vote. The boycott of the parliamentary elections by most opposition parties in December 2013 had given his government a free reign in parliament. In November, the internationally known anti-slavery activist and presidential candidate Biram Ould Abeid was arrested after leading a peaceful protest against slavery in the south of the country. Although international media and the UN had urged Mauritania to fight slavery and its consequences more effectively, the government did little to heed that call.

In the Gambia, President Jammeh showed that, despite widespread dissatisfaction, his grip on the regime remained strong. His outbursts against homosexuals and Western donors continued to dominate official government discourse. Jammeh survived an alleged coup attempt in December and subsequently cracked down brutally on individuals who his government claimed had participated.

It should be noted that protest and opposition movements existed in all three of these remaining autocracies, perhaps most visibly in Togo, where the churches, civil society and the donor community managed to find common ground. Nevertheless, all three governments were clearly in control of domestic events throughout the year, and the human rights situation remained precarious across all three countries.

Two West African nations embarked on a *transition process*. After weeks of protest against his attempts to stay in office for an unconstitutional third term, Burkina Faso's long-term autocrat, Blaise Compaoré, was ousted by the military in late October. In early November, the Burkinabe military allowed a civilian-led democratic transition. Civil society, religious leaders, business associations, civilian politicians and members of the former governing party agreed on a transition charter. Michael Kafando, a retired diplomat with extensive international experience, was selected as transitional president. The transitional government, with a majority of civilian representatives, received a year-long mandate with responsibility for organising legislative and presidential elections before November 2015.

Guinea Bissau's transition process reached its next phase. The successful elections in April and May replaced the widely criticised 2012 post-coup transitional government. The international community declared the elections free and fair. Although the 'Partido para a Independência da Guiné e Cabo Verde' (PAIGC) had an absolute majority in parliament, it formed a government inclusive of all parties with parliamentary representatives. Former finance minister and businessman José Mário Paz (PAIGC) won the presidential elections with a decisive majority in the second round. The new government replaced the former general chief of staff and 'éminence grise', António Indijai, with Biague Nantam, who was believed to have a stronger commitment to democratic norms.

Socio-Economic Developments

According to the AfDB, West Africa's projected *growth rate* in 2014 was 7.4%, which made it the fastest growing sub-region on the continent, at 2% above the continental average. Economic performance varied by country, however. A closer analysis of the 2014 HDI for each country reveals that, with the notable exceptions of Ghana and Cabo Verde, all West African nations remained stuck at the bottom of the index. However, Ghana's economic performance gave rise to concern and called into question the ability of the Mahama administration to improve the macroeconomic situation. The 2014 budget indicated that inflation had escalated to 16.9%, while its revenues fell short of expectations. Ghana's public debt stood at a staggering 60% of GDP, an increase of 5% compared with the previous year. Erratic power supply on unprecedented scale contributed to the economic meltdown. Cabo Verde's economic growth also slowed. As a major tourist destination, it proved less resilient than anticipated in the face of the euro crisis.

After rebasing its nominal GDP in April, Nigeria emerged as the continent's biggest economy. This confirmed Nigeria's regional *economic hegemony* and its potential to become an increasingly important player on the global stage. Simultaneously, however, Nigeria remained unable to improve its energy infrastructure, despite the fact that the government had accelerated deregulation. Nigeria managed to swiftly contain the Ebola virus, which brought the country international recognition. Two other larger markets, Senegal and Côte d'Ivoire, saw encouraging signs of economic recovery. Senegal's growth rate was projected to be 4.5%, an increase of 1% compared with the previous year, and Côte d'Ivoire's growth rate was estimated to stand at 8.7% as its cocoa production increased by around one-third. The World Bank stated that Côte d'Ivoire was among the top ten economies in the world for drastic improvement in their business environment. Both Senegal and Côte d'Ivoire invested in their *infrastructure* by trying to improve nationwide access to electricity.

The economies of the four Sahel states, Mali, Niger, Mauritania and Burkina Faso, belong to the poorest in the world. In 2014, all four showed solid growth rates of between 4% and 6%. This was particularly positive for Mali, which in the two previous years had seen instability and large-scale conflict. In all four countries, *Chinese enterprises* were involved in large-scale infrastructure projects. Although all four had to prepare for a possible Ebola outbreak, only Mali reported two cases of infection and it was quickly able to contain the virus.

By contrast, in Guinea, Sierra Leone and Liberia, the *Ebola outbreak* brought the economies to a complete halt, eradicating whatever tiny socioeconomic progress these countries had achieved over the last decade. The Guinean government announced the Ebola outbreak on 22 March and the virus reached the capital, Conakry, only a few days later on 27 March. It rapidly spread to the two neighbouring countries. Rumours of a Western plot, or a conspiracy by the national governments to attract aid, local superstitions and beliefs in witchcraft greatly undermined the containment of the virus. Across the three countries, official figures put the number of *people infected* at 20,206, with 7,907 deaths reported by the end of the year. According to WHO, half the cases were in Sierra Leone, while half the deaths were in Liberia. Around 80% of flights to the Ebola-ravaged countries were cancelled and all borders remained closed for a considerable period of time. The mining sectors were particularly affected as the areas where mines were located were put under quarantine. In Liberia, the virus killed 80% of national healthcare workers. Although there is no comparable data for Sierra Leone or Guinea, it is beyond doubt that all three nations will have to rebuild their national health services. The

World Bank estimated the total economic loss caused by the outbreak in all three countries to be around $ 500 m. At the end of the year, the projected annual growth rate for Guinea stood at 0.5%, for Liberia at 1.8% and for Sierra Leone at 4%, all considerably lower than in previous years. By late December, infection rates had dropped in Liberia and Guinea, but Sierra Leone was still waiting for the epidemic to peak.

The smaller economies of Togo, Guinea-Bissau and Gambia experienced very different trajectories, although all three remained heavily dependent on IMF funding and donor goodwill. Of the three, Togo stood out as the most promising, with an estimated average GDP growth of 6%. The government initiated the expansion of the port of Lomé, one of its largest infrastructure projects in recent years. Questions remained, however, as to how sustainable such high public investment would be in the future. Guinea-Bissau's estimated annual growth rate of 2.7% was comparatively small. The World Bank paid the salaries of all teachers and healthcare workers from January to June and the whole of the public sector continued to be affected by strikes, which went on throughout the year. The Ebola outbreak forced Guinea-Bissau to close its border with Guinea between August and December. Gambia's estimated annual growth rate was negative (-0.7%), largely due to a 22% contraction in agricultural production. Probably unlike any other West African country, Gambia also remained dependent on trade with China, which accounted for 57% of its exports and 30% of its imports. The IMF claimed that Gambia had failed to reduce its budget level and its domestic borrowing as previously recommended. Despite government efforts to deter them, large numbers of Gambian youths left the country for Europe via North Africa.

Regional Cooperation and Foreign Affairs

Across all five of the major regional organisations in which West African states participate, ECOWAS, the Community of Sahel-Saharan States (CEN-SAD), the West African Monetary Union (WAMU), the Mano River Union (MRU), and the Liptako-Gourma Authority, there were attempts to either foster regional cooperation or to rejuvenate those groupings where cooperation had stalled.

In March, during the 44th ordinary meeting of *ECOWAS* heads and states in Yamoussoukro, the Ivorian political and administrative capital, Ghanaian President John Mahama was elected as the new head of ECOWAS, taking over from his Ivorian counterpart, Alassane Ouattara. In July and December, ECOWAS heads of state and government met for two additional ordinary sessions in Accra (Ghana) and Abuja (Nigeria). At the July meeting, the ECOWAS heads of state signed an *EPA* with the EU that provided ECOWAS members with continued free access to European markets, but forced them to open their markets to European goods over the course of the next 20 years. ECOWAS leaders agreed to sign, even though several powerful member states (including Nigeria) expressed doubts about the extent to which the EPA benefited African economies. The July meeting also abolished residence permits for ECOWAS nationals living in another member state; it was from then on sufficient for foreign ECOWAS citizens to produce a biometric identity card. The December summit extended the mandate of the ECOWAS mission in Guinea-Bissau (*ECOMIB*) for an additional six months. The ECOMIB mandate was to help the newly elected government of Guinea-Bissau to assert its authority. The mission had been established in 2012 with an original mandate to facilitate the return of Angolan soldiers and to organise free and fair elections. Since then, the mandate had changed several times.

On 6 November, ECOWAS heads of state and government met for an extraordinary summit in Accra to discuss the situation in Burkina Faso after Compaoré had been forced to resign. Prior to the summit, ECOWAS had sent the presidents of Senegal, Ghana and Nigeria to help mediate between Burkina's military and its civilian elites. The ECOWAS summit passed a declaration calling for a civilian to lead the *transition process*.

Between 19 May and 3 June, the third *ECOWAS parliament* held its first session. ECOWAS parliamentarians criticised the lack of compliance with past rulings of the ECOWAS Court of Justice, as several member states had still not ratified the protocol establishing the court. They further passed a resolution on the security situation in Nigeria, condemning terrorist violence by Boko Haram. The ECOWAS Court did not try any further cases.

CEN-SAD, whose major aim remained confined to the creation of a free trade area between its 29 member states, remained paralysed due to the internal security crisis in Libya. The organisation had long been associated with the deposed Libyan leader Muammar Kadhafi. The ratification of its revised 2013 community treaty remained a work in progress. The revised treaty foresaw the creation of a permanent peace and security council. By February 2014, only Togo had ratified it, but on 4–6 May Burkina Faso hosted a meeting of legal experts, who were in the process of *harmonising* all CEN-SAD legal documents.

On 20 October, *WAEMU* celebrated its 20th anniversary in Ouagadougou (Burkina Faso). Although WAEMU was arguably the most advanced regional organisation with regard to the establishment of a free trade area, a common currency union and the establishment of macro-economic convergence criteria, the IMF criticised the low prudential standards in the *banking sectors* of its eight member states; a significant number of banks were seriously underfunded.

The heads of state of the *MRU* (Côte d'Ivoire, Guinea, Liberia and Sierra Leone) met on 4 May in Conakry (Guinea) and called for greater cooperation between the MRU and ECOWAS. The meeting passed the annul budget of around $ 6 m and agreed to re-launch the regional airline Air Mano.

The otherwise dormant *Liptako-Gourma Authority* (Mali, Burkina Faso and Niger) organised a meeting for representatives of national border authorities in May in Ouagadougou, which discussed security risks on the borders of the three member states. Indeed, all West African states increased regional and/or bilateral cooperation on *border security* issues and on terrorism.

All countries of the region fostered trade relations with *China*. However, this did occur at the expense of long-standing relations with the EU, or with individual EU member states. All West African presidents participated in the US-Africa Leaders' Summit held in Washington, DC, in August.

As in previous years, Nigeria, Ghana, Senegal, Benin and Burkina Faso were the region's most diplomatically active countries. In June, Nigeria set up a joint intelligence response unit with the US, the UK and France to focus on *terrorist threats* in the West Africa region. Although Nigeria remained at the forefront of regional consultations on Islamist terrorism, its relationship with the US cooled significantly after Washington blocked the Nigerian purchase of US-made Chinook helicopters from Israel. The Americans cited human rights violations by the Nigerian army in northern Nigeria as the reason for this. Throughout the year, there were signs of growing American disenchantment with the manner in which the Jonathan administration dealt with the threat from Boko Haram. Benin developed into a major troop provider for *UN peacekeeping* missions. By the end of the year, Benin had deployed 1,261 troops (496 in the DRC, 421 in Côte d'Ivoire and 267 in Mali).

Senegal also kept a high profile in the region. President Sall headed the facilitation group on the negotiations between ECOWAS and the EU on the EPA. His government also increased Senegal's contingent in the *UN Multidimensional Integrated Stabilization Mission* (MINUSMA) in Mali to 800 troops. In November, Senegal ratified its border with Mali. In line with Senegal, Ghana promised the contribution of 850 troops to UN missions in South Sudan in January. Burkina Faso maintained one of the largest African military contributions to MINUSMA.

Benin, Mali, Niger, Burkina Faso and Mauritania remained heavily involved in various anti-terrorism initiatives. In February, Burkina Faso, Mali, Mauritania, Niger and Chad set up the *G5*, a loose organisation intended to better direct regional initiatives for development and security policies. In May, the G5 interior ministers met in Niamey (Niger) to intensify their cooperation in the fight against organised crime in the Sahel. Niger became the host of the G5 secretariat. In February and March, Niger hosted *Operation Flintlock*, a US-led annual military exercise in West Africa. In August, France began *Operation Barkhane*, a French-led anti-terrorist operation in the Sahel region. Operation Barkhane was the successor to Operation Serval in Mali and involved 3,000 French troops, of whom around one-third would be permanently based in Mali. French surveillance missions would be based in Niger and Burkina Faso. Their main purpose was to prevent all forms of trafficking and to crack down on violent jihadi forces in Mali, Chad (where the operation had its permanent headquarter) and Niger.

Benin

Alexander Stroh

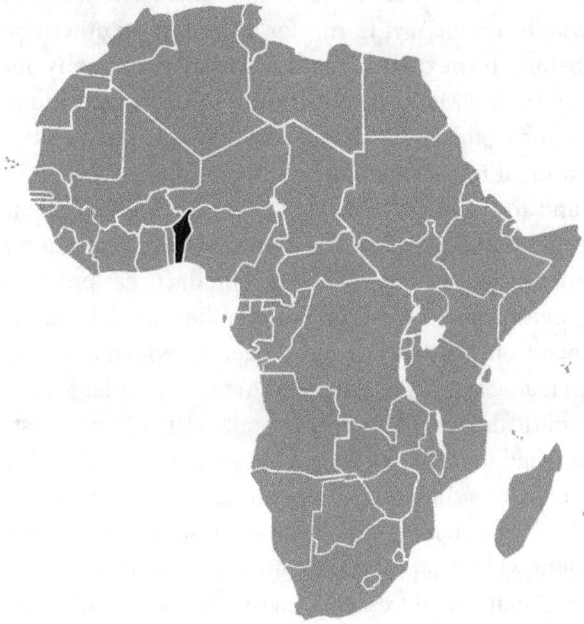

While most people in Benin were concerned about the rising cost of living, the political and societal elite continued to fight a war of words about the political intentions of incumbent President Yayi. Since his re-election in 2011, the opposition had assumed that his initiative to reform the country's constitution was aimed at permitting him another re-election despite Benin's two-term limit. Yayi constantly denied this in public. The third-term issue dominated the political debate and thus led to neglect of urgent socio-economic and security issues such as commodity production, port effectiveness and Boko Haram in neighbouring Nigeria.

Domestic Politics

In 2013, the parliamentary opposition had used its majority to defeat the budget in a secret ballot. The Constitutional Court declared the secrecy of the voting procedure used to be unconstitutional, but the National Assembly refused to acknowledge this judgement, much less to rectify the procedure. Because the 15 January judicial deadline for the correction of this procedural error failed to be met, President Thomas Boni Yayi was allowed to pass the *national budget* by presidential decree. This was a

 | DOI 10.1163/9789004305052_005

first indicator that the year would be full of political conflict and this, overall, led to the concessions forced upon the president outweighing the political gains he made.

As in previous years, the most important political controversy focussed on the question of whether the president was aiming to eliminate the *two-term limit* on presidential mandates, as laid down in Article of 42 of the Constitution. Only a constitutional amendment would permit Yayi to run for a third term; otherwise, he would have to step down before the next elections and, with parliamentary and presidential elections in April 2015 and March 2016 respectively, the constitutional amendment debate heated up during the year. Critics of the president claimed that the actual goal of his constitutional reform agenda was not to follow through on international commitments and to make the political system more efficient, but to circumvent Article 42. The fact that Yayi repeatedly denied any ambition to run for a third term – most prominently in his address on 31 July on the occasion of the national holiday – impressed neither the opposition nor members of civil society. Since its promulgation, the 1990 Constitution had never been amended and, over the decades, it had become an iconic symbol of democratic stability for large parts of the intelligentsia and the political elite, who were generally wary of any constitutional change. Yayi, however, had contributed to the increasing lack of trust in him. For example, municipal elections should have been held in 2013 but had not taken place and, because of the failure to revise the much-contested computerised electoral roll (LEPI), the elections were postponed until after 2014, even though the president had asserted in his national day address that they would take place by the end of the year.

On 21 July, Yayi appointed the new president of the 'Haute Autorité de l'Audiovisuel et la Communication' (HAAC) – a *media supervision* body with the capacity to sanction those who breached Benin's media regulations. Other members were appointed by various actors including media representatives. On 29 October, HAAC President Adam Boni Tessi – a former member of the presidential movement in parliament – released a statement in which he urged the media not to report negatively on the controversial process for the revision of the electoral roll in order to protect social peace. Journalists and civil society protested in large numbers against Tessi's interference with press freedom and immediately projected their anger on Yayi. On 4 December, Tessi publicly apologised for his behaviour.

In August, the first permanent board of the 'Commission Électorale Nationale Autonome' (CENA) was appointed. The *electoral commission* had previously been an ad hoc body; newly appointed for every election. On several occasions, the late appointment of the commission had led to organisational flaws that resulted from the lack of adequate preparation time. After a long debate about how to reform the commission, decision-makers finally agreed to create a permanent body with a five-year mandate. Alongside the Constitutional Court, which declares the final results and adjudicates in electoral disputes, the CENA is the most important actor in Beninese elections. Yayi appointed Emmanuel Tiando, a former minister and secretary-general of the presidential office, as head of the formally independent body. Like Tiando, two other members of the CENA board, Moïse Bossou and Geneviève Boko Nadjo, were also considered close to the president, while the remaining two members, Freddy Houngbédji and Basile Fassinou, were seen as politically independent. Some opposition forces thus alleged that the CENA board was biased in favour of the president. These accusations created even more suspicion of Yayi's political intentions, even though the new commission had not yet had the chance to prove its capacities and integrity.

In addition, criticism of the LEPI review process run by the 'Conseil d'Orientation et de Supervision' (COS-LEPI) continued. In November, demonstrations against financial and technical issues related to COS-LEPI coincided with political events in neighbouring Burkina Faso, where massive street protests eventually forced President Blaise Compaoré to step down. This gave the *protests* against COS-LEPI greater impetus. In response, the Yayi administration, after blocking financial resources for months, immediately released CFAfr 3.15 bn (approx. € 4.8 m) to COS-LEPI.

On 19 August, the Constitutional Court, one of Benin's most powerful and most active political players, reconfirmed and broadened its previous ruling on the two-term limit, stating that revision of the limit could not be part of a constitutional reform process because it belonged to the fundamental values set by the National Conference in 1990. According to earlier constitutional adjudication, it could not be altered unless a similarly broad consensus emerged. On 20 November, the court specified that, due to the initial weight of the National Conference's consensus, any amendment made by a state organ born of that consensus would be unable to create a '*new republic*' (francophone legal terminology denoting the start of a new constitution). A 'new republic' would thus imply that the old constitutional order was obsolete. The opposition feared that Yayi intended to use this legal trick to begin a 'new' republic, which, even if it inherited the same two-term limit, would entitle him to run for two further terms.

Two Constitutional Court decisions expressed the major concern of Benin's democratic elite about the vulnerability of public opinion to political manipulation. Paradoxically, in order to reaffirm the special protection of Article 42 and others that guaranteed regular democratic change in the highest executive office, the court substantially limited *freedom of speech*. In the first case, Minister of Agriculture Fatouma Amadou Djibril, speaking on Canal 3's popular talk show 'Zone Franche' on 20 July, had sympathised with the argument that the democratic rights of the people should include the right to decide how many terms the president should serve. In the second case, an ordinary citizen had published an open letter to the head of state in several newspapers, urging Yayi to run for a third term. The Constitutional Court ruled both public statements to be unconstitutional, thereby setting the institutional consensus of 1990 above individual democratic rights.

On 20 August, the day after the court's ruling on the minister of agriculture's public statement, Yayi sacked her and six other ministers. He had already, on 14 April, dismissed two senior government and police officials, also for political misconduct, but in relation to public sector strikes. The strikers had held the prefect and the police commissioner of Cotonou responsible for a violent crackdown on a union demonstration in late 2013. Among the ministers dismissed in August was Jonas Gbian, the brother of retired army general Robert Gbian (Général Gbian Robert, known as GGR). GGR was positioning himself as a presidential candidate for 2016. He had previously served as Yayi's chief military advisor but in December GGR aligned himself with Issa Salifou's opposition party the 'Union Pour la Relève' and politicians from Sacca Lafia's party, the 'Union pour la Démocratie et la Solidarité nationale', which had recently split from the presidential movement to establish the 'Alliance Soleil'. This electoral alliance was immediately blamed for perpetuating and deepening of the country's political north-south divide, as its leading members – including GGR – were 'northern' politicians. The *cabinet reshuffle* left long-standing Minister for Higher Education and Research François Abiola, Development Minister Marcel de Sousa (the president's brother-in-law) and Foreign Minister Nassirou Bako-Arifari as the new strongmen. All three were seen as potential successors to Yayi in the 2016 elections.

On 14 May, Yayi gave a *presidential pardon* to a group allegedly involved in an attempt to poison him and organise a coup in 2013. They included exiled businessmen Patrice Talon and Olivier Boko, as well as one of Yayi's nieces and his former personal doctor, who had both been on remand in Benin. Yayi was clearly attempting to pacify another long-standing political conflict. Talon was still a politically well-connected and wealthy actor who was expected to exert influence in the upcoming electoral contest and at the donors' round table that took place in Paris – Talon's place of exile – on 19–21 June. The Benin government was well aware that Western governments including France had been sceptical about the content and management of the 'Talon Affair'. Meanwhile, Talon, who denied the allegations, had expressed regret for the destabilising impact of the affair on his home country. The major consequences had been a slowdown in economic reforms that Talon's companies had advocated (port administration, cotton production) and a further deterioration in Yayi's relations with the opposition. The Cotonou Court of Appeal had dismissed the case against Talon in 2013, but the Supreme Court overruled this decision on 2 May on the grounds that it did not conform with legal procedure. The case remained pending till 1 August, when the Cotonou Court of Appeal confirmed its original decision. In October, local newspapers reported that Talon and Boko had met with difficulties in renewing their passports. The Talon Affair thus unveiled deep political controversies and mistrust.

Foreign Affairs

Benin's small size and heavy dependence on international cooperation meant that foreign policy continued to focus on donor and trade relations and stayed away from conflict-prone power politics. However, *regional security* challenges ranging from Boko Haram in Nigeria to pirates in the Gulf of Guinea and al-Qaida terrorism in Mali forced Benin to contribute to the response to these threats.

France remained Benin's most important international partner and this was evident in all relevant fields of cooperation, including close military relations. The French military trained soldiers and naval forces on numerous occasions over the year. Paris also urged the government in Cotonou to become more active in regional security affairs. President Yayi attended a high level summit on the fight against *jihadist terrorism* in the region on 17 May in Paris. In June, a follow-up summit took place in London, where the foreign ministers of Benin, Cameroon, Chad, Niger and Nigeria committed themselves to establishing a 'Regional Intelligence Fusion Unit' and joint military activities. The UK announced support for these regional intelligence efforts, although critics raised doubts about the effectiveness of the initiative after earlier efforts such as CEMOC (Regional Command for Joint Counter Terrorisms Operations based in Tamanrasset [Algeria]) had largely failed to function. On 13 October, shortly after another meeting in Niamey (Niger), the five African foreign ministers met again in Abuja (Nigeria) to discuss an appropriate legal framework for future joint security operations.

Benin contributed to eight UN *peacekeeping* missions and had deployed 1,261 troops by the end of the year, being particularly engaged in the DRC (496), Côte d'Ivoire (421) and Mali (267). Benin also contributed low-cost solutions to regional conflict resolution efforts. For example, at the request of ECOWAS, Benin granted political asylum to Michel Djotodia in January. Following François Bozizé who had arrived the previous year, Djotodia was the second former president of the CAR to have gained and lost power by unconstitutional means and been accepted by Benin. Even though Benin enjoyed a longstanding democratic reputation domestically, democratic norms were not driving its foreign policy agenda.

China's relations with Benin continued to gain importance in the course of the year. Two new aid agreements worth CFAfr 25.5 bn were signed, 16.7% of this sum being granted by China, and the rest provided in the form of a non-interest-bearing loan. In October, Chinese Ambassador Tao Weiguang inaugurated the Vocational Training College of Sino-Beninese Friendship in Akassato (around 30 km north of Cotonou). On 18 November, the two countries signed an agreement to strengthen bilateral cultural cooperation and, on 10 December, Ambassador Tao received the honours of a Commander of the National Order before leaving Cotonou after three years' service.

President Yayi received a number of foreign presidents throughout the year. During a visit on 20–21 February, President of the European Council Herman van

Rompuy laid the foundation stone of the information and coordination centre of the West African Power Pool, which was established to enhance regional cooperation in the energy sector. On 8 April, the presidents of Togo and Niger arrived in Cotonou to celebrate the start of construction of the Niamey-Cotonou-Lomé railway line. Other official visits included one by President Ernest Bai Koroma of Sierra Leone on 15–16 July, when the first mixed cooperation commission linking the two countries was set up.

Socioeconomic Developments

Political protests against President Yayi also affected the relationship between the government and organised labour. In January and February, *public sector strikes* affected the court system, public administration, schools and the health sector. The government played down the impact of the strikes and claimed that only a small proportion of the workforce had participated. The unions offered their own interpretation, well knowing that strikes in the education sector always had a high potential to create unrest. Eventually, the government took the strikes more seriously than originally reported. In early April, it raised the monthly minimum wage by over a quarter to CFAfr 40,000 (approx. € 61). It was a common government strategy to first imply that it would ignore the strikes and then suddenly to give in and make financial concessions.

On 8 May, the IMF published the staff report on its sixth review under the ECF, which expired in June. The report drew a generally positive picture of Benin's efforts, stating that all performance criteria had been met. It reported a recovery of growth rates at the sub-Saharan average level (somewhat above 5%) during the ECF programme period (2010–14). The level of public debt had stabilised at below 40% of GDP. Diplomatically phrased criticism pointed to the stagnation of tax revenues and problems in the cotton sector. The report urged the Benin government to enhance tax administration reform and to address the vulnerabilities of the banking sector. Concerning the cotton sector – the second largest GDP contributor after the port of Cotonou – the report mainly criticised the lack of management transparency, a criticism which also referred to the government's opaque conduct of the Talon Affair. Before the alleged poisoning, Talon had owned the largest production company in the cotton sector. He lost his market share to state-run enterprises after being accused of attempting to murder President Yayi and mastermind a coup.

The *cotton* sector was in trouble early in the year. Cotton ginners voiced their anger about the management of the season, which had seen production fall by half. The effectiveness of the cotton harvest was dependent on the quality of the management of the complex multiplayer process in which individual farmers, cotton ginners and marketing agencies needed to be coordinated. Optimistic estimates reported 70,000 tonnes of production volume in mid-February, with the harvest season usually ending in March. Surprisingly though, the government's minimal target of 300,000 tonnes was exceeded by 6,000 tonnes, a 30% increase on the previous season. However, local experts argued that the goal was attained at a high cost. The government had ordered 3,000 security personnel to assist the cotton harvest and had heavily subsidised fertilizers, pesticides and prices.

On 17–19 June, a *fund-raising* conference on Benin's development from 2014 to 2018 took place in Paris. The government met with state donors and foreign private investors but the domestic employers association, the 'Conseil National du Patronat du Bénin', boycotted the conference, voicing concerns about the government's lack of respect for contractual obligations and the rule of law. The conference nevertheless managed to secure donor and investment pledges worth CFAfr 5.6 trillion (about € 8.5 bn). Although this was roughly double what the government had expected, it failed to cover the CFAfr 8 trillion estimated costs of Benin's ambitious public investment programme, and no donor or investor in Paris made definite funding commitments. The conference identified the transport and energy sectors as two top priority areas for funding, in line with the IMF's recommendations for a medium-term strategy. The priority planning in the energy sector envisaged a tenfold increase in electricity production from the current 200 MW to 2 GW. Plans in the transport sector included work on all major traffic routes.

In early April, Yayi and President Mahamadou Issoufou of Niger launched the construction of the Niamey-Cotonou *freight railway*. The project was in line with the IMF's recommendation to raise more money via public private partnerships. The project was run by a multinational company in which Benin and Niger each held a 10% share while the private sectors of both countries held 20%. French-owned Bolloré Africa Logistics invested in the remaining 40% and was responsible for managing the project. According to the UN's 'Africa Renewal' news platform, experts estimated the cost of the Niamey-Cotonou line at $ 1.6 bn. It was envisaged that the railway would boost trade by providing improved access to ports on the Atlantic coast. The project was part of an ambitious plan to construct a full West African railway loop by connecting Niamey to Abidjan (Côte d'Ivoire) via Ouagadougou (Burkina Faso) and finally closing the loop along the coastline. While Benin's biggest public private partnership in the transport sector started with construction between Niamey and Dosso in Niger, engineering work in Benin was scheduled to start in 2015.

Following years of severe *flooding*, which affected housing and agriculture, Benin secured an agreement with the World Bank on 5 June for CFAfr 25 bn in new funding to extend a flood defence project in urban areas of the south; it was ratified by parliament on 17 November. In September, heavy rainfall destroyed about 100 houses the northern village of Boko (near Parakou), reminding the government that the ongoing establishment of early warning systems needed to be accelerated.

Burkina Faso

Daniel Eizenga

The defining moment of 2014 in Burkina Faso was, without doubt, the end of the 27-year rule of former president Blaise Compaoré. The demise of the Compaoré regime occurred after months of opposition and civil society demonstrations against the government, and particularly against attempts to change Article 37 of the Constitution to allow Compaoré to stand in the presidential elections scheduled for 2015. A popular insurrection prevented the National Assembly from voting on a proposed modification to presidential term limits and forced Compaoré to resign from office on 31 October. After the fall of the Compaoré regime, some international actors threatened sanctions. Burkina Faso also increased its commitment to regional counter-terrorism operations by joining new regional organisations and military operations. Burkina's economic growth slowed due its reliance on the mining sector, while the cotton sector experienced a robust harvest for the second year in a row. Optimistic forecasts and government planning for potential risks in this volatile sector offered encouraging signs for future economic development.

 | DOI 10.1163/9789004305052_006

Domestic Politics

Domestic politics in 2014 revolved around the modification of *Article 37*, which stipulates that the president may serve a maximum of two five-year terms. On 4 January, 75 of around 400 national members of the presidential party, 'Congrès pour la Démocratie et le Progrès' (CDP), *resigned*, among them three key figures: Roch Marc Christian Kaboré, a former prime minister and president of the CDP, Salif Diallo, former political advisor to Compaoré and his close political ally until a falling-out in 2008, and Simon Compaoré (no relation to the president), former mayor of the capital, Ouagadougou. The resignation letter explicitly rejected the party's plans to amend Article 37 and criticised the CDP's lack of internal democratic procedures.

On 18 January, the *political opposition*, led by Zéphirin Diabré the president of the 'Union pour le Progrès et le Changement', organised peaceful *demonstrations* across the country in protest against Compaoré's efforts to remain in power and calling for the retention of Article 37. The event drew tens of thousands of participants in Ouagadougou, Bobo Dioulasso, Koudougou, Fada N'Gourma, Dédougou and Kaya. After participating in these protests, former members of the CDP created the opposition party, the 'Mouvement du Peuple pour le Progrès'. The party had 117 members, all of whom were former CDP national party members. Kaboré was named the president, Diallo first vice president, and Simon Compaoré second vice president.

Political parties were not the only organisations to engage in *civil disobedience*. *Unions* mobilised their members against the government, organising protests, strikes, and sit-ins. On 4 February, 33 public sector unions formed an alliance called 'Unité d'Action', and launched a coordinated 48-hour strike throughout the country. The unions' primary grievances concerned a simplification of the benefits system, which the government had agreed to adopt by July 2013, but which had not yet been implemented. On 14 February, the 'Syndicat des Travailleurs de la Commune de Ouagadougou' held a march, and in May staged a series of random sit-ins, against the government's failure to meet promised salary increases. On 19–20 May, the 'Syndicat National des Agents des Ministère de l'Industrie, du Commerce, et de l'Artisanal' staged sit-ins in front of the ministry in Ouagadougou and its regional offices over frustrations that had been unaddressed since 2011. A sit-in led by the 'Syndicat National des Agents des Finances' took place on 12, 13 and 14 June because Minister of Finance Lucien Marie Noël Bembamba had failed to adopt a series of benefits decreed by Prime Minister Luc-Adolphe Tiao in 2012. The union of clerks of court held a five-day strike from 9 to 13 June after the Ministry of Justice failed to respond to a 72-hour sit-in in February and a 72-hour strike in May. These mobilisations focused on the inability of Minister of Justice Dramane Yaméogo to adopt a standardised protocol specifying the responsibilities attached to the clerks various positions.

The level of union activity in 2014 was notably higher than in recent years, when the government had attempted to compromise with the unions. The failure of the government to implement its promises aggravated the already delicate political situation in which the Compaoré regime had found itself. In this atmosphere of political dissatisfaction, violent acts of civil disobedience occurred even outside the capital in the months leading up to the popular insurrection that ended the Compaoré regime.

On 30 July, the police department in Houndé, 250 km south-west of Ouagadougou in Tuy province (Hauts-Bassins region) was burned to the ground. Two girls had been accused in suspicious circumstances of the attempted kidnapping of two young boys and sent to the provincial police headquarters for questioning. This event triggered public outrage and protests against Houndé's security forces. According to the regional section of the 'Movement Burkinabè des Droits de l'Homme et des Peuples' based in Houndé, the demonstrations were the result of *dissatisfaction with the justice system* because of a series of mishandled cases, and the abuse of human rights. State forces arrived and repressed the demonstrators after the burning of the police department. Twelve out of the 30 people accused of the deliberate destruction of public property and illegal protest were found guilty and sentenced to up to 12 months in prison.

In Djibo, more than 200 km north of Ouagadougou in Soum province (Sahel region), *youth associations* mobilised against the failure of the government to repair the road between Djibo and Ouagadougou. On 1 September, they held a sit-in at the High Commission, during which their leaders presented renewed demands for the road to be repaired. Failing to receive a plan for immediate action from local authorities, the associations decided on 2 September to block the roads that gave access to the town. Several hundred people used their bodies and a variety of debris to create a blockade at the town's entry points. The blockade was planned for a period of three days along with a *public march* and the closure of all shops on 3 September. The governor of Sahel region, Boureima Yiougo, arrived the same day to resolve the situation. The associations asked him to hold a public meeting in the town square, but he refused and broadcasted a radio appeal to the public. During the night of 3 September, elements of the 'Compagnie Républicaine de Sécurité' (CRS) were deployed from the surrounding area to re-establish order. The CRS launched an assault on the demonstrators, using tear gas to disperse the crowd from the blockade on the morning of 4 September. Several protesters returned to the centre of Djibo and committed acts of vandalism throughout the town. The protesters were violently repressed by the CRS, restoring relative calm but leaving one dead and five seriously injured. These events in Houndé and Djibo underscored the disenchantment of Burkinabé with their government, but it also demonstrated the continued willingness of the regime to *repress* acts of *civil disobedience*.

Events organised and led by the political opposition and other civil society organisations in the capital proved more difficult to stamp out. On 23 August, opposition leaders organised a public demonstration against the *modification of presidential term limits*, which they claimed involved over 100,000 in Ouagadougou. The demonstrators marched for 8 km without any violent encounters with police or military and no damage to property was reported. Subsequently, a period of relative calm took hold in Ouagadougou as a number of civil society and religious leaders endeavoured to use negotiations to resolve tensions between the presidential majority and the opposition. These mediated negotiations failed, however, when the legislative group of the CDP proposed that *Article 37* be amended by passing a bill of law in the National Assembly.

On 21 October, a cabinet meeting was held to discuss the possible modification of presidential term limits. During this meeting, the government decided that, rather than holding a public *referendum*, a bill would be put to the floor of the National Assembly to modify the term limits. If the bill received a simple majority, it would then proceed to a public referendum – a guaranteed outcome since the CDP alone held 70 of the 127 seats at the National Assembly. If the bill received three-quarters of the votes, however, it would pass without a referendum. The law was scheduled to be voted upon on 30 October. Three parties were expected to support the bill: the CDP, the 'Convention des Forces Démocratiques', and the 'Alliance pour la Démocratie et la Fédération – Rassemblement Démocratique Africain' (ADF-RDA). The ADF-RDA was crucial to the vote because it took the presidential majority above the three-quarters threshold, thereby avoiding the need for a referendum.

The decision to propose the bill ignited public outrage. The government closed all schools on 23 October to deter student protests on campuses. On 28–29 October, much of the population of Ouagadougou camped out in public places such as La Maison du Peuple, La Place de la Nation, and the UN Round Point. Crowds blocking streets were consistently dispersed by heavily armed security forces. On the morning of 30 October, crowds descended upon the National Assembly to prevent representatives from voting on the bill in what was later called a *popular insurrection*. The protesters overwhelmed security forces breaking into the National Assembly and setting it on fire. The crowds later looted and burned the Ministry of Communication, the CDP party headquarters, and several private residences of government officials and Compaoré family members.

While many buildings were being looted and burned, several demonstrators were led by retired General Kwamé Lougué towards the presidential palace. The 'Régiment de Sécurité Présidentielle' (RSP), considered an elite force within the military, prevented protesters from reaching the presidential palace. Under the supervision of General Gilbert Diendéré, head of the RSP, Lougué headed a delegation of protesters to a meeting with President Compaoré. Afterwards, Compaoré announced on national radio an 'état de siège' throughout the country and declared the beginning of negotiations with the political opposition. He also officially cancelled the proposed modification of presidential term limits and dissolved the government. These dramatic efforts did not return Ouagadougou to calm but rather incited protesters to continue their *calls for the president's resignation*.

On the morning of 31 October, protesters demanded a *meeting with the heads of the military* at their headquarters in Ouagadougou. The crowd remained united by a single goal – the resignation of Blaise Compaoré. Leaders of the demonstration, Professors Augustin Loada and Luc Marius Ibriga of the 'Front de Résistance Citoyen', Hervé Ouattara of 'Collectif Anti-Referendum', Sams'K la Jah, Smockey and, and Guy Hervé Kam of 'Balai Citoyen', and Casimir Sawadogo of 'Réseau d'Action pour la Démocratie', were invited to discuss the situation with the heads of the security forces. Present for the discussion were both General Honoré Traoré, military chief of staff, and Lieutenant Colonel Issac Zida, the deputy head of the RSP and official spokesperson of the military to the demonstrators.

After hours of discussion, the leaders returned to the crowd and Zida announced *Compaoré's resignation*. Confusion quickly mounted over who was the *interim head of state*. Traoré declared himself interim president to the international community, but later that afternoon Zida announced the suspension of the Constitution and that he was interim head of state. The following day, a letter, signed by Traoré, declared Zida interim president with the unanimous support of the security forces. By this time, Compaoré had already fled the country with a convoy led by a contingent of the RSP. He eventually reached Côte d'Ivoire with the alleged support of Ivorian and Western military forces.

During the popular insurrection of 30–31 October, more than 20 persons were killed by bullets and tear gas, and over 200 individuals were injured. Demonstrations, looting, and general civil disobedience in protest against the proposed bill were strongest in Ouagadougou, but similar events took place throughout the country, including in Bobo Dioulasso, Zinairé the hometown of former president Compaoré, Ouahigouya, Tenkodogo, Léo, and Dédougou. The events of these two days represented the most wide-scale, coordinated and effective protests that Burkina Faso had experienced in recent history.

On 2 November, thousands led by Zéphirin Diabré again assembled in Ouagadougou's Place de la Nation, urging the military to allow a *civilian-led democratic transition*. Zida began negotiations with the opposition on 3 November and discussed the transition with representatives of the former presidential majority, religious leaders, trade unions and business associations. On 4 November, Zida affirmed that he had no intention of remaining in power any longer than was necessary to establish a *transitional government*. By the end of 5 November, the broad aims of the transition were agreed upon between the military, the political opposition and civil society. Opposition party leaders, civil society representatives and military officers agreed on the details of a year-long transitional government on 13 November.

The agreed *Transition Charter* stipulated that the transition be led by a civilian president with a 25-member cabinet and a legislative body known as the 'Conseil National de la Transition' (CNT). After hours of closed-door consultations between Zida, opposition leaders and civil society representatives, Michel Kafando, a retired diplomat with extensive international experience as a former foreign minister and ambassador to the UN, was selected as *transitional president* and inaugurated on 18 November. Kafando's nomination was put forward by the military in the presidential selection process and he in turn nominated Zida to be prime minister on 19 November. The 90-member CNT was designed to maintain a civilian majority of representatives. The charter provided 30 seats for former opposition parties, 25 for the military, 25 for civil society organisations, and 10 for former parties of the presidential majority. On 27 November, Cherrif Sy, the founder of an independent weekly newspaper, 'Bendré', and head of the national editors' association, won a three-cornered internal election for the presidency of the CNT with 71 votes. The transitional government received a year-long mandate with responsibility for organising legislative and presidential elections before November 2015.

Foreign Affairs

Burkina Faso increased its *military cooperation* with regional and Western countries, especially France. It maintained one of the largest military contributions to the *UN peacekeeping mission*, 'Mission Multidimensionelle Intégrée des Nations Unies pour la Stabilisation au Mali' (MINSUMA), in neighbouring Mali. In mid-February, five Sahelian countries (Burkina Faso, Chad, Mali, Mauritania and Niger) agreed to set up a regional security and development organisation, '*G5 du Sahel*', based in Nouakchott (Mauritania), with the aim of better directing regional initiatives to combat poverty and support development. These goals are also part of the wider *counter-terrorism* objective to reduce the influence of armed groups in the Sahel.

Similar objectives to prevent terrorist expansion in the Sahel contributed to the creation of a new military operation, Operation Barkhane, led by *France*. The ongoing operation, with headquarters in N'Djamena (Chad) and a Special Forces division stationed in Ouagadougou, involves the deployment of roughly 3,000 French military personnel, six fighter jets, 20 helicopters and three drones in six Sahelian countries (Burkina Faso, Chad, Mali, Mauritania, and Niger). This increased military cooperation with France came after the US and French military established intelligence and logistics bases in Ouagadougou during Operation Serval, the 2013 French military intervention in Mali.

Given the close cooperation between the Compaoré regime and Western counter-terrorism operations, some observers were surprised by statements made by the US ambassador to Burkina Faso, Tulinabo Mushingi, following the massive social demonstrations against the modification of presidential term limits. He expressed the *US government's apprehension* over the increasing political tensions prior to the popular insurrection that forced Compaoré's resignation. Mushingi stressed that democracy is reinforced through strong institutions only when the government 'respects the constitutional process'. His statements were welcomed by the political opposition in Burkina Faso as an unusually direct criticism of the Compaoré regime.

Following the popular insurrection, *international organisations and donor countries*, including the UN, the AU, ECOWAS, the US, France and others expressed doubts over whether Colonel Zida would hand power over to a civilian government. The AU insisted he do so by mid-November or face *sanctions*. ECOWAS sent the presidents of Senegal, Ghana and Nigeria to help mediate negotiations between the military and civilian leaders. At least one donor country, Canada, sanctioned Burkina Faso by suspending economic assistance. Nevertheless, as the transition talks advanced, international pressure abated. When acting AU President Mohamed Ould Abdel Aziz of Mauritania visited on 10 November, he said that he was not there to sanction the country, and the US ambassador also said that it was too soon to speak of sanctions. The implementation of a transitional government with a majority of civilian representatives ensured that Burkina Faso avoided major sanctions.

Socioeconomic Developments

Burkina Faso remained one of the least developed countries in the world. Its HDI rose marginally from 183rd in 2013 to 181st out of 187 countries. Real *GDP growth* slowed with the Economist Intelligence Unit estimating it to be 5.2%, more than a full percentage point lower than in 2013. The 2014 MDG report acknowledged, in an assessment of performance based on effort, that Burkina Faso had achieved a higher level of acceleration than any other African country participating in the MDGs, but went on to note that, despite this remarkable *progress*, it remained highly unlikely that Burkina Faso would attain the *MDGs* by 2015.

The Compaoré government had drafted a new mining code, which, among other measures, aimed to increase revenue from the *mining sector* by reducing tax exemptions and advantages and setting a 20% capital gains tax on transfers of mining titles. However, given the depressed gold prices, the government decided to delay its implementation in order to avoid further stress on the sector, which is Burkina's largest export sector. *Gold* prices fell from $ 1,700/oz in 2012 to $ 1,300/oz at February 2014. Many mining companies also experienced production setbacks during the first half of the year, including Endeavour Mining, Avocet Mining and Amara Mining, which ceased operations at the Kalsaka/Sega mine. However, other companies experienced increased production and the general forecast for gold in Burkina Faso remained positive throughout the year. Gold generated around 20% of fiscal revenue and three-quarters of total *export earnings*.

Given the continued deterioration of gold prices and the resultant negative trend in Burkina Faso's export performance, the government began pursuing projects aimed at *diversifying the country's economy*. One such effort was the granting of a licence to Pan African Minerals for the Tambao manganese mine in northern

Burkina Faso. The government hoped this development might offset losses due to the February suspension of open-pit mining operations at the Perkoa zinc mine. The Transitional Government promised a full-scale audit of the mining sector in 2015, which alleviated anxiety for mining companies. Regardless of the recent negative trend in export performance due to the falling price of gold, and the planned audit of the sector, the robust performance of the cotton sector caused economic forecasters to predict moderate growth for 2015.

Cotton production recorded robust *growth* with 766,000 tonnes of raw seed cotton, surpassing the target of 730,000 tonnes set by the 'Union Nationale des Producteurs de Coton du Burkina' (UNPCB). In a parliamentary address in April, Prime Minister Tiao remarked that the country had experienced abundant harvests of both cereals and cotton, with cotton production increasing by 26%. Growth in the cotton sector was attributed to the utilisation of genetically modified cotton. The 'Association Interprofessionnelle du Coton du Burkina' (AICB), which includes the UNPCB, the three cotton marketing companies and the government, set a target of 800,000 tonnes for the 2014–15 season. Some forecasters feared that cotton production might decline due to a slight reduction (from $ 0.47 per kg to $ 0.45 per kg) in the minimum purchase price for the forthcoming season, but the government agreed to subsidise the cost of fertilizer and the AICB authorised a $ 0.02 per kg bonus for all cotton farmers due to recent growth in the sector.

In July, a deal was signed between the Burkinabè government and the Canadian company, Windiga Energy, to construct a *solar power* station in Zina, 200 km north of the capital. With Burkina Faso's reliance on thermal power to meet its energy needs, investing in the solar sector was expected to dramatically improve the country's electricity grid. A large-scale project to rehabilitate the road from Lomé (Togo) to Ouagadougou commenced on 23 October. The projected consequent increase in *trade flows* would benefit both countries, since Burkina Faso already contributed over 37% of transit volume at the port in Lomé.

The annual march in remembrance of *Norbert Zongo*, an investigative journalist found killed alongside three colleagues in mysterious circumstances, took place on 13 December, after the African Court on Human and People's Rights, based in Tanzania, issued a ruling on 28 March that was highly critical of the Burkinabè authorities' investigative and judicial handling of his assassination in 1998. The commemorative march brought together tens of thousands of demonstrators in the 'Place de la Nation', where transitional Prime Minister Zida promised that the Zongo case would be reopened in 2015 and justice would be done for the crimes of the Compaoré regime.

Cabo Verde

Gerhard Seibert

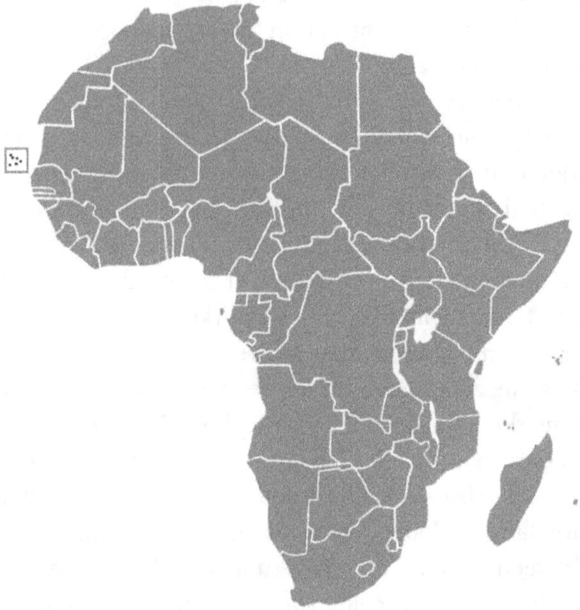

In March, the central bank reduced the principal interest rates in an attempt to halt the downward trend of economic growth. The number of tourists dropped by 2.6%, though this was partly compensated for by only a 0.6% reduction in nights spent by the visitors. Following strong protests against the nomination of a former minister as the new governor of the central bank, in November, Prime Minister José Maria Neves gave in and appointed another candidate. In mid-December, the 36-year old Janira Hopffer Almada, minister of youth, employment and human resources development, achieved a convincing victory in the direct elections of the ruling 'Partido Africano da Independência de Cabo Verde' (PAICV) and succeeded Neves as party leader.

Domestic Politics

In response to a call of the 'União Nacional dos Trabalhadores de Cabo Verde – Central Sindical' (UNTC-CS), one of the country's two trade union federations, on 20 January, thousands of *people demonstrated against the government's labour policies*, rising unemployment, scheduled changes to labour regulations and low wages.

 | DOI 10.1163/9789004305052_007

In addition, the UNTC-CS demanded that the 'Plano de Cargos, Carreiras e Salários', a career development programme for employees in public administration, should also be applied to the private sector. Before the demonstrations, on 10 January, Prime Minister Neves had held talks with trade union leaders Júlio Ascenção Silva (UNTC-CS) and José Manuel Vaz of the 'Confederação Cabo-verdiana dos Sindicatos Livres' (CCSL) in an attempt to prevent the protests, but the negotiations failed. The unions threatened further demonstrations and announced a general strike for 29–30 April. On 28 April, however, CCSL leader Vaz postponed the general strike, as many union members had allegedly been intimidated and persecuted by employers and members of the government. UNTC-CS leader Silva, in turn, blamed Vaz for the postponement and accused him of corruption.

On 19 September, *Prime Minister Neves reshuffled his cabinet.* Huberto Brito was replaced as minister of tourism, industry and energy by Leonesa Fortes, hitherto director of the 'Instituto Nacional da Previdência Social'. At the same time, the ministry was renamed as the Ministry of Tourism, Investments and Business Development. Minister of Defence Jorge Tolentino succeeded Jorge Borges as foreign minister, while the minister of parliamentary affairs, Rui Semedo, added the defence portfolio to his responsibilities. Minister of Marine Resources Adalberto Vieira was dismissed and his portfolio was taken over by Sara Lopes, till then the minister of infrastructure and maritime economy. Démis Lobo was appointed minister of the Presidency, the Council of Ministers and media. Maria de Jesus Mascarenhas, hitherto ambassador in Brussels, became secretary of state for foreign affairs and Esana Carvalho became deputy secretary of state for finance and planning. The parliamentary leader of the opposition 'Movimento para a Democracia' (MpD), Fernando Elísio Freire, criticised the reshuffle as a mere redistribution exercise. All the ministers who had lost their positions were appointed to new jobs in public administration. The new ministers had already served in previous PAICV governments.

The nomination of Humberto Brito, hitherto minister of tourism, industry and energy, as the *new governor of the central bank* on 29 September provoked fierce criticism from the MpD, which argued that, under existing legislation, former members of government were barred from taking up positions in regulatory bodies for two years. In addition, MpD leader Ulisses Correia e Silva argued that the new central bank governor should be politically independent. Neves initially argued that the central bank was not a regulatory agency, but was in charge of monetary policy. In addition, he gave a reminder that both the outgoing governor, Carlos Burgo, and his predecessor, Olavo Correia, had been government ministers before their appointment. However, on 11 November, Neves, gave in and nominated João Serra, a former finance minister and former president of the 'Sociedade de Desenvolvimento Turístico Integrado da Boa Vista e do Maio', as central bank governor. The prime minister now argued that the question of incompatibility had divided the legal community. On 24 November, the attorney-general ('Procuradoria da República') confirmed the legality of the government's initial position: Brito's nomination had been legal as the central bank was not considered a regulatory agency.

On 14 December, 36-year-old Janira Hopffer Almada, the minister of youth, employment and human resources development, succeeded José Maria Neves as PAICV leader. She won *the ruling party's leadership election* with 51.2% of the votes. Voter turn-out was less than 50% of the 29,300 registered members. Hopffer Almada, daughter of the prominent lawyer, David Hopffer Almada, a former minister of justice, became the fourth leader of the PAICV after Aristides Pereira (1981–90), Pedro Pires (1990–2000), and José Maria Neves (2000–14). Her victory meant that she would be the party's candidate for the premiership in the 2016 legislative elections. José Maria Neves, in power since 2001, had already announced that he would not run for a fourth term. Hopffer Almada promised to strengthen the party and address the country's economic problems in order to win the legislative elections. Felisberto Vieira (Filú), parliamentary leader of the PAICV, came second with 40.3% of the vote, and Cristina Fontes Lima, the health minister, came third with 8.5%. In response to her defeat, Fontes Lima resigned from her ministerial post on 17 December, followed five days later by Foreign Minister Jorge Tolentino, who had been the representative ('mandatário') of Fontes Lima's candidature.

Foreign Affairs

On 14 February, *EU Commissioner for Development* Andris Piebalgs declared on an official visit that the EU would provide technical support for the development of renewable energy in order to contribute to the government's objective of producing 50% of Cabo Verde's electricity from renewable sources by 2020. He also pledged a development package of € 55 m for the period 2014–20. Piebalgs was received by President Fonseca and Prime Minister Neves, with whom he discussed the 4th EU-Africa Summit and Cabo Verde's special partnership with the EU.

On 17 February, Finance and Planning Minister Cristina Duarte paid a three-day visit to Luanda (Angola), where she was assured of *Angolan budgetary support* to the tune of € 10 m to finance infrastructure projects on the archipelago. Duarte also called on Angola's business community to increase their private investments in Cabo Verde. On 5 June, Neves also visited Luanda, where he was received by President Eduardo dos Santos. Neves and his delegation expressed their strong interest in the participation of Angolan investors in the privatisation of the Cabo Verdean state-owned companies Transportadora Aérea Cabo-verdiana (TACV), Electra – Empresa de Electricidade e Água, and Empresa Nacional de Administração dos Portos (ENAPOR).

On 5 March, *Senegal's President Macky Sall* arrived for an official visit and was warmly welcomed at Praia's Nelson Mandela Airport by hundreds of Senegalese immigrants. He held talks on bilateral cooperation and questions concerning a number of regional issues with Neves and Fonseca. Mall and Fonseca exchanged national honours medals – Cabo Verde's Amílcar Cabral Order and Senegal's Lion Order. Sall also received the keys to the city of Praia from Mayor Ulisses Correia e Silva during a solemn session of the municipal assembly. He addressed the National Assembly and expressed his hopes for the consolidation of diplomatic relations between the two countries. He stated that regional integration within ECOWAS would bring many challenges, which both countries could overcome together.

On 28 March, Neves participated in the 44th ordinary session of the *ECOWAS* heads of states and government meeting in Yamoussoukro (Cotê d'Ivoire). In his address, he stressed the particular nature of Cabo Verde's integration into the community, given its status as an island. Neves then paid a two-day visit to Abidjan (Côte d'Ivoire), where he signed four agreements on bilateral cooperation, covering investment and maritime and air transport. On 2–3 April, Fonseca represented his country at the *4th EU-Africa Summit* in Brussels (Belgium), which was attended by 60 European and African leaders. The aim of the conference was to strengthen economic and political cooperation between the two continents. During the summit, Fonseca held bilateral meetings with the president of the European Commission, Durão Barroso, the presidents of Senegal and Seychelles, Macky Sall and James Michel, and Spanish Prime Minister Mariano Rajoy.

On 16 June, Fonseca began a four-day official visit to the *Seychelles* to participate in the commemoration of the 38th anniversary of Independence in Victoria. Fonseca, whose delegation included Minister of Tourism, Industry and Energy Humberto Brito and the mayor of Praia, Correia e Silva, was received by his counterpart Michel. He also addressed the national parliament in Victoria. The two heads of state stressed the geographic, cultural and structural commonalities of the two Creole island nations and various bilateral cooperation agreements covering tourism, fishing and renewable energy were signed.

Local *Cabo Verdean tourism investors* visited the Seychelles together with the presidential delegation to learn from the experience of their counterparts in the Indian Ocean archipelago. The mission was organised by the Ministries of Finance and Planning, and Tourism, Industry and Energy and was financed by the World Bank. The visit resulted in a series of recommendations, including a call for institutional reform of the tourism sector with clearly defined competences for each unit, the creation of a mechanism for effective participation in tourism development by the private sector, the establishment of mechanisms to provide access to finance for private investment in the sector, the development of a programme of sustainable tourism management, and a study on the applicability of the Seychelles Secret brand, which groups together small high-quality holiday properties in Cabo Verde.

On 4–6 August, Fonseca participated in the *US-Africa Leaders Summit* in Washington DC. In a communiqué on the eve of the event, he referred to the longstanding ties between the two countries: Cabo Verdeans had first settled in the US during in the early 19th century. He stressed his country's desire to strengthen bilateral relations with the US in maritime security and other sectors of mutual interest.

On 25 September, and on behalf of seven countries, Cabo Verde formally submitted a request for the *extension of the continental platform* beyond the existing 200 miles to the UN Division of Ocean Affairs and the Law of the Sea. The process was a regional initiative and included Gambia, Guinea-Bissau, Guinea-Conakry, Mauretania, Senegal and Sierra Leone. It had started in 2009 and was coordinated by Cabo Verde. Norway provided technical support.

Socioeconomic Developments

The national airline TACV continued its *financial restructuring process* initiated in 2013. On 14 February, TACV returned the 174-seat Boeing 737–800 leased in August 2012 to International Lease Financing Corporation, claiming that it lacked sufficient customers for three Boeing planes. It was expected that this would save the company around $ 5 m per year. On 8 May, the government separated handling and ground services off from TACV and established a new company, Cabo Verde Handling, with a stock capital of CVE (escudos) 188 m, as full a subsidiary of TACV. On 31 October, TACV sold two of its three ATR 72 planes in an attempt to further reduce its debts. This cut the company's fleet to one Boeing 757 and one Boeing 737–800 for international flights and one ATR 72 for domestic flights. The reorganisation of TACV was aimed at reducing its debts to enable the airline's privatisation, which had been announced since 2002, but had failed because of its financial problems. In early November, Minister of Infrastructure and Maritime Economy Sara Lopes announced that the privatisation of both TACV and the port authority ENAPOR would take place by mid-2015.

On 1 March, the *central bank, 'Banco de Cabo Verde'* (BCV), reduced three of its principal interest rates in an attempt to stimulate economic growth. The policy rate was cut from 5.75% to 4.25%, the standing lending facility from 8.75% to 7.25%, and the rediscount rate from 9.75% to 8.25%. The lower interest rates were expected to bring down the lending rates of commercial banks and to make cheaper credit available to the private sector. Critics argued that these steps were insufficient to accelerate economic growth if they were not accompanied by other structural measures to boost local consumption. On 30 December, the BCV announced that in January 2015 it would bring into circulation new banknotes in denominations of CVE 200, CVE 500, CVE 1,000, CVE 2,000 and CVE 5,000. The new CVE 2,000 and CVE 5,000 notes would depict the singer Cesária Évora (1941–2011) and Cabo Verde's first president, Aristides Pereira (1923–2011).

On 6 June, Prime Minister Neves laid the foundation stone of *Cabo Verde's first Hilton Hotel,* located in Santa Maria, Sal Island. The investment of € 46 m was jointly financed by Batuque SA (60%), a local subsidiary of the Hilton Group, and a consortium of five local banks (40%). The local company Sociedade de Construções was chosen by the investors to construct the five-star 240-bed hotel, including three restaurants, a spa, a casino and a business centre. The project was expected to create 360 jobs and the hotel was scheduled to open in March 2016.

On 23 November the *volcano on Fogo Island* began to erupt after almost 20 years of inactivity. Immediately after the eruption, the government called an emergency cabinet under the leadership of Prime Minister Neves to provide those affected with medical assistance and food, energy and water supplies. The eruption was severe. Lava and ash destroyed the nearby town of Châ das Caldeiras and its 1,200 inhabitants had to be evacuated from their homes. Parts of the vineyards on the island and the headquarters of Fogo's National Park, only inaugurated in March, were also destroyed by lava streams. The local airport of São Filipe remained closed until the end of the year because of the emission of volcanic ash.

On 29 November, the National Assembly approved the *2015 budget* by 36 votes of the governing PAICV to 26 votes of the MpD and two of the 'União Cabo-verdiana Independente e Democrática'. The budget set out total revenue of CVE 44 bn (€ 401.3 m) and expenditure of CVE 55.9 bn (€ 510.8 m), of which CVE 12.9 bn (€ 118.2 m) were allocated to investment projects. The budget predicted economic growth of 3–4% in 2015, a budget deficit of 7.5% and public debt amounting to 112% of GDP. Felisberto Vieiro, the parliamentary leader of the PAICV praised the budget for including expenditure of CVE 83 m for vocational training and CVE 48 m for social housing projects. The parliamentary leader of the MpD, Fernando Elísio Freire, rejected the budget since it lacked clear measures to adequately address the problem of increasing unemployment.

During the year, the number of hotel units in the country increased by 3.2% from 222 to 229. Santiago (51) and Santo Antão (41) led the *national tourism statistics* in terms of hotel units, but Sal (51.5%) and Boa Vista (26.0%), the two islands dominated by large hotels and tourist complexes, represented the major share of available beds. The number of people employed in the hotel sector increased by 9.2% (up from 5,755 to 6,282). The total number of visitors was 539,621, a fall of 12,523 (2.3%) compared with 2013. However, the total of nights spent in the country dropped by only 0.6% (21,279) to 3,441,832 nights. The UK contributed 18% of visitors, followed by Germany (12.8%), France (11.5%) and Portugal (11.1%). In the same period, the port of Praia received 32 cruise ships with 26,186 passengers, a drop of seven ships and 399 visitors compared with 2013. ENAPOR related the fall to the Ebola virus epidemic in neighbouring Guinea-Conakry, Liberia and Sierra Leone.

Côte d'Ivoire

Alfred Babo

For Côte d'Ivoire, 2014 was a year of mixed hope and anxiety. The post-war reconciliation process produced modest and limited results. The year was also marked by the trial of prominent members of the former regime, including the former first lady, Simone Gbagbo. However, nobody from President Alassane Ouattara's side was indicted by the national judicial system or the ICC. The country was torn by disputes about the upcoming 2015 presidential elections. The two main political parties, the 'Parti Démocratique de Côte d'Ivoire – Rassemblement Démocratique Africain' (PDCI-RDA) and 'Front Populaire Ivoirien' (FPI) were deeply divided about the election and its procedures.

The country continued to improve its economic performance, largely due to the government's impressive investment in infrastructure, which was generally recognised as a success in post-war recovery. Throughout the country, Ouattara inaugurated new bridges, highways, etc. Investment was encouraged by the improvement in general security, particularly in Abidjan, and by measures that upgraded the business environment.

Despite these successes, international financial institutions underscored the low impact of recent growth on people's lives because poverty and unemployment

 | DOI 10.1163/9789004305052_008

remained high. In addition, the government still had to deal with the aftermath of the war, especially mutinies and the failure of security sector reforms.

Domestic Politics

Domestic politics in Côte d'Ivoire was shaped by the ups and downs of the government-opposition dialogue, negotiations on political participation, the return of exiles, malfunctions of justice and mismanagement of the reconciliation. There also were debates and tensions within the major political parties.

Talks between the 'Rassemblement des Houphouëtistes pour la Démocratie et la Paix' (RHDP) *government* (a coalition of four parties: the 'Rassemblement des Républicains' [RDR], the PDCI-RDA, the 'Mouvement des Forces d'Avenir' [MFA] and the 'Union pour la Démocratie et la Paix en Côte d'Ivoire' [UPDCI]) *and the opposition FPI* began in January in Abidjan and were made possible by a number of measures taken by the government: individuals on bail could now access their bank accounts again and numerous individuals were reinstated as public sector workers. The two parties agreed on the need to ensure security for political leaders and freedom of political action for the opposition, oversight of party political finance, and the evacuation of illegally occupied houses. In spite of this progress, the dialogue was suspended on 29 March after the FPI criticised the government's failure to implement points agreed measures. Tension also rose when the opposition party called for a *boycott of the general census* and accused the government of trying to naturalise foreigners in order to influence future elections. In addition, the transfer of Charles Blé Goudé, former leader of the Young Patriots, to the ICC on 22 March led to the opposition's *withdrawal* from the discussion. The Ivorian government kept appealing to the opposition to return to the negotiating table and, thanks to Aïchatou Mindaoudou, the UN Secretary-General's special representative, the dialogue was resumed in May.

President Alassane Ouattara regularly called on exiled Ivorians to return and, in response to these appeals, a dozen *prominent exiled supporters of the ousted president Laurent Gbagbo* came home. The first returnee was Marcel Gossio (former CEO of Abidjan Port) in January. Notable other examples included Alain Dogou (former defence minister), Voho Sahi (former special adviser to Gbagbo), Koumoué Koffi Augustin (former minister of mines and petroleum), and Navigué Konaté (president of the youth wing of the FPI), who all returned to Abidjan in January and February. They were followed by another dozen executives including three former ministers (Hubert Oulaye, Odette Sauyet and Assoa Adou) and Michel Guédé Zadi (former CEO of Hotel Ivoire) and, in November, another group including former MP William Atteby and the former minister of culture, Lia Bi Douayoua. Even though the FPI agreed to these returns, it was still concerned because they took place outside the national framework for dialogue and commitment, which envisaged not only an organised return of exiles but also the release of prisoners. Both were seen as critical conditions for national reconciliation.

The Ivorian justice system was criticised during the year for beings politically biased. It continued to indict individuals who had sided with Gbagbo while former supporters of current President Ouattara walked free. In December, a joint report issued by the International Federation for Human Rights, the 'Mouvement Ivoirien des Droits Humains' and the 'Ligue Ivoirienne des Droits de l'Homme' stated that individuals suspected of human rights crimes by NGOs enjoyed special protection and therefore never appeared before the 'Cellule Spéciale d'Enquête et d'Instruction' (CSEI), an investigation team set up by the government. Most of them had fought for Ouattara during the post-electoral war of 2011. In addition, they had been promoted by the regime to the very the top of the country's military and administrative hierarchy. The ongoing legal proceedings were very slow. The first trial for post-election crimes, set to be held in October, was postponed indefinitely. As a result, more than *300 pro-Gbagbo detainees* in Abidjan prison initiated a hunger strike in protest against their three years of imprisonment without trail, demanding that they be tried or released. In early December, the trial of *Simone Gbagbo*, the former first lady, who had been indicted by the ICC, and 82 others got underway at the Abidjan Criminal Court.

Institutions such as the CSEI and the 'Commission Dialogue Vérité and Reconciliation' (CDVR), which had been created to overcome the post-election crisis and advance national reconciliation, did not operate effectively. The CSEI ran into budget issues, while the CDVR concluded its work in October without proposing a clear methodology. The Commission failed to explain the various stages of its work, which most people were not familiar with. In addition, important parts of the dialogue process were not implemented. For example none of the 70,000 victims' hearings (around 80 public hearings) were televised. On 21 November, the president of the CDVR submitted the *final report* to president Ouattara, but did not disclose any of the content to public.

Military reforms also failed, leading to *two major mutinies* by former 'Forces Nouvelles' soldiers, who had been integrated into the 'Forces Républicaines de Côte d'Ivoire' (FRCI). The first mutiny occurred in November in Bouaké and Abidjan but soon ended when the government offered negotiations. However, serious unrest broke out in December in military camps in Abidjan, Bouake, Korhogo and Daloa and lasted two days. The rioting units claimed that the government had not complied with promises made after the first mutiny, including the payment of salary arrears and their integration into the national army. Taking this threat seriously, on 18 December, the government arrested a *former warlord Traoré Salif*, known as 'Commandant Tracteur'. The authorities accused Traoré of being the instigator of the mutiny because most arrested mutineers were linked to his unit and some of those interrogated implicated him. Instability among the military worsened the Ivorian political crisis.

After the reorganisation of the 'Commission Electorale Independandante' (CEI) in May, some civil society organisations and political parties (especially the pro-Gbagbo 'Alliance des Forces Démocratiques' [AFD], an opposition coalition that included the FPI) alleged that the CEI was tailored to favour Ouattara. Although allied with other small parties in the AFD, the FPI, as the principal opposition party, continued to act independently, while the others increased their negotiating power by appointing a joint representative. By splitting their representation in this way, the AFD coalition seemed to increase its chances of controlling the CEI. Various opposition groups either wanted to appoint the *chair of the CEI* themselves or called on the government to appoint a chairperson acceptable to all parties. Despite their protest, *Youssouf Bakayoko*, a member of the PDCI-RDA and former president the CEI during the 2010 crisis, was re-elected by 12 to 17 CEI members in September. Various opposition leaders, including Fr Boni Martial, representative of the Catholic Church, Koné Marguerite Yoli Bi from the non-confessional NGOs, Anaky Jacob, representative of the MFA, Alain Doghou, representative of FPI, and Bertin Ganin N'Goran of the AFD,) boycotted the election. The FPI representative then claimed that the government was not committed to reaching a consensus and that it had re-elected a CEI president who had been a prominent figure in the post-electoral war of 2010. As a result, the FPI suspended its participation in the CEI in September, but returned in November, after the government modified its structure by including representatives of the opposition on the executive board.

Crises also broke out within the two most important political parties, the PDCI-RDA and the FPI. Inside the PDCI-RDA, a member of the governing RHDP alliance, criticism of the party president, *Konan Bédié*, grew after he *decided unilaterally to support Ouattara*. On 17 September, Bédié used the occasion of Ouattara's visit to his village, Daoukro (Centre), to address a message to PDCI-RDA activists, asking them to endorse Ouattara as the only RHDP candidate in the 2015 presidential election. This became known as the *'appel de Daoukro'* and it triggered sharp reactions from prominent party leaders, including the representative Kouadio Konan Bertin, who accused Bédié of betraying the resolutions of the 2013 party congress, which stated that the PDCI-RDA should appoint one of its own members as the presidential candidate. In the wake of this protest, three party leaders, Essy Amara (former minister, former president of the 49th UN General Assembly and former secretary of the AU), Konan Banny (former prime minister) and Kablan Brou declared their intention to stand as *PDCI-RDA candidates in the 2015 presidential election*. Bédié denied their right to be supported by the party and stated that if they wanted to run, they would have to do so without the PDCI-RDA.

The FPI was also torn by internal conflicts. In July, pro-Gbagbo members contested the authority of the party's president, Pascal Affi N'Guessan, when he modified the composition of the FPI's national bureau and dropped some influential members who had refused to engage in dialogue with the government as long as Gbagbo was detained at the ICC. Three years after its fall from power, the *FPI remained profoundly divided*. The crisis heated up after Gbagbo's mother died a few days after she had been sent back to Côte d'Ivoire from her exile in Ghana and reached its height when militants called for Gbagbo to stand for party president. Affi N'Guessan argued that Gbagbo's candidacy would go against the FPI constitution and its bylaws. The party's central committee, which was responsible for party elections, nevertheless allowed Gbagbo to run for the party presidency during the party convention, scheduled for December. In response, Affi argued that the letter of interest presented by the pro-Gbagbo activists was a fake and he filed a lawsuit in the Abidjan civil court on 18 December. The court banned the convention and asked the protagonists to wait for the court to arrive at a decision. On 29 December, the *court rejected Gbagbo's candidacy*.

Foreign Affairs

Côte d'Ivoire intensified its cooperation with SSA and the rest of Africa. President Ouattara's term as chairman of ECOWAS ran until March. In addition to its active role in the war against terrorism in Mali, the Ivorian government signed *several bilateral agreements with SSA countries*. On 28 January, Côte d'Ivoire and Nigeria signed a number of cooperation agreements. On 31 March, the Prime Minister of Cabo Verde visited Côte d'Ivoire. On 29 July, Ouattara went to Ouagadougou to attend the 4th Conference of the Treaty of Friendship and Cooperation between Burkina Faso and Côte d'Ivoire. Côte d'Ivoire further strengthened its relations with the Kingdom of Morocco and King Mohammed VI was in Côte d'Ivoire for the second time in February, following an earlier visit in March 2013. These visits led to 26 cooperation agreements and Ouattara visited Morocco in October. High-ranking Ivorian officials, including the president of the National Assembly, made official visits to Equatorial Guinea, Gabon, and the Republic of the Congo.

France remained one of Côte d'Ivoire's major trading partners, and French trade with Abidjan intensified. French President François Hollande spent two days in Côte d'Ivoire in July, and signed several agreements on debt relief and development. Ouattara participated in the August commemoration of the 70th anniversary of the allied landing in Provence and met with Hollande in France in December. As a sign of this good relationship, the French embassy offered computer equipment to Côte d'Ivoire's universities within the framework of France's 'support for university governance and reform of higher education'.

In Europe, in addition to France, Côte d'Ivoire made efforts to revitalise its cooperation with *Italy*, with which it has partnerships in the infrastructure, food and energy sectors, and received the Italian minister of foreign affairs in January. Côte d'Ivoire further deepened diplomatic relations with *Turkey*. In August, President of the Ivorian National Assembly Guillaume Soro attended the inauguration of the new Turkish president. The partnership with Turkey envisaged cooperation in the field of political and military intelligence and preferential trade agreements were signed to strengthen the presence of Turkish business groups in Côte d'Ivoire.

Partnerships with China, South Korea, Japan and India were also invigorated. With *China*, a visa abolition agreement for official passport holders was signed in December. In addition, the China Eximbank provided a loan of CFAfr 395 bn to the Port Autonome d'Abidjan to finance the first phase of its major infrastructure construction projects. With *South Korea*, cooperation was strengthened through mutual visits by officials from both countries. In January, the government of South Korea opened the office of the Korean International Cooperation Agency (KOICA) in Abidjan, signalling an increasingly positive relationship between the two countries. At the end of the year, KOICA agreed to provide technical assistance to Côte d'Ivoire to improve the water distribution system in Abidjan. A Japanese-Ivorian summit took place in January in Abidjan attended by Japan's Prime Minister Shinzo Abe. Also in January, two major bilateral cooperation agreements were signed with *India*, when Deputy Minister of Foreign Affairs Pareenet Kaur visited Côte d'Ivoire.

Côte d'Ivoire worked to improve its relations with the USA and Canada. In December, the country was selected to benefit from aid to the value of CFAfr 6 bn to CFAfr 11 bn within the *Millennium Challenge Corporation 'Threshold' programme* funded by the US Congress to promote inclusive and sustainable economies in Africa. In addition, Côte d'Ivoire collaborated with the US government on issues of regional maritime security and border terrorism in Mali.

Apart from bilateral cooperation, Côte d'Ivoire benefited from the *financial support of several international institutions* to advance social stability and economic recovery. In June, the AfDB granted CFAfr 20 bn to support various programmes for peace and social cohesion and an additional CFAfr 22.2 bn for the CDVR, the National Social Cohesion Programme and the Observatory of Solidarity and Social Cohesion. The World Bank provided CFAfr 18 bn to partially fund the development and rehabilitation of the Boulevard de France and the Lagoon Boulevard in Abidjan and, in December, approved a credit of $ 70 m (CFAfr 35 bn) to strengthen public administration and foster private sector growth.

In June, the IMF approved a disbursement of CFAfr 37.5 bn as part of its support for the Ivorian *post-crisis reconstruction programme*. Following a performance review in December, the IMF scheduled payment of a further $ 94.7 m, bringing the total allocated to Côte d'Ivoire to $ 615.9 m. In addition, the IMF granted an extension to the Ivorian credit line (up to $ 190 m).

Socioeconomic Developments

According to the IMF, Côte d'Ivoire's macroeconomic outlook was positive at the start of the year. In March, Michel Lazare, deputy director of the IMF's Africa department, announced that, with an *8.7% growth rate* and a controlled inflation rate of 2.5% in 2013, Côte d'Ivoire offered *strong positive economic prospects*. Annual growth was estimated at 9% by the Ivorian government, the high rate being due to strong public investment. From January to December, the Centre for Promotion of Investments in Côte d'Ivoire recorded the creation of 5,983 companies, which generated a total investment of CFAfr 400 bn. As in previous years, an Investment in Côte d'Ivoire Forum took place from 29 January to 1 February to attract international investments and business. This Forum revealed that 38 projects totalling CFAfr 1,694 bn had successfully completed. This economic performance grew out of a *series of government measures* taken to facilitate entrepreneurship and improve the business environment.

According to Reuters, between October 2013 and January 2014, Ivorian *cocoa production increased* from around 721,000 tonnes to 932,000 tonnes. The 28% increase in production was an important economic indicator and the country continued to be the world's leading cocoa producer. According to the International Coffee and Cocoa Organization, about 520,000 tonnes of cocoa (30% of national production) were processed within the country during this same period, 10% more than during the previous season. This performance placed the Côte d'Ivoire just behind the Netherlands for cocoa processing.

In addition, Côte d'Ivoire *increased its energy production* (oil, natural gas) and privatised a mining company as part of its development strategy. Oil production amounted to 37,000 b/d, far behind the 100,000 b/d forecast for 2014. In January, the *sixth gas turbine* of the Ivorian Electricity Production Company (CIPREL) was inaugurated and was expected to bring capacity up to 111 MW without any additional consumption of natural gas. The completion of both phases of CIPREL IV would add 222 MW to the installed capacity. The mining sector experienced disengagement from the Ivorian state. The government viewed *the privatisation of the mining sector* as an economic growth strategy. In January, the Mining Development Corporation sold 9.1% of its activities to the La Mancha Precious Metals group. Important infrastructure improvements took place, although investment in basic infrastructure remained limited. The new section of the 'highway of the North' from the village of Singrobo to Yamoussoukro, the country's political capital, had opened in December 2013 and the first supplementary section was renovated at a cost of CFAfr 35 bn, which was provided by local donors. Another major project, the Abidjan-Bassam Highway, was completed after 30 months of construction. It was financed (CFAfr 63 bn) by the BTP China Machinery Engineering Corporation and the Ivorian state. Two major bridges were built: the so-called '*third bridge*' or Henri Konan Bédié Bridge, built at a cost of CFAfr 125 bn, opened in Abidjan in December, and Marahoué Bridge, located in the town of Bouaflé, completed towards the end of the year at a cost of CFAfr 9 bn.

The Ivorian government concluded negotiations with a French-Korean consortium including the Bouygues group, Dongsan Engineering, and Hyundai Rotem Company to build a *city train* in Abidjan. The asphalting work for the Bouna-Doropo road (91 km) in north-east Côte d'Ivoire was launched in October. This work was projected to cost CFAfr 33.5 bn. Only two out of 12 scheduled *drinking water* infrastructure projects had secured funding by the end of the year. The government announced a CFAfr 9.4 bn project for the construction of a second national heart centre in Bouaké. Although the building of healthcare facilities was a major government concern, the sector received little investment.

According to the World Bank's Doing Business 2015 report, Côte d'Ivoire was *among the ten economies that drastically improved their business environment* in 2014. However, the country was ranked 147th, which was only a mild improvement (from 158th in 2013). According to TI, Côte d'Ivoire had become slightly less corrupt and was now listed at 115th out of 175 countries with a score of 32 out of 100. After several controversies in 2013 about the procurement of public contracts, the government set up a new system.

In addition, the government took a series of initiatives to reduce social inequalities. For example, salaries for 121,382 out of a total public sector workforce of 153,021 increased by an average of 12%. The increase in the minimum wage would cost the Ivorian state CFAfr 78.9 bn according a statement by the previous minister of public service and administrative reform, Gnamien Konan on 16 January. The government also paid bonuses to health personnel and lowered the cost of fuel.

Despite some economic progress, the HDI ranked Côte d'Ivoire 171st out of 187 countries, reflecting the country's *weak medical and educational systems*. According to the World Bank, nearly 50% of the population remained poor. The increase in the minimum wage failed to increase purchasing power, because over 90% of the employed population worked in the *informal sector*. Furthermore, the state was unable to enforce the implementation of the minimum wage or fight illegal and/or exploitative employment. The *unemployment* rate remained a major challenge. The official unemployment rate stood at 5.3%, but international estimates put it at 25% or more.

The government's support for small businesses remained limited. Even though around 15% to 20% of the annual budget was spent on fostering small businesses, the government was heavily criticised for not doing more. The repayment of the *national debt* accumulated between 2000 and 2010 remained a contested issue. In total, the Ivorian debt stood at CFAfr 784 bn. The state's failure to service its debt had placed numerous companies, including the national oil and gas company, PETROCI, under considerable financial strain. For example in October, the FRCI failed to pay off an estimated CFAfr 20 bn for gas supplied by PETROCI. In response, PETROCI looked for cash from financial partners such as the trader Glencore to solve its difficulties.

Following the catastrophic flood of 2013, the government evacuated large parts of the population from Abidjan's at-risk neighbourhoods such as Attécoubé. At the end of the year, *997 families had been evacuated*, a total of 3,623 people. Although these evictions were a positive move because they aimed at saving people's lives, those displaced complained that they were left without better housing. There was no resettlement scheme in place.

Gambia

Alice Bellagamba

Throughout the year, opposition media and diasporic civil organisations denounced President Jammeh's repressive regime, but events showed that, despite increasing popular disaffection, his grip on the country remained strong. In the early hours of 30 December, the Presidential Guard rapidly countered an attack by a group of armed men on the Presidential Palace in the capital, Banjul. Repression of alleged dissidents and civilians started immediately after the foiled attack. The closure of the border with Senegal in the first part of the year had economic consequences for both the Gambia and the Casamance. The late beginning of the rainy season compromised crop production. Rising food prices and an annual inflation rate of 6.1% seriously reduced the spending power of Gambian households.

Domestic Politics

Patronage and brutal repression continued to give President Yahya Jammeh and his party, the Alliance for Patriotic Reorientation and Construction Party (APRC), a

 | DOI 10.1163/9789004305052_009

firm grip on the army and the population. As before, Jammeh shuffled his cabinet regularly in order to prevent potential rivals from consolidating a power base, with appointments dependent on the individual's capacity to demonstrate his personal support for Jammeh, and the slightest suspicion of disloyalty leading to prompt demotion. Zero tolerance of critics of the regime was on-going, implemented through a strong network of informants and secret agents who exploited personal relationships.

On 10 July, Jammeh shocked the nation by refusing the repatriation from Senegal of the body of Boubacar Baldeh, former minister of the First Republic of the Gambia, which had been requested by his family. Baldeh had been managing editor of the government-controlled 'Daily Observer' newspaper from 2000 to 2002 and had also acted as orgainser of APRC political campaigns. Repeated arrests had forced him to leave the Gambia in 2006. In Dakar (Senegal), he was an active member of civil organisations that mobilised for the restoration of democracy in the Gambia. This episode illustrated Jammeh's determination to prolong the persecution of his opponents even after their death, and his willingness to make their families suffer.

Fear and suspicion also loomed large among the Gambian diaspora. Imprudent statements against Jammeh risked retaliation against relatives at home. Migrants returning to visit the country reported that as soon as they left the airport, their families and friends warned them against expressing their opinions about the state of the country. This well-organised repression did not, however, stop the growth of popular disaffection with Jammeh's regime both within and outside the country. Opposition media based abroad, such as 'Freedom Newspaper', 'Gainako' and 'Kibaro', continued to gather and spread information on Jammeh's business relations, his private life and his relations with the army. These online newspapers also provided a radio service countering the propaganda statements of government-controlled media, such as the 'Daily Observer', national television and national radio. In January, for instance, 'Freedom Newspaper' reported that two Gambian Americans, Alhagie Mamut Ceesay and Ebou Jobe, who had disappeared while visiting the Gambia in December 2013, had been killed by security forces. The Chief of the Gambia's intelligence service, Chief Yankuba Badjie, denied the allegations.

There was no change in Jammeh's policy of countering the international community's pressure for an improvement in the Gambia's poor human rights record with *harsh anti-Western propaganda*. On 6 February, he dismissed Chief Justice Mabel Maame Yamoah Agyemang, whom he had appointed in 2013 and who had a reputation for independence. The abrupt end of Agyemang's tenure was the result of her differences with the president. On radio and television, Jammeh denounced her as a "thief and a criminal" who took orders from an unspecified foreign country and had sought protection in one of the Banjul embassies. The Ghanaian Embassy announced that she had safely travelled to Ghana. Agyemang's dismissal was just one example of a series of political interventions by the executive, which in recent years had dominated the Gambian judiciary. Humiliation and attacks usually followed judges' decisions that were seen as against the government's interest.

On 18 February, Jammeh's presidential address on Independence Day attacked the human rights culture as resulting from "coercive and dictatorial pressures by some foreign powers" that had "one set of standards for themselves, and another for the rest of mankind especially Africans". He then attacked homosexuality in name of Gambian traditional values and religious sensitivity: "We will fight … homosexuals or gays the same way we are fighting malaria-causing mosquitoes." Momadou Lamin, the president of the Gambia's Islamic Supreme Council and a strong supporter of discrimination against homosexuals, endorsed Jammeh's declarations. Both the EU and the US published statements condemning this anti-gay rhetoric. On 6 March, at the swearing in as chief justice of Ali Nawaz Chowhan, an internationally renowned Pakistani jurist who had served for three years at the International Criminal Tribunal for the Former Yugoslavia in The Hague and acted as legal advisor of the President of Pakistan, Jammeh stated that the Gambia would soon drop the use of English as its official language, as this was a "colonial legacy". He also made clear that judges were part of government. At the same ceremony, former acting chief justice Emmanuel Fagbenle was sworn in as the new president of the Gambia Court of Appeal, and Oledi Uko Uduma as a High Court judge.

In August, the National Assembly passed a bill that amended the criminal code by introducing a life sentence for "aggravated homosexuality". Homosexual acts were already punishable by up to 14 years in prison under a Gambian law that had been amended in 2005 to apply to women as well as men. Jammeh signed the "aggravated homosexuality" bill on 9 October and it came into force on 19 November. According to AI, the security forces started to crack down on alleged homosexuals: four men, one 17-year-old boy and three women were arrested and threatened with torture and sexual violence if they did not confess their homosexual orientation.

In November, the auditor general announced that the audit of the 2011 government accounts showed serious mismanagement of public funds. The irregularities took place before the launch of the 2012–15 Program for Accelerated Growth and Employment, whose target includes tackling corruption. In July, Jammeh had announced that he would soon create a National Anti-Corruption Commission but no concrete steps in that direction were taken during the year.

The year's most dramatic event was an *attack by a group of armed men on the Presidential Palace* – apparently an attempted coup – in the early hours of 30 December. Troops loyal to Jammeh beat off the attack. Residents of Bangui reported gunfire in the night and that soldiers blocked the way of people trying to reach their work places in the morning. Banks and other offices were closed throughout the day, and national radio played traditional music. The government downplayed the event by denying that there had been a coup attempt. Jammeh, who was in Dubai for a private visit at the time, rapidly returned to the country.

The attack was led by Lamin Sanneh, ex-army colonel and commander of the Presidential Guard. Fearing arrest by the National Intelligence Agency, Sanneh and his family had left the Gambia in 2012 and sought refuge in the US. Sanneh had teamed up with other Gambian expatriates to overthrow Jammeh. He was killed in the coup attempt together with three other plotters, including Njaga Jagne, a US army reservist (and captain), who lived in Kentucky. A fourth man, Modou Njie, was arrested but died the following day, while the rest of the group apparently escaped across the border into Senegal. Fears spread that Jammeh would launch a purge among the army and the population and arrests of current and former military figures and of civilians started almost immediately. Jammeh's new year statement on the night of 31 December portrayed the foiled coup as a terrorist attack by Gambian dissidents based in Germany, the UK and the US. According to the official version of the event, the weapons came from the US, and the attackers had no accomplices in the Gambian army, whose loyalty was undisputed. "No human can attack the Gambia", Jammeh stated, as "we are blessed by God". Gambia would not be colonised by foreign countries "that smile at you and then stab at your back".

Foreign Affairs

Gambian foreign policy continued to be contingent on Jammeh's erratic behaviour. The *relationship with Senegal*, although unlikely to break down given the strong social and economic interdependence of the two countries, remained unstable, with two unresolved causes of animosity: Senegal's accusation that Jammeh supported the Casamance rebels, and Jammeh's resentment that Senegal hosted Gambian political dissidents. From January to 16 April, the Senegalese Transportation Union blocked the border with Gambia in protest against increases by the Gambian Port Authority to the ferry tariff to cross the River Gambia. Private cars were allowed to cross using the bridge, but all public transport was put on hold, forcing travellers to cross the border foot and find another transport in Senegal. The border closed again for unknown reasons on 19–25 April. These blockages affected the economies of both the Gambia and the Casamance.

In an effort to foster cooperation, Senegal's President Macky Sall made his second visit to the Gambia on 10 October. He was invited to participate in the celebrations of the 20th anniversary of the 22 July revolution that had brought Jammeh to power. On 11 November, the two countries finally signed an agreement that paved the way for the construction of the trans-Gambia bridge. Jammeh had attempted several times to halt the project as he feared that greater mobility between the two countries could comprise the security of his regime. Co-financed by the AfDB (99.1%) and the governments of the Gambia (0.2%) and Senegal (0.7%) the bridge would be the first phase of a *trans-West African Coastal Highway*, scheduled to link 12 West African coastal nations, from Mauritania to Nigeria. There would be one-stop border posts in line with the ECOWAS decision to support intra-community trade and cross-border movement. The second phase would see the rehabilitation of the road from Ziguinchor (Senegal) to Senoba (the Gambia).

In order to signal Jammeh's willingness to cooperate with EU migration policies, the government sent a team of Gambian immigration officials to various European countries in July in order to identify and repatriate Gambians living illegally in Europe. In the same month, the Gambia received a € 2.6 m grant from the EU to improve justice and access to legal education in the country. Relations with the EU worsened, however, as a consequence of the Aggravated Homosexuality Bill, European development assistance to the Gambia being contingent on its progress in the field of human rights and democracy, monitored twice a year by the government and EU representatives. The Gambia postponed the meeting scheduled for 11 November and, on 26 November, Jammeh suspended all discussions with EU. In December, the EU announced that it would not disburse € 13 m in development aid because of systematic abuses of human rights and the US suspended the Gambia's participation in AGOA.

Socioeconomic Developments

Although the government remained committed to macro-economic stability, it significantly missed the target it had set in 2012 to qualify for a three-year extension of an IMF credit facility of $ 28.3 m. An IMF delegation visited the country in September and found that the government had failed to reduce the budget level and the level of domestic borrowing. One of the causes was the National Water and Electricity Company's financial problems. The implementation of VAT measures introduced in 2013 was also limited. The meticulous record keeping needed for this form of indirect taxation proved difficult in a predominantly informal economy like the Gambia's. VAT resulted in price increases without businessmen really understanding what they owed to the state.

The reform of several parastatals seemed unlikely to take place in the short term. According to the Gambia Bureau of Statistics, real GDP contracted by 1.4% following the 22% contraction in agricultural production caused by the late rainy season and the impact of fears connected with the Ebola epidemic on the tourist sector. The inflation rate stood at 6.1%, and in December the exchange rate stood at $ 1:44.7 dalasi. A number of factors accounted for the decline in value of the national currency: excessive liquidity, lack of confidence in the government and lack of fiscal discipline. Jammeh refrained from trying to control the currency rate, which he had done in 2013. These previous attempts had undermined the confidence of investors and he was not prepared to take that risk again. Agriculture continued to be the major source of income for the rural population. The late arrival of the rainy season compromised the harvest and further restricted the purchasing power of Gambian households. In spite of government efforts to deter them, Gambian youths showed an ever-growing determination to leave the country and reach Europe by the 'back road' through North Africa. The Gambia remained depended on China for 57% of its exports and 30% of its imports. The second most important trading partner was India, with an average 30% of exports and 6.7% of imports.

Ghana

Nancy Annan and Kwesi Aning

The growing economic meltdown was the main feature of 2014 as many complained of the failure of the Mahama government to deliver on its promise of 'Building a Better Ghana'. Politically, inter-party tensions were minimal while there were many cases of intra-party controversy. Increasingly irregular power supplies, contested policies, numerous outbreaks of fire and high inflation further increased public agitation. As a result, there were widespread civil and political demonstrations across the country. Corruption continued to be a major challenge for the government, as ministers, parliamentarians and state workers were accused of diverting state resources.

Politics

The year began with the *first anniversary* of the installation of President John Dramani Mahama's government on 7 January. To mark the day, Mahama organised a press conference on the theme 'One Year of Responsible, Transparent and Accountable Governance'. Throughout his first year in office, the president had

 | DOI 10.1163/9789004305052_010

faced heavy public criticism for his inability to deliver on his campaign promises and the increasing allegations of corruption in his government, despite his promise to curb it. He met with the media to respond to criticisms and used the opportunity to reassure Ghanaians of his ability to fulfil all his campaign promises, despite a turbulent 2013.

As the president celebrated his first year in office, the country's 275 parliamentarians were simultaneously summoned back to parliament on 7 January to discuss the sale of the state-owned *Merchant Bank* to Fortiz Equity Fund, a Ghanaian company allegedly owned by the president's brother, Ibrahim Mahama. There were heated debates as the parliamentary Minority, led by the National Patriotic Party's (NPP) Osei Kyei Mensah Bonsu, argued that the deal was not transparent because the South African First Rand company, which had been in the running to win the bid, had been rejected in favour of Fortiz Equity Fund. The parliamentary speaker, Doe Adjaho, dismissed the objection. On 10 January, the Minority organised a news conference venting their disapproval of the speaker's ruling and threatening a "self-imposed enquiry" into the Merchant Bank sale. They further accused the speaker of "double standards", citing two situations in which he had given a ruling, even though the matter was before the court.

Assessments of the president's first year in office were generally mixed. While some praised him for his efforts, others were critical. On 7 January, a private legal clerk, Nii Armah Quaye, commended the Mahama government for initiating infrastructural projects and for boosting the country's security. Similarly, the regional chairman of the ruling National Democratic Congress (NDC) party, Joseph Kobina Ade Coker, indicated that, despite the challenges faced by the president, "his performance in office is far better than a pass mark". Conversely, on 9 January, one of the country's senior journalists rated Mahama's first year as "the most difficult year for ordinary Ghanaians", since he had failed to meet expectations. On 15 January, the NPP hosted a media conference dubbed "2013 in Retrospect", where they reviewed the *president's performance*. They claimed that he had performed poorly, as the economy continued to plummet. The party criticised the growing number of power fluctuations, the public debt, which stood at $ 23 bn in 2013 (compared with $ 8 bn in 2008), the low salaries of public workers and the contested Merchant Bank deal.

On 25 February, Mahama delivered his State of the Nation Address in accordance with Article 67 of the 1992 constitution. Among other things, he promised to increase the number of beneficiaries of the Livelihood Empowerment Against Poverty initiative to 100,000 (from 74,000 beneficiaries in 2013); to complete the construction of the Upper West Regional Hospital in Wa; to launch the GHS (cedi) 10 m Youth Enterprise Support programme to assist Ghanaian youth in business and other ventures; and the commencement of construction of 50 schools by 3 March.

On 10 March, Alban Bagbin, a veteran MP for the Nadowli-Kaleo constituency of the Upper West Region and former Majority leader, accused his fellow parliamentarians of taking *bribes*. This allegation was rejected on the same day by some members of the house, including Minority leader Osei Kyei Mensah-Bonsu. On 11 March, parliament agreed to investigate the claims. To support the investigation, on 15 March, the Majority leader, Benjamin Kunbuor obliged the house to take all necessary steps to verify the assertions. While many MPs criticised Bagbin for his statement, some sections of the population believed that there was some truth in his accusations. On 12 March, Ken Kuranchie, editor of the 'Daily Searchlight' newspaper, endorsed Bagbin's allegations and a former NPP presidential candidate, Kobina Arthur Kennedy, followed suit on 28 April, labelling, the country's parliament "corrupt and selfish".

Following numerous criticisms of ministers' incompetence, the Mahama government underwent some *ministerial reshuffles*, the first on 3 March, when the president reshuffled regional ministers. Subsequently, between May and early July, the president dismissed and appointed several new ministers.

Corruption allegations once again dominated the national discourse. The most controversial issues were cases related to the Commission on Human Rights and Administrative Justice (CHRAJ) and the National Service Scheme (NSS). On 16 September, CHRAJ Commissioner Laurette Vivian Lamptey was accused of spending over GHS 180,000 on her accommodation, of renting an apartment for $ 4,500 per month and of failing to return 20 Toyota vehicles, funded by the Danish International Development Agency, to regional offices. Her actions led to a public demonstration by the Alliance for Accountable Governance (AFAG) on 24 September and, on 25 September, Osei Kyei Mensah Bonsu called for her resignation. As a result, on 11 October, Mahama authorised Chief Justice Georgina Theodora Woode to investigate. In a subsequent issue, the national director of the NSS, Alhaji Alhassan Mohammed Imoro, was reprimanded on 15 October by the Accra Circuit Court for defrauding the state of a total of GHS 86.9 m between September 2013 and July 2014. According to the Bureau of National Investigations, the NSS headquarters had inflated the service database with some 22,612 ghost names, costing the state about GHS 7.9 m in July 2014 alone.

Political and civil demonstrations were rife through the year due to the collapsing economy and increasing power supply problems. The first round of protests took place on 13 January, led by the Progressive People's Party (PPP), against corruption. According to the leader of the protest, Paa Kwesi Nduom, many public officials engaged in corruption with impunity because there were no mechanisms for investigating them. The second round was organised by the Coalition for Farmers Rights and Advocacy against Genetically Modified Organisms on 28 January in protest against the government's introduction of genetically modified foods and the Plant Breeders Bill. The grass roots association, made up of farmers, labour unions and religious, political and civil society organisations, saw the bill as overriding the rights of farmers as the premier breeders and as contributing to increasing poverty among the already marginalised agricultural workers. The NPP also organised a demonstration under the slogan 'Ya ye dien?' (What have we done?), when thousands of people marched in Kumasi on 10 June protesting against the country's economic meltdown. This was followed by an 'Occupy Flagstaff House' demonstration on 1 July, organised by Concerned Ghanaians for Responsible Governance. The protesters called on the Mahama government to address "corruption, infrastructural decay, worsening economy and the deteriorating conditions in the country". On 8 July, the offices of two leaders of the protest were attacked by unknown individuals who stole laptops, hard disks and a tablet. Defying these attacks, the group launched a new campaign, called 'Red Friday', on 11 July. The campaign asked its followers wear red in their traditional Friday attire and post pictures, comments and videos on social media. Three weeks after 'Occupy Flagstaff House', two groups – railway workers in Accra and the Industrial and Commercial Workers Union in Tema – demonstrated simultaneously on 22 July against poor working conditions. This was immediately followed on 24 July by a nationwide strike by the country's Organised Labour Union under the Trade Union Congress, demanding that the government implement economic reform. Ghanaians in the diaspora also took to the streets to protest against Mahama's leadership. On 11 August, Ghanaians in Washington DC vented their frustrations in a demonstration, carrying placards with slogans such as "Mahama is a thief" and "Ghana's president is damn corrupt". The last protest of the year was the 'Agbe wor' (They are killing us) demonstration, organised by AFAG on 12 November against corruption and decadent economic policies.

With the 2016 elections around the corner, *smaller political parties* began assessing their policies and strategies and engaging in dialogue about merging. On 19 May, the Convention Peoples Party (CPP) and the People's National Convention revisited their talks about uniting their parties. They had first discussed a merger in 2010 but internal disagreements meant that it did not take place. By 12 August, other parties such as the Ghana Consolidated People's Party and the PPP joined the debate. The CPP chairperson, Samia Nkrumah, daughter of Ghana's first president, Kwame Nkrumah, threatened on 25 September to resign if the party's leadership did not agree to the merger.

Most parties conducted internal elections for constituency, regional and national executives as well as for *presidential candidates* for the 2016 elections. The process sparked numerous controversies and intra-party conflicts. The controversial election of the NPP candidate in the Ho constituency was a case in point. The election was brought to a standstill when the party's constituency secretary, Francis Boafo, accused the national executive of meddling in local voting procedures. Likewise, the NDC also experienced great internal tensions. On 24 August, an aspiring NDC executive member, Bossman Oduro-Fosu, dragged the party to court. His intention was to have paragraph 6(c) of the party's constitution withdrawn. He claimed that this paragraph, which states: "In addition, a member of the party shall not qualify to vie for a regional executive committee position unless the member has prior to seeking elections held an executive position in the constituency", had not gone through the appropriate channels before its approval. A similar court case was issued against the party on 29 September by NDC member Linus Njonolah, who accused the leadership of not respecting their term limits as party officials.

Perhaps the election of NPP presidential candidates was the most contentious as the party was divided into two camps: supporters of Nana Akuffo-Addo and supporters of Alan Kyeremanten. Unfortunately, the division sometimes resulted in aggressive verbal exchanges and violence between party members. On 21 August, for example, the party headquarters was attacked by angry supporters with weapons during a press conference organised by the chairman, Paul Afoka, and general secretary, Kwabena Agyapong. The attacks resulted in several casualties. Despite these altercations, the NPP organised its congress on 18 October and elected Akuffo-Addo as its presidential candidate for the third time, with over 117,413 votes (94.4%), over Kyeremanten, a former state minister under the Kufour government (5,908 votes [4.8%]), and Addai Nimoh, an NPP veteran (1,128 votes [0.91%]).

The political year ended with the NDC's *8th National Congress* at the Baba Yara Stadium in Kumasi on 20 December. The congress had been scheduled for 25 October but was delayed by the numerous court injunctions issued against the leadership by party members.

Foreign Affairs

President Mahama began his *diplomatic engagements* on 9 January, with a bilateral discussion with Chinese Foreign Minister Yi Wang, who paid him a courtesy call. At the meeting, the president requested the release of a $ 3 bn loan from the China Development Bank. Mahama indicated that although only $ 600 m of the total amount had been released, Ghana was paying commitment fees on the whole loan. Although the loan had been agreed in 2011, *China* was reportedly still not satisfied with the terms. It was speculated that the delay was due to Ghana's deportation of over 4,500 Chinese miners in 2013. At the meeting, Mahama made efforts to explain that this harsh action had been taken against these illegal small-scale Chinese miners because their activities were affecting Ghana's natural resource sector as well as the security of local communities.

Problems in the *energy security* were one of the main motivations for Mahama's foreign engagements in 2014 as the country had continued to experience incessant power failures since he took office. On 19 January, he travelled to Abu Dhabi for a two-day visit. The focus of the trip was on renewable energy, water and the environment. Among other things, the president anticipated strengthening partnerships with experts from the *UAE* to share best practice in electricity supply. He also participated in the Abu Dhabi Sustainability Week Conference, and met with business partners and investors. On 17 March, the president sent Minister of Energy and

Petroleum Emmanuel Armah-Kofi Buah to *Nigeria* to broker a deal with the leaders of the West Africa Gas Pipeline to supply more natural gas, which was needed to power Ghana's thermal plants, as the Nigeria Gas Company had failed to meet its promise to deliver the agreed amount of gas. This was followed by a deal with *Turkey*'s Karadeniz Energy Group on 11 October to construct *two energy generating ships* to produce 450 MW of power. On 1 December, on a three-day visit to *Qatar*, Mahama had a discussion with Qatar Petroleum International about investment in Ghana's liquified natural gas in order to improve the country's electricity supply.

Ghana continued to deepen its obligations to its regional and continental partners. Between 15 and 17 January, Mahama was represented by Vice President Amissah-Arthur at the West Africa Regional Consultations of the Eminent Persons Groups of the ACP. The aim of the meeting was to develop strategies to address poverty. At the continental level, Amissah-Arthur and Minister of Food and Agriculture Clement Humado attended the 22nd Ordinary Session of the AU in Addis Ababa (Ethiopia) on 30 January.

Perhaps the highlight of the country's regional engagement occurred on 28 March, at the 44th Ordinary Session of the ECOWAS Heads of State and Government on 28–29 March in Yamousoukro (Côte d'Ivoire), when Mahama was elected *Chair of ECOWAS* for a year, taking over from his Ivorian counterpart President Allasane Ouattara. In his acceptance speech, Mahama indicated that his one-year term would focus on three key issues: regional security (the fight against Boko Haram); economic integration and development, through continuous discussions with the EU on the EPAs to boost trade in the sub-region; and finally infrastructural expansion and development, with a strong focus on the West African Gas Pipeline to improve the supply of energy. Immediately after taking office, Mahama turned his attention to the region's security dilemmas by organising the ECOWAS Intelligence Chiefs Meeting on Anti-terrorism at the Kofi Annan International Peacekeeping Training Centre in Accra on 22 May. The president was represented by Minister of Foreign Affairs Hannah Tetteh. The meeting aimed at developing strategies for dealing with *Boko Haram* in Nigeria and rescuing the 200 school girls who had been there abducted. In addition, on 30 May, Mahama hosted and chaired an Extraordinary Session of ECOWAS Heads of State and Government in Accra. The meeting focused on security challenges in northern Mali and Nigeria. Following the civil uprising in *Burkina Faso* on 31 October, which had resulted in the collapse of Blaise Compaoré's 27-year presidency, Mahama travelled there on 5 November in his capacity as ECOWAS chair to negotiate a peaceful democratic transition with the interim military leaders.

In mid-2014, Liberia, Sierra Leone and Guinea experienced an outbreak of the *Ebola virus*. According to the Centre for Disease Control and Prevention, a component of the US Department of Health and Human Services, the alarming epidemic had led to the death of over 7,800 people in these three West African countries by

31 December. Consequently, Mahama, in his capacity as ECOWAS chair, embarked on a one day 'Ebola tour' on 15 September to support the affected countries. During the tour, he used the opportunity to hold discussions with fellow African leaders on strategies to address this fatal virus. In addition, he met with the UN country team in Ghana on 18 October to discuss UN initiatives on Ebola. Ghana agreed to allow the UN to use the country as its logistics base for its emergency response to Ebola in the West African region. On 6 November, Mahama held an emergency meeting of ECOWAS to consider ways of addressing the Ebola virus in the region.

Internationally, Ghana continued to strengthen its commitment to global politics and trade. For instance, after a request from UN Secretary General Ban Ki-moon, Mahama promised to contribute 850 *troops* to the UN mission in South Sudan. He disclosed this in a meeting with Ethiopian Foreign Minister Tedros Adhanom Ghebreyesus at Flagstaff House on 15 January. On 22–25 January, he attended the World Economic Forum meeting in Davos (Switzerland), under the theme 'The Reshaping of the World: Consequences for Society, Politics and Business'. There, Mahama pledged to stop illegal mining, which had been a matter of concern for some time. On 2–4 April, Mahama attended the 4th EU-Africa Summit in Brussels (Belgium) to discuss the progress of the joint Africa-EU strategy adopted in Lisbon (Portugal) in 2007. The meeting was attended by around 40 African and 20 European leaders and took the theme 'Investing in People, Prosperity and Peace'. At the end of the meeting, leaders agreed to a strategic roadmap for 2014–17, addressing, among other issues: global security; sustainable development; democracy and good governance; and continental integration. As part of the trip, Mahama had a meeting with President of the EU Commission Jose Manuel Barroso on 2 April with the aim of strengthening *Ghana-EU relations*. The president encouraged the EU to allocate € 64 m in multi-donor budgetary assistance to Ghana. The president then travelled straight to Medellin (Columbia) to attend the UN-led World Urban Forum on 5–11 April. This biannual event brought together experts on the environment and heads of organisations to discuss global urban challenges. During his opening address, Mahama emphasised his commitment to promoting sustainable development on the continent in collaboration with other African heads of states.

The president attended the annual UN General Assembly on 22 September. In his address at the 69th session on 25 September, he drew attention to the challenges in Africa, including violent extremism in Nigeria and Kenya and the Ebola epidemic in Liberia, Sierra Leone and Guinea.

With the increasing depreciation of the Ghana cedi and the reluctance of investors to trade with the country, the government announced on 3 August its decision to accept a *bailout from the IMF*. This decision was the outcome of Mahama's meeting with his presidential advisory committee on economy on 1 August. Some saw this move as a much needed measure to boost the national economy. Others wondered whether turning to the IMF was a good idea, as Ghana's relations with the IMF in the past had been disastrous. Despite this criticism, on 10 October, the president dispatched Vice President Amissah-Arthur and senior ministers to Washington DC to negotiate details of the IMF bailout. The three-year $ 940 m loan would focus on five goals: wage bill reduction; expenditure cuts and improvement mechanisms; revenue mechanisms; debt stock; and improved social development and protection policies. The IMF was not the only global organisation that offered support to Ghana. On 16 and 28 April, the World Bank pledged $ 24 m to increase funding in the science, technology and higher education sector, $ 30 m for public/private partnership projects and $ 100 m for a five-year commercial agricultural project.

The relationship with *South Africa* was consolidated when Mahama demonstrated his support for President Jacob Zuma by attending the latter's investiture ceremony on 24 May after he won a second five-year term on 7 May. Aside from South Africa, the president had several other bilateral engagements. On 20 October, Mahama and First Lady Lordina Mahama visited the *UK* to pay a courtesy call on Queen Elizabeth II. As part of his trip, the president had discussions with the All Party Parliamentary Group at the House of Commons on Ebola and security in the West African sub-region. He also chaired investment meetings at Chatham House and the Royal African Society. The president then visited *Denmark* for a two-day bilateral visit with Danish Prime Minister Helle Thorning-Schmidt and Crown Prince Federick on 21–22 October. In Denmark, Mahama also delivered a keynote address at the 4th Green Global Growth Forum's (3GF) meeting on 'Facing the Consumers/Citizens: Transforming our Consumption Habits'. The president's next stop was in *Norway* on 27 October, where he met with businessmen and investors in order to boost Ghana's international trade and commerce.

The president's busy diplomatic schedule led to severe *criticism*. For example on 28 October, the MP for Manhyia (Ashanti Region), Matthew Opoku Prempeh described Mahama's travels as "wasteful", accusing him of constantly leaving the country while "Ghanaians are languishing in abject poverty".

Socioeconomic Developments

The year started on a sad note when the death of *Komla Dumor* at the young age of 41 was widely reported on 18 January. The demise of the inspirational Ghanaian journalist, who had worked with the BBC, came as a shock to many. On 20 January, there were tributes from President Mahama, former president John Agyekum Kufuor, Kofi Annan and other dignitaries and well-wishers. Unfortunately, Komla Dumor was not Ghana's only illustrious son to be lost in 2014. On 17 May, P.V. Obeng, a career statesman, also died, of a heart attack. Obeng had served as the Chairman of the Committee of Secretaries during the rule of former president Jerry Rawlings's Provisional National Defence Council from 1982 to 1992 and was presidential adviser on governmental affairs under Rawlings's NDC from 1992 to 1997. Before his death, Obeng was one of Mahama's senior presidential advisors.

In the midst of national grief, Ghanaians found excitement in the *Fifa World Cup*, which took place from 12 June to 13 July in Brazil, as they were full of hopes for *Ghana's national team, the Black Stars*. However, their enthusiasm and high expectations were brought to a halt when the Black Stars failed to impress and dropped out of the competition on 26 June. The country's poor performance was caused by tensions within the team. On 24 June, two players, Kevin Prince Boateng and Sulley Muntari, verbally and physically assaulted thee national coaches, Kwesi Appiah, and some state officials. Their actions led to their indefinite suspension on 26 June. Upon the team's return to Ghana on 29 June, the public called on the president to investigate the planning committee led by Minister of Youth and Sports Elvis Afriyie Ankrah. The national football team (or the planning committee?) was accused of misappropriation of state funds. In response to the public outcry, a three member Commission of Enquiry made up of Justice Senyo Dzamefe, lawyer Moses Foh-Amoaning and sports enthusiast Kofi Anokye Owusu-Darko was established on 4 August. The commission's task was to investigate the preparation of the Black Stars in the run-up to the World Cup tournament as well as the financial activities of the national team. The Commission completed its work in December, but had not met with the president by year's end.

There were problems in the *education sector*. On 14 January, all 83 senior high schools in the three northern regions remained closed as the administration had not paid its contribution to the school canteens. On 1 February, there was a clash between the University of Ghana and the National Security Taskforce over the former's quest to collect tolls at the university's entrance to defray its GHS 8 m debt. As tensions rose between the university and the state, on 17 February, National Security Coordinator Lieutenant Colonel Larry Gbevlo-Lartey (rtd), ordered the demolition of the toll booth, describing it as a "public nuisance". According to rumours, Gbevlo-Lartey's involvement in the destruction of the booth led to his dismissal by Mahama on 29 April. After several criticisms for failing to implement his 200 school building project, Mahama finally had a success story on 3 March, when he led the opening ceremony for the first batch of 50 of the 200 government schools (as promised in his 2012 presidential manifesto) at Nyanoa in the Eastern Region.

On 12–15 May, the National Economic Forum took place at the Royal Senchi Hotel, Akosombo (Eastern Region). At the end of the three-day workshop, the 140 participants, including representatives from organised labour, the private sector, financial institutions, security institutions, political parties, civil society organisations and government ministries, as well as religious and traditional leaders, parliamentarians and academics, adopted a 22-point roadmap dubbed the 'Senchi Consensus' towards sustainable development in the country.

The 2015 National Budget presented by the president on 19 November indicated that, as of October 2014, *inflation* had escalated to 16.9% (from 16.5% in September and 13.5% in December 2013). This increase was linked to the depreciation of the cedi, petroleum and utility price modifications and a reduction in *exports* (down by 2.8% compared with 2013) and imports (down by 17.8%). The amount of *gold* exported was $ 3,369.3 m, compared with $ 3,708.9 m in 2013. The revenue from the export of *cocoa* beans and product, on the other hand, saw an increase to $ 1,921.7 m, 11.4% up from 2013. According to the budget, the country's total *revenues and grants* for the year amounted to GHS 17,670.2 m, falling short of the anticipated GHS 18,414.1 m. In contrast, *public debt* (domestic and external) stood at GHS 69,705.9 m ($ 21,733.5 m), representing 60.8% of GDP, compared with 55.5% in 2013.

Erratic power supply contributed to the country's economic meltdown and increased public frustration with the state and the Electricity Corporation of Ghana (ECG). On 13 January, the ECG was ordered to pay compensation of about GHS 36,327.7 to 15 consumers whose equipment had been damaged as a result of power fluctuations. This was one of the biggest challenges to the Mahama administration. In order to resolve the issue, Mahama signed a deal with the UAE on 22 May for the production of 5,000 MW of electricity by 2016. The project was expected to produce 100,000 m^3 of desalinated water. The energy challenge was partly blamed on the state's involvement in the electricity sector so, on 17 December, the chair of the Stakeholders Consultations Commission on Energy, Frank Ocran, announced plans to privatise the ECG by mid-2015.

Drinking water remained a challenge, especially in the three northern regions. On 21 January, Mahama inaugurated a seven-year drinking water project under the Northern Region Small Town Water and Sanitation Scheme for the Bunkpurugu community. The C$ 30 m project, jointly funded by the governments of Ghana and Canada, was intended to provide drinkable water to several communities in the north.

An increasing number of *road accidents* were another challenge. On 15 January, the explosion of a petroleum tanker in Kwahu-Fodua (Easter Region) led to the death of eight people mainly women and children, with 13 others injured, and 37 houses destroyed. According to the National Road Safety Commission, the country had by September experienced about 10,061 crashes involving 15,600 vehicles with a total of 1,441 deaths and 8,802 injuries.

During the year, the number of *fire outbreaks* also increased. Between February and November, there were four fires in Kumasi Central Market. The fires destroyed goods worth millions of cedis, with more than 500 traders losing their sources of livelihood. In Accra, on 28 March, Makola market saw a fire in which 200 shops burnt down and 2,000 traders lost their sources of income.

Ghana continued to combat *drug trafficking*. On 7 January, two people were sentenced to 35 years in jail for importing 414 kg of cocaine worth $ 60 m. The most publicised case was that of Ruby Adu Gyamfi alias Nayele Ametefe, who was arrested at Heathrow airport on 10 November for carrying 12.5 kg of cocaine worth $ 3.5 m. She had previously been arrested for being in possession of 10 kg heroin at

Kotoka International Airport (KIA) on 14 April. Investigations revealed that she had travelled through the KIA diplomatic lounge. On 27 November, she pleaded guilty to drug trafficking charges in a court in the UK. This case raised critical questions about the effectiveness of state agencies, in this case the Ministry of Foreign Affairs. Many observers were left wondering how someone not employed in the diplomatic service could possess a diplomatic passport.

Guinea

Anita Schroven

After a promising economic start, popular hopes for social and political improvements, which had been much expected after years of governmental reforms, were disappointed. Guinea suffered from political and economic stagnation due to the outbreak of Ebola, which undermined the fledging economic progress. Local elections that had been scheduled for 2014 were postponed, causing tension amongst the political elite and fuelling lack of trust in the government and the security forces amongst wide sections of the population.

Domestic Politics

The parliament, which had been elected in 2013, was scheduled to hold its first session on 13 January under the presidency of Claude Kory Kondiano of the 'Rassemblement du Peuple de Guinée' (RPG), President Alpha Condé's party. Parliament focused on preparations for the upcoming presidential election. Very little time was spent debating the decline in state income that had resulted from the global slowdown in the mining economy. In June, opposition parties temporarily withdrew from parliament in protest at the government's cancellation of a previously authorised meeting of the 'Union des Forces Guinéens' (UFG) party.

 | DOI 10.1163/9789004305052_011

Cabinet reshuffles on 21 January and 4 February removed more politicians of the late president Lansana Conté's era, while retaining trusted allies, such as Prime Minister Mohamed Saïd Fofana. Naby Youssouf Kiridi Bangoura remained secretary general of the president's office, along with other trusted hands. Energy Minister Papa Koly Kourouma was made minister of state – advisor to the president. Justice Minister Christian Sow was dismissed; the much lauded Kerfala Yansané was transferred from the Ministry for Economy to the Ministry of Mines. Yansané had begun a thorough restructuring in the Ministry for Economy, which remained unfinished. After the dissolution of the Ministry for Religious Affairs, the number of ministries totalled 34. On 22 October, another cabinet reshuffle took place. Energy Minister Idrissa Thiam (only appointed to this post in January) was appointed minister at the Presidency, while former Kaleta-Hydroelectric general manager Malick Taliby Sylla became energy minister. Mahmoud Cissé took over the Ministry of Security and Civil Protection from Madifing Diané.

On 8 August, an embarrassing blow was dealt to the government and the Central Bank by the seizure of a private plane that was carrying around $ 8 m in cash from the Central Bank to Dubai. No further details were made public, but this mode of transport was allowed to continue, with the government's approval. Opposition parties accused the government and the Central Bank of corruption and lack of transparency. Amadou Oury Bah, who had recently returned to the largest opposition party, the 'Union des Forces Démocratiques de Guinée' (UFDG), from exile in France, used this occasion to criticise the government for involvement in corrupt activities.

Local elections scheduled for 2014 were delayed without a new date being set. Talks on the preparation for the 2015 presidential elections began on 26 June, after which opposition spokesperson Aboubacar Sylla ('Union des Forces Républicaines') lauded the good will of all parties. Justice Minister Cheick Sacko announced a new, consensual election road map on 5 July. However, the opposition failed to sign the document because there were contradictory interpretations of its content. The parties did not reach an agreement on the composition of the electoral commission (CENI), its mandate, the composition of its oversight committee or whether or not the CENI should continue to cooperate with the two controversial companies, Sabari and Waymark, which had been contracted for the facilitation of the 2010 presidential elections. Instead of signing the new accord, the opposition parties presented an alternative draft. On 21 August, the opposition rejected all the activities that the CENI had undertaken since July. On 7 November, the opposition repeated its demands and set the government a deadline of 15 December to sign their version of the election accord. President Condé responded by stating that he would not tolerate any demonstrations in the midst of the Ebola outbreak (see below). On 21 November, Minister of Interior and Territorial Administration Alhassane Condé updated parliament on the electoral preparations. He reiterated the government's position and urged the opposition parties to sign the July draft. He gave assurances that Justice Minister Cheick Sacko, who had chaired the July meetings, would soon approach all parties involved to sign a more accommodating draft of the agreement. On 8 December, Cellou Dalein Diallo, runner-up in the 2010 presidential elections and head of the UFDG, stressed the need for full transparency in the electoral process, even if this meant delaying the elections by several months. He reiterated his doubts of the neutrality of the Guinean judiciary in light of the controversial decisions regarding the 2010 and 2013 election results.

Throughout the year, the government insisted that the debate about electoral reform should be held in parliament, which had refused to honour a 2013 agreement between the government and opposition parties. While the government stressed that its priority was to fight the Ebola outbreak, the opposition accused the government of perpetually stalling local and presidential elections and of waiting for an economic recovery that would sway the population to favour the ruling coalition.

In comparison with previous years, fewer political demonstrations took place. A protest on 10 February was motivated by repeated power and water cuts in Conakry, in spite of the government's promises to fix these problems. The protestors were met by police, who had been instructed not to use lethal force; 21 persons were injured. In a subsequent demonstration on 18 February, two people were killed and 33 injured. On 27 February, demonstrators denounced the death of two teenagers who had been shot by police in Fria and broke into the local prison, releasing at least 20 inmates. The population of Kankan demonstrated on 22 March against the increase in violence in the city and in the same month, women protested peacefully against the recruitment policies of a palm oil factory in Diécké in the Forest Region. Security forces violently dispersed the protest and the subsequent popular unrest left five people dead.

The funeral of prominent UFDG-member Amadou Oury Diallo on 26 September turned into a political rally attended by several leaders of the opposition. Cellou Dalein Diallo, president of the UFDG, implied that Amadou Oury Diallo's murder on 15 September was a political assassination intended to deter political protest.

Although there was little progress with the prosecutions in connection with past human rights violations, the judiciary took at least some steps towards the prosecution of certain individuals. In connection with the 2009 stadium massacre known as 'Bloody Monday', more than 400 victims were interviewed as well as several key witnesses, including high-level members of the security forces, who retained their official positions and privileges and in many cases also the support of parts of the population. In February, an ICC delegation visited Guinea in order to maintain pressure on the judiciary to deliver results.

The Reflective Commission, set up by presidential decree in 2011, made little progress towards launching a truth and reconciliation process. The Human Rights Ministry under Gassama Kalifa Diaby remained comparatively inefficient overall but was continuously active in promoting human rights.

The security services used excessive force, but no gross human rights violations took place. On 29 September, the Ibrahim Index of African Governance ranked Guinea 42nd out of 52 countries, lauding its improvement in transparency and governance since the military take-over in 2008. Freedom House maintained Guinea's previous rating of 5.0 while the World Press Freedom Index ranked Guinea at 102nd (of 180 countries), a sharp drop compared with previous years.

President Condé was lauded for keeping the army in check while slowly gaining control over its internal structures and retiring 10,000 soldiers. The government did not increase the army's economic privileges and continued to support the EU-led security sector reform. However, due to military deployment to control population movement in the wake of the Ebola outbreak, relations between the military and civilians became more strained. This was especially the case in the Forest Region, where the military arrested tens of people after disturbances following Ebola interventions.

Ethno-regional tensions increased further and political parties continued to mobilise along ethnic lines. In previous years party demonstrations had often turned violent, but very few such demonstrations took place during 2014 and they remained relatively small. July saw the publication of the long-awaited census, which did not include information about ethnicity. Its regional population estimates conflicted with the electoral lists for the 2013 parliamentary election, which led to suspicions of possible fraud during past and future elections and contributed to the worsening of ethnic tensions.

Foreign Affairs

The UN, the EU, France and the USA remained Guinea's biggest donors. On 27 January, the EU released € 140 m for reforms in the transport, justice and security sectors – funds that had been frozen due to the delay of the elections. As a sign that the EU-led security sector reform (in cooperation with the UN Peace Building Commission) was considered sustainable, the EU lifted its arms embargo, which had been in place since the military coup in 2008. Guinea remained a key hub for the trafficking of South American drugs, so concerns persisted about the willingness of the military and the government to cooperate fully with international security partners.

At an AU meeting in January, Guinea agreed to support the controversial plans for the African Capacity for Immediate Response to Crisis force planned by the AU. At the same meeting President Condé supported UN engagement in the CAR.

In March, Condé welcomed Mali's President Keita for a three-day visit, during which they signed cooperation agreements on energy, agriculture and the free movement of people. In order to facilitate free movement, the Milo River was to be dredged to open up commercial shipping possibilities. On 22 April, a Guinean soldier was wounded in a bomb attack on UN peacekeepers in Mali, but the government still announced its intention to expand Guinean involvement there. On

17 October, ECOWAS and Canada agreed to cooperate in future electoral monitoring missions, including the 2015 Guinean presidential and local elections.

Throughout the year, President Condé and many government members participated repeatedly in WHO, ECOWAS and MRU-level meetings for the Ebola response (see below), strengthening regional public health integration and infrastructure.

Socioeconomic Developments

After several suspicious deaths in the eastern Forest Region, the Guinean government announced an outbreak of Ebola virus disease (EVD) on 22 March. The first suspected victim had died in December 2013. Several members of his family, as well as health workers who had taken care of him, died shortly thereafter. Health Minister Colonel Rémy Lamah banned the consumption of bats and other wildlife. On the same day, 'Médecins Sans Frontières' (MSF) announced the shipment of 33 tonnes of medication and isolation equipment to help curb the outbreak. On 27 March, the first EVD case in the capital, Conakry, was diagnosed, raising alarm about the spread of the virus.

On 14 April, Foreign Minister Lounceny Francois Fall announced that the EVD outbreak had been brought under control, but by 17 April, about 24 healthcare workers were suspected of having been infected with the Ebola virus and at the end of the year 70 health workers had died. On 4 May, the Mano River Union met to discuss joint efforts against EVD, as well as further regional integration in cross-border security and economic cooperation.

A meeting of regional health ministers was held in Accra (Ghana) on 2–3 July to address the challenges involved in fighting the disease. The proposal to close the border caused profound disagreements among the participants. Although Senegal closed its border to Guinea, a Guinea student travelled to Dakar to seek treatment for EVD. This sparked attacks on Guinean citizens and affected trade at border markets. Most airlines stopped their commercial flights to Conakry and other regional airports.

On 6 August, WHO declared the EVD outbreak a "public health emergency of international concern", opening up more possibilities for international agencies to intervene in affected countries. The Guinean government declared a national health emergency on 13 August. Among other measures, it prohibited moving bodies, put travel restrictions in place and increased border controls. At this point, more than 1,550 EVD deaths had been confirmed, mainly in the Forest Region bordering Sierra Leone and Liberia. While transmission rates were slowing down in Guinea itself, many healthcare professionals were infected (80 by 23 October), which weakened the public health sector even further. The general lack of trust in the government and its information policy was a major challenge in the fight against EVD. International medical personnel were suspected of harvesting and trafficking organs of the deceased, of experimenting with dangerous drugs and of collaborating with the government to allow a drop in the population in opposition strongholds.

This mistrust was evident in N'Zerekoré, where the spraying of disinfectants caused a riot that spread across the city on 29 August. A 24-hour curfew was imposed to quell the unrest. On 16 September, eight members of a health education team were killed in Womey in the Forest Region. The security forces arrested 11 individuals and dispersed large parts of the local population into the forest. On 11 November, a group of activists went on hunger strike, demanding the return of those who had been arrested.

The government and opposition parties blamed each other for using the outbreak for their own benefit. At the same time, domestic tensions between various ethnic groups increased, especially in the Forest Region. In many places, the local population banned foreigners and the government from accessing their villages, often resorting to violence. On 2 September, the president held a national meeting with civil society and political actors, urging them all to remain united for the period of the EDV epidemic. He named Dr Sakoba Kéita as national coordinator of the EVD efforts.

In September, FAO warned that the disappointing harvest was threatening the food security of 500,000 people and that the country was experiencing increased market prices for basic staple foods. At the same time, border closures began to inhibit cross-border trade and seasonal labour migration. On 25 September, the UN General Assembly considered steps to be taken for the implementation of the first UN mission during a health emergency. Throughout this period, the government was criticised for its slow response to the crisis. On 26 September, the IMF granted Guinea emergency financial assistance of $ 40 m, while the World Bank granted $ 25 m for Ebola containment measures.

The UN Mission for Ebola Emergency Response (UNMEER) was set up in Ghana and started to coordinate UN efforts across the region. In October, 165 Cuban medical doctors arrived in Conakry to help treat the growing number of Ebola patients. The total number of those infected reached 1,667 at the end of September, including 1,018 deaths. On 21 October, the National Assembly increased the Health Ministry's budget by 2.3%.

In November, WHO assessed the EVD outbreak in Guinea as having stabilised. While the situation in Conakry and other areas of the west and north of the country was improving, in the eastern Forest Region infection rates remained steady while the population continued to resist interventions in many parts of the country.

In mid-November, MSF announced that research for treatment would be conducted in three sites: Guékédou, Donka in Conakry, and an undetermined location that was later re-located to Liberia. On 28 November, French President Hollande visited Conakry, underlining his country's support. France pledged $ 125 m to the

UN fund and installed several isolation units and treatment centres across Guinea, as well as training centres for health workers.

On 3 December, ECOWAS dispatched its first batch of volunteer healthcare workers to the three most affected countries, including Guinea. UN Secretary-General Ban Ki-moon, Margaret Chan (WHO), David Nabarro (UN special envoy on Ebola) and Anthony Banbury (head of UNMEER) visited Conakry on 20 December.

At the end of the year the total number of EVD victims in Guinea was estimated to have reached 2,707, of whom 1,708 had died (and in West Africa as a whole, 20,206 infected and 7,905 deaths).

In February, the IMF concluded its third economic review under the ECF and disbursed $ 28.2 m, bringing the total amount of the scheme to $ 112.8 m. Labour-intensive infrastructure projects were implemented with the support of the AfDB, which calculated the unemployment rate at 61% in June. In September, the World Bank loaned Guinea $ 20 m to counter youth unemployment and improve the agricultural sector. On 17 December, AfDB announced a transport infrastructure programme for the Mano River Union to benefit trade and investment. Guinea's share was $ 11,774,000.

The government conducted a World-Bank-financed census of its civil servants and found that about 11,080 of a total of 101,689 listed staff were missing or non-existent. Freezing these salaries would save about $ 1.7 m per month. In an effort to curb the high unemployment rate, the government announced plans to hire up to 10,000 new civil servants and was budgeting accordingly for the following year.

In 2013, the World Bank had forecast an annual growth rate of 4.5% for 2014. Owing to the consequences of EVD, this was lowered to 2% in October and, at the end of the year, the World Bank put the annual growth rate at 0.5%. These calculations were partly influenced by the drop in agricultural production as farmers fled the fields in Ebola-affected areas. Production of rice – Guinea's staple food – was estimated to have fallen by 40%.

While revenue forecasts were lowered by $ 93 m, spending increased by $ 106 m (3% of GDP), which was one indicator that the government had ceased budgetary austerity for the year, regardless of the public health emergency. Non-Ebola-directed spending was cut as $ 10 m was diverted to the Ebola response plan. The plan totalled $ 90 m and was adopted to facilitate logistics and acquisition of food and equipment, as well as to cover salaries. The adjusted budget, including the negative balance of -$ 286 m, was fully financed with the help of budget support by the IMF ($ 41 m), the World Bank ($ 50 m) and the AfDB ($ 32 m), announced in September. Inflation fluctuated in the course of the year, with an overall average of 10%. Despite these negative factors, Guinea retained its position on many international indices; for example, it stayed at 179th on the HDI. The World Bank kept Guinea at 168th in its 'Doing Business' report. On 3–5 February, the annual African mining conference Indaba in Cape Town (South Africa) ranked Guinea as 'Top Spot' in its investment category. In July, the Extractive Industry Transparency Initiative deemed Guinea to be fully compliant with their regulations, further adding to the government's positive track record on making mining revenues more transparent.

Production in mining, Guinea's biggest economic sector, did not shrink significantly, despite international staff being recalled because of the Ebola outbreak. Some local staff started to be laid off at the end of the year, however. Most mines were located in low-infection areas and could therefore maintain operations. Due to the global economic downturn, the IMF and the World Bank expected the mining sector to shrink by 3% and, with the Ebola outbreak, this was adjusted to 4%. The biggest mining project, Rio Tinto's Simandou explorations, was at a standstill, as was the Vale and Benny Steinman Group Resources (BSGR) joint venture on the northern half of the site. On 9 April, a government-initiated mining-review panel recommended stripping the company of its rights to the site because indications of corruption in the title's acquisition had come to light. In the USA, some of the company's representatives were being charged with corruption involving the late president Conté's wife, Mamadie Conté, and her brother Ibrahima Sory Touré, who headed BSGR's Guinean subsidiary. While Vale was cleared of this accusation, BSGR had plans to sue the Guinean government over these proceedings, demanding international arbitration instead. After the decision was made public, Rio Tinto sued BSRG, Vale and some Guinean individuals, amongst them former mining minister Mahmadou Thiam, for damages in connection with their Simandou dealings since 2005. In September, Benny Steinmetz accused President Condé of rigging the narrowly-won 2010 presidential elections with the help of South African politicians and business men, citing allegations that had long been made by Guinean opposition parties against the South Africa-based election firm Waymark. In the long-term, the dispute had the potential to secure BSRG an opportunity to regain the concession. With the weakness of the global iron ore market, no other company had yet presented a bid for the Simandou concession.

Meanwhile, Rio Tinto reached an agreement with Chinalco and International Finance Corporation on a $ 20 b investment framework for its Simandou concession on 27 May. The agreement needed parliamentary approval as Guinea held a 7.5% stake in the project.

Artisanal mining, especially for gold, remained a security problem. On 16 April, seven people were killed at a gold mine near Siguiri. On the southern coast, a boat with 61 persons on board sank after colliding with a mining vessel in high seas on 12 October. Twenty persons were reported dead.

Guinea-Bissau

Christoph Kohl

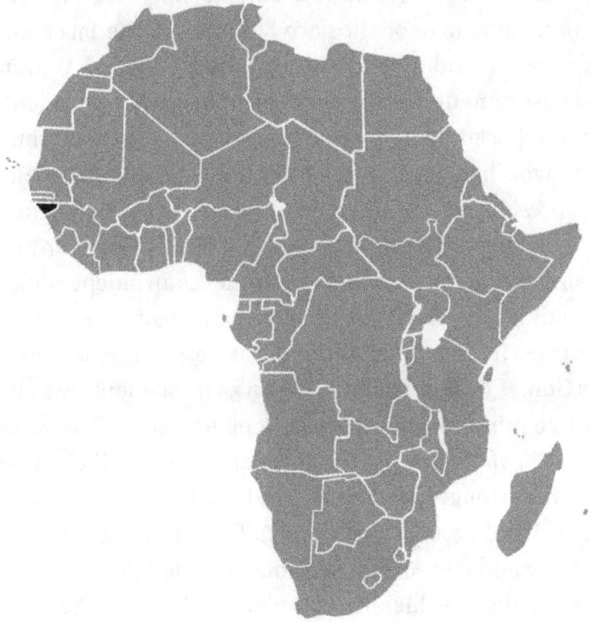

The year was marked by democratic general elections in April and May, leading to the replacement of the unpopular and corrupt 2012 post-coup 'transitional government'. The 'Partido para a Independência da Guiné e Cabo Verde' (PAIGC) obtained an absolute majority in parliament and won the presidency. Despite its majority, the PAIGC formed a government inclusive of all parties represented in parliament. In the aftermath of the elections, political tensions decreased, helped by the unexpected death of long-time political agitator, former state-president Kumba Yalá (PRS) in April and the dismissal of the controversial general chief of staff, António Indjai, in November. Both were believed to be behind the 2012 military coup. International relations normalised, sanctions were lifted, and financial and development cooperation was resumed.

Domestic Politics

After the *elections* had been postponed twice (originally scheduled for April 2013), they finally took place on 13 April. A lack of organisational resources hampered the registration process. After numerous delays, registration was completed on

 | DOI 10.1163/9789004305052_012

10 February. The 'transitional government' (dominated by the 'Partido da Renovação Social' [PRS]) and the military reportedly attempted to influence the registration in favour of the PRS and politicians close to former president Kumba Yalá. At the PAIGC congress in early February, former 'Comunidade dos Países de Língua Portuguesa' (CPLP) secretary-general Domingos Simões Pereira competed successfully against businessman Braima Camará to be the party's prime ministerial candidate and party leader. Both the PAIGC and the PRS were internally divided. Within the PAIGC, a pro-'transitional government' wing around the transitional president, Manuel Serifo Nhamadjo, was opposed by a wing of supporters of former prime minister Carlos Gomes Júnior, who had been deposed in the 2012 coup. The PRS nominated Abel Incada as its presidential candidate, but former party leader Yalá and military circles supported businessman Nuno Gomes Nabian. The former PRS heavyweight and speaker of parliament, Ibrahima Sory Djaló, ran as an independent. Among the 13 presidential candidates were former World Bank economist Paulo Gomes (independent) and former finance minister and businessman José Mário Vaz (PAIGC), an ally of Carlos Gomes Júnior. The PAIGC won 55 parliamentary seats (out of 100), the PRS 41 and three minor parties together took four seats. The voter turn-out on 13 April was high (89% of 775,508 registered citizens). A runoff election between Vaz (who emerged as the strongest candidate) and Nabian was scheduled for 18 May; Vaz won with a majority of 62% (364,000 votes). The international community declared the elections free and fair. Although Nabian claimed that electoral irregularities had taken place, he did not file any complaints. Cipriano Cassamá (PAIGC) was elected speaker of parliament on 17 June, and announced the (re-) creation of an ethics commission to fight political corruption. The newly elected President Vaz was sworn in on 23 June. Despite its majority, the PAIGC formed an all-party government, reportedly to preclude potential opposition and resistance to security sector reform from amongst the military. Criticism within the PRS against this settlement began to spread in October, with calls for the PRS to withdraw from the government.

Headed by Domingos Simões Pereira, the *new government*, composed of 16 ministries, was sworn in on 4 July. Parliament unanimously approved the government programme on 23 September. The new heads of the national and regional administrations, as well as the new heads of the state media, were progressively appointed thereafter. On 6 June, Vaz announced that the controversial attorney-general, Abdu Mané, had been dismissed; Hermenegildo Pereira became his successor on 2 October. António Artur Sanhá, the former prime minister and leading member of the PRS, was dismissed as mayor of Bissau on 22 September. Having been involved in the killing of a girl in 2001, Sanhá was accused of bad governance. Adriano 'Atchutchi' Gomes Ferreira, a cultural activist and ally of the late president João Bernardo 'Nino' Vieira, was nominated as his successor. A setback for the government was the resignation of Interior Minister Botche Candé on 28 November. Candé had visited the northern border areas and unwittingly crossed the border into Senegal, where he and his entourage were surrounded by Casamance rebel fighters.

Army general chief of staff and éminence grise António Indjai was dismissed on 15 September and replaced by Biague Nantam, the previous head of the presidential guard. Nantam had a good relationship with Vaz and was believed to have a stronger commitment to democratic norms. Indjai was appointed as presidential advisor, which stripped him of any political influence. Convicted military officials allegedly involved in a coup attempt on 21 October 2012, including the reported spearhead and Indjai ally, Pansau Ntchama, were released by the government on 9 September. They were granted amnesty on 30 September. On 29 July, Defence Minister Cadi Seidi prohibited the wearing of *military* uniforms off duty, underlining the subordination of soldiers to civilian rule.

According to TI, *corruption* increased in 2013 as a result of political instability. The Ibrahim Index of African Governance ranked Guinea-Bissau 48th (out of 52) in September. Simultaneously, Attorney-General Mané was accused of embezzling € 23,000 that had been confiscated in 2013. On 19 March, the lawyer of the former head of Bissau's port authority was arrested after he tried to bribe an investigating prosecutor. In June, accusations against the Bissau-Guinean embassy in Lisbon became known; € 26,000 had disappeared. The embassy had survived without any funds from Bissau for decades. Vaz's presidential decree of 7 July required all civil servants who had been employed since the 2012 military coup to leave the presidency. This triggered a debate about inflationary promotions in the security forces and the drastic increase of the civil service after the 2012 coup. In fact, the transitional interior minister António Suka Ntchama had promoted more than 200 officials on 25 February and General Chief of Staff Indjai had created several new battalions. The government promised to put an end to illicit police road blocks, which the police had used to extort money. In August, it was reported that Foreign Minister Mário Lopes da Rosa (PRS) had misappropriated technical equipment from a fishery project. As a result, Prime Minister Pereira asked his cabinet on 28 August to disclose their assets in order to improve transparency. On 15 September, the Interior Ministry announced that it had reimbursed € 51,000 that had been 'lost' when former civil servants had not been removed from the payroll. In October, more than 160 municipal officials were dismissed. All of them had been employed since the coup, thus contributing to the growing burden of the public sector salaries. Trade union protests were the consequence. On 27 November, the EU announced its intention to invest € 555,000 in a UN project on public accountancy.

On 5 January, civil society demanded the trial of those responsible for the 2012 coup. The coup had long-term effects on *human rights*. In the search for exiled former prime minister Gomes, armed police, military and National Guard officials invaded the regional UN Integrated Peace-Building Office in Guinea-Bissau (UNIOGBIS) branch in Buba on 16 January, responding to intelligence service rumours. Military and police forces with alleged links to organised criminals repeatedly interfered in criminal investigations being carried out by the Judicial Police. In February, members of the intelligence service vowed the death of two minor party politicians. On 20 March, a former soldier and PRS political activist was beaten and arrested by the military for alleged desertion. In May, PAIGC members were attacked and beaten by a small crowd in Bafatá. In September and October, several former and current officials, among them the former minister of the interior Ntchama and former prime minister Rui Barros, were interrogated about the beating of the transitional transport minister, Orlando Viegas, in November 2013.

On 14 and 30 January, several members of the military and the national guard were sentenced to long prison sentences for assassinating a Chinese businessman in Bafatá in September 2013. This dealt a blow to the general feeling that the security forces enjoyed impunity. However, despite some progress, police officials continually violated basic rights and freedoms and were involved in corruption and crime. The regional police superintendent of Bafatá was dismissed in August because he was allegedly involved in the concealment of a crime and the misappropriation of rice and oil that the government had set aside for police lunches.

The *media* came under attack from the government: in February, Attorney-General Mané pressed charges against several print journalists for violating his and the Supreme Court president's 'dignity'. In March, a new media law came into force.

Although Guinea-Bissau is officially a mine-free country, a *landmine* from the colonial period killed 22 people on 30 September.

The former head of state, *Kumba Yalá*, died unexpectedly on 4 April.

Foreign Affairs

The international community, notably the UN, the EU, Portugal, Timor, New Zealand and ECOWAS supported and accompanied the electoral process. After the elections, *international relations* normalised: Brazil and the EU re-launched bilateral cooperation in July, and Portugal did the same in November. Relations with Cabo Verde were also normalised. In December, the government expressed its interest in Timor opening a consulate in Bissau, given Timor's financial and technical engagement. Diplomatic relations with Angola were normalised, although human rights activists lamented the disappearance of several Bissau-Guinean citizens in Angola. On 18 June, Guinea-Bissau was readmitted to the AU and on 29 December the USA reinstated Guinea-Bissau as a preferential trading partner.

Drug-trafficking remained a challenge. The police confiscated cannabis in the Cacheu Region and 2 kg cocaine and 27 kg cannabis at Bissau's international airport in September; several individuals were arrested. Former navy chief of staff José Américo Bubo Na Tchuto, who had been arrested by the US Drug Enforcement Administration in 2013, pleaded guilty to drug-trafficking at a New York court in May.

His aid Papis Djemé was sentenced to six-and-a-half years in prison in September, and his bodyguard Tchamy Yalá to five years in December.

The former president of São Tomé e Príncipe, Miguel Trovoada, was appointed as the new UN Special Representative and Head of *UNIOGBIS* on 14 July, succeeding José Ramos Horta. On 29 May, UNIOGBIS's mandate was extended until 30 November and again on 25 November until 28 February 2015.

Various international actors continued to support *security sector reform*. This took various forms, including the rehabilitation of police stations, the renovation of courts and the provision of security equipment. This was particularly important in the interior, where livestock theft, assassinations, and armed attacks occasionally occurred. Prior to the elections, UNIOGBIS and Brazil provided security training for 1,500 police and military officials. This occurred in cooperation with the ECOWAS Mission in Guinea Bissau (ECOMIB), which strengthened its presence in the country. On 11 March, the media reported that some progress was being made with regard to the pension fund, as about 900 military officials intended to retire, while the government announced in November that the number would be around 2,000. The police training centre that had been financed by Brazil was officially inaugurated on 19 November; the building for this had been handed over to the government in 2011. In December, plans to enable the military to grow its own food emerged as part of security sector reform. On 14 December, ECOWAS recommended the extension of ECOMIB's mandate for a further six months (until 30 June 2015).

Socioeconomic Developments

The international community provided essential *financial support*. From January to June, the World Bank paid the salaries of teachers and health workers ($ 15 m) and also pledged to pay all salary arrears that were owed in the public sector. The contract between the government and the World Bank was signed 3 April. The IMF urged the new government to restore budgetary discipline, avoid arrears, and improve the business environment. The Central Bank of West African States granted a credit worth € 23 m. According to press reports on 13 August, Timor donated $ 6 m. On 29 October, the EU provided budgetary assistance of € 20 m. On November 3, the IMF approved an emergency assistance package worth € 4 m as part of its rapid credit facility.

According to the IMF, food insecurity and poverty increased during the rule of the transitional government. The World Bank's International Development Association provided $8.2m, the EU €10m, and WFP €5m in early 2014 in order to improve *food security*. The EU and Guinea-Bissau renewed their *fishing* protocol (2014–17), which meant an annual income for Guinea-Bissau of €9.2m. On 30 November FAO announced that *rice* production was expected to fall by 36% due to irregular rainfalls. The price f rice doubled, prices for other agricultural goods. Although the prices for *cashew* (the country's main cash-crop) recovered in 2014, the country's export (68,000t) due to smuggling (production: 250.000t) as the state Fund to Promote Industrialization of Agricultural Products charged high taxes. The IMF demanded the funds suspension. The West African Development Bank continued to finance several development projects. In November Portugal promised to implement various development projects worth €6.8m.

Guinea-Bissau ranked 177th (of 187 evaluated countries) in the 2014 *HDI* and was unable to achieve the *MDGs*. Although the fight against malaria showed positive results, the HIV/AIDS prevalence rate was at an alarming high. On 13 August, the government announced the provision of free health insurance for pregnant women, children and the elderly. Due to the *Ebola* outbreak, the country closed its borders with neighbouring Guinea between 12 August and early December. Public gatherings were prohibited and public awareness campaigns about the dangers of Ebola, as well as disinfection and cleanup campaigns, began. In September, the World Bank pledged $ 750,000 for an Ebola prevention plan.

In February, the Finance Ministry announced that tax revenues had fallen. On 3 December, President Vaz declared that the transitional government had accumulated a total public debt of € 15 m in 2013. In February, the IMF reported that the country's fiscal deficit (for 2013) stood at 2.2% of GDP. The new government reported revenue increases in September. With the exception of the Safim control post (outside the capital), the government disbanded all fiscal checkpoints in July. New checkpoints were scheduled to open in 2015. On 26 August, the government reported that peasant products were tax exempted up to a certain threshold. In July, the IMF estimated the annual growth rate at 2.5%. Parliament unanimously approved the *annual budget* (€ 183 m) on 29 September, recording a deficit of € 95 m. The 2015 budget of € 225 m was approved on 9 December, recording a deficit of € 87 m.

Minor *infrastructure* improvements included the rehabilitation of roads in Cacheu province (March). In June, the World Bank announced $ 17.2 m worth of support for a *water and electricity* supply project. The government promised on 29 October to increase the electricity capacity by December and to construct a new power station by the end of the election period; the generators arrived in December. Bissau had suffered from energy shortages for years, but the electricity and water supply had deteriorated even further during the rule of the transitional government. In July, the WADB gave € 116 m for infrastructure projects. State-run *Guiné Telecom* ceased to operate in early 2014, leaving the country without land lines. Two private mobile operators now dominated the telecommunications market. In December, the US company Securiport took over security control at Bissau's international *airport*. On 14 November, EuroAtlantic started to directly link Bissau and Lisbon; the Portuguese carrier TAP had suspended its activities in 2013. On 30 October, China invested $ 20 m in the construction of a new palace of justice.

As in previous years, the whole of the public sector (ministries, schools, hospitals and state media) were affected by *strikes*. In most cases, public sector employees were calling for the payment of their salaries and social security contributions. As a result of an extended period of strikes in the education sector, the government cancelled the 2013–14 school year in May. Strikes in the state media sector put a temporary end to the broadcasting of election campaigns. After July, the new government paid all regular salaries and, with international assistance, also covered the most recent salary arrears.

Illegal logging, timber exportation and awarding of logging licences particularly by the military had boomed under the transitional regime. Impoverished communities and poorly paid officials benefitted from bribes, mostly paid by Chinese operators. President Vaz announced a review of existing licences in June. The government prohibited the export of timber in July and logging in the capital in August, but these measures were difficult to enforce. *Illegal fishing* remained an issue. In January, the Senegalese authorities captured a Russian vessel with 20 Bissau-Guineans on board. One Senegalese and five Chinese ships were seized in November. It was revealed in January that offshore *petroleum* resources were larger than expected. *Heavy mineral sands* exploitation by the Russian enterprise Poto, working with a five-year government licence in north-western Guinea-Bissau, started in May. The local populations were heavily opposed to this and expressed ecological and economic concerns. The government suspended the explorations in July, but the project continued in November. The Angolan company *Bauxite* Angola (BxA) restarted its activities in September, intending to exploit deposits in the eastern part of the county. With Portuguese assistance, the country's internet top level domain *.gw* was up and running from November.

Liberia

Lansana Gberie

The country was overwhelmed for most of the year by a devastating Ebola epidemic, which struck Liberia like a biblical plague in March. Efforts to eliminate the virus overtook all other state priorities and nearly led to political instability. The despatch of 4,000 US troops to build dozens of treatment centres and provide other support helped stabilise Sirleaf's faltering regime. The death toll from the disease rose to over 3,600 by year's end, making Liberia the country most affected by the outbreak. The toll on the country's economy was also dramatic. Growth dropped from about 6% at the beginning of the year to only 1% by year's end, and inflation reached double digits.

Domestic Politics

On 24 January, a Supreme Court decision exonerating *Mary Broh* promised months of excitement for the country's sensationalist media and unruly political class. Broh, an unusually effective and feisty former mayor of Monrovia and a close friend of President Ellen Johnson Sirleaf, had been suspended from office by Sirleaf in February 2013 after House of Representative members accused her of contempt and

 | DOI 10.1163/9789004305052_013

of being "arrogant, disrespectful, and disobedient" by protecting a colleague from being arrested on the orders of the House. Sirleaf had appointed Broh to the lucrative position of director general of the General Services Agency in September 2013, and critics said the president's apparently easy capitulation to the lawmakers called her judgement into question. For weeks, the local media connected this to a series of past *missteps by Sirleaf*, including several unresolved corruption allegations against senior officials in her government, until it was replaced by another scandal around a damning report into most sectors of the country, written for USAID by the Washington consultancy firm Chemonics International. Leaked in early March, the report, entitled "Liberia Governance Stakeholders Survey", asserted that *corruption* was deep-rooted in the Liberian state and society, and blamed public servants "at all levels". It claimed that 4,100 schools listed as receiving financial support from the government did not exist, and that 9,000 employees had been suddenly added to the Education Ministry's payroll just before the 2011 elections. The 118-page report examined the political economy of the government payroll and was intended to recommend measures to help strengthen governance reform. It claimed that the government payroll was "dominated by syndicates of corruption that operate at all levels of the public administration" and that a large number of the employees were 'ghosts'.

In May, the National Legislature conducted public hearings on the *General Audit Commission*'s reports on state entities between 2006 and 2010, which Sirleaf's government had ignored. The audit reports had exposed numerous instances of graft and misuse of state funds. However, when IMF findings concluded that contracts were issued by key service delivery government ministries without budgetary allocations or proper procurement procedures, Sirleaf announced an investigation into all contracts between the Ministry of Works and construction companies. The investigation had not been concluded by year's end.

Following the Audit Commission's reports, the usually inert Liberia *Anti-Corruption Commission* increased the number of audits and investigations of corruption cases, and reviewed several asset declarations. The Commission investigated two cases involving former government officials, but failed to take action against 30 individuals believed to have misrepresented their assets during a verification conducted in 2013.

The USAID report excited considerable public comment, until the *outbreak of Ebola virus disease* (EVD) made such a scandal look trivial. EVD was first confirmed in Guinea, near the Liberian border, on 22 March, and quickly spread to Liberia, which reported its first cases in Lofa County, close to the Guinean epicentre, by mid-March. By 10 April, 26 suspected and confirmed cases were reported, with 13 deaths, some of them in the Monrovia area. On 15 April, about a month after the outbreak, the government launched its first testing facility, in Kakata, close to Monrovia. On 1 July, Samuel Muhumuza Mutoro, a Ugandan surgeon at the John F. Kennedy Hospital (JFK) in Monrovia, Liberia's largest hospital, died after being diagnosed with Ebola. About three weeks later, a prominent Liberian doctor and JFK's main expert on Ebola, Samuel Brisbane, succumbed to the virus. This was followed by an announcement by the American charity Samaritan's Purse that an American doctor, Kent Brantly, was in quarantine with Ebola at Monrovia's ELWA Hospital. He was sent to the leading Center for Disease Control and Prevention in Atlanta, USA.

The ravages of the virus and its toll on state capacity were exacerbated by *security concerns*. On 3 July, over 500 people took part in a violent protest at the multinational ArcelorMittal iron ore company in Nimba County, claiming that the company was not complying with its social commitments. The overwhelmed Liberia National Police reportedly used firearms, though no one was killed. Company property worth millions of dollars was destroyed. Only the intervention of the UN police prevented further escalation. The government arrested 57 persons and charged them with kidnapping and terror threats. Sirleaf described the demonstration as "an attack on the Liberian economy". Close to 80% of Liberia's poorly equipped and poorly trained police force of about 5,000 were deployed around the capital, Monrovia, and the incident at AcelorMittal mines demonstrated its reliance on the UN police to prevent the frequent protests in the capital – by oppositionists, students and former soldiers who had served ex-president Charles Taylor's regime – from escalating into violence. Moreover, HRW accused the Liberian police of being "riddled with corruption and a lack of professionalism and accountability" and acting as "predators" on citizens.

The security implications of EVD itself soon became evident when on 23 July, a man claiming that an Ebola-stricken relative was not being given proper treatment set fire to the main conference hall of the Ministry of Health and Social Welfare in Monrovia, causing around $ 200,000 worth of damage. Then, on 27 July, irate members of a community in Lofa took bodies of Ebola victims from the makeshift hospital to give them a traditional burial, which the government had persistently warned against. They burnt a government ambulance, which they thought had been responsible for introducing the disease to the area. By 30 July, a total of 383 cases had been reported in Liberia, resulting in 216 deaths, including of health-care workers.

That day, Sirleaf declared a *state of emergency*; security officers were deployed to quarantine infected areas and all non-essential state employees were sent on 30 days' leave. The disease continued to spread rapidly, particularly in Monrovia, and confused and fearful residents began throwing dead bodies on the streets. The government set aside $ 20 m for a special fund to combat the outbreak, about 60% of which was allocated to the security agencies. Under Operation White Shield, declared on 8 August, Sirleaf deployed hundreds of troops across the country. This did not stop residents in the slum district of West Point from looting an Ebola holding and treatment centre on 16 August, stealing mattresses and other equipment and letting all the patients go – further helping to spread the disease in the densely populated city. On 19 August, Sirleaf announced a *nationwide curfew* to be enforced by the armed forces and the national police.

Her minister of defence also promptly deployed troops to quarantine West Point, triggering a shooting incident on 20 August, in which three civilians were seriously wounded, and one, a 15-year-old boy, killed. Sirleaf went to the area a few days later and apologised for the incident.

Political uncertainty and *allegations of a coup plot* to force Sirleaf, now almost universally reviled in Monrovia, to resign and bring in a transitional government led by Vice President Joseph Boakai, added to the confusion. The allegations first surfaced in the 'National Chronicle', a Monrovia tabloid, which in August began running a series that implicated Boakai, along with many prominent Liberians at home and in the USA. The paper described a secret meeting between US President Barack Obama and Boakai, when the latter visited Washington in early August to lobby for support in Liberia's battle against Ebola. Soon after publication, police raided the paper's offices in downtown Monrovia and arrested the editor, Philipbert Browne. The paper was also temporarily banned. Boakai remained silent on the matter, though it was reported that he would be interrogated by Colonel Clarence Chris Massaquoi, the inspector-general of Liberia's national police.

Meanwhile, on 9 September, Minister of Defence Brownie Jeffrey Samukai Jr described the Ebola crisis to the UNSC as "existential". That same day, President Sirleaf wrote a letter to President Obama appealing for support to combat the epidemic, noting that without support "we will never break the transmission chain and the virus will overwhelm us". In a mark of the influence she still wielded in the international community, Sirleaf's letter elicited an immediate response from Obama, who announced the *despatch of 4,000 US troops* to build dozens of treatment centres. Crucially, they also introduced faster tests for the virus and provided other support to Sirleaf's government, which stabilised the political situation. Over 80 health workers, seven Armed Forces of Liberia soldiers, and two UN employees, including a Sudanese doctor, had by then died of Ebola. The epidemic in Monrovia began to subside in September, by which time over 2,800 Liberians had died from the disease.

The persistent allegations of *Sirleaf's nepotism* resurfaced in early October amidst the EVD crisis, when Minister of Justice Christiana Tah resigned, citing in a letter to Sirleaf her inability to investigate corruption in the National Security Agency, headed by Sirleaf's stepson Fumbah Sirleaf. Tah wrote: "I cannot be the minister of Justice and not supervise the operations of the security agencies under the Minister of Justice to independently investigate allegations of fraud against the National Security Agency."

By year's end, Liberia was reporting few new EVD cases, but the virus had already killed close to 4,000 people. The US, China and other partners built treatment centres in every county and half a dozen in Monrovia, though nearly half did not receive a single patient. ECOWAS contributed doctors and funds. Better and faster tests, as well as safer burial (introduced by the US army, which set up several dozen burial teams, replacing an earlier – and problematic – policy of cremation of victims that Sirleaf had introduced as part of the emergency measures) slowed the rate of infection considerably. The UN placed on hold its transition out of the country: by year's end, it was maintaining 4,415 troops, 1,466 police personnel, and 1,621 civilian staff.

This allowed the National Elections Commission (NEC) to conduct *Senate elections* on 20 December for 15 of the 30 seats in the Senate. Originally scheduled for 14 October, as mandated by the constitution, the elections were first postponed to 16 December, and then to 20 December, due to the EVD epidemic. Sirleaf banned campaign rallies, afraid that they might spread the now almost contained Ebola virus. The NEC had in January and March updated the electoral roll and registered 104,710 new voters, well short of its target of 400,000. The NEC attributed this to public apathy. Just over 1.9 m Liberians were registered to vote, 49% of them women. The government allocated $ 13.6 m for the elections. Of the 14 political parties that entered, Sirleaf's Unity Party won the most seats (four), but she received what amounted to a personal blow to her prestige and popularity when her son and former key adviser, Robert Alvin Sirleaf, was overwhelmingly defeated for a senate seat in Monserrado by Sirleaf's old rival, former football star George Weah. The fact that Robert had stood as an independent appeared to make no difference in the perception among Liberians that his defeat amounted to a vote of no confidence in Sirleaf's government. Only two incumbents – Prince Yormie Johnson, a warlord during the civil war, and Jewel Howard Taylor, the estranged wife of former president Charles Taylor – were re-elected, indicating a slight shift in the political landscape. The Unity Party now had ten seats in the 30-member Senate, and 25 of the 73 seats in the House of Representatives. The National Patriotic Party, which was set up by former President Charles Taylor, had six seats in the Senate, the second highest; but only three in the House of Representatives. Weah's Congress for Democratic Change had ten seats in the House of Representatives, the second highest, but only three Senatorial seats. Eleven parties, apart from Independents were represented in the Legislature.

Foreign Policy

Sirleaf demonstrated her international clout when she attracted massive support from the *USA* to combat the EVD crisis. She was also active in getting support from the *AU* and *ECOWAS* and continued to be seen as a major state leader in both organisations. Relations with neighbouring *Côte d'Ivoire*, strained in the past as a result of alleged armed incursions into that country from the porous Liberian border, considerably improved after both countries closed their borders as a result of the EVD crisis. There were reported attacks in March on the Ivorian villages of Fete and Grabo, in which several Ivorian security agents were killed, but no such deadly attacks occurred after the borders were closed in July.

Socioeconomic Developments

The economic outlook, already bleak at the beginning of the year, worsened as a result of the EVD crisis. From January up to the beginning of the Ebola outbreak, GDP *growth slowed* from 8.1% in 2013 to 6.8%, largely because of falling global commodity prices, in particular that of iron ore, Liberia's chief export. *Inflation* rose to 9.8% in April owing to exchange rate depreciation. By April, the Liberian dollar had depreciated by 6.5% (and fell by over 21% by December), resulting in reduced spending by poorer citizens. By year's end, growth had fallen to 1%, and inflation rose from 7.1% at the beginning of the year to 13% by year's end. Around 80% of all flights to Liberia were cancelled, and several service sector businesses were boarded up.

This weak outlook triggered heated exchanges between the president and the legislature, which summoned the minister of finance and planning twice in May, requesting an explanation for revenue shortfalls that were impeding the implementation of the 2013/14 budget. On 16 May, Sirleaf submitted to the legislature a proposed 2014/15 *national budget* of $ 529 m, approximately $ 54 m less than for 2013/14. During these discussions, legislators seized on the USAID report, which had claimed that the government "does not know how much money it should be collecting" in taxes, and that logging concessions alone were responsible for a shortfall of $ 34 m. This criticism, however, was not in line with the way international financial institutions rated Liberia. In 2012, for example, the IMF compared 23 SSA countries and noted that Liberia had performed best in tax collection, at 23% of GDP, compared, for example, with South Africa (at 22%), and Sierra Leone (only 10%). Since 2006, Liberia had attracted the highest FDI per capita in Africa.

The *USAID report* (see above) blamed revenue shortfall on *systemic corruption*. It said that "a culture of impunity, political patronage, and family ties, ethnicity and religion, gender, and corruption" were culpable and that "formal institutions, or the lack thereof, play a key role, enabling informal institutions to thrive. These include a strong executive enabled by a lack of checks and balances, weak enforcement and regulatory bodies, ineffective rule of law institutions, poor systems of accountability, an incomplete legal framework, and unimplemented laws."

All *education* institutions were closed down as a result of the emergency measures announced on 30 July and schools, universities and technical training institutions remained closed at year's end.

The World Bank reported in September that the *agricultural sector*, which accounts for about one-quarter of Liberia's GDP and nearly half of the total employed workforce, was severely affected by the crisis. The production and shipment of rubber, Liberia's most important agricultural export, was seriously disrupted by both the reduced mobility of workers and the difficulty in getting products to ports because of Ebola quarantine restrictions. Rubber exports, estimated at about $ 148 m in 2014, were estimated to have dropped by 20% by year's end. Investments in palm oil production by large corporations including by Sime Darby were disrupted due to the evacuation of managerial and supervisory personnel, and the focus shifted to maintenance. Sime Darby postponed its planned construction of a $ 10 m modern palm oil mill, which had been due to be completed by July 2015. Local food production was also severely affected because the main food growing areas were in Lofa County in the north-west of the country, which was the original locus of the Ebola pandemic. Farms were abandoned.

Mali

Bruce Whitehouse

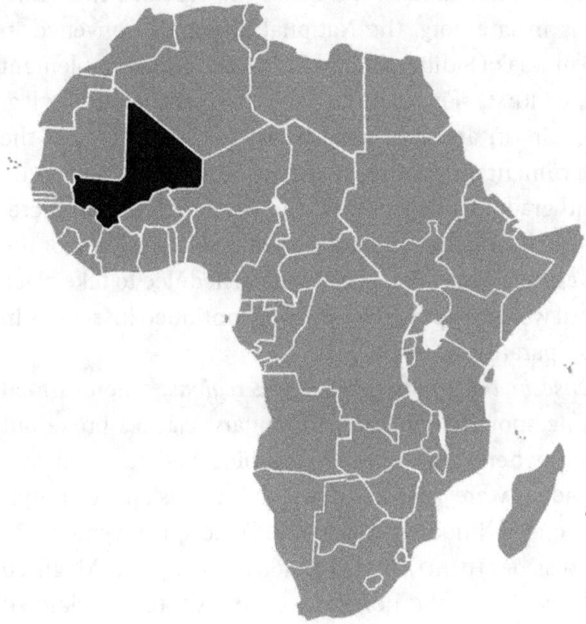

While a 2013 international military intervention brought a measure of stability to the country, old threats persisted within Mali's borders and new ones emerged in 2014. Low-intensity terrorist violence and sporadic clashes between government troops and rebels in the north, corruption scandals and a dramatic outbreak of the deadly Ebola virus in the capital ensured that Mali would stay in the international spotlight throughout the year. The Malian government remained heavily dependent on support from its Western partners but diversified its sources of support by forging new ties with non-Western states. Economically, Mali showed on-going signs of gradual recovery but continued to rely on two primary commodities for its export earnings.

Domestic Politics

Public opinion, according to an Afrobarometer survey conducted in December 2013, was optimistic as President Ibrahim Boubacar Keita's government, established the previous September, began its work. The survey showed that 83% of Malian respondents regarded the 2013 elections as free and fair, while two-thirds felt that

 | DOI 10.1163/9789004305052_014

their country was now moving in the 'right direction'; 92% expressed support for national unity, and 65% felt that a peace agreement between the Malian government and northern rebels would probably permit sustainable peace in the country.

Constitutional order was re-established early in 2014 as many of Mali's political institutions returned to normalcy after the disruptions of the previous two years. Following legislative elections in late 2013, the National Assembly convened in January under the leadership of Issaka Sidibé, a member of Keita's 'Rassemblement Pour le Mali' (Rally for Mali, or RPM). Five months later, party switching by legislators enabled the RPM to gain an absolute majority with a total of 75 of the Assembly's 147 seats. The government also established a new commission for truth, justice and reconciliation, and gradually began to fill the administrative void created in northern regions after many officials and judges had fled in the wake of the 2012 rebel takeover there. Nevertheless, municipal elections scheduled to take place throughout the country in April were postponed because of continued insecurity in some areas and insufficient preparation at the local level.

The *situation remained tense in the country's northern regions*, where armed groups continued to perpetrate sporadic violence. In January, clashes broke out among rival factions in Kidal, where ambushes, kidnapping and targeted killings of rebel fighters and leaders were reported. Two militant Islamist groups, the 'Mouvement pour l'Unicité et le Jihad en Afrique de l'Ouest' (Movement for Oneness and Jihad in West Africa, or MUJAO), and al-Qaida in the Islamic Maghreb (AQIM) stepped up terrorist activity in the north. In February, MUJAO claimed responsibility for the abduction of five civilians, including four employees of the International Committee of the Red Cross, in the Gao region. The five were freed by French troops two months later. Rocket attacks on UN, French, and Malian military bases in the north also occurred with increasing frequency, as did explosions of improvised explosive devices. On average, peacekeeping troops participating in the UN's Multidimensional Integrated Stabilisation Mission in Mali (MINUSMA) were killed or wounded every four days, making it the deadliest UN mission in the world, with 44 deaths and over 100 injuries reported by year's end since the mission began in July 2013.

Political scandals engulfed President Keita's regime beginning in March, when reports emerged in the French media of the president's close association with Michel Tomi, a 67-year-old Corsican businessman with ties to organised crime. The French authorities were investigating Tomi for money laundering, fraud and corruption of public officials stemming from his business activities in multiple African countries, including Mali where he owned a casino. Tomi paid for the training of Keita's personal security detail, and introduced several business associates to Keita after the latter assumed office in 2013. One of these associates helped arrange the purchase of a new presidential jet through a series of opaque transactions that drew the attention of the IMF in May. The IMF, which had granted the Malian government a credit facility worth some € 30 m in return for commitments to transparency and good governance, said that the aircraft purchase (worth roughly € 20 m) was not in Mali's national budget, and demanded an explanation from the Malian Ministry of Finance. The IMF was equally concerned by two no-bid contracts for over-invoiced military equipment awarded to the president's associates totalling more than € 100 m. In May, the IMF and other major donors announced that they would delay transferring funds to the Malian government; the IMF asked the Malian government to publish audits of its irregular spending and tighten its procurement procedures. After the government had met these conditions, aid payments resumed in December. At no time did Keita or his associates admit to any wrongdoing, but his regime was significantly damaged in public opinion by the revelations of improper spending.

The president's poor performance led Prime Minister Oumar Tatam Ly to resign on 5 April, and issue a brief letter suggesting that Keita was unwilling to make necessary reforms. Ly was replaced by Moussa Mara, whose *new government* was installed on 17 April. Mara, 39, was a former presidential candidate and leader of a small political party allied with Keita's RPM; he had served as minister of urban planning in Ly's cabinet. Shortly after he took office, Mara defended Keita's policies, including the acquisition of the new presidential jet, before the National Assembly.

Relations between the Malian government and northern separatist rebels deteriorated throughout early 2014, with no meetings conducted to organise the disarmament of rebel fighters. On 17 May, intense fighting broke out between rebels and government troops in Kidal following a surprise visit by Mara to the rebel bastion, where the Malian government had maintained a largely symbolic presence for several months. Rebel forces captured and killed eight Malian officials and then, on 21 May, defeated a Malian army offensive and ultimately expelled all elements of the Malian security forces and administration from Kidal and three other northern towns. Dozens of Malian soldiers were killed, wounded, or captured in the fighting. A cease-fire was brokered by the UN and the AU on 23 May to prevent further hostilities. Although Mara resisted calls for his resignation, Defence Minister Soumeylou Boubèye Maïga resigned on 27 May.

In the wake of its military reversal in Kidal, the Malian government committed itself to *reinvigorating the stalled peace process*. After concluding, with Algerian mediation, an exchange of prisoners, the government and rebel groups sent representatives to Algiers to work out a 'roadmap to peace'; this roadmap, which reiterated the support of all sides for maintaining Mali's unity and territorial integrity, was signed on 24 July. Formal peace talks began in Algiers on 1 September and continued through November, with discussion of a series of proposed agreements. The draft accord that emerged in November proposed ceding considerable authority to Mali's regions by replacing regional governors, hitherto appointed by the central government, with elected executives, establishing regional legislatures and local police forces, creating a national senate to give an official role to Mali's traditional and religious authorities, and shifting 30% of state revenue from the national to the local level. While this proposal was strongly backed by the international community, it was criticised by many government loyalists who feared that it would pave the way to Mali's eventual partition, and by rebel supporters who pressed their leaders to hold out for an explicitly federal system. The Malian government, for its part, continued to reject any solution that would grant autonomy to the north. Opposition to the proposals was heightened by the exclusion of Mali's civil society groups from the negotiating process, even though they had been guaranteed a role in the talks. The content or status of a final agreement was uncertain by the end of the year, but five rebel groups announced in December that they were 'favourable' to the latest proposal issued in Algiers.

Spurning the peace process, *Islamist militants* continued to mount attacks against the Malian government and its foreign allies throughout 2014, and to hold a number of European hostages. In April, MUJAO announced the death of Gilberto Rodrigues Leal, a Frenchman it had captured in November 2012. Serge Lazarevic, another French hostage captured by AQIM in late 2011, was freed in December in exchange for the release from Malian government custody of his two suspected kidnappers and two other alleged terrorists. Lazarevic's release meant that there were no longer any French citizens being held in the Sahel, but the prisoner exchange was severely criticised by human rights groups for weakening the rule of law in the country. Ansar Eddine, a Tuareg-dominated Islamist faction, claimed responsibility for carrying out a rocket attack that targeted French, UN and Malian troops in Tessalit on 29 December; this was the group's first such claim in nearly a year. French troops, sometimes working in conjunction with Malian and UN forces, mounted regular missions during 2014 to locate and capture Islamist fighters and leaders, and weapons hidden across northern Mali.

Foreign Affairs

The Malian state continued to rely heavily on foreign support to protect it from various threats, as it had since the massive international military intervention in 2013, and President Keita made at least 40 international trips in the course of the year. The Keita regime's perceived unwillingness to strengthen transparency and good governance, however, complicated its relations with key partners abroad.

In May, Prime Minister Mara estimated that about half of the € 3.25 in *international financial assistance* pledged at a 2013 donor conference had already been disbursed. Mara encouraged donors to route more of their funding through the Malian state treasury, which he said was bypassed by two-thirds of all foreign aid spending in the country, but donors' faith in Keita's administration waned due to suspicions of financial mismanagement, lack of accountability, and corruption that surfaced around the acquisition of the presidential plane and the military equipment contracts in the year's second quarter. The freezing of fund payments announced by the IMF, the World Bank, the EU and other major donors in June was evidence of growing distrust between the international community and the Malian government. IMF Director Christine Lagarde, during a visit to Bamako in September, asked Mali's finance minister to cancel certain dubious contracts. The flow of aid was generally restored by the end of the year, but donors remained sceptical of Keita's commitment to reform.

Foreign support for the Malian military, which had been extensive prior to the 2012 coup d'état, was largely limited to the *EU* Training Mission (EUTM), which saw the formation and graduation of two additional Malian army battalions in 2014, to add to the three battalions trained the previous year. In April, the EUTM's mandate was renewed for another year and extended to include training of Malian police and gendarmes. The EU also budgeted € 40 m for humanitarian assistance (including emergency food aid, water and sanitation projects) to Mali in 2014, up € 5 m from the previous year, and committed other funds to road construction, education and heritage preservation projects. EU leaders planned to allocate a total of € 615 m for aid to Mali over the six years beginning in 2014.

The *UN* continued to play an active role in attempting to alleviate the conflict in northern Mali, most notably through its MINUSMA peacekeeping mission, but MINUSMA was plagued by a number of problems in 2014. One was the issue of inadequate staffing: the mission, while authorised to comprise over 12,000 uniformed personnel, had just over 9,000 by year's end. It also lacked sufficient numbers of armoured vehicles to protect its troops on operations, and helicopters to transport them to conflict spots. UN peacekeepers in Mali were therefore mainly limited to protecting the main towns in the north where their garrisons were located, and where they were subject to regular rocket and suicide bombing attacks by Islamist militants. Although Senegal and the Netherlands increased their contingents in MINUSMA by roughly one-third early in 2014, the government of Chad, whose troops taking part in MINUSMA had sustained heavy losses, protested that Chadian soldiers were paying too high a price and receiving inadequate support in their operations in Mali. In October, the governments of Mali and France criticised what they perceived as MINUSMA's inadequate and tardy deployment on the ground. Also in October, the mission suffered a leadership crisis when Bert Koenders left his post as the Secretary-General's Special Representative for Mali and head of MINUSMA after being named foreign minister of the Netherlands. He was replaced in December by Mongi Hamdi, who at the time of his appointment had been serving as foreign minister of Tunisia.

Mali's relations with *France* were overshadowed by the corruption scandals that afflicted Keita's regime, most notably the 'Tomi affair' (see above). After reports of the French investigation appeared in the French newspaper 'Le Monde', alleging that

Keita had received gifts and financial support from Tomi, Keita threatened to sue 'Le Monde' for defamation. While acknowledging his friendship with Tomi, Keita denied that there had been any financial dealings between them. Tensions between the French and Malian governments delayed the signing of an important bilateral defence pact until July. Winding down its 'Operation Serval' military mission in Mali that month, France launched a new mission, called 'Operation Barkhane', with a more regional scope. Three thousand French troops were deployed to the Sahel (including in Burkina Faso, Chad, Mali, Mauritania and Niger) as part of Barkhane, with 1,000 of those troops based in Mali. Soumeylou Boubèye Maïga, Keita's former defence minister, was arrested by police in Paris on 3 October and briefly detained in connection with the ongoing investigation into the Tomi affair.

North African states pursued closer ties with the Malian government. Algeria notably expanded its role in the conflict resolution process by mediating in peace talks between the government and rebel leaders, after having ceded that role to Burkina Faso in 2013. Two of the three Algerian diplomats taken hostage by Islamist militants in the city of Gao in 2012 were released in August, the third hostage having died of illness while in captivity. The government of Morocco also vied for influence in Bamako, where King Mohamed VI paid an official visit in February. Bilateral agreements between the Malian and Moroccan governments established provisions for greater cooperation in agriculture, mining, petroleum exploitation and other areas of investment, and Morocco offered training opportunities for Malian soldiers and imams. In return, Malian officials voiced support for Morocco's position on the disputed Western Sahara. The Malian government also signed multiple cooperation agreements with the government of Tunisia, which extended to agriculture, mining, energy, cultural and religious affairs, education and broadcasting.

Mali also strengthened relations with a number of *partners in Asia*. In May, the government of Japan resumed its aid to Mali, which had been suspended since 2012. In June, Keita was the guest of honour at the annual US-Islamic World Forum held in Qatar, his second visit of the year to the Persian Gulf emirate, and Qatari businessmen were courted in Bamako. In September, the government of China signed 34 agreements with the Malian government during a visit by Keita to the World Economic Forum in Tianjin. Although few details were made public, the agreements were believed to cover over € 8 bn of infrastructure investment, and reportedly included the rehabilitation of the railway between Bamako and Dakar (Senegal), the construction of a new rail link between Bamako and Conakry (Guinea), the construction of a new bridge over the Niger River in Bamako and the expansion of Mali's road network.

Socioeconomic Developments

In October, after the *Ebola virus* had raged in neighbouring Guinea, Liberia and Sierra Leone for several months, Mali confirmed its first case of Ebola infection, a two-year-old girl who had recently entered the country from Guinea. She died on 24 October, but no subsequent infections were traced to her. The next confirmed case came in November after an imam from Guinea was treated at a private clinic in Bamako. The imam's death was not immediately diagnosed as stemming from Ebola, and seven more infections were later traced to him, including two clinic personnel who had treated him. In total, eight cases of Ebola were diagnosed in Mali in late 2014, resulting in six deaths. Despite the relatively low number of cases, the disease's spread highlighted weaknesses with Mali's health infrastructure, and generated significant public and international concern, and schools were closed in some areas for several days. WHO assisted the Malian authorities in tracing contacts of those infected, which resulted in 90 people being placed in quarantine. By the end of December, no new cases had been identified in Mali and no one remained in quarantine.

Mali's *macroeconomic outlook*, which had been seriously weakened by political instability and insecurity in 2012 and 2013, gradually became more optimistic in 2014, with growth for the year estimated at approximately 5% according to the IMF, up from 2% the previous year. Prices of consumer goods in most of the country settled after having spiked in 2013. In the north, however, where violence continued to threaten, economic activity remained at a standstill, and the temporary suspension of major donors' aid from June to September added to economic uncertainty, prompting the government to levy new taxes, including one on livestock exports. The IMF reiterated earlier advice to the Malian government, asking it to make a number of structural reforms to increase tax revenue, tighten controls on spending, and better manage debt. The national budget operated at a 5% deficit for the year, according to state sources.

In the *mining sector*, industrial gold production fell slightly from the year before, down from 47 to 45.8 tonnes as older mines began to exhaust their deposits. Officials estimated that a further 4 tonnes were produced by artisanal miners, and Mali remained the third-largest gold producer on the continent, behind South Africa and Ghana. Construction began in June of the country's first gold refinery, a joint venture between Swiss Bullion Company and Pan African Minerals Beneficiation Consultants worth € 45 m, with production expected to begin in mid-2015. In July, the Malian government cancelled 130 mining permits, about 30% of existing permits, in areas where no mining had been undertaken. The government planned to issue permits to new investors in hopes of spurring activity in these areas, and sought ways to diversify its mineral exports beyond gold. It cancelled 12 petroleum exploration agreements for the Nara and Taoudeni basins, promising to grant exploration permits to companies with the capacity to pursue exploration.

In September, the government announced plans by a Chinese company to develop a new iron mine and steel plant in western Mali, developments that would capitalise on improved rail links to be built by Chinese firms.

In the *agricultural sector*, production of cotton (Mali's second most important export after gold) reached record levels by year's end, standing at 552,000 tonnes, compared with 440,000 tonnes the previous season. Favourable rains and increased state subsidies to inputs, part of a five-year government strategy to boost production, contributed to the rise.

Mauritania

Claes Olsson and Helena Olsson

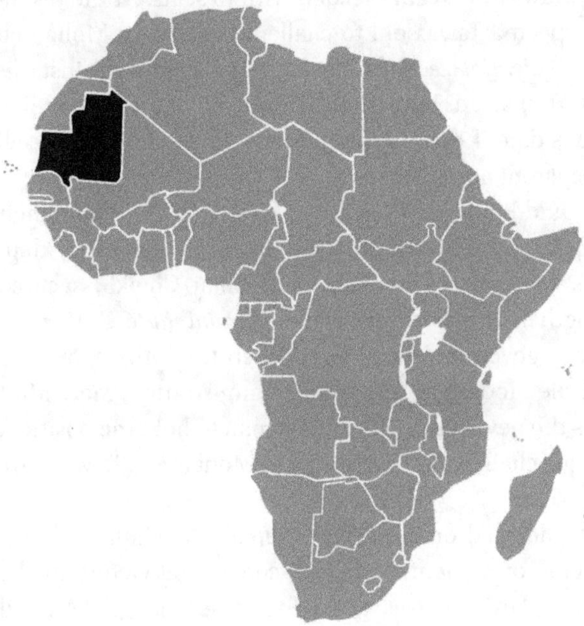

Ensuring political stability and tackling high rates of poverty and unemployment, as well as unequal growth, were the biggest challenges to President Aziz. The president benefited from the UPR's domination of parliament and the fact that the opposition alliance, the 'Forum National pour la Démocratie et l'Unité (FNDU), was fragmented and hardly represented in parliament. The moderate Islamist party, Tawassoul, established itself as the main opposition force. Progress towards the abolition of slavery continued to be slow, notwithstanding the government's attempts to follow the road map to that end.

Mauritania's participation in the UN-led peacekeeping mission in Mali strengthened its role in the war against terrorism in the Maghreb area and possibly secured rewards in the form of increased Western aid. Aziz's electoral victory was welcomed by Algeria and also by Western countries, including the USA and France, which saw him as a reliable partner in the struggle against extremist groups in the Sahel region. Mauritania also strengthened its role as a regional mediator.

 | DOI 10.1163/9789004305052_015

Domestic Politics

Following the opposition's boycott of the parliamentary elections in December 2013, the ruling party, the 'Union pour la République' (UPR) strengthened its position. The moderate Islamist party, 'Tawassoul', came second with 16 seats. At the beginning of the year, observers expected Tawassoul to challenge President Mohamed Ould Abdel Aziz in the June *presidential elections*, but the party decided against this and joined the opposition FNDU instead. Tawassoul claimed that it was impossible to keep to the 21 June elections date if the intention was to hold elections that all participants regarded as transparent and fair.

On 29 January, Mohamed Ould Boilil (UPR) replaced Messaoud Ould Boulkheir as the speaker of the National Assembly, with the support of 89 out of 137 deputies. Tawassoul's candidate, Mohamed Ghoulam Ould Elhaj Cheikh, secured 34 votes. The UPR also strengthened is position in the '*Communauté Urbaine de Nouakchott*', the local authority governing the capital, when the former minister of public service, labour and the modernisation of the administration, Maty Mint Hamady (UPR) was elected as the new mayor, the first woman to hold the position. She received 25 votes while her challenger, Elhacen Ould Mohamed (Tawassoul), secured 12.

Quite surprisingly, the UPR decided on 4 March to replace its chairman, vice chairman and secretary general, only months after its convincing victory in the parliamentary elections. No explanation was given for these changes. Ahmed Ould Isselkou Izid Bih, a former minister, was appointed as the new chairman and Minister of Communication and Relations with Parliament Sidi Mohamed Ould Maham was appointed vice president of the party. Elmoudir Ould Bouna replaced Oumar Ould Maatalla as secretary general.

A number of civil society groups joined the 'Coordination de l'Opposition Démocratique' (COD) and formed together the opposition FNDU, which included a total of 17 parties, ten unions, and several civil society groups. Negotiations between the opposition and the ruling UPR on the procedure for the presidential elections collapsed on 21 April, following a presidential decree fixing 21 June for the first round and 5 July for the presidential run-off. The collapse in the negotiations resulted in a boycott by the major opposition groups: Tawassoul, the 'Alliance Populaire Progressiste' and the FNDU.

President Aziz was re-elected for another five-year term on 21 June with 81.9% of the vote. The well-known anti-slavery campaigner and leader of the 'Initiative pour la Résurgence du Mouvement Abolitioniste en Mauritanie' (IRA), Biram Ould Dah Ould Abeid, received 8.7%, Boydiel Ould Houmeid El Wiam (regarded as close to the exiled former president Maaouya Ould Sid'Ahmed Taya) received 4.5%, and Ibrahima Moctar Sarr ('Alliance pour la Justice et la Démocratie'/'Mouvement pour la Rénovation') received 4.4%. The only female candidate, Lala Meriem Mint Moulay Idriss, received 0.5% of the vote. Ould Abeid launched a legal case contesting the elections, but the Constitutional Council ('Conseil Constitutionnel de Mauritanie') confirmed the election result on 29 June. Nevertheless, Ould Abeid's relative success gained him some influence against the authorities' pressure to marginalise his vigorous campaign for black rights. For the only female candidate, Lala Idriss, the election offered a chance to put the issues of Mauritanian women centre stage.

On 20 August, Aziz appointed former transport minister Yahya Ould Hademine as prime minister and a *new government* was announced on 22 August. It was largely comprised of members of the UPR and was made up of 27 ministers, seven of them women. Divisions between the government and the COD widened, although the opposition remained fragmented. Instead of resuming the negotiations that had started in April, the government and the opposition engaged in a war of words, calling each other forces of evil.

On 26 August, the UN special rapporteur on modern forms of *slavery*, Gulnara Shahinian, presented her report from the follow-up mission to Mauritania on 24–27 February. She applauded the government's adoption of the road map to end slavery but concluded that "further efforts are necessary in order to fully implement the road map" and specifically pointed out that the government lacked definitive data on the nature and incidence of slavery in Mauritania. Boubacar Messaoud, leader of a campaign group, SOS-Esclave, and representatives of other human rights organisations repeatedly claimed that the phenomenon still persisted on a large scale, even though slavery had been formally abolished in 1981 and criminalised in 2007.

Public protests against slavery and in support of land rights continued. On 29 April, thousands of representatives of the Haratin, the descendants of former slaves, staged a protest march in Nouakchott to demand more rights and the enforcement of existing laws against slavery. The protestors also drew attention to the anniversary of the publication of a manifesto on their political, economic and social rights. On 11 November, the former opposition presidential candidate, Biram Ould Dah Ould Abeid, organised a peaceful land rights protest, 'La caravane de la liberté', near the town of Rosso. The protest was brutally put down and Abeid and nine other activists, all members of the IRA, were arrested. They were charged with disrupting public order, encouraging the organisation of an illegal gathering, rebellion, and membership of an unregistered organisation, and remained in custody for rest of the year. The prosecution sought five-year prison sentences, a fine and the confiscation of all IRA property. The incident was a clear indication that the country's human rights record was deteriorating – remarkable for two reasons. First, Abeid was one of the few opposition candidates who had participated in the elections and thus had contributed to the credibility of the presidential poll. Second, the incident stood in clear contrast to the peaceful atmosphere that had surrounded the presidential election.

Mauritania remained top of the list for the prevalence of slavery on the Walk Free Foundation's Global Slavery Index 2014.

Foreign Affairs

International attention to the country's inability to handle the slavery issue, together with the crackdown on the IRA in November, was a problem for the country's international image. However, President Aziz maintained and tried to improve relations with neighbouring SSA countries, especially in West Africa, and also in the Maghreb. The regional terrorist group, al Qaida in the Islamic Maghreb (AQIM), continued to be a major security threat in Mauritania and in the region as whole.

On 30 January, Aziz was elected president of the AU. In his acceptance speech, he highlighted the importance of *regional cooperation*. As an example, he referred to the potential for exploitation of the Senegal River to generate hydroelectric power across the borders of *Senegal, Mali* and Mauritania. Through his position as AU president, Aziz played a key role in a number of negotiations, including the ceasefire agreement between Mali's three main *Tuareg* separatist groups, the National Movement for the Liberation of Azawad, the High Council for the Unity of Azawad and the Arab Movement of Azawad. The ceasefire with the Malian government was signed on 20 May, after intensive talks facilitated by Aziz and the UN special representative in Mali, Albert Koenders.

On 15–17 February, Aziz chaired a summit of five Sahel states, Mauritania, Mali, Burkina Faso, Niger and Chad, which agreed on an institutional framework for the coordination and monitoring of regional cooperation in development and security, the *G5 Sahel* (G5S).

On 11 February, Mauritania participated in a conference in Algiers at which African police chiefs agreed on establishing the African Mechanism for Police Co-operation (*Afripol*), a body for cooperation between police forces on the continent, based in Algiers. The commitment to set up Afripol was seen as a part of wider efforts to increase security cooperation among AU members.

Relations with the USA remained good and mainly focused on US military training of local troops as part of concentrating the *US counterterrorism strategy* on the training of local forces rather than the commitment of US troops. Significant quantities of weapons from Libyan army arsenals that had been raided after the downfall of the Kadhafi regime had come into the possession of numerous groups, including AQIM, the Movement for Oneness and Jihad in North Africa and 'Ansar Dine'. These groups continued to pose a serious security threat to the Sahel region. ('Sahelistan').

Socioeconomic Developments

Generally speaking, the government's *macro-economic policy* was based on the country's third poverty-reduction strategy paper (PRSP-3), which runs for the period 2011–15. The IMF praised Mauritania's efforts to improve its fiscal position through stronger fiscal and external buffers. There was a marked increase in public spending on *infrastructure projects*, such as an overland electricity line, a water supply system and a new airport. *Real GDP growth* was estimated at 5.4% (compared with 6.4% in 2013). Consumer price inflation stood at 4.4% and the exchange rate was regarded as moderately overvalued. The IMF estimated that the overall fiscal balance, including grants, deteriorated to a deficit of 4.1% of non-oil GDP. The average annual inflation was estimated at 4.4% and the general downward trend in non-oil commodity prices dampened inflationary pressures. The *current-account deficit* increased to $ 1.6 bn (compared with $ 1.4 bn in 2013) partly as a result of lower official transfers and higher spending on the imports of goods and services.

The national *iron ore* company, the 'Société Nationale Industrielle et Minière' (SNIM), maintained a dominant position. Its income accounted for 25% of GDP and nearly half of the country's exports. During the first half of 2014, SNIM produced 6.7 m tonnes of iron ore from the Zouerate mine, which indicated an 8.5% year-on-year increase in production. However, following the 30% drop in the price of iron ore, the company launched a cost-reduction programme in July, including 30% cuts in spending.

The distribution of wealth remained highly unequal. According the World Bank, 42% of the population (3.8 m people) were living in poverty. WFP estimated that 20%-30% of the population were still suffering from high food insecurity. The *unemployment rate* remained high. According to national employment strategy documents, it stood at slightly above 30%. The informal sector absorbed a significant number of job seekers. Renewed problems in the global economy and economic uncertainties in the US and the euro zone continued to constitute risk factors in the already vulnerable economy.

On 20 February, EU Development Commissioner Andris Piebalgs announced € 195 m of support for Mauritania in the areas of food security, rule of law and healthcare for the period 2014–20. The commissioner met both President Aziz and Prime Minister Moulaye Ould Mohamed Laghdaf during his visit. Their discussions focused in particular on ongoing cooperation projects between the EU and Mauritania in the areas of security, development and fishing. The meeting also considered EU support for security measures in the Sahel.

In its implementation completion and result report on Mauritania, produced on 19 November, the World Bank expressed concern over the country's public procurement system. The Islamic Development Bank expressed concern over the conditions for the extension of the dual fuel power station in Nouakchott. The contract (worth $ 67.7 m) was awarded to the Wartsila Group without going through a competitive tender.

The fishing sector continued to be important. A Moroccan group, Unimer, secured a contract to build a $ 28 m fish-processing plant in Nouadhibou and began work in October. The plant was expected to create 1,000 jobs and to stimulate the creation of an additional 500 jobs in businesses that would profit from the plant. It was estimated that the plant would process 100,000 tonnes of fish per annum. European fishing boats were ordered to halt operations temporarily in late June because of a breakdown in negotiations between Mauritania and the EU on an extended fishing agreement. As a consequence of a compromise, demersal and tuna fleets had to stop fishing on 31 July. Shrimpers and small pelagic fleets were able to continue fishing until the end of the year.

The central bank supported the government's efforts to keep inflation at a moderate level and continued to manage a flexible exchange rate regime. Early in the year, the central bank governor, Sid'Ahmed Ould Raiss, confirmed that T-bill sales had been reduced after a record increase in the country's foreign reserves in 2013. On 10 September, the central bank organised a meeting to consider the planned *stock market* in Nouakchott. Specialists from the Arab stock market association participated in the meeting in order to channel available private funds into the financing of commercial and production activity. Raiss affirmed that Mauritania was committed to establishing a national stock market as soon as possible.

In late August, the government announced the adoption of a national strategy to fight *corruption*, followed on 11 September by the formation of a national commission to fight corruption and mismanagement. The 15-member commission included five representatives from the public administration, five from civil society organisations and five from the private sector. According to Minister of Economic Affairs and Development Sidi Ould Tah, the committee had a mandate "to watch the monitoring of the national strategy on corruption and take measures conducive to its application". Critics within COD/FNDU considered this an attempt by President Aziz to placate the opposition.

Mauritania was ranked 124th out of 175 countries in TI's Corruption Perception Index, and came 174th out of 189 countries in the World Bank's Doing Business 2014. This was only a small improvement, although the country had improved its credit information system by lowering the minimum threshold for loans to be included in the registry's database and by eliminating the fee to obtain a tax identification number.

The UNDP Human Development Report 2014 ranked Mauritania 161st out of 187 countries, and UNDP *Gender Equality* ranked Mauritania 140th out of 149 countries. Female participation in the labour market stood at 28.6%, compared with 79.0%for men. The percentage of female parliamentarians was 19.2%, and participation in secondary level or higher education was 8.0% for females and 20.8% for males. The maternal mortality rate was 510 for every 100,000 live births.

The *Ebola epidemic* in neighbouring countries in August forced the government to start implementing an action plan. The administration tried to stop the spread of the virus by securing its boundaries and on 24 March the authorities decided to close all crossings along the 1,790 km Senegal River with the exception of the Rosso and Diama border posts. Weekly markets in the border region were also closed. On 25 October, the Gogui Zemma border crossing with Mali was closed after Mali's first Ebola case was confirmed. The authorities were criticised for acting too slowly and too late in educating the public about the Ebola epidemic and its implications.

Niger

Klaas van Walraven

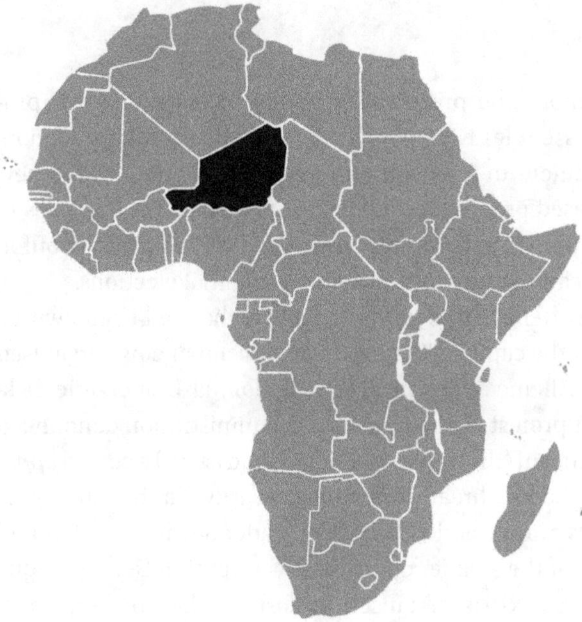

Politics remained conflict-ridden and subject to unpredictable changes in political alliances. Thus, the 2013 rupture between President Mahamadou Issoufou and National Assembly chair Hama Amadou led to a complete disintegration of their relationship in the run-up to the 2016 presidential challenge. Ultimately, Issoufou came out of this conflict as the stronger party as Amadou lost his Assembly presidency and appeared to be heading for the political wilderness. The government put the heat on opposition elements, and the country's image was tarnished by demonstration bans, attacks on politicians' residences and arrests of opposition supporters. By year's end, the situation had calmed down. The realignment of forces led to a rapprochement between Issoufou and Mamadou Tandja (the former president who had been overthrown by the military in February 2010 after refusing to step down after two terms in office). This had the potential to permanently incorporate elements of Tandja's divided party, the 'Mouvement National pour la Société de Développement' (MNSD), into Issoufou's camp. Negotiations with French nuclear energy group Areva on a new uranium contract finally led to an agreement that largely met government demands. This reinforced the domestic standing of the president, who also boosted his international reputation as a key partner in the regional battle against Sahel jihadists. There were a couple of attacks on Nigérien targets, which must be seen as spill-over effects from the Malian theatre. Concern

 | DOI 10.1163/9789004305052_016

rose over the worsening violence of Nigeria's Boko Haram. Rains led to flooding but stopped prematurely. As in the previous year, this resulted in a deficient cereal harvest.

Domestic Politics

In an interview on 18 December, the president claimed success in the '3N' programme ('les Nigériens nourissent les Nigériens') to boost agricultural production. He also asserted overachievement in job creation targets and pointed to the new Areva contract, whose increased proceeds could help him to keep his promises in the social and infrastructural domains. Towering over his neutralised rivals, Issoufou declined to speak out on his candidature for the 2016 presidential elections.

This self-confidence came after a turbulent political year that had begun with a peaceful opposition march in the capital Niamey in late December 2013. Organised by the opposition coalition 'Alliance pour la Réconciliation, la Démocratie et la République' (ARDR), this first protest against Issoufou's administration denounced the government's authoritarianism (the previous month it had issued a ban on *opposition marches* – pointing to jihadist threats to national security – although a court later lifted the ban). The rally was attended by MNSD leader Seyni Oumarou and Mahamane Ousmane, leader of the smaller opposition 'Convention Démocratique et Sociale' (CDS). On 5 January, NGOs organised protests in the northern town of Agadez, demanding jobs and better services. Taken by surprise, the government responded on 27 January by arresting several journalists and activists, who were charged with insulting the president and threatening state security. On 8 February, the coalition of government parties staged a counter-rally in Niamey in support of the administration.

The *political climate deteriorated* further when students rioted against grant payment delays (20–21 May), leading to dozens of injuries and arrests. The government claimed the protests had been instigated by Hama Amadou's party, the 'Mouvement Démocratique Nigérien' (Moden-Lumana). On the first day of the protests, assailants shot at the house of Ben Omar Mohamed, 4th vice president of the Assembly and member of one of the lesser parties in the government coalition. There were no casualties. Three days later, the offices of Issoufou's 'Parti Nigérien pour la Démocratie et le Socialisme' (PNDS) were attacked; three people were injured, one of them seriously. Police arrested some 40 Moden members on suspicion of destabilising the country and working towards an army coup d'état. Among those arrested was Hama Amadou's son.

A planned ARDR march was banned, and a coalition of NGOs called 'Collectif Sauvons le Niger' accused the government of *abusing its power*. On 3 June, police released the majority of detainees, including Amadou's son and one of his cabinet staff. Six people were kept in detention on charges of threatening state security, including two former cabinet ministers and the former mayor of Niamey. All were Moden members close to Amadou, still widely seen as Issoufou's main rival in the 2016 polls. Whatever the veracity of the charges, Amadou claimed that the arrests had been orchestrated against his party and that he had been the victim of a poison attempt. On 15 June, the opposition responded with a big rally in the capital. All the principal opposition leaders (Amadou, Oumarou and Ousmane) took part. A rally planned in Niger's second city, Zinder, on 27 June was broken up by police.

These displays of organised discontent and authoritarian reflexes formed the backdrop to a strategy of confrontation. The urgency of a *showdown* became obvious when Amadou increasingly used the Assembly presidency to taunt Issoufou's administration. Secure in his parliamentary immunity (not unimportant in a political system where fallen leaders have frequently been imprisoned), he began to bring accusations of misdemeanours, not all of them convincing, against the government. Early in the year, the government began to take counter-measures, such as effecting changes in Amadou's security retinue. Amadou, who had not spoken to the president since he led Moden's partial departure from the government the previous year, claimed his house was shot at on 16–17 February; the interior minister denied an attack had taken place. Since the government did not command the two-thirds majority needed to depose Amadou, other steps seemed necessary – incongruous ones, yet frequently resorted to in Niger's political arena.

With the physical attacks on a government politician and the PNDS headquarters, the opposition overstepped the mark. The government struck back in late June, mentioning one of Amadou's wives in a baby-trafficking scandal. This involved women in Nigeria giving birth in a 'baby factory' and their off-spring being sold to childless couples in Niger and Benin. Seventeen people were arrested, including Amadou's wife, who was said to have played a central role but denied the charges. On 26 August, the government sought the Assembly's permission for Amadou to be questioned, whereupon the latter secretly left the country for France. The next day, a parliamentary committee decided to *lift* the *chairman's immunity*, an act sanctioned by the Constitutional Court in early September; later that month, an arrest warrant was issued. Amadou claimed the affair was politically motivated and gave fear of assassination as the reason for his flight. The existence of the trafficking ring appeared to be true, however. Among those arrested was Agriculture Minister Abdou Labo. It was widely speculated that Labo, a close ally of Issoufou but a member of the CDS, was sacrificed to counter charges of political motivation.

With Amadou out of the way, Issoufou's electoral prospects improved, though the longer-term consequences of Amadou's political elimination were unclear. As the Moden party was divided between pro- and anti-government wings, Issoufou had little to fear from them, and he faced no threat either from the *new Assembly president*, Amadou Salifou, an MNSD member who the previous year had broken with his party leader, Oumarou, and joined the government majority.

Salifou's election provided Issoufou with an opportunity to drive a bigger wedge into the ranks of the MNSD. Against this background, a *rapprochement* took place between *Issoufou* and the deposed Mamadou *Tandja*, who still played an important role in MNSD affairs. The previous year, Tandja had given his blessing to MNSD secretary-general Albadé Abouba to participate in government – leaving MNSD president Oumarou out in the cold. In a get-together with MNSD supporters in October 2013, Tandja was overheard saying that, when he was deposed from power in 2010, there had been some CFAfr 400 bn in the state's coffers – an amount that could not be accounted for and led opposition elements to accuse Issoufou's administration and the preceding military transition regime (2010–11) of graft. The government, however, used this to put pressure on Tandja. On 26 June, the Supreme Court lifted his ex-presidential immunity, and used this threat to conclude an entente with the man who had dominated Nigérien politics during the previous decade. On 2 July, Issoufou received Tandja at the palace and on 13 November the ex-president, sick with cancer, was flown to Morocco in the new presidential jet for treatment.

Although the courts were still able to restrict government encroachment on *civil liberties*, the administration's actions broke with the enlightenment of the preceding years: one of the worst offenders with regard to media freedom, Issoufou had made Niger an example by becoming the first head of state to sign the 2007 Table Mountain declaration calling for the decriminalisation of defamation in Africa laws.

With the stepping up of attacks in border areas, Niger recorded a first confrontation with *Boko Haram* fighters. An army patrol was ambushed 20 km from the eastern city of Diffa in the first week of May. Several people were wounded and 14 suspects apprehended. Earlier, in February, 20 people in Diffa, where youths had joined Boko Haram mainly for financial gain, were arrested on suspicion of planning attacks across Niger; they were all of Nigerian origin. In Zinder, too, militants were arrested with bomb-making material for an attack on local markets; they were said to have planned to kidnap the governor to press for the release of fellow fighters. The government continued its cautious policy of surveillance and patrols of the porous frontiers without engaging militants across the border unless they were attacked. However, in early November Boko Haram took control of the Nigerian border town of Malam Fatori, causing Nigerian soldiers to flee across the border into Niger. Military personnel from Chad and Niger, part of a Multinational Joint Task Force established in the 1990s to combat arms smuggling, had also been involved in the fighting, and Niger pulled back some of its men. No further incursions into Nigérien territory took place, but this seemed essentially due to Boko Haram prioritising attacks elsewhere.

The number of *Nigerian refugees* entering Niger increased dramatically. After an attack on the Nigerian village of Gashkar on 16 January, the Nigérien border town of Gueskérou took in 7,000 people who crossed the Komadougou-Yobé River (the frontier between the two countries). In August, some 10,000 refugees crossed into Niger, and in October–November a further 30,000. The total number rose to 100,000 by year's end. On 24 November, Boko Haram attacked the Nigerian border village of Damasak and 3,000 villagers crossed the Komadougou. UNHCR was asked to establish reception centres, 50 km from the border, as local absorption capacity had reached its limit. On 12 December, the government appealed to the international community for help.

On 30 October, men said to belong to the 'Mouvement pour l'Unicité et le Jihad en Afrique de l'Ouest' (MUJAO) in *Mali* launched simultaneous attacks on Malian refugees 60 km from the border, the prison at Ouallam, and a military patrol in Bani Bangou. The government reported that nine soldiers and policemen were killed, along with two of the assailants and one innocent civilian. Ninety of the 118 detainees in the Ouallam prison escaped and fours assailants were captured. On 19 November, another MUJAO attack took place in Bani Bangou, with assailants cutting telephone lines, killing a non-commissioned officer and wounding two. Some of the captured assailants were ethnic Peuls. In the past, several had joined 'Gandakoye' vigilante groups in Mali targeting Tuaregs in acts of ethnic cleansing; in previous years, they had flocked to MUJAO in an effort to get even with Tuaregs pursuing a separatist agenda. The government played a constructive role in the release of the last French hostage in the hands of al-Qaida in the Islamic Maghreb (AQIM), on 9 December. As a quid pro quo, four AQIM detainees in Bamako, including two of the kidnappers, were released. It seems likely that money was also exchanged, although Issoufou officially denied any knowledge of a ransom payment.

The *defence* budget was set at $ 150–200 m (out of a total budget of $ 3.8 bn) – a fourfold increase over four years. While social expenditure had increased significantly, Foreign Minister Mohamed Bazoum admitted that revenue streams originally budgeted for education and social services had been diverted to the security budget. On 22 October, the government announced the purchase of a reconnaissance plane valued at $ 10.5 m, which was supposed to limit dependence on French and American intelligence gathering. On 20 October, a US drone crashed at Niamey airport for unknown reasons. Ten days earlier, French troops launched a raid against vehicles carrying arms from southern Libya to Mali via the Salvador mountain pass in Niger. French troops established themselves at a desert base in Madama, a colonial fort guarding the border with Libya. The French intended to establish a military presence stretching from Tessalit in northern Mali to Faya-Largeau in Chad. This would enable them to monitor armed elements in the desert, including southwest Libya. France's presence in the Sahara-Sahel was projected to be increased to 3,000 troops, around 1,000 of them to be stationed in Niger. The future headquarters would be in the Chadian capital N'Djaména.

Foreign Affairs

Niger's role in resisting Islamist forces, in addition to facilitating the release of Western hostages, reinforced Issoufou's international position, notwithstanding his government's violations of civil liberties earlier in the year. He toured *Europe* early in April, attended the 4th EU-Africa summit, spoke at the European Parliament and participated in a donor conference for the CBLT, currently under his presidency, in Bologna (Italy).

Relations with *France* were still under pressure resulting from negotiations on Areva's mining contract but improved after the conclusion of a new deal, confirmed by the signing in July of six agreements in various development sectors worth some € 74 m. On his first African tour, new French Prime Minister Manuel Valls visited Niger on 23 November, when he had talks with President Issoufou, met Areva officials and called on the French air base in Niamey.

The *USA* also enjoyed good relations with Niamey, given Niger's geostrategic importance for American military operations in the Sahel. Operation Flintlock, a US-led annual military exercise in West Africa focusing on anti-terrorist activity, took place in Niger (19 February–9 March). Around 1,000 men from 18 African and European countries participated in the joint operations in the regions of Agadez, Tahoua and Diffa. As a consequence, American Air Force personnel increased in number to 200 men over the year. On 7 August, Issoufou received US Under-Secretary for Defence, Robert Work, and the commander of Africom, General Rodriguez. They agreed to establish a second base for unarmed intelligence drones, in Agadez.

The government decided to extradite associates of the former Kadhafi regime to *Libya*, including a son of Muammar Kadhafi, Saadi. Niger had initially refused to deport him on the grounds that he could face the death penalty. Niger had had good ties with Col. Kadhafi, whose mediation in conflicts with Tuareg communities had afforded him an important role in Nigérien affairs. Ex-military from the Kadhafi regime could move freely in Niamey and enjoyed free telecommunications access – thus angering Libya's official central government. With south-west Libya turned into a launch pad for operations by jihadist fighters, Niger felt forced to change tack. This was made easier when the Kadhafi men were suspected of subversive operations in the Sebha region (on 6 May, six Nigérien migrants were killed there by militias). In late January, Issoufou's government handed over 16 Kadhafi officials, and on 6 March it returned Saadi Kadhafi to the Libyan authorities. As the chaos in Libya escalated, Niger called for Western intervention. On 5 February, Niger's Interior Minister Massoudou Hassoumi reminded Washington and Paris of their responsibility for Libya's current situation. On 13–14 July, the foreign ministers of Libya's neighbours, including Niger's, met in Tunisia to discuss the flow of arms and fighters coming out of Libya, and on 18 December Issoufou reiterated the call for Western intervention. Obviously, this caused new anger in Tripoli.

In mid-February, the *Sahelian countries* (Chad, Niger, Mali, Mauritania and Burkina) agreed to establish a regional security network called 'G5 du Sahel', with its nerve-centre in the Mauritanian capital, Nouakchott. Niger would provide its secretariat. This was followed by another summit in Mauritania in late December, which Issoufou attended.

On 17 May, the president participated in a summit in Paris to discuss *Boko Haram's regional implications*. A ministerial meeting on the same topic in London on 12 June followed. The foreign ministers of Niger, Nigeria, Chad, Benin and Cameroon agreed to set up a Regional Intelligence Fusion Unit. This would involve joint patrols for which each country would provide a batallion. Much of this discussion took place within the framework of the CBLT. On 17–18 March, its defence members met in Yaoundé (Cameroon) to discuss the regional force. A summit meeting in Niamey on 6–7 October, to which Benin was also invited, elaborated the details, announcing that the force would be deployed in November. However, the troops involved in the battle over Malam Fatori in November were part of the Multinational Joint Task Force, which was established by Nigeria in 1994 to combat banditry and in 1998 saw the inclusion of contingents from Chad and Niger. In contrast to Niger, Nigeria did not allow neighbouring armies to cross the border in pursuit of Boko Haram fighters. Issoufou used the Boko Haram crisis to press donors for development funds, in this case pointing to the social implications of the ecological deterioration of the Lake Chad basin.

Socioeconomic Developments

At the end of the year, the government set its *growth* forecast at 5.6%. The IMF thought 6.3% more likely. The 2013 growth rate was retrospectively adjusted down to 4.1%.

In view of the previous year's cereal deficit (estimated at 343,566 tonnes, i.e. 9% of total consumption), *food provision* became an issue of concern. WFP warned that around 2 m people faced severe food shortages and USAID's early warning network showed that several areas – including Tillabéri in the west and Zinder and Diffa in the east – were suffering 'food stress'. Some 23% of the population were estimated to be at risk of severe hunger. Malnutrition among children remained widespread and admission to nutritional recovery centres increased sharply. Donors were asked for $ 80 m in assistance. The government began to sell cereals at subsidised prices early. The failure of the government to feed its population once more led to criticism of Issoufou's much-acclaimed '3N' agricultural policy. However, some claimed that the policy at least lessened famine. The rains stopped prematurely, thus leading to deficient cereal harvests. In August and September, large parts of the country were flooded, affecting more than 50,000 people.

During the negotiations for a new *uranium mining contract*, Niger asked Areva to conform to the mining code of 2006. This meant an increase in royalties from 5.5% to 9–12%. The government further insisted on the lifting of several tax exemptions and for more contributions to the country's infrastructure. On 1 February, Areva resumed production (which had been suspended one month earlier). On 6 February, hundreds of people took to the streets of Niamey to protest against

Areva's perceived violation of national laws. Shortly thereafter, the French development minister told the National Assembly in Paris that Niger's demands were 'legitimate'. On 26 May, the new mining contract was signed. The company committed itself to the 2006 mining code, raising royalties to 12–15% (depending on profits), which it was estimated would bring an additional € 30–35 m into state coffers. Areva would hire Nigériens to head its two mines, build a new headquarters in Niamey and provide $ 123 m for renovation of the 'route de l'uranium', the motorway built for the evacuation of yellow cake to the port of Cotonou in Benin. Niger accepted further delays in the opening of the Imouraren mine, which would be good for 5,000 tonnes of yellow cake and make it the world's second largest uranium producer; the negative impact on uranium prices of the disaster at the Fukushima nuclear reactor in Japan in 2011 still prevented a viable operation.

On 27 June, the president launched the construction of a 600 MW coal power plant north-west of Tahoua. The project, funded by a US company, included coal mining operations and the generation of electricity on a site covering 30 km². It was intended to ameliorate the perennial power shortages, reduce logging for fire wood and combat desertification. Another important development in the field of *infrastructure* concerned the extension of the Cotonou railway. On 8 April, Issoufou, in the presence of his counterparts from Benin and Togo, formally launched the project, which would link Niamey with the Parakou-Cotonou railway in Benin, a dream project since independence. Niger selected the French Bolloré firm as strategic partner; 80% of Niger's freight is exported through the port of Cotonou, transported over derelict roads. Orange-Niger signed a deal with the US firm Intelsat for the use of broadband capacity to extend its mobile phone network further into rural areas. Celtel was given a licence to develop a 3G network (July–August). Niger had some 7 m mobile phone subscribers in 2013. Finally, the country purchased a new presidential jet, a € 30 m Boeing 737. This was criticised by the opposition and civil society groups. Pilots said the old plane, which had been built in the 1970s, was no longer safe to operate.

Despite the extension of *social services*, improvement of service delivery remained urgent. According to recent Afrobarometer data, most Nigériens regarded the government's performance in power generation, water delivery and sanitation as bad or very bad. The government performed better in basic health care and primary education. *Child marriage* continued to be a problem. In May, a 63-year-old man was given a four-year prison sentence and fined for taking a young girl as his so-called 'fifth wife', an illegitimate form of concubinage that dated back to Tuareg masters selling the off-spring of their slaves. The money from the fine went to the anti-slavery NGO Timidria, which had taken up the case.

Nigeria

Heinrich Bergstresser

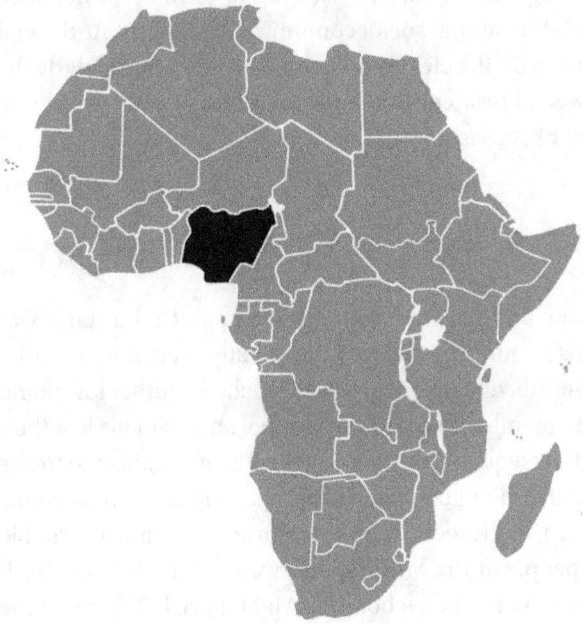

Throughout the year, Nigeria had to face up to enormous security and political challenges. Despite the fact that democratic institutions were quite stable, the president and his government dealt with the endless deterioration of the security situation in the North with brinkmanship. Clashes between security forces and factions of the Islamic sect Boko Haram took place almost daily with a high death rate on both sides. Almost unnoticed, Boko Haram had changed its name, and now called itself 'Jama'at ahl al-sunna li-l-da'wa wa-l-jihad 'ala minhaj al-salaf' (Community of the people of the Sunna who fight for the cause of Islam according to the method of Salaf). Several hundred people, including innocent persons and security personnel, as well as alleged members and sympathisers of the sect, died in bomb attacks, suicide bombings, indiscriminate killings, rape and deadly raids on barracks, police stations, mosques, churches, schools, hide-outs, villages, outdoor refreshment stops, markets and prisons. The sheer number of attacks, counter attacks and sectarian clashes makes an accurate account of these events all but impossible. At year's end, Boko Haram was ranked second of the top ten terrorist groups worldwide. Over 2,000 people had lost their lives, bringing the number to around 12,000 victims (a modest estimate) since the Islamist insurgency started in the aftermath of the killing of the Boko Haram leadership by security forces in 2009. In addition,

 | DOI 10.1163/9789004305052_017

Nigeria's human and civil rights record was mixed at best. These developments notwithstanding, Nigeria experienced another year of remarkable economic growth, particularly in the prosperous and booming South. This, together with financial stability, consolidated the Nigerian economy as one of the leading economies in Africa, although the plummeting oil price in the last quarter of the year heralded what would probably be painful structural socioeconomic adjustments. At the end of the year, however, all eyes were on the elections due in early 2015, particularly the battle for the presidency between President Goodluck Jonathan and his challenger, Muhammadu Buhari, a repeat of the last election in 2011.

Domestic Politics

The *state of emergency* in Borno and neighbouring Adamawa and Yobe states was extended in May for a further six months. However, the already precarious security situation in the North-East continued to deteriorate and reached another low point. Almost every day, Boko Haram members, security personnel and civilians lost their lives in numerous attacks and subsequent counter-attacks. The most affected towns in Borno State were the capital, Maiduguri, as well as other towns such as Bama, Chibok, Damboa, Dikwa, Gwoza and Konduga, turning Borno State into a veritable battlefield. On 14 January, as people of the Muslim faith were celebrating the birth of the Prophet, a suicide bomber detonated a bomb in Maiduguri, killing more the 40 persons. The city's 'Monday Market' was hit by a car bomb on 1 July, which killed dozens, including a group of vigilantes, known as the civilian joint task force. Soon afterwards, towards the end of July, the city's famous Eid Durbar, a three-day festival marking the end of Ramadan, was cancelled for the third year running for security reasons. Earlier in the year, on 16 February, suspected Islamists, armed with sophisticated weapons, gunned down at least 90 people in the village if Izge near the Cameroonian border; three days later some 80 died in Bama, where properties worth several million naira were destroyed, including the palace of the Shehu of Bama. On 14 March, the notorious Giwa barracks in Maiduguri, which also served as an illegal prison camp, was attacked by hundreds of militants who were able to free many alleged Boko Haram members and sympathisers. Within hours, in a cruel act of revenge, the security forces re-arrested suspects by the dozen and, according to AI, executed more than 600, burying them in mass graves. These extra-judicial killings were seen as a tipping point, further fuelling the unprecedented brutality on both sides.

One of the cruellest incidents in Borno State was the abduction of more than 270 *female students in Chibok*, a town in the southern part of the state with a significant Christian population. The students, aged 16–18, were about to sit their final year exams. On 14 April, late at night, gunmen in a convoy of vehicles stormed the school hostel and abducted them. Some of them managed to escape when the truck they were in had a problem and slowed down. For more than two weeks, President Goodluck Jonathan and his government ignored the incident, an act of gross negligence. Hundreds of mainly women protesters marched through the Nigerian capital, Abuja, to press for the release of the abducted students and to put pressure on the government to act, including initiating some form of dialogue with factions of Boko Haram or at least an exchange with some of the sect's imprisoned members. Their campaign received international attention, particularly in Europe and the US, and exposed a helpless and rather embarrassed leadership. On 2 June, the police banned the ongoing rallies, calling them a security problem, but immediately backpedalled when a court order in favour of the protesters was about to be issued.

The security forces did not perform much better than the government, despite their claims that they would stand up to the insurgency and the *terrorist threat*. Interestingly, the sect's self-proclaimed leader, Abubakar Shekau, who, according to the security forces, had died after a military raid at Sambisa Forest in June 2013, appeared in video messages. As with similar videos in 2013, the military authorities once again dismissed them as fakes, or insinuated that the videos showed Shekau's double, but their claims were not verified. On 24 August, he declared his claimed territory an 'Islamic Caliphate'. A second video showing the abducted schoolgirls was a further rebuke to the handling of the crisis by both the military and the government. More was to come when, in mid-October, the federal government announced that the schoolgirls were about to be released. Soon, however, it became clear that there was no truce, and neither had negotiations with Boko Haram succeeded.

The *relentless killings* went on unabated and, on 5 May, at least 300 people including more than a dozen policemen were killed in Gamboru, a town on the Cameroonian border and headquarters of Ngala local government. On 30 May, the insurgents struck again, killing the Emir of Gwoza, Alhaji Idrissa Shehu Tinta, who was on his way to the burial of the Emir of Gombe. Shortly thereafter, on 1–2 June, villages in Gwoza local government such as Attagara, were raided and up to 200 people, mostly Christians, killed.

On several occasions, the insurgents overran strategically important villages and communities in areas such as Damboa, where they hoisted the sect's flag on 18 July. Gwoza, home to a police mobile training academy, was taken over in mid-August and more than two dozen of its police officers were reported missing. Soon afterwards, Boko Haram fighters attacked the barracks near Gamboru and seized parts of the border town for the second time, forcing almost 500 soldiers to flee to neighbouring Cameroon. On 1 September, the sect overran Bama town and hoisted its flag. Only on 5 September did the military leadership commence a 'special operation', including an aerial attack, which had some success in dislodging the insurgents from major towns including Bama, Damboa, Gamboru and Gwoza. In the strategic town of Konduga, east of Maiduguri, on 12 September, security forces killed more than 200 insurgents marching to capture the capital. Two weeks later, on 25 September, troops repelled another advance on Konduga and the town of

Benesheik, some 70 km west of Maiduguri. During the weekend of 24–25 October, the *Multinational Joint Task Force* (MNJTF), made up of Nigerian troops and reinforcements from neighbouring Niger and Chad, based in Baga, re-captured the town of Abadam, close to the Nigerien border and Lake Chad, which had fallen under insurgent control the previous week. However, the MNJTF had little impact on the security situation in the area. On 12 November, insurgents invaded the headquarters of the 174th motorised battalion, deployed from its base in the South-West, forcing the remaining soldiers to withdraw. On 20 November, a group of fish traders on their way to Chad to buy fish were attacked and killed near the village of Doron Baga. Towards the end of November, the National Assembly refused President Jonathan's bid to have the state of emergency extended for another six-month period. On 13 December, Boko Haram attacked the village of Gamsuri, some 70 km south of Maiduguri, killing more than 30 and kidnapping more than 150 persons.

Yobe State fared no better. Late at night, on 25 February, the Federal Government College in Buni Yadi, the headquarters of Gujba local government area, south of the state capital Damaturu, was raided by suspected Islamists; 59 students, all boys, died in the raid. On 27 May, the town was targeted again and a security camp attacked; close to 50 security personnel and almost a dozen civilians fell victim to the insurgents, who arrived in several Hilux vans and on motorcycles. Earlier, on 5 April, neighbouring Buni Gari was targeted when gunmen opened fire on a mosque, killing some 20 worshippers and seriously injuring others. During the FIFA World Cup, on 17 June, a bomb blast rocked a centre in the state capital, where football spectators were watching a match; several spectators died in the blast and dozens were hurt. Potiskum, Yobe's largest city and its commercial hub, was seriously hit in a blast on 3 November, when a suicide bomb killed ten members of the Muslim Brethren, who call themselves 'Shiites', as they celebrated the Islamic new year (there are no recognised Shiites in Nigeria, but the group admires the model of the Iranian revolution). On 10 November, another suicide bomber, disguised in a school uniform, killed almost 50 students of the senior science secondary school. Damaturu was attacked again on 1–2 December; almost 40 police officers, a few soldiers, some 60 insurgents and more than 100 civilians died when the army, backed by air force helicopters, repelled the attackers.

Adamawa State, with a significant Christian population, became a veritable battlefield as a result of both the Boko Haram insurgency and, to some extent, a serious leadership crisis in the state; Governor Murtala Nyako was impeached on 15 July. Two of the larger towns, Michika and Mubi, and the surrounding areas were for a short period in the hands of Boko Haram fighters. Only after several fierce battles, with hundreds dead on both sides, were the insurgents driven out in the final quarter of the year. One of these battles, in which vigilantes and local hunters joined the troops, took place in the towns of Gombi, Hong and Pella and lasted for four days (16–19 November); more than 400 insurgents were killed but the government remained very tight-lipped about the number of victims among the security forces.

At the same time, in a night-time attack, local vigilante groups, popularly called 'Yan Tauri' (meaning in Hausa 'those who resist/are invulnerable [to wounds]'), drove most insurgents out of Mubi. By 5 December, the remnants were dislodged by military forces and the emir of the town, Abubakar Ahmadu, re-entered his palace on 12 December, after a two-month temporary exile. In neighbouring Gombe State, on 6 December, military forces repelled a strong attack on the town of Ashaka, where the main objective was a dynamite store. Ten soldiers fell to the attackers, who lost some 70 fighters. It was the second time within a month that the town had been targeted.

Kano city, capital of the state of the same name and one-time hub of the north, became another focus of the spread of violence, experiencing several grisly incidents. On 18 May, a car bomb explosion rocked the urban quarter of Sabon Gari ('New Town'), causing some 15 deaths. The quarter is made up of a mixture of indigenous ethnic Hausa-Fulani Muslims and migrants from other parts of the country, many of them Christians. The following month, on 23 June, an explosion struck the Kano School of Hygiene and at least eight students lost their lives. Towards the end of July, within the space of five days, three bomb attacks on a Catholic church (27 July), a petrol station and a kerosene queue at a storage facility of the National Nigerian Petroleum Corporation (NNPC) (28 July) left seven people dead and many more injured. The newly enthroned Emir Muhammad Sanusi II remained defiant and, despite the blasts, he performed the traditional evening 'Sallah Durbar' on 28 July. Despite the president's reluctance, the kingmakers and Governor Rabiu Kwankwaso, who had fallen out with Jonathan, enforced the enthronement of the former governor of the Central Bank to succeed Kano's longest sitting emir, Ado Bayero, who had passed away on 6 June.

In the weeks and months that followed, *deadly attacks* continued. On 17 September, a twin explosion at both the old and new campuses of the federal college of education caused the deaths of at least 15 students. Dozens sustained various injuries and both suicide bombers lost their lives. On 14 November, a petrol filling station in the Hotoro area was targeted, and six people, including three policemen, were killed. The ugliest incident, however, happened on 28 November, when, during Friday prayers, gunmen set off three bombs and opened fire on worshippers at the central mosque close to the emir's palace. At least 130 people died and many more were wounded. Once again, the emir, by cutting short his lesser hajj trip to Saudi Arabia the same day, and leading the evening prayer at the site of the bombed mosque the following day, set an example, standing up to the suspected Islamists.

Nor was the *Federal Capital Territory Abuja* spared by the Islamists. On 14 April, during morning rush hour, two blasts hit a crowded bus station in the suburb of Nyanya, claiming more than 70 lives and injuring scores more. Rather surprisingly, the following day, Jonathan flew to the city of Kano for a People's Democratic Party (PDP) jamboree. Less than three weeks later, on 2 May, another bomb explosion ripped through the same area, resulting in the deaths of at least 19 people; 60 more were injured. More than 20 people were killed and many more wounded on 25 June, when another blast hit the EMBA Plaza shopping centre in Wuse II, close to the city centre. The incident forced Jonathan to cut short his trip to the AU summit in Equatorial Guinea. This attack fuelled further speculation that corruption was widespread within security circles and that millions of dollars had been wasted on purchasing inoperative security devices such as video surveillance equipment.

Late in the year, a number of events embarrassed the government. On 24 August, Shekau announced the *'Islamic Caliphate'* in the territory controlled by Boko Haram. On 5 September, a private jet chartered by the Nigerian intelligence apparatus, with $ 9.3 m on board for the purchase of weapons, was seized at Johannesburg airport; some three weeks later, a further $ 5.7 m was impounded. However, in late October, after several controversial discussions, the National Assembly finally granted the president's request for a $ 1 bn loan to intensify the fight against the Boko Haram insurgency.

The *Middle Belt*, particularly Plateau, Benue, Gombe, Nasarawa, Taraba and Kaduna states, was another focal point of sectarian and ethnic clashes that claimed many victims. One of the most devastating attacks occurred in the Plateau state capital Jos, which was seriously hit by twin blasts on 20 and 24 May, with more than 120 and half a dozen people killed, respectively. And in Kaduna State, on 23–25 June, several villages were raided by alleged Fulani herdsmen, leaving some 250 people dead. As in previous years, however, these states were the scene of serious political and socioeconomic conflicts concerning the fragile local political power and leadership structure, distribution of revenues, rights over fertile farmlands, housing and cattle rustling.

On 31 March, a *peace accord* was signed in Makurdi. It had been drafted by the presidential peace committee, a conflict resolution and peace building committee and the Fulani socio-cultural organisation 'Miyetti Allah Kautal Hore'. It was agreed that the Fulani could freely use the grazing areas but should do so in cooperation with the farmers. In addition, a joint committee, made up of Fulani herdsmen, ethnic Tiv and some Agatu (related to the ethnic Idoma), was to check criminal activities on both sides of the divide. In the end, the agreement had little impact on the volatile situation. This also applied to similar efforts in Taraba and Nasarawa, where on 5 April and 8 November, respectively, peace accords were signed or negotiated. In the Taraba state capital Jalingo, representatives of ethnic Tiv, Jukun, Hausa-Fulani and Fulani signed the accord presided over by the deputy inspector general of police Michael Zuokumor, representing the presidential peace committee. The negotiations in Nasarawa, however, were overshadowed by a cruel assault when, in a classic case of irony, gunmen ambushed and killed almost 40 participants returning from the peace summit convened by the traditional ruler of the Akriya chiefdom, Alhaji Usman Babba.

The precarious security situation eventually took its toll on *key positions in the military*. At the start of the year, on 16 January, three new service chiefs were appointed in a sweeping shake-up. Lieutenant General Onyeabo Azubuike Ihejirika, the army chief of staff, Vice Admiral Ola Sa'ad Ibrahim, chief of the defence staff, and Rear Admiral D.J. Ezeoba, the naval chief of staff, were replaced. The survivor of the purge in the military high command was the air force chief of staff, Air Vice Marshal Alex Sabunduh Badeh, who became the new chief of the defence staff. His portfolio was taken over by Air-Vice Marshal Adesola Nunayon Amosu. Major General Tobiah Jacob Minimah became the new army chief of staff and Rear Admiral Usman Jibrin the new naval chief of staff, being subsequently promoted to admiral. The appointments were confirmed by the senate on 30 January, in line with a 2013 decision of the Abuja Federal High Court that such confirmation was mandatory under the Constitution.

Soon afterwards, on 12 February, 107 senior officers, including six newly-appointed *General Officers Commanding* (GOC), were redeployed. Major General K.C. Osuji took over the GOC 1 Division based in Kaduna, Major General Emanuel Abejirin the GOC 2 Mechanized Division in Ibadan and Major General John Zaruwa the GOC 3 Armoured Division in Jos. Major General T.I. Dibi emerged as commander of the GOC 81 Amphibious Division, garrisoned in Lagos, and Major General S. Yusuf as the new GOC 82 Airborne Division commander in Enugu. The GOC 7 Infantry Division, garrisoned in Maiduguri and created the previous year against the backdrop of the Boko Haram insurgency in the North-East, had been led by four commanders within just nine months, which suggested internal wrangling and serious structural problems within the military as a whole. The latest appointment was made on 16 May, when Brigadier M.Y. Ibrahim emerged as acting commander, succeeding his controversial predecessor Major General Abubakar Mohammed. In mid-August, the air force experienced a shake-up in its high command with the appointment of new Air Force Officers Commanding and, on 24 November, 16 officers were promoted to the rank of air vice marshal and 35 others to air commodore. On 9 December, the navy followed suit and carried out a far-reaching redeployment of senior officers.

All was not well at the top of the military hierarchy. 14 May was seen as the beginning of a chain of mishaps within the military and its fight against the Islamist insurgents. On that day, aggrieved soldiers who had been ambushed in a deadly attack the previous night on their way from the Chibok area to Maiduguri staged a *mutiny in Maimalari cantonment* against the then commander of the 7 Infantry Division, Abubakar Mohammed. They were said to have pleaded for their return to be delayed until dawn because moving at night was a risk, which proved to be true. Abubakar Mohammed was almost immediately relieved of his command and 12 mutineers were court-martialled and sentenced on 15 September to death by firing squad. Abubakar Mohammed was quietly retired in August. On 17 December, a court martial imposed the death sentence on another batch of 54 soldiers who had allegedly refused to obey orders on 4 August. In the Nigerian legal system, any sentence handed down by a court martial can be challenged in the two highest secular courts of the land.

Shortly after, it was revealed that another batch of 15 soldiers had been given prison sentences of four years for their refusal to go to the front line in northern Adamawa. These verdicts heralded a massive investigation of the rank and file and of both non-commissioned and commissioned officers for alleged offences such as 'cowardice' and 'disobeyed deployment directives'. In the weeks that followed, a few hundred were arrested, *court-martialled* behind close doors and sentenced, with the aim of countering the indiscipline that was allegedly spreading within the armed forces. These efforts notwithstanding, this purge also served as a cover-up for widespread corruption within the upper ranks, which, to a large extent, had long denied the combatants the necessary equipment, maintenance and training to successfully fight the insurgency.

The *police forces* also underwent major changes. On 1 August, Suleiman Abba emerged as the new inspector general of police. He succeeded Mohammed Abubakar, who took statutory retirement after 35 years of service. Prior to that, on 26 February, the police service commission promoted more than 5,100 policemen to the rank of assistant superintendent. On 20 August, 19 commissioners of police rose to the rank of assistant inspector general and eight to the rank of deputy inspector general following a redeployment of 36 senior officers.

At the start of the year, the *embattled president* tried to regain the initiative to show that he and his government were still in charge. The controversial chairman of the ruling PDP, septuagenarian Bamanga Tukur, held partly responsible for the party's internal wrangling, was forced to resign in mid-January. On 20 January, the respected former Bauchi state governor, Adamu Mu'azu, emerged as the new party chairman. On 11 February, Goodluck Jonathan sacked his chief of staff, Mike Oghiadomhe, and appointed retired Brigadier Jones Oladehinde Arogbofa. In the days that followed, more ministers suffered the same fate, including Ms Stella Oduah (aviation), Godsday Orubebe (Niger Delta), retired Navy captain Caleb Olubolade (police affairs) and the governor of the Central Bank, Lamido Sanusi.

Unexpectedly, the septuagenarian Aliyu Mohammed Gusau, a retired lieutenant general, became minister of defence. He had served as *national security adviser* to the former president, Olusegun Obasanjo, as well as to Jonathan. Soon afterwards, on 5 March, a career diplomat, Aminu Bashir Wali, was made minister of foreign affairs. On 3 June, Godwin Emefiele took over the Central Bank's top position and, in the weeks that followed, the education, aviation and national planning portfolios were given to Ibrahim Shekarau, Osita Benjamin Chidoka and Abubakar Sulaiman, respectively. Abdul Jelili Adesiyan was appointed to oversee the Ministry for Police Affairs, Steve Oru became minister for the affairs of the Niger Delta and, on

13 August, Danladi Kifasi became the new head of the federal civil service, following Abubakar Goni Aji's retirement after 35 years of service.

On 17 April, Ms Zainab Bulkachuwa became the first female president of the Court of Appeal. On 20 November, Mahmud Mohammed became Nigeria's chief justice, succeeding Ms Aloma Mariam Mukhtar, who had reached the mandatory retirement age of 70.

With regard to the planned 2015 elections, the *Independent National Electoral Commission* (INEC) released the election timetable on 24 January, with presidential and national assembly elections due to be held on 14 February 2015, and governorship and state elections scheduled for 28 February 2015. At year's end, some 68 m voters were registered. By December, however, the INEC had failed to issue all the permanent voter cards as planned, and was forced to extend the deadline for them to be collected until shortly before the elections. The question of IDP suffrage remained unresolved at year's end, since the law stipulated that voters had to cast ballots in their home constituencies.

On 21 June and 9 August, *gubernatorial elections* took place in Ekiti State and Osun State, respectively, In Ekiti, the PDP candidate, Ayodele Fayose, who had been governor during the second legislative period (2003–7) and impeached in 2006, defeated the incumbent governor Kayode Fayemi of the All Progressives Congress (APC). While many observers considered the election to have been largely free and fair, the PDP had, in fact, frequently used federal and security machinery to intimidate their political opponent in the run-up to the election. In Osun however, the sitting APC governor Rauf Aregbesola was returned, confirming the APC's hold on the ethnic Yoruba dominated southwest.

In the meantime, it became clear around mid-year that all the attacks and challenges from within and without the ruling party to prevent Jonathan from seeking re-election were failing to materialise. On 11 December, at the *PDP convention* in Abuja, Jonathan emerged as the sole candidate keeping Vice President Namadi Sambo as his running mate. Earlier, on 15 July, Murtala Nyako, governor of Adamawa State, had been impeached by the state assembly, largely orchestrated by the federal government, and the speaker Umaru Fintiri had been sworn in as acting governor. Nyako was one of five PDP governors who had defected to the APC in 2013, which the presidency feared might have a decisive impact on the presidential election. Although it was said that the deputy governor, Bala James Ngilari, had resigned, the Abuja Federal High Court, shortly before the gubernatorial election scheduled for 11 October, declared the parliament's action invalid and Ngilari the legal governor, a verdict decision accepted by all.

At the same time, under its new chairman, John Odigie Oyegun, an old-hand politician from Edo State in the South-South geo-political zone, the *APC* was still struggling to establish a platform acceptable to all. Finally, on 11 December, at a convention in Lagos, the party endorsed the candidature of retired Major General

Muhammadu Buhari, a former military dictator and three-times unsuccessful presidential candidate. On 17 December, and after intense discussion within the APC's top hierarchy, Yemi Osinbajo, a former Lagos state attorney general and commissioner for justice, was named as his running mate. This sealed a strong alliance between the North-West and South-West, which Nigeria had last seen on the eve of the civil war. Earlier in the year, on 23 July, Buhari had escaped unhurt when his convoy was attacked in Kaduna by a car bomb, but his chances of becoming the APC's presidential candidate were still vague at that time.

Nigeria's *human and civil rights record* during the year was mediocre at best. To a large extent this was due to the precarious security situation in the North, which had made more than 3 m people homeless, although the government claimed that Nigeria only had about 1 m IDPs. On 10 January, a presidential directive forced the defence headquarters to release more than 165 suspects apprehended in the course of the anti-terror campaign in the North-East and more suspected terrorists were released during the year, including a group of 42 detainees on 6 November. These actions, however, contrasted with the severe criticism of government policy, illustrated, for example, in the AI report "Welcome to hell fire: Torture and other ill-treatment in Nigeria", published on 18 September, which focused on illegal detention centres and the brutal behaviour of the security forces. The governing council of the National Human Rights Commission had previously, on 15 June, labelled Boko Haram's activities as war crimes and crimes against humanity and had expressed concern over detention centres run by unauthorised persons.

A serious incident occurred in the ancient city of Zaria, when soldiers opened fire on 25 July during a 'Qud's Day' procession that had caused serious congestion on a major road. Three sons of Shaykh Ibraheem Zakzaky, founder of the *Muslim Brethren*, a sect that calls itself Shiite, and more than 30 other members of the group lost their lives.

The precarious security situation in the North also had serious consequences for the *private media*. On 6 June, security agencies, particularly the military, laid siege to the offices of leading newspapers such as 'Daily Trust', 'Leadership', 'Nation', 'Punch' and 'Vanguard', closing their distribution depots in the major cities. The government justified the clampdown by citing intelligence reports that indicated the movement of materials with serious security implications. The government's arguments were not substantiated and after around five days all the newspapers returned to the newsstands.

The movie "Half of a Yellow Sun", an adaptation of Chimamanda Ngozi Adichie's famous novel about the Biafran War, filmed by the Nigerian-born British director Biyi Bandele, was set to open in Nigerian cinemas in late April, having premiered on 8 April in London. Following a directive of the State Security Service (or Department of State Services), the *Nigerian film and censors board* initially refused its release on security grounds. After heated debates and severe criticism, the board backed down on 4 July, realising that the movie was listed for online viewing in the US.

On 7 January, Jonathan signed into law the controversial legislation banning same sex-marriage, despite strong criticism from Western counties and the UNCHR.

Organised crime persisted and kidnappings, piracy, bank raids and killings frequently took place, although Lagos state governor Babatunde Fashola declared on 10 September that Lagos city, Nigeria's economic hub, had not seen a successful armed bank robbery in the past six years.

The security forces killed and arrested a significant number of gang members, particularly in the southern parts of the country where the economy was booming. In April alone, *police forces broke up seven gangs* in Anambra, Delta, Lagos, Ogun, and Rivers states. Among those arrested were the kidnappers of Anglican Archbishop Ignatius Kattey and his wife, who had been abducted in September 2013 and released after payment of a NGN (naira) 10 m ransom. A further success was the capture of a gang that had kidnapped the owner of a private school and a chief executive officer of a micro bank, Ms Edith Aliyu, on 29 June. Although a NGN 2 m ransom was paid, she was still killed. The gang was paraded in Abuja on 23 July. In most cases, kidnap victims were released when a ransom was paid. Generally speaking, the amounts involved were eventually revealed, as in the case of human rights activist Mike Ozekhome, who been abducted in 2013 and had paid NGN 40 m to regain his freedom. Wealthy churches were increasingly targeted after it became clear that quite a number of them were making billions of naira every year. One such was the Assemblies of God Church, which suffered an assault on its senior staff in Abakaliki in early December.

Piracy along the coast was on the increase and, according to the International Maritime Bureau, Nigerian pirates accounted for 31 of 51 attacks in the West African region.

As in the previous years, the government's *anti-corruption campaign* did not yield too many results, due in part to the Economic and Financial Crimes Commission's incompetence in providing sufficient evidence, or to controversial government decisions such as the presidential pardon granted to Diepreye Alamieyeseigha, former governor of Bayelsa State. Overburdened courts and lack of administrative capacity also stood in the way of an effective anti-corruption policy. For example, on 17 January, the Supreme Court confirmed a judgment of the Appeal Court, which said that Mohammed Abacha, son of the late dictator Sani Abacha, had to face trial in a lower court for retaining properties allegedly stolen by his father while in office. The court held that the father's immunity in office did not extend to his son, as was claimed. On 18 June, however, to expedite the proceedings, which had been going on for several years, the government withdrew the suit in favour of a compromise settlement. In return, Abacha and his family withdrew their case at the European Court of Human Rights for alleged infringements of their right to a fair trial and the peaceful enjoyment of their property. This case had delayed the return of the funds for several years. The deal enabled the Abacha family to retain quite a portion of their wealth but, immediately after the agreement, the Principality of Lichtenstein transferred $ 227 m to the Nigerian government.

Towards the end of the year, the Fiscal Responsibility Commission released a report on massive *fraud within ministries*, departments and agencies, pointing out that the NNPC and the capital market regulator, Securities and Exchange Commission, led the field. This report and the already widely believed allegations about stolen funds worth several billion dollars within the NNPC only increased the public's increasing mistrust of the president and his government.

Foreign Affairs

Over the course of the year, Nigeria's domestic security crisis shaped its foreign policy. Relations with the *USA* cooled significantly because of disagreement on how to tackle Boko Haram and in the wake of serious cuts by the US of oil and gas imports. At the start of the year, on 18 January, Nigerian soldiers received training in counter-insurgency tactics, organised by special units from both sides. General James Lindner, commander of Special Operation Command Africa, was one of the key resource persons. On 18 February, during the two-day meeting of the US-Nigeria Binational Commission in Abuja, US Assistant Secretary for African Affairs Linda Thomas-Greenfield was still expressing confidence in Nigeria's ability to defeat Islamist insurgents. At the second meeting on 4 September, however, her remark that the reputation of the Nigerian military was at stake indicated an undercurrent of tension between Nigeria and the US.

Against the background of increasing *piracy and oil theft*, a joint multinational maritime security exercise tagged 'Operation Obangame' took place on 19 April. Apart from the US and Brazil, 20 African and European countries participated in the off-shore exercise.

In June, the US government announced the speedy installation of a 24-hour satellite television channel in Kano as part of its campaign against Boko Haram, although the project had not been implemented at end of the year. Meanwhile, on 10 June, the US, the UK, France, Nigeria and its neighbouring countries set up an *external intelligence response unit on terrorism*. This was in line with a US pledge to spend $ 110 m annually over a period of three to five years to support peacekeeping forces that could be rapidly deployed to deal with terrorist threats and other crises. This commitment was to some extent negated, however, by the fact that, in late June, Nigeria had only received non-lethal transportation, communication and force protection equipment. In September, it was even revealed that any effort by the Nigerian military to purchase US-made Chinook helicopters from Israel would be blocked by the US. This freeze was triggered, according to the then ambassador, James Entwistle, by severe human rights abuses committed by Nigerian troops in the North. His remarks, made on 9 October, during a visit to the American University of Nigeria, located in the Adamawa state capital Yola, did not go down well with the Nigerian government and its Washington representative, Ambassador Adebowale

Ibidapo Adefuye, sharply criticised the US administration's attitude when he appeared before the Council on Foreign Relations on 10 November. Furthermore, on 1 December, the US cancelled a planned joint training programme.

Against the background of these disagreements on security and the expansion of fracking in the US, Nigeria did not export a single barrel of crude oil to the US after July – the first time this had happened since records began in the early 1990s. The US had previously been one of Nigeria's most important trading partners, importing about half of its total crude exports of some 2.2 m b/d and significant quantities of liquefied gas. *India*, already a major employer in Nigeria's economy, became the leading customer for its crude oil. Despite the cooling of relations, the US was still a major destination for Nigerian students, with more than 7,300 studying there.

Nigeria's *ailing power sector* remained a lucrative magnet for huge US investments. In May, the US Secretary of Commerce Penny Pritzker led a high-level delegation of investors, including General Electric, who, in December, signed an MoU for the implementation of a $ 1 bn investment plan. In addition, Nigeria's rapidly growing fast food sector and its shopping malls attracted companies such as Proctor & Gamble, which had established a factory in Ogun State. Against this background, Nigeria's president joined African leaders at the US-Africa Leaders' Summit in Washington on 4–6 August. The following day, after a court ruling, the US government revealed that it had taken control of more than $ 480 m looted by the late dictator Sani Abacha and would return the money to the Nigerian government in due course.

Legal issues also shaped relationships with *Britain*. At the start of the year, the two governments finalised an agreement to allow the transfer of prisoners between their countries. In September, Jeffry Okafor was arrested in Asaba and extradited to the UK, charged with a murder committed in 2009. He had fled to Nigeria using a passport belonging to his brother, who had already been prosecuted and jailed for four years. The case went to trial in London on 7 November. On 26 February, two young British nationals of Nigerian ancestry, Michael Adebolajo and Michael Adebowale, were found guilty of the murder in 2013 of Lee Rigby, a British soldier out of uniform; they were eventually sentenced to life imprisonment and life with a minimum of 45 years, respectively.

In April, there was another twist in the James Ibori saga. In 2012, the former governor of Delta State had been sentenced to 13 years in prison for fraud and money laundering. The case was somehow closely related to a pending complicated *confiscation of assets hearing*. £ 80 m had been temporarily confiscated from Ibori and his associates and frozen. The British crown prosecutor, however, called for a re-trial of the entire case and Southwark Crown Court adjourned the hearing, this time to April 2015. On 4 November, the Metropolitan Police disclosed that the British government was set to return another £ 6.8 m to the Nigerian government, having already transferred £ 1.2 m. It was not known whether the money had been handed back to the true owner and beneficiary, the Delta state government.

In April, the Nigerian Access Bank commenced the implementation of the judgment of a British court against its former manager, Erastus Akingbola, with the sale of two of his properties, which fetched more than £ 13 m. In 2012, he had been ordered by a British court to the pay Access Bank £ 654 m for *fraudulent practices* while in charge of the now defunct Intercontinental Bank, which Access Bank had later acquired. On 8 April, following the UK court judgement, the Lagos Federal High Court ordered him to pay the bank NGN 212 bn. In addition, Akingbola was facing trial for allegedly stealing depositors' money to the tune of NGN 47 bn.

Between September and November, British branches of two of *Nigeria's charismatic mega churches* were under investigation by the UK Charity Commission. After an altercation between the founder, Chris Oyakhilome, and his wife Anita, the Commission opened a statutory inquiry into a controversial payment of more than £ 3 m to the Christ Embassy. At the same time, the famous Winners' Chapel International was investigated following its request to establish an independent school, which would teach 'biblical truths' in each subject, and because of its methods of exorcising children believed to be witches or possessed by evil spirits.

In mid-May, Mark Simmons, the UK's Foreign Office minister for Africa, was in Abuja exploring long-term solutions to the Boko Haram issue. On the occasion of the global *summit to end sexual violence in conflict* held in London on 12 June, the foreign ministers of Nigeria and its neighbouring countries, the US, the UK, Canada and a representative of the AU re-affirmed their strong commitment to defeating Boko Haram and securing the safe return of the Chibok students. In addition, the UK promised to increase its military and educational aid, thereby setting aside possible cuts in aid due to Nigeria's anti-gay law. During a meeting of the Nigeria-UK Honorary International Investment Council in London on 21 November, the country's anti-terrorism campaign took centre stage, with President Jonathan attending in person.

Jonathan's attendance at the World Economic Forum in Davos (Switzerland) on 22 January was a prelude to the World Economic Forum on Africa, which took place in Abuja on 7–9 May. At this summit, economic *cooperation with China* was furthered by the presence of Chinese Prime Minister Li Keqiang, who was on a four-nation tour of the continent. Subsequently, on 20 November, the China Railway Construction Corporation signed a deal worth some $ 12 bn to build a railway along the coast connecting Lagos in the west with Calabar in the east.

Jonathan's two-day pilgrimage to *Israel* on 25–26 October, the first by a sitting Nigerian president, underlined Nigeria's close relationship with Israel. It was alleged that the relationship was instrumental in Nigeria's abstention in the crucial vote on the status of Palestine at the UNSC on New Year's Eve. On 6 January, both sides had already signed a bilateral air services agreement.

All of Nigeria's *diplomatic activities on the African continent* were shaped by Boko Haram. Even the centenary of the country's founding – the then colony of Nigeria came into existence on 1 January 1914 – celebrated in February, was turned into a conference on security and even saw French President François Hollande attending. On 17 May, Jonathan joined a security summit in Paris, hosted by his French counterpart. Nigeria's president attended the AU's Peace and Security Council meeting in Nairobi (Kenya) on 2 September, held talks with his Chadian counterpart Idriss Deby on 8 September, took part in an extraordinary meeting in Niamey (Niger) on 8 October and was a member of a three-man ECOWAS delegation on 5 November, which helped to resolve the crisis in Burkina Faso. Earlier in the year, in January, the president participated in the AU summit in Addis Ababa but had to cut short his attendance at the summit in Malabo (Equatorial Guinea) in June. At the beginning of the year, Nigeria took its seat as a non-permanent member at the UNSC for a two-year period. On 24 September, Jonathan addressed the UN General Assembly and on 27 November, Minister for Petroleum Ms Diezani Alison-Madueke was elected as the first female president of OPEC; soon afterwards, on 16 December, she emerged as president of the gas exporting countries forum.

Socioeconomic Developments

Oil prices, well above the $ 100 per barrel mark, remained high only until mid-year, while production levels in the Niger Delta were kept fairly stable at about 2.3 m b/d. The last four months of the year saw a *dramatic decline in oil prices*, which at the end of the year reached the $ 60 per barrel mark. Against this background, foreign reserves were under pressure, standing at $ 35 bn in December, while the Excess Crude Account, a rather controversial financial instrument used to share some of the windfall profit from oil and gas at federal and state level, stood at $ 3.5 bn. The national currency was under pressure as well and, in November, the Central Bank slightly devalued the naira to an exchange rate of NGN 168:$ 1. On 19 December, the rate fell to NGN 187:$ 1, partly due to the approaching Christmas and New Year celebrations and to currency speculation, with the latter probably having the greater impact. The depreciation however, heralded a further decline of the naira in the coming year.

As of 30 September, the *total debt* of the federal government, the 36 federal states and the Federal Capital territory Abuja stood at $ 69.6 bn, being $ 9.5 bn of external debt and $ 60 bn of domestic debt. The states' share, however, was some $ 10 bn domestic and $ 3 bn external debts.

Nevertheless, in April, after it had rebased its nominal GDP, *Nigeria emerged as the biggest economy on the continent*, with an estimated $ 509 bn for the year 2013, up from $ 285 bn, thereby overtaking South Africa by a clear margin. The sectoral distribution put services on top with 52%, of which retail and wholesale emerged with 20% and the booming telecommunication market with 8%. Industry, still dominated by the production and export of oil and gas – the main source of foreign exchange proceeds – and agriculture followed at 25% and 22% respectively.

As in previous years, the signing of the *federal budget* into law was delayed. The 2014 budget, totalling NGN 4.695 trillion ($ 29.3 bn) based on a benchmark of $ 77.5 per barrel of crude oil, a production of some 2.4 m b/d and an exchange rate of NGN 160:$ 1, was not signed by the president until 21 May. Unsurprisingly, the lion's share of the budget, NGN 968 bn, went to the security sector, to include the military, police, the office of the state security advisor and paramilitary services. On 17 December, the government presented its 2015 budget proposal of NGN 4.358 trillion, based on a benchmark of $ 65 per barrel of crude in the expectation that prices would average about $ 65 to $ 70 in 2015. The exchange rate was pegged at NGN 165:$ 1, although the rate was already falling towards the NGN 190:$ 1 mark.

There was little or no real improvement with regard to the supply of electricity, despite the fact that the government had allegedly accelerated deregulation. Gas shortages and inadequate distribution infrastructure continued to depress both power generation and supply output from the national grid with an average of less than 4,000 MW. According to local estimates, private generators produced around 6,000 MW. Interestingly, some private companies such as the Dangote Group and other cement, food and beverage manufacturing plants across the country had built their own power plants and were generating more than 15,000 MW for the exclusive use of their own companies. Against this background, it was no wonder that, in April, the US firm General Electric, one of the world's leading power companies, considered Nigeria a significant power market. This was in line with the commitment of the World Bank, which, in May, supported Nigeria's power sector reform programme with $ 700 m over the next few years. In addition, on 18 November, the Central Bank signed a NGN 213 bn ($ 1.3 bn) memorandum of understanding with the Ministry of Petroleum Resources, the Ministry of Power and the Nigerian Electricity Regulatory Commission on the CBN-Nigeria Electricity Market Stabilisation Facility. Its aim was to resolve the power sectors' liquidity challenges. Local observers, however, regarded this agreement as yet another source of enrichment to some dubious players in the field.

On 20 July, the Liberian-US citizen Patrick Oliver Sawyer, working for ECOWAS, arrived at Lagos airport knowing that he carried the *Ebola virus*. On arrival, he collapsed and was admitted to a private hospital, where he died on 24 July. Although Sawyer denied being infected, consultant physician Ms Ameyo Stella Adadevoh was able to establish that Sawyer was Nigeria's first Ebola patient. On 28 July, all flights to and from Monrovia (Liberia) and Freetown (Sierra Leone) were suspended and, on 9 August, Nigeria's president declared the outbreak of Ebola "a national emergency" and all schools were closed until October. Unfortunately, the physician, the protocol officer who had received Sawyer, and five other individuals also succumbed to the disease. A dozen confirmed cases survived the outbreak. WHO officially declared Nigeria free of Ebola on 20 October and Nigeria won praise for its swift containment of the disease at a very early stage. In early December, the president signed the National Health Bill into law.

On 18 June, the *Aare Musulmi of Yorubaland*, Alhaji Abdul-Azeez Arisekola-Alao, passed away in London at the age of 69. The Ibadan-based religious leader, wealthy businessman and military contractor had played a dubious and controversial role in the aftermath of the botched democratisation process in the 1990s under the then military dictators Ibrahim Babangida and Sani Abacha.

Senegal

Emmanuelle Bouilly and Marie Brossier

At the midpoint of his first term, President Macky Sall went through a difficult time. The few achievements in the socio-economic field (falls in the price of staple foods and the cost of rent, the overfunding of the 'Plan Sénégal Émergent' (PSE), and the revival of the peace process in Casamance) did not compensate for the disruptive return of former president Wade, the controversies over the trial of Wade's son, rumours of nepotism in the presidential entourage, divisions within the presidential coalition, and growing social unrest.

Domestic Politics

The trial of Karim Wade, son of the former president and ex-minister, before the 'Cour pour la Répression de l'Enrichissement Illicite' (CREI) dominated the political scene. Wade's lawyers contested the CREI's constitutionality and challenged the decisions of its investigation commission. They argued that the CREI did not have jurisdiction to prosecute a former minister as this was the prerogative of the High Court of Justice. Accordingly, Wade's lawyers filed several motions to terminate the trial before the Dakar Appeal Court, which on 21 January declared itself

 | DOI 10.1163/9789004305052_018

incompetent to judge the case. On 6 February, the Supreme Court granted Wade's request and referred the matter to the Constitutional Council. On 5 March, the Constitutional Council ruled that the laws prohibiting illicit enrichment and governing the CREI were consistent with the Constitution. On 7 March, human rights organisations such as the 'Ligue Sénégalaise des Droits de l'Homme', AI Sénégal and the 'Rencontre Africaine pour la Défense des Droits de l'Homme' alleged that Wade's detention was irregular and not in compliance with the international conventions ratified by Senegal.

After two years in France, *former president Abdoulaye Wade returned to Senegal* on 23 April. The Senegalese authorities banned the welcome meeting organised by his party, the 'Parti Démocratique Sénégalais' (PDS), at Place de l'Obélisque. By 28 May, Abdoulaye Wade still had not set foot in Rebeuss prison, where his son was in detention, although his wife Viviane Wade had been visiting him there on a regular basis. On 12 June, PDS members demonstrated outside the CREI asking for permission to visit Karim Wade in prison. Several PDS officials including the party's national coordinator, Oumar Sarr, were arrested. On 17 June, the financial prosecutor in Paris decided to drop the corruption file lodged by the Senegalese government against Karim Wade in 2012. In Senegal, his trial opened on 31 July. The prosecution objected to the presence of former ministers (Souleymane Ndéné Ndiaye, Amadou Sall, Alioune Badara Cissé) on his defence team. On 5 August, the defence counsels challenged the CREI's jurisdiction but, on 18 August, the CREI was declared competent to judge Karim Wade and his co-defendants. Two days later, his lawyers filed an appeal in the Court of Cassation. On 23 August, the authorities banned a demonstration planned by the PDS and, on 7 May, AI expressed its concern that a significant number of demonstrations had been banned.

The trial resumed on 1 September with the appearance of Bibo Bourgi, one of Karim Wade's alleged accomplices. The prosecution of the seriously ill Bourgi raised controversy. On 12 November, Alioune Ndao, the CREI special prosecutor in charge of the Wade case, was dismissed by President Sall. Cheikh Tidiane Mara took over his position. According to some commentators, Ndao's mismanagement of Bourgi's medical record explained Sall's decision. The CREI waited until December to grant Bourgi permission to leave Senegal to seek medical care in France, even though the Ministry of Justice had requested this on 1 October. Karim Wade's trial was suspended and started again on 1 December, immediately after the end of the 15th OIF Summit, held in Dakar. On 21 November, Sall had banned a demonstration organised by the PDS and its allies in support of Karim Wade in order not to disrupt the Summit but, confronted with the risk of national unrest, he eventually allowed the demonstration. On 29 December, the CREI rejected a request for Wade's provisional release on the grounds that it was likely to disturb public order. On the margins of the trial proceedings and debates on the CREI's jurisdiction, the justice system was reformed. On 27 October, regional and departmental courts became 'Tribunaux de grandes instances et d'instances', and new criminal chambers were created.

In addition to Wade, *other prominent PDS members were indicted on corruption charges.* On 27 April, former Senator Aïda Ndiongue and Abdul Aziz Diop, former chief of staff of Senegal's minister of housing and urban development, were officially accused of illicit enrichment to the tune of CFAfr 47 bn. Both had been in pre-trial detention since December 2013. They were alleged to have misappropriated funds from the 'Plan Jaxaay', a government programme meant for the construction of social housing and slums-upgrade. Ndiongue appeared before the judges on 11 June, but the trial was postponed several times. On 11 February, Farba Senghor, once special adviser to former president Wade and former minister in charge of PDS propaganda, was summoned by the 'Division des Investigations Criminelles'. On 11 August, after the expiry of the notice, the mayor of Ziguinchor, Abdoulaye Baldé, also appeared before the CREI. His assets were seized on 24 December.

Sall's 2012 election promises to raise moral standards in the political arena led to the establishment of the 'Office National de Lutte contre la Fraude et la Corruption' on 3 January. The government also passed a law on the declaration of assets on 20 March. On 13 February, the 'Commission Nationale de Réforme des Institutions' (CNRI) chaired by Amadou Mahtar Mbow presented a preliminary proposal for a new constitution. Proposals included the reduction of the presidential term from seven to five years (renewable only once), a prohibition on the merging of the functions of president and political party leader, and the imposition of an age limit of 70 years for presidential candidates.

The press highlighted the existence of a *'Faye-Sall' dynasty* that facilitated access to positions of power for members of their families (Aliou Sall, Mansour Faye, Adama Faye, Abdoulaye Thimbo), including high-level positions within the presidential party, the 'Alliance Pour la République' (APR) in the run-up to the June local elections. On 20 July, First Lady Marième Faye and her foundation 'Servir le Sénégal' were reported to the CREI prosecutor over allegations that it had enriched the individuals in charge of the organisation. The 'Association des Jeunes Marabouts Citoyens' accused Faye of having received a CFAfr 650 m donation from the 'Banque Marocaine du Commerce Extérieur' in order to finance a modern 'Daara' (Qur'anic school). The interference of the first lady in the Senegalese political arena was strongly criticised when ministers such as Mbagnick Ndiaye (minister of culture) confirmed that they owed her their position.

The adoption of the 'Code Général des Collectivités Locales' marked the beginning of the *3rd Act of the decentralisation reform programme* for better governance and an efficient 'territorialisation' of public policies. The law attracted a lot of criticism. Mayors, including Dakar's Mayor Khalifa Sall ('Parti Socialiste' [PS]), saw it as a government strategy to reduce their power as it meant they would lose resources and competencies. On 20 January, a technical committee representing all political stakeholders (the 'G50') was established to review the electoral code. The committee struggled to decide on the voting system for local elections. The government called for a majority rule process but the opposition argued in favour of the existing proportional representation voting system. On 7 April, the new electoral code was finally adopted as part of an emergency procedure privileged by Sall in order to keep to the electoral calendar. The lists remained controversial. On 7 April, the APR National Secretariat expressly forbade any alliance with opposition parties, while, on 17 April, people such as lawyer Mame Adama Gueye heavily criticised the exclusion by the electoral law of independent candidates ahead of the local elections.

The pre-electoral period and the election campaign (which officially began on 16 June) *were marked by violence* (stone throwing, fights between activists of different parties) and resulted in nearly 40 people being injured. More than 2,700 electoral lists competed with each other, which indicated differences within the governmental coalition 'Benno Bokk Yaakar' (United in Hope) between the APR and the PS. For some, this was a sign that the coalition was disintegrating. At the local elections on 29 June, the APR lost many cities including Ziguinchor and Dakar, where the incumbent mayor Khalifa Sall defeated Prime Minister Aminata Touré. However, the ruling party took cities such as Fatick, Linguere, Kaolack and St Louis, sometimes amid controversy (as in the case of the victory of Mansour Faye, President Sall's brother). Following the disappointing results, President Sall fired Prime Minister Touré on 4 July, and appointed Mahammed Dionne (previously responsible for monitoring the PSE) on 6 July. A new government of 40 ministers was formed. While Sall wanted to investigate the losing candidates, the press reported on 8 August that numerous former ministers (including Mor Ngom, Benoit Sambou, Abdou Aziz Mbaye) had been appointed as personal presidential advisers. During his 11 November policy speech before the National Assembly, Prime Minister Dionne insisted on the implementation of the PSE, which the government had launched on 1 January. The PSE incorporated elements of the 'Yoonu Yokute' and the Economic and Social Development Strategy and focused on three main objectives: restructuring of the economic production infrastructure, improvement of the quality of human resources, and good governance. The government said it wanted to reach these objectives by 2035.

The local elections in June offered *political parties the opportunity to reorganise*. In late September, Sall changed strategy and moved closer to the leaders of 'Benno Bokk Yaakar' coalition and 'Macky2012'. On 19 September, he rejected the CNRI's draft constitution, which proposed a major institutional reform of the parliamentary system. Nevertheless, Mbow (chair of the CNRI) requested Sall's resignation as head of the APR on 18 September arguing that the presidency and leadership of the ruling party could not be merged. On 20 October, Sall announced that a referendum on the reduction of the presidential term would be held in 2016. The PS held its 15th Congress on 6–7 June in Dakar. Ousmane Tanor Dieng, supported by the mayor of Dakar, was re-elected as the party's secretary general with 95% of the votes. His opponent, Aïssata Tall Sall, withdrew her candidacy and refused to recognise the result of the election. She announced her intention to run in the 2017 presidential election. Inside the PDS, the lack of a party congress exacerbated tension in July. A number of PDS candidates for the presidential election in 2017 were announced, including Souleymane Ndéné Ndiaye, who had served as prime minister under former president Wade. On 28 December, the PDS announced that its congress would be held in July 2015, when a new secretary general would be elected. Within the 'Rewmi' party, its leader Idrissa Seck reshuffled his national secretariat on 4 September, and Déthié Fall became the party's vice president.

After his return to Senegal, Abdoulaye Wade renewed his relationship with several *religious leaders*. In April, he visited the religious leaders of the holy cities of Touba and Tivaouane and met with the head of the Catholic Church, Cardinal Theodore Adrien Sarr. On 25 August, the General Caliph of the Mourides, Serigne Cheikh Sidy Mokhtar, sent his son to play a mediating role and calm PDS militants who wanted to defy the ban on demonstrations at the Place de l'Obélisque. When visiting Serigne Cheikh Sidy Mokhtar in Dakar, President Sall was booed by the caliph's disciples. On 15 September, Sall promised to complete the work begun by Wade in Touba and to modernise the city. On 4 December, a crowd of Mourides responded to Mokhtar's order to welcome Sall in Touba but, two days later, Wade was warmly received there without any formal instruction ('ndiggel' in Wolof) by the caliph. On the Christian side, Cardinal Theodore Adrien Sarr left his post as Archbishop of Dakar and was replaced by Bishop of Kaolack Benjamin Ndiaye on 22 December.

Significant progress was made with regard to the continuing *separatist conflict in the south-western Casamance* region. On 4 January, in Guinea-Bissau, the warlords César Atoute Badiate and Ibrahima Compasse Diatta met to reconcile the two opposing factions of Senegal's main separatist movement, the 'Mouvement des Forces Démocratiques de Casamance' (MFDC) and to prepare for negotiations with the Senegalese authorities. Sall's visit to Ziguinchor on 17 March launched the Casamance Development Pole Project, which envisaged an investment of. over CFAfr 20 bn in the revitalisation of the local economy. Sall spoke of "reconciliation, reconstruction and sustainable development" and offered peace negotiations. On 28 April, Salif Sadio, the rebel leader of the most radical faction of the MFDC and the preferred partner of the Catholic Sant'Egidio Community (based in Rome) in the peace process in Casamance, announced a unilateral ceasefire on the radio. This was perceived as a sign of goodwill, following negotiations through Sant'Egidio on 22 February. However, Sadio refused to engage with the faction led by César Atoute Badiate. On 3 June, Cardinal Sarr met a delegation of MFDC fighters, close to Badiate. Further negotiations were conducted in Rome in mid-July between representatives of the government and the MFDC. On 24 November, after clashes between rebels, the interior minister of Guinea-Bissau urged the MFDC to leave Guinea-Bissau within 72 hours. The publication on 18 July of Colonel Abdul Aziz Ndaw's book 'Pour l'honneur de la gendarmerie sénégalaise', in which he accused the former head of the gendarmerie (General Abdoulaye Fall) of nepotism and complicity with the MFDC, led to a major controversy and Fall had to resign as Senegal's ambassador to Portugal on 3 August. Ndaw was summoned to appear before the High Command of the Gendarmerie on 10 August. He left his position as Senegal's military attaché in Rome, and was detained for 60 days on 13 August.

Foreign Affairs

Senegal kept its high profile in the region. As the head of the facilitation group carrying on the negotiations between ECOWAS and the EU on EPAs, Sall achieved a minimal compromise on 7 February, and reached an agreement on 10 July. He attended several regional and international meetings: the NEPAD conference in Addis Ababa (Ethiopia) on 29 January, where he launched the AfDB's Africa 50 Fund; the 22nd Ordinary Session of the AU in Addis Ababa on 30–31 January; and the US-Africa Leaders Summit in Washington on 3–6 August, where he met President Obama for the third time. Senegal also hosted major events: NEPAD's Financing Summit for Africa's Infrastructure in Dakar on 14–15 June, the 15th OIF Summit on 29–30 November, and its first Economic Forum on 1 December.

February was a particularly important month. On 12–13 February, European Commissioner for Development Andris Piebalgs launched in Dakar the 11th European Development Fund of € 347 million for 2014–20. After the Chinese minister of foreign affairs signed a memorandum of understanding on diplomatic and political issues on 11–13 January in Dakar, President Sall visited *China* on 19–22 February. He was accompanied by a major delegation including seven members of the government, five employer representatives, two union leaders, and numerous businessmen. He met Chinese President Xi Jiping and Prime Minister Li Kepiang, whom he praised for China's worldwide economic success and its non-alignment policy. The two states signed five economic cooperation agreements on the construction of the Thiès-Touba highway, Sine Saloum University and the 'Cité du Savoir'. China was also funding joint ventures in agriculture and automobile assembly plants, and the development of industrial parks for the relocation of Chinese firms in Senegal. Discussions were held on the possibility of upgrading the Dakar-Bamako railway and building a new national wrestling arena. China was committed to exempting Senegalese diplomatic and service passport holders from visa requirements, and to listing Senegal as an authorised tourist destination. After visiting China, Sall flew to France to meet with the Paris Consultative Group for Senegal (24–25 February), where he looked for an additional funding of the PSE and managed to secure CFAfr 3,729.4 bn in loans and grants over five years, much more than the CFAfr 1,853 bn expected. He then travelled to Qatar, where he met Emir Sheikh Tamim Bin Hamad Al Thani on 25–27 February to discuss funding for a 'Cité des Affaires' and two luxury tourism projects.

Senegal maintained its *regional diplomacy*. President Sall began the year by increasing the Senegalese contingent in the Multidimensional Integrated

Stabilization Mission in Mali (MINUSMA) to 800 troops. Dakar welcomed Malian President Keita on 14 April and he and Sall confirmed their commitment to fighting organised crime and cross-border terrorism, and to solving operational problems at the Dakar-Bamako corridor. On 12 November, Sall promulgated a decree ratifying the treaty delineating the Senegalese border with Mali.

Sall made regular visits around *Africa*. He went to Cabo Verde (5–7 March), Côte d'Ivoire (29–30 March), and Gabon (8–10 December). Senegal and Côte d'Ivoire confirmed their warming diplomatic ties: on 19 March, the joint commission, which had not met for 17 years, signed 16 cooperation agreements on a wide range of sectors such as health, environment, education, agriculture and sport. On the margins of the AU summit, Ghana and Senegal agreed on 29 January on the establishment of a joint cooperation committee. In October, Sall strongly denied rumours regarding his putative support for President Blaise Compaoré of Burkina Faso and he flew on 5 November to Ouagadougou, where he was appointed by ECOWAS to chair the Burkina Faso contact group.

These positive diplomatic relations were marred by *tensions with Gambia and Guinea*. On 1 January, Senegalese passengers and freight hauliers boycotted the Gambian ferry in protest at its high prices. Negotiations on prices lasted over four months. After the Gambian authorities closed the border for one week, business relations gradually returned to normal at the end of April. The diplomatic climate became tense again when Gambia's President Yahya Jammeh charged Dakar with complicity in sheltering the perpetrators of an attempted coup against him on 31 December. The outbreak of the Ebola virus complicated the relationship with Guinea. Senegal closed its land border twice: first from 30 March to 6 May, and then on 21 August after a Guinean student infected with Ebola travelled to Dakar and became the country's first confirmed case. This hampered cross-border commutes and trade and Guinea's President Alpha Condé strongly criticised the Senegalese action. The only routes open between Senegal and Guinea, Sierra Leone and Liberia were air corridors for the delivery of humanitarian aid. On 25 October, an ECOWAS extraordinary summit asked Senegal to reopen its frontiers and air borders alone were reopened on 7 November. Tension with Guinea was increased when Senegalese customs seized an undeclared sum of CFAfr 10 bn in transit from the Guinean Central Bank to Dubai on 26 August.

The *EU* and Senegal remained close partners. On 7 January, Dakar hosted Italian Minister of Foreign Affairs Emma Bonino. Both governments declared their mutual support for their respective applications for non-permanent membership of the UNSC. Bilateral cooperation in fields related to economic affairs, migration and culture was reinvigorated. On 31 March, President Sall met German Chancellor Angela Merkel to speak about their economic partnership. Germany increased its financial support for local development and good governance to CFAfr 4 bn. On 11 March, the EU and Senegal signed a judicial cooperation agreement, which allocated € 2 m for the organisation of the trial of former Chadian dictator, Hissène Habré, due to take place in the Extraordinary African Chambers in Senegal in 2015. A new agreement between the EU and Senegal on fishing licences was officially signed in Brussels on 21 November, replacing the previous agreement, which had been suspended since 2006; 40 European vessels were authorised to catch 14,000 tonnes of tuna and 2,000 tonnes of hake per year in return for a total payment of € 15 m over a five-year period. The agreement also envisaged support measures designed to ensure the sustainability of the fisheries sector. On 26 November, a joint programming document was signed allocating CFAfr 785 bn to coordinate cooperation between Senegal, the EU and its member states. On 19 November, Sall met Pope Francis in Rome.

The situation of the *Senegalese diaspora* was a key issue. In January, the government provided CFAfr 700 m for the repatriation of 630 Senegalese from the war-torn CAR. As Senegalese citizens were regularly victims of assault, murder and xenophobia in Italy, Spain, Morocco, Libya and the USA, the government announced increases to specific funds to secure and support them (the 'Caisse de Secours' from CFAfr 40 m to CFAfr 540 m, and the 'Fonds d'Appui à l'Investissement des Sénégalais de l'Extérieur' from CFAfr 300 m to CFAfr 1 bn), and CFAfr 1.5 bn was granted to support women in the diaspora.

Socioeconomic Developments

Senegal's progress towards *economic recovery* was confirmed despite the *Ebola outbreak and a bad harvest.* GDP growth reached 4.5% (compared with 3.5% in 2013). Pressures on some foods (onions and meat) and petrol prices did not reverse the overall *deflation* (–0.8%). On 22 January, the National Assembly passed a law to regulate and lower *rents,* which drove down housing costs by around 10%. The structural trade deficit fell to an estimated CFAfr 1,730.9 bn thanks to a 3% increase in exports. The current account deficit fell from 10.8% of GDP to 9.6%. On 24 July, the authorities successfully borrowed on the international market by issuing Eurobonds worth CFAfr 1,733 bn.

The *state budget* increased from CFAfr 2,527 bn in 2013 to CFAfr 2,685 bn, while the budgetary deficit went down to an estimated CFAfr 396 bn (5.1% of GDP). State revenues increased through improved collection of fiscal and non-fiscal revenues (especially taxes on oil products), and a CFAfr 32 bn increase in grants. An out-of-court settlement of litigation between Arcelor Mittal and Senegal provided additional income: in June, Mittal paid CFAfr 150 bn, of which CFA 45 bn was dedicated to funding the 2014 budget. A reduction in current expenditure (from CFAfr 687 bn in 2013 to CFAfr 659.2 bn) offset the increase in staff and investment expenditure (1,000 staff and 500 midwives in the public health sector were hired).

President Sall highlighted his intention to increase the country's *economic attractiveness* by boosting *investment* and developing the *national infrastructure.* In January, he launched two funds (the 'Fonds Souverain d'Investissement Stratégique' and the 'Fonds de Garantie des Investissements Prioritaires'), and the 'Banque Nationale de Développement Economique', the last of which is dedicated to supporting the SME sector. On 11 February, the BOT Bill (Build, Operate and Transfer) was passed to foster public-private partnerships. On 8 May, an inter-ministerial council was created to enhance the country's business environment and improve its Doing Business ranking. Apart from major infrastructure projects in the Dakar region, the government invested in the connectivity and electrification of rural areas through two projects (launched in February and August).

Growth was mainly driven by the *tertiary sector* (+5.6%). However, tourism suffered as a result of the Ebola epidemic, with tourism professionals estimating the loss at CFAFr 3 bn. The government's efforts to save the bankrupt Senegal Airlines paid off; it was taken over by Skyjet, a UAE company, on 12 June. The upturn in the *secondary sector* continued (+3.3%). The chemicals, power and building material sectors reported growth (up by 2.3%, 6.5% and 11.5%, respectively) while extractives and refining industries reported a decline (down by 16.6% and 4.1% respectively). The chemical industry improved slowly, particularly due to the privatisation of 'Industries Chimiques du Sénégal' on 6 June, and its recapitalisation on 21 August; an Indian firm, Indorama, invested CFAfr 50 bn, and became the main shareholder. The construction sector grew significantly thanks to large scale infrastructure projects, and the public housing programme. The rehabilitation of three power plants, the building of a coal-fired plant in Sendou, and important investments boosted the energy sector. On 4 August, Senelec and Contour Global, an American firm, signed a contract worth $ 100 m for the construction of a power station.

The *primary sector* went through a difficult time. Artisanal fisheries declined because of adverse weather conditions, over-fishing and the on-going conflict with Mauritania over fishing licences. *Late rainfalls* resulted in the plummeting of the cereal harvest (except for rice), and the reduction of land available for grazing, which adversely affected livestock and meat production. The government responded by giving out short season seed, lowering fertilizer prices, and providing CFAfr 13 bn to safeguard livestock. On 16 May, an emergency plan was implemented to address *food insecurity* in rural areas and 67,500 families had received CFAfr 16 bn worth of food aid by 31 August.

The *social climate deteriorated* markedly. Doctors and tax officers went on strike on 20–21 February and 26–28 February, respectively, and road hauliers' unions went on strike on 18 November. Street vendors frequently demonstrated against eviction programmes in Dakar and regional urban centres. Public *education* suffered seriously from strikes. Despite a memorandum of understanding with teachers on 17 February, threats to carry out strikes and sit-ins continued to affect education between September and December. Higher education students began the year by protesting against the increase in tuition fees and high school graduates demanded university enrolment. On 11 February, the government set up a steering committee for the construction of a second university in Dakar, which would take

30,000 students by 2016. On 21 May, riots occurred on the Dakar university campus, with students protesting against the non-payment of their school grants, and the introduction of a selection process for masters degrees. Students looted the rector's and accountant's offices. The police intervened, leading to 125 people being injured; 22 students were arrested, but they were finally discharged on 28 May. The violence reached a climax when a student, Bassirou Faye, was shot dead by police on 14 August. On 16 August, former president Wade received a student delegation, and expressed his support. On 18 August, students demanded the resignation of the ministers of higher education and the interior as a condition for entering into any negotiation. The next day, President Sall visited some of the injured and urged everyone to remain calm. In order to avoid an 'année blanche' (nullifying the whole academic year), a single session of examinations was scheduled.

Civil society and professional organisations strongly criticised the EPAs and fishing agreements with the EU through the media and various conferences, claiming that the negotiation process had been undemocratic and untransparent. They also saw the agreements as licensing the plundering of resources and against the national interest. The building of a new Turkish embassy on the Dakar coast was another hot topic. On 12 April, the police put down a demonstration against land-grab, and 20 people were arrested, including the leaders of the 'Y en a marre' movement, which continued to assume its watchdog and spokesperson role by organising the second 'Foire aux Problèmes' ('luma djafé djafé yi' in Wolof) on 10 May.

The government tried to ease social tensions by announcing the creation of a High Council for Social Dialogue on 15 April. The government also lowered the retirement age to 60 and increased pensions by 10%, effective from May. On 28 August, the 'Agence pour la Promotion de l'Emploi des Jeunes' was launched with a budget of CFAfr 8.158 bn to encourage self-employment, facilitate access to credit, and provide 40,000 internships and jobs for young people.

Sierra Leone

Krijn Peters

According to all estimates, Sierra Leone had been expected to finish the year with impressive financial growth. Instead, due to the Ebola epidemic, 2014 turned out to be one of the worst years since the civil war ended in 2002. Following the first Ebola death in late May, the virus spread uncontrolled and by the end of the year the country had 10,000 reported cases. The death toll for the Mano River Union countries, Sierra Leone, Liberia and Guinea, was put at nearly 8,000. The crisis eventually triggered a huge international response, but prior to the international intervention the country suffered from months of inaction, which proved to be disastrous and costly. By the end of the year, the epidemic had still not peaked. It was expected that it would be well into 2015 before the country could be declared Ebola free. The human loss would be in the thousands and the economic loss in the hundreds of millions of dollars. The Ebola crisis and its consequences thus clearly dominated developments in Sierra Leone in 2014.

 | DOI 10.1163/9789004305052_019

Domestic Politics

On 13 March, *former president Ahmad Tejan Kabbah died* at the age of 82, following a long illness. Kabbah was born in 1932 and started his career as a civil servant in 1959. In the late 1960s he had become the youngest permanent secretary, serving in various ministries. Following the defeat of the Sierra Leone People's Party (SLPP) in the 1968 elections, his political career came to a temporary halt. He moved abroad and subsequently worked for more than 20 years for UNDP. One year into the Sierra Leone civil war, Kabbah became president of Sierra Leone's National Consultative Council. In 1996, he was elected president in the first free elections in decades and in November that year brokered a peace-accord with the rebel Revolutionary United Front of Sierra Leone. The following year, he was ousted by a coup and fled to neighbouring Guinea. He returned in 1998 and won the 2002 elections, which allowed him to rule for another five years. Kabbah has been widely perceived as the president who ended the civil war and brought peace to the nation.

On 14 April, a military court charged a captain and 13 soldiers with mutiny after they were arrested for planning a protest against President Ernest Bai Koroma in August 2013. All pleaded not guilty. The accused faced either demotion or, in the worst (but unlikely) case, execution by firing squad.

On 20 September, the 2014 Ibrahim Index of African Governance was published, ranking Sierra Leone ranked 25th of the 52 listed countries with an improved overall score of 51.1, up 3.9 points since 2009. To illustrate both the country's sustained progress and the considerable challenges it faced, the overall score in 2000 had been only 34.0.

Foreign Affairs

At the start of the year, Sierra Leonean military troops were still in *Somalia* as part of the African Union Mission in Somalia (AMISOM) to fight against al-Shabaab militants. Following the arrival of about 4,000 Ethiopian troops, the Sierra Leonean troops were now part of a 22,000 strong UN-backed force. On 2 June, Sierra Leone's military chief of staff, General Samuel Omar Williams, arrived in Mogadishu. He met with the AMISOM commanders and visited Sierra Leonean troops stationed in the Juba region. One month before his visit, the first phase of the construction of an ECOWAS military depot, close to Sierra Leone's international airport in Lungi, was completed. Stocked with military equipment donated by the USA, it would allow the regional body to respond quickly to emergencies and conflicts in the West African region.

In January, Italian Foreign Minister Emma Bonino visited Sierra Leone as part of a six nation tour, to explore closer links between the two countries. Opportunities for collaboration of a predominately economic nature were discussed. On 17 May,

Koroma met with the presidents of Equatorial Guinea, Libya and Congo-Brazzaville in Oyo (Republic of Congo) as a part of the AU Committee of Ten tasked to formulate a united Afican position in its campaign for a permanent seat on the UNSC. The campaign was scheduled to be launched in 2015 and coordinated by Koroma.

On 10–11 July, Koroma attended the ECOWAS summit meeting in Accra. The main topics discussed were security, migration and the Ebola crisis. The ECOWAS leaders established a solidarity fund of $ 10 m to help those countries worst affected by the virus. On 15 December, the 46th ECOWAS Heads of State and Government Summit ended in Abuja (Nigeria). Koroma, who had stayed in Sierra Leone to monitor the Ebola crisis, sent Ebun Strasser-King, Sierra Leone's deputy minister of foreign affairs and international cooperation, to attend in his place. The Ebola crisis in the Mano-River countries dominated the Summit's agenda.

Socioeconomic Developments

In early 2014, several cases of death from a highly contagious disease were reported in south-eastern Guinea, close to the borders with Sierra Leone and Liberia. On 22 March, French scientists established that the virus responsible for the mysterious epidemic was the Ebola virus. There was little to indicate at that time that this would become the worst Ebola crisis ever. By March, more than 60 people had died in Guinea, and Liberia and Sierra Leone reported their first suspected cases. Given the lack of a vaccine, a mortality rate of between 25% and 90%, and the fact that Ebola virus disease (EVD) is highly contagious, national and international efforts to stop its spread were shockingly minimal. On 26 May, Sierra Leone confirmed its first Ebola death. In June, Médecins Sans Frontières (MSF) stated that the Ebola epidemic was "out of control", although MSF had 300 specialists and WHO had 150 experts on the ground. Over 60 different outbreak hotspots were recorded.

On 2–3 June, the health ministers of Guinea, Sierra Leone, Liberia, the Gambia, Guinea Bissau, Senegal, Mali and Côte d'Ivoire attended a meeting organised by WHO in Accra (Ghana). The ministers of Uganda and the DRC were also invited, as those countries had experienced Ebola outbreaks in the past. The meeting's aim was to find "the best way of tackling the crisis collectively as well as develop a comprehensive inter-country operational response plan". Meanwhile, the government of Sierra Leone announced that "it is a serious crime to shelter patients infected with the Ebola virus who are in hiding". By 20 July, the death toll had risen to 660 across the three countries, with Sierra Leone witnessing 182 deaths and 405 confirmed cases, and a mortality rate of around 60%. In all likelihood, these figures significantly under-represented the true numbers of Ebola cases and deaths. Rumours of a Western plot, or of a conspiracy by the governments of the affected countries to attract aid money, as well as superstition and local beliefs in witchcraft, greatly undermined efforts to fight the spread of the virus. According to the World Bank,

90% of the outbreak's cost was caused by "irrational attempts of the public to avoid infection". Traditional practices such as touching and washing the bodies of the deceased at funerals exposed many people to contamination. Widespread suspicion of expatriate doctors and the fact that local populations often put their trust in traditional medicines further complicated the fight against the virus. In light of this, a particular set-back was the death of Dr Sheik Umar Khan, a Sierra Leonean doctor in charge of the fight against Ebola. Dr Khan, a virologist and expert on the deathly Lassa fever, was diagnosed with Ebola and admitted to Kailahun hospital. He died on 29 July. On 18 December, Khan was named by 'Nature' as one of ten "people who mattered in 2014". President Koroma described him as a "national hero". A week before his death, nurses at the government hospital in Kenema town went on strike in response to the death of three of their colleagues. Delays in the payment of danger money and the lack of proper protective clothing, such as gloves, masks and protective goggles, were other issues that led to the strike.

Although the area around the epicentre of the disease was declared an isolation zone on 1 August, the virus spread uncontrollably. Following a summit in Washington attended by 35 African presidents, the World Bank pledged $ 200 m and the AfDB a further $ 60 m to support the fight against EVD. By 26 August, the death-toll had risen to 1,552 – including 120 health workers – with more than 3,000 people infected. Of those who died, 422 were Sierra Leoneans. The wider availability of treatment – by the supply of intravenous drips, for example – led to a drop in the mortality rate from 60% to 52%. On 28 August, WHO, which had declared the Ebola epidemic a "public health emergency of international concern" on 8 August, issued a roadmap "to guide and coordinate the international response to the continuing outbreak of EVD in West Africa." It now estimated that up to 20,000 people could become infected and also highlighted the broader socio-economic impact for the sub-region, which was increasingly under lock-down and suffering from a fall in cross-border and international trade. Nearly all airlines temporarily suspended flights to and from the three worst-affected countries. WHO criticised their decision as the restrictions limited the arrival of medical staff and supplies. On 8 September, the AU called for the travel ban to be lifted. Farmers had abandoned their fields and local businesses had been closed. A separate UN-wide operational platform was created to provide basic services, such as sanitation and water, primary health care and food. On 25 August, the UN Secretary-General's senior Ebola coordinator, Dr David Nabarro, described the fight against EVD as a war. He said: "The effort to defeat Ebola is not a battle but a war which requires everybody working together, hard and effectively." On 12 August, WHO allowed the (limited) use of unapproved and experimental drugs in order to contain the outbreak.

By September, the epidemic had worsened. Figures released on 23 September put the number of those infected at over 6,500 and the death-toll at more than 3,000 (double the August figure); 605 of those deaths were in Sierra Leone. On 18 September, the UNSC declared the Ebola outbreak a "threat to international peace and security" and unanimously adopted UNSC Resolution 2177, which urged UN member states to provide more resources to fight the outbreak. Subsequently, the UNSC created the first ever UN mission for a public health emergency, the UN Mission for Ebola Emergency Response (UNMEER). President Obama referred to the outbreak as a "threat to global security". Fortunately, Senegal and Nigeria, which had seen a handful of cases the previous month, did not announce any new cases. On 26 September, the IMF executive board approved emergency financial assistance to the three affected countries. It allocated £ 40 m to Sierra Leone. The EU increased its Ebola aid to $ 183 m. On 10 September, the Bill and Melinda Gates Foundation announced the allocation of $ 50 m for the fight against Ebola. The World Bank added $ 28 m for Sierra Leone, in addition to the $ 200 m it had pledged in the previous month. The UN estimated that funds close to $ 1 bn were needed – ten times the amount estimated in the previous month. A number of Western countries responded to the appeal, including Canada ($ 27 m) and France ($ 70 m). On 19 September, a three-day country-wide lock-down took place. The intention was to isolate cases and allow health-workers and 30,000 volunteers to search houses and educate people on preventing the spread of the virus, although this measure was criticised by MSF, who feared that it would force people underground and destroy trust. On 22 September, the government confirmed 150 new cases and the discovery of the bodies of 70 previously unreported victims. On 25 September, the president announced that he had decided to extend the quarantine to districts that had so far been only lightly affected by Ebola. The new quarantine zones affected an additional 1 m people. One of these districts was Port Loko, the site of multi-billion-dollar iron ore mining operations, and the quarantine measures resulted in a huge economic loss to the country. Many of the expatriates working in mining and other industries had already left the country. FAO stated that the crisis had led to food shortages, price increases and panic buying in the three worst-affected countries. Cash crops such as coffee and cocoa were left rotting in the fields. According to an IFAD report, more than 40% of agricultural land had been abandoned by farmers. On 10 September, Finance Minister Kaifala Marah revised the annual growth estimates for 2014 down from 11.3% (the World Bank had even forecast 14.4%) to 7%. The next day, the deputy spokesman of the IMF, William Murray, estimated a financing gap for Sierra Leone of between $ 100 m and $ 130 m.

At the start of October, Britain pledged its former colony $ 190 m to support a range of Ebola-related health interventions. It had also deployed 350 troops on the ground to help the country fight the crisis. On 8 October, the World Bank warned in a newly released report that, if the epidemic was allowed to spread to neighbouring countries, "the cumulative two-year impact could reach $ 32.6 bn by the end of 2015" for the West African region. A price tag of $ 359 m for 2014 and $ 129 m for 2015 was given if the epidemic was controlled by the end of the year, with figures for Sierra Leone of $ 163 m and $ 59 m, respectively. However, it was estimated that the medium-term impact on Sierra Leone if the crisis was not brought under control by the end of the year would be $ 809 m. On 23 October, WHO confirmed more than 10,000 probable and suspected cases of Ebola and 4,922 reported deaths, although Christopher Dye, WHO's strategy chief, stated that around 5,000 deaths may not have been included in this count because villagers often buried victims without informing the authorities to prevent interference with burial ceremonies. October was the first month in which Ebola had spread to all the districts of Sierra Leone. In addition to the Mano River Union countries, a few EVD cases – all linked to the three affected countries – had been reported in Mali, Spain, the USA, Nigeria and Senegal. The infection of Western health workers seemed to prompt Western countries to step up their efforts in combating EVD in Sierra Leone, Guinea and Liberia. Prior to the infection of Western health workers less than $ 400 m of the $ 1 bn requested by the UN had been provided by Western governments. Former UN Secretary-General Kofi Annan said he was "bitterly disappointed" and that "if the crisis had hit some other region it probably would have been handled very differently". By now, the AfDB had increased its pledges to $ 210 m, with the head of the bank, Donald Kaberuka, warning donors not to repackage aid money already pledged for other development projects in the Ebola affected countries.

Less than a month later, on 18 November, the death toll had risen to 5,459 in the three countries, with more than 15,000 reported cases of EVD. According to the head of UNMEER, Anthony Banbury, isolated rural areas in Sierra Leone, the Northern provincial capital, Makeni, and the north-western town of Port Loko were of particular concern. More generally, the situation in Sierra Leone continued to worsen. MSF stated that the situation "was not under control" and expressed its concern that ambulances, transit facilities, holding facilities and healthcare facilities could all act as transmission points. The Ebola infection rate in Guinea stabilised, while in Liberia it began to drop significantly towards the end of the month. This provided evidence that it was possible to effectively fight the virus.

On 2 December, the World Bank estimated the economic loss caused by the crisis to be around $ 500 m for Liberia, Guinea and Sierra Leone. The World Bank's Ebola Economic Impact Update projected contracting or negative growth for these countries in 2015 and put the growth figure for Sierra Leone at 4%, a drop of 4% from October estimates. On 3 December, ECOWAS sent a first group of ECOWAS volunteer workers to the three worst-affected countries. The last WHO report of 2014 – released on 29 December – stated that there were just over 20,000 suspected, probable and confirmed cases of Ebola, including 7,842 fatalities. By now, Sierra Leone accounted for nearly half of the 20,000 cases. In the first week of December alone, the country reported nearly 400 new cases. Upon his return from Sierra Leone, the Director of the London School of Hygiene and Tropical Medicine, Peter Piot, who had discovered the Ebola virus in 1976, stated that the epidemic was likely to peak in Sierra Leone in the next few weeks, but warned against complacency, saying that it could have a "very long tail and a bumpy tail". Half of the population was now under quarantine and on 10 December the diamond mining district of Kono, in eastern Sierra Leone, was put under a two-week lock-down. On 12 December, the government announced a ban on all Christmas celebrations.

Togo

Dirk Kohnert

The upcoming presidential election set for 2015 dominated political discussion. The ruling elite clearly lacked the will for constitutional and electoral reforms, which the opposition, civil society and international donors regarded as precondition for free and fair polls. The donor community nevertheless increased their aid because of concerns about growing instability and terrorism in the sub-region and Togo's role as a willing supplier of troops for UN-missions. Promising growth prospects were overshadowed by increasing poverty, inequality and youth unemployment.

Domestic Politics

Urgently needed reforms of electoral institutions and the constitutional framework in the run-up to the *upcoming presidential election* in March/April 2015 dominated political discussions throughout the year. The inter-party dialogue 'Cadre Permanent de Dialogue et de Concertation', begun in 2009 between government and opposition but suspended since 2012, formally resumed on 19 May. Because of irreconcilable differences, the talks between the two camps stalled again in early June. Correcting the biased electoral system was one of the opposition's most

 | DOI 10.1163/9789004305052_020

salient demands for electoral reform prior to the next election. The political accord of 2006 ('Accord Politique Global', APG) had endorsed a return to the 1992 constitutional two-term limit on incumbent presidents and its implementation would have put an end to 47 years of autocratic rule by the Gnassingbé clan. The government accepted the APG in principle but wanted to apply the constitutional term-limit only from 2015 onwards, enabling Faure Gnassingbé to remain in office for a third and ultimately also a fourth term.

After the break-down of the interparty dialogue, the government of Prime Minister Ahoomey-Zumu, in a surprise move on 24 June, tabled a *draft reform bill* in order to accommodate some of the opposition's key demands. The bill envisaged (among other things) a partial return to the 1992 Constitution (adapted to the needs of the ruling Eyadéma regime in a 'constitutional coup' of 2002) by re-establishing a presidential term limit and a return to a two-round majority system for presidential elections. Further proposals included the institution of a second chamber, the Senate (already provided for in the Constitution but never established), a reform of the Constitutional Court, a redefinition of the prerogatives of the prime minister and new conditions for eligibility for the presidency. Although the bill did not meet all the opposition's demands, notably the limitation on the presidential mandate with retroactive effect, the opposition was nevertheless ready to enter into negotiations with the government. In fact, this coup stunned not only the opposition and the general public but also international donors, who acted as facilitators of the dialogue. However, only one week later it appeared that the government's initiative was yet another trick to outmanoeuvre the opposition and not a genuine offer. On 30 June, the majority of the ruling 'Union pour la République' (UNIR) in parliament voted against its own president's draft bill, while the opposition voted in favour.

But if the president had surmised that the opposition and the international community would nevertheless recognise him as a moderniser who was impeded by hardliners in his own party, his plan did not work. The stance of the major donors (the G5, i.e. France, Germany, US, EU, UNDP) vis à vis the government hardened. Thus the G5's support for a consensus and for the APG meant that the donors de facto supported the opposition.

The *stalemate* following the imbroglio in parliament went on for months. In a joint statement on 1 October, Togo's three churches (Catholic, Presbyterian and Methodist) appealed to the political actors to resume the dialogue. The churches also decried the fact that the parliamentary majority had rejected the bill drafted by the ruling party. Ten days later the donor communities supported the churches' joint stance

Minister for Territorial Administration and Decentralization Gilbert Bawara, who was responsible for the organisation of elections, responded by asserting that electoral reforms could not be carried out before the 2015 presidential election. He was seconded by the president of the Constitutional Court, Aboudou Assouma, who, on 5 October, declared the APG void. Assouma referred to the advent of a functioning pluralist parliament and stated that "the page of reforms had been turned definitely since 30 June by the refusal of the parliamentary majority of the draft reform bill". This statement of the most senior judge in the land reinforced once more the lack of trust on the part of the *opposition and civil society* in the impartiality of the justice system. Shortly before, in mid-September the head of state and his UNIR parliamentary majority, had re-elected largely the same (seven of nine) notorious judges as members of the Constitutional Court who had been chosen for the same posts in 2007. The president himself, on a state visit to Accra (Ghana) on 25 November), reaffirmed that the Constitution (of 2002) would be rigorously respected in the run-up to the 2015 presidential election, thus indirectly refusing to commit to any reforms before that election. Instead he proposed to put in place a new expert commission with a mandate to elaborate on proposals for political reforms. In so doing, he neutralised the mandate of the already established Truth and Reconciliation Commission (CVJR) of Mgr Barrigah, which had already tabled its proposals on these issues. In early April, the government itself had adopted a draft bill for a White Book concerning the implementation of the 68 recommendations for reconciliation based on the CVJR's final report, issued in 2012. In October, 26 local development projects througout the country were identified, on the basis of CVJR recommendations, within the framework of the 'Projet d'Appui à la Société Civile et à la Réconciliation Nationale' (founded in 2012) in collaboration with the EU and local civil society organisations.

In line with the president's attempts to move the debate about critical election issues into commissions, Bawara, the minister responsible for election organisation, had appointed on 21 October an expert committee to develop a roadmap for the *local elections*. This had been postponed several times since the last elections in 1987 due to the ruling elite's lack of political will to devolve powers to the regions and districts. The government also feared that it might lose ground to the opposition in the urban centres and the south. Shortly before, Prime Minister Ahoomey-Zunu had ruled out local elections taking place before the upcoming 2015 presidential election.

On 17 September, parliament nominated the 17 members of the Independent National *Electoral Commission* (CENI), without any major disagreement between government and opposition. However, the nomination of the expert committee, including the re-nomination by the ruling party of former CENI-chef Taffa Tabiou (UNIR) as CENI president proved much more controversial. This was a strategy of the government to maintain its hold over the CENI.

A national uprising at the end of October against President Compaoré in neighbouring Burkina Faso after 27 years of autocratic rule encouraged the Togolese opposition in turn to take a firmer stand against the ruling regime. It caused the opposition alliance, Arc-en-Ciel, to end its quarrels with the more radical 'Collectif Sauvons le Togo' to create a *common opposition alliance* called 'Combat pour l'Alternative Politique en 2015' (CAP 2015). On 31 October, the two parties agreed to nominate Jean-Pierre Fabre, the head of the main opposition party, 'Alliance Nationale pour le Changement' (ANC), as the sole opposition candidate in the upcoming presidential election. According to Afrobarometer data in October, about two-thirds of the population thought that the current electoral system allowed the electorate neither to vote the president out of office nor to vote for deputies who reflected their will.

The *reorganisation of the military* continued in December with the aim of reinforcing the power of the head of state vis-à-vis hardliners within his own ranks. Two battalions of a Rapid Intervention Force had already been created by presidential decree on 9 October. Raymond Germanos, Gnassingbé's dubious military advisor, a retired French five-star general, supervised the establishment of these battalions, which consisted of 550 well-equipped troops with headquarters in Lomé and Kara. Colonel Awoki Panassa, former head of the National Gendarmerie, became the president's chief of staff, replacing Néyo Takougnadi, who became the head of the National Navy. A fundamental reform of the National Gendarmerie, with the creation of two regional directorates, was announced at the same time. Yotroféi Massina, the chef of the controversial intelligence agency ('Agence Nationale de Renseignements'), accused of torture in 2012 by the National Human Rights Commission (CNDH), became head of the Gendarmerie. In mid-October, the protection of the electoral process, which had been hitherto the task of the national police under the command of the minister in charge of security and civil protection, Colonel Yark Daméhame, was transferred to the Ministry of Defence and thus de facto to the head of state himself. In addition, a special force ('Force Sécurité Élection Présidentielle', FOSEP 2015) composed of elements of the gendarmerie and the police was created to secure the presidential election, as in previous elections.

Corruption, money laundering and *illicit financial flows* continued to influence domestic politics. Lomé attracted all sorts of merchandise from all over central Africa, such as ivory (four tons in January alone), which was then re-exported clandestinely in huge quantities to Vietnam and China. According to a report by the US non-profit think tank Global Financial Integrity, published in April and put before the general public in Togo in August by the ANC, illicit outflows from Togo averaged $ 1,847 bn between 2002 and 2011, with a peak in 2008 when it amounted to 160% of GDP, more than four times the state budget. The ANC was quick to point to the Gnassingbé regime as the main beneficiary, claiming that this explained its reluctance to implement political reforms.

In September, ECOWAS launched a maritime piloting zone to fight *piracy* in the coastal waters of Nigeria, Benin and Togo. The deep water harbour of Lomé emerged as the primary African destination for US petroleum exports, partly as a way to thwart pirates.

The *human rights* situation remained precarious Although Togo's Freedom House rating improved from 'not free' in previous years to 'partly free', this was mainly due to the peaceful conduct of the 2013 legislative elections. The elections were free, but not fair. On the democracy index of the Economist Intelligence Unit for 2013, Togo had improved by two places compared with 2012 to rank 128th out of 167 countries. However, Togo's low score of 3.45 out of 10 remained unchanged and the country thus continued to be classed as an 'authoritarian regime'. In the ranking of the Paris based Reporters Without Borders, Togo improved from 83rd out of 179 countries in 2013 to 76th. A delegation of the New York-based Parliamentarians for Global Action visited Togo at the end of June. The purpose of the trip was to persuade the government to sign up to the ICC in The Hague. The mission failed and Togo thus remained the only ECOWAS member that is not a member of the ICC.

Urban centres were characterised by an increasing lack of security. A series of murders took place in Lomé: for example, on 28 September, a group of traders on their way to China were ambushed at the airport by robbers, who made off with about € 4.5 m in cash. Deplorable *prison conditions* attracted international attention. According to a report by the US-based Open Society-Justice Initiative published on 1 September, Togo counted among the 20 countries worldwide with the highest percentage of pre-trial detainees, amounting to 65% of the total prison population in 2012. Detainees were housed in prison cells of about 35–50 m^2, which held up to 55 inmates, and had to rely on their families for basic food and drinking water. Prison staff delegated much of their authority to trusties, who effectively controlled and terrorised their co-inmates. Torture to extract confession remained widespread at police and gendarmerie stations.

Foreign Affairs

On a visit to Lomé on 27 November, the UN's West African special envoy, Mohamed Ibn Chambas, urged all political players to reach a consensus on the presidential term limits. He thus reconfirmed the position of the international donor community, notably that of the *EU*, whose representative in Lomé, Nicolàs Berlanga-Martinez, had underlined on 10 July that, contrary to the Gnassingbé government, the EU was not of the opinion that the reform question was off the table.

Nevertheless, *major donors* increased their support for Togo because of geostrategic considerations: Togo supports regional peace-keeping operations, e.g. as a troop provider. In October 2013, the EU had already agreed to raise its financial support to $ 292 m for the funding period 2014–20 within the framework of the 11th EDF. This constituted an increase of 70% compared with the previous period (2008–13). Within this framework, the EU signed a National Indicative Programme on 10 October, which provided € 216 m for state consolidation and security, water, sanitation and energy. Another € 16.7 m of EU budget support had been already approved in February. *Germany* nearly doubled its aid to € 40 m for two years (2014–15) on 5 June. In July, IFAD provided a loan of $ 39.6 m to promote rural entrepreneurship.

The World Bank, the International Bank for Reconstruction and Development and IDA approved $ 40 m for operations in 2014. The first *IMF*-financed three-year ECF, which had expired in 2011, was not extended, due to Togo's reluctance to implement IMF recommendations. In July, the US entered into a military State Partnership Program aimed at internal and border security, in addition to a $ 1.8 m construction and humanitarian assistance US Africa Command (AFRICOM) programme. The *US-Africa Leaders' Summit* in Washington DC on 4–6 August, hosted by president Obama and attended by leaders from 50 African states, among them the Togolese president, focussed on 'aid by trade', investment and international security. One of the key issues was the extension of AGOA, due to expire in September 2015, but the US Congress would not make a decision till 2015 at the earliest. *France*, which was still keen to keep its special relationship with Francophone Africa, followed the line of the EU, UNDP, Germany and the USA and insisted on political reforms before the 2015 presidential election. Paris continued its aid and military assistance programme, including the provision in July of urban guerrilla warfare equipment for the Togolese army in order to enhance its peacekeeping capabilities. *China* continued its economic cooperation, with major infrastructure projects financed by Chinese aid, e.g. the construction of a new Lomé international airport ($ 141 m), with double the capacity of the former airport, by the China Airport Construction Group, which was completed on 25 December.

Apart from aid, *remittances* from the Togolese diaspora played a significant role in development, although there was no apparent link between remittances and economic growth. According to OECD statistics, Togo ranked high on a global scale both for ODA per capita ($ 91 in 2011, ranked 17th) and remittances per capita ($ 52 in 2011, ranked 7th), together amounting to franc CFA 182 bn ($ 333 m) in 2014.

Negotiations on the controversial EU-West African *EPAs*, which had dragged on since 2002, were increasingly under pressure by the EU, which wanted to sign the agreement by 1 October at the latest. African civil society organisations and churches, including the secretary general of the Fellowship of Christian Councils and Churches in West Africa, the Liberian Rev. Dr Tolbert T. Jallah, a well-known anti-EPA campaigner, cautioned ECOWAS against premature conclusions and criticised the secrecy surrounding the negotiations. Despite the pressure applied on all ECOWAS members to sign the EPAs, at least five countries, among them Nigeria and Togo, refused to do so, even though the ECOWAS head of states had endorsed the negotiations at the ECOWAS 45th ordinary session in Accra (Ghana) on 10 July.

The *Ebola* pandemic posed a new risk to Togo. In early October, epidemiology studies carried out by North-Eastern University in Boston (MA, USA) and Oxford University placed Togo among the ten African countries most likely to be exposed to an outbreak of Ebola. Shortly before, China had granted $ 0.8 m for Togo to buy Ebola screening equipment. During an extraordinary ECOWAS meeting in Accra on 6 November, which focused on Ebola, Faure Gnassingbé was elected ECOWAS coordinator of Ebola related activities. At a West African Economic and Monetary Union summit in Lomé shortly before (on 25 September), member states had been urged to reinforce the health system in order to prevent the spread of the fever.

Socioeconomic Developments

Economic *growth* remained promising. The annual growth rate was expected to stand at 6.0% in 2014 and 6.3% in 2015, the increase being largely the result of heavy assistance by the international donor community. Because of falling global oil and food prices, inflation remained well below 3%, despite a rise in domestic fuel prices in January. This was the result of government efforts to reduce subsidies. In February, the government finally established a new and more efficient revenue authority ('Office Togolais des Recettes'), thereby merging customs and tax directorates, a measure that had been delayed since December 2012. Overdue *privatisation* of parastatals remained an issue and suffered from lack of transparency. Two of four state-owned banks still remained to be sold and the tender to sell the phosphate mines ('Société Nouvelle des Phosphates de Togo' joint-venture) was still pending at the end of year. Ailing phosphate production increased by 3.4% to 900,000 tonnes in 2013. Cotton production, the most important cash crop managed by the 'Nouvelle Société Cotonnière du Togo', fell by 18% compared with the previous cropping season to 67,000 tonnes in 2013/14. Major investments included the extension of the deep water *port of Lomé* by a third container terminal, financed with € 457 m by the French Bolloré group. The extension was completed in October and allowed for the processing of 1.2 m containers per year. A supplementary fourth private container terminal was also nearing completion. Its even bigger capacity of 2.2 m containers meant that Togo would now serve as a logistical hub for the West African coast. The extension was the result of a Chinese-Dutch joint-venture with an overall cost of $ 420 m financed in conjunction with the IFC which acted as facilitator. Other projects included road construction and the huge $ 250 m clinker and cement grinding plant under construction by German HeidelbergCement. From 2015, up to 1.5 m tonnes of clinker a year would be produced in Tabligbo, 80 km north-east of Lomé, and up to 200,000 tonnes of cement per year from 2016 in Dapaong in the far north.

The current account *deficit* remained high (13.4% of GDP) because of growing public investment, which in turn resulted in higher imports, while exports of major foreign exchange earners and transfer inflows lagged behind. Because of high public investment and election-related expenses, the fiscal deficit was forecast to increase from 5.6% of GDP in 2014 to 5.9% of GDP in 2015.

According to an IMF poverty reduction strategy paper published in July, the government's 'Strategy for Boosting Growth and Promoting Employment' (SCAPE,

2013–17), focused too much on the coastal region and was unsustainable because of high vulnerability to external shocks. The IMF further claimed that the programme was not inclusive of the country as a whole and had led to regional *inequality* and an increase in extreme poverty. Despite a small drop in monetary *poverty* since 2006, the depth and severity of poverty increased. About 81% of the population were vulnerable to falling into the poverty trap. The regional distribution varied from 91% of people living below the poverty line in the northern Savanes region to 33% in Lomé.

Youth unemployment continued to be a concern to the government because of its potential political repercussions. The programme for unemployed school leavers (PROVONAT – 'Programme de Promotion du Volontariat au Togo', backed by UNDP) became in June the 'Agence Nationale de Volontariat au Togo'. According to official figures, about 65% of Togolese school leavers did not find employment. Up to 4,280 volunteers had participated in the PROVONAT programme since 2011 and 44% of its participants found employment.

The ambitious *budget* (franc CFA 815.9 bn) for 2015 was adopted by parliament on 30 December, with the opposition voting against. The increase of 12% over the 2014 budget was justified by citing fiscal reforms and promising economic growth perspectives. The opposition accused the government of wishful thinking and argued that the 2014 budget had already suffered from a budget shortfall of 13%. The IMF had warned the government in May to control the growing public debt, especially external debt, which was forecast to reach 22% of GDP by 2016. African traditional religions, notably *vodun* in the southern regions and occult beliefs throughout Togo, continued to play an important role in everyday life, with priests often acting as conflict mediators at the local level. In October, 'Jeune Afrique' named Ni-Mantche, the grand master of the vodun goodness Maman Kole in southern Togo, as one of the 15 most influential religious leaders in Africa and one of the most celebrated African vodun priests.

PART 4

Central Africa

Andreas Mehler

With the CAR crisis and Boko Haram spilling over into Cameroon and Chad, security issues were again impacting on the lives of many people and were also high on the agenda of Central Africa's decision-makers. Both aspects showed how permeable frontiers were and how strongly crises in the neighbourhood could affect the entire sub-region.

Democracy and Elections

The sub-region again fared worst in comparison to West, Eastern and Southern Africa in terms of democratic standards, as evidenced by ratings from Freedom House or all other available indicators. However, in contrast to previous years, some new impetus combined with growing organisational capacity brought civil society organisations more to the fore.

Relevant elections took place in only one country of the sub-region – *São Tomé and Príncipe* (legislative and local elections), where the legislative elections of 12 October again brought major changes to the composition of the National Assembly: the 'Acção Democrática Independente' won an absolute majority by increasing its seats from 26 to 33 (out of 55) and Miguel Trovoada became prime minister for the third time in November. The quickly changing majorities in the country attested on the one hand to the extraordinary openness of the political system, but were, on the other, evidence of some instability. An earlier sign of widespread unease was the refusal of the presidential guard to report for duty when President Manuel Pinto Da Costa returned from an official trip, which led to the resignation of the chief of defence staff on 13 February. In the *CAR*, preparations for a constitutional referendum and elections (formally ending an interim period) made only slow progress, not least because of the on-going insecurity in the country. This meant that the transition calendar had to be updated; elections were postponed from February 2015 to summer.

The overthrow of Burkina Faso's Blaise Compaoré after a phase of popular revolt sent clear signals to Central Africa. Both President Sassou Nguesso (*Congo*) and President Joseph Kabila (DRC) were interested in seeking a further term in office, though this was prohibited by their countries' existing constitutions – the same scenario as in Burkina Faso. Supporters of Sassou Nguesso campaigned throughout the year for an obviously unpopular change to the Constitution to allow him to run for a third seven-year term after 2016. Taken together Sassou had already held presidential power for 30 years, interrupted only from 1992 to 1997. The influential Catholic

 | DOI 10.1163/9789004305052_021

Church openly expressed its opposition to such a move and dissent was even expressed within the ruling party. However, the party's politburo finally endorsed Sassou's ambition to change the Constitution on 31 December.

The frontline in neighbouring *DRC* was similar. The Catholic Church opposed a change in the legislation to allow the president to stand for a third term in office in 2016 (having already been elected in 2006 and 2011). Some political veterans such as Kengo wa Dondo, speaker of the Senate, were equally openly against such a move. Opposition parties organised a protest march in Kinshasa on 4 August, leading to the arrest of an opposition leader, later sentenced to one year in prison. Civil society engagement was certainly more impressive than on the other side of the Congo River, with almost all reputable domestic NGOs signing a declaration against constitutional revision.

Gabon, a rather mild electoral autocracy, witnessed a new wave of contestation. Unexpectedly, on 19 February, Jean Ping, formerly a chairman of the AU Commission (and earlier the influential foreign minister under the late Omar Bongo) announced his resignation from the ruling party and joined the opposition to President Ali Bongo. Ping and former prime minister Eyeghe Ndong were among the participants in an anti-regime protest on 20 December, which government forces quelled with the use of tear-gas.

In *Equatorial Guinea*, by all standards the most authoritarian regime of the sub-region, the government offered some timid steps towards political openness at a national dialogue, held on 7–16 November. The event followed the formation of a coalition of 12 parties and associations in the diaspora in January, but the diaspora groups were absent from the national dialogue, as was the most vocal opposition party, based in Malabo, which attended only the first day.

Neither large-scale protest nor reforms were observable in Cameroon or Chad, potentially because both presidents had managed long ago to change the constitutions to allow them to stand for elections as they wished. In *Chad*, the regime also appeared more solidly established than ever. In May, the opposition platform 'Coalition des Partis Politiques pour la Défense de la Constitution' called off its boycott of the political dialogue framework offered by the government. *Cameroon*'s governing elites feared a violent regime change more than elections, as was attested by a nervous debate about the backers of the Boko Haram movement within Cameroon.

Instability, War and Peace

The deployment of more peacekeepers to the *CAR* (in three separate missions: the French Sangaris, a UN-led mission replacing an AU mission, and an EU mission) gradually improved the security situation in the western part of the country. However, it came too late to prevent a good part of the *Muslim minority* from leaving the country under threat or from settling in a few moderately secure spots. The conquest of Bangui by the Séléka rebels in 2013 had proved unsustainable, as had Michel Djotodia's hold on power. In a spirit of revenge, the so-called anti-Balaka militias attacked Muslim neighbourhoods in the capital and secondary cities, irrespective of whether their inhabitants had shown sympathy with the Séléka rebels or not. In the countryside, nomadic Fulani (Mbororo) were attacked but they also retaliated. Many of their youth joined a faction of the Séléka movement. One source of concern in diplomatic circles was the visible fractures within both the Séléka and the anti-Balaka camps, making it nearly impossible to come to an overall peace agreement. Instead, a ceasefire agreement was signed on 23 July – and immediately contested by non-signatories. Séléka factions controlled most of the territory in the eastern half of the country and invested in establishing a diamond- and gold-based war economy; similar moves by anti-Balaka leaders were observed in the west.

The Lord's Resistance Army (*LRA*) continued to operate, mostly in the CAR, but also in the DRC and South Sudan. The government of Sudan was suspected of supporting the LRA and of providing a safe-haven in Kafia Kingi, an area disputed between Sudan and South Sudan; Khartoum later denied such allegations, which came from UN Secretary-General Ban Ki-moon. The US administration decided to deploy military aircraft and more personnel to provide enhanced air mobility support to African forces. US military advisers spread defection messages by various means; some 81 LRA fighters in fact defected during the year. In November, the Regional Task Force was 2,284 soldiers strong (1,437 from Uganda, 447 from South Sudan and 400 from the DRC – far below the 5,030 troops that had originally been pledged), while the LRA was thought to be composed of only 150–200 armed elements, split into several highly mobile units. Despite such massive international efforts, LRA leader Joseph Kony remained at large. The effectiveness of the military task force engaging with the LRA suffered mainly from the prevailing insecurity in both the CAR and South Sudan; the security forces of both countries were either not operational or absorbed by the civil war. Kony reportedly continued to be in effective command of his fighters. According to some defectors, Kony had ordered his fighters to loot diamonds and gold from artisanal miners in eastern CAR and had also established good contacts with the Séléka rebels there. Subsequently, the LRA moved most of their forces back to north-eastern DRC, where they engaged in wildlife poaching.

With the defeat of the M23 rebellion in late 2013, the *DRC* had entered a new phase of a long drawn-out pacification strategy, i.e. on the one hand more seriously promoting DDR efforts, and on the other coming to terms with smaller insurgencies operating in the east. Progress on the DDR front was very limited and fears persisted that M23 would reorganise in Rwanda (with bilateral relations between Kinshasa and Kigali again rather tense). Government forces failed to attack the pro-Hutu 'Forces Démocratiques de Libération du Rwanda' (FDLR) rebels, who were aiming at toppling the Rwandan government and were operating on Congolese soil.

This also applied to the 3,000-strong Force Intervention Brigade (FIB) which was meant to complement the UN Stabilization Mission in the DRC (MONUSCO) and had in 2013 showed its effectiveness in combating M23. Unrelated armed attacks also occurred in Kinshasa and Katanga. Attacks in January on diverse government installations such as the National Radio and Television building were attributed to the self-declared prophet Joseph Mukungubila. The security forces killed attackers and followers of Mukungubila (officially 103 people, but possibly many more). The Kata Katanga movement, demanding a bigger share in resource exploitation income in the mineral-rich southern province, clashed several times with security forces and burnt down some villages.

Cameroon clearly suffered from the insecurity in the CAR; incursions by armed groups and abductions occurred on its soil and refugees had to be given safe haven. One overarching concern was that the inter-communal cleavages in the CAR might also affect relations in Cameroon – not necessarily in terms of Christian-Muslim conflict, but on a lower level of local coexistence. The nomadic Mbororo, a prime target of anti-Balaka groups in the CAR, had until recently been relatively well integrated in Cameroon, though tensions with some adjacent settler communities always existed. Cameroon faced even greater repercussions from the *Boko Haram* revolt, originating in Nigeria but clearly seeking a second theatre in northern Cameroon. After an upsurge in abductions during the first part of the year, including the kidnapping of foreigners and prominent local persons, massive attacks on villages close to the border followed. The government deployed more troops to the north and sought new recruits. Speculation as to the motives and connections of Boko Haram's Cameroon mission abounded, but very limited reliable information on the confrontation was available. According to official sources, 40 soldiers and almost 1,000 Boko Haram fighters had been killed by November. *Chad* was ready to become more engaged in fighting Boko Haram and other Islamist rebel organisations, both by offering a base for the new French military mission Barkhane and by strongly supporting the idea of regional military coordination within the CBLT framework. This firm stance followed the failure of talks during September and October in N'Djamena between the government of Nigeria and representatives of Boko Haram (facilitated by the Chadian authorities) to reach a ceasefire. Chad clearly claimed a prominent role in diplomatic and military affairs touching the sub-region.

Bilateral relations between the *two Congos* made headlines. Over a period of four months, the Congolese authorities deported about 250,000 DRC citizens, frequently employing brute force. Officially, this action was part of a campaign to combat growing criminality, not at all well received in Kinshasa. The tensions led to the temporary introduction of mutual entry visa requirements. It was unclear whether the Congolese security forces' attack on a private villa, leading to the killing of exiled Kabila opponent and rebel commander Udjani Mangbama on 10 May, was related;

Brazzaville had previously steadily refused to extradite him. However, relations improved during the summer. Kabila and Sassou Nguesso met on 19 September, and a few days later the visa requirements were lifted.

UNHCR statistics indicated an overall rise in the number of *refugees* as a result of the lack of security. The on-going violence in both Sudan and the CAR had repercussions for Chad, which now hosted 454,882 refugees, far more than the neighbouring countries. Cameroon came second (226,368) and the DRC third (117,907). CAR nationals accounted for the highest number of refugees, with 135,000 having fled to Cameroon, 22,000 to the DRC, 20,000 to Chad and 10,000 to the Congo. Refugees from the DRC continued to be assisted to return from Congo (Brazzaville), reducing the number of refugees there to 49,192. The largest number of *IDPs* in Africa were again found in the DRC, where there were over 2.6 m, a figure that has remained quite constant for years. The number of IDPs in the CAR grew at an alarming rate, from 400,000 to about 500,000 by the end of 2014.

Human Rights

Not surprisingly, armed conflicts formed the principal context for the most serious human rights violations during the year; both state and non-state actors committed serious crimes and frequently went unpunished. Major reports by human rights organisations documented the atrocities committed during two years of turmoil and armed conflict in the *CAR*. AI devoted two reports to the situation: "Central African Republic: time for accountability" focused on human rights violations committed not only by anti-Balaka and Séléka forces (and individuals within both camps), but also by the Chadian contingent of the AU-led peacekeeping mission. The earlier AI report, "Ethnic cleansing and sectarian killings in the Central African Republic", documented mainly the merciless attacks by anti-Balaka militias on Muslim communities, which led to a mass exodus of Muslims to neighbouring countries. The same topic was taken up by a report from various fact-finding missions issued jointly by the International Federation for Human Rights (FIDH) and its associated local organisations 'Ligue Centrafricaine des Droits de l'Homme' and 'Observatoire Centrafricain des Droits de l'Homme' (entitled "They must all leave or die: answering war crimes with crimes against humanity"). Both reports directly criticised the failures of the international community to halt mass killings and of the national and international justice system to deal with them effectively. The US-based 'Enough' project, organised around expert analyst John Prendergast, which focused on ending genocide and crimes against humanity, published a more analytical report on those confrontations titled "Behind the headlines: drivers of violence in the Central African Republic", pinpointing the economic agenda of perpetrators of violence. One hotly debated issue, less in Bangui than in Western capitals and New York, was whether the killings and forced displacements of Muslims were to be rightly described as genocide. The UNSC's investigation commission did not confirm this view and stood in opposition to many human rights activists who had used the term, potentially for its capacity to mobilise media attention. Earlier, during a visit to the CAR in April, UN Secretary-General Ban Ki-moon had warned that peacekeepers could be "overwhelmed", and that this might lead to a repeat of the Rwandan genocide. This view was arguably instrumental in securing UNSC approval for a substantial UN peacekeeping mission.

The second main theatre of armed conflict was equally a focus of international NGOs. An Oxfam report ("Secure insecurity: the continuing abuse of civilians in eastern DRC as the state extends its control") pointed to on-going risks for the population in the eastern *DRC* after the end of the major confrontation between the security forces – supported by the UN peacekeeping operation – and the M23 rebels. In particular, the authors portrayed the competition for scarce land resources as a potential source of further violence. Far away from the armed conflict, the Kabila regime was accused of abusing human rights in a HRW report ("Operation Likofi: police killings and enforced disappearances in Kinshasa"). It alleged that, in a three-month operation against criminal gangs (Operation Kuluna; December 2013–February 2014) in the capital, the security forces tortured and killed mere suspects, instilling a climate of fear, with youths aged 14–17 among those killed.

A joint report by the FIDH and the 'Observatoire Congolais des Droits de l'Homme' ("République du Congo: tortures, persécutions politiques et attaques contre les libertés syndicales") placed a rare focus on the intimidation of trade union activists in *Congo* (Brazzaville). Torture and unfair trials were frequent and were taken as a sign of a deteriorating political climate in Congo. This accusation was in line with complaints about the persecution of journalists covering protests against the regime's plan to change constitutional rules to allow President Sassou Nguesso to run for a further term.

Homophobia remained a serious problem in the sub-region, particularly in Cameroon where seven men were arrested on homosexuality-related charges on 1 October. The authorities showed little inclination to inquire seriously into the background of the murder of the lesbian, gay, bisexual, transgender and intersexual (LGBTI) rights activist Eric Ohena Lembembe in 2013.

The *ICC* continued to follow events in the Central African sub-region closely, including recent developments in the CAR. However, the older case-loads were only slowly dealt with and the main trial, in the case of Jean-Pierre Bemba, formerly a DRC prime minister, for crimes against humanity committed by his militia in the CAR, dragged on; closing statements were made on 12–13 November. The ICC proved slightly more effective in its trial of Germain Katanga, who was found guilty on 7 March of a crime against humanity and four counts of war crimes committed in 2003 during an attack on a village in the Ituri district in the DRC (while he was acquitted of other charges); on 23 May, he was sentenced to 12 years' imprisonment.

On 9 June, an ICC Chamber confirmed charges of both crimes against humanity (including forcible transfer of population, rape and sexual slavery) and war crimes (including conscription of child soldiers) against Bosco Ntaganda, all allegedly committed in eastern DRC. Ntaganda had voluntarily given himself up in 2013.

There was also some good news: Equatorial Guinea suspended the death penalty as a condition for joining the CPLP and Chad's new Penal Code included the complete abolition of the death penalty.

Socioeconomic Developments

With two exceptions, the economies of the sub-region fared well according to the IMF's World Economic Outlook (published in April 2015). Substantial progress was calculated for the DRC (GDP *growth* of 9.1%). Chad (6.9%), Congo (6.0%), Gabon (5.1%) and Cameroon (5.1%), and São Tomé and Príncipe (4.5%) followed. The CAR, after experiencing a dramatic downturn following the new civil war (–36% GDP per capita) in 2013, saw a small 1% rise in GDP, representing more or less a stand-still at a very low rate of growth – and feeding doubts as to how quickly the country could recover to an already low pre-war standard. At the opposite end of the GDP per capita list within the sub-region, Equatorial Guinea as the only country experiencing a fall in GDP scored low again (–3.1 %); the IMF even projected a further substantial decline of GDP in 2015, in contrast to Malabo's high economic and political ambitions. The sub-region's generally good growth prospects contrasted starkly with the generally low rankings in the Index of Economic Freedom (Heritage Foundation), which had three countries falling into the 'mostly unfree' category (Gabon, São Tomé and Príncipe, and Cameroon) and five in the worst category of 'repressed' economies (Chad, CAR, DRC, Congo and Equatorial-Guinea – ranking between 165 and 173 out of 178). The World Bank's "Doing Business" report contained similar messages, with the first three countries placed in the same order, but those in the worst category in more or less reverse order, with the CAR ranking 187th out of 189. Insecurity was clearly also detrimental to business. The cost of war (against Boko Haram) was not yet fully felt in Cameroon and Chad, but also presented an economic risk.

Illicit trade flourished in these circumstances and was an incentive to, *inter alia,* poaching activities. On 13 February, presidents Bongo (Gabon) and Déby (Chad) attended the Conference on Illegal Wildlife Trade in London and pledged – along with their counterparts from Tanzania and Botswana – to respect a 10-year moratorium on the sale of their ivory stockpiles as one measure to protect elephants. Poaching nevertheless continued in the sub-region. In one instance, 187 elephant tusks were found in a military car in Cameroon's capital Yaoundé. A high-level meeting co-organised by Gabon and Germany on 26 September on the margins of the UN General Assembly addressed poaching and wildlife trafficking.

Inflation continued to be *low or moderate* in most countries: Congo (0.9%), the DRC (1.0%), Chad (1.7%) and Cameroon (1.9%) scored low; Equatorial Guinea (3.0%) and Gabon (4.6%) still had moderate levels. Less reassuring were the inflation rates in São Tomé and Príncipe, which dropped from 8.1% in 2013 to a still considerable 7.0%, and in the CAR (15%), principally as a result of food shortages with the war-led destruction of harvests and widespread insecurity preventing the population from going to their fields.

With the 2015 endpoint in sight, a provisional balance sheet on the MDGs was drawn up. Overall, the international *poverty reduction* agenda made progress, but not as strongly as expected in the sub-region. The AfDB, in its MDG report published in November, listed all seven countries of the sub-region as having made insufficient progress in under-5 mortality rates. Similarly disappointing was the reduction in maternal death rates, with Central Africa reducing the incidence by 38% – significantly less than both West and Eastern Africa, and translating into a depressing 500 maternal deaths per 100,000 live births (in 2013).

Sub-regional Organisations

The usual undecidedness with regard to which would be the more prominent sub-regional organisation (CEEAC or CEMAC?) gave way to a clearer picture: regional initiatives were taken at the CEEAC level, while *CEMAC* was not able to hold a summit scheduled for 23 May, which was called off at the last minute. Instead, only ministers representing their heads of state went to Libreville (Gabon) at that time to hold a meeting at the margins of the big business meeting New York Forum Africa. The only exceptions were the host (Ali Bongo) and the CAR's new interim president, Catherine Samba-Panza – in her case not unexpectedly as the summit was meant to discuss the crisis in the CAR. Earlier (on 12 March), it was decided to temporarily relocate the CEMAC headquarters from its insecure location in Bangui to Libreville; these circumstances may have contributed to the overall impression of inertia.

CEEAC leaders, by contrast, met for two extraordinary summits and a council of ministers, which prepared for an ordinary summit. The 9–10 January extraordinary summit in N'Djamena had a direct impact on the CAR crisis. The main political actors, including the interim president (Michel Djotodia), the interim prime minister (Nicolas Tiangaye) and the entire interim legislative body (135 members) were summoned to the Chadian capital, where the pressure on Djotodia and Tiangaye was so strong that they were forced to resign forthwith and the summit also appealed to the international community to offer stronger support to the International Support Mission to the CAR (MISCA). Senior officials and representatives of the USA and the AU and the UN Secretary-General's special representative for the CAR also attended. An informal meeting of CEEAC leaders was held in Malabo on 27 June at the margins of the AU summit. Again, the CAR crisis took centre-stage. The heads of state wanted to revive the slow transition process in the CAR and expressed support for a national reconciliation forum. A more explicit roadmap towards political and social stability plus consolidation of security forces was called for. The participants condemned the violence in the CAR, but also armed conflicts in the Great Lakes region more generally. The CAR's Catherine Samba-Panza was more or less summoned to the meeting. The summit preceded ceasefire negotiations in Brazzaville that led to the signature of a corresponding document on 23 July.

A certain reconfiguration of CEEAC was in the offing. Rwandan Foreign Minister Louise Mushikiwabo was invited to a military exercise ('Loango 2014') undertaken in Congo under CEEAC auspices. She explained on 27 October why Rwanda wanted to become a member again after having left CEEAC in 2007. While *Rwanda* clearly continued to have more commercial ties with the East (i.e. the EAC), it now hoped to regain influence with the West. CEEAC Secretary-General Ahmad Allam-Mi (Chad) was also present on this occasion. Within CEEAC, a certain competition for influence between Chad's President Idriss Déby and his Congolese counterpart Sassou Nguesso developed (leaving Gabon's Bongo on the sidelines). A council of ministers was held in the Chadian capital on 21–22 November, focussing on the political and humanitarian situation in the CAR, as well as on terrorism and other factors in the security situation. It ended with resolutions on the institutional reform of CEEAC that called for a revision of all major statutes with a view to their harmonisation with the AU, but obviously also bearing in mind a potential future merger between CEMAC and CEEAC. However, the ordinary summit was postponed sine die and with no reasons given shortly before it was due to start; the re-admission of Rwanda thus had to wait.

The *CBLT* showed some signs of revival, not unrelated to the security threats posed by Boko Haram to all member states. Ministers of defence, chiefs of staff and heads of security and intelligence services of the member states (plus Benin) met in Niamey (Niger) on 27 July. A follow-up council of ministers was held on 1–4 December, again in Niamey, to prepare for joint military action.

Members of the *ICGLR*, under Angolan chairmanship, met frequently at ministerial or summit level throughout the year with a strong focus on monitoring the situation in the DRC; emphasis was put on urging military action against the FDLR by both the Congolese army and MONUSCO. ICGLR members sometimes met in conjunction with their SADC counterparts, following the same agenda (while the CEPGL appeared mostly dormant). This was a further expression of institutional overlaps. In fact, with Joseph Kabila taking over the chairmanship of COMESA and issuing invitations to a summit in Kinshasa on 26–27 February, it became clearer than ever that countries in the sub-region had even further links to organisations focussed more strongly on neighbouring sub-regions.

Cameroon

Fanny Pigeaud

The serious security crisis in the north of the country, characterised by repeated attacks and officially attributed to the Nigerian-based Boko Haram movement, was the main concern throughout the year, mobilising the army and raising controversies domestically and internationally. Linked to this issue, the relationship between the regime of President Paul Biya, in power since 1982, and France, the former colonial power, continued to deteriorate, though not in public.

Domestic Politics

After several abductions in 2013, the Far North region faced even greater security challenges: towns bordering Nigeria were targeted by armed attacks, which were officially attributed to *Boko Haram* and became increasingly frequent as the year progressed. In February, Nigeria announced the closure of a part of its border with Cameroon to stop Boko Haram from moving between the two countries. Towards the end of the same month, the village chief of Goumouldi was abducted and had

 | DOI 10.1163/9789004305052_022

his throat cut by presumed elements of Boko Haram. At the beginning of March, a military confrontation broke out near Fotokol between Cameroonian soldiers and armed men identified as Boko Haram members. Seven people were killed, including a Cameroonian soldier. Weeks later, reports revealed that numerous transfers of weapons were taking place between Chad and Boko Haram in Nigeria, through Cameroon. Other reports alleged that hundreds of young men, most of them Kanuri from Nigeria, were being recruited by Boko Haram and leaving their villages to join training camps, indicating escalating violence.

On 5 April, two Italian priests and a Canadian nun were abducted in Tchere, about 20 miles from Cameroon's border with Nigeria. Boko Haram was once again suspected, although the terrorist group did not make any claim to responsibility. On 17 May, a Chinese worksite near the Waza national park was attacked; at least one Cameroonian soldier was killed and ten Chinese workers were kidnapped. Ten vehicles belonging to their company, China's state-run construction company Sinohydro, which was working on road maintenance, were also taken, although the worksite was protected by elements of the 'Bataillon d'Intervention Rapide' (BIR), an *elite unit of the army*. After these two events, President Biya decided to deploy more troops to the north. Official sources announced the addition of 2,000 soldiers, bringing the number of men present to about 3,000 in the three northern regions. The army divided the front line into two areas: the southern, held exclusively by the BIR, and the northern, held by the BIR in conjunction with several other army units. The Canadian nun and the two Italian priests were finally released in June, but the circumstances of their seizure and detention remained mysterious: no responsibility for their abduction was ever claimed.

In July, despite the military reinforcements, the *assaults* became more intensive and violent. A gendarmerie brigade was attacked in Bomberi, 5 km from the Nigerian border: a policeman was wounded and the attackers seized ammunition and a pickup truck. At the end of July, a dozen people, including the wife of Deputy Prime Minister Amadou Ali and a 'lamido' (a traditional chief), were abducted in two attacks on Kolofata, in the Far North Region, Amadou Ali's village. There were again numerous unresolved questions and disturbing details concerning this event: some reports said that some of the attackers were Cameroonians. A few days later, Biya dismissed several officers, including the commander of the Gendarmerie Legion for the north. No public reason was provided for these decisions, but informal sources spoke of the officers' potential complicity with the attackers.

A few weeks before, rumours had already started to circulate about the *identity of the funders, leaders and elements* of Boko Haram, after a statement made by Cavaye Yeguie Djibril, the speaker of the National Assembly. Cavaye Yeguie, third in command in state protocol (after the president of the Republic and the speaker of the Senate), stated in the opening speech of the plenary session of the National Assembly that Boko Haram members were in high places in Cameroonian society. "We know them very well. Many of them are amongst us; some in hiding and others in active service, and in their hypocrisy do pretend to be supporting the state authorities to fight the sect; with the ulterior motive of destabilizing the state and setting it on fire," he said. Cavaye Yeguie was not publicly questioned on his assertions, but as a traditional ruler in the Far North Region and a man very connected in the region and the country, it was clear to everybody that he knew exactly what he was alluding to, though his motives were unclear.

A few weeks later, Anicet Ekane, of the opposition party 'Mouvement Africain pour la Nouvelle Indépendance et la Démocratie' (Manidem), and the Social Democratic Front, the main opposition party, in turn made statements pointing to the existence of a Cameroonian *armed rebellion acting under the cover of Boko Haram*. Unofficial sources in Biya's security services also referred to a rebellion sponsored by political elites from the north and members of the regime, talking of a 'Cameroonian Boko Haram' linked with the Boko Haram terrorist group in Nigeria. According to these sources, the aim of this Cameroonian rebellion was to destabilise Biya or even to overthrow him. Some members of the ruling 'Rassemblement Démocratique du Peuple Camerounais' also issued a public letter denouncing a "rébellion du Grand Nord". Because all of them were from the Lekié department in Centre Province, their statement gave rise to many criticisms and attempts at political exploitation of ethnic divisions, a tactic frequently used by the Biya regime. In October, the ten Chinese workers who had been kidnapped in June and the 17 people abducted in Kolofata, including Amadou Ali's wife, the lamido of Kolofata and some gendarmes, were all released, once again in very mysterious circumstances. In December, the archbishop of Douala, Samuel Kleda, publicly claimed that those who were attacking northern Cameroon were killing Muslims and Christians indiscriminately, and seeking to seize power, and that the Boko Haram issue was above all a political matter. However, no official made any public statement confirming this accusation, which was not surprising since the regime had always depicted Biya as a man who managed to keep Cameroon in peace. To publicly admit that the president was facing an armed rebellion would have destroyed the myth of "Biya, man of peace".

In the second half of the year, the Biya regime also had to deal with serious security threats at the border with the CAR, over which several people were arrested in August. Among them were Aboubakar Sidiki, president of a very small and unknown opposition party, the 'Mouvement Patriotique du Salut Camerounais', and Abdoulaye Harissou, a notary based in Maroua, member of the opposition party 'Union Démocratique du Cameroun' and known to be close to the former general secretary of the Presidency and former minister of interior Marafa Hamidou Yaya, who had been in prison since 2012. According to the authorities, Harissou and Sidiki were in contact with armed groups originating from the CAR. Harissou was accused of trying to recruit rebel factions in Chad, the CAR and Sudan to destabilise Cameroon, of having written speeches *calling for a popular uprising*, and of having sent journalists a document threatening state security. He was charged with insulting the president, hostility to the homeland and revolution, complicity in murder and illegal possession and carrying of weapons of war. He was detained in the Secretariat of State for Defence, the headquarters of the Gendarmerie, where other "very important prisoners" such as Marafa Hamidou Yaya were detained. However, these arrests did not prevent armed attacks along Cameroon's eastern border with the CAR. In September, clashes between armed groups and the security forces erupted in the area of Ngaoui Adamawa, and a businessman was killed in Saboua. Cameroon closed the border between the two countries. At the same time, an armed group attacked and kidnapped eight people in Garoua-Boulaï. Other battles took place in October between the Cameroonian army and rebels from the CAR who were trying to enter Cameroon via Garoua-Boulaï. The identity of the attackers was not officially announced, but according to some media, they may have been members of the armed group 'Front Democratique du Peuple Centrafricain' (FDPC) of warlord Abdoulaye Miskine, who had been in jail in Cameroon since September 2013.

At the end of November, the minister of defence announced that Cameroon had lost about 40 soldiers and killed almost 1,000 Boko Haram fighters. These figures were not verified by independent sources. There were generally serious *difficulties in obtaining reliable information* on what was going on at the battlefront. Unofficial reports also revealed numerous abuses, such as summary executions, committed by the army. Others indicated that the soldiers on the field were lacking resources. There were allegations of embezzlement of war funds and resources by the top brass in the Ministry of Defence. As in the Bakassi conflict, many years before, it clearly appeared that the war was a business opportunity for several actors.

At the beginning of December, the security situation finally drove Biya to take legal measures. Legislators voted on the draft of an *anti-terrorism law* prescribing the death penalty for all those guilty of carrying out, abetting or sponsoring acts of terrorism and allowing the punishment of people and companies found guilty of promoting terrorism, as well as various fines and prison terms for those who gave false testimony to the administrative and judicial authorities in matters related to terrorism. This law provoked anger within civil society and the opposition, who both accused the government of seeking to use the law to criminalise any opposition to Biya. Minister of Justice Laurent Esso replied that Cameroon would never be complicit with those whose only agenda was to destabilise the normal functioning of the state. Cameroon had not carried out any executions since 1997.

In February, Biya celebrated the *50th anniversary of the reunification* of Cameroon in Buea (South-West Region), three years later than planned. Although a cabinet reshuffle had been announced on several occasions throughout the year, it never took place. A few events that made the headlines showed the *lack of coordination* that existed at the highest levels of the state. For example, Minister of Secondary

Education Louis Bapes Bapes was arrested in April and taken into custody without being dismissed from his post. He was released 24 hours later without explanation.

Foreign Affairs

The relationship between President Biya and *France*, already quite bad in 2013, continued to deteriorate. Biya finally gave in to the French government's pressure for the release of the French-Cameroonian businessman Thierry Michel Atangana. In February, on the occasion of the 50th anniversary of the reunification of Cameroon, Biya signed a decree granting remission to some individuals convicted for crimes including embezzlement of public funds. One of the articles of this decree seemed to have been tailored specifically for Atangana and his former mentor, Titus Edzoa, once general secretary of the Presidency and a former close collaborator of Biya. Both had been sentenced to 15 years in prison in 1997 and to a further 20 years in 2012 for corruption. Atangana and Edzoa were released and Atangana immediately left for France. Biya made no comment about French pressure.

In May, Biya attended a summit organised by France (in Paris) dedicated to the *fight against Boko Haram*, which brought together the presidents of Nigeria, Chad, Niger and Benin, as well as representatives of the USA, the UK and the EU. On this occasion, Biya publicly declared war on Boko Haram. Behind the scenes, bilateral relations were deteriorating: at the highest level of state, Cameroonian officials were sure that France was plotting against Biya and wanted to get rid of him and might even be supporting Boko Haram for that purpose. The messages delivered by media close to the Presidency provided an idea of this inside thinking: there were indeed regular accusations that France was a supporter of Boko Haram. In response, the French embassy in Yaoundé issued denials on several occasions. Cameroonian commentators noted that French President François Hollande visited Chad in July but did not go to Cameroon. At the end of the year, the tension was at its height, and many Cameroonians were now convinced that France was acting under the cover of Boko Haram. In late November, Biya went to the OIF summit in Dakar (Senegal). Although he had a meeting with Hollande there, reports noted that the Cameroonian regime disliked the French president's speech welcoming the "beautiful demonstration" of people in Burkina Faso that had ousted Blaise Compaoré from power. Some media close to the Presidency quickly established a link with the growing fears in Yaoundé and expressed regret that the French president praised popular uprisings.

One of the factors that further aggravated relations with France was certainly to be found in Biya's aim to diversify Cameroon's commercial partners and to forge closer relationships with *China* in particular. Since Biya's state visit to China in 2011, Exim Bank, the Chinese public financial institution that acts as the secular arm of Chinese investment abroad, had become Cameroon's largest donor, funding most of the country's major infrastructure projects: the Memve'ele dam, the deep water port of Kribi, the Yaoundé-Douala highway, the optic fibre network, etc. In 2012, China had become Cameroon's top donor and subsequently also its leading customer, being the destination for 15% of Cameroonian exports. Chinese Minister of Foreign Affairs Wang Yi made an official visit to Cameroon in January. More importantly, in October, the Cameroonian government signed an agreement with China for an equipment grant in the amount of CFAfr 2.5 bn for the Cameroonian navy.

Since *Chad* had become France's most important African ally, President Idriss Déby Itno was viewed with suspicion by the Cameroonian authorities. In May, after the Paris summit on the fight against Boko Haram, Déby visited Cameroon, ostensibly for a "working and friendship visit" with Biya. On 27 November, the *CAR* warlord Abdoulaye Miskine, leader of the FDPC, a minor element in the Séléka rebel alliance, was released after being under house arrest in Cameroon for more than a year. This came in response to the release of the Polish priest Mateusz Dziedzic, who had been abducted mid-October in western CAR by FDPC fighters. Twenty-six other hostages, including 15 Cameroonians who had been detained since September, were released simultaneously. Media reports said that the President Denis Sassou Nguesso of Congo had played a mediating role in this exchange.

Socioeconomic Developments

The *economic cost of the war* was obviously heavy, even though there was no concrete assessment of how much was spent. According to unofficial sources, the war effort cost the government about € 1 bn in 2014. The trade, agriculture, transport, tourism and livestock sectors were the most affected by the armed attacks. Customs revenues dropped sharply, as the border custom posts in the Far North Region were closed down; they had preciously provided a monthly income of CFAfr 700 bn. At the end of the year, there were about 137,000 refugees from the CAR and 41,000 from Nigeria in Cameroon.

According to Prime Minister Philemon Yang, the *GDP growth rate* rose to 5.8%, a slight increase from 2013. It was also slightly higher than the CEMAC average of 5.7%. However, this result was actually lower than the 6% target initially set. According to Yang, this development was due to the sluggish global economic conditions and the security concerns in the north and east of the country.

Budgetary expenditure and revenues had both been fixed at CFAfr 3,312 bn, an increase of CFAfr 76 bn compared with the 2013 fiscal year. This small increase was intended to be used to support additional expenses, such as the salaries of a contingent of 25,000 new public sector recruits, the remuneration of traditional leaders and the costs of the recently created Senate. Expended revenues were CFAfr 1,985 bn from non-oil resources and CFAfr 718 bn from oil, an increase of CFAfr 13 bn overall. The government planned to issue bonds worth CFAfr 280 bn and also expected CFAfr 658 bn in loans and donations. The government earmarked CFAfr 2,01 bn (62.1% of the budget) for direct operating costs, CFAfr 1,000 bn for investment and CFAfr 302 bn for debt repayment (compared with CFAfr 314 bn in 2013).

For the third year running, the country's *oil production* increased, reaching 27.5 m b/d, compared with 24.2 b/d in 2013. This increase was due to the intensification of exploitation of a major offshore field and to the commissioning of three new fields. *Gas exploitation* was up by 124% according to the 'Société Nationale des Hydrocarbures'. The improvement was due to the Sanaga South field, whose production was constantly growing, and to the Logbaba field, which was exploited by Rodeo Development, a subsidiary of the British Victoria Oil & Gas. The gas potential was also revalued upward from 144 bn m^3 to 154 bn m^3. This increase of 10 bn m^3 followed new exploration work in some petro-gas fields by operators under contract to the state.

Pushed by the IMF and the World Bank, Biya had to take unpopular measures: he decided to revise upwards the *prices of fuel and cooking gas* early in July, making a litre of super cost CFAfr 731, 14.2% up from the previous CFAfr 650; these prices had been frozen by the government since 2008. The cumulative loss to the state amounted to CFAfr 1 357 bn (€ 2 bn) over the years, according to the government.

To mitigate the effects of this measure, Biya increased the *salaries of civil servants* by 5%. This decision, following the increase in fuel prices at the pump, was expected to cost about CFAfr 30 bn (€ 45 m) annually and affected more than 200,000 people. The government also reviewed the fuel price structure, reducing *inter alia* the special tax on petroleum products ('taxe spéciale sur les produits pétroliers'; TSPP) and some taxes paid by trucks. The fall in TSPP would impact on the public finances to the tune of about CFAfr 15 bn. In late July, the *guaranteed minimum wage* ('Salaire Minimum Interprofessionnel Garanti'; SMIG) was also increased by about 30%, from CFAfr 28,216 to CFAfr 36,270 (€ 55) per month. The last SMIG increase occurred in June 2008 (when it had been CFAfr 23,000 [€ 35]), after the riots of February 2008.

In early December, Biya launched a CFAfr 925 bn three-year '*emergency plan*' (2015–17), financed by Deutsche Bank, 'Banque Gabonaise et Française Internationale', Ecobank, Atlantic Bank and Standard Chartered Bank. Through this 'emergency plan', the government planned to invest in various projects in agriculture and livestock (seed distribution, slaughterhouses and cold storage), health (general hospitals and rehabilitation of technical facilities), social housing (1,000 units to be built in the country's ten regions), infrastructure (roads, construction of police stations and border posts, water supply in cities and in rural areas, public lighting in Yaoundé and Douala …).

In July, the National Assembly and the Senate succumbed to European pressure and approved the *ratification of the interim EPA* with the EU. This agreement, signed by the government in 2009, provides for a tariff dismantling over 15 years between Cameroon and the EU, as well as the liberalisation of 80% of imports from Europe.

Some Cameroonian employers denounced this agreement, saying it was one-sided and emphasised that the government had estimated the losses for Cameroon to be about CFAfr 1,500 bn (€ 2.3 bn) in 2020 and CFAfr 2.5 bn (€ 3.8 bn) in 2030.

Some changes occurred in (former) *parastatal* companies. In September, the national electricity company SONEL changed its name to Energy of Cameroon (ENEO). Owned since 2013 by the British Actis, ENEO had a portfolio of more than 900,000 customers and an installed capacity of 935 MW and was employing 3,600 people. The company was planning to invest CFAfr 170 bn (€ 260 bn) over the next five years. In September, the government issued a 3G license to the national telephone company Cameroon Telecommunications (Camtel) and to MTN (South Africa), Orange (France) and Nextell (Vietnam). This decision put an end to Nextell's monopoly on 3G. Nextell, which launched its operations only in September 2014, asked in vain for the extension of its previously agreed privilege beyond the expiry date of 31 December. With about 1 m subscribers, Camtel had only a 5.7% market share in the Cameroonian telecoms market (land line and mobile), behind MTN (57%) and Orange (37%).

An important change on the *mining* front was the announcement in October by the Anglo-Australian mining group Rio Tinto that it would relinquish ownership of its share in Alucam at the end of 2014. Created by the French group Pechiney, Alucam had produced aluminium since 1957. Rio Tinto had held 46.7% of its capital since 2006 (in equal shares with the State of Cameroon, the remainder being held by employees and the 'Agence Française de Développement'). Rio Tinto explained that Alucam's business plan was no longer in line with its strategic priorities, but that it would assist the government in finding a buyer and would maintain technical and administrative assistance contracts. This decision came as Alucam had started several development projects, including the extension of its aluminium factory in Edea to increase capacity to 300,000 tonnes per year. This extension was linked to the development of the Lom Pangar dam and the Nachtigal dam. It was also planning to set up another aluminium factory near Kribi to produce 800,000 tonnes from 2021. This project was conditioned by the construction of the Song Mbengue dam (930 MW). With 570 employees, Alucam had an annual production capacity of 100,000 tonnes. All ambitious expansion plans were seriously endangered by the Rito Tinto move.

The *anti-corruption campaign* 'Opération Epervier' (Operation Sparrowhawk) produced few headlines. There was only one major arrest: Gervais Mendo Ze, former director of Cameroon Radio Television for 17 years and former minister for communication, was arrested in November. Sacked from the government in 2005, he had been repeatedly under the spotlight for all kinds of alleged wrongdoing during his time in office. One detainee convicted of corruption, the former Cameroonian ambassador to the USA, Jerome Mendounga, died in custody in November. He had been imprisoned in 2009 and convicted of embezzlement in 2012 in the case of a purchase of a presidential plane called 'Albatros'.

Central African Republic (CAR)

Andreas Mehler

The CAR witnessed another difficult year, starting with more armed violence throughout the country, including in the capital, Bangui. But a change in the interim leadership, massive deployment of peacekeepers and some initial negotiations between belligerents provided hope. Without the strong engagement of the international community it would have been impossible to lower tensions and mitigate the humanitarian crisis. A ceasefire agreement was signed, albeit not a full peace agreement, which seemed difficult to reach in light of the lack of cohesion of the various armed movements. The mostly Muslim Séléka alliance split into three major factions, and the Christian anti-Balaka movement was even more decentralised – local militias used the label, but would not obey orders from self-proclaimed leaders. International efforts to involve former presidents Bozizé and Djotodia in peace talks surprised the interim government in Bangui and appeared inconsistent with the sanctions regime.

 | DOI 10.1163/9789004305052_023

Domestic Politics

The year began with a major change in *government*. In reaction to substantial international pressure, interim President Michel Djotodia, the former Séléka leader, and Prime Minister Nicolas Tiangaye resigned on 10 January. On 12 January, initial celebrations by the Christian majority in Bangui turned into mob violence targeted at mosques and shops owned by Muslims. After deliberations within the transitional parliament, the 'Conseil National de Transition' (CNT), Catherine Samba Panza, a civil society representative (and a Christian), took over as the CAR's first female (interim) president on 20 January and appointed as prime minister André Nzapayeké, who had made a career in international finance. At the time of his appointment, he was the vice president of the 'Banque de Développement des Etats d'Afrique Centrale' (BDEAC). Within his government, announced on 27 January, technocrats took most positions. Seven female ministers were among the 21 members of the cabinet. Two Séléka officials held ministerial positions and Herbert Gontran Djono Ahaba, close to Djotodia, remained minister of public works. The anti-Balaka commander Léopold Narcisse Bara became minister of youth and sports.

The *security situation* at the beginning of the year was catastrophic. In Bangui, roughly 100,000 IDPs were stranded at the airport M'poko. In Bozoum (capital of the Ouham-Pende prefecture; North-West), bloody clashes between anti-Balaka and ex-Séléka groups continued in January with heavy casualties. In Boali, 95 km north of Bangui, anti-Balaka groups targeted Muslims who were regrouping to flee to neighbouring Chad. French soldiers and a local priest intervened to stop the killings in January. Similar confrontations were recorded in Bouar, and in the villages of Bossemptele and Guen (West). In Boda (South West) and Yaloké (West) thousands of threatened Muslims had to be protected by peacekeepers. Several hundred Muslims were killed during mob violence and by organised attacks in the first three months of the year. The Séléka forces reacted and tried to regroup outside Bangui (while 2,114 were guarded by peacekeepers in preparation for their demobilisation – officially 'relocation' – in three camps in the capital). On 2 February, peacekeepers regained control over the strategically located Sibut (Kémo prefecture), where hundreds of fighters had gathered; the Séléka fighters now moved further east to Bambari. In a retaliation attack after the killing of an allied Fulani chief, Séléka fighters destroyed the village of Goussima (Centre) in May, killing 66 people and burning houses and coffee plantations. In addition, 18 people (three aid workers and 15 community leaders) died in a Séléka attack on a hospital run by 'Médecins Sans Frontières' in Boguila (North) on 26 April. Earlier, clashes had erupted in the same village when a convoy carrying peacekeepers was attacked – resulting in a temporary exodus from Boguila. Atrocities of a smaller magnitude occurred in several other places. One particularly noteworthy event was a grenade attack on 28 May on the church of Notre Dame de Fatima in Bangui, where thousands of refugees had gathered; between 15 and 20 people were killed, including the priest. The backlash against the Séléka conquest of Bangui in March 2013 was ferocious. It had been interpreted as a take-over of state affairs by the *Muslim minority* (or in some cases, strangers from neighbouring countries). Now every Muslim – whether related to the rebels or not – was seen as a target throughout the country, including in Bangui. In the spring, several convoys of trucks, protected at first by Chadian peacekeepers, carried the majority of the Muslim residents out of the city towards the Chadian border. Some smaller cities such as Bossangoa were abandoned by the Muslim community after fierce attacks by anti-Balaka forces. Pastoralists, mostly Mbororo Fulani, were associated with and had voluntarily sided with the Séléka rebels. The pattern of confrontations in the countryside was (mostly Christian) settlers, organised into militias, against cattle-herders (largely Muslim), supported by Séléka forces. Former bandits were found on both sides and specialised in cattle theft and highway robbery. Many cattle-herders had armed long before these escalations. Direct confrontations between anti-Balaka and Séléka forces were rare and concentrated in Batangafo (July/August) and Bambari. The centrally-located *Bambari* (Ouaka prefecture) first became a powderkeg when 'foreign' anti-Balaka forces (coming from Bangui) entered the city in June. Tensions grew when an internal rift between Séléka wings became very obvious. A major Séléka assembly on 9–10 May in Ndélé was attended by 1,200 participants and saw the movement's military wing renamed as the 'Forces Républicaines'. It was led by Joseph Zoundeiko, who wanted to impose his rule in Bambari, with the help of ethnic Gula fighters, while the local zone commander, Ali Darass, a former lieutenant of the famous Chadian warlord Baba Laddé, tried to hold onto his position with the help of Fulani fighters. The Séléka infighting resulted in dozens of deaths in August, with international peacekeepers unable to stop the violence. The disarmament measures used earlier had been only partially effective and the situation deteriorated: Noureddine Adam, believed to be the most powerful Séléka leader, unilaterally suspended the internal coordination mechanism and organised an assembly of Séléka leaders in Birao (6–10 July). A subsequent communiqué announced that the movement had become the 'Front Populaire pour la Renaissance de la Centrafrique', with a politbureau to be led by Djotodia. Zacharia Damane, leader of the least visible Séléka faction, the 'Rassemblement Patriotique pour le Renouveau de la Centrafrique', continued to control Bria, an important diamond-producing zone.

It became obvious that the new government was not able to stop the violence, while the international peacekeeping forces were still being built up and were not yet operating at full capacity. The need for a peace agreement was therefore strongly motivated by external actors. However, with the anti-Balaka movement being a strongly decentralised group and the *Séléka split* into three major factions (and many smaller sub-units), bringing all relevant actors to the negotiating table became a huge challenge. At the end of a tumultuous peace forum in Brazzaville (Congo), a *ceasefire agreement* was signed on 23 July. The Séléka faction led by Moussa Dhaffane took part in the meeting, but the potentially strongest faction, led by Noureddine Adam, who was under international sanctions and in hiding in Birao to avoid arrest, did not attend. Noureddine (first vice president) later unilaterally deposed Dhaffane (second vice president) and also fell out with Zoundeiko. Further meetings of various factions confirmed the deep split, and Darass created his own 'Unité pour la Centrafrique' on 25 October. Patrice Edouard Ngaissona, a minister under former president Bozizé and increasingly seen as the most powerful spokesperson for the *anti-Balaka* movement, signed the ceasefire agreement on their behalf. It is important to note that Ngaissona was believed to be directly implicated in attacks against MISCA ('Mission Internationale de Soutien à la Centrafrique sous Conduite Africaine') peacekeepers in March. He faced strong competition from other ambitious individuals within this extremely heterogeneous movement. Leaders of two smaller rebel movements also signed the text.

Following the Brazzaville ceasefire agreement, the Nzapayeké government resigned on 5 August and, on 10 August, Samba-Panza chose a *new prime minister*: Mahamat Kamoun, a Muslim and former close associate of Djotodia. Many Séléka leaders rejected Kamoun as they had not been consulted before his appointment. It was obvious that the Séléka leaders expected some sort of compensation for their loss of power only a few months after their conquest of Bangui. On 22 August, Kamoun formed a government that gave the armed movements more symbolic representation. In fact, three Séléka members became ministers (for transport, telecommunications and cattle-breeding). The anti-Balaka movement was given two positions (environment and tourism). Armel Ningatoloum Sayo, the leader of the small rebel movement, 'Révolution et Justice', operating mostly around Paoua, became minister of sports and youth. Armed movements were therefore well represented in the interim government. Twelve members of the former government remained in the new team, but five of them changed posts (including the former interior minister, Aristide Sokambi, now minister of defence); the government grew to 31 members.

A new round of *confrontations in Bangui* erupted in October, when anti-Balaka groups erected barricades in response to murders allegedly committed by Séléka elements. This led to violence that cost dozens of lives and 6,500 civilians were forced to abandon their homes. In Zémio, intercommunity violence in November resulted in the exodus of 80% of the population, and 20,000 inhabitants of Kouango crossed the Oubangui River when new confrontations between anti-Balaka forces and Fulani cattle herders erupted in December.

As progress on the preparations for a constitutional referendum and elections was slow, the *transition calendar* had to be revised several times. Elections were now scheduled for the summer of 2015 (instead of February). The transition had originally been set to last not more than 18 months with an option to extend the process by a further six months, but it was only on 24 June that the president signed a decree on the organisation and functioning of the National Electoral Authority. The transitional government and the CNT struggled to deliver tangible public benefits and clearly lacked legitimacy. Some parties were already prepared for elections; they included the 'Mouvement de Libération du Peuple Centrafricain', which selected former prime minister Martin Ziguélé as its candidate on 22 November. On 22 December, the CEEAC mediator, Congolese President Sassou Nguesso, after receiving the green light from the UNSC, agreed to extend the transition period and four days later Prime Minister Kamoun announced a new transition calendar with a constitutional referendum planned for May and legislative and presidential elections scheduled for July and August 2015. The CNT adopted an amended electoral law on 27 December, but it had not been promulgated by the end of the year. A local consultation process on the constitution and the envisaged peace order started in December (ahead of a national forum) with government ministers deployed to the provinces.

A number of additional conflict risks were far from eliminated. The Lord's Resistance Army (*LRA*) in the south-east of the country had not yet surrendered. On 29 June, an attack on the Ugandan army stationed in Bakouma that was attributed to the LRA allied to some Séléka splinter groups resulted in three dead. Cross-border raids by smaller rebel movements active in Chad and the CAR, or Cameroon and Chad, were still able to trigger violence as was the involvement of the official security forces of both countries.

The planned *redeployment of the state administration* throughout the country proved very difficult. Some of the prefects installed in the provincial headquarters with the help of international peacekeepers immediately boarded a plane back to Bangui after the official ceremonies. Séléka forces even prevented the installation of a new prefect in Ndélé. The limitations of the state administration became clear when a joint CAR and Sudanese army contingent had to leave Birao in response to an ultimatum set by Noureddine on 26 June. In both Birao and Ndélé, the establishment of prefects ultimately failed (formally 50 out of 71 sub-prefects were reinstalled). At one point, a document leaked to the press indicated that some Séléka leaders were considering splitting of the country in two.

Foreign Affairs

Pressure on the *UNSC* to act on the CAR crisis grew constantly. The AU-led *MISCA* peacekeeping mission, mandated and established in December 2013, was perceived as not well-enough equipped and staffed (starting with 4,500 soldiers and intended to grow to 6,000). Burundi and Chad (850 soldiers each) provided the largest contingents. The mission was mainly funded by the EU with € 125 m from its African Peace Facility, covering allowances, accommodation and food. It was clear to most New

York-based diplomats that MISCA should only be a temporary arrangement until a UN mission became operational. In early March, UN Secretary-General Ban Ki-moon recommended a 12,000-strong UN peacekeeping operation and MISCA peacekeepers in Bangui came under fire from anti-Balaka groups several times during the same month. With Resolution 2149, passed on 10 April, the UNSC finally approved the 'Mission Multidimensionnelle Intégrée des Nations Unies pour la Stabilisation en République Centrafricaine' (MINUSCA), to be formed of 10,000 military and 1,820 police personnel. MINUSCA finally took over from MISCA on 15 September and had at that time 7,500 operatives. In the meantime, an EU-sponsored mission was also in the making. On 20 January, EU foreign ministers agreed to launch the ninth EU military operation, and quickly received a UNSC mandate (on 28 January). In mid-April, the EU Force (EUFOR) mission became operational, reaching full operational capability on 15 June with 700 troops. France contributed by far the largest contingent (and the force commander). Other EU members (Spain, Finland, Georgia, Germany, Italy, Latvia, Luxembourg, Netherlands, Poland and Romania) contributed smaller contingents. The EUFOR mission was mostly assigned to provide security at Bangui airport and in two districts of Bangui, thus making it possible for MISCA (later MINUSCA) and the French Operation Sangaris to reach out to the hinterland. On 20 October, the UNSC extended the EUFOR mandate for a further six months until 15 March 2015. The European Commission and individual EU member states scaled up their humanitarian aid from € 20 m (in 2012) to € 128 m.

France was now more involved militarily than it had been since downsizing its presence in the late 1990s. Its Operation Sangaris was crucial for security in Bangui, and France also contributed troops to MINUSCA and EUFOR. On 4 January, the French government reported that the situation had calmed. Gradually, containment activities spread from the capital to the hinterland, starting with the control of the Bangui-Bossangoa axis and the road link to Cameroon. On 25 February, after a visit by French Defence Minister Jean-Yves Le Drian, the French National Assembly approved the expansion of Operation Sangaris by 400 to 2,000 men (including 50 policemen). France's involvement proved effective in the western part of the country. Sangaris commander Francisco Soriano also engaged in diplomacy by meeting religious and civilian authorities; he was dismissed in June, when French media reported that the operation was collaborating closely with some anti-Balaka units. By the end of the year, Sangaris had lost two soldiers, and 120 had been injured since the start of the operation a year before. In December, the French government announced its intention to reduce Sangaris to 1,500 soldiers, as the security situation had improved (despite a surge in criminal activities); this clearly did not reflect the on-going insecurity in the centre of the country and the very limited control exercised by peacekeepers over the east.

The immediate precursor of Djotodia's resignation was a special *CEEAC* summit convened by President Idriss Déby of Chad on 9–10 January. The entire CNT was invited to the Chadian capital, N'Djamena. Djotodia decided to step down at the end of the summit. *Chad*'s involvement in both the civil war (first on Bozizé's side, and then in support of Séléka) and peacekeeping efforts remained highly controversial. A Chadian MISCA company was attacked upon arrival in Bangui on 28 March and the Chadians allegedly indiscriminately shot at civilians in retaliation, creating even more unrest. In response, on 3 April, Chadian President Déby decided to withdraw the Chadian contingent from MISCA without prior consultation. While mostly welcomed on the ground, this created logistical problems and further unease. The Chadian contingent was one of the strongest numerically and was responsible for security in Bossangoa. With the departure of the Chadians, 540 Muslims under their protection had to leave with them for Chad. Armed incursions from Chad into northern CAR, most probably with consent, if not orders, from N'Djamena, continued and the border was officially closed on 4 May. In one instance, the sub-prefect of Markounda was arrested and taken to the Chadian capital for interrogation.

Cameroon felt the effects of the on-going crisis as armed groups from the CAR entered Cameroonian territory in September and October, leading to a temporary closure of the border. The 'Front Democratique du Peuple Centrafricain' was probably the initiator of some of these actions, as their leader, Abdoulaye Miskine, had been held in Cameroon since 2013. After mediation by Sassou Nguesso, Miskine was released on 27 November in exchange for 26 abducted hostages, including a Polish priest. The *Ugandan army* clashed with Séléka troops at the end of June, killing 15 fighters; a spokesman for the Ugandan Army stated that Séléka had forced civilians to give food and medicine to the LRA and that they were also jointly engaged in trade in ivory and minerals. This escalation meant that it would be difficult for Ugandan soldiers to join UN peacekeeping forces, as Kampala had wished.

A *UN panel of experts* continued to work on the CAR situation. In their final report, they attributed killings of civilians, including humanitarian aid workers, in the period 5 December 2013–14 August 2014 to Séléka (617) and anti-Balaka (861), with total casualties estimated at 3,000. The experts also looked into the illicit trade in and exploitation of natural resources (gold, diamonds and timber) and reported on the use of forced labour in gold mines involving Séléka commanders in their strongholds; in addition, individual Séléka commanders were engaged in diamond smuggling. Anti-Balaka members were doing the same in the western part of the country. A debate (mostly carried on outside the country) as to whether the targeting of the Muslim minority would meet the *criteria for genocide* played a part in attracting attention to a forgotten crisis. However, some direct implications of this quarrel were also felt on the ground. In December 2013, the UNSC had established an *investigation commission* into human rights violations, led by the highly respected Cameroonian lawyer Bernard Muna, formerly the deputy prosecutor at the International Criminal Tribunal for Rwanda. The commission was only able to start investigations in April because of the highly hostile environment. Its first provisional report was issued in July and stated: "The fact that there is an anti-Muslim propaganda from certain non-Muslim quarters does not mean that genocide is being planned or that there is any conspiracy to commit genocide or even a specific intent to commit genocide," This was not well received by international human rights NGOs. The final report followed the same line and was issued on 19 December. It argued that government forces under Bozizé, as well as the Séléka and the anti-Balaka groups, had been involved in serious violations of international humanitarian law and gross abuses of human rights. The commission could not establish genocidal intent by any party to the conflict but stated that this did not diminish the seriousness of crimes committed or give any reason to assume that in the risk of future genocide had subsided. A pattern of ethnic cleansing had been executed by the anti-Balaka in the areas in which Muslims had been living, amounting to a crime against humanity. Not unrelated to such investigations were strong actions: on 9 May the UNSC Committee decided to impose targeted *sanctions* on François Bozizé, the anti-Balaka leader (and close aid of Bozizé), Lévy Yakité, who had been involved in numerous atrocities, and Noureddine Adam. US President Barack Obama extended the sanctions to Michel Djotodia and warlord Abdoulaye Miskine. Yakité later died in a road accident in France. The French government froze the French assets of Jean-Francis Bozizé, son of the former president, when suspicions arose that he was planning a coup d'état in November. In a resolution on 18 December, the UNSC threatened to extend sanctions to other individuals. On 24 September, the *ICC* formally opened an investigation into crimes committed since 2012. While many observers welcomed this initiative, its short-term effect was questionable, given that the ICC had not ended proceedings in the case of Jean-Pierre Bemba, who was awaiting judgement for crimes committed in the CAR back in 2001. In December, much to the surprise of the government, mediator Sassou Nguesso together with the Kenyan government initiated *parallel peace talks* in Nairobi (Kenya) involving Djotodia and Bozizé.

Socioeconomic Developments

The misery of the population continued as a result of the dire security situation. Towards the end of the year, UNHCR reported that there were about 410,000 IDPs and 420,000 refugees – nearly a fifth of the population and four times as many as after the last round of hostilities (2008). According to the UN Office for the Coordination of Humanitarian Affairs (OCHA), 2.7 m Central Africans (out of a total population of 4.6 m) were *in need of assistance* at the end of the year. Apart from security, the establishment of a minimum level of material well-being was also a target of the international community. As of 31 December, donors had committed $ 376.4 m (68%) of the $ 555 m requested within the CAR Strategic Response Plan. OCHA noted that early recovery, education and emergency shelter would be the least funded sectors. The peacekeeping missions concentrated part of their efforts on keeping the Bangui-Douala corridor open to allow *humanitarian aid* to come through. State revenues were very limited and mostly used to pay the security forces, while the World Bank ensured the payment of civil service salaries. The IMF approved financial assistance worth close to $ 13 m under a Rapid Credit Facility to support emergency recovery programmes. The IMF took a critical look at the *economic prospects* and projected that the scarcity of basic consumer goods would translate into a steady rise in prices, leading to an inflation rate of 11.6% at the end of the year (according to UN figures even 15.3%) – well above the convergence criterion adopted by CEMAC. Most of the population lacked access to food. The local *cattle market* was completely distorted, with anti-Balaka groups stealing cattle from Fulani nomads, and selling meat in the larger cities at lower prices. Some Fulani had to leave their cattle behind when they fled the country. Prospects for stabilising that market were grim. Agricultural projects funded by international partners benefitted only 110,000 households.

The state finances were in a difficult situation. Internal revenue receipts totalled $ 92 m (against a projected $ 103 m). The entrenched *war economy* structures were partly responsible: the CAR had been temporarily suspended from the Kimberley Process Certification Scheme in May 2013, resulting in a ban on official diamond exports. This had immediate effects. While the accredited merchants in Bangui continued to purchase diamonds, *diamond smuggling* – probably via neighbouring states (Cameroon and Sudan) – rose to an estimated additional 140,000 carats (worth $ 24 m). Some were seized in Belgium. The UN panel of experts suggested their origins lay in Sam-Ouandja and Bria, a zone under Séléka control. Diamond zones in the west, such as Boda, were in the hands of anti-Balaka groups. Séléka commander Ali Darass was reportedly able to build up a parallel taxation system in his stronghold of Bambari and its surroundings. The UN panel of experts estimated that he would be able to raise $ 150,000 per year in taxes from local gold production, and a similar amount from the coffee trade (from Bambari to Sudan).

Chad

Ketil Fred Hansen

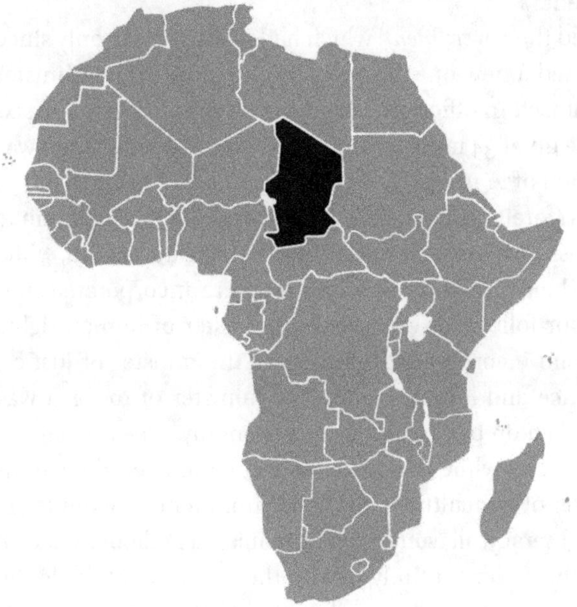

While Chad offered little attraction to external investors, the country strengthened its image as an effective military partner for US anti-terror units and a key ally in France's military engagements in the Sahel region and Central Africa. Actively participating in two UN peacekeeping missions, taking an active stance against Boko Haram and acting as a base for the new French military operation, Barkhane, Chad's army had seriously developed its capacity to protect security since the attempted coup in 2008 and had what was counted as one of the best-trained and equipped armies in Africa.

Economic growth was high, despite falling oil prices on the world market, but the developmental results of this growth were not tangible for the Chadian population, and the human rights situation equally saw only minor improvements.

Chad hosted an increasing number of refugees from neighbouring Sudan, CAR and Nigeria.

 | DOI 10.1163/9789004305052_024

Domestic Politics

President Idriss Déby Itno, often only called IDI by the populace, ruled the country firmly throughout the year. With the 1,661 presidential decrees issued during 2014, Déby severely curtailed the constitutional powers of both the elected members of parliament and the government.

On 20 April, Déby dismissed the *government*, which had been in place only since 17 October 2013, and established a new one, formally proposed by Prime Minister Kalzeubet Pahimi Deubet (himself in office only since 21 November 2013). The six-month-old government, made up of 34 ministers and seven secretaries of state was replaced by a new, smaller team of 21 ministers and six secretaries of state. Four of the most important ministers (foreign affairs, finance, national defence and public security) remained in their positions. Only six new ministers were appointed, while 19 were dismissed. Most of their former responsibilities were incorporated into already existing ministerial portfolios. For example the minister of human rights was dismissed and his portfolio incorporated into that of the minster of justice, who became minister of justice and human rights. The minister of tourism was dismissed and his portfolio taken on by the minister of economy, now minister of economy and tourist development, while the portfolio of the minister of environment went to the new minister of agriculture and the environment. The ministers of micro-finance, women and literacy, all women, were dismissed and not replaced. Of the six states secretaries, three were entirely new to the government while the former minister of aviation and meteorology was demoted to the position of secretary of state with the same portfolio. On 11 September, the minister of justice and human rights was replaced and one new post (re)created: Mme Issa Sokoyote Ester Woïbogo was appointed minister of women and social action. Chad's government then consisted of three women ministers and 19 men, while five of the six secretaries of state were women. All governors and prefects were men.

Another major replacement, this time among the top *administrators*, took place on 24 November, when Déby replaced five (out of 22) regional governors and five (out of 22) regional general secretaries. On the same day, he also replaced a large number of prefects and sub-prefects in the various counties (Départements) throughout the country. In Moyen Chari, in particular, all three prefects of the region's three counties were replaced, as well as nine of the 19 sub-prefects. One of the most high-profile prefects in that region, Abdel Kader *Baba Ladde* in Grande Sido county, was among them. This former rebel, who had opposed the Déby regime from 1998 to September 2012, was appointed prefect on 19 July only to be removed in the big reshuffle on 24 November. From his base in the town of Mora, only a few kilometres from the CAR frontier, he had already gained popularity for organising football matches and mediating between farmers and stockbreeders, raising suspicion in N'Djamena. The replacement created tensions in the town and the Chad gendarmerie arrived in Mora on 1 December with orders to remove Baba Ladde by force. He managed to escape but was arrested on 8 December by the peacekeeping forces in the CAR, where he was held in custody until the end of the year.

Although the removal of Baba Ladde created a stir and received a lot of media attention, all 22 of the Chad regions experienced significant changes in their administration at that time. Given the personalisation of politics and the personal power of state representatives in Chad, this shake-up changed the dynamics of power relations in them all. It was not possible, however, to find the political or ideological reasons that lay behind most of these replacements. Taken together, the high number of presidential decrees, the constant ministerial changes and the dismissal and replacement of numerous high-level territorial administrators indicated Déby's increased control over the state machinery to the point that it appeared almost *totalitarian*. He also continued to appoint trusted *family members* to powerful positions. For example, on 20 November, his youngest son, Mahamat Idriss Déby Itno (at 29 already a military general), was appointed general director of Chad's internal security force, the Directorate of Security Services and State Institutions. Another son, Zakaria Idriss Déby, retained the position of cabinet director at the presidential palace, while a younger brother, Saleh Déby Itno, remained general director of customs. The president's brother, Daoussa Déby Itno, had entered the government as minister of post, communication and information technology in 2013. The list of Déby's close relatives, including his in-laws, who held important public posts was even longer and his policy of employing family members continued, to the frustration of large parts of the population.

Insecurity remained a priority issue for Chadian citizens. Politically motivated threats and violence occurred, but purely criminal violence was also widespread. The police had a reputation for heavy-handed repression and were also accused of involvement in crime. On 1 April, the special intervention force within the police ('Groupement Mobile d'Intervention de la Police'), swooped on N'Djamena and indiscriminately imprisoned 200 persons for 72 hours for interrogation. A further source of concern were mines remaining from the war against Libya in the 1980s, which represent a genuine danger in border areas. On 13 February, for example, five people were killed and nine wounded when their trucks ran over mines near the border town of Wour.

After years of discussion, resistance and delaying tactics and reluctance to open a case against former Chadian president *Hisséne Habré*, the Senegalese parliament had in 2013 created an Extraordinary African Chamber tasked with prosecuting "the person or persons most responsible" for international crimes committed in Chad during Habré's presidency (1982–90). Habré, who had lived in luxury near the Senegalese capital since 1990, had been in pre-trial prison detention since July 2013. Pressured from various sides, the Chamber discussed whether Habré should stand a trial all through 2014. The AU, the EU, the current Chadian regime and a number of international human rights organisations, HRW being the most insistent, lobbied actively for the trial to take place. On 2 November, 141 African human rights groups from 32 African countries published an open letter expressing support for Senegal's efforts to prosecute and the trial was set to start in mid-2015.

Newspaper and radio editors were at risk of being censored by the regime. On 8 October, for example, the High Council suspended the community radio station FM Liberté for seven days. The station had broadcast a statement signed by 12 human rights NGOs critical of the shortage of fuel. Blogs and online papers hosted outside the country became more influential, as the Internet was not censored.

Foreign Affairs

Chad gained a seat on the *UNSC* for two years starting in January. This was controversial in many quarters since the Déby regime had disregarded the UNSC's warrant for the arrest of Sudan's President Omar al Bashir for crimes against humanity. Déby even hosted al-Bashir in Chad during the year. As a consequence, critics asked how a state that did not respect the rulings of UNSC could become one of its ten rolling members. Some realpolitik seemed to prevail. In fact, Chad's active engagement in UN peacekeeping operations in both Mali and the CAR and its international collaboration in fighting terrorism probably gave Chad the votes needed to secure its seat.

Déby also continued to play a role in trying to mediate peace in *Darfur*. On 26–30 March, his officials organised the second Forum for Peace, Security and Peaceful Co-Existence in the Chadian border town Um Jaras as a follow-up to the first Forum, organised in October 2013. Various Sudanese rebel leaders and representatives of numerous ethnic groups met with al-Bashir and Déby to discuss the conflicts in Darfur. Coming up with a list of 23 recommendations, the Forum urged all "arms holders to respond to the call for peace and uphold the values of dialogue, tolerance, forgiveness, rejection of war and violence, and tribal fanaticism". Both Déby and al-Bashir wholeheartedly supported the recommendations. However, many of the rebel groups, including the Justice and Equality Movement (JEM) and the Sudan Liberation Movement, denounced the Forum for being biased and for consolidating tribalism. Déby nevertheless went on to meet the chairperson of the JEM, Gibril Ibrahim, in Paris on 5 April to discuss further the recommendations from the Forum. On the initiative of the Chadian government, leading members of three important Sudanese rebel groups met in N'Djamena on 1 November with the Chadian foreign minister and others for further discussion of the Darfur peace process.

Chad felt strongly the backlash of the never-ending conflict in Darfur. Some 360,000 Sudanese *refugees* were living in Chad and, by the end of the year, refugees from the region being hosted in the country totalled 460,000, making Chad one of the world's foremost receivers of refugees. During the first four months of the year, some 30,000 new refugees arrived from Sudan, fleeing from conflict in Darfur. In addition, some 93,000 refugees from the CAR and some 2,000 from Northern Nigeria were living in Chad, many of them having arrived during the course of the year. Most of them were living in about 20 camps near the CAR or Sudanese border.

In addition to the refugees, around 200,000 Chadians had returned from Libya and the CAR in recent years; many of them were still living in camps and in need of humanitarian aid, including shelter, water and sanitation, food and health care.

France continued to maintain good and intense diplomatic relations with Chad. President François Hollande received Déby in Paris on three occasions over the year, on 14 February, 4 April and 17 May, when a main theme of their discussion was the fight against Boko Haram and other terrorist groups in the Sahel. On 19 July, Déby received Hollande on an official visit to Chad and they met for a two-hour tête-à-tête at the presidential palace. Déby also received the French Prime Minister Manuel Valls in N'Djamena on 22 November mainly to discuss further anti-terror collaboration. On the military level, collaboration with France also intensified. The military cooperation agreement (signed in 1976 and amended in 1990) remained in force. The agreement contained the loaded formulation that France would "ensure the sovereignty of the Chadian state", but there was some dispute as to what exactly this implied. On 10 February, Déby accepted an extension of the French military presence in Chad and the creation of a new base near the town of Zouar, in addition to the two already existing in Faya and N'Djamena. He also welcomed the stationing in Chad of Operation Barkhane, consisting of 3,000 French soldiers and military equipment. Beginning on 1 August, this French contingency force was meant to serve French security interests in the Sahel and Central Africa from its bases in Chad. Barkhane was also seen as a central element of the French contribution to the fight against terror organisations, including Boko Haram and others in the Sahel. By the end of the year, Barkhane consisted of 3,200 troops, 200 more than originally planned. However, some 1,000 of them were stationed in the town Gao in Northern Mali as Operation Serval ended there when Barkhane began. Chad remained economically insignificant to France. Apart from crude oil, 97% of the value of exports to France came from gum Arabic. In contrast, France was economically very important to Chad. France continued to be the third largest contributor of FDI, after China and the US, construction, food (especially sugar and beer) and banking being the main receivers of French investment, in addition to oil. France also continued to be Chad's most important bilateral donor of long-term development assistance.

Boko Haram's activities in Northern *Nigeria* meant that landlocked Chad was completely encircled by armed conflicts in neighbouring countries: in the north by post-Kadhafi insurgencies in Libya since 2011, in the east by the Darfur conflict since 2003 and in the south by the civil war in the CAR since late 2012.

In the battle against terror treats, including Boko Haram, in the *Sahel region*, Chad participated in many regional and bi-lateral anti-terror and security initiatives. The CBLT member states (Chad, Cameroon, Niger and Nigeria) seemed even more occupied with security than with demanding environmental issues, particularly the shrinking volume of Lake Chad (reduced in the past 50 years from a surface area of 25,000 km² to less than 2,000 km²). During their summit meeting in Niamey (Niger) on 7 October, all CBLT member states announced the formation of a joint

2,800-strong joint task force to act against Boko Haram, but this force had not materialised by year's end.

On 16 February, Chad, Burkina Faso, Mali, Mauritania and Niger established a new regional organisation, named G5 Sahel. From its headquarters in Niamey, G5 Sahel, encompassing the five countries the UN Secretary-General had presented (on 14 June 2013) as the target countries in the UN's anti-terror Sahel policy, would enhance regional security, focusing on both the acute security situation and the root causes of conflict in the region. Its proposed budget of $ 14.8 bn (sought from international funders) included the cost of governance, security, economic resilience and infrastructure. In July, the UN, the EU, the World Bank and the AfDB, as well as bilateral donors (including France, the US and the UK) expressed hopeful interest in the G5 Sahel's Priority Investment Program. The establishment of the G5 Sahel was instrumental in Chad's acquiring a more central position in global and regional initiatives in the Sahel security architecture after being previously somewhat sidelined. For example, Chad had been excluded from the EU Sahel initiatives (because the EU prioritised Mauritania, Mali and Niger), and from the regional Joint Military Staff Committee of the Sahel Region (which included only Algeria, Mauritania, Mali and Niger).

Chad also gained a central place in the *US anti-terror commitments* in the Sahel under its Africa Command (AFRICOM) programme. On 21 September, Chad and the US signed a renewal of the military Acquisition Cross Servicing Agreement, which permitted the rapid and uncomplicated exchange of many types of military services, equipment and supplies between the two nations. During the year, the US military also trained both troops and military medical personnel and, in May, the US deployed 80 troops, mostly Air Force personnel, to conduct surveillance flights in the search for the Nigerian schoolgirls taken hostage by Boko Haram.

The UN, the AU and various human rights groups strongly criticised Chad when Chadian troops taking part in the International Support Mission to the *CAR* (MISCA) opened fire at a market in Bangui on 29 March, killing 30 civilians and wounding around 300 more. Déby decided to withdraw his troops from MISCA immediately; by 13 April, all Chadian solders had left and Chad formally closed its border with the CAR on 11 May.

By contrast, Chad continued to contribute to the UN Multidimensional Integrated Stabilization Mission in *Mali* (MINUSMA) and even received international acclaim for its troops' courage and quality. However, Chad accused the MINUSMA headquarters of neglecting to support the Chadian contingent in Mali, after ten solders from Chad were killed there in September.

Socioeconomic Developments

In March, Chadians working for the local branch of the China National Petroleum Corporation went on strike to protest about their working conditions and demand a pay rise and, on 21 March, the Chadian authorities fined the company $ 1.2 bn for environmental damage. When the company refused to pay, Chad forced the company to suspend operations in May and the Oil Ministry withdrew five exploration permits from the company on 9 August. What happened thereafter remained unclear, but by the end of the year the joint venture Djarmaya refinery (60% owned by *China* and 40% by Chad) was producing its regular 15,000 b/d and relations with the Chadian authorities were restored.

A multi-ministerial commission tasked with checking the existence and qualifications of all *public sector employees* was established in February. The commission found that 10,223 state employees (about 12%) were fictitious and existed only on the payroll. This assessment meant that some $ 40 m per year would be cut from the public sector wage bill. Those who had benefited from this fraud now had to reduce their standard of living or find other means of maintaining it, so fighting corruption created tensions among state agents and politicians. Some observers praised the commission's report as a success story in the fight against fraud and corruption; Chad was ranked 154th (out of 174 countries) in the TI Corruption Perceptions Index.

Tensions also occurred elsewhere. On 11 November, important rallies took place in N'Djamena, Sarh and Moundou. They began as a teachers' protest against the non-payment of their promised examination bonuses, but this was rapidly followed by others protesting against the high *cost of living*. In Moundou, there were also demonstrations against the lack of petrol and diesel in the town, resulting in attacks on an empty Total petrol station. It was ironic and indicative of the level of maladministration that people living very close to oil fields that were producing 130,000 b/d did not have steady access to fuel. Moreover, the consumer price of oil products, when they were available, increased steeply after August, even though the world price of oil fell dramatically during the same period. It appeared that a significant amount of the oil refined at the Djermaya plant 32 km north of N'Djamena, which was designated for the national market, had in fact been smuggled out and sold in northern Cameroon and the CAR at prices much higher prices than the normal CFAfr 500 per litre in Chad, where the petrol shortage resulted in black market prices of up to CFAfr 1500 per litre. Oil revenues made the Chadian economy grow faster than average African economies, but without apparent positive consequences for ordinary citizens.

Food prices fluctuated widely according to season and across different locations, but generally speaking saw steep rises over the year. In July, a 25 kg bag of maize bag cost CFAfr 25,000, compared with CFAfr 14,000 in January and 5 litres of cooking oil cost CFAfr 7,500, compared with CFAfr 5,000. Even sugar, produced by a state owned company that received government subsidies to keep prices low, increased in priced from CFAfr 750 for a 1 kg packet to CFAfr 1,100. Many families were permanently food insecure, and weather conditions in some areas made the situation even worse. In the Salamat region, heavy rains in February wiped out all food production in 61 villages. Close to 10,000 persons lost all their crops and about 1,000 were made homeless.

Access to the *Internet* remained restricted by illiteracy, poverty and inadequate infrastructure. One cell phone company, AIRTEL, operating as Tigo-Tchad, was granted a licence to deploy 3G and 4G platforms on 8 April and the 4G network was inaugurated on 17 July. By the end of the year, these services were functioning in N'Djamena, Abeche, Sarh and Moundou, but prices made Internet use on mobile phones a luxury only available to a few of the wealthiest elite. Around half of the adult population in Chad owned at least one mobile phone, but only 2.4% had access to the Internet. The state-controlled telecommunications company Sotel started working towards privatisation on 13 February, but, parliament voted against privatisation on 30 May thereby stopping the process.

On 3 June, the ministers of transport of Chad and in Cameroon signed an agreement for planning an extension of the *railway* from its current endpoint at Ngaoundere in Cameroon to N'Djamena, a distance of roughly 750 km – an ambitious project with the potential to substantially ease access to land-locked Chad. Currently, around 80% of imports and exports travel 1,600 km, mostly on dirt roads, to and from N'Djamena through Cameroon to the port of Douala. Discussions on the railway extension had begun in December 2010 but had been delayed for technical and financial reasons.

Humanitarian organisations suggested that some 2.4 m people were food insecure at the end of the year. UNICEF estimated that 553.000 children were suffering from severe or moderate acute *malnutrition*. Close to half of them, some 245,000, were treated for malnutrition in one of the 480 nutritional centres. There were fewer than 500 Chadian doctors for the entire population, which made it hardly surprising that Chad had the third-highest maternal mortality rates in the world, with 1,100 mothers dying per 100,000 births. Diseases such as malaria, measles and meningitis, however, are the most common cause of death. Throughout the year, around 1 m people contracted malaria, which caused some 15% of all deaths in hospitals and clinics. A reported 10,000 people were infected with measles, while the incidence of cholera had declined; only 172 cases were reported, compared with 17,000 in the 2011 epidemic. UNDP classified Human Development in Chad among the lowest in the world (184th out of 189 countries).

In the World Economic Forum's Global Gender Gap rankings for 2014, Chad was placed 140th (out of 142 countries), above only Pakistan and Yemen, thus making it the *most gender-unequal country in Africa* with regard to economic participation, health issues, political empowerment and educational opportunities for women. Furthermore, 35% of girls were married before the age of 15 and more than 40% of girls underwent genital mutilation, adding to doubts regarding the authorities' concern for women's rights.

Congo

Brett Logan Carter

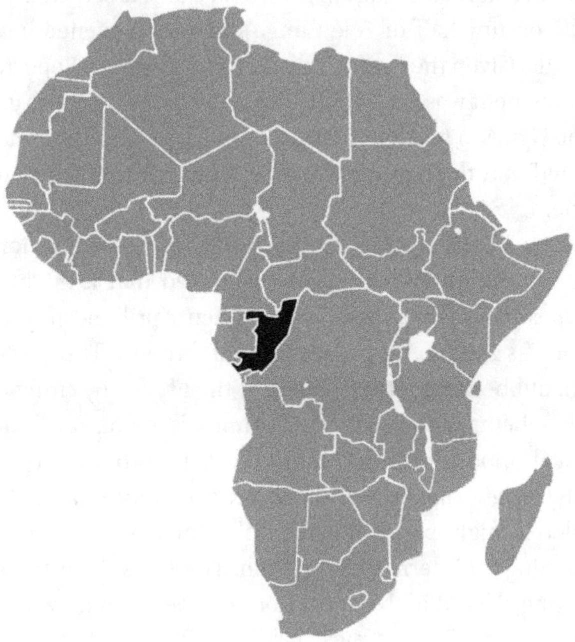

Congo's political climate was marked by new tensions, as President Denis Sassou Nguesso continued his efforts to engineer a constitutional revision that would enable him to retain power beyond 2016. The local and senatorial elections of September and October, respectively, highlighted the political opposition's weakness. With most citizens overwhelmingly opposed to the constitutional revisions, Sassou Nguesso sought to deter protests by demonstrating the regime's capacity for violence. Abroad, he attempted to fashion himself as the region's elder statesman, mediating in the conflict in the CAR and amplifying his efforts to curry favour in Paris and Washington. Although these endeavours met with limited success, they acquired greater urgency following the revolution in Burkina Faso, which swept President Blaise Campaoré from power as he contemplated a similar constitutional revision. Amid declining oil production, the government held a series of conferences in Brazzaville to attract foreign investors. But enshrined corruption, a poor regulatory framework, and the spectre of political instability limited their success. Congo's GDP growth rate continued to fall, and its citizens' living standards remained among the world's lowest.

 | DOI 10.1163/9789004305052_025

Domestic Politics

The year began auspiciously for the Sassou Nguesso government. In late January, Euronews announced that it would launch its *Africanews* subsidiary in Brazzaville in late 2015. The announcement marked a diplomatic victory for Sassou Nguesso. Africanews would reportedly occupy half of Télé Congo's newly christened headquarters in northern Brazzaville. Given the regime's declining rating from Reporters Without Borders, the announcement was met with widespread surprise; it also generated suspicions that Sassou Nguesso had lured Euronews with a significant financial subsidy. Euronews insisted that the pan-African news network would espouse an independent editorial line.

Sassou Nguesso's supporters began openly campaigning for a constitutional revision in April. As public criticism grew, the regime signalled that it might be willing to employ *violence to suppress mass protests*. Between April and July, the government deported as many as 250,000 DRC citizens, often brutally. The government justified the operation, dubbed Operation 'Smack of the Elders', by citing the crime rate, DRC nationals often being regarded as petty criminals in Brazzaville and Pointe-Noire. But the political opposition interpreted the deportations very differently and considered that, by ignoring appeals from UN Secretary-General Ban Ki-moon, the regime signalled it might be willing to employ force against protesters, even at the risk of becoming an international pariah. The mass deportations devastated Brazzaville's working class. With National Route 1 – between Brazzaville and Pointe-Noire, and thus crossing Congo's most fertile agricultural land – still devastated by the 1997 civil war, the urban poor had historically purchased food imports from Kinshasa (DRC). When the borders closed following the deportations, the cost of food increased fivefold.

The regime soon targeted Congo's few *independent journalists* and most ardent pro-democracy activists. Elie Smith served as the chief reporter for the MNTV television channel – owned by Maurice Nguesso, the president's elder brother and one of Congo's wealthiest citizens – from which he occasionally criticised the constitutional revision On 10 September, five armed men broke into Smith's Brazzaville home, physically assaulted him, and raped his younger sister. Smith was expelled to his native Cameroon on 26 September. Sadio Kante Morel, a stringer for Reuters who reported the assaults, was expelled to Mali on 22 September, although she was born to West African parents in Brazzaville and entitled to Congolese citizenship. In October, a group of 35 opposition activists who comprised the Citizen Movement for the Respect of Constitutional Order were arrested and held, without trial, for four weeks. Patrick Eric Mampouya, well known for the opposition website he had once run from Paris, was among them.

On 28 September, voters went to the polls to elect *departmental and municipal counsellors*. With several prominent opposition leaders, including Mathias Dzon and Clement Mierassa, calling for a boycott, Sassou Nguesso's 'Parti Congolais du

Travail' (PCT) claimed a crushing victory. Of 850 seats, the PCT alone claimed 402. The 'Union Panafricaine pour la Démocratie Sociale' (UPADS), founded by former president Pascal Lissouba and the only significant remaining opposition party, won but 54 seats. The remaining seats were divided among political parties allied with the PCT. Senatorial elections were held on 12 October, and again the PCT dominated. Of 38 seats, the PCT claimed 30. Of the remaining eight seats, PCT allies received six, leaving but two for the opposition. Both went to UPADS. In the wake of defeat, several prominent UPADS figures formed a new party, the 'Congrès Africain pour le Progrès'.

André Okombi Salissa, a deputy from Lekana, Plateaux and perhaps Congo's most viable *opposition* leader, returned to Congo in June after 15 months of voluntary exile in Paris. He came back ostensibly to attend a budgetary session in the National Assembly, but virtually all observers interpreted his return as confirmation that he would seek the presidency in 2016. During a trip to the USA in May, Okombi Salissa had signed a contract with Rasky Baerlein Strategic Communications, a public relations firm that would be responsible for burnishing his relationships with American policymakers. This would be critical, as most State Department officials regarded him as a leading architect of Sassou Nguesso's mass violence in Brazzaville following the 1997 civil war. Okombi Salissa remained the unofficial leader of the Téké axis, which included Colonel Ntsourou, Dzon and Jean Martin Mbemba, formerly Sassou Nguesso's justice minister.

The *PCT* political bureau was expected to formally announce its support for a constitutional revision following its 8 November meeting. Having watched Burkina Faso's President Compaoré fall to a mass uprising in late October, however, Sassou Nguesso quietly deferred the PCT's decision to 31 December. On 8 December, the Catholic Church, long opposed to the regime, criticised the constitutional revision in unusually harsh terms. Even some within the PCT openly dissented. Dubbed the party's 'intellectual' wing, this group quietly advocated not only Sassou Nguesso's departure in 2016, but also a demographic shift in the party's leadership away from the Mbochi ethnic group. Led by long-time minister Isidore Mvouba and Charles Zacharie Bowao, Sassou Nguesso's former defence minister, this 'intellectual' wing attracted support from Likouala and Plateaux natives. In July, Bowao even published an essay that criticised the PCT's "ethnocentrism" and "tribalism", serious accusations in a country that had fought a series of civil wars along ethnic lines less than 20 years before. Although the PCT ultimately endorsed the constitutional revision on 31 December, the spectre of an alliance between this 'intellectual' current and the Téké axis – in conjunction with the mass revolt that brought down Compaoré in October – had the potential to compel Sassou Nguesso to eventually jettison the constitutional revision.

The year witnessed several *important political appointments*. Bonaventure Engobo, former National Protocol director, became adjoint secretary general of the National Security Council, the regime's chief domestic intelligence service. In July,

Sassou Nguesso appointed Louis Patrice Ngagnon, an ethnic Téké and an engineer by training, to head the national water distribution company. With the 50th African Games coming to Brazzaville in 2015, the city's frequent water scarcities threatened to become a serious embarrassment for the regime. In October, Pascal Ngotene, an ethnic Mbochi, was named head of the Pointe-Noire port authority, replacing Jean-Marie Aniélé, who had occupied the post since the 1997 civil war. Ngotene's appointment marked the persistent influence of Minister for Great Projects Jean Jacques Bouya, Sassou Nguesso's nephew. Bouya also successfully positioned his brother, Bernard Serge Bouya, as Ngotene's deputy. In November, Sassou Nguesso named Benjamin Makaya, a native of Pointe-Noire, as adjoint director general of the 'Société Nationale des Pétroles du Congo' (SNPC) to oversee production.

Foreign Affairs

Diplomatically, Sassou Nguesso sought to establish himself as *Central Africa's elder statesman* by positioning himself as the chief mediator for the *CAR crisis*. On 20 January, Catherine Samba-Panza, regarded as the 'civil society candidate', succeeded Michel Djotodia as CAR president. She had been vocally supported by Sassou Nguesso and her victory marked a triumph for him and secured him a strategic partner in Bangui. Moreover, by advocating for a candidacy that most donors viewed as a milestone for civil society activism and gender equity, he hoped to earn a measure of goodwill in Paris and Washington in advance of the constitutional revision. His efforts were not entirely in vain. Virtually reviled by the government of French President François Hollande upon its election in 2012, by July Sassou Nguesso had emerged as France's indispensable partner in the CAR. But even so, his efforts were not as successful as he had hoped. In November, France prevailed upon Sassou Nguesso's African counterparts to elect Michaëlle Jean as secretary-general of La Francophonie, rather than Henri Lopès, Sassou Nguesso's long-standing ambassador to France and effectively the dean of the African diplomatic community in Paris.

Sassou Nguesso also sought to play kingmaker in *Gabon*. In April, he met discretely with Jacques Adiahénot, a minister in several governments of the late Omar Bongo, president of Gabon until 2009, and former head of the 'Parti Democratique Gabonais' (PDG) of current President Ali Ben Bongo. On 6 March, Adiahénot resigned from the PDG to help coordinate Jean Ping's nascent presidential campaign to unseat Ali Bongo. Observers in Brazzaville and Libreville alike interpreted the meeting as a signal of support for Ping's candidacy, despite the long-standing alliance between the Bongo and Sassou Nguesso families. The meeting came less than a month after Ali Bongo had chosen not to attend an event in Oyo to mark the fifth anniversary of Edith Lucie Bongo's death; the first lady of Gabon until her death in 2007, Edith Lucie was also Sassou Nguesso's eldest daughter. Ali Bongo's absence was made all the more conspicuous by the host of African presidents who chose to attend: Teodoro Obiang Nguema of Equatorial Guinea, Ibrahim Boubacar Keïta of Mali, and Ernest Bai Koroma of Sierra Leone.

Unsurprisingly, the spring deportations damaged Congo's bilateral relations with the *DRC*, and with Joseph Kabila's few allies. Angolan President José Eduardo dos Santos, whose military support during the 1997 civil war had been decisive for Sassou Nguesso's victory, cancelled their meeting in Luanda on 23 April. Just two weeks later, in an effort to calm tensions, Congolese security forces captured Udjani Mangbama, a former DRC rebel leader and long-time rival of Kabila. A close ally of Jean-Pierre Bemba, currently imprisoned in The Hague for crimes against humanity, Mangbama had fled the DRC for Brazzaville in 2010 and had been sentenced to death in absentia by a Kinshasa court in August 2011; Sassou Nguesso's government refused Kinshasa's request for extradition. Mangbama died from wounds suffered during his capture in Brazzaville on 10 May. The bilateral relationship had recovered somewhat by August, when Sassou Nguesso and Kabila were photographed touring Kinshasa, hand in hand.

In August, Sassou Nguesso attended the US-Africa summit in *Washington* hosted by President Barack Obama. He arrived a full week before the summit began. He hoped to generate support in Washington for his constitutional revision, an effort that included a speech at the National Press Club. By all accounts, the project failed, as the US State Department remained resolutely opposed to the revision and Congressman Eliot Engel, a Democrat from New York, called on Sassou Nguesso to step down in 2016. This diplomatic failure coincided with the Congo National Conference for Democratic Alternance, a four-day affair in *Paris* that was hosted by several prominent opposition leaders in the Congolese diaspora. Held at a small Catholic church in the 13th arrondissement, the Conference attracted just over 100 people; Dzon was not among them, for the prominent opposition leader had been detained at Brazzaville's Maya-Maya airport by Sassou Nguesso's security services, forbidden to leave the country. The summit was designed as much to unify the Paris-based opposition as to mobilise support within the French government, which was represented at the summit by several officials from the Quai d'Orsay. In response, Sassou Nguesso dispatched PCT Secretary General Pierre Ngolo to Paris immediately after the Conference ended. Along with several other high level representatives, Ngolo held a 'citizen meeting' with Sassou Nguesso's partisans in France on 22 June. The meetings took place at the Hotel Pullman Paris-Bercy, bordering the Seine, a setting that underscored the vast financial disparity between Sassou Nguesso and the opposition.

With bilateral relationships with Paris and Washington still tense, *China* continued to emerge as perhaps Sassou Nguesso's most important ally. In June, he visited China for nearly two weeks, ostensibly to celebrate the 40th anniversary of diplomatic relations between the two countries. On 30 September, the PRC government celebrated the 65th anniversary of its founding. The event was toasted in Brazzaville by the Chinese ambassador, surrounded by a handful of Sassou Nguesso's most trusted ministers, including his uncle Aimé Emmanuel Yoka.

Socioeconomic Developments

Congo's GDP reached $ 14.09 bn, representing a growth rate of 3.4%. This was a significant decline, for just four years earlier, in 2010, it had reached nearly 9%. Congo's *slowing growth rate* was driven almost entirely by its declining oil reserves and global market prices. Oil production continued its long-term decline, down to 265,000 b/d, from 305,000 b/d in 2010, although Congo was still Africa's fourth-leading oil producer, behind Nigeria, Angola and Equatorial Guinea. With most analysts anticipating an even further decline, the government accelerated its search for new reserves. It focused on the 16,000 km^2 Ngolo block in the Cuvette basin, with Eni responsible for exploration. The oil sector again accounted for approximately 90% of Congolese exports, with timber and cement comprising the balance. Congo's total exports continued to decline as well, from $ 10.53 bn in 2013 to $ 9.91 bn. China and the USA remained Congo's chief export partners, accounting for just over 50% of total exports. After it reached the HIPC completion point in 2010, Congo's external debt was largely forgiven by bilateral and multilateral creditors. The country's external debt now totalled $ 3.45 bn, or roughly 25% of GDP. Its inflation rate increased rapidly, reaching 6% after a low of 1.3% in 2011.

Sassou Nguesso sponsored a series of international conferences that sought to attract *foreign investors*. In February, he welcomed the first Build Africa Forum, a two-day event billed as an opportunity for international investors, donors and NGO leaders to discuss how infrastructure improvements might stimulate sustainable growth across the African continent. The Forum was organised by Richard Attias, the Moroccan businessman who had been organising the New York Forum AFRICA each year in Libreville (Gabon). Attended by potential investors from Brazil, Nigeria, South Africa and other middle-income countries, it was an extended advertisement for Congo's economic potential and part of Sassou Nguesso's ongoing bid to shift the economic centre of Central Africa from Libreville. In late July, Sassou Nguesso welcomed the Forbes Africa Forum, at which he persuaded former French president Nicholas Sarkozy to speak, as well as other well-known French media personalities.

Notwithstanding these conferences, Congo's business climate remained among the least attractive in the world. The World Bank found that firms could expect to spend 602 hours per year – or fully 75 working days – filing taxes alone. The effective tax rate was nearly 60%. Enforcing a contract in the Congolese court system cost, on average, nearly 55% of the total claim. Reflecting this, Congo's FDI continued to decline, falling to roughly $ 2 bn from a high of just over $ 3 bn in 2011. The government did little to ameliorate these persistent weaknesses. As a result – and despite the country's vast oil wealth – Congolese citizens remained mired in poverty. Life expectancy held constant at 58 years, while nearly 73% of the population subsisted on less than $ 2 per day. The government continued to neglect public services, allocating just 2.5% of GDP to health care and 6% of GDP to education. Congolese citizens continued to migrate to Brazzaville and Pointe-Noire from the rural hinterlands, pushing the country's urbanisation rate to 65%.

Democratic Republic of the Congo

Claudia Simons

The year was marked by a fierce political battle around the question whether President Kabila was aiming to run for a third term in 2016 and a polarising debate over a potential constitutional revision. It was only at the end of the year that the government of national cohesion – promised more than a year before – was formed. In one of the most far-reaching army reforms since the Sun City peace agreement of 2003, three defence zones were set up and important posts filled with notorious individuals close to Kabila. With regard to the security situation in the east of the country, national and international attention turned from the defeated M23 to the Ugandan rebel movement Allied Democratic Front (ADF) and to the Rwandan Hutu militia 'Forces Démocratiques de Libération du Rwanda' (FDLR). Whereas the DRC army engaged in a large-scale military operation against the former, the government's approach towards the latter was marked by negotiations and reluctance to engage in military action. The FDLR started a half-hearted demobilisation process and talks with the DRC government, the UN and international partners. Kinshasa's approach towards the FDLR led to fierce criticism by Rwanda and relations between the DRC and Rwanda deteriorated further. Despite enduring relief after the victory against the M23 in late 2013, the humanitarian situation

 | DOI 10.1163/9789004305052_026

remained challenging due to on-going fighting by other rebel movements in the east and a deteriorating security situation in Katanga province. Transparency and development in the mining sector remained the most discussed economic issue throughout the year.

Domestic Politics

In the course of the year, the question of whether President Joseph Kabila would run for a *third term in 2016* became the biggest political issue in the DRC. Article 70 of the Constitution only allows for two terms and Article 220 explicitly prohibits any revision of the term limit. Various means to prolong Kabila's hold on power – most importantly a revision of the Constitution – were discussed throughout the year, polarising the political debate in Kinshasa. Supporters and opponents of a third term were not easily located in either the presidential or opposition camp, but could be found on both sides. Among the loudest supporters were Evariste Boshab, the head of Kabila's 'Parti du Peuple pour la Réconstruction et la Démocratie' (PPRD), Monseigneur Marini Bodho, the head of the largest Protestant church, the 'Eglise du Christ au Congo', and Kin-Kiey Mulumba, the minister of telecommunications. The president of the Senate, Léon Kengo wa Dondo, openly opposed a *revision of the constitution*. So did the Catholic Church, first and foremost Cardinal Monsengwo, who had repeatedly in the political history of the DRC openly challenged ruling elites and advocated for democracy. The political opposition launched a coalition against any constitutional revision under the slogan 'Don't touch my constitution'. On 4 August, important parliamentarian opposition parties such as the 'Union pour la Nation Congolaise' (UNC) and the 'Union pour la Démocratie et le Progrès Social' (UDPS) organised a demonstration in Kinshasa, after which the UNC's General Secretary Jean-Bertrand Ewanga was arrested and sentenced to one year in prison for contempt of state institutions. In September, around 650 Congolese NGOs, including the most important associations, signed a declaration against a constitutional revision and protesters took to the streets. Kabila himself remained silent on the issue. However, many political manoeuvres suggested that he planned to stay in power – among others a reshuffle in the military that allowed for his closer personal *control over the armed forces*, as well as the eventual establishment of a government of national cohesion, meant to strengthen Kabila's own coalition and satisfy opponents of a third term (see below).

Given the polarised situation concerning a potential third mandate, the publication of the first part of the *electoral calendar* on 26 May by the national election commission ('Commission Electorale Nationale Indépendante' – CENI) caused a controversy. The political opposition criticised the electoral calendar on various fronts. The document was silent about presidential and legislative elections and only presented a strict time schedule for the election of councillors and mayors.

Local elections had been promised since 2006 but had been repeatedly postponed. Despite the fact that the opposition and international partners had for years been urging the government to keep this promise, they feared that the financial and organisational challenge of local elections in 2015 would be used as a reason to postpone the presidential and parliamentary elections of 2016, effectively prolonging Kabila's hold on power. The opposition claimed that the first elections to be held should be the provincial elections, but it was not even clear whether the basis for elections would be the current 11 provinces or 26 provinces as foreseen in the constitution of 2006. CENI also remained silent on the question of a national census, as recommended by the national consultations of 2013. Instead, CENI's only comment on the problem of the hitherto chaotic and unreliable electoral register – and the de facto absence of a voters' register on the local level – was that voter registration should be externally monitored. This was especially worrisome to parts of civil society, as they feared that simmering communal conflicts would be exacerbated by badly planned local elections. In fact, it was only in November, that the 'Office National d'Identification de la Population' (ONIP) was created, staffed and tasked with conducting a national census. According to the head of ONIP, Adolphe Lumanu, the census would only take one year but would cost around $ 500 m. He said the Chinese company Huawei EximBank would carry out the census with financing from the state-lender ChinaEximBank. The plan immediately came under heavy criticism by the opposition. They feared that the census would take many years because of logistical and financial constraints and so would be used as yet another means to delay presidential elections for many years. In a reaction to the publication of the electoral calendar, the special envoys of the UN, the AU, the EU and the USA, as well as the EU election observer mission, urged the government to publish a complete and detailed calendar. However, the head of CENI, Apollinaire Malu-Malu, said in July that he was waiting for the election budget to be passed before announcing the complete calendar. Kabila assured the opposition and the international community on 15 December that all elections would take place according to the Constitution. However, no complete calendar had been presented by year's end. On 21 September, two important opposition parties, Vital Kamerhe's UNC and Etienne Tschisekedi's UDPS, and their allies announced the suspension of their participation in all CENI activities as well as promising their presence in parliament whenever the electoral law or calendar was discussed.

On 7 December, Kabila announced a major *government reshuffle*, 13 months after his promise of a government of national cohesion. Prime Minister Matata Ponyo kept his post, contrary to much speculation. He had initially enjoyed a good reputation as a result of his pragmatic stance towards economic reform, but had come under criticism for not being able to handle the M23 crisis in the east. The posts of three deputy prime ministers were created and given to the secretary-general of the ruling PPRD, Evariste Boshab, the 'Mouvement de Libération du Congo' secretary-general, Thomas Luhaka, and the permanent secretary and speaker of the

'Parti Lumumbiste Unifié', Willy Makiashi. The political opposition got some high-ranking positions in terms of protocol, most notably the state minister for budget (Michel Bongongo, 'Union des Forces du Changement'), but the most powerful ministries were given to political heavyweights from the 'Alliance pour la Majorité Présidentielle' coalition and Kabila's home base of Katanga was over-represented. This was largely interpreted as a means to strengthen the coalition, satisfy political allies and appease potential troublemakers. The new government replaced the rather technocratic no-name government that had been warmly supported by international partners. Only three women were appointed to the new government, which consisted of 38 members (the prime minister, his deputies, and ministers, not including vice ministers). Notably, key positions related to the question of a third term for Kabila were filled by Kabila loyalists: Boshab became minister of the interior (combined with his position as deputy prime minister), a key position in the run-up to elections in 2016; Tryphon Kin-Kiey Mulumba became minister for relations with Parliament – the latter being the institution that would be decisive for an eventual constitutional amendment.

The early days of January were marked by the aftermath of simultaneous *armed attacks* on the national television station, the military headquarters and the international airport of N'djili in Kinshasa province, as well as attacks in Lubumbashi (Katanga) and Kindu (Maniema). The government attributed the attacks to followers of the self-proclaimed prophet and presidential candidate of 2006, Joseph Mukungubila, who denied any involvement. According to the government, 103 people – most of them attackers – were killed during the clashes. In a report published on 22 May, the Paris-based human rights organisation 'Fédération Internationale des Ligues des Droits de l'Homme' (FIDH), together with the DRC NGO 'Ligue des Électeurs', accused the security forces of killing more than 250 followers of Mukungubila, arresting more than 100, wounding dozens of civilians and pillaging many homes on 30 December 2013 and the days that followed. On 2 January, the federal secretary of the UDPS in Kasai-Orientale, Bruno Kabangu, was arrested in Kinshasa for complicity with Mukungubila and sentenced to 12 months in prison on 20 June. On 15 May, Mukungubila, in exile in South Africa, was briefly detained under an Interpol arrest warrant and had his first hearing before a court in Johannesburg on 15 July.

On 18 September, Kabila announced a major reshaping of the 'Forces Armées de la République Démocratique du Congo' (FARDC). Instead of organising the army in 11 provincial commands, three broad *defence zones* were established in the west, south and east. Gabriel Amisi Kumba would now command the west, Jean-Claude Kifwa the south and Mushale Tshipamba the east, all three being close allies of Kabila. The head of the ground forces, François Olenga Tete, was replaced by Dieudonné Banze Lubundji, the former head of the Republican Guard – Kabila's de facto private army. It was not till 16 November that Kabila announced the appointment of Ilunga Kampete Gaston-Hugues as the new head of the Republican Guard, after months of rumours as to whether the former head of police, John Numbi, would be appointed to the post. The appointment of General Amisi was particularly noteworthy. Amisi, better known under his war name 'Tango Fort', was an influential ex-'Rassemblement Congolais pour la Démocratie-Goma' rebel commander who had fought against the Kabila government in the second Congo war, but had then become integrated into the FARDC. He had been commander in chief of the land forces, but had been suspended in late 2012 over accusations of providing arms to rebel groups, basically helping M23 rebels to capture Goma in November 2012. A military commission presided over by Kabila acquitted him of all charges in late July. Amisi had been accused of orchestrating a massacre in Kisangani in 2002 and repeatedly mentioned by the UN Group of Experts (UNGoE) in the context of large-scale corruption and illicit mineral exploitation. Kifwa had also been under UNGoE observation for his relations with the Mai Mai Morgan rebel group and his involvement in illicit resource trafficking. The reshuffle was largely interpreted as a means to tighten Kabila's direct control over the FARDC and thereby as a potential sign that he would not leave power in 2016. Furthermore, the reform was a serious reversal with regard to the professionalisation of the FARDC. Many reform-oriented officers – such as Olenga, who had been instrumental in the success against the M23 – were replaced by notoriously corrupt individuals close to Kabila, including the above mentioned Kifwa and Amisi, as well as many others, who were returning after their temporary removal, which in 2013 had spread hope of improved army performance.

Furthermore, the reform came after the death of two other officers key to improving professionalism, discipline and performance within the FARDC – Mamadou Ndala and Lucien Bahuma. The *Ndala Affair* was especially sinister. On 2 January, the commander of Operation Sokola, carried out by the FARDC, was killed in Beni. His murder was quickly attributed to the rebel group ADF and on 17 November a military court in Beni ruled that the ADF had made common cause with elements of the FARDC. The court sentenced Colonel Nzanzu Birocho and a number of rank and file soldiers and members of the ADF (including in absentia the ADF leader Jami Mukulu) to death or long prison terms. According to the court, the ADF had paid army officers to kill Ndala in order to prevent the offensive against the ADF, but lack of evidence and the sudden death of a key witness in October fuelled the perception that the trial was staged and that the assassination was related to internal power struggles within the FARDC. On 30 August, Major General Lucien Bahuma Ambamba, the army commander of the military region covering North Kivu and a key player in the reformist wing of the FARDC died – allegedly from a stroke – causing rumours that his death was not as natural as officially announced.

On 2 May, one-and-a-half years after the *mass rape* of around 130 women and girls in Minova by FARDC soldiers, a military court in Goma handed down the verdict. Of the 39 indicted troops, only two low-ranking soldiers were found guilty for rape; 23 were convicted of pillage and 13 were acquitted. Human rights organisations, such as the FIDH and the United Nations Joint Human Rights Office denounced the judgement as weak and discouraging for rape victims. The UN Secretary-General nevertheless stated in his report of 24 September that the judgement offered constructive lessons for future prosecution of crime in the region.

After the defeat of the *M23* and separate declarations by the rebel movement and the DRC government of December 2013 (in Nairobi, Kenya), progress in dealing with the remaining M23 ex-combatants and implementing the *Nairobi Declarations* was slow. According to the UNGoE's interim report of 25 June, the exact numbers of ex-combatants remaining in Uganda was still unclear due to inconsistencies in the lists drawn up by Ugandan officials and the M23 themselves. It was only after months of delay that the DRC government became involved in identifying M23 combatants through a technical team sent to Uganda and Rwanda in April and July. Evidence emerged that the M23 were reorganising in Uganda. Furthermore, dozens were said to have fled from camps in Rwanda. In November, M23 president Bertrand Bisimwa stated from exile in Uganda that the M23 were willing to continue fighting if the DRC government did not fulfil its part of the peace deal. One crucial accusation was that the government had not complied with the *amnesty* agreement and continued to detain M23 fighters in prison. Exiled M23 combatants would therefore not be willing to return to the DRC. The granting of amnesty had been part of agreements between the government and the M23 in 2013, in which, however, the concrete procedure for granting amnesty remained ambiguous. On 11 February, parliament passed a law granting amnesty on a case-by-case basis to members of armed groups for crimes committed between February 2006 and December 2013 (except in the case of genocide, war crimes and crimes against humanity). The deadline for applications was set to mid-August, but applications were still considered afterwards due to delays in the process. The government published several lists of individuals subject to the law, naming M23 elements, including many, but not all, of those who were awaiting repatriation from Uganda. The lists also included combatants of the Kata Katanga rebel group, members of the 'Armée de Résistance Populaire' of Faustin Munene and Mobutists close to Honoré Ngbanda, as well as individuals implicated in attacks in Kinshasa on 27 February 2011. The M23 criticised the procedure as violating the agreements of December 2013; they requested a general amnesty for their members and rejected the government's right unilaterally to decide who would be granted amnesty. The amnesty law also included political offences, as agreed during the national consultations in October 2013. The law did not apply, however, to most political opponents facing legal prosecution, as they had usually been charged for real or invented criminal offences and not on political grounds.

Following the defeat of the M23, the UN Stabilization Mission in the DRC (MONUSCO) and the FARDC turned their attention to *other rebel groups* operating in the DRC. Although the FDLR were supposed to be at the centre of operations, the second large joint offensive by the FARDC and the UN Force Intervention Brigade

(FIB), called Operation Sokola, was launched against the Ugandan rebel group ADF. The offensive – now under the command of General Muhindo Akili Muondos – started on 16 January and by 13 March the army had declared victory against the group. The ADF had for years held relatively stable strongholds in Beni territory in North Kivu and had extended its reach during 2013. Despite the declared victory, over 80 civilians were allegedly killed by the ADF in Beni during a series of attacks in October. The massacres were largely seen as revenge attacks by surviving ADF elements, whose command and control apparatus had remained intact, despite the dismantling of operational bases. Also, after the trial in the Ndala murder case began, a series of attacks on civilians in Beni occurred without much interference by either the army or the UN soldiers deployed in the city. Contrary to earlier assumptions, the UNGoE found no links between the ADF and al-Shabaab or al-Qaida. With the support of MONUSCO, the FARDC also launched operations against 'Ndumba Defense of Congo'/Cheka, Raia Mutomboki and May-May Kifuafua elements in Walikale (South Kivu), as well as making smaller efforts to dislodge some FDLR splinter groups in Rutshuru (North Kivu) and marginal moves against FDLR road blocks. However, no large-scale operations against the FDLR took place during the year.

In fact, since the military victory by the FARDC and the FIB over the M23 in late 2013, the *FDLR* had become increasingly nervous and was keen to hint at voluntary disarmament before becoming the next target of military action. On 30 December 2013, the FDLR had already declared their willingness to lay down their arms and engage in a political struggle. On 12 January, the group announced the "start of activities" of the new alliance 'Front Commun de Libération du Rwanda' (FCLR-Ubumwe), founded in 2012 and intended as an umbrella for (exiled) Rwandan opposition parties. On 30 May and 9 June, 193 FDLR fighters – a small segment of the militia, which was suspected to have around 1,500–2,500 troops – handed in their weapons. After these first two disarmament events, a Joint Technical Commission of the DRC government, the FDLR and MONUSCO was set up for the Kivu provinces, tasked with overseeing the *demobilisation process*. While the FDLR had repeatedly stressed their willingness to disarm, they continued to insist on peace talks with the Rwandan government, while the latter continued to refuse any negotiations with the rebels. On 26 June, however, *negotiations* took place in Rome between an FDLR delegation, the head of MONUSCO, the special envoy of the UN Secretary-General for the Great Lakes, the special envoys of the US, Belgium and the EU, along with delegates of the DRC government, marking the highest level talks with the FDLR since their creation. SADC, the ICGLR, the AU and Rwanda rejected the invitation. The FDLR presented their political demands, including dialogue with the Rwandan government and integration into the Rwandan security forces. The event was facilitated by the French UN Under-Secretary General responsible for peacekeeping operations, Hervé Ladsous, at the invitation of the Sant' Egidio religious community, which had already been involved in talks with the FDLR in

2005. The acting president of the FDLR, Victor Byiringiro, was also brought from Goma to Kinshasa by MONUSCO in order to go on to Rome. However, a request from the UN Department for Peacekeeping Operations (DPKO) for the lifting of the UN travel ban on Byiringiro, who had been under sanctions since 2010, was effectively blocked by Rwanda and rejected by the UN Sanctions Committee. Rwanda fiercely criticised the action of the UN and threatened in a letter to the UNSC of 26 June to withdraw from the Framework Agreement if the DPKO continued to "sanitize the FDLR genocidaires".

On 28 December, another round of *disarmament* operations took place in North and South Kivu, where 151 FDLR combatants voluntarily disarmed and handed over 67 weapons. As in May and June, the surrendering combatants were of low rank and the weapons old, suggesting that the rebels were not serious about demobilisation. Also, the time schedule agreed on by the Joint Technical Commission was not met. The DRC government nevertheless gave much publicity to all disarmament events.

On 14 April, the leader of the *Mai Mai* Morgan rebel group operating in Ituri, Paul Sadala, was killed after surrendering together with 42 fighters. The incident, in which several more Mai Mai and two FARDC soldiers were also killed, occurred while he was being transferred by the FARDC to Bunia. According to the government, Sadala tried to escape. However, the exact circumstances of his death remained unclear and the UNGoE found evidence for disproportionate use of force and mistreatment by the FARDC. Sadala was known for his close links to FARDC officers in Beni territory with whom he had traded resources for arms, including Jean-Claude Kifwa, who was appointed commander of the western military region in September (see above). The incident sparked wide-spread criticism as it discouraged combatants from surrendering.

Disastrous *conditions in a demobilisation camp* in Kotakoli in Equateur Province added to this impression. According to HRW, over 100 ex-combatants and their family members had died of starvation and many more had been affected by serious illnesses in the camp as of October. The fighters came from various armed groups and had been transferred from the east of the country to Kotakoli in September 2013. They were meant to stay there for only three months before being integrated into the armed forces or put into a DDR programme. The remoteness of the area and the poor infrastructure hindered adequate provision for the camp residents. The special representative of the UN Secretary-General and head of MONUSCO, Martin Kobler, visited the camp on 11 September.

There were security problems in other parts of the country, too. The southern province of *Katanga* had already made headlines in 2013, with increasing attacks by various rebel groups (most notably the Kata Katanga under the command of Kyungu Mutanga) and clashes between a self-proclaimed prophet and security organs that had caused the death of around 40 people on 30 December 2013. On 10 January, more clashes between rebels associated with the Kata Katanga and security forces occurred. The rebels became known for their 'scorched earth' policy, in which whole villages were burnt to spread fear. Kobler stated in February that MONUSCO would look at deploying more troops to Katanga but underlined that the problem had to be solved by the DRC government. By year's end, MONUSCO had presented neither a timetable nor figures for the reinforcement of the 450 blue helmets already deployed from Benin. Conflicts in Katanga revolved around the sharing of income from natural resources between the province and the central state. The resource-rich province is not only the economic engine of the country but also the stronghold of Kabila and his regime, so unrest in Katanga has long had a strong influence on national political stability.

State failure to prevent man-made disasters was also a source of unrest. On 13 December, a *boat accident* on Lake Tanganyika left at least 129 people dead. The boat was going from Kalemie (Katanga) to Uvira (South Kivu). Only ten days later, more than 30 people died and hundreds went missing when a boat from Kisangani to Isangi (Orientale Province) capsized. In reaction, riots occurred in Isangi, with youths setting fire to government buildings. Accidents of this kind had long been common, due to poor maintenance of the vessels, frequent overcrowding and a lack of life jackets – a particular risk, as many people do not know how to swim.

Foreign Affairs

Progress with the implementation of the sub-regional *Peace, Security and Cooperation Framework Agreement* (PSCF) was mixed. The agreement, signed by 11 countries of the region in Addis Ababa (Ethiopia) in February 2013, addressed two main points: the non-involvement of neighbouring countries in the DRC's internal affairs and the reform of DRC institutions, notably the security and justice system and local administration. On 12 July, the National Oversight Mechanism, established in May 2013, developed more than 50 benchmarks and 300 indicators of progress to monitor the implementation of the commitments of the DRC government within the PSCF. However, apart from the approval of a national DDR plan and other minor developments, important aspects of the commitments as laid down in the agreement, such as decentralisation and sustainable security sector reform, remained unfulfilled. With regard to the commitments of the regional partners, the UN Secretary-General stated in his report of 24 September that, despite hints to the contrary, leaders in the region by and large adhered to the principles of non-interference and refrained from supporting armed groups within the DRC.

UNSC Resolution 2147 of 28 March extended the mandate of *MONUSCO* and the FIB to 31 March 2015. The focus of MONUSCO now turned towards the electoral process, which led to a souring of relations with the FARDC. However, the FIB continued to support the FARDC in their fight against armed groups in the troubled east of the DRC, albeit with less direct combat involvement. Shortly after the declared victory against the ADF, the FIB supported the FARDC in operations against the

'Alliance des Patriotes pour un Congo Libre et Souverain' with aerial attacks. The rebel group clashed with other Mai Mai groups in Masisi (North Kivu) in February. Up to the end of the year, MONUSCO repeatedly confirmed its readiness to engage in military action against the FDLR but made it clear that the FIB would only take action if explicitly mandated by the government. The FIB had been created in March 2013 with around 3,000 troops from South Africa, Tanzania and Malawi and tasked with neutralising armed groups in the DRC.

Relations with both the *ICGLR* and *SADC* revolved around the approach to rebels in the Kivus, most importantly the FDLR. Both *South Africa* and *Tanzania* – who were providing the bulk of troops to the FIB and had tense relations with Rwanda – supported the DRC's approach of voluntary disarmament and political negotiations between the FDLR and Rwanda. On 3 July, the second joint ICGLR-SADC ministerial meeting in Luanda (Angola) gave the FDLR a six-month ultimatum to disarm. In light of the lack of progress in disarmament, the ultimatum was reiterated in August and October. It was said that, in case of non-compliance, military action would follow in January 2015. *Rwanda* (together with Uganda and Kenya) was highly sceptical of this strategy, and pressured the government and the UN to take military action. The conflict over what approach to take towards the FDLR brought to the fore the fragility of the cohesion of multilateral organisations – which formed the basis of the Addis Ababa Framework Agreement signed in 2013. Throughout the year, Rwanda criticised Kabila for not doing enough against the FDLR, while the DRC opposition accused Kabila of having been too 'pro-Rwanda' in his stance against the M23 (and former Rwandan-backed rebel groups). At the 20 years genocide commemoration event in Kigali (Rwanda) on 7 April, President Kabila was persona non grata. On 11–12 June, the *DRC and Rwandan armies clashed at the border north of Goma* (North Kivu). Both sides reported fatalities and accused each other of initiating the battle. At year's end, the exact circumstances of the clashes remained unclear. The ICGLR Expanded Joint Verification Mission reported that they had found five dead DRC soldiers on Rwandan territory and that Rwanda had occupied parts of DRC territory prior to the incident. Rwanda's government strongly criticised the report, while the DRC government even claimed the dead soldiers had been taken alive to be murdered in Rwanda. New visa requirements for Rwandan citizens (see below) added to the already tense relation between the two countries.

Relations with *Angola* also soured after they had seemed to improve in 2013. The long-simmering row over their maritime border heated up when DRC Foreign Minister Raymond Tshibanda wrote a letter to the UN Secretary-General rejecting a map drafted by Angola in December 2013 to clarify rights to territorial waters. The UN Commission on the Limits of the Continental Shelf had to postpone any assessment of the map scheduled for July and September due to the ongoing dispute. At stake in the conflict between the two countries were large offshore oil fields.

Rumours of the presence of the *Burundian* army in South Kivu, as well as the arming of the Imbonerakure – the youth wing of Burundi's ruling 'Conseil National pour la Défense de la Démocratie – Forces de Défénse de la Démocratie' (CNDD-FDD) party – on DRC soil caused much debate in the east. In October, the UN Secretary-General's deputy special representative to the DRC, Abdallah Wafy, confirmed the presence of the Burundian army in Kiliba (South Kivu) in an interview with Radio France International. The government acknowledged that information exchange had taken place but denied any long-term presence of the Burundian army on its territory. On 30 December, around 200 unidentified armed fighters tried to cross the border from South Kivu into Burundi but immediately clashed with the Burundian army. The ensuing fighting lasted around five days and left about 100 rebels dead. Burundian rebels – mostly of the 'Forces Nationales de Libération' (FNL) – had been present in South Kivu since the 1990s and repeatedly formed alliances with other rebel groups, such as the FDLR. The December attacks, however, were probably not related to the FNL but to internal frictions in the CNDD-FDD and the Imbonerakure.

The conflict in the *CAR* continued to have its spill-over effects in the northern part of the DRC. CAR soldiers and defunct Séléka elements fleeing across the border into Orientale province created an atmosphere of insecurity. The number of refugees from the CAR increased, reaching an estimated 75,000 by the end of the year. Most refugees were stranded in Zongo (Equateur Province), which is situated directly across the border from the CAR capital, Bangui. From December 2013, the DRC had 850 soldiers and 150 police in the CAR as part of the international force 'Mission Internationale de Soutien à la Centrafrique' (MISCA). The deployment gave rise to some polemic within the DRC, as a part of civil society considered the intervention unimportant given the DRC's own problems with armed groups. The situation in the CAR and the DRC's on-going support for MISCA was the main topic at a meeting between Kabila and French President Hollande in Paris on 21 May.

Relations with the neighbouring *Republic of Congo* revolved around the mass deportations of DRC citizens across the Congo River from Brazzaville to Kinshasa. On 4 April, a large-scale operation against crime and illegal immigration started in Brazzaville and continued for several months. An estimated 400,000 DRC citizens, around 10% of the city's population, were said to be living in Brazzaville, many of whom, according to the Congo government were involved in crime and disturbing public order. The exact numbers of deportees remained unclear because, when the expulsions began, many DRC citizens crossed the border voluntarily in fear of being deported. In a press statement on 26 May, the UN spoke of 130,000 people and urged Brazzaville to stop the forced deportations. Kobler visited a transit camp close to Kinshasa and said he was shocked by the many accounts of human rights violations committed by the Congolese authorities during the deportations. Thousands of deportees were stranded in the national stadium in Kinshasa, lacking adequate provision of food, health care and sanitation. The deportations caused a veritable diplomatic crisis between the DRC and Congo.

On 4 May, *US* Secretary of State John Kerry visited Kinshasa – the first time a secretary of state had been in the country since 2009. Kerry acknowledged the progress made with regard to the demobilisation of armed groups in the east, but called on Kabila to respect the Constitution and leave office in 2016. He promised a $ 30 m grant earmarked for funding the elections. On 5 June, US Special Envoy to the Great Lakes Region Russ Feingold reiterated the negative US position on a potential third term.

The investigations against DRC rebels at the *ICC* made some progress during the year. On 10–14 February, a hearing took place to confirm the charges against Bosco Ntaganda. On 9 June, the pre-trial chamber of the ICC confirmed 13 charges against him of war crimes allegedly committed in Ituri between 2002 and 2003, and sent the case to trial, to start on 2 June 2015. The notorious rebel leader, who was key in founding the M23 in 2012 and had been wanted by the ICC since 2006, had surprisingly turned himself in to face charges in the Hague in late 2013. On 1 December, the ICC confirmed the 14-year prison sentence on Thomas Lubanga, who had been found guilty in 2012 of enlisting child soldiers in his rebel group 'Union des Patriotes Congolais'. Lubanga appealed after the verdict on grounds of breach of his right to fair process. On 23 May, Germain Katanga was sentenced to 12 years' imprisonment on one count of crimes against humanity and four counts of war crimes committed in 2003 in Ituri. On 13–14 November, the closing oral statements were read in the case against Jean-Pierre Bemba (a DRC war-lord and Kabila's fiercest opponent in the 2006 presidential elections, but tried for atrocities committed in the CAR in 2001). The verdict was pending.

Investigations into the FDLR leadership in exile continued throughout the year. On 5 December, a court in Düsseldorf (*Germany*) sentenced three individuals to four, three and two years in prison for participation in and support of a terrorist organisation (the FDLR). All three were German citizens of Rwandan origin and had been arrested in Germany in December 2012. According to the court, they had helped with propaganda after the arrest of former FDLR president Ignace Murwanashyaka and vice president Straton Musoni in 2009, whose trial for crimes against humanity and war crimes, begun in 2011 in Stuttgart, continued throughout the year.

Socioeconomic Developments

Macroeconomic development continued to show positive trends, with low consumer price inflation at 1.6% and a constantly high GDP growth rate of 8.5%, largely due to a continuous rise in mining outputs, especially copper. Tax revenues were projected to increase in the budget planning of 2014, but essentially fell owing to lack of control, resulting in an increased fiscal deficit. The year also saw a rise in foreign investor caution, given the unstable political environment and lack of transparency in economic decisions. The fact that the DRC did not have an economic programme with the IMF – after it was first temporarily suspended in 2012 and the suspension confirmed in 2013 – had a serious negative effect on the investment climate. In the World Bank's 'Ease of Doing Business' index, the DRC fell from 183rd in 2013 to the bottom place, at 189th.

The *humanitarian situation* remained extremely challenging throughout the year while external funds remained limited. Only around 35% of the humanitarian appeal for the year could be funded. After the military defeat of the M23, many *IDPs* in North Kivu voluntarily returned to their homes. However, continued fighting by other armed groups in the area caused new waves of IDPs. As of December, the UNHCR estimated the number of IDPs in North Kivu at 890,000. The total number of IDPs at the end of the year was estimated by UNHCR at 2.6 m. Displacement figures increased most rapidly in Katanga due to fighting between the FARDC and armed groups (including the Kata Katanga). Numbers of DRC *refugees* in other countries remained high, with an estimated 430,000 residing mainly in Uganda, Rwanda, Tanzania and Burundi. This was despite the repatriation of large numbers of refugees from Congo (120,000) and the CAR (20,000).

On 24 August, the government confirmed an *Ebola outbreak* in Equateur province. On 27 August, WHO spoke of 24 suspected cases of Ebola; 13 of the victims had died. By 9 August, the number of reported cases had risen to 64, including 35 deaths. The strain was said to be independent of the virus in West Africa and easily controllable due to the remoteness of the area and the experience of the DRC with small scale Ebola outbreaks in recent years.

On 25 June, the DRC tightened its *visa regime*. While citizens of the neighbouring countries of the Economic Community of the Great Lakes Countries (DRC, Burundi, Rwanda) had previously been able to travel with laissez-passer papers, the new requirements introduced relatively high visa fees for students, traders and workers. The changes seriously disturbed the very lively cross-border relations between the DRC and Rwanda, which are essential for the survival of small-scale businesses, and were met with criticism from affected people (students, traders), Rwandan border personnel and the UN special envoy to the Great Lakes Region. The move was largely interpreted as a reaction to the clashes between DRC and Rwandan forces earlier in June (see above). On 10 July, Rwanda hit back by making DRC citizens wait for hours at the new Rwandan immigration hall of the main Goma-Gisenyi border post. Although the DRC government later postponed the full enforcement of the visa regime, cross-border movement continued to be disturbed.

Transparency continued to be an issue in the *mining sector* – the most important driver of growth in the DRC, with cobalt and copper alone making up around 98% of exports and 44% of nominal GDP. On 2 July, the DRC became a full member of the Extractive Industries Transparency Initiative. The DRC's candidate status had been suspended for a year in April 2013 due to flaws in its 2010 report, which it had since addressed. On 20 January, the DRC launched its certification programme under the regional certification mechanism of the ICGLR's Regional Initiative on Natural Resources, intended to align due diligence in supply chains for cassiterite, wolframite, coltan and gold in the region. Later in the year, other international efforts to achieve greater transparency in the mining sector came under criticism. On 14 August, the cabinet director of DRC's mining minister, Joseph Ikoli Yombo Y'Apeke, criticised international legislation aimed at greater transparency in the mining sector, such as the US American Dodd Frank Act, for being a "de facto embargo" on mining exports. On 11 September, the renowned Goma-based Pole Institute research centre published an open letter signed by 70 DRC and international experts and academics criticising international legislation – in particular again the Dodd Frank Act – for misinterpreting the resource-conflict link and having disastrous effects on the local economy. The ongoing debate about a *revision of the mining code* continued throughout the year without tangible results. A statement by Prime Minister Ponyo in February that the government aimed to almost double tax revenues from minerals caused widespread criticism among mining companies.

On 26 July, the head of the state-run mining company Gécamine, Ahmed Kalej Nkand, was sacked for mismanagement. Gécamine had repeatedly come under criticism for dubious asset sales. The ousting occurred in the midst of a restructuring process that was supposed to increase *copper* production and required stable investments, and only two months after workers in the important Kolwezi mine in Katanga went on strike for a week over delays in salary payments. However, the dismissal seemed to be more a political account-settling than a move towards more transparency and good governance.

On 20 March, the World Bank agreed a $ 73 m grant to the DRC government to develop an expansion of the *Inga Dam* – highly controversial due to lack of transparency concerning the financing and the final share of benefits, as well as outstanding compensations for the relocation of whole villages. South Africa and Katanga-based mining companies had expressed particular interest in the project, hoping for an ease in power shortages.

In early June, the UK-based oil company Soco International announced that it would not drill for *oil* in Virunga National Park for the time being, although they remained ambiguous about future endeavours. The UNESCO World Heritage Site in eastern DRC is home to endangered mountain gorillas and UNESCO, conservationists and human rights groups had repeatedly warned of the ecological and human consequences – including armed conflict exacerbation – of oil drilling in the area.

Equatorial Guinea

Joseph N. Mangarella

Following a landslide victory in the legislative elections in 2013, President Obiang and his ruling PDGE maintained the regime's grip on internal affairs. In response to a growing chorus of criticism from exiled dissidents and the international community, increased foreign judicial scrutiny of the president's son, who was his second vice president, and falling revenues from the aging oilfields, the regime relied on its usual resource-backed brinksmanship. Lavish summits were staged, dissidents were threatened or jailed, journalists were silenced, and lip service was paid to democracy and diversification, while the regime pursued its gradual shift from an oil-driven to a gas-fueled export economy.

Domestic Politics

In January, a group of *12 diaspora associations and political parties* formed the 'Coalition d'Opposition pour la Restauration d'un État Démocratique' (CORED) and publicly called on President Teodoro Obiang Nguema Mbasogo to resign or take steps towards democratic reform. CORED, based in France and Germany, highlighted in a manifesto the political and human rights abuses that had taken place

 | DOI 10.1163/9789004305052_027

during 44 years of dictatorship, 35 of which had been under the sitting president. The 'Convergencia para la Democracia Social' (CPDS), the only legal domestic opposition party, which had two seats in the legislature, joined the pro-regime parties in inviting the repatriation of CORED members for a national political dialogue, while also deploring CORED's alleged aim of destabilising the nation. The CPDS, under the new leadership of Andres Esono Ondo, was regularly attacked by diaspora groups as a false opposition, thereby frustrating the development of a robust domestic front to the ruling 'Partido Democrático de Guinea Ecuatorial' (PDGE).

On 27 March, exiled dissidents attended an event organised by the World Council of Churches in Geneva (Switzerland), where representatives from various groups attempted to draw UN and international attention to the growing political crisis. The attendees' allegations of *patronage* were validated in April when Obiang appointed 50 more presidential advisors, bringing the number of senior members of government to over 350. On 27 June, CORED and NGOs such as EG Justice and HRW publicly repeated their demands for a democratic transition as the AU summit in Malabo concluded.

On 29 August, Obiang embarked on a series of conciliatory gestures to build a democratic image. Under moderate pressure from abroad, he announced a *national political dialogue* to discuss the country's socioeconomic and political shortcomings, which was to be held in November. The president uncharacteristically invited banned and exiled groups such as CORED and the 'Partido del Progreso de Guinea Ecuatorial' (PPGE), the self-declared government-in-exile led by Severo Moto in Madrid (Spain), both of which expressed *deep scepticism*. In his statement, the president required all parties, both foreign and domestic, to register as legal parties, a status denied to activist Avelino Mocache and his new formation less than a month later. Moreover, the convictions in absentia of exiled politicians for political crimes gave exiled opposition leaders further cause to avoid returning to Malabo. In February, as a result of international pressure, the teacher Agustín Esono Nsogo was released from the infamous Playa Negra prison; he had been detained without a warrant in October 2012, held incommunicado for a week, and subjected to torture. On 27 September, the dissident, Leoncio Abeso Meye, was tried in absentia, while five others were sentenced by military courts to between 15 and 27 years imprisonment without legal representation. According to AI and HRW, their associate, former army colonel Cipriano Nguema, had been in prison since December 2013 on charges of embezzlement and plotting a coup, and was thereafter tortured at the National Security Headquarters in Malabo.

On 21 October, Obiang signed *a decree granting amnesty* to persons convicted of or facing trial for political crimes, without indicating specific crimes or names. The unprecedented 'pardon' was only one of the preconditions laid down by opposition groups for their participation in the national dialogue. Others went unheeded, such as the PPGE's demand that an impartial mediator be appointed and the insistence by several parties that Obiang should resign before they would attend. The national dialogue, held from 7 to 16 November in the absence of the major diaspora groups, nevertheless appeared to grant *limited concessions to opposition parties*, including the abolition of a CFAfr 30 m registration fee for new parties and more access to state media by non-PDGE parties. The CPDS, however, withdrew from the dialogue on the first day, declaring it a one-sided "monologue" and citing the continued detention of political prisoners.

The regime's nominal concessions failed to divert attention from repressive measures taken to quell dissent. In summer, the Economist Intelligence Unit published its 2013 democracy index, which ranked Equatorial Guinea 161st out of 167 countries, confirming the government as one of the most authoritarian in the world. On 7 July, the UN General Assembly's Human Rights Council published its *2nd Cycle Universal Period Review of Equatorial Guinea*. The report made no less than 191 recommendations, including accession to the Statute of Rome and other conventions as well as measures to combat arbitrary detention and torture, increase fiscal and political transparency, strengthen the rule of law, remove the death penalty and enhance the freedom of the press. The repression of media rights remained a major concern, as in January two 'Financial Times' journalists were detained without formal charges and taken to the Ministry of National Security, where their equipment and records were confiscated.

Foreign Affairs

Facing international scrutiny for various abuses, the government sought to promote external legitimacy, while state visits were undertaken with the intention of attracting foreign investment. In March, the *French authorities* launched a formal investigation into alleged money-laundering and misuse of public funds by 'Teodorín' Nguema Obiang Mangue, President Obiang's son and second vice president. The 'biens mal acquis' case, first brought in 2009, both dampened Teodorín's prospects of succeeding his father and soured Franco-Equatoguinean relations. On 5 March, the highest court in France rejected the regime's appeal against judicial asset seizures ordered in 2012 in the absence of evidence that its high-value Parisian apartment blocks were used for diplomatic purposes. In mid-March, an absentee Teodorín finally made contact with the French authorities and had his arrest warrant lifted, but the ongoing investigations prompted a 21 March communiqué by the Equatoguinean government accusing France of seeking to destabilise the country. The French judicial authorities, undeterred, went further in May by investigating 'Société Générale de Banques en Guinée Equatoriale', the local subsidiary of 'Société Générale', on suspicion that it had aided and abetted Teodorín's transfer of funds to France. In addition, in early July a French court dismissed Teodorín's defamation action against the French weekly 'L'Express'. In a final blow to the second vice president's international and domestic image, Teodorín agreed in October to settle a case brought by the US *Department of Justice* in 2011 under the US Kleptocracy Asset Recovery Initiative for having used stolen wealth to acquire assets in the US. The settlement forced the liquidation and appropriation by charities of Teodorín's $ 30 m mansion in California, and his Ferrari and Michael Jackson memorabilia. Teodorín's troubles were compounded in June, when HRW obtained a damning medical report about Italian businessman Roberto Berardi, a former associate of the second vice president, who had apparently been detained since 2013 and mistreated for his sensitive knowledge of Teodorín's financial dealings.

A series of cosmetic gestures began in February with Equatorial Guinea's signed commitment to the AU's Africa Peer Review Mechanism, a name-and-shame initiative with limited influence. On 20–27 June, the country hosted the annual *AU summit in Malabo*, during which Obiang was commended by foreign dignitaries and organisations, such as UN Secretary-General Ban Ki-moon and FAO, for contributing $ 30 m to the African Solidarity Trust Fund. Spanish Prime Minister Rajoy attended the summit, becoming the first Spanish prime minister to visit the former colony since 1991. On 23 July, amidst protests by officials and activists in Portugal, Equatorial Guinea was *admitted to the CPLP*, which claims that it bans members with oppressive regimes. Repeatedly denied admission to the CPLP since 2006, the regime had obtained the critical diplomatic support of its oil-producing counterparts Angola and Brazil. In September, the government agreed for the second time to host the Africa Cup of Nations (in 2015), while in late November it welcomed leaders for the Africa-Turkey summit.

Other diplomatic events underscored the regime's desire to solicit FDI and conclude hydrocarbons sales. On 2 February, the regime opened a two-day 'investment summit' in Malabo. In August, Obiang travelled to Washington for the US-Africa Leaders Summit and participated in a forum to advertise investment opportunities in Equatorial Guinea, an *invitation-only event* co-sponsored by the Corporate Council on Africa and the prominent law firm Greenberg Traurig LLP. Notable bilateral trade talks were concluded between Obiang and representatives of several regional states throughout the year, e.g. Swaziland in January, Egypt in May, Rwanda in July, Côte d'Ivoire in October and South Africa in September. During September's UNESCO-Equatorial Guinea awards ceremony, which recognised research achievements in life sciences, Obiang and Kenya's President Kenyatta reportedly discussed building trade links.

Some regional engagements were driven by multilateral crisis management and Equatorial Guinea's own perceived security interests. In February, Equatorial Guinea joined CEEAC in pledging funds and mediators for the CAR crisis. Only weeks after drawing criticism in mid-August for refusing visitors from suspected Ebola-affected countries, Obiang donated $ 2 m to WHO to help combat the Ebola outbreak. In measures to protect its markets and border integrity, the government inaugurated a warship in June dedicated to *countering maritime piracy* in the Gulf of Guinea while enforcing its policy of regional immigrant deportation, particularly of those from Cameroon seeking work on oilfields.

Socioeconomic Developments

Real GDP contracted by estimates of 2.3%–2.5% (according to the Economist Intelligence Unit and the IMF, respectively), a relative improvement from negative real GDP growth of -4.8% in 2013. Steeper economic decline was moderated by an expansion in both natural gas output and the services sector (increasing its share of GDP by 6.0%), which partially offset *diminished crude oil production* estimated at 34.3% of GDP. Hydrocarbons sales made up 95% of all exports in goods, while total exports accounted for roughly 80% of GDP (in 2013). Even as the country's trade surplus reached $ 6.0 bn (nominal GDP was estimated at $ 14.6 bn), the current account balance was roughly -$ 2 bn, as over $ 5 bn left the country through income transfers and investment. While Equatorial Guinea again recorded the *highest per capita income* in Africa at an estimated $ 32,601 (PPP), reports suggested at least two-thirds of its 800,000 citizens were impoverished.

With oil production having fallen from 276,000 b/d in 2013 to 254,000 b/d, and oil receipts having comprised approximately 90% of government revenue, the regime continued its limited steps towards *mid-term diversification*, a stated goal under the 2007 National Economic Development Plan (Horizon 2020). During its international investment conference in early February, the government announced before roughly 250 companies that it would set aside $ 1 bn towards a three-year economic diversification fund, which was intended to support investment in non-hydrocarbon areas such as agriculture, fishing, mining, tourism, petrochemicals and financial services. Despite protests from international financial institutions, support would primarily come through public expenditure on infrastructure, and not human capital. In October, the regime announced plans to invest $ 2 bn to promote the manufacture of cables, transformers and aluminium in the mainland city of Mbini, but no details of the project were disclosed. Past experience meant that such projects were likely to stall in the planning stages for logistical reasons. Using local data collected through 2014, the World Bank in its 'Doing Business 2015' report found that connecting to the electricity grid took an average of 106 days and cost over 500% of income per capita.

The regime proved active in furthering hydrocarbons development, leaving no indication that it was willing to depart from its root source of political sustenance. Efforts continued to be made to promote the country's upstream and downstream oil and *liquified natural gas (LNG) sectors*, emphasising LNG as a gradual replacement for maturing oilfields. Substantial gas discoveries by the UK-based Ophir Energy on Block R drew Equatorial Guinea into talks with Côte d'Ivoire and Ghana in February to lay out plans for a joint operation, formed in May, which would lead to Equatorial Guinea exporting LNG. Sonagas, the gas parastatal, was frustrated in plans to sell LNG in July, when unfavourable prices fixed by contract led the Japanese Mitsui to sell its 6.5% share in the LNG plant at Punta Europa. Mitsui's decision also highlighted the country's difficulties in obtaining feed-gas to supply its plant, a factor which further promised to stall plans for a second LNG 'train', a plant's facility for liquefying and purifying dry gas. In August, the government signed gas sales agreements with hydrocarbons operators including US-based Noble Energy and Nigeria-based Atlas petroleum in Blocks I and O, which included the newer Aseng and Alen oilfields. Part of the government's efforts to boost downstream operations, the gas was to service a planned petrochemical complex at Riaba on Bioko Island. Thus in September, Equatoguinean officials celebrated Ophir Energy's discovery of recoverable gas reserves on Block R, bringing the block's total to 3.4 trillion ft^3 and ranking it among the biggest on the continent.

Oil initiatives fared worse as *efforts to offset declining production* in older fields such as Zafiro met with little success. In January, the government entered into talks with officials in Côte d'Ivoire to purchase a 20% stake in SIR, the Ivorian refining company, in an attempt to diversify GEPetrol's parastatal operations, while later in the month Energy Minister Gabriel Obiang Lima offered to jointly explore São Tomé's bordering exclusive economic zone. The closure of a new licensing round for 15 blocks, originally announced for September by the Ministry of Mines, was delayed several times for apparent lack of interest by major companies. While the outcome of the licensing round tempered hopes of new oil discoveries, Africa Energy Intelligence reported Ophira Energy as having expressed interest in acquiring new fields for its ongoing development of the country's LNG sector.

Public expenditure fell by 15.2% of GDP from 2013, in line with the drop in oil revenues. Although this may have helped preserve the country's solvency – external debt fell slightly to $ 1.4 bn (13% of GDP) – low social spending, corruption and high-profile prestige projects could not have improved Equatorial Guinea's *abysmal human development record*, which had been one of the poorest among high-income, non-OECD countries, according to sources such as the HDI and UNICEF's statistics on childhood malnutrition. On 5 May, WHO alerted governments to the spread of polio, citing Equatorial Guinea's exposure and inadequate vaccination.

Several projects granted to the China Road and Bridge Corps (CRBC) by President Obiang were completed during the year, including a road and port extension servicing the new PDGE headquarters, itself nearly completed by CRBC in October. Along with misappropriation of public funds within those projects, failures to address social needs were partly credited to *endemic corruption*. In April, one internal investigation by Monaco-based Single Buoy Moorings, a partner to GEPetrol in developing the Aseng field, revealed that the company had paid Equatoguinean officials $ 18.8 m in bribes between 2007 and 2011.

Gabon

Douglas A. Yates

A cabinet reshuffle in January reflected President Bongo's commitment to maintaining his economic policies. But the summer oil-price collapse clearly threatened his ambitious 'Gabon Emergent' programme, and triggered anti-regime protests, violently repressed, which foreshadowed a coming fiscal crisis. Efforts to offset falling crude oil revenues included a major new manganese deal with India.

Domestic Politics

On 24 January, a *cabinet reshuffle* started the government calendar. *Daniel Ona Ondo* was named prime minister by President Ali Bongo, replacing Raymond Ndong Sima. Ondo, a former minister of both education and culture, before becoming the first deputy speaker of the parliament, had legislative experience useful in implementing Ali Bongo's 'Gabon Emergent' public-spending programme (i.e. moving Gabon into the 'emerging countries' category). Both Sima and Ondo came from the country's largest ethnic group, the Fang, and both were loyalists within the ruling party.

 | DOI 10.1163/9789004305052_028

But Ondo's appointment was also influenced by a longstanding unwritten tradition. The president's father, Omar Bongo was a Téké, a minority ethnic group. In order to legitimise his rule, he had long made it his practice to appoint as prime minister a Fang from the Estuary region. His son Ali had followed this tradition to some extent, but had deliberately chosen his two prime ministers – first Sima and now Ondo – from the Fang of the Woleu N'Tem region. This move could be seen as part of the president's long-term strategy to undermine his strongest and most vocal opponents, among them his father's former prime ministers, such as presidential contenders Andre Mba Obame and Jean Eyeghe Ndong, who came from the long-influential Fang of the Estuary region.

On 19 February, *Jean Ping*, long-term foreign minister under the late Omar Bongo, one of the best-known Gabonese politicians and former chairman of the AU Commission, submitted in writing his resignation from the ruling 'Parti Démocratique Gabonais' and *joined the opposition*. With his international connections and domestic celebrity, gained from his long service to the elder Bongo, Ping quickly became the most serious potential challenger to Ali Bongo. Before 2014, Ping had avoided making any political public declarations, but now he stated, "I have decided to break that silence, and make it clear that I have nothing, absolutely nothing to do with the powers that be."

The opposition press continued to be censored and intimidated. On 2 September, two private newspapers, 'La Loupe' and 'L'Aube', were pirated, with counterfeit printed editions distributed in the kiosks. Their front pages contained editorials praising the Bongo government, although both periodicals were strident critics of the regime. Subsequently, the editors of 'L'Aube' accused the president's men of having mounted this pirating operation, pointing their finger at the influential Maixent Accrombessi, Bongo's chief of staff. On 19 December, investigative journalist Jonas Moulenda was arrested, detained and questioned after publishing an article in 'Echos du Nord', one of the best-known newspapers close to opposition parties, about ritual murders in the country that had gone unpunished. His article was highly critical of the Bongo regime, the defence forces and the police. The National Communication Council suspended publication of the newspaper's letters-to-the-editor – just one example of press censorship and intimidation.

On 10 November, the Gabonese government filed a complaint against French investigative journalist *Pierre Péan* after the publication of his book entitled '*Nouvelles Affaires Africaines*' declared that the president of Gabon, Ali Bongo, was not the natural child of former president Omar Bongo but an adopted Biafran orphan from Nigeria. The book claimed that Ali had produced a fake birth certificate in 2009 when he filed his candidacy for the presidential elections, giving his name as 'Ali Bongo Ondimba', although it is well known that he did not use the first name 'Ali' until his conversion to Islam in 1973 and, like his father, only added the patronymic 'Ondimba' around the turn of the century. The president appeared on

French television news station France24 three months later and denied these scandalous accusations. But the damage to his hereditary legitimacy was done.

On 20 December, several hundred opponents gathered in the streets of Libreville to *protest against the regime*, chanting "Ali, get out! 50 years is too long!" Jean Ping was among them. Despite having served Bongo's father for decades, and having been married to the president's sister Pascaline for many years (thus being Ali's ex-brother-in-law), Ping styled himself as the president's main challenger. This protest was illegal, and had been forbidden by the Interior Ministry, so the forces of order were called onto the streets. Special units of the gendarmerie and police used their weapons to quell the protestors, reportedly resulting in three deaths. (The government claimed one.) Around 100 people, including ten foreigners, were arrested. Both Ping and Eyeghe Ndong were tear-gassed. This was the largest protest in the country since 2011, when the opposition candidate Mba Obame had rallied his supporters in a failed attempt at an 'African Spring'.

Foreign Affairs

The conduct of foreign relations was reduced to a series of personal trips by the president with his entourage. Foreign Minister Franck Emmanuel Issoze-Ngondet remained in post under the new Ondo government. He had previously served as Gabon's permanent representative to the UN – and ex-officio president of the UNSC in 2010 – but neither he nor his president, both in their early fifties, had been able to acquire the international influence wielded by their predecessors. Gabon was increasingly overshadowed by Denis Sassou Nguesso's *Congo* as the most active diplomatic player in Central Africa.

On 3 January, President Bongo received French Defence Minister Jean-Yves Le Drian at the presidential palace in Libreville in an effort to coordinate responses to the *conflict in the CAR*. Le Drian recognised the country's contribution of some 500 troops to the French-backed peacekeeping operation 'Mission Internationale de Soutien à la Centrafrique sous Conduite Africaine' (MISCA) and called Gabon one of the countries essential for resolving the conflict. On 10 January, as ex officio president of CEMAC, Bongo was involved in negotiations to install the Samba Panza government in Bangui at the 6th extraordinary ECCAS summit of heads of state and government held in Chad. In the end, however, it was Congolese President Sassou-Nguesso, and not Bongo, who mediated the ceasefire talks between the rebels and the defence forces in June.

In another effort at high-level personal diplomacy, Bongo represented Gabon at the *3rd Nuclear Security Summit*, held in The Hague, The Netherlands, on 24–25 March, attended by 53 heads of state including US President Barack Obama, to work on solutions to the problem of the spread of nuclear weapons technology and material to terrorists. From 2011 to 2012 Gabon had held a UNSC seat and helped push through two of Obama's most difficult UN votes: sanctions against Iran's nuclear programme and support for the removal of Moammar Khadhafi. Bongo actively allied himself with the USA on the containment of Iranian nuclear weapons-making capacity as part of his larger diplomatic effort to move his dependency away from France.

On 23–25 May, 1,500 foreign businessmen attended the 3rd *New York Forum Africa*, hosted in Libreville, a showcase for Bongo and his wife Sylvia, which involved extraordinary expenditure. Four major new projects were signed at this summit. French Foreign Minister Laurent Fabius signed an infrastructural investment deal designed to protect houses in Libreville from flooding. The Korean firm Samsung signed a deal to renovate the Mandji oil refinery of Port-Gentil. The AfDB based in Tunis agreed to create an incubator for small businesses. A Moroccan businessman agreed to create a Microsoft IT Academy in Gabon.

On 3 August, President Bongo and First Lady Sylvia Bongo travelled to Washington DC to participate in the *USA-Africa Leaders Summit*. Invitations were extended to all African leaders 'in good standing' with the US and the AU. Although Bongo had met personally with Obama at the White House in 2012, his request for a personal meeting was denied this time. Despite having a continued interest in Gabon's oil sector, the White House appeared to be keeping a guarded distance from Bongo himself because of a Justice Department investigation into alleged corruption and illegal money laundering by the Bongo family. The investigation was stepped up in the first half of 2014 with a probe into assets linked to Bongo and his chief of staff Maixent Accrombessi, initiated after one of Bongo's former hairdressers was found to be carrying $ 150,000 in a suitcase through Los Angeles International Airport in 2013, but could not explain where it came from.

Bongo announced at the World Parks Congress, a decennial meeting of environmental scientists and government decision-makers held in Sydney (Australia) on 12–19 November, that he had decided to create a network of marine parks where no commercial fishing would be permitted. Following recommendations from marine biologists seeking to maintain *biodiversity*, Gabon's marine park boundaries would increase from 1% to 23% of the protected ocean territory. The rest of the exclusive economic zone, the president explained, would be divided into community and commercial fishing areas and petrol exclusion areas, where industrial fishing would not be permitted. Gabon had been trying to eliminate illegal fishing in its territorial waters for some time. Lack of naval forces had reduced the country to accepting patrol boats and training from foreign coast guards, leaving it open to expanding piracy in the Gulf of Guinea coming from as far away as the Niger Delta.

Socioeconomic Developments

World *oil prices* started to plummet in mid-June and fell from $ 100 to under $ 50 per barrel, provoking the above-mentioned political crisis. On 15 October, the government, ignoring the price collapse, issued a communiqué announcing that the budget for 2014 would increase by 5.8% over the previous year. Bongo had staked his re-election on the ambitious 'Gabon Emergent' plan. Spending priorities in 2014 included the national infrastructure master plan with continuation of the work being undertaken on the Lalala-Port Môle-Libreville axis being given special emphasis. Other priorities included an increase in teaching facilities, digital infrastructure and modernisation of prisons, barracks, police stations, hospitals, courts and provincial airports. The communiqué insisted that increased fiscal spending would be paid for from increased mining revenues, particularly in the manganese sector.

Early in the year, the oil sector had already made headlines. On 22 January, after signing a ten-year production sharing agreement with Gabon Oil Company (GOC), the Chinese oil firm Addax (Sinopec) agreed to pay $ 400 m in back taxes to the Gabon fiscal authorities. The government had withdrawn Addax's licence because of non-compliance with the terms of its contract concerning the payment of customs and duties. But after detaining its employees at Obangué for six months under the aegis of the GOC, the government eventually agreed to sign a new production-sharing contract with the Chinese oil firm.

In February, the cabinet presented a bill for a *new oil code*, a text that had been awaited for three years, which set the rules for customs and taxes as well as for changes in exploration and production activities and transport of oil products. It was meant to replace the old 1962 oil law, which was inspired by the French mining code, and numerous revisions already made to it in 1983. But since the new code, published in the Official Gazette on 25 April, was not validated by the National Assembly deputies before the end of the ordinary session on 30 June, it became null and void (all texts published in the Official Gazette must be approved by the legislature during the current ordinary session or they lose their juridical value).

For this reason, the new code had to be discussed again, from 1 to 15 July, and substantial modifications were made to the draft already published. A special commission was piloted by the 'Direction Générale des Hydrocarbures' within the Ministry of Mines, Petroleum and Hydrocarbons, but directed by presidential advisor Michel Alilat Antseleve Oyima. The Ministry had wanted to get the final version in order after having published a document different from that released in the presidential ordinance of 19 February. Oil Minister Etienne Ngoubou had to clarify the textual morass regulating the oil sector. This was how, after several years of discussions, the two different versions of the code were now followed by a third government version, substantially different from the other two.

The government's final version, published in the Official Gazette on 8 September, was much more demanding of the oil companies, as it said the *state would take a 20% share* in all the Gabonese affiliates of foreign oil companies. Adding this 20% participation that all partners in a bloc had to grant to the state to the 15% reserved for the GOC meant that Libreville would control up to 35% of new permits. The text also set new taxes, notably for the environment and for the national parks, to be imposed on all companies, not only those that operated in ecologically sensitive sites. It also foresaw that the state's share of production would be 55% (instead of the 50% currently taken) for the shallow-water offshore fields, and 45% (instead of 40%) for deep-water offshore concessions. Seven foreign oil companies were in the exploration-and-production phase. In January, Perenco took over Marathon's oil activities, making it the most productive leasing company (at 60,000 b/d) followed by Total Gabon (56,900 b/d), Shell Gabon (44,000 b/d), Maurel and Prom (20,000 b/d), Vaalco Gabon (11,000 b/d) and Addax Petroleum Gabon (9,000 b/d).

Gabon was the world's third-largest producer of *manganese* ore in 2014, behind South Africa and Australia. The Moanda mine, exploited by Comilog (owned by Eramet) contains reserves estimated at more than 150 m tons. Comilog was the second-largest company in Gabon, and operated the country's only railway, the Transgabonais. A new actor, Gabon Manganese and Ferro Alloy (GMFA) emerged in June with the signature of an 85/15% joint venture between India's Navodaya Trading and Gabon's new state company, 'Société Equatoriale des Mines'. The Indian company thereby acquired concessions that had previously been granted to Brazil's Vale by Bongo's father, the late Omar Bongo, in 2005. While the deposit at Okondja in eastern Haut-Ogooué was modest compared with the Comilog reserves, GMFA's plans to construct a processing plant that would expand local industrial capacity were in line with the president's resource nationalisation strategy.

A presidential spokesman announced in late January that the state had acquired the whole capital of the Chinese 'Compagnie des Mines de Belinga' (Comibel), which had been established in the final years of the Omar Bongo era to exploit the *iron reserves of Belinga* in the north-east quarter of the country. For over a decade, the Belinga iron project had been heralded as the most important foreign investment project in the country, and Omar Bongo had often said that he estimated it would help to replace the declining oil sector. Comibel was also a symbol of the major Chinese entry into Gabon, and the promise of freedom from the conditionality imposed by international financial institutions for better governance and transparency in the extractive industries sector.

But Ali Bongo instructed his government to completely rewrite the production convention his father had signed with Comibel (75% owned by the Chinese Machinery Engineering Corporation, CMEC). It was agreed through an amicable settlement that CMEC would be compensated for some $ 33.9 m expenditure it had undertaken over the past decade on geological studies at Belinga, one of the world's largest untapped iron ore mines. China had promised major infrastructural projects, and that its steel companies would purchase all of the iron ore mined, but negotiations became bogged down over environmental concerns, and then declining steel production in the wake of the world financial crisis. The break-down of the Belinga contracts revealed that *disenchantment* may have set in concerning China.

São Tomé and Príncipe

Gerhard Seibert

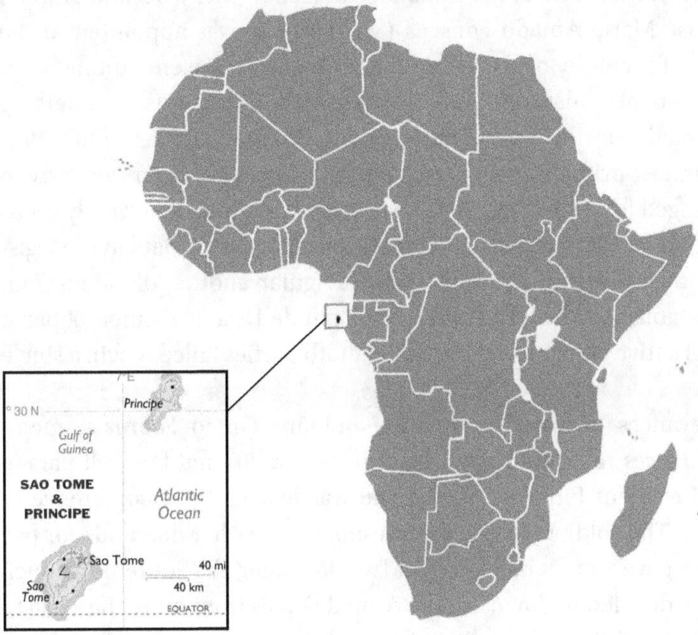

In June, Taiwan formally expressed concern when President Pinto da Costa paid a private visit to China in search of private investments for his country. In October, Patrice Trovoada returned to power with an absolute majority in parliament when his 'Acção Democrática Independente' (ADI) won a surprising landslide victory in the legislative elections. One of Trovoada's first decisions was to cancel an agreement on a huge urbanisation scheme signed with a Chinese company by the previous government.

Domestic Politics

At the beginning of the year, Prime Minister Gabriel Costa was forced to *reshuffle his cabinet* in response to scandals. On 2 January, Health Minister Leonel Pontes (of the 'Movimento Democrático Força de Mudança', MDFM) resigned following revelations that he had paid illegal subsidies to his wife and a brother living in Angola. On 20 January, Osvaldo Abreu ('Movimento de Libertação de São Tomé e Príncipe',

 | DOI 10.1163/9789004305052_029

MLSTP/PSD), the minister of public works, infrastructure and natural resources, was dismissed when it became known that he was one of the five shareholders in a private investment company established in November 2013. On the same day, Maria Tomé (MDFM) replaced Pontes as minister of health, Fernando Maquengo (MLSTP/PSD), hitherto executive-director of the National Oil Agency (ANP), became Abreu's successor, while José Maria Amado Fonseca (MLSTP/PSD) was appointed to the newly-created post of secretary of state for infrastructure and the environment.

Following a period of consecutive quarrels with the MLSTP/PSD leadership headed by Jorge Amado, during a party meeting on 24 January, Rafael Branco, former party leader and ex-prime minister, *declared his withdrawal* from the party to which he had belonged for more than 30 years. On 23 April, Branco formally registered his own 'Partido de Estabilidade e Progresso Social' to participate in the legislative elections. At the same time, António Quintas Aguiar, another dissident from the MLSTP/PSD, established the 'Plataforma Nacional de Desenvolvimento' party. However, in the legislative elections on 12 October both parties failed to win a single seat in parliament.

Substantial grievances persisted within the military. On 10 February, members of *the Armed Forces* refused to participate in the traditional farewell parade at the airport for President Pinto da Costa, who was leaving for a conference in Brazzaville (Congo). The soldiers hoped for a response to earlier demands for pay increases, which the government had ignored. Two days later, the Supreme Council of National Defence decided to downsize the Armed Forces from more than 800 to 600 men and condemned the indiscipline of the soldiers involved, but recognised the legitimacy of the military's demands. As a result of this affair, Chief of Staff of the Armed Forces Brigadier Felisberto Maria Segundo resigned on 13 February. He was replaced by Brigadier Justino Lima, who took office on 18 February.

At the suggestion of President Pinto da Costa, a *National Dialogue* took place in São Tomé on 24–29 March to discuss crucial national questions. The various sessions were attended by ordinary citizens and representatives of civil society groups and all political parties, except the opposition ADI, whose leadership considered the forum unconstitutional. The forum approved a series of non-binding recommendations, including the re-establishment of voting rights for citizens from other Portuguese-speaking African countries resident in São Tomé, the strengthening of democracy, fighting vote-buying and corruption, the limitation of political mandates, improvement of the functioning of the judiciary, and revision of the country's current administrative division.

On 15 June, from his voluntary exile in Portugal, Patrice Trovoada (who had been prime minister in 2010–12) lodged a criminal complaint at the *ICC* in The Hague against President Pinto da Costa, Prime Minister Costa, President of the National Assembly Alcino Pinto, Defence Minister Óscar Sousa and Police Chief Roldão Boa Morte, alleging persecution of political opponents. In São Tomé, Trovoada's unusual action was interpreted as a reaction to criminal investigations related to his supposed implication in the laundering of € 600,000 when he was prime minister. In fact, São Tomé's public prosecutor called Trovoada to appear for interrogation on 17 July. Instead of Trovoada, who remained in Portugal, his lawyer Agostinho Fernandes attended, but he was not received by the public prosecutor.

A total of 12 parties participated in the legislative elections on 12 October, while the 'União de Mudança e do Progresso do Príncipe' (UMPP) competed only in Príncipe's regional elections. For the first time, *legislative and local elections* were held simultaneously. After almost two years of voluntary exile in Portugal, Trovoada returned to São Tomé only on 3 October, after the beginning of the two-week election campaign. He had invited four Portuguese parliamentarians to accompany him, allegedly to discourage any possible action against him by the judicial authorities. However, such concerns proved to be unfounded. Unexpectedly Trovoada's ADI won an absolute majority in parliament by increasing its seats from 26 to 33. The MLSTP/PSD was reduced from 21 to 16 seats, while the 'Partido de Convergência Democrática' (PCD) lost two of its seven seats. The MDFM of former president Menezes lost its single seat to the 'União para a Democracia e Desenvolvimento', the party of Prime Minister Costa. The announced turn-out was lower than expected, but still respectable at 74.4% of the 92,790 registered voters. Trovoada apparently benefitted from both the failures of his adversaries and his long absence abroad, which allowed him to return as national saviour. This was the third time that Trovoada had become prime minister, the first two occasions being in 2008 and 2012, and his ADI was the third party to gain an absolute majority of seats in parliament. Unlike the PCD in 1991 and the MLSTP/PSD in 1998, the ADI may become the first ruling party to serve a full term, since the constitutional revision of 2003 meant that the president could no longer easily dismiss the government. In the local elections, the ADI won all six districts in São Tomé Island except Caué, where the MLSTP/PSD remained in power. The UMPP won the regional elections in Príncipe for the third time in a row. After the newly elected national deputies were inaugurated on 22 November, José Diogo (ADI) was elected president of the National Assembly. On 29 November, President Pinto da Costa swore in the members of Trovoada's new government. Nine of the 13 ministers had participated in Trovoada's previous executive, which was dismissed in November 2012.

Foreign Affairs

The evolution of bilateral relations with Taiwan and Angola dominated diplomatic activity. On 24 January, *Taiwan's President Ma Ying-jeou*, accompanied by a delegation of more than 100, arrived for a 24-hour visit to São Tomé. During the official banquet for Ma Ying-jeou, President Pinto da Costa expressed thanks for Taiwan's generous development assistance, praised his country's geo-strategic potential for Taiwanese private investments and accepted Ma's invitation to visit Taipei. In turn, Ma promised to increase his country's development assistance and private investments in the two-island republic, one of three African countries that continued to maintain bilateral ties with Taiwan. Ma's visit silenced speculation that São Tomé might re-establish full diplomatic relations with China, which had been broken off in 1997. On 8 April, Taiwan's Ambassador Jack Chen and Foreign Minister Natália Umbelina signed a $ 15 m annual aid agreement that focused on the agriculture, health and tourism sectors.

On 6 June, Pinto da Costa left for a *private visit to China*, the first by a Sãotomean president, since the country established diplomatic ties with Taiwan in 1997. Despite Pinto da Costa's claims that his visit was in search of private Chinese investments for his country's planned deep-sea harbour, the Taiwanese Foreign Ministry formally expressed serious concerns about the presidential visit to China. In response, Pinto da Costa promised Ma Ying-jeou in a letter that his visit would not jeopardise relations with Taiwan, since it was strictly private with the sole objective of seeking Chinese investments. Besides, in mid-June, Pinto da Costa sent the head of his presidential office, Amaro Couto, on a four-day visit to brief the Taiwanese on his China trip, and he was received in Taipei by his Taiwanese counterpart, Timothy Yang, and Foreign Minister David Lin.

On 18 February, Prime Minister Gabriel Costa left for a one-day visit to Luanda (Angola), where he was received by President Eduardo dos Santos. Costa discussed details of the disbursement of the first tranche of the three-year loan of $ 180 m promised by *Angola*. Diplomatic activities between the two countries were strengthened. On 10 March, a delegation of the parliamentary group of the MLSTP/PSD arrived in Luanda for a three-day visit to sign a cooperation agreement with the parliamentary group of the ruling 'Movimento Popular de Libertação de Angola' (MPLA). On 25 May, an MPLA delegation arrived in São Tomé for a three-day return visit to hold talks with MLSTP/PSD leader Jorge Amado, the president of the National Assembly, Alcino Pinto, and the parliamentary group of the MLSTP/PSD headed by José Viegas. In addition, the MPLA delegation had courtesy meetings with President Pinto da Costa and Prime Minister Costa. On 1 July, Fernando Dias da Piedade dos Santos, president of Angola's National Assembly, with a delegation of five deputies, paid a three-day visit to São Tomé. Piedade dos Santos signed a cooperation agreement between the two parliaments, held meetings with the parliamentary leaders of the MLSTP/PSD, ADI, and PCD, and met with members of the resident Angolan community in São Tomé.

On 20 March, the London-based Chatham House held an international conference on *maritime security in the Gulf of Guinea region* in São Tomé. On this occasion, the British destroyer HMS Portland anchored in São Tomé to train members of the local coast guard. It was the first visit by the British navy in São Tomé since 1985. On 9 April, the Portuguese frigate Bartolomeu Dias commenced a two-day exercise in São Tomé, including the on-board training of the local coast guard and surveillance operations in the country's territorial waters. On the same day, the Brazilian navy vessel Oceânico APA paid a three-day visit to São Tomé to supply weapons, ammunition, computer equipment and uniforms destined for the coast guard's first unit of marines, who were to be trained in São Tomé by ten Brazilian marines over the course of one year. Subsequently, the three navies participated in the fourth Obangame Express annual maritime surveillance exercise in the Gulf of Guinea region, which commenced on 16 April. On 30 June, the Brazilian navy donated to São Tomé's coast guard one LAPE 10 motor launch, the Águia, and two more boats to strengthen its surveillance capacity in the archipelago's territorial waters.

Prime Minister Costa travelled twice to the USA. On 4–6 August, he participated in the *US African Leaders Summit* in Washington DC, the first such meeting to be held by the US administration. The summit, which was attended by 50 African heads of state, focussed on trade and investment and stressed the US commitment to the continent's security. On 29 September, Costa addressed the 69th UN General Assembly in New York, when he stressed the importance of Brazilian cooperation with regard to maritime security and vocational training and emphasised the support received from Portugal, the EU and the UN in the organisation of the elections.

Socioeconomic Developments

On 9 January, the National Oil Agency (ANP) invited oil companies to submit bids for blocks 1 and 6 in the archipelago's Exclusive Economic Zone (EEZ) after Blue Skies World Group, a private US holding company, and London Global Energy had shown interest in the two blocks. By the 30 January deadline, only two other oil companies, Petróleos de Portugal (Petrogal) and the Jersey-based New World Oil and Gas, had declared their interest in participating in the auction. The *restricted bidding round* was launched on 10 March and closed on 20 June. However, the ANP had not announced any results by year's end. In late June, ERHC Energy and the ANP had concluded the final terms of a production sharing contract (PSC) for EEZ Block 11, which, together with Block 4 had already been awarded signature-bonus free, in February 2010, as part of ERHC's preferential rights shortly before the first EEZ licensing round.

On 14 January, the majority of deputies of the ruling parties, the MLSTP/PSD, PCD and MDFM, approved the *2014 annual budget* of $ 159 m. against the votes of the 26 deputies of the opposition ADI. Levy Nazaré, ADI secretary-general and deputy, explained that his party did not trust the budget submitted by the Costa government, alleging that various social projects had only been included in response to demands by members of parliament of the three governing parties. The scheduled budget privileged expenditure in the social sectors and the country's infrastructure.

Approximately 90% of the budget depended on external financing, mostly from non-Western countries.

On 20 March, the Nigerian press reported that, during a hearing at the House of Representatives Committee on Cooperation and Integration in Africa, Foreign Minister Nuruddeen Mohamed had described the *Joint Development Zone* (JDZ) with São Tomé and Príncipe as a loss-making venture, since oil production had never got off the ground, and the chairman of the Committee, Abukar Momoh, had declared that Nigeria could not continue to finance a joint-venture that was of no economic benefit. He said that Nigeria would, in consequence, revoke the treaty signed with São Tomé in 2001. Obviously prompted by the Nigerian threats, on 27 March, the executive directors of the Joint Development Authority in Abuja (Nigeria), Luís dos Prazeres and Kashim Tumsah, claimed that, thanks to the use of innovative drilling techniques, oil production in JDZ block 1 could probably start within 18 months.

On 22 May, President Pinto da Costa inaugurated a *vocational training centre* conceived by Brazil's National Service for Industrial Training (SENAI) and financed by the Brazilian Cooperation Agency (ABC) to the tune of $ 4 m in the Quinta de Santo António neighbourhood. The centre, which had been constructed and fully equipped between January 2012 and March 2013 with a capacity to receive 800 students per day and to train 3,200 students per year, would provide professional training in construction, car and motorbike mechanics, blacksmithing, welding, food processing, electrical engineering and information technology.

On 5 August, President Pinto da Costa laid the foundation stone of a *housing project* located in the town park of Trindade, Mé-Zochi district. The project, financed by the Angolan company PROCONGEC, included 52 housing units, a commercial area for 16 shops, playing fields and leisure spaces. The 18 local shop owners who had to leave the park after running their businesses there for 40 years contested the amount of compensation proposed by the local municipality, since it would not cover their financial losses.

On 1 October, the Costa government and the Chinese company Guangxi Hydroelectric Construction Bureau signed an agreement for the construction of a 211 ha-large *urbanisation project* called Gongá Expo involving investments of $ 300 m and located between São Tomé town and Roça Bela Vista. On the same day, Fernando Maquengo (MLSTP/PSD), the minister of public works and natural resources, laid the foundation stone of the project, whose construction was expected to last for 58 months. However, in early December, shortly after assuming office, Prime Minister Trovoada publicly announced the cancellation of the huge project, arguing that his government would prefer to give priority of improving infrastructure in the existing capital city.

PART 5

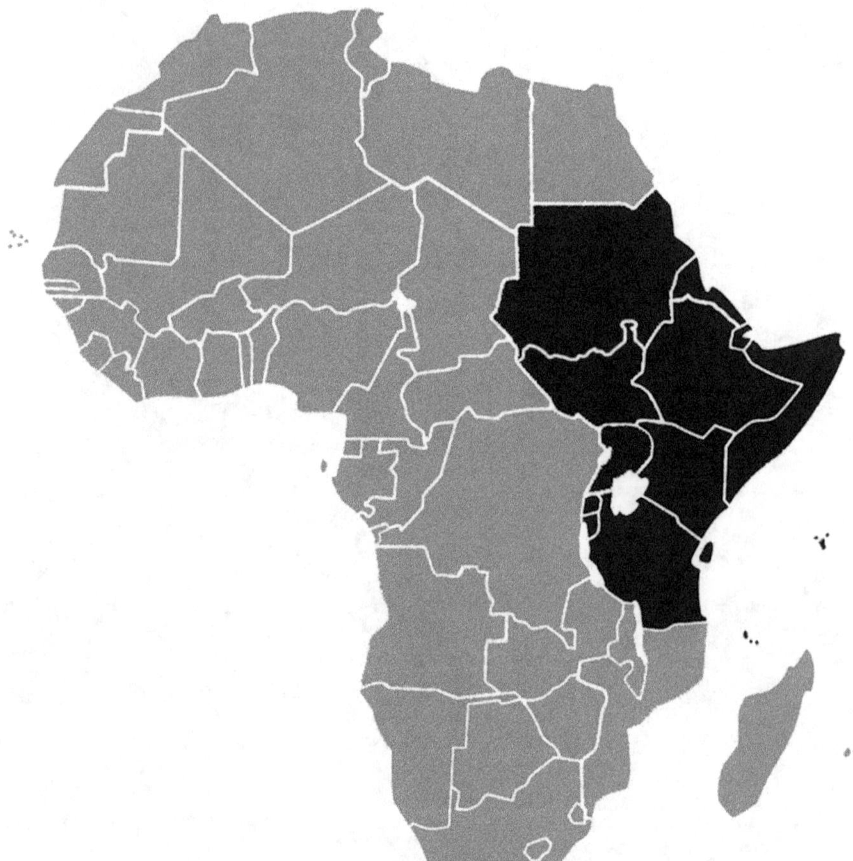

Eastern Africa

Rolf Hofmeier

Throughout the year, most international attention on the Eastern Africa sub-region was centred on the civil war in South Sudan, a continuation of low-key conflicts in various parts of Sudan and the persistent fears of Islamist terrorist attacks in the wider Horn of Africa region, while the threat of Somali piracy activities in the Indian Ocean had all but disappeared and faded to a haunting memory of the recent past. Regional mediation efforts to resolve the vicious conflict in South Sudan proved futile, with no lasting peace agreement in sight. The Somali federal government in Mogadishu made little further progress with the consolidation of its authority, while the Islamist terror groups were by no means defeated and were able to carry out surprise attacks. In all other countries of the sub-region, it was, by and large, a fairly 'normal' year, almost without major upheavals or unexpected developments. The sub-region was also spared of any extraordinary natural calamities.

The year saw practically no changes in the prevailing political situation in the sub-region. No national elections were held, but a number of countries were already gearing up for important elections in 2015 or 2016, thereby markedly raising the temperature of political debates. Scheduled elections in Comoros were postponed to early 2015. At the very end of the year, an unexpected reconciliation agreement between the authoritarian regime and the opposition in Djibouti raised hopes for a new opening of political space. According to Freedom House assessments, the sub-region still encompassed four of the globally worst-rated political regimes: Eritrea, Somalia, Sudan and South Sudan.

The sub-region's macroeconomic performance was again quite mixed and, by and large, relatively satisfactory. The majority of countries achieved about the same or slightly higher GDP growth rates than in 2013; only Seychelles and South Sudan experienced a marked deceleration of economic growth. By far the best economic performer was once again Ethiopia with around 10% growth, followed by Tanzania with 7%. Most other countries only achieved relatively modest growth rates of 3%–6%, with Eritrea trailing with less than 2%. The majority of countries succeeded in containing inflation rates at acceptable levels of less than 7%; only South Sudan and Eritrea were struggling with exceptionally high inflation rates.

No formal institutional changes occurred with respect to the various sub-regional organisations. South Sudan's and Somalia's applications for membership of the EAC were again deferred. The sharp tensions that had emerged between two camps of EAC member countries during 2013 were generally overcome; a pragmatic approach prevailed, which allowed the pursuit of joint infrastructural ventures by member countries outside of the formal EAC framework. After more than a decade of controversial negotiations, a full EPA between the EU and the EAC was at last

 | DOI 10.1163/9789004305052_030

concluded in October. The launch of an envisaged extensive tripartite FTA (made up of COMESA, the EAC and SADC) was again deferred and the idea was given little attention. Again no progress was made on reaching a permanent new agreement on the sharing of the water resources of the River Nile among all riparian states.

Political Developments

The political scene in *Sudan* was largely absorbed by debates around the run-up to the next elections, scheduled for April 2015. Attempts to find a rapprochement between the governing regime and various opposition groups remained unsuccessful, thus making an election boycott by the opposition and a clean sweep by the president and his ruling party very likely. Again, no permanent peace solutions were in sight for the decade-old conflict in Darfur and the other more localised conflicts in areas near to the border with South Sudan in Blue Nile and South Kordofan provinces. President al-Bashir continued to be subject to an ICC warrant on charges of crimes against humanity in Darfur. The population in *South Sudan* suffered enormously throughout the year from the civil war that had broken out in December 2013 as a result of a power struggle between President Salva Kiir and his former deputy, which had quickly escalated into a confrontation between ethnic groups. Mediation efforts under IGAD auspices brought no tangible results and no end of the tragic conflict was in sight.

Again, no change was discernible with respect to the domestic situation in *Eritrea*. The authoritarian regime remained in undisputed control and showed no sign of permitting even limited public debate on political issues, while an already substantial refugee exodus gained even more strength. Political developments in *Ethiopia* related mainly to the taking of positions ahead of crucial elections, slated for May 2015. The powerful dominant regime was able to maintain full control over all public affairs at the centre and in the provinces, but allowed some limited space for fledgling opposition groups. Fundamentally, however, there was no genuine change in the repressive political climate or the government's general development strategy, which was geared towards high growth and rapid modernisation. All hopes of a partial liberalisation of the authoritarian political situation in *Djibouti* seemed to have been put on hold after 18 months of on-off negotiations between the ruling and opposition coalitions brought no results, but a reconciliation deal was surprisingly struck at the end of December, bringing a flicker of optimism, although the well entrenched power of the president and government was not seriously challenged and remained unperturbed.

The federal government of *Somalia*, installed in Mogadishu since 2012, continued to make modest progress with the consolidation of its authority, although this only applied to some parts of the country. The government was recognised internationally and received support from many sides; there was a noticeable further upsurge in economic activity and urban reconstruction in Mogadishu, largely undertaken by returning Somalis and financed by remittances from the Somali diaspora. Radical Islamist groups, particularly al-Shabaab, nevertheless continued to subject considerable parts of the population to their draconian rules and to launch armed attacks and bombings against all representations of formal state institutions. Little progress was made with the creation and/or consolidation of federal states with a degree of autonomy from Mogadishu. The internal situation in *Somaliland* remained stable, allowing for the normal functions of a regular state, despite continued failure to achieve full international recognition as an independent state. In practice, *Puntland* also maintained its status as a semi-autonomous state.

Kenya experienced a relatively normal political year after the excitement around the tight elections in March 2013 and the installation of a new government, led by President Uhuru Kenyatta. The challenges of implementing a new politico-administrative state structure (devolution) brought about by the 2010 constitution continued to be felt. The creation of a Senate and 47 new counties had enforced the devolution of a hitherto highly centralised state and led to new forms of political battle between various authorities, not always necessarily in line with party loyalties. Critical observers accused the government of pursuing a strategy of gradual reversal of the devolution principles and of curtailing the freedom of the media and civil society voices. The political opposition remained in some disarray after its election defeat, thus allowing the governing coalition to exercise relatively undisputed control. To Kenyatta's relief, the ICC had to stop the pursuit of his indictment for responsibility for the 2008 post-election violence.

Most political debates in *Tanzania* were focused on the on-going constitutional review process and on early speculation around the prospects for the upcoming elections in October 2015. The deliberations in the Constituent Assembly became so acrimonious that a coalition of opposition groups boycotted the process and left the field to the government majority, which eventually adopted the text of a revised constitution that was intended to be submitted to a referendum in April 2015. By far the most contentious issue was the future structure of the existing asymmetrical Union arrangement between the mainland and the semi-autonomous *Zanzibar* archipelago. Despite strong demands for a revision of this structure, the status quo was in the end retained. The long-ruling dominant party remained in undisputed control of all political institutions, while the opposition was in search of a joint strategy for the election year.

In *Uganda*, the government was able to maintain full control over all public affairs, but faced considerable public discontent and sympathy for opposition protests. The authoritarian tendencies of the entrenched ruling system and intimidation of outspoken critics remained very evident. Rumours abounded about the next presidential elections in 2016: whether President Museveni would run again or who would be groomed as his successor. Increasingly numerous critical voices were also raised from within the ruling party and groups of MPs, who were no longer willing always to follow the prescribed party line and presidential directives. This culminated in the sudden dismissal of the prime minister (and party secretary general), who was considered a potential rival to the president.

The domestic political situation in *Rwanda* remained largely unchanged. President Kagame and his ruling party exercised absolute control over all aspects of public life and firmly suppressed all potentially dissenting voices. There were already debates about whether Kagame should run again for the presidency in 2017, although he was constitutionally barred because of an existing two-term limit. Despite the outward appearance of extreme stability and unity in the political system, signs of internal dissension and cracks in the inner circles were occasionally discernible. Rising foreign criticism by long-term donors led to a reduction of aid funding and a need to pressurise the population into mobilising more local resources for the government's ambitious and often technically impressive development programmes.

The political temperature in *Burundi* rose considerably with the approach of the next general elections (on all state levels) in mid-2015. No reconciliation was yet in sight between President Nkurunziza's ruling party and the alliance of opposition parties that had boycotted the 2010 elections. The opposition was left in a weak extra-parliamentary position and also without any influence on the local level, while the government secured its position by using strong-arm tactics of harassment and, allegedly, even the extra-judicial killing of suspected opponents. Growing tensions emerged between the dominant ruling party and its junior coalition partners, and uncertainties remained over whether Nkurunziza would be constitutionally eligible to run again for a third term.

The year 2014 was a rather uneventful political year in the *Seychelles*, with President Michel and his long-ruling government party dominating all spheres of public life. The opposition again remained weak and appeared resigned to their fate of being unable to gather more popular support in the face of a successful socioeconomic government performance. Politics in *Comoros* was fully focused on the parliamentary and communal elections, originally scheduled for November and December, but eventually adjourned to early 2015 due to failures of the election administration. Despite the existence of a plethora of small parties, a clear confrontation between two opposing camps emerged: the supporters of President Dhoinine were faced by the followers of his predecessor (and former mentor) Ahmed Abdallah Sambi, who had created his own party in 2013 and pursued ambitions to regain the presidency in 2016. Not all traditional inter-island rivalries were eliminated, but a relatively cooperative style prevailed and enabled the government to operate normally, although severely hampered by financial shortages and public discontent over recurring power and water outages.

In the entire *Eastern Africa sub-region*, there were some noticeable changes in *Freedom House*'s annual assessment of *political rights* and *civil liberties*, and they all indicated a downward trend without a single case of improvement. Burundi and Uganda were pointedly downgraded from the category 'partly free' to 'not free', due to reductions by one point for political rights in Burundi and for civil liberties in Uganda. Reductions by one point also applied to political rights in South Sudan and to civil liberties in Rwanda. None of the 13 sub-regional countries scored top points (on a scale of 1 at the top to 7) in the 'free' category, and altogether nine countries were now listed as 'not free' (Burundi, Djibouti, Eritrea, Ethiopia, Rwanda, Somalia, South Sudan, Sudan and Uganda). Eritrea, Somalia and Sudan remained among the ten lowest-rated countries in the world (with scores of 7 for both political rights and civil liberties); South Sudan, however, was only slightly better with a score of 6 for civil liberties. Only four countries were categorised as 'partly free' (with both political rights and civil liberties in the 3–4 point range). Of these, Seychelles and Tanzania were again judged the best (with 3 points in each category), followed by Comoros (3 for political rights and 4 for civil liberties) and Kenya (4 and 4). Somaliland, with its unique status, was also assessed as 'partly free' (4 points for political rights and 5 for civil liberties).

TI's Corruption Perception Index for 2014 once again revealed wide discrepancies between the countries in the sub-region. Of the 175 countries listed, Seychelles and Rwanda achieved outstanding positions (among the top 100) with overall rankings of 43rd and 55th, respectively, and scores of 55 and 49 (out of 100). Seychelles moved up a few places, while Rwanda fell, but the general assessment changed relatively little and both countries were well ahead of the rest of Eastern Africa. All other countries had scores markedly below 50 points, which was the threshold indicating the incidence of serious corruption. Somalia was rated as the worst country (ranked last with 8 points), while Sudan (11 points) and South Sudan (15 points) were also at the very bottom of the list. The remaining countries, like most SSA countries, had scores between 34 and 18 points and ranged between positions 107 and 166 in the following order: Djibouti, Ethiopia, Tanzania, Comoros, Uganda, Kenya, Burundi and Eritrea.

Similar divergences between countries were discernible with regard to *press freedom*, as indicated in the 2015 World Press Freedom Index by *Reporters Without Borders* (with scores ranging from 0 to 100). Of 180 listed countries, Eritrea for the eighth consecutive year ranked last in the world (scoring an unchanged 85). Sudan (ranked 174th), Somalia (172nd), Djibouti (170th) and Rwanda (161st), with scores ranging from 72 to 57, were also again judged to be general offenders against the principles of freedom of the media. Practically no change had been observed compared to 2013. The relatively best marks were given to Comoros (ranked 50th, score 25) and Tanzania (75th, score 28), by and large confirming a little changed situation. Seychelles and Uganda (both ranked 96th, score 32) moved up several positions in the ranking, while Kenya for the second year running had fallen another ten places (ranked 100th, score 32) as a result of a clear hardening of the government's media policies. Press freedom was also judged as highly restricted in South Sudan, Ethiopia and Burundi (scoring 38, 42 and 43, respectively). From a global perspective, most countries in the sub-region were again considered to be stagnating towards the bottom of the list.

Transnational Relations and Conflict Configurations

Again, no substantial progress was made towards bringing the *Darfur* conflict in *Sudan*, on-going since 2003, closer to a sustainable solution. Limited fighting between various rebel factions and government forces continued throughout the year, and around 2 m people were still forced to remain in IDP camps. Widespread lawlessness and banditry prevailed in the absence of regular state structures. The large hybrid UN-AU Mission in Sudan (*UNAMID*) remained tasked with protecting the civilian population and performing a peacekeeping role, but its effectiveness was severely restricted. After the independence of *South Sudan* in 2011, new conflict zones had emerged along the border, which was in large parts as yet undefined. A promised referendum to determine the disputed status of the oil-rich *Abyei* area was still not held, and a UN Interim Security Force for Abyei (*UNISFA*) remained deployed to prevent the outbreak of full hostilities. In parts of Southern Kordofan and Blue Nile states, local population groups favouring an association with South Sudan continued to carry out rebel activities against the Khartoum authorities.

South Sudan had in mid-December 2013 been suddenly faced with the outbreak of a vicious armed conflict between government forces and rebel groups loyal to former vice president Riek Machar, who had been dismissed a few months earlier by President Salva Kiir. Initially a classical political power struggle, the rebellion quickly escalated into a full-blown *civil war* with a confrontation between the country's largest ethnic groups, the Dinka and the Nuer. Heavy fighting, particularly for control of key oil-producing areas, involved large parts of the country and turned many thousands of civilians into IDPs or refugees. Regular agricultural production was severely curtailed by dislocation and fighting. This situation remained unchanged throughout the year, with the intensity of fighting fluctuating with seasonal climatic changes. Several negotiated cease-fire agreements were quickly broken by both sides, and at year's end no lasting solution to the conflict was in sight. The situation also had threatening implications for all the neighbouring countries, and *IGAD* had been quickly identified as a suitable body for mediating between the opposing parties. Lengthy rounds of peace agreements were held under IGAD auspices in Addis Ababa (Ethiopia), but without any tangible results. Kiir's government obtained primary support from Sudan and Uganda, both key neighbours. A military contingent was quickly sent by *Uganda* to stabilise the situation in Juba (South Sudan) and in the end stayed on much longer than at first foreseen. The UN Mission in South Sudan (*UNMISS*) was initially completely overwhelmed by the outbreak of the conflict and took some time to increase in strength, but its attenuating impact on the situation remained rather limited.

The population in remote areas in the triangle between *South Sudan*, the *CAR* and the *DRC* continued to be victimised by small remnant groups of the *Lord's Resistance Army* (LRA), which had terrorised large parts of northern *Uganda* until

2006, but had since been completely driven out of that country. Although the LRA was no longer a domestic Ugandan issue, the Ugandan military was still pursuing LRA leader Joseph Kony in the CAR and DRC in the context of an AU regional task force and with logistical support from US military advisers, but Kony and his fighters remained elusive.

Eritrea remained seriously isolated in the sub-region and at loggerheads with all other governments, with the partial exception of Sudan. There was still no permanent solution in sight for its border conflicts with either *Ethiopia* or *Djibouti*. There were no open military confrontations along the disputed borders, but no agreement on mutually accepted frontiers, either.

The insecurity and turmoil in *Somalia* had significantly affected all its neighbouring countries and they had been greatly relieved by the installation of an internationally recognised new government in Mogadishu in 2012. But radical Islamist groups still controlled considerable parts of the countryside and repeatedly launched armed attacks on installations and representatives of the government. With EU and US support, a new Somali police force and army continued to be trained and to expand its operational capacities, but had yet to become an effective force against al-Shabaab. Security protection by the large AU peacekeeping mission (*AMISOM*) therefore remained essential. AMISOM was composed of troops from Burundi, Djibouti, Ethiopia, Kenya, Uganda and Sierra Leone plus further staff from more African countries, and had a total strength of about 22,000 military and police personnel. *IGAD*, the relevant sub-regional organisation for the Horn of Africa, continued to fully support the federal government in Mogadishu, but was considerably less involved in pursuing Somalia's political developments than in previous years. *Kenya* remained particularly affected by an overspill of the Somali conflict through terrorist attacks by al-Shabaab adherents and in view of the presence of very substantial numbers of Somali refugees. Other neighbouring countries also increasingly feared becoming potential targets of terror attacks as al-Shabaab was losing ground in Somalia, but apparently intent on widening its terrorist activities geographically. In contrast, the threat from *Somali pirates* to international shipping in the Gulf of Aden and along the East African coast practically vanished in continuation of the previous year's trend. In 2014, only 11 piracy incidents were reported, and no ships were successfully highjacked.

The *Great Lakes Region*, with its wide-ranging significance across several national borders, continued to witness the complex interplay of many groups and interests from various countries in two sub-regions: Eastern Africa and Central Africa. In 2013, 11 African countries (all ICGLR members, apart from South Africa) had signed a UN Peace, Security and Cooperation Framework for the region that focused mainly on reform of the DRC's state and army and the neutralisation of all perceived 'negative forces' (i.e. various rebel groups) active in *eastern DRC*, and included the creation of a 3,000-strong Force Intervention Brigade (FIB) to complement the long-existing but rather ineffectual UN Stabilization Mission in the DRC (MONUSCO). The FIB, with troops from South Africa, Malawi and Tanzania, had in November 2013 defeated the M23 rebel group, which was allegedly supported by Rwanda. Against this background, the Rwandan government demanded with increasing impatience throughout 2014 that other rebel groups still active in eastern DRC, particularly the 'Forces Démocratiques de Libération du Rwanda' (FDLR), should now also be removed. Several calls for the surrender of the FDLR remained without response, and both the Congolese army and MONUSCO failed to take action against the FDLR, prompting *Rwanda* to accuse them, and thus indirectly South Africa and Tanzania, of tacit complicity with the rebels. Eventually a six-month ultimatum (until 2 January 2015) was given for the FDLR's surrender; in case of non-compliance they would be pursued militarily.

Bilateral relations between *Rwanda* and *Tanzania* remained rather frosty, since the Rwandan government accused the Tanzanian leadership of being too sympathetic with the FDLR, viewed in Kigali as responsible for the 1994 genocide and as retaining a genocidal ideology. In 2013, a public suggestion by Tanzanian President Kikwete that the Kigali government should engage in dialogue with the FDLR was furiously rejected by President Kagame. The FIB's reluctance to act against the FDLR and alleged contacts of Tanzanian officials with FDLR leaders further confirmed Rwanda's suspicions about Tanzania's positions. However, this did not significantly undermine their cooperation within the EAC context, and towards the end of the year there were signs of an easing of the bilateral tensions.

UN peacekeeping activities in the sub-region continued to face severe constraints. The large *MONUSCO* contingent in the DRC had in the past only achieved limited success in containing an overspill of rebel raids (FDLR, LRA, Allied Democratic Forces) into neighbouring East African countries and in stabilising the situation in eastern DRC. The *FIB*, with its unusually robust mandate, had proved to be considerably more effective against the M23 in 2013, but remained largely passive throughout 2014. *UNMISS* in South Sudan had been completely overwhelmed by the sudden outbreak of the civil war in late 2013 and, despite an increase in strength, remained relatively ineffective in containing the hostilities and their disastrous consequences for the civilian population. The large hybrid *UNAMID* also continued to struggle rather ineffectually to fulfil its peacekeeping role in the decade-old conflict in Sudan's Darfur region. *UNISFA* persevered in preventing the outbreak of open hostilities in the disputed Abyei border area between Sudan and South Sudan.

The indictment of Sudanese President al-Bashir for crimes against humanity in the Darfur conflict, issued by the *ICC* in 2009 and still in force, again had few practical consequences other than restricting his international travel. In December, similar charges against Kenya's President Kenyatta in connection with Kenya's post-election violence in early 2008 were withdrawn for lack of enough hard evidence. In October, Kenyatta had made history as the first accused sitting head of state to attend ICC hearings in person. In contrast to Kenyatta's case, proceedings against his vice president, William Ruto, continued.

Socioeconomic Developments

The *macroeconomic performance* of countries in the sub-region was again quite diverse, but on the whole reasonably satisfactory. They continued, by and large, to weather the effects of the persisting global economic and financial weaknesses relatively well, and most countries managed to achieve a slight acceleration in economic growth. Climatically, it was a relatively normal year, which led to average harvests almost everywhere. In an expression of growing confidence, Ethiopia and Kenya were able to issue maiden sovereign bonds (Eurobonds) on the international financial markets.

According to preliminary IMF figures for April 2015, the *2014 GDP growth rate* for SSA was 5.0% (against 5.2% in 2013); excluding the heavyweights Nigeria and South Africa, the average growth rate for all other countries was estimated at 5.6%. Eastern Africa was more or less in conformity with this general SSA trend. Ethiopia once again managed to achieve an outstanding growth rate of 10.3%, by far outperforming all its sub-regional neighbours and consolidating a record decade of exceptional growth. Tanzania (7.2%) and Rwanda (7.0%) again maintained their relatively stable successful growth paths. Djibouti (6.0%), South Sudan (5.5%), Kenya (5.3%), Uganda (4.9%) and Burundi (4.7%) recorded more or less average growth, while Sudan (3.4%), Comoros (3.3%), Seychelles (2.9%) and Eritrea (1.7%) performed less well. The five-member EAC block as a whole was estimated to have slightly accelerated its growth rate to 6% (from 5.8% in 2013). Taking into account the corresponding population growth, the *real per capita GDP growth rates* were, of course, generally much lower, e.g. for the EAC block 2.9%.

Most countries pursued cautious monetary policies and modest *inflation* targets, and they were by and large successful in containing average consumer price increases at acceptable levels. The IMF's preliminary estimate of average SSA inflation for 2014 was 6.3% (excluding Nigeria and South Africa it was 5.3%). Not surprisingly, the track records of individual countries differed widely, with some far exceeding the continental average. Once again, Sudan (36.9%) and Eritrea (12.3%) were clearly top of the list with practically the same high inflation rates as in the two preceding years. All other countries managed to keep their inflation rates close to or below a threshold of an annual average of 7%. Ethiopia (7.4%), Kenya (6.9%) and Tanzania (6.1%) were thus slightly above the SSA average, while the remaining countries had very moderate rates of less than 5%. South Sudan even experienced an astounding negative inflation rate (-0.7%) after zero in 2013. The EAC block brought down inflation from 6.2% (in 2013) to 5.8%.

Practically all countries in the sub-region (except Eritrea and South Sudan) again had considerable negative *current-account* balances, in contrast to the only slightly negative SSA average of -3.3% of GDP (due to surpluses on the part of major oil and mineral exporters, which strongly skewed the average). Djibouti (27.4% of GDP), Seychelles (22.5%), Burundi (17.6%), Rwanda (12.0%), Comoros (10.6%) and Tanzania (10.2%) had current-account deficits of more than 10% of GDP, while the remaining countries were below this threshold. Eritrea and South Sudan proved to be exceptions with practically negligible current-account deficits.

A good measure of the intensity of domestic development efforts, without simply relying on the inflow of aid funds, was the volume of *government revenue* (excluding grants and expressed as a percentage of GDP). Most countries in the sub-region remained below the yardstick of the IMF's projected 2014 SSA average of 19.1% (excluding Nigeria and South Africa it was 22.2%). The EAC as a group was estimated to have achieved only 16.2%, which was nevertheless a continuing small improvement over previous years. Only Seychelles (32.0%), in line with a long-standing past record, Djibouti (28.8%), South Sudan (24.7%) and Kenya (20.0%) were able to demonstrate high domestic revenue generation above the SSA average. In contrast, particularly low rates were estimated for Sudan (11.2%), Uganda (12.3%), Burundi (13.7%), Tanzania (13.8%) and Ethiopia (14.0%), followed by Comoros (14.6%), Rwanda (16.5%) and Eritrea (16.9%).

UNDP's 2014 *HDI* (with 2013 data) again clearly highlighted considerable variations in the sub-region in respect of general socioeconomic development levels. With the exception of Seychelles, all Eastern African countries (out of 187 listed) appeared in the 'low' human development category. Seychelles, with a recalculated HDI value of 0.756 and ranked 71st, was the third-highest-ranked African country (after Libya and Mauritius), at the bottom of the 'very high' human development category. Kenya (HDI value 0.535, ranked 147th) and Rwanda (0.506, ranked 151st) had a slightly higher HDI value than the SSA average of 0.502. Comoros and Tanzania (both 159th), Uganda (164th), Sudan (166th), Djibouti (170th), Ethiopia (173rd), Burundi (180th) and Eritrea (182nd) showed a lower-than-average ranking. Somalia and South Sudan were not listed.

According to the World Bank's *Doing Business Report*, Rwanda (ranked 46th, down 14 places) and Seychelles (65th, up 15 places) were as of mid-2014 considered the most business-friendly economies in Eastern Africa, while Eritrea and South Sudan, at the bottom of the list, were clearly in the opposite category of countries that largely obstructed private business ventures. The remaining countries, ranging from Tanzania (131st) to Sudan (160th), all belonged to an intermediate group of countries that in principle wanted to foster more business activity, but were still hampered by an overly burdensome bureaucracy, legal weaknesses and other impediments.

The World Economic Forum's *Global Competitiveness Index 2014–15* provided a somewhat similar attempt to compare the attractiveness of a total of 144 listed countries (including only seven from Eastern Africa). Again, Rwanda (ranked 62nd) was considered to have the most competitive economic environment, followed by Kenya (90th) and Seychelles (92nd). Ethiopia (118th), Tanzania (121st), Uganda (122nd) and Burundi (139th) were all grouped in the lowest quarter of the global ranking.

Sub-regional Cooperation and Sub-regional Organisations

The *EAC*'s 12th extraordinary *summit* on 30 April in Arusha (Tanzania) was mostly devoted to routine business. At the request of the South Sudanese government (in view of the internal crisis situation), the pending issue of South Sudan's application for EAC membership was postponed. The council of ministers was directed to initiate the process of drafting a constitution for the envisaged East African political federation and to develop a relevant roadmap. In reaction to growing concern about the threat of more terrorist attacks by the Somali al-Shabaab in all member states, the council was also directed to implement a regional counter-terrorism strategy as a matter of urgency. The 16th ordinary *EAC summit*, scheduled for 30 November, was postponed at the last moment due to Tanzanian President Kikwete's inability to attend shortly after having undergone an operation in the USA. Kikwete was expected to assume the annually rotating EAC chairmanship, which thus remained with Kenya's President Kenyatta. On 29 November, a 3rd EAC retreat on infrastructure development and financing held in Nairobi (Kenya) was attended by about 400 participants. By year's end, all member states had duly ratified the protocol on the *East African Monetary Union* that had been signed in November 2013. In May, the East African Payment System was launched (initially between Kenya, Tanzania and Uganda), which greatly facilitated monetary transfers between the countries. Tanzania also loosened its remaining capital controls on foreign ownership, thus removing restrictions for EAC citizens on the Dar es Salaam stock exchange. The *Single Customs Territory* (SCT) agreement got off to an only partially successful start in July; the joint collection of taxes under the SCT was intended to ease very cumbersome documentation procedures and to facilitate the cross-border movement of goods. A host of non-tariff barriers still continued to severely hamper the functioning of a genuine Common Market. This came out clearly with the launch of the East African Common Market Score Card in February, which showed that Burundi and Tanzania still retained the highest number of restrictions on cross-border trade and intra-EAC FDI flows.

On 5 June, the *East African Legislative Assembly* (EALA) approved the *EAC budget* for 2014/15 to the tune of $ 124 m, down from $ 130 m and $ 140 m, in 2013/14 and

2012/13, respectively. It prioritised the operationalisation of the SCT and measures for the full implementation of the EAC Common Market Protocol and an industrialisation policy. The budget was still heavily donor-dependent, with 59% of the total expected to come from contributions from external development partners. It allocated 61% of expenditure to the EAC secretariat in Arusha, 12.5% to the EALA, 10.8% to the Lake Victoria Commission, 7.5% to the Inter-University Council and the rest to the East African Court of Justice and other minor institutions. Months of internal bickering among its members gave the EALA, the third in the EAC's history, a bad and almost farcical image, even culminating in calls for its early dissolution; in a climate of paralysis, most EALA sessions failed to carry out their regularly assigned responsibilities. The debacle started in late March with a censure motion against the EALA speaker, Margaret Nantongo Zziwa, for alleged incompetence, poor leadership, etc. Intricate procedural manipulations dragged on throughout the year, until Zziwa was finally removed by a clear majority vote on 17 December and her Ugandan compatriot Daniel Kidega was two days later elected unopposed as the EALA's fourth speaker.

During the latter half of 2013, major *divergences between key leaders of the EAC* partner states had temporarily threatened to undermine the level of integration that had been achieved. A trilateral group (Kenya, Rwanda, Uganda) had convened three top-level summits to discuss and promote plans for a number of major infrastructure projects in the so-called Northern Corridor, while Burundi and Tanzania were not invited to participate. The trilateral group, quickly labelled the *Coalition of the Willing* (CoW) in the media and by the general public, was seen as propagating a two-speed approach to the integration process in East Africa, leaving an apparently reluctant Tanzania somehow apart. The acrimony had already cooled considerably by the end of 2013, but nevertheless continued to be occasionally felt less sharply. One concrete result was the introduction of a single tourist visa by Kenya, Rwanda and Uganda in February; a later inclusion of Burundi and Tanzania remained uncertain. During the year, four more Northern Corridor Integration Project summits were held without being regarded with suspicion by Burundi and Tanzania, who now participated as observers. A common understanding had been reached that partner states were free to make their own arrangements to pursue projects in which they had a shared interest as long as these did not clash with provisions of the EAC treaty. It was foreseen that similar infrastructural arrangements for the Central Corridor in Tanzania would be pursued.

After more than a decade of difficult discussions, the protracted controversy over an *EPA* between the EAC and the *EU* finally ended on 14 October with the signing of an EPA text. The EAC only very reluctantly succumbed to strong pressure from Brussels, primarily to save Kenya from the dire consequences of a refusal to sign, while the other EAC countries, as 'least developed countries', were not so directly affected. Since the negotiations were not concluded before the final deadline

30 September, the EU immediately started to levy customs duties on all Kenyan exports to the EU. They were only lifted on 26 December when the EPA was prematurely declared effective; but it still needed to be ratified by the EALA and the national parliaments.

COMESA held its 17th summit in Kinshasa (DRC) on 26–27 February, with Congolese President Kabila assuming the rotating chairmanship. Uganda's President Museveni, the outgoing chairperson, underscored in his address his efforts to engage COMESA more strongly with major emerging economies (e.g. the BRICS group), particularly with regard to investing in crucially important infrastructure. The DRC, Ethiopia and Uganda again pledged to complete their full accession to *COMESA's FTA* before the year's end, while the envisaged *COMESA Customs Union* remained quite uncertain, since most of the 19 member states were slow to align their national tariffs with agreed common external tariffs. Beyond public gaze, progress on the technical level was made with regard to the ambitious plan to create a grand *Tripartite FTA* (TFTA) made up of all 26 member states of COMESA, the EAC and SADC, stretching from the Cape to Cairo. The TFTA was expected to be formally launched during a 3rd tripartite heads of state summit in mid-December in Egypt, but it was postponed at short notice to June 2015, apparently due to South African reservations.

In 2012 and 2013, the *ICGLR* had gained enhanced international recognition as the most appropriate sub-regional institution to deal with the continued conflict situation in eastern DRC and the ensuing tense relations between the Congolese, Rwandan and Ugandan governments. This continued to be the case throughout 2014. On 15 January, the 5th ordinary ICGLR summit in Luanda (Angola) passed the chairmanship from Uganda's President Museveni to Angola's President dos Santos; subsequently, most meetings on the conflicts in the Great Lakes region were held in Luanda. On 25 March, a mini-summit of leaders from six member states, constituting the committee in charge of monitoring the situation in the DRC, decided to approve urgent military action against the FDLR by the Congolese army and MONUSCO. A *joint meeting* of *ICGLR* and *SADC* foreign and defence ministers on 2 July dealt exclusively with the FDLR problem and demanded the voluntary disarmament and surrender of the FDLR within six months. Another ICGLR mini-summit on 14 August confirmed this ultimatum, as did the regular SADC summit on 17–18 August. An informal meeting of ICGLR leaders on 22 September in New York (on the margins of the UN General Assembly) reiterated the demand for the FDLR's unconditional surrender, and the UNSC expressed concern about the lack of visible progress (with only 200 FDLR fighters having been disarmed). A third joint ICGLR and SADC ministerial meeting on 25–26 October threatened to use force against the FDLR rebels, but no decisive action had been taken by year's end. Rwanda's government became increasingly impatient and accused South Africa and Tanzania in particular of lacking the political will to act resolutely against the FDLR.

Again, only limited progress was made towards the revitalisation of the *CEPGL*, which continued mostly with support from Belgium and the EU. A two-day policy dialogue in January deliberated on the substantial economic potential of the grouping. Cooperation agreements were signed with the EAC in March and with CEEAC in April. No summit had been held for over two decades, which severely hampered a vigorous new beginning. The DRC's President Kabila, as current chairperson, hinted at the convening of a summit, but this did not materialise.

IGAD was primarily occupied throughout the year with attempts to mediate in the conflict in South Sudan, focussing much less on Somalia than had been the case in the past. Five extraordinary IGAD summits were held in Addis Ababa to discuss the South Sudan conflict, plus a mini-summit on 22 October in Juba. An IGAD mediation team, led by Seyoum Mesfin (Ethiopia) and Lazaro Sumbeiywo (Kenya), held endless discussion rounds in Addis Ababa with representatives of the rival camps, but to practically no avail, since several seemingly agreed peace agreements were almost immediately broken. A special IGAD summit on drought emergencies, held on 27 March in Kampala (Uganda), discussed joint initiatives to tackle the recurring severe drought problems in the sub-region.

The *IOC* celebrated its 30th anniversary on 10 January in Victoria (Seychelles), where it had been founded. During the 29th ministerial council meeting on 10–11 April in Moroni (Comoros), the rotating IOC presidency was belatedly passed on from Comoros to Madagascar, which had emerged from years of political crisis. Comoros drew great prestige from the fact that a rare heads of state summit (only the fourth) with the participation of French President Hollande was held on 23 August in Moroni. The short gathering did not set out any new initiatives, but simply reconfirmed the IOC's modest cooperation activities with a focus on improved connectivity and environmental and security issues. Comoros resisted a proposed name change of the organisation to Community of Indian Ocean Islands (or States), fearing that this might open the door for the inclusion of the French département Mayotte, regarded in Moroni as an integral part of Comoros.

Remarkable progress was made towards the establishment of the *Eastern Africa Standby Force* (*EASF*) as one of the five components (with military, police and civilian elements) of the AU's envisaged African Standby Force. The EASF announced its full operationalisation, ready for deployment on peace operations, with a strength of 5,000 personnel by the end of the year, one year ahead of the original target date. Ten countries actively participated in the EASF: Burundi, Ethiopia, Kenya, Rwanda and Uganda committed the bulk of the troops, while Comoros, Djibouti, Seychelles, Somalia and Sudan only played a minor role and Tanzania remained apart from the EASF. The funding of potential future deployments, however, remained an unresolved challenge.

The 20 *IORA* member states (including eight from Eastern and Southern Africa) met for their 14th ministerial council meeting on 9 October in Perth (Australia), the second time during Australia's two-year chairmanship. Recent progress was maintained, with a noticeable invigoration of the organisation, which had long seemed almost moribund. Top priority was given to the issue of maritime security and to strengthening the blue economy by making productive and sustainable use of the Indian Ocean and its resources.

The water ministers of the ten *Nile Basin Initiative* (*NBI*) member states held their 22nd council meeting on 19 June in Khartoum. The NBI called on Egypt to restart its activities in the initiative, which it had frozen since 2010 in protest over the signing of the text of a *Cooperative Framework Agreement* (CFA) by six upstream countries. The Nile riparian states remained split over the CFA, with Egypt and Sudan fearing negative effects on their historical share of Nile waters (based on colonial era treaties), while the upstream countries demanded a new formula for a more equitable utilisation of the water resources. Only Ethiopia and Rwanda had already ratified the CFA, thus leaving its implementation and the envisaged creation of a fully-fledged permanent Nile River Basin Commission undecided.

Burundi

Stef Vandeginste

The coalition government, one of the pillars of Burundi's power-sharing arrangement, was increasingly dominated by the party of President Pierre Nkurunziza. In the run-up to the 2015 elections, new electoral legislation was adopted. The national electoral commission (CENI) was strongly challenged by the opposition parties. Tensions increased within the dominant party around Nkurunziza's alleged third term presidential ambitions. The number of breaches of security was on the rise. The government's human rights record was negatively affected by some internationally very visible cases. A truth and reconciliation commission was established. Relations with the UN and with neighbouring Rwanda became increasingly tense. Students at the University of Burundi went on strike on several occasions. Some efforts were made to diversify Burundi's economy.

 | DOI 10.1163/9789004305052_031

Domestic Politics

In early 2014, a pillar of Burundi's post-conflict institutional stability came under serious threat. In line with the Arusha Peace and Reconciliation Agreement of August 2000 and the Constitution of 18 March 2005, a *coalition government* had ruled the country for the past decade. The two main partners in this coalition government were the dominant political party 'Conseil National pour la Défense de la Démocratie – Forces de Défense de la Démocratie' (*CNDD-FDD*) of *President Pierre Nkurunziza* and the much smaller 'Union pour le Progrès National' (*UPRONA*). This internationally negotiated cohabitation between the former predominantly Hutu rebel movement and the former predominantly Tutsi single party had been remarkably smooth between the 2005 elections and early 2014. In January, however, Interior Minister Edouard Nduwimana (CNDD-FDD) informed UPRONA chairperson Charles Nditije of his interpretation of a ruling of the Administrative Chamber of the Supreme Court and argued that Nditije could no longer be officially recognised as party leader. This was generally perceived as a reaction against the successful reunification of the UPRONA party under Nditije. The UPRONA leadership, as well as First Vice President Bernard Busokoza (UPRONA), rejected the interior minister's interference with internal party matters. Without consulting the president, Busokoza annulled the interior minister's decision. The crisis between the two coalition partners reached its peak when, 24 hours later, Nkurunziza dismissed his first vice president. As a result, UPRONA withdrew its ministers from the coalition government and UPRONA members of parliament no longer supported the CNDD-FDD majority. *Government instability* was, however, resolved when a new party leadership, under chairperson Concilie Nibigira, took over from Nditije at the interior minister's request. A new first vice president, Prosper Bazombanza, and new UPRONA ministers were appointed. The political crises within UPRONA persisted, however, with the so-called 'legal' and 'legitimate' wings of the party opposing each other for the rest of the year. Former chairperson Nditije accused the new party leadership of planning to assassinate him in July. The *UPRONA dispute* was brought to the attention of the East African Court of Justice, which delivered a ruling in November. Although ruling in favour of the applicants (the Nditije wing), the judgment had no immediate effect on the composition of the party leadership. Five months before the legislative elections, scheduled for May 2015, UPRONA remained deeply divided. Although these developments seriously affected the political dimension of power-sharing in Burundi, it was important to note that they did not jeopardise military stability – also based on a power-sharing accommodation between former government forces and the former rebel movement.

A second major crisis occurred in November, with the removal of two of Nkurunziza's most *influential aides*, General Alain-Guillaume Bunyoni, chief advisor to the president, and General Adolphe Nshimirimana, administrator-general of the 'Service National des Renseignements' (SNR – the national intelligence service). This came as a major surprise because both generals had been close allies of the president since the early days of the rebellion. Both Bunyoni – accused of corruption and embezzlement – and Nshimirimana – accused of gross human rights violations – had become the subject of significant domestic and international criticism. Although some observers questioned the real motives and sincerity of this *apparent 'palace revolution'*, their dismissal was perceived as a sign of flexibility on the part of Nkurunziza vis-à-vis the moderate wing within his CNDD-FDD. The new head of the SNR, General Godefroid Niyombare, former chief-of-staff of the armed forces and former ambassador in Nairobi, was widely perceived as a more moderate successor to Nshimirimana. By appointing Niyombare, the president clearly also had the intention of co-opting, and thus silencing, one of the most outspoken opponents of his alleged ambition for a *third presidential mandate*. Throughout the year, it became increasingly clear that not only civil society, the opposition parties and some international partners but also part of the CNDD-FDD leadership opposed a third term for Nkurunziza. While the president did not openly announce his intention to run again for president in 2015, internal resistance increased throughout the year. By the end of the year, it had become clear that the two generals remained influential and that their apparent removal from the spheres of power had not quelled the internal unrest within CNDD-FDD. At the same time, the popularity of the president in rural areas remained unquestioned, making him by far the safest option for the party at the 2015 polls, despite the *Catholic Church*'s remarkable declarations opposing a third term. The letter of the Constitution left room for interpretation as to whether the two-term limit included in the Arusha Peace and Reconciliation Agreement applied to the first post-conflict – indirectly – elected president. Nkurunziza did not therefore necessarily need the constitutional amendment that his government had tabled at the National Assembly, which was rejected in February when UPRONA members of parliament voted against it, preventing the required four-fifths majority in favour.

In the run-up to the 2015 elections, the *opposition* remained *extremely divided*, both within the parties themselves and within their fragile and ever-shifting alliances. Like UPRONA, almost all other parties were internally divided. Furthermore, the opposition also faced major difficulties as a result of the judicial proceedings initiated against some opposition leaders. Vague statements by the spokesperson of the CENI regarding the eligibility of persons who had judicial cases against them pending fuelled the perception of a judicial anti-opposition campaign. One of the three leading parties within the 'Alliance des Démocrates pour le Changement au Burundi' (*ADC-Ikibiri*) opposition coalition, the 'Front pour la Démocratie au Burundi' (*FRODEBU*), did not reunify. Instead, in September, former state president Domitien Ndayizeye was excluded from the party, following disagreements with FRODEBU leader and ADC chairperson Leonce Ngendakumana. Ngendakumana himself was prosecuted for falsely accusing the CNDD-FDD and the government-friendly radio station Rema FM of inciting ethnic hatred. In October, he was sentenced to a one-year prison term. Pending his appeal, the implications for his candidacy at the 2015 elections remained unclear. Frédéric Bamvuginyumvira (FRODEBU), a former vice president and potential ADC-Ikibiri candidate at the 2015 presidential elections, who had been arrested on charges of adultery and corruption in December 2013, was provisionally released in March, but it was widely presumed that he would be convicted by the anti-corruption court in order to jeopardise his presidential ambitions.

A second key player within the ADC-Ikibiri coalition was the 'Mouvement pour la Solidarité et la Démocratie' (*MSD*) of former journalist Alexis Sinduhije. The MSD headquarters were the scene of a serious breach of security in March, when a politically sponsored sports event was violently broken up by the police and two police officers were temporarily taken hostage by MSD youth. During the violent clashes, more than 70 party members were arrested. In April, 21 of them were sentenced to life imprisonment for endangering the security of the state. MSD leader Sinduhije once again fled the country; he was arrested on arrival at Brussels airport in Belgium but released soon after. By the end of the year and despite his presidential ambitions, he had not returned to Burundi.

A third important party within ADC-Ikibiri was the 'Forces Nationales de Libération' (*FNL*) of Agathon Rwasa. Although Rwasa was no longer officially recognised as the chairperson of the FNL, as political leader of the 'dissident' FNL wing he was widely perceived as having more legitimacy than the officially recognised FNL leader Jacques Bigirimana, whom the government had formally 'appointed' as opposition leader. On several occasions, however, Rwasa hinted at his possible departure from the ADC-Ikibiri coalition, thus undermining attempts at building a more unified opposition. Like his former spokesperson Pasteur Habimana, Rwasa was prosecuted for his alleged involvement in the 2004 massacre of Banyamulenge refugees at the Gatumba refugee camp. Both Habimana and Rwasa denounced this political instrumentalisation of the judiciary and invoked the temporary immunity that had been granted to them under the peace accords (but which, in reality, did not cover crimes against humanity like that committed in Gatumba). More important than his legal immunity, however, was the 'popular' immunity offered to him by his supporters. In December, when the prosecution department called for his appearance, thousands of Rwasa supporters marched through the streets of the capital, Bujumbura, a highly unusual event in Burundi where public demonstrations had till then been extremely rare. The demonstration was symbolic of the growing capital-based resistance against the political dominance of the CNDD-FDD.

Although not yet successful, attempts to reunify the 'Union des Patriotes Démocratiques' (*UPD*) of former CNDD-FDD strongman Hussein Radjabu – who continued to serve a long prison sentence – were more promising than was the case for the other opposition parties. None of the opposition parties, nor the ADC-Ikibiri coalition, presented an alternative electoral manifesto. The main electoral strategy of opposition elites was to encourage divisions within the CNDD-FDD, particularly around the issue of the third presidential mandate. In doing so, the opposition found inspiration in the CNDD-FDD's own policy of 'Nyakurisation' (the creation of so-called 'original', but in reality government-friendly dissident wings) of political parties.

The calendar for the 2015 elections was announced in July. Despite their lack of cohesion, all the opposition parties denounced the role played by the national *CENI* in the *preparation of the 2015 elections*. According to the opposition, the CENI operated on the orders of the CNDD-FDD and the president's office. The process of voter registration was marred by irregularities. In the CENI's view, these were minor incidents that could be remedied by extending the deadline for voter registration, but according to the opposition and other observers, the irregularities amounted to gross pre-electoral fraud. In particular, the process for distributing national identity cards, a requirement for the registration of voters, was problematic in several ways. The CENI was also accused of refusing to enter into a real dialogue with 'political actors', the term used to indicate those politicians who were no longer formally chairing their parties (such as Nditije and Rwasa). ADC-Ikibiri coalition parties withdrew from the local-level divisions of the CENI in protest against the alleged irregularities. Nevertheless, the opposition at no point announced a *boycott* of the 2015 elections. In 2010, their electoral boycott had turned out to be a major strategic error, paving the way for CNDD-FDD control of parliament. In August, a new administrative code was adopted, reducing the number of municipalities in Bujumbura. While the government put forward good governance arguments to justify this reform, other observers interpreted it as an attempt at legally engineering the 2015 election results in the capital, the main electoral support base of the opposition parties. In their *opposition to a third presidential mandate*, the opposition (as well as civil society) repeatedly referred to developments in Burkina Faso, where President Compaoré had been forced by popular pressure to resign. Despite the tense pre-electoral climate, an important positive step was taken in May, when a new *Electoral Code* was adopted by consensus. Furthermore, in June, under the auspices of the 'Bureau des Nations Unies au Burundi' (BNUB), a roadmap with General Principles for the Conduct of the 2015 Election was agreed upon by all parties. But the winding up of the BNUB (see below) in December meant that an oversight mechanism monitoring the implementation of the General Principles was no longer available. While offering significant financial support to the CENI and for election preparations more generally, Burundi's *international partners* (the USA, France, the EU, Belgium, the Netherlands and other donors) repeatedly expressed grave concern and called for a peaceful and inclusive electoral process. In addition to an increasing number of security-related incidents involving the party's youth division (see below), the CNDD-FDD was accused of intimidating civilians and forcing them to make a financial contribution to the party.

Although Burundi did not experience a return to civil war or to widespread political violence, the year saw an important rise in the number of incidents *undermining peace and security*. Also, there was a continued fear for terrorist attacks because of Burundi's military involvement in Somalia (see below). The main source of insecurity was said to be the CNDD-FDD youth division *Imbonerakure* ('those who see from afar'). There were increasing signs that the Imbonerakure not only engaged in political activities to support the CNDD-FDD throughout the country but also acted as a para-military militia, assisting or even replacing the regular law enforcement bodies. In March, some 30 Tutsi civilians from northern Kirundo province fled to Rwanda, accusing the Imbonerakure of plans to assassinate them. In April, a leaked confidential BNUB report to UN headquarters documented the distribution of arms and police and military uniforms to the Imbonerakure. The report also stated that the militia operated with full impunity and in collusion with local authorities. This gave rise to a major diplomatic incident and, in an immediate reaction, the BNUB chief security advisor was declared persona non grata by the government. Leaked around the time of the official commemorations of the start of the genocide in neighbouring Rwanda, 20 years earlier in 1994, the report was used by the opposition parties and by civil society to warn the international community of Rwanda-like scenarios. Major controversy arose when human rights organisations accused the government of arming and training the Imbonerakure across the border, on the territory of the neighbouring DRC. This gave rise to, among other things, the arrest of human rights activist Pierre-Claver Mbonimpa in May (see in more detail below). In July, armed Imbonerakure members who had attacked and robbed citizens in Bubanza province were given (mild) prison sentences, an unprecedented judicial confirmation of the criminality of their behaviour. More frequently, CNDD-FDD strongly rejected allegations made by the media, national civil society groups and international human rights watchdogs concerning the crimes and insecurity attributed to its youth division.

Major *armed insurgency activities* were reported on two occasions. In March, an FNL faction based on Congolese territory claimed responsibility for an attack on an army position on the Burundi-DRC border, in which seven government soldiers were allegedly killed. More seriously, at the end of December, heavily armed insurgents invaded Cibitoke province. No one claimed responsibility for the armed attack. Some government sources attributed responsibility to the MSD, denouncing its intention to set up a military basis in the Kibira forest in order to disrupt the 2015 electoral process. Almost 100 insurgents and some 15 military personnel died during the violent confrontation, which went on for five days. Several media and human rights organisations reported that war crimes were committed by the army which, allegedly with the support of the Imbonerakure, executed several rebels, most of them teenagers or in their early twenties, who had surrendered to the security forces. The prosecutor general announced the establishment of a commission of inquiry, which was also requested by most of Burundi's international partners.

Burundi's *human rights* record was primarily marked by the arrest, in May, and prosecution of *Pierre-Claver Mbonimpa*, chairperson of the 'Association pour la Protection des Droits Humains et des Personnes Détenues' and an internationally celebrated human rights defender. Mbonimpa was charged with endangering the security of the state after publicly accusing the government of arming and training young Burundians on the territory of the DRC. A national and international campaign was launched in his support. A public demonstration by civil society organisations was prohibited by the mayor of Bujumbura, who accused the organisers of insurrectional intentions. In September, the European Parliament adopted a resolution on Burundi, with particular regard to the Mbonimpa case, calling for his immediate and unconditional release. US President Barack Obama also stepped up diplomatic pressure on Burundi for Mbonimpa's release. At the end of September, he was provisionally released on medical grounds, but was ordered not to travel outside Bujumbura. Shortly after, the UN Independent Expert on the situation of human rights defenders visited Burundi, expressing regret that the government considered them to be political opponents. In September, *three Italian nuns* were assassinated in their convent in Kamenge, a suburb of Bujumbura. Although the circumstances remained unclear, some journalists accused the intelligence service and the police of involvement. In June, the UN *Committee against Torture*, in the first ever case brought before it against Burundi, found that Burundi had violated the torture convention when a night guard was seriously ill-treated in a prison cell. On several occasions, the Burundian government denounced the reports published by HRW, AI and other international organisations, such as the ICG, accusing them of conspiring against the authorities.

On 15 May, Nkurunziza promulgated the law establishing a *truth and reconciliation commission* (TRC) for Burundi. The law was only adopted by MPs of the CNDD-FDD, however, which negatively affected the TRC's perceived independence. Eleven national commissioners were appointed in December, but there was a general expectation that no public hearings would be held until after the 2015 elections. Also, necessary complementary legislation on the protection of victims and witnesses was not yet adopted. A highly respected clergyman, Monseigneur Jean-Louis Nahimana, was appointed as the TRC chair. Because the establishment of the TRC was not based on a prior agreement with the UN, several donors hesitated to pledge their support for it. The UN Special Rapporteur on the promotion of truth, justice, reparation and guarantees of non-repetition visited Burundi in December, welcoming the establishment of the TRC but insisting that its truth telling mandate should not be replaced by overemphasising the pardons procedure. Meanwhile, the *land commission* ('Commission Nationale Terres et Autres Biens', CNTB) continued to operate. Mandated to settle land-related disputes between (mainly Hutu) returnees and (mainly Tutsi) occupants of the land, the CNTB remained a source of controversy. In September, the government established a Special Land Court ('Cour Spéciale des Terres et Autres Biens'), with the exclusive jurisdiction to deal with appeals against CNTB decisions.

Foreign Affairs

In February, the UNSC extended the *BNUB* mandate until the end of the year. After ten years of embodying the – initially also military, later solely political – presence of the UN, the mandate of the BNUB and of UN Secretary-General's Special Representative Parfait Onanga-Anyanga came to an end in December. Preparations were made for the UN Electoral Observation Mission (MENUB) to start its activities in early January 2015. A UN Secretary-General Special Envoy, former president of Mauritius Cassam Uteem, was appointed as head of *MENUB*. His senior diplomatic rather than technical profile was greeted with dissatisfaction by the government. Also, disagreement about MENUB's precise mandate – was it merely to observe elections or also to 'validate' the results? – constituted a source of tension between the UN and the government. In addition to the regular UN country team presence, the government accepted a country office of the UN High Commissioner for Human Rights on the basis of a 1995 host country agreement. In his final report on BNUB to the UNSC, UN Secretary-General Ban Ki-moon expressed concern at the risk of a violent derailment of the electoral process against the background of a gradual erosion of the Arusha Agreement.

Relations with *Rwanda* were negatively affected by a number of developments. In August, a disputed number of corpses – various sources referred to between five and 40, – were found in Lake Rweru, a natural border between Rwanda and Burundi. A mixed commission of investigation, with the technical support of the US FBI, was announced but failed to materialise. In October, Prosecutor-General Valentin Bagorikunda stated that the bodies had originated from Rwanda, an allegation that was immediately rebutted by Rwanda's Foreign Minister Louise Mushikiwabo. Throughout the year, government officials also became increasingly suspicious of possible Rwandan support for Burundian opposition parties and civil society groups. Furthermore, developments within the *EAC* also affected bilateral relations with Rwanda. In January, a regional EAC defence pact was signed by Rwanda, Kenya and Uganda (the self-declared 'coalition of the willing' within the EAC), but not by Tanzania and Burundi. During a parliamentary debate in August, Minister Léontine Nzeyimana, in charge of Burundi's integration in the EAC, denied allegations that Burundi was about to withdraw from the EAC. Instead, the government proposed to recognise English as an official language. This proposal was approved in parliament in October. Burundi was also seen as siding with *Tanzania* in its diplomatic row with Rwanda after the Tanzanian foreign minister referred to the 'Forces Démocratiques pour la Liberation du Rwanda' (FDLR) as 'freedom fighters' with whom Rwanda should negotiate. In October, Tanzania granted citizenship to over 160.000 'old caseload' Burundian refugees. The position of EAC member states regarding Nkurunziza's possible candidacy for a third presidential term was a constant subject of speculation and advocacy. In December, Tanzania's ambassador in Bujumbura formally denied media reports that Tanzania approved a third presidential term.

Burundi continued to provide over 5,400 troops to the AU Mission in Somalia (*AMISOM*) peace keeping force. In September, Burundian AMISOM force commander Silas Ntigurirwa rejected a report published by HRW on sexual exploitation and abuse by AMISOM personnel. Training of Burundian AMISOM forces continued to be carried out by the US State Department led African Contingency Operations and Training Advice (ACOTA) operation.

Bilateral relations with *China* and *Iran* intensified. With both countries, Burundi concluded visa exemption agreements for holders of diplomatic or service passports. Nkurunziza visited China in August and was awarded a Certificate of Honorary Professorship at the Nanjing Sport Institute. China also reiterated its support for the construction of a new presidential palace in Bujumbura. In November, Nkurunziza went to *South Africa*, where an agreement was signed to structure bilateral trade and other relations through a joint commission for cooperation. Burundi also strengthened its trade relations with *Dubai*. From September onwards, Flydubai operated two flights a week between Bujumbura and Dubai via Entebbe (Uganda). Burundi actively – though not successfully – supported former president Pierre Buyoya's candidacy as secretary-general of '*la Francophonie*', the International Organisation of Francophone states.

Socioeconomic Developments

The *fight against corruption* remained high on the government's agenda. A high-level conference with international partners in October suggested additional legal reforms and efforts to improve coordination in the investigation and sanctioning of corruption. Nevertheless, civil society groups reported that ambitious zero tolerance action plans and legal and institutional reforms had so far not yielded significant results. In September, the chairperson of the 'Observatoire de la Lutte contre la Corruption et les Malversations Economiques' (OLUCOME) was briefly arrested for trying to organise a public demonstration against corruption and illegal enrichment. Burundi's position on TI's Corruption Perceptions Index – already worse than its neighbouring countries – fell slightly.

A National Committee for Social Dialogue started operating in February. Nevertheless, throughout the year, several social and economic sectors were affected by *strike movements*. A protest campaign against sharp rises in the price of consumer goods was particularly tangible in the capital city. Repeated strikes by university students were occasioned by a number of reforms that were badly conceived or poorly communicated by the government. New legislation on study grants was adopted in January. Although introduced in order to promote transparency and independence in the selection of beneficiaries, the measure – which lacked the necessary transition modalities – was perceived as intended to benefit students affiliated to the dominant political party. Some 12,000 students who went on strike against the annulment of their grants were suspended from university in March and were invited to re-enrol, waiving their right to strike. In October, a new strike was occasioned by protests against the introduction of the bachelor-master system. In December, the vice-chancellor of the public 'Université du Burundi' was replaced.

In August, hospitals faced a severe *shortage of blood*. The National Blood Transfusion Centre attributed the shortage to budget cuts and administrative complications in ordering blood bags. A medical workers union blamed poor governance at the level of the Ministry of Health. During a parliamentary debate, the ministers of health and finance rejected these allegations and instead attributed the shortage to the holiday period.

Tea exports increased to $ 21.3 m (an increase of 2.4% compared with 2013). The 2013–14 *coffee* season saw a 50% fall in production, which the 'Autorité de Régulation de la Filière Café' (ARFIC) attributed to a shortage of fertilizer and negative weather conditions. At the same time, ARFIC expressed concern, in July, at the illegal coffee trade across the Rwandan border. In May, in an effort to diversify Burundi's exports, a tea producing company together with a Chinese investor launched STEVCO, a joint venture investing in *stevia* plantations in Mwaro province. In October, a new *mining* company, 'Burundi Musongati Mining', was established, charged with exploiting nickel. The Musongati site in Rutana province had an estimated desposit of 150 m tonnes of nickel.

A new *Commercial Code* was promulgated in November. The legal reform was carried out in order to harmonise Burundian trade law with EAC regulations and to further ease business registration. A new *Investment Code* was discussed at the level of the council of ministers, but not yet adopted in parliament. Consolidating its position in the World Bank's 2015 *Doing Business Report*, Burundi was ranked 152nd (out of 189 countries). Its performance stood out positively as far as starting a business and registering property were concerned. On the downside, Burundi scored poorly when it came to access to credit, access to electricity, legal enforcement of contracts and cross-border trade. In the *Global Competitiveness Index* 2013–2014 of the World Economic Forum, Burundi was ranked 146th (out of 148 countries). In terms of technological readiness, it was ranked bottom. In August, an agreement was signed with China to launch a 'Burundi Broad Band Project' in 2015. Also in

August, the World Bank launched the first *Economic Update report* for Burundi, calling for urgent economic growth acceleration.

Macro-economic performance was marked by an estimated *GDP growth* of 4.7% (compared with an actual 4.6% growth in 2013). *Consumer price* inflation fell to 4.4 % (compared with 8.1% in 2013). For the third year in a row, taxes collected by the '*Office Burundais des Recettes*' (OBR, Office of Burundi Revenue) increased, reaching $ 416 m, up 17% on 2013. In June, OBR Commissioner General Kieran Holmes (of Ireland) was replaced by Domitien Ndihokubwayo. In July, Ndihokubwayo announced a new action plan against fraud and corruption as well as the launch of an electronic single window to smoothe customs procedures and controls. In December, a *budget* for 2015 was adopted in the National Assembly. Expenses were budgeted at $ 982 m, compared with $ 918 m in December 2013 (an increase of 6.9%). Donor contributions were expected to increase by 3% over 2014.

Comoros

Rolf Hofmeier

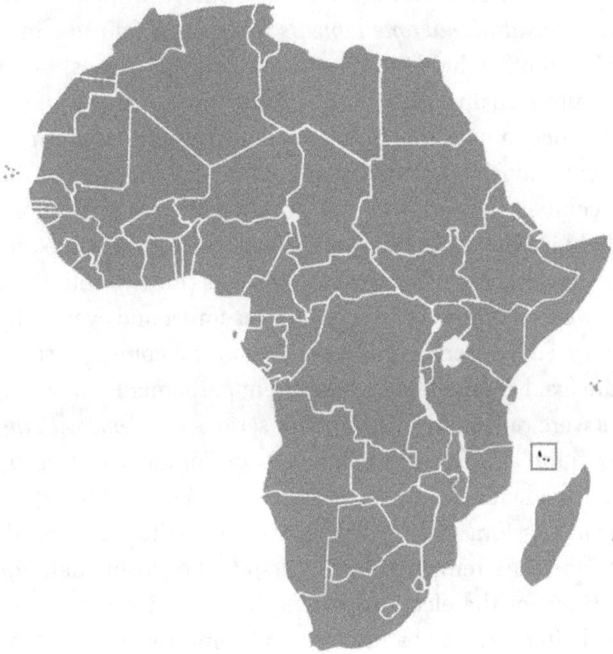

Throughout the year, the political scene was dominated by the run-up to expected triple elections (National Assembly, island councils, local communities), which were eventually postponed to early 2015 as a result of severe preparation problems. Various political alliances were already gearing up for the next presidential elections in 2016. President Dhoinine's camp was mainly confronted by the renewed presidential ambitions of his predecessor and former mentor, Sambi. Despite some signs of a possible re-emergence of the vicious political confrontations that had long characterised the country during its often turbulent past, 2014 turned out to be another year of relatively calm political normalcy without any major upheavals. The long-existing frictions between the three islands of the 'Union des Comores' and their political elites continued unchanged, but caused no immediate problems. A rare IOC summit was held in Moroni, but this international highlight did not bring about any change in the ambivalent relationship with France, given the enduring contentious Mayotte issue. Economically, it was a difficult year, with recurring power and water outages and the return of salary arrears in the public sector. The government's socioeconomic performance was considered rather unsatisfactory.

 | DOI 10.1163/9789004305052_032

Domestic Politics

Months of controversial discussions in 2013 had ended with a compromise agreement to hold *harmonised elections* for three levels of representatives, and the necessary changes to Article 20 of the constitution had been passed in parliament on 26 December 2013. These *constitutional amendments* were also confirmed by a meeting of all 'grands élus' (top office holders from Union and the islands) on 14 February and then formally approved on 25 February by a two-thirds majority of the councillors from the islands. These amendments extended the parliament's term to five years (as for the president and island councils) and prolonged the term of the current legislature to 22 December (instead of April). Simultaneous triple elections were thus expected to be held in November, while presidential elections were due in 2016. Election dates were decreed on 2 August, but the dates (for two rounds of voting) were subsequently twice postponed to the end of December and eventually to January and February 2015. Few observers raised fears about a coming institutional vacuum in view of the fixed expiry date of the current parliament.

From September, doubts were repeatedly raised about serious *problems with the preparation of the elections*, quite a familiar phenomenon in Comoros, caused by insufficient funds, technical inadequacies and quarrels and delays in setting up an independent electoral commission. Attempts to alter the constituency boundaries for the 24 directly-elected MPS remained unsuccessful. The closing date for the submission of candidatures for the elections was 24 November. A number of candidates were disqualified after scrutiny by the electoral commission and/or by the Constitutional Court. According to the electoral commission, 275.000 voters (fewer than in 2010) had been registered under a new biometric system and a total of 805 candidates were allowed to enter the electoral contest (204 for the National Assembly, 353 for the island councils and the rest for the municipal councils). The official campaign period started on 25 December in a rather lacklustre atmosphere. Twenty-three political parties, most of them of only marginal importance, and a substantial number of independent candidates entered the fray for the first election round.

In mid-April, 28 political parties and civil society organisations, representing practically all members of the political class, had agreed on and signed a '*historical consensus*' on common principles for the running of public affairs in Comoros, placing particular emphasis on the safeguarding of national unity. Nevertheless, the *political scene* remained characterised by a plethora of small parties, practically all based on loyalty to particular individual leaders and not on articulated party programmes or specific ideologies. Only a few of the political parties were of significant importance at the national level, although they had varying degrees of support on particular islands. The political groups supporting *President Ikililou Dhoinine* had in 2013 joined forces as the 'Union pour le Développement des Comores' (UPDC), while the president's predecessor, *Ahmed Abdallah Sambi*, had six months later created his own party 'Juwa' (Sun). Another former president (and a putsch leader in 1999),

Azali Assoumani, was in turn the leader of the 'Convention pour le Renouveau des Comores' (CRC), which had been a main opposition party during Sambi's period in office. The 4th CRC congress in early May confirmed Assoumani's renewed political ambitions, but internal quarrels also led two of his close collaborators to create a splinter group, the 'Rassemblement pour un Développement Harmonisé et Integré' (RADHI). Mouigni Baraka, the governor of Ngazidja, was the undisputed leader of the 'Rassemblement Démocratique des Comores' (RDC), while Mohamed Daoud, aka Kiki, had formed his 'Orange' party to pursue his personal ambitions (as MP and/or mayor of Moroni). UPDC, Juwa, CRC and RDC were considered to be the main contenders in the coming 2015 elections, with RADHI and Orange having lesser prospects.

All political discussions and the formation of personal and party alliances were already strongly focused on the upcoming *presidential elections* in *2016*. President Dhoinine was constitutionally barred from seeking another term and the field for any potential candidates appeared wide open. The constitutional principle of a presidency rotating among the islands had been adhered to in one full cycle with consecutive presidents from Ngazidja, Anjouan and Mohéli; the next president was consequently expected to hail from Ngazidja. In 2013, former President *Sambi* had started to strongly criticise the performance of Dhoinine's government and went on to clearly voice his ambition to return to the presidency; a good showing by Juwa in the parliamentary election was to buttress this goal. Hailing from Anjouan, Sambi was constitutionally not eligible to be the next president, but there were rumours that he might try to force another change in the constitution (as he had before) if Juwa won a parliamentary majority. Assoumani had also expressed his intention to run for the presidency, while Baraka was expected to have the same ambitions. Changing alliances ahead of the parliamentary elections were strongly linked with the strategies of the main presidential contenders. Juwa was only aligned with several minor parties, while UPDC, CRC, RADHI and Orange intended to form shifting alliances at the local constituency levels for the second round elections.

Anjouan governor Anissi Chamsidine had initially joined Juwa and supported Sambi, but fell out with the latter during the year and eventually backed his own candidates for the elections. This was partially linked with a regrouping of followers of the secessionist leader *Mohamed Bacar*, who had been defeated in 2008 by the Sambi-initiated invasion and forced into exile in Benin. Speculation arose about Bacar's eventual return and there were indications of a rapprochement between Chamsidine and Bacar's followers, who even created their own political party, 'Génération Nouvel Ensemble Comorien Rénové', which desisted, however, from fielding candidates in the election. Dhoinine appeared undecided about Bacar's possible return, while the antagonism between Bacar and Sambi clearly lingered in the background.

In May, in response to the refusal by the island commissioners to answer councillors' questions, a majority of the *Ngazidja* councillors expressed their dissatisfaction with the island government in a vote of no confidence and presented Baraka with an ultimatum to change the team of commissioners. In mid-June, however, the Constitutional Court declared the censure motion null and void since it had not been passed by the necessary quorum.

No visible progress was made with the investigations into the foiled *coup attempt* in April 2013. Several dates for court hearings were postponed. On 31 December, the Supreme Court rejected an objection brought by the defence lawyers against the continued detention without trial of the 13 suspects.

Foreign Affairs

The key international event was the *IOC summit*, held on 23 August in Moroni. This rare meeting of heads of state and government was the first for nine years. During a ministerial council meeting in April, Comoros had passed on the IOC chairmanship to Madagascar, but had retained the privilege of hosting the summit. The most prominent participant was French President *François Hollande*, who stayed in Moroni for only a few hours. In the run-up to the summit, Comoros strongly objected to proposed suggestions that the name of the IOC should be changed to the Community of Indian Ocean States (or Islands), fearing that this might enable Mayotte to become a separate member as an autonomous French entity. The question was postponed for further deliberations. The summit declaration underscored the value of deepening the connectivity between IOC members and of further enhancing their cooperation, particularly with respect to environmental and security issues, but did not launch any significant new initiatives.

The summit changed nothing regarding Comoros' long-standing conflict with *France* over the status of *Mayotte*, the archipelago's fourth island. The issue continued to be a national focus, but without materially jeopardising the delicate relations with the former colonial power. As of 1 January, Mayotte was fully recognised by the EU as its 9th peripheral region. Although all Comorian governments had always insisted that Mayotte remained an integral part of the Comoros under international law, the completion of Mayotte's integration into France and the EU had by now been reluctantly accepted as inevitable by most politicians and the general population. Bilateral *Comorian – French relations* thus continued to be characterised by considerable ambivalences between the Mayotte conflict and a traditional substantial dependence on France as a major economic partner and aid donor. A meeting of a new 'Haut Conseil Paritaire', intended as a dialogue platform, was very discretely held in December in Paris. In his speech at the UN General Assembly in September, Dhoinine focused as usual on the Mayotte issue, but equally stressed the existing good relations between Comoros and France.

Within the generally very limited scope available to it, the government continued to pursue an *open-door policy* and attempted to maintain equally cordial relations with Western powers (particularly France and the USA) and with China, Iran and many Arab countries in the expectation of attracting aid or commercial investments from these diverse sources, although not many investments had so far actually materialised. Efforts were made to strengthen links with Arab countries, such as by opening an embassy in Qatar and welcoming resident ambassadors from Qatar and Saudi Arabia in Moroni. Regarding its *geographical neighbours*, cooperation agreements were concluded with Mauritius (January) and with the French Overseas Département Réunion (October), in the latter case deliberately signed by the three island governors and not by the government for fear of creating a diplomatic precedent with France. A high-profile visit by the Zanzibar President Ali Mohamed Shein in September underscored the close cultural and historical links with that semi-autonomous island; Dhoinine had attended the 50th anniversary celebrations of Zanzibar's revolution in January. In February, Comoros hosted the 18th policy organs meetings of the East African Standby Force and a unit of 150 men was later declared ready to serve under the Force. In July, the government signed a military cooperation agreement with the USA. During the year, Dhoinine participated in the AU, Arab League and AU-EU summits and attended the conference of the Small Island Developing States in Samoa (September) and the UN climate conference in Peru (December).

November brought the announcement of a proposed deal between Comoros and *Kuwait* by which tens of thousands of stateless residents of Kuwait (known as Bidun) would be offered Comorian passports under the Economic Citizenship Program, while continuing to live with work permits in Kuwait. The plan flopped miserably, however, since the Bidun were not willing even to consider this offer.

Socioeconomic Developments

Although the Comorian economy continued to grow slowly and key macroeconomic indicators turned out to be moderately satisfactory, it was nevertheless a difficult year for most of the population. Dissatisfaction grew markedly with what was widely perceived as poor government performance. The *GDP growth rate* was projected to have slightly slowed down to 3.3%, but was still close to the 3.5% rate in 2013, which had been the highest for a decade. The average *inflation* rate for the year was estimated at 2.9%, somewhat higher than in 2013, but considerably down from 5.9% in 2012. This was again largely due to the restraining effect of membership of the franc zone, whereby the franc comorien (FrC) remained pegged to the euro and supported by France (at FrC 492:€ 1). Record *remittances* from the large Comorian diaspora (contributing 26% of GDP) and inflows of aid revenue remained essential to counterbalance the traditional enormous *structural trade deficit*. The value of imported goods and services was about 3.5 times higher than export income (practically all from cloves, vanilla and ylang-ylang), and remittances were considerably higher than export proceeds. The import bill was mainly burdened by Comoros' heavy dependence on importing food staples and all of its energy requirements. The *current-account* deficit was forecast to fall to 7.4% of GDP (compared with 11.3% in 2013) as a result of a contraction in the cost of imports (due to lower global fuel prices and a reduced volume of investment goods) and higher remittances. Foreign exchange reserves of around $ 170 m continued to provide a comfortable safety cushion of almost six months import coverage. Comoros' risk of debt distress was re-assessed by the IMF and the World Bank as moderate rather than high (as before) due to the full inclusion of remittances and the comprehensive 2012 debt relief.

In the 2014 *HDI*, Comoros was ranked 159th (out of 187 listed countries) in the 'low human development' category. The nominal per capita income was given as $ 923. With an annual population growth rate of around 3%, economic growth in per capita terms was only minimal. The incidence of poverty was considered quite severe, but no valid poverty data had been assembled for a decade. There was nevertheless some evidence of modest improvements in some social indicators (primary education, health) in recent years. Comoros' practically unchanged position in the World Bank's Doing Business 2015 report (159 out of 189) was again indicative of the country's enduring unfavourable business climate. Only a fraction of remittances were therefore invested in productive activities. A new second-generation PRSP 'Stratégie de Croissance Accélérée et de Développement Durable' for the period 2015–19 was in the final stages of preparation. The strategy aimed to achieve economic stability and inclusive growth, promote sectors with high growth potential, strengthen governance and social cohesion and enhance human development. The critical challenge remained a realistic implementation approach.

IMF missions assessed the Comoros' financial and economic performance, but no new ECF arrangement was concluded after the previous ECF expired in December 2013. The IMF acknowledged that the country had made notable progress in recent years and that macroeconomic policymaking and economic performance had improved since the adoption of the new constitution in 2009, but underlined that much remained to be done to consolidate and accelerate inclusive economic growth through continued focus on policies that emphasise macroeconomic stability and improvements in infrastructure, and foster structural reforms that improve the competitiveness of the economy and strengthen the business environment.

Sticking to agreed *fiscal policy* goalposts and implementation of the *2014 budget* proved a major challenge for the government, particularly after mid-year. While revenues were broadly on target, finance was inadequate to cover the higher-than-budgeted wage bill resulting from an increase in teacher salaries (approved in March) and other un-budgeted expenditure (such as IOC summit and elections).

State-financed investment projects had to be curtailed and debt-service obligations and *public sector salary payments* ran temporarily into arrears. This had been a quite common feature in the past, but its recurrence was a major cause of popular dissatisfaction. August salaries were not paid until late October. Recurrent government spending for the year was projected to be about 20% higher than budgeted. A better balance between available financial resources and expenditure clearly had to be found.

Frequent *outages of electricity and water*, sometimes for several weeks, made life difficult for most of the population and were another major cause for dissatisfaction with the government. On 30 September, several civil society organisations organised a *peaceful protest march* in Moroni and formulated a petition to the government about the power and water problem. On 29 October, various NGOs organised a successful operation '*île morte*' (dead island) on Ngazidja, which brought public life to a standstill. In late May, in a measure to obtain more revenue, the government unexpectedly introduced a *new 5% tax* on the purchase of cell phone credit cards. This was met by wide public protests and was consequently quickly withdrawn.

Again, no tangible progress was made on a fundamental reform or privatisation of notoriously badly managed *parastatal companies*, particularly key public utilities (electricity, water and telecoms). This had been demanded by the IMF and the World Bank for years, but without success. Renewed efforts to restructure and improve the performance of *Ma-Mwe*, the ailing power and water company, remained futile throughout the year and could not prevent the repeated failure of Ma-Mwe's standard services. The situation was further aggravated by the difficulties of the 'Société Comorienne des Hydrocarbures', the public oil importer and distributor, which ran temporarily out of supplies and was hard put to pay for the needed oil imports. The long-planned and very controversially discussed privatisation of '*Comores Télecom*' was once again blocked by continued resistance from politicians and trade unions, who feared the inevitable loss of up to 1,000 jobs. The government finally capitulated and withdrew the relevant bill from parliament in late April. No further initiative was undertaken during the rest of the year. In May and June, a new conflict arose over the controversial import of alcohol, which ended with a deregulation of the prevailing restricted system.

Neither was any marked progress made with regard to hopes for eventual success in *oil and gas* exploration in Comoros' extensive coastal waters. Expectations had recently risen following substantial hydrocarbon finds along the East African coast, but the start of concrete exploration activities was very slow to materialise. In March, new exploration licences were awarded to two consortiums for six offshore blocks, but dreams of a possible bonanza had to be extended into a distant future.

Djibouti

Rolf Hofmeier

The year opened with continued deadlock between the government and the coalition of opposition parties in the aftermath of the strongly disputed February 2013 parliamentary elections. Insisting that massive electoral fraud had taken place, elected opposition candidates persisted in refusing to take up their seats in parliament. Throughout the year, several attempts were made to re-open political dialogue and to find a workable agreement, but they stalled despite intermittent signs of apparent progress. It was only on 30 December that a formal accord was finally signed, opening vaguely optimistic prospects for some advances towards introducing limited democratic elements into a political system hitherto dominated by the authoritarian regime of President Guelleh and its undisputed full control of all aspects of public life. Intimidation of dissidents and repression of opposition activists continued during the year. The government further pursued the vision of transforming the small and resource-poor state into an important commercial hub by taking advantage of its strategic geographical location. Cooperation with Ethiopia was further intensified and raised speculation about closer political links. On the back of continued investment inflows, a number of ambitious infrastructural

 | DOI 10.1163/9789004305052_033

projects were under way or planned, with general economic performance remaining relatively satisfactory.

Domestic Politics

Throughout the year, the political scene was fully occupied by the continued standoff between the long-ruling regime of *President Ismail Omar Guelleh* (widely dubbed IOG) and the opposition coalition '*Union pour le Salut National*' (USN). At the root of this vicious confrontation were the heavily disputed parliamentary elections of February 2013, in which various opposition parties, united under the USN coalition, had participated for the first time after a decade of repeated election boycotts caused by an unfair electoral system. The USN leaders had not accepted the official election results and alleged serious election fraud. Ten USN candidates had been elected as MPs, but all but one had refused to take up their seats in the National Assembly. The 55 MPs of the governing '*Union pour la Majorité Presidentielle*' (UMP) coalition thus remained *de facto* in undisputed control of the parliament, which was in any case only of minor political importance compared with Guelleh's absolutely dominant role. Attempts to initiate a dialogue between the government and the opposition had been started in July, but had remained unsuccessful until the end of 2013, and this situation was carried forward into 2014.

The parliamentary speaker had threatened that the nine elected USN MPs would lose their mandates by 31 January at the latest, if their *boycott of parliament* persisted, but this threat was never executed, and the situation was deliberately left in limbo. On 29 January, one more USN MP attended a parliamentary session, while the rest maintained their boycott throughout the year. Aden Robleh Awaleh, the first USN MP to have broken the boycott in June 2013 and a prominent politician of long standing (a former rival of Guelleh for the presidency), died on 31 October.

Throughout the year, repeated efforts were made at *political dialogue* between the government and the USN and to reach a consensus for an accord between the two camps. These efforts took place in phases and had the appearance of several on-and-off sequences of talks, mostly conducted by a few key individuals and not detectable by the general public. Agreement seemed imminent and was rumoured to have been found several times, but then the process stalled again. It seemed that Guelleh himself was vacillating between a desire to improve the country's international democratic reputation (in reaction to some modestly applied pressure from Western countries) and warnings from his own ranks about making too many concessions to the opposition and possibly endangering his hitherto unrivalled dominance of the political scene. During an unofficial meeting between Guelleh and a USN leader on 1 February, a list of USN demands was handed over and expectations were raised for a new opening of the political space, but no agreement on a timetable for formal negotiations was reached and all hopes were soon dashed again. Street demonstrations by USN activists were partially suppressed, and in mid-March the USN reported that 35 of its members (including elected officials) and supporters were currently in prison.

A new round of *informal talks* began in July between Guelleh and USN Vice President Ismael Guedi Hared (leader of the 'Union pour Démocratie et Justice', one of the five registered opposition parties that constituted the USN coalition). The talks were described by IOG as very inclusive and were apparently conducted in an atmosphere of mutual trust, but no details were publicly disclosed. On 2 September, Guelleh announced that a political agreement was imminent, but this bounced once again and in an unusual press conference on 7 October three cabinet ministers dismissed the USN demands and called Hared's alleged new requirements irrational. Negotiations nevertheless continued without public attention and finally culminated in a grand ceremony on 30 December with the signature of an *accord between the government and the USN*. Guelleh expressed a sense of pride at having eventually found a solution after a difficult 18-month process without external mediation. The deal foresaw the entry of nine new USN MPs into parliament in the following week (thus representing an official opposition for the first time since independence) and the creation of a commission, with equal numbers from each side, tasked to draft jointly agreed reform measures, which would still need to be submitted for parliamentary approval. Some USN leaders did not support the accord, however, since it did not include firm agreements on key USN demands (i.e. the status of the opposition and creation of an independent electoral commission). After many years of continuous political confrontation, a new dispensation finally seemed to have been ushered in, but the future role of the opposition still remained to be concretely determined.

Guelleh reiterated several times that he did not intend to seek re-election in 2016. Frequent speculation nevertheless continued in view of the absence of any apparent heir and of Guelleh's persistent domination of the political scene, despite signs of failing health. In late May, he underwent surgery in a military hospital in Paris. Guelleh's own party '*Rassemblement Populaire pour le Progrès*' (*RPP*), the core element of the ruling UMP coalition, celebrated its 35th anniversary on 5 March and re-elected IOG as its president for another four-year term. Prime Minister Abdoulkader Mohamed Kamil and Finance Minister Ilyas Moussa Dawaleh were confirmed as RPP vice-president and secretary-general, respectively. The RPP's supremacy remained without any apparent challenge.

A suicide *bomb attack* by Somali Islamists on 24 May in a popular restaurant in the centre of Djibouti-Ville (which killed three and wounded 15) came as a shock and led to an intensification of security measures. A few isolated incidents in northern Djibouti, home of the minority Afar ethnic group, were a reminder of the continued existence of the illegal armed wing of the 'Front pour la Restauration de l'Unité et de la Démocratie' (*FRUD*) and of its recurrent, but limited, threat to security. Harassment and intimidation of government critics continued to some extent throughout the year, and several activists were imprisoned for various terms. In contrast, as a placatory gesture towards the opposition, three religious leaders who had been sentenced to 18 months in prison in 2013 were released and amnestied in August. They represented the non-registered 'Mouvement pour le Développement et la Liberté' (*Model*), which advocated a moderate Islamist orientation and was aligned with the USN; the government feared its links with the Muslim Brotherhood and the spread of fundamentalist tendencies. The government's legal battles to confiscate assets of the businessman Abdoulrahman Boreh, a former close associate of Guelleh and since 2008 an exiled dissident and active supporter of the opposition, continued on several international fronts, still with no end in sight. In April, a Dubai court rejected a request for Boreh's extradition.

Foreign Affairs

Priority attention continued to be focused on relations with neighbouring countries in the conflict-ridden Horn of Africa region, on strengthening Djibouti's strategic position in the wider regional context and on supporting international antiterrorism activities in the region. Again, no progress was made towards a final demarcation of the contested border with *Eritrea* and a few Qatari military observers continued to monitor the frontier. In an incident that showed the persistence of tensions, a Djiboutian officer was captured on 25 July by Eritrea in the demilitarised zone and only released after six weeks. In mid-April, Djibouti had released 266 Eritrean detainees (deserters and prisoners of the 2008 war) and handed them over to the UNHCR. Djibouti's government continued to take a close active interest in the complex political developments in *Somalia*, its ethnically closely linked and turbulent neighbour. A pledge had been made in 2013 to augment the existing Djiboutian military contingent under the AU peacekeeping mission in Somalia by another battalion, but this was not confirmed during the year. The Djiboutian unit was apparently not considered to be very effective; in March it suffered fatal losses at the hands of the al-Shabaab Islamist militia. The bomb attack in May was in retaliation for Djibouti's military involvement in Somalia. In December, Guelleh acted as facilitator for a third round of direct discussions between the presidents of Somalia and *Somaliland* about the future of the country. Djibouti continued to fully support the Somali government in Mogadishu, but also maintained its friendly relations and close cooperation with the self-declared Republic of Somaliland, for which Djibouti served as a vital link to the outside world.

Of singular importance was the further intensification of close and cordial relations with *Ethiopia*, Djibouti's large dynamic neighbour and a hegemonic player in the sub-region. Several large projects were under way or at the planning stage to improve the infrastructural and trade links on which both countries depended. An emerging tendency towards economic integration had in recent years become ever more pronounced. At an important ceremony in mid-May, Ethiopia's Prime Minister Hailemariam Desalegn launched nine new vessels of the Ethiopian Shipping Enterprise, thereby underlining the overriding importance of Djibouti's ports for his country. Various bilateral commissions also demonstrated actual areas of close cooperation. On several occasions, Guelleh even hinted at possible scenarios for moving further into some kind of closer political arrangement, although most Djiboutian economic and political actors would probably not welcome coming even further under Ethiopia's dominance. No concrete suggestions were made, but the possibility of such an eventual move was raised on various occasions.

The *USA* continued to attach great importance to its *military base*, Camp Lemmonier, due to Djibouti's ideal strategic geopolitical location. A new 10-year lease agreement for the base was concluded during Guelleh's visit to the USA in early May, when he met with President Obama. The rent for the base was increased by 66% to an annual $ 63 m, but there were also commitments to substantial US investments and support for Djibouti's security forces. About 4,000 US personnel, military and civilian, were stationed at the Camp, while *France* announced a planned significant reduction (in 2015) of its force of around 1,900 troops due to budget constraints. Given the small *Japanese military camp* and the presence of navy personnel from the *EU's anti-piracy Atalanta mission*, Djibouti was probably the most internationalised military zone in the world. Similar *Chinese* and *Russian* installations also seemed to be in prospect for the near future. In January and February, in quick succession, the Chinese foreign and defence ministers visited Djibouti, and a security and defence agreement was signed that included the construction of a Chinese naval base, while some naval facilities were also under discussion with Russia. In early February, Djibouti hosted the second meeting of the Gulf of Aden *Counterterrorism Forum*, a US-sponsored platform on security issues in the region.

Djibouti continued to benefit from *aid programs* and inflows of *private foreign investments* from a diverse spectrum of sources, thanks to its valuable strategic location in an international conflict zone and from its role as the most suitable base for coordinated international anti-piracy activities. These programs were still considered important and therefore maintained, despite an almost total factual collapse of the piracy threat. All external partners again largely refrained from openly expressing any sharp criticism of the authoritarian regime and its civil rights violations, but some tacit pressure may have had an influence on coming to the political reconciliation. *China* had taken the lead position not only as investor in all types of infrastructural projects, but also as executing contractor. The *Arab Gulf states* also remained important economic partners, particularly Qatar and the UAE (despite tensions with Dubai over the Boreh affair and the port management contract of DP World). *Iran* obtained a high profile by the construction of a flashy new parliament building that was inaugurated in November.

Despite apparent health problems, Guelleh again had a full international travel schedule and chose to personally represent his tiny nation at many *international forums*, such as the AU, Arab League, COMESA, EU-Africa summit, US-Africa summit, etc. All these undertakings were in pursuance of Guelleh's declared ambition to increase Djibouti's visibility around the world. The most prominent visitors to Djibouti during 2014 were UN Secretary-General Ban Ki-moon and World Bank President Jim Yong Kim in late October during a joint tour of the Horn of Africa.

Socioeconomic Developments

Within the last decade Djibouti's *economy* had experienced a *substantial transformation* that changed the structural features of its formerly sleepy backwater appearance, and this trend continued unabatedly throughout the year. This development was primarily driven by large inflows of FDI for major infrastructural projects and by service earnings that benefited primarily from the sustained economic boom in Ethiopia. However, capital-intensive investments and construction activities continued to have little impact on the alleviation of the structural persistence of very high levels of poverty and unemployment among the population.

The overall *macroeconomic performance* in 2014 was again mixed, but generally satisfactory, confirming the recent trend of gradual improvement. The *GDP growth rate* was estimated at 5.6%, a further acceleration compared with 2013 (5.0%) and the highest rate ever achieved. Consumer price *inflation* was successfully contained at 2.9%, compared with 2.4% in 2013. The current-account deficit remained substantial (forecast at around 23% of GDP) at about the same level as in 2013, again largely as a result of substantial capital goods imports for infrastructure projects; the shortfall was comfortably financed by FDI and external borrowing. Foreign exchange reserves were further augmented to about $ 380 m in September to allow a healthy import coverage of six months. The Djibouti franc (Dfr) remained pegged to the US dollar under a currency board arrangement (at a rate of Dfr 177:$ 1). Estimated exports (in fact mostly re-exports) of $ 120 m continued to be dwarfed by further substantially increased imports of around $ 800 m, thus maintaining the traditional huge structural trade deficit. The *budget* outturn for 2014 was expected to show an increased fiscal deficit of around 3% of GDP, thus again failing to achieve a promised surplus target. Extensive tax exemptions for FDI projects continued to undermine the government's revenue mobilisation efforts. There seemed to have been some slight improvement in the general business environment, but Djibouti remained ranked 155th (out of 189 listed countries) in the World Bank's 'Doing Business 2015' assessment. The World Bank supported several programmes to improve the local business climate.

The last ECF arrangement with the *IMF* had been completed in mid-2012 and, despite the government's request for a follow-up arrangement, there was again no indication that this would materialise. The IMF apparently still felt that the government's general performance was weak and that there was no agreement on the principles of a new ECF. The IMF continued to be mainly concerned about the persistence of fiscal deficits and the need for stringent fiscal reforms, the growing high risk of debt distress (resulting from new, mainly Chinese, credits for infrastructural expansion), the slowness of structural administrative reforms in the public sector and, above all, failure to make noticeable progress in the fight against *poverty* and an alarming level of *unemployment*: 42% of the population were assessed to be living in extreme poverty, and the unemployment rate was estimated at over 50%. About one-third of the population was in need of humanitarian assistance. After four consecutive years of drought, the food situation was precarious; in June several NGOs launched a famine alert. The exodus from rural areas continued, with 85% of the country's population already living in the greater Djibouti-Ville area. Djibouti's generally deficient socioeconomic standard was clearly reflected in its low 2014 *HDI* ranking (170th out of 187 countries). In June, the government launched a strategic long-term development outlook, '*Djibouti Vision 2035*', which proclaimed highly ambitious goals. A national investment programme, presented in March, similarly focused strongly on the eradication of poverty. A new World Bank Country Partnership Strategy 2014–17 was strongly based on the 'Vision 2035'.

The recent ambitious expansion of Djibouti's *infrastructure* was vigorously pursued, with many major projects either under way or at the planning stage. In mid-August, construction contracts were signed with two Chinese companies for a $ 580 m expansion of the Doraleh container terminal (seven new berths) and for the Damerjog livestock port. On-going construction activities included *inter alia* two smaller new ports and a range of significantly improved links with Ethiopia (two railway lines, roads, electric power lines, water pipeline, etc.).

In July, the government revoked its 20-year *management contract* with *DP World*, based in *Dubai*, for the Doraleh container terminal, claiming that DP World had been unfairly favoured by the then port director, Boreh. The case was submitted for an arbitration ruling in London in October 2015, while DP World continued its regular operations. Another long-standing commercial dispute re-emerged in December with the government insisting on claiming substantial *compensation for damages* from the French *Total* oil company. This referred to a major oil pollution incident in the port area in 1997, caused by Total's local subsidiary. The Supreme Court had in June upheld an earlier decision that damages of around $ 125 m should be paid, but the local Total company had in the meantime claimed insolvency.

Eritrea

Nicole Hirt

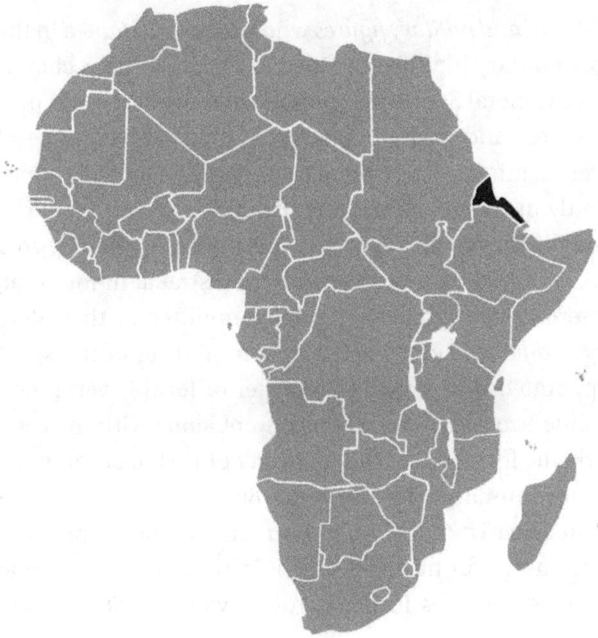

Eritrea's firmly entrenched autocratic political system and its command economy persisted, while the mass youth exodus accelerated rapidly. The four Catholic bishops harshly criticised the government's policy of militarisation and demanded reforms, and passive resistance to forced conscription increased. The long-standing conflicts with Ethiopia and Djibouti remained unresolved and the UN sanctions against Eritrea remained in place. The government tried to strengthen political ties with Egypt and Russia, whereas relations with Qatar cooled significantly. European governments were worried about the increasing influx of Eritrean refugees, but failed to pressure the Eritrean government to address the root causes of their flight. Eritrea reportedly reached the health-related MDGs, but food insecurity still prevailed and basic commodities remained scarce.

Domestic Politics

The political system retained its *autocratic character*. In a speech on the occasion of Independence Day on 24 May, *President Isaias Afewerki* announced the launch

 | DOI 10.1163/9789004305052_034

of a constitution drafting process, disregarding the fact that the implementation of Eritrea's ratified constitution of 1997 was still pending. At the end of the year, Isaias declared the existing constitution null and void, claiming on EriTV that "as everybody knows, there is no constitution". He said that a body had been formed to draft a new constitution.

The prominent *Muslim political and military figures* who had been *detained* in the aftermath of the January 2013 military mutiny remained in prison without charge. Long-term minister of defence General Sebhat Ephrem was removed from his post and appointed minister of energy and mines, replacing Ahmed Hadj Ali, one of the detainees. No new defence minister was appointed, but General Philippos Weldeyohannes was apparently in charge of handling the ministry's business. The post of minister of information had remained vacant since the defection in 2012 of former minister Ali Abdu, who had requested asylum in Australia. In mid-year, Woldenkiel Abraha, a long-term member of the central committee of the ruling *People's Front for Democracy and Justice* (*PFDJ*) and a former minister of transport and communication was appointed to the post of minister of local government. According to the unimplemented constitution, this post went along with the vice-presidency. Tesfaselassie Berhane, formerly general manager of EriTel, became the new minister of transport and communication. Nesredin Bekit, who had formerly worked for the PFDJ-owned Red Sea Trading Corporation, was appointed minister of trade and industry. He was known for his involvement in the contraband trade and the establishment of smuggling hubs in the border towns of Tessenei and Girmaika.

On 14 March, the remnants of the *PFDJ's central committee* met for the first time after the crackdown on PFDJ reformists in 2001. State media reported a meeting of the 'central office', a term that had not previously been used. About two-thirds of the 37 former central committee members were either in jail or had been forced into exile. The cabinet of ministers met twice during the year, in April and October.

On 6 March, Major General Gebregziabher 'Wuchu' Andemariam died, only shortly after having been appointed chief-of-staff of the defence forces. On the occasion of his funeral, the *restructuring of the military operational command zones* and the reallocation of several posts were made public. The eastern operational command zone was now headed by Brigadier General Musa Raba, while General Teklai Kifle 'Manjus' retained command of the western zone. The central operational command zone was headed by Brigadier General Simon Okbe and the command of the militias was awarded to Brigadier General Gebrehiwet Zemichael; neither of the last two had played a prominent military leadership role before. *Philipos Weldeyohannes* established himself as the strongman among the military leadership; he was promoted to the rank of full general and appointed as the new *chief-of-staff of the army*. He also headed the sprinter operational command, an emergency standby force. About 7,000 soldiers of the *Tigray People's Democratic*

Movement, an Ethiopian opposition group based in Eritrea, were deployed near Asmara, reportedly with the task of protecting President Isaias. Major General Haile Samuel 'China' seemed to have fallen out of favour and lost his post as a military operational zone commander. *Rifts within the military leadership* became manifest when Teklai 'Manjus' was apparently put under house arrest for several weeks in June and had several of his personal staff arrested by General Philipos in October.

The *mass exodus of the younger generation* to avoid conscription or to flee the potentially unlimited national service *accelerated sharply during the year* and the number of new arrivals of Eritrean refugees in Ethiopia and Sudan increased markedly. The total number of Eritreans in both countries rose to 216,000 registered refugees, plus substantial numbers who preferred to stay out of refugee camps and so were not registered. In October alone, 5,000 Eritreans crossed the border into Ethiopia. *People smuggling and trafficking* of Eritreans carried out by the Rashaida tribe and Sinai Bedouins with the complicity of Eritrean, Sudanese and Egyptian officials continued and many refugees were abducted in Eastern Sudanese refugee camps. An estimated 1,000 refugees, mostly Eritreans, remained trapped in trafficking compounds on the Egyptian Sinai Peninsula. From 13 to 16 October the AU, UNHCR, IOM and the Sudanese government held a joint conference with the aim of tackling people trafficking and smuggling in the Horn of Africa. On this occasion, Eritrea's ambassador to the AU claimed that the generous asylum policies of various Western countries were the main push factor for Eritrean refugees.

In May, the country's four *Catholic bishops* published a *Pastoral Letter* titled "Where is Your Brother", in which they deplored the mass exodus of the young and middle-aged and pointed out that this was due to the imposition of indefinite periods of conscription. They stated that current living conditions were unbearable and that the youth would not leave a country in which it was possible to make a living and where peace, justice and freedom of expression prevailed. They openly criticised the PFDJ's ideology of national sacrifice, stating that the country was made for the people and not the people for the country. They concluded that "the pillar that holds our social life is been uprooted and … we are heading towards utter collapse". The letter was widely distributed in secret throughout the country. The government did not retaliate against the bishops, who were backed by the Vatican, but on 20 September the commander of the Eritrean Police Force held a meeting with 150 religious leaders and warned them not to interfere in political issues.

Religious freedom remained *severely restricted*. Patriarch Antonios of the Orthodox Church, who had been replaced by Bishop Dioscoros in 2007 after having criticised government interference in religious affairs, remained under house arrest. An estimated 1,500 Christians and similar numbers of Muslims were in detention for their faith. Sunni Islam and Orthodox, Catholic and Lutheran Christianity were the only permitted religions, while adherents of Pentecostal churches, Jehovah's Witnesses and Muslims opposed to the government-appointed mufti were considered as 'radicals' and faced persecution. In April, police forces arrested four Lutheran Christians who were to be ordained to pastoral ministry. The government did not accept the holding of a clerical post as justifying exemption from military service. *Freedom of the press* was *non-existent*, and Eritrea continued to be ranked last worldwide in the Reporters Without Borders press freedom index.

The *Warsay-Yikealo Development Campaign*, which forced all Eritreans of working age (18 to over 40) to serve in the military or do national service for unlimited periods, continued. The conscripts worked for pocket money in infrastructure projects, on military-owned agricultural enterprises, in the administration and in public services. According to state media, 500,000 people had so far been trained at the Sawa military training camp, which also served as a boarding school for the twelfth and final school year. About 6,000 mostly female conscripts who had gone through military training earlier had been held at Heday military camp near the town of Afabet without any work assignments and with little food for more than a year. Their fate contributed to growing *passive resistance against forced conscription*, and increasing numbers of young people who were supposed to report for military training or national service refused to do so and went into hiding or fled the country. Similarly, members of the '*people militias*', elderly citizens aged between 50 and over 80 years who had been forced since 2012 to undergo military training and to patrol their neighbourhoods carrying guns, increasingly refused to perform their duties and to attend training sessions. The *resistance group Arbi Harnet* ('Freedom Friday'), which had been founded in the diaspora, strengthened its base inside Eritrea and was involved in several acts of civil disobedience. It published an underground magazine called 'MeqaleH Forto' (Echoes of Forto), a reference to the failed military uprising of January 2013. In August, members of the group distributed about 5,000 nakfa notes carrying the message "exodus is not the solution, rise up" during the annual festival at the Expo compound in Asmara. Diaspora members of the movement made telephone calls to Eritrea, encouraging parents not to send their children back to the Sawa military training camp after the summer break.

Eritrea's *judicial system* remained in disarray, with a poorly organised formal court system that often suffered from government interference. Imprisonment for political reasons as well as arrests for alleged criminal offences mostly took place without respect for legal process, and those affected were arbitrarily kept in prison and subsequently released without having been brought before a court of law. Civil cases were handled by traditional elders and mediators on the basis of customary law or by community courts headed by government-picked lay judges. *Corruption* was endemic and practised by military officers, PFDJ cadres and state employees with little government interference. TI's Corruption Perception Index ranked Eritrea as 'highly corrupt' (166th out of 174 countries). The surviving *members of the G15*, a group of prominent PFDJ members who had demanded political reforms and were detained in September 2001, remained in custody without charge. The same applied to the *journalists of the free press* who had been arrested along with them, including Dawid Issak, a Swedish-Eritrean national. On 15 April, 17 Muslims from the Keren area who had previously served as local administrators, security officers or doctors were released after several years' imprisonment. They had been neither accused of a specific crime nor brought before a court of law.

On 13 May, the *UN Special Rapporteur on the situation of human rights in Eritrea*, Sheila Keetaruth, presented a report in which she spoke of rampant human rights violations related to the indefinite national service and unlawful arrest and detention. As a consequence, the *UN Human Rights Council* established a Mission of Inquiry on 27 June with a mandate to further investigate human rights violations in Eritrea. On 25 September, Eritrea became a signatory to the UN Convention against Torture and Other Cruel, Inhuman or Degrading Treatment or Punishment, possibly as a reaction to the UN's scrutiny. However, in the absence of any human rights monitoring mechanisms in the country, it was highly doubtful that this step would bring an improvement in the prevailing human rights situation.

The *political opposition parties in the diaspora remained fractured* and generally inactive throughout the year. The National Council of the *Eritrean National Conference for Democratic Change* (*ENCDC*), an umbrella organisation of the political opposition and some civic society groups, met in Bishoftu (Ethiopia) on 17 December to address the current ENCDC impasse and to prepare a congress for the following year. *Human Rights Concern Eritrea* lobbied for the rights of Eritrean refugees around the globe, and in April the organisation's director, Elsa Chyrum, went on a three-day hunger strike in Geneva in support of 267 Eritreans who were being held in Djibouti in prison-like conditions. The Djiboutian government consequently handed them over to the Red Cross. On 3 February, a group of *prominent PFDJ dissidents*, among them ambassadors Andeberhan Wolde Giorgis and Abdela Adem, launched a *Forum for National Dialogue* in London with the aims of serving as a catalyst for pro-democracy Eritreans and preparing a political programme for the post-Isaias era. In April, the *Eritrean Lowlanders League* was founded in London as a forum to articulate the interests of the various lowland societies, who comprised the majority of the non-Tigrinya groups in the country.

Foreign Affairs

The *targeted sanctions* imposed on Eritrea by the UNSC in December 2009 (resolution 1907/2009) and December 2011 (resolution 2023/2011) *remained in place*. In a letter dated 13 October, the *UN Somalia Eritrea Monitoring Group* stated that it had found no further evidence that Eritrea supported the al-Shabaab militias in Somalia. However, the group asserted that Eritrea had imported weapons and ammunition from South Sudan, and that these activities had been coordinated by Nusredin Ali

Bekit, the manager of the Tessenei branch of the PFDJ-owned Red Sea Corporation, who was promoted to minister of trade and industry in mid-2014. Furthermore, *Eritrea continued to support armed Ethiopian opposition groups*, namely the Ogaden National Liberation Front, the Tigray People's Democratic Movement (based inside Eritrea) and Ginbot Sebat. The UN monitoring group confirmed that Eritrea was still holding 17 Djiboutian prisoners of war and that the conflict between the two countries remained unresolved. In addition, the Eritrean government continued to coerce Eritreans and persons of Eritrean origin in the diaspora to pay a 2% income tax, contrary to the provisions of the 2011 sanctions resolution.

Relations between the Eritrean government and *Qatar* cooled significantly after the abdication of Emir Sheikh Hamad bin Khalifa al-Thani in 2013, because Eritrea constantly undermined Qatari efforts to mediate in its conflict with Djibouti. When President Isaias visited Qatar on 2 March, he was not received by Emir Sheikh Tamim bin Hamad al-Thani, but only by the minister of municipality and urban planning. In early August, the Eritrean military detained a *Djiboutian officer* who had accompanied a Qatari military contingent in the demilitarised zone between the two countries; Qatar was monitoring the contested territory under a 2010 tripartite agreement between Djibouti, Eritrea and Qatar. The officer was released later in the year, but Eritrea continued to refuse to hand over Djiboutian POWs.

The *political stalemate* and the no-war-no-peace situation between *Eritrea and Ethiopia continued*. During Sudanese President Omar al-Bashir's visit to Asmara in mid-January, the Sudanese ambassador to Eritrea announced that al-Bashir had begun to hold indirect talks with President Isaias and Ethiopian Prime Minister Hailemariam Desalegn in the hope of bringing them to the negotiation table at a later stage. However, these efforts did not produce any results. Both governments retained their respective positions, Asmara insisting on the implementation of the Eritrea-Ethiopia Boundary Commission's 2002 decision, according to which the contested border area around Badme had been awarded to Eritrea, and Ethiopia insisting on the need for dialogue prior to the demarcation of the border. There were no military incursions from Ethiopia into Eritrean territory, with the exception of one assault carried out by two Ethiopia-based Eritrean opposition groups, the Red Sea Afar Democratic Organization and the Democratic Front for Eritrean Unity, who attacked a military base in the Adi Quala subzone on 22 December, reportedly killing seven Eritrean intelligence agents.

Relations with *Sudan* remained close. On 5 April, presidential advisor Yemane Gebreab travelled to Khartoum to deliver a message from Isaias. President al-Bashir visited Isaias for a second time on 22 June to discuss regional issues, including relations between Sudan and South Sudan. During al-Bashir's January visit to Asmara, he and his Eritrean counterpart had announced their support for the South Sudanese government, but there were unconfirmed allegations by US human rights activist John Pendergast that both Eritrea and Sudan were clandestinely supporting South Sudanese opposition forces.

The Eritrean government tried to establish close relations with *Egypt*'s new president, Abdelfattah al-Sisi, and on 9 September President Isaias, Foreign Minister Osman Saleh and presidential adviser Yemane Gebreab travelled to Cairo to hold talks with al-Sisi and various high-level government officials. The Eritrean regime considered Egypt a valuable ally due to its conflict with Ethiopia over the construction of the Grand Ethiopian Renaissance Dam and its share of the Nile water.

In another attempt to overcome its international isolation, the government tried to improve its relations with *Russia*. On 17 February, Foreign Minister Osman Saleh visited Moscow and both parties signed a cooperation agreement on trade and investment. On 5 June, an Eritrean delegation headed by the foreign minister and Yemane Gebreab visited the Crimea Peninsula at the invitation of the Russian Federation, purportedly to attend celebrations marking 215 years since the birth of Alexander Pushkin, who was believed to have Eritrean ancestors. The Ukrainian ministry of foreign affairs criticised the visit, calling it "an unfriendly step" and "blatant disrespect of international law" and a violation of Ukrainian sovereignty.

Israel continued its hostile policy towards Eritrean refugees, and in late August about 2,000 Eritreans and Sudanese were held in the Holot facility in the Negev desert in prison-like conditions. According to HRW, 367 Eritreans had been coerced to return home as of March; their fate upon reaching Eritrea was unknown.

Eritrean embassies, consulates and government middlemen around the globe continued to collect a *2% diaspora tax* levied by the regime on diaspora Eritreans' incomes from either work or social welfare. There were no further attempts by host countries to stop these activities, which were restricted under the 2011 sanctions regime. Throughout the year, large numbers of *Eritrean refugees* reached *Europe* via the Mediterranean on boats provided by people-smuggling rings. On 2 July, Italy's Deputy Foreign Minister Lapo Pistelli met Isaias in Asmara, stating that it was time for a new beginning in relations between the two countries. The reported aim of the visit was to encourage Eritrea to enter into constructive regional relations, to boost economic cooperation with Italy and to enter into a shared commitment to human rights. It seemed that the Italian government implicitly hoped that this policy shift would reduce the numbers of Eritreans fleeing their country. On 14 November, a UNHCR spokesperson reported that the number of Eritreans arriving in Europe had nearly tripled in 2014 and amounted to 37,000 individuals, 34,000 of whom had arrived by boat, the second-largest group after Syrians. The increase was partially facilitated by Italy's 'Mare Nostrum' operation, which increased the chance of reaching Europe safely by boat from Libya. The majority of the refugees filed asylum claims in Sweden, Switzerland and Germany, but other countries were affected as well. The rising numbers of *Eritrean asylum seekers* provoked discussions in several European countries, questioning the practice of granting automatic protection to those who left Eritrea illegally in order to escape national service. On 25 November, the Danish Immigration Service published a report largely based on a short mission to Eritrea and on talks with various diplomats and international NGO representatives, which concluded that the situation on the ground had improved and collective protection was no longer necessary. However, the report was heavily criticised by HRW and the UNHCR.

Eritrea's relations with the *USA* remained poor. On 29 January, the Ministry of Foreign Affairs published a press release in which it summarised all the USA's alleged wrongdoings against Eritrea and stated that "US hostility not Eritrean rigidity" were responsible for sour relations. Neither the US embassy in Asmara nor the Eritrean embassy in Washington DC had ambassadors assigned.

Socioeconomic Developments

Eritrea's *faltering command economy* remained under the firm control of the ruling PFDJ and the high-ranking military. The exchange rate to the dollar remained fixed at a severely overvalued rate of 15 Eritrean nakfa (ERN) to $ 1. The *black market* therefore continued to thrive, and diaspora Eritreans who changed hard currency during a visit to the homeland received a black market change rate of about 55 ERN:$ 1, while money sent through the informal hawala system was changed at a rate of about 50 NRN:$ 1. Black market activities were under the control of government agents. Regular *electricity blackouts* continued and Asmara had no electricity supply for extended periods throughout July and August; fuel was only available on the black market. No investments were made in Asmara's deteriorating infrastructure, including the sewerage system, and running water was hardly available.

Chronic food insecurity continued in spite of good rains in the highlands. A potential bumper harvest was wasted since large amounts of ripe crops could not be gathered because older farmers were called to participate in military training during harvest time, while younger Eritreans were absent from their villages on national service. UNICEF published no updated nutrition data for 2014 but indicated that malnutrition rates had increased during the past years in four of the six Eritrean regions, namely Anseba, Gash-Barka, Southern Red Sea and Ma'ekel (Central Region). The Global Hunger Index rated the *nutritional situation* as '*extremely alarming*', Eritrea and Burundi being the only remaining countries worldwide in that category. In September, the UNDP and the government published a report related to the *health-related MDGs*, which stated that MDGs 4 to 6 had been achieved. According to the report, under-five mortality had fallen to 50 per 1,000 live births and maternal mortality to 380 per 100,000 births, while mortality due to malaria had been reduced by 90% and HIV/AIDS had almost been eradicated. However, it was unclear whether these data were accurate, since non-governmental organisations had no access to the countryside and an independent assessment of data accuracy was impossible. There were no reports concerning the remaining five MDGs, none of which was likely to be achieved. Hunger and extreme poverty (MDG

1) had only been reduced by 13% since 1990 and, according to the 2014 Africa MDG Report, Eritrea had the lowest school enrolment in Africa (38% in 2011) and the second-lowest primary school completion rate, at 33%.

Reliable economic and financial data were hard to come by due to the government's constant lack of transparency. The authorities did not publish a state budget and nothing was known about the use of revenues from the mining sector, estimated at $ 1 bn since 2011. The inflation rate remained stable at 12.3% and the current-account balance was estimated at 0.3% of GDP. The African Economic Outlook (AfDB, OECD) corrected its earlier estimate for 2013 and stated that *economic growth* in that year had been only 1.1% instead of an assumed 7%, and estimated the *2014 growth rate* at 1.9%. This was due to shrinking economic activity in all sectors, with the exception of the mining industry. Growth was largely driven by *copper production* at the Bisha mine, a joint venture of the Canadian Nevsun Mining Corporation and the Eritrean National Mining Corporation (ENAMCO). On 20 November, three Eritrean individuals who had fled to Canada sued Nevsun for complicity in the use of forced labour under its local sub-contractor, the PFDJ-owned Segen construction company. The plaintiffs stated they had been forced to work at the Bisha mine against their will and that they had been subjected to cruel and degrading treatment.

According to the AfDB, the influx of *remittances* gathered through the 2% diaspora tax levied by the government had *declined sharply* to about 10% of GDP due to the implementation of the 2011 UN sanctions, which required diaspora host countries to scrutinise the methods by which the tax was collected.

While Lufthansa did not resume flights to Eritrea, *Turkish Airlines* launched a route from Istanbul to Asmara on 19 August and *Qatar Airways* commenced flights from Doha on 5 December.

Ethiopia

Jean-Nicolas Bach

Politically, the year was marked by preparations for the fifth general elections, scheduled for May 2015. So-called 'right-wing multinational' groups failed to create a broad coalition to counter the ruling EPRDF and appeared weakened by internal struggles (doubtless exploited by the EPRDF) in the run-up to the elections. A four-party front of ethnic and multinational parties nevertheless maintained its candidacy and thus represented the first coalition to contest two successive general elections. The young Blue Party, created in January 2012, was to take part in its first election.

The end of 2014 brought an opportunity for evaluation of the EPRDF's performance. Economically, it was the moment to present visible results of the first Growth and Transformation Plan (2010–15). Prime Minister Hailemariam Desalegn announced the achievements made in terms of infrastructures. The drafting of the next five-year plan began. Although the first versions were not made public, the government continued to pursue the objective of furthering the industrial transition of the country through major infrastructural projects, large-scale agricultural schemes and the development of a narrowly controlled private sector. But the relatively posi-

 | DOI 10.1163/9789004305052_035

tive economic situation could not hide a dramatically deteriorating socio-political situation: as many inhabitants said, "one cannot eat rails" and there was social discontent over persistent poverty, the high cost of living, recurring water and electricity shortages, and what many denounced as increasing corruption. The tense relationship between the EPRDF and parts of the Muslim community eased, but problems were 'solved' by threats and imprisonments rather than by negotiation. Demonstrations in the Oromo region were harshly repressed by the security services. Demonstrations organised by political opposition parties multiplied throughout the year; most were peaceful, but some were marked by imprisonments of party activists and leaders, and sometimes by violence. The macroeconomic growth rate remained strong, officially at 11.4%, largely attributed to the government's spending on infrastructure and various mega projects, substantial remittances, FDI (mainly from China, India and Turkey) and agricultural schemes.

The government maintained the long pursued strategy concerning its regional policies, intervening diplomatically and militarily in order to prevent conflicts spilling over and affecting Ethiopia's economic gains. It thus maintained a strong diplomatic involvement in the resolution of the crisis between Sudan and South Sudan, and also with regard to South Sudan's civil war. About 4,000 Ethiopian troops officially joined the AU Mission in Somalia. The tense relationship with Egypt over the construction of the massive dam on the Blue Nile showed signs of improvement. Relations with Eritrea were still blocked by both sides due to a lack of political will to negotiate.

Domestic Politics

The political sphere remained fully under the undisputed hegemony of the *Ethiopian People's Revolutionary Democratic Front* (*EPRDF*), and had a good chance of remaining so after the 2015 elections. However, deep tensions existed within the Front. Relations between its four constituent components (the *Tigray People's Liberation Front* [*TPLF*], the Amhara National Democratic Movement [ANDM], the Oromo People's Democratic Organization [OPDO], and the Southern Ethiopian Peoples' Democratic Movement [SEPDM]) and within the dominant TPLF itself were likely to need redefinition after the elections. In fact, although the TPLF still controlled the economic, security and military apparatus, tensions had been increasing since the death of the dominant prime minister Meles Zenawi in 2012. An '11-day tour' organised by some veteran TPLF figures in May in Tigray found evidence of discontent among local population and elites, who accused the current regional and national leadership of 'bad governance' and 'corruption'. It also revealed increasing tensions between older members of the TPLF and younger cadres. In addition, tensions increased between the leaders in Addis Ababa and in the

Tigray region, the former fiefdom of the TPLF, where demands for more autonomy were emerging.

Further intensification of such competition within the TPLF had the potential to endanger the *balance of power within the EPRDF*, where relations between the various political groups also became more tense during the year; this was described by one observer as a "leadership in disarray". As the TPLF remained dominant, the ANDM was claiming a greater share of power, partly citing its support of Meles' group during the 2001 TPLF crisis. While the SEPDM remained relatively weak within the EPRDF and supportive of its head and prime minister Hailemariam Desalegn, the OPDO was shaken by the EPRDF's repressive response to demonstrations in the Oromo region in May.

The story began with the new '*Addis Ababa and the Surrounding Oromo Special Zone Integrated Development Plan*' (known as the 2014 '*Masterplan*'), made public by the Addis Ababa City Administration in May. As its administration expanded into the surrounding Oromo territories, many Oromos feared that the fast development of the capital would prevent them from accessing their land or even force them to move, as had been the case in the Western Gambella region. (Addis Ababa, itself a city-state within the federal system, is situated in the middle of the Oromo region, which is the biggest region and is home to the largest ethnic group, the Oromo, representing about 35% of Ethiopia's population.) By integrating eight towns administered by the Oromo region, the 2014 Masterplan was denounced as expanding Addis Ababa illegally. Many Oromos took to the streets in various regions, and especially on university campus (as in Ambo and Weda Walabu). The reaction of the security services was very harsh, as *dozens of demonstrators were jailed* and 11 were officially acknowledged to have been killed by security agents (30 according to AI, up to 65 according to Oromo political leaders). This reaction had a profound impact within the ruling OPDO, as many members contested the policy of the EPRDF. OPDO members and TV journalists lost their jobs because of their 'narrow political views'. What happened in the Oromo region during the spring not only illustrated the tensions within the ruling EPRDF, but was also indicative of the readiness of the government to use violence to deal with discontent. It marked a turning point in the year, as the government attitude towards opponents clearly hardened from then on.

This development could be observed in the government's attitude toward *opposition parties*. The political opposition had been permitted to organise peaceful demonstrations since 2013. In February, Unity for Democracy and Justice (UDJ) and the All-Ethiopia Unity Party (AEUP/'Mähihad'), two of the largest opposition parties, organised a major demonstration in Bahir Dar in Amhara Region to denounce the 'insulting' declaration of the region's vice president, a member of the ANDM, concerning displaced Amhara peoples in the Beni Shangul region. Peaceful demonstrations were held by the AEUP in Sewela (Southern Region), and the Blue Party, notably in the capital city and in Gonder (Amhara region). The Ethiopian Federal

Democratic Unity Forum ('Medrek') also held markedly successful demonstrations in Addis Ababa and Hawassa. However, the last *demonstrations turned violent*: in December, the Blue Party called for a demonstration in the capital, where UDJ and the AEUP also took part. Many members were arrested and spent several days in jail, including the Blue Party leader, Yilkal Getent. With the election date drawing closer, pressure on opposition activists increased and they were regularly detained for a few hours, a few days or a few weeks. Others, accused of being linked with foreign-based terrorist groups such as 'Ginbot 7' or the Oromo Liberation Front (OLF), remained in jail.

The year was also characterised by the *failed merger between UDJ and the AEUP*. In an attempt to recreate a united 'right-wing multinational' opposition similar to the 'kinijit' coalition in 2005, UDJ and the AEUP signed a 'pre-merging agreement' in June – by so doing, UDJ de facto left the 'Medrek' coalition with which it had gained one parliamentary seat in the 2010 election. But irregularities were soon exposed by internal dissent in the AEUP, and the National Electoral Board (NEBE) eventually rejected the legality of the merger. This left both political formations deeply divided by internal factionalism. Unexpectedly, dissident groups within each party overthrew their respective presidents and assumed the leadership in October–November, but the NEBE once again rejected the legality of these changes; by year's end no decision had been taken on the status of the previous leaderships. Many UDJ dissidents decided to join the Blue Party to campaign as its candidates, but this was once again rejected by the NEBE. The entire opposition suffered from this failed merger and entered the electoral campaign in a clearly weakened position. UDJ and the AEUP were now isolated and could not properly register their candidates. 'Medrek' lost a strong member with deep roots in the strategic Amhara region. The Blue Party remained stable for its first participation in an election, although many of its candidates had been rejected by the NEBE.

Press freedom also suffered dramatically during the year. Six private media outlets were closed, and many journalists were arrested or forced to flee the country. According to HRW, during the year "22 journalists, bloggers, and publishers were criminally charged, and more than 30 journalists fled the country in fear of being arrested under repressive laws". Among the cases that received most international attention, Eskinder Nega and Reyot Alemu (both arrested in 2011 and remaining in jail) were representative of many journalists who were forced to self-censor out of fear of being charged. In October, Temesgen Desalegn was sentenced to three years in jail for his articles published two years before in 'Feteh'. Still waiting to be judged, the *Zone9 bloggers* were representative of the closing space of the press in 2014, symptomatic of the application of the Anti-Terrorism Proclamation, and illustrative of the increasing fear among the EPRDF leadership of infiltration into Ethiopia by 'Ginbot 7'. The blog, founded in 2012 with the motto "we blog because we care", published challenging critical views of EPRDF policies. Of the nine bloggers, six were arrested in April, along with three journalists who were close relatives. They were later charged with terrorism, and more specifically with being 'Ginbot 7' agents in Ethiopia. The other three bloggers escaped and were now operating from abroad (USA and Sweden). These recent measures against journalists explained why Reporters Without Borders' 2015 World Press Freedom Index ranked Ethiopia 133rd out of 179 countries.

The *human rights situation* also generally worsened. A Freedom House summary published in February 2015 said: "Ethiopia is rated Not Free in Freedom of the World 2014, Not Free in Freedom of the Press 2014, Not Free on the Net 2014." AI also contributed to the growing international concern and criticism of the Ethiopian government by publishing a report in October that referred to the arbitrary detention in Addis Ababa and in the provinces of several tens of thousands of activists, journalists and opponents; according to the report, some 5,000 Oromos had been arrested between 2011 and 2014. Local activists were arrested in the regions: the Oromo Federal Congress, for instance, denounced the arbitrary detention of several hundred of its activists since the demonstrations in the Oromo region in spring. Blue Party members also became victims of repeated harassment, as in March, when ten members were detained for up to ten days for shouting political slogans on the occasion of International Women's Day in Addis Ababa. Preventive arrests of activists took place to thwart demonstrations and deter opponents from informing the public about future gatherings. Weynshet Molla, head of financial affairs of the Blue Party, was detained for about a month during the summer for her participation in a Muslim protest in Addis Ababa. Muslim demonstrations continued during the year, but the situation was less tense than previously – although jailed Muslim leaders remained in prison, charged with terrorism. In sum, local activists as well as leaders of the Oromo Federalist Congress, the AEUP, UDJ, the Blue Party, the Ethiopian Democratic Party and Arena Tigray (a member of 'Medrek') were repeatedly arrested and some of them charged, along with journalists, under the 2009 Anti-Terrorism Proclamation.

One of the most widely reported and debated political events of the year was the arrest of *Andargachew Tsige*. He had British citizenship and was the general secretary of 'Ginbot 7', which was labelled a terrorist organisation by the government and led by a former prominent politician, Berhanu Nega. The movement was operating partly from the USA – through its media outlet, ESAT – and partly militarily from Eritrea. The Eritrean government offered sanctuary and allowed the armed wing of 'Ginbot 7' to train – the movement claimed to have about 18,000 trained soldiers. Andergatchew was arrested in Yemen in June while in transit to Eritrea. He was then extradited to Ethiopia, where he remained detained at an unknown location. This was not an isolated case: in January, two representatives of the Ogaden National Liberation Front (ONLF; another armed group based in the Somali Region in eastern Ethiopia) were arrested in Nairobi (Kenya) and handed over to Ethiopia. The Andargachew case provoked many reactions within Ethiopia and in Ethiopian social media networks abroad, where he was often considered a 'hero', but it was also a reminder of the reality of the 'terrorist' threat in the region, its support by the Eritrean government and its regional ramifications. Relations between Western countries and Ethiopia became quite ambiguous. The British government – which was denied access to Andargachew several times – cancelled a fund previously directed to supporting the formation of police forces. Relations with the USA also became tense as Washington hosted 'Ginbot 7' leaders and Ethiopian political exiles. US Secretary of State John Kerry found himself in an uncomfortable position when it emerged that a young student he had met and congratulated publicly was arrested a few months later as one of the Zone 9 bloggers. However, the apparent absence of any strong international criticism of the Ethiopian government during 2014 was striking. The EU, silently, did not plan to send an election observation mission for the 2015 election. This eloquent diplomatic silence was clearly due to the fact that Ethiopia still represented a pivotal ally in one of the world's most unstable regions.

Foreign Affairs

The projects implemented by the Ethiopian 'Democratic Developmental State' extended far beyond the national borders: hydroelectric dams, irrigation schemes, roads and railways were drawing new economic boundaries. The EPRDF was well aware that any lasting national development within Ethiopia depended on a minimal degree of regional stability. As Defence Chief of Staff Samora Yenus noted, Ethiopia had to remain involved militarily in order to defend its development. The Ethiopian leadership thus continued to pursue its agenda of working hard militarily and diplomatically to stabilise its borders.

In April, Global Firepower ranked Ethiopia as the third-strongest *military power* in Africa. Ethiopia in effect allocated $ 7.5 bn of its budget to defence – a sector that was becoming a powerful branch within the Ethiopian economy. Ethiopia had for a number of years maintained strong involvement in a very unstable region targeted by heavy terrorist attacks. Militarily, it continued its involvement in operations under international mandates in the Horn of Africa: in *Darfur* (Sudan) in the hybrid UN-AU mission (UNAMID) to which Ethiopia contributed around 2,400 soldiers, and in *South Sudan* under the UN Interim Security Force in Abyei (UNISFA), in which it was practically the sole troop-contributing country, having sent around 4,500 soldiers since 2011. Ethiopia became the fourth-largest contributor to UN missions in 2014.

In January–February, Ethiopia's regional security policy took a dramatic turn as Prime Minister Hailemariam Desalegn announced the integration of Ethiopian troops into the AU mission in Somalia (*AMISOM*). Ethiopia had been intervening regularly in Somalia since the fall of the Barre regime in 1991, most heavily between

2006 and 2009 against the Union of Islamic Courts, and since then intermittently in support of AMISOM. But Addis Ababa's interventions in Somalia had been conducted without an international mandate. The new move thus represented a radical change for Ethiopia's regional involvement in Somalia, at least officially – as the country remained de facto quite independent with regard to its operations in the field. Furthermore, by contributing to AMISOM, Ethiopia had now become a leading troop-contributor to internationally mandated missions worldwide. Ethiopia's participation in AMISOM could be seen as partially motivated by financial considerations, since AMISOM was financially and logistically supported by the UN and the EU, but this would be too simplistic an explanation. Being part of the mission allowed the government to obtain a perspective from within. In this regard, Nairobi's decision to contribute Kenyan troops to AMISOM in 2012 may have been decisive. Tensions remained between Addis Ababa and Nairobi in 2014 concerning the fate and management of the borderland region of Jubaland in south-west Somalia. Joining AMISOM may also have helped the Ethiopian regime in terms of building a positive international image, especially in the context of the coming election and the dramatic narrowing of political space.

The difficult relations with *Eritrea*, Ethiopia's northern neighbour, did not improve. The UN Border Commission's 2002 decision to recognise disputed territories (including the town of Badme) as part of Eritrea had made the withdrawal of Ethiopian troops from 'its' territory a precondition for negotiations. The UN Monitoring Group on Somalia and Eritrea accused Eritrea of hosting armed groups opposed to Ethiopia ('Ginbot 7' and the Tigray People's Democratic Movement), and of supporting others within Ethiopia (the ONLF and the OLF), while Addis Ababa hosted Eritrean opposition parties (the most important being the Eritrea National Council for Democratic Change and the recently founded Eritrean Youth Solidarity for National Salvation) and provided them with offices, conference venues, and some funding.

Addis Ababa was also deeply involved diplomatically in the *Sudanese peace processes*, hosting many peace conferences in the Ethiopian capital, notably under the auspices of IGAD. As tensions between Khartoum and Juba eased, armed conflict had erupted within South Sudan in December 2013. Within *South Sudan*, the opposing camps, the SPLM and SPLM-In-Opposition, signed several ceasefires that were never adhered to and conducted peace talks almost throughout the year in Addis Ababa, with IGAD as the forum for mediation. But the mediating team, led by the veteran Ethiopian TPLF leader Seyoum Mesfin (Ethiopia's ambassador to China), failed to persuade the belligerents to accept a minimum compromise by the end of the year and no solution was in sight.

Due to these ongoing conflicts in neighbouring countries, Ethiopia became the leading refugee-hosting country in Africa. In collaboration with international humanitarian agencies, Ethiopia offered assistance and protection on its territory to more than *600,000 refugees*, mainly originating from South Sudan, Eritrea and Somalia. The vicious conflict in South Sudan that broke out in December 2013 had displaced more than 1.5 m people and, according to UNHCR, around *190,000 South Sudanese* refugees were hosted by Ethiopia in 2014; the same source indicated that there were about 100 new arrivals from South Sudan every day. The expanding camps for South Sudanese refugees in Gambella Region in western Ethiopia, already facing tensions due to land grabbing and local population displacements, threatened to further increase socioeconomic problems there.

The antagonism between Ethiopia and *Egypt* over the Grand Ethiopian Renaissance Dam on the Blue Nile was not yet finally resolved, but seemed to be drawing closer to an amicable agreement. The situation between the two countries remained stalled, as Egypt still feared the negative impact of the dam on the downstream flow of water. But in contrast to earlier open threats, the new Egyptian government of President al-Sisi adopted an increasingly pragmatic approach to negotiations. In October, both countries agreed to commission further independent studies to assess all direct and indirect consequences of the dam and to prepare a trilateral memorandum of understanding between Egypt, Ethiopia and Sudan. Ethiopia left no doubt about its resolve to complete the building of the dam, as it had become a matter of national pride and was considered essential for providing electricity to other infrastructural and development projects.

Socioeconomic Developments

Ethiopia's *population* officially reached 89.7 m according to the Central Statistical Agency, and around 95 m according to international financial institutions (IMF, World Bank). Population growth rate continued to be high, as the last census, in 2007, had estimated a population of about 74 m. According to the World Bank, *poverty* had been reduced by 33% during the previous decade – although it estimated that 37 m Ethiopians were still poor or vulnerable to falling into poverty. This contrasted with a recent study by the Oxford Poverty and Human Development Initiative (OPHI), which ranked Ethiopia among the poorest countries in the world. OPHI's Multidimensional Poverty Index categorised 87.3% of the population as "poor", 58.1% as "poor and destitute" and 36.8% as poor with less than $ 1.5 per day. Ethiopia's *Gini* coefficient was 0.336 and the *HDI* 0.435. Poverty thus remained hard to fight, although 60% of government expenditure in recent years had been oriented toward pro-poor economic growth (agriculture, education, health and road development), and despite an impressive sustained GDP growth rate.

Prime Minister Hailemariam Desalegn officially announced an 11.4% *economic growth rate* for the fiscal year (clearly outpacing the SSA average). International institutions also estimated that real GDP growth had remained very solid in 2014, but nevertheless considered the Ethiopian figures to be overestimates. The *IMF*, for instance, gave a growth rate of 10.3%. The official *GDP per capita* in 2014 was about $ 630.

The service sectors and remittances were estimated to contribute about 9% and 10% of GDP, respectively, but *key drivers of growth* remained national investments in transport infrastructure (roads, rail), energy (hydroelectric power generation through dams) and agriculture. *Agriculture* officially grew by 8.5%, taking advantage of the transformation of subsistence smallholders into commercial farmers, helped by the development of roads, power supplies and market networks. However, the agricultural sector's development was constrained by unfavourable international commodity prices for important cash crops (such as coffee).

Manufacturing industries (23% of GDP) continued to benefit from public investment. Rumour had it that the government would invest $ 20 bn in the power-generating sector for the second *Growth and Transformation Plan* (2015–20). The Plan had not yet been made public, but was expected to follow the path of the previous plan, with massive investment in infrastructure and a strong state-led economic policy. Finance Minister Sufian Ahmed told Reuters in December that "without investing in infrastructure, it is now abundantly clear that Africa cannot sustain growth".

The pace of *infrastructural 'mega-projects'* continued, although not quite as fast as the initial ambitious schedules had foreseen. These projects included 159,000 condominium houses that Hailemariam said were under construction. The road network expanded further (road-building accounted for almost one-third of the national budget). The government officially announced the start of construction of a 220 km road linking the north-east of the country to the port of Djibouti. China consolidated its predominance in financing these roads, as well as the impressive new Addis Ababa Light Railway, one line of which was expected to be tested in February 2015; 87% of the Light Railway project was already completed, as well as 80% of the Addis Ababa-Dewole railway. India also increased its involvement in the construction of infrastructural projects, notably in the field of railway construction. The government announced ambitious plans for the construction of 5,000 km of railway lines in the coming years, and also the expansion of Addis Ababa's international airport.

Among key infrastructural works, the construction of *dams for hydroelectric power generation* continued to be pursued with impressive speed. Electricity was expected to partly support domestic economic development and infrastructure projects (such as electric trains), but was also foreseen to be exported to neighbouring countries. In 2014, Djibouti was already benefitting from Ethiopian hydroelectricity. Construction of the Gibe III dam was 89% completed, and of the Genale dam 66% completed. But the most impressive project under construction remained the *Grand Ethiopian Renaissance Dam*, 43% of which was already completed. Started in 2013, the construction of the $ 4.2 bn dam was planned to finish in 2017 and was expected to then produce 6,000 MW (the government announced that 700 MW would be produced as early as 2015). The Ethiopian Electric Power Corporation issued Millennium Bonds to finance the project to enable the Ethiopian populace to remain the sole financier of the dam, which had become a symbol of national pride. The issue of more bonds by the government in December was intended to raise finance for infrastructural projects for which sufficient funding seemed to be lacking.

The government further confirmed its gradual turn towards market-oriented economic policies, issuing its first *Eurobond* in December after an international investors roadshow. The 'B1' or 'B' assigned to Ethiopia by rating agencies Moody's and Standard & Poor's, respectively, in their short-term and long-term financial risk assessment, combined with the IMF's September declaration that the risk of debt distress was low, enabled the government to issue securities for the first time. Ethiopia had till then been shut out of the international bond market. In this respect, 2014 represented a radical turn that should be seen as the culmination of constant government attempts to enter the global financial markets, as Hailemariam declared in December that this was not a new government policy. He said that international institutions had not previously allowed Ethiopia to apply for commercial loans in the capital market, but this had now changed. The $ 1 bn loan would run over a period of ten years at an interest rate of 6.625–6.675%. By issuing a debut international bond, Ethiopia confirmed its economic improvement and gained recognition of its ongoing success by international public and private institutions. Nevertheless, many socioeconomic challenges still remained.

Inflation was further controlled and was brought down to a low 5.6% in September. The government was thus able to confirm the substantial reduction of inflation that had been accomplished in 2013 (8.1%) as compared with 22.9% in 2012 (with average inflation of 16.1% over the previous five years). This reduction was due to the pursuance of a tight monetary policy and the positive effect of a good primary harvest on domestic food prices. However, the continuing drop in global raw material prices, the fiscal deficit (about 3% of GDP) and a falling exchange rate, still threatened to keep inflationary pressure high. The government also used the exchange rate as a policy tool, seeking to devalue the national currency (birr; ETB) with the aim of maintaining export competitiveness. This supported sustained economic growth, but kept the risk of inflation high (the average exchange rate in 2014 was ETB 21.1:$ 1). Furthermore, export growth was still outstripped by that of imports and the current-account deficit was projected to have widened to 7.3% of GDP in 2014. The fall in key commodity prices (e.g. coffee, horticulture) led to a drop in Ethiopian export revenue of an estimated $ 60 m. The volatility of agriculture, which still represented almost half of the economy's gross value added, and the sector's exposure to climatic hazards (drought, flooding) also remained as restraining elements.

Another challenge for the Ethiopian authorities was the stable and pervasive level of *corruption* in the country, as documented by *TI*'s Corruption Perceptions Index. Ethiopia had been ranked 111th out of 177 countries in 2013, and was ranked 110th out of 175 countries in 2014. Even more critically, Ethiopia was ranked ninth of the ten African countries with the highest illicit financial outflows (between 1970 and 2008), as documented by the AU High-Level Panel on Illicit Flows led by South Africa's former president Thabo Mbeki. The panel reported that Ethiopia could have lost about $ 16.5 bn in this way in the period 1970–2008, substantiating IMF and World Bank reports that estimated Ethiopia to have lost more than $ 11 bn in illicit outflows during the 2000s.

Kenya

Gabrielle Lynch

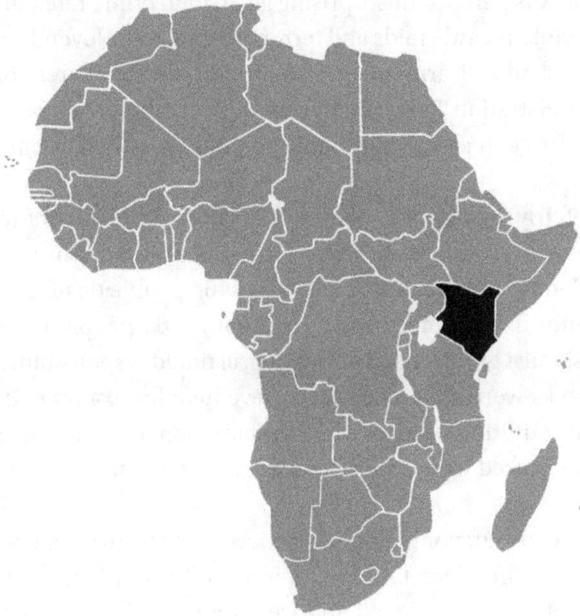

Dominant issues in 2014 were insecurity, devolution and the ICC. Insecurity led to a significant loss of life and property, and slowed an otherwise buoyant economy. It also exacerbated political divisions, as the Jubilee Alliance called for unity and blamed local opposition forces for increasing tensions and encouraging violence, and the principal opposition coalition and prominent activists argued that the government was using insecurity as an excuse to limit political freedoms. The government and opposition also came into direct conflict over devolution, which remained broadly popular and introduced new levels of political competition, but also proved expensive and exacerbated inter-ethnic tensions. Finally, the year was characterised by uncertainty about whether President Uhuru Kenyatta would have to stand trial at the ICC. This was clarified in December, when the ICC withdrew charges against him. The year therefore ended with only two Kenyans facing charges of crimes against humanity at the ICC: Deputy President William Ruto and the Kalenjin vernacular radio presenter Joshua arap Sang.

 | DOI 10.1163/9789004305052_036

Domestic Politics

The 2013 elections had been characterised by a pervasive 'peace narrative', which called upon Kenyans to vote and accept election results in peace. In 2014, this narrative was adapted by the new Jubilee government to call for *unity* in the interests of *peace and development*. This was perhaps unsurprising given high crime rates, an increase in wildlife poaching, violent cattle raids and terrorist attacks. In November, the Kenya Defence Forces launched a disarmament operation in the Pokot areas of Baringo County, after 19 Administration Police officers were killed by Pokot raiders in Kapedo following an upsurge in cattle raids between the Pokot and Turkana communities.

Terrorist attacks included fairly regular but relatively small-scale incidents in parts of Nairobi, Coast and northern Kenya, as well as a series of attacks in and around Mpeketoni in Lamu County in June, which left at least 60 people dead, and two attacks in Mandera County in November, in which another 64 people were killed. *Al-Shabaab*, a radical Islamist group based in Somalia, claimed responsibility for the casualties. Several attacks were apparently also prevented; for example, in March, four empty boxes of ammunition were found in the basement of a shopping mall in Nairobi, while a vehicle packed with explosives was discovered in Mombasa the same month.

In December, and in the face of burgeoning public criticism, Inspector General of Police David Kimaiyo and Cabinet Secretary for Interior and Coordination of National Government Joseph ole Lenku resigned and were replaced. This change in personnel was long overdue. However, the *national security* shortcomings were clearly greater than these two individuals. Indeed, throughout the year, the government's heavy-handed response helped fuel Islamic radicalisation and undermined efforts to prevent attacks and infiltrate terrorist cells by further alienating Muslims across the country.

Following ole Lenku's dismissal – and in a clear attempt to minimise complaints of ethnic marginalisation coming from his Maasai community and to simultaneously blur the executive/opposition divide – the government appointed a Maasai retired *army general* and opposition Orange Democratic Movement (ODM) MP, Joseph Nkaissery, to head national security. However, it soon became clear that Nkaissery's socialisation into military culture outweighed his opposition allegiance, when his public statements revealed an ongoing commitment to heavy-handed security tactics. Nkaissery's appointment also continued a government trend towards the selection of trained military officers for key political positions. Other examples included the appointment of Major General (Rtd) Gordon Kihalangwa as director of immigration in August, and Major General (Rtd) Philip Kameru as director general of the National Intelligence Service in September.

The government's *counter-terrorism strategy* – which included a number of seemingly arbitrary arrests and the closure of several mosques – was the source of particular criticism. Most notable was *Operation 'Usalaama Watch'*, which was launched in April and led to the round-up and screening of thousands of ethnic Somalis and the arrest of more than 650 residents in Nairobi's Eastleigh area. The operation was marred by allegations of harassment, bribery and looting by some of the 6,000 security personnel deployed, while human rights activists drew attention to the appalling conditions at Kasarani Stadium in Nairobi, which was temporarily commandeered as a detention centre.

The operation also strained relations within the ruling *Jubilee Alliance* as Aden Duale, an ethnic Somali, prominent member of Deputy President William Ruto's *United Republican Party* (URP), and majority leader of the National Assembly, openly criticised the scale and severity of the crackdown, which prompted calls for his removal by some of his counterparts from Kenyatta's *The National Alliance* (TNA). Yet, tensions within the Jubilee Alliance extended far beyond security to include relations between Kenyatta's and Ruto's Kikuyu and Kalenjin communities, who had been brought together for the first time in a multi-party election in 2013.

A number of *Muslim clerics* were killed during the year. This included the shooting of prominent radical preacher Sheikh Abubakar Shariff 'Makaburi' outside Shanzu Law Courts on 1 April – which was widely attributed to the state's *Anti-Terrorism Police Unit* (ATPU) – and the subsequent assassination of Sheikh Mohammed Idriss, a lead campaigner against Islamic radicalisation, who was generally believed to have been targeted by al-Shabaab in retaliation for ATPU killings.

Terrorist attacks were also associated with a further deterioration in relations between the government and the political opposition. This relationship had been tense since former prime minister Raila Odinga and the *Coalition for Reform and Democracy* (CORD) had accused Jubilee of rigging the presidential election in 2013. Then, in June 2014, President Kenyatta blamed local opposition forces for the Mpeketoni attacks. This was despite the fact that al-Shabaab claimed responsibility for the attack, while analysts suggested that al-Shabaab had become more effective at using local grievances to facilitate recruitment and build alliances with leaders at the local level. Kenyatta's carefully chosen language rendered it unclear whether he had accused Odinga, local Lamu politicians or coastal radicals. However, the fact that Kenyatta's pronouncement followed a series of high profile CORD rallies – which had been timed to coincide with Odinga's return from an American lecture tour and the anniversary of a famous 1991 pro-democracy rally on 7 July – led many to conclude that Kenyatta had accused national opposition politicians.

Prior to the 2013 election, most losers in presidential elections had secured seats in the National Assembly. However, the separation of powers that attended the new 2010 constitution meant that unsuccessful aspirants – such as Odinga and his running mate, Kalonzo Musyoka – held no elected office. CORD also suffered from a poor party whip system in the National Assembly, and the opposition alliance only managed to mobilise a clear political line in opposition to a highly contentious *security bill*. The bill was nevertheless passed on 18 December amidst an orchestrated disruption of debates, which prompted CORD to challenge the constitutionality of the bill through the courts.

With no elected office, CORD leaders came to rely on political rallies and other public performances to display their relevance. By mid-2014, these efforts had come to focus on the government's alleged undermining of the 2010 constitution and associated reforms, most notably the *devolution of power* to *47 new county governments*. County governments had been formed after the 2013 elections when governors, members of county assemblies (MCAs), senators and county women's representatives were elected for the first time. It was therefore unsurprising that the year was characterised by much debate and uncertainty, as different levels of government sought to clarify their roles, responsibilities and budgets; or that the political opposition and county governments claimed that the central government was trying to block full devolution, and that more resources needed to be allocated to the county level to ensure that devolved governments met their development mandates.

In July, CORD leaders launched a national *referendum campaign* – dubbed '*Okoa Kenya*' or 'Save Kenya' – which demanded an increase in county government budgets. However, as the coalition crisscrossed the country to collect the requisite number of signatures to initiate the long-winded process of a popular constitutional referendum, the campaign lost steam. This was partly due to developments around a second referendum campaign – '*Pesa Mashinani*' or 'money to the grassroots' – which was launched by county governors soon after 'Okoa Kenya', and which also demanded that more resources be allocated to county governments. The fact that county governors felt unable to campaign alongside CORD leaders, despite their having similar agendas, reflected high levels of political polarisation. Nevertheless, the number of governors who initially came together – and the fact that they were led by URP governor Isaac Rutto – revealed the relevance of this new tier of government as a check on the national government. In response, Jubilee stalwarts turned the referendum issue into a party issue: support for a referendum was presented as pro-CORD, and resistance as pro-government or Jubilee. At the same time, Jubilee enticed governors with promises of increased funds, which ensured that the governors' campaign ultimately achieved its aims without a referendum ever having to be held.

The willingness of governors to mobilise across party lines also reflected high levels of competition between elected officials at the county level, as governors sought to defend their position against ambitious *senators* and truculent *MCAs*. Indeed, a central characteristic of domestic politics during the year was fierce contests between governors and other locally elected officials, which saw a series of governors threatened with impeachment and the removal of a number of county executives in numerous counties. Governors were under attack from several angles. First, a number of senators and MPs came to set their sights on the governorship and the control of associated funds, and sought to undermine incumbents. Second, many MCAs used their powers to impeach governors and sack county executives to negotiate for special funds, contracts and other perks, which often brought them into opportunistic alliances with the senators or area MPs. Moreover, as with senators and governors, many MCAs sought to position themselves to vie for parliamentary seats in the next election, which brought them into direct conflict with sitting MPs. Such efforts reflected the powers of new county governments, but they also encouraged unnecessary competition, duplication and corruption at the county level. One example was *Nairobi County*, where Senator Mike Sonko launched a range of projects despite not having a development portfolio or budget. They included the 'Sonko Rescue Team', which promised to provide a range of services to Nairobi residents, who Sonko claimed had been left to fend for themselves by the county's allegedly 'ineffective' governor, Evans Kidero.

Increased competition for resources, positions and boundaries at the county level also exacerbated *inter-ethnic tensions* in a number of areas. For example, violent clashes in Mandera County during the year were linked to contests between the majority Garre and minority Degodia communities, as the latter argued that Garre sought to control the county, while Garre presented the Degodia as encroachers who sought to expand into their ethnic strongholds. Even in ostensibly peaceful counties, majority and minority groups often came into conflict over the question of who should benefit from political nominations, recruitment drives, employment policies and settlement schemes at the county level. For example, reports from Bungoma County suggested that Bukusu resented the number of positions and amount of power that they had shared with Sabaot neighbours in the 2013 election; while in Kericho County, the fact that only one nominated MCA represented minority groups fostered a sense of marginalisation amongst those who felt excluded.

In many areas, local-level conflicts pitted members of the same political parties and coalitions against each other, which helped to counterbalance tense relations between Jubilee and CORD at the national level. Both *Jubilee* and *CORD* also suffered from *internal divisions*. In Jubilee, divisions centred on complaints by some Kalenjin politicians that they had not received a fair distribution of resources, the executive's questionable commitment to devolution, and the uncertainty that surrounded the Alliance's future if ICC charges were dropped against Kenyatta but Ruto was successfully convicted. CORD in contrast, suffered mainly from power struggles within the coalition's largest party – ODM – as to whether party members should unite behind Odinga's leadership or seek to foster internal party democracy. The latter came to the fore in February, when rival camps coalesced around Senator Agnes Zani and MP Ababu Namwamba. In the same month, *ODM elections* were disrupted by mysterious 'men in black', who were widely rumoured to have been brought in by Odinga allies to avoid the defeat of Zani's team. Failed party elections were followed by the formation of a ten-person executive committee, and then, in November, by the selection of new officials. The line-up of both – together with the decision to avoid potentially divisive elections – highlighted the importance of personalities and ethnic identities, even in the ostensibly reformist opposition.

The government faced strained relations with *civil society organisations* and *media* outlets due to a widespread perception that the government was using the threat of insecurity to close the political space. In fact, so bad did relations become, that a Cold War developed between prominent human rights activists and the government, as the former organised protests and claimed harassment, arbitrary arrests and intimidation, and the latter sought to present their detractors as stooges of Western donors. In contrast, disagreements between the government and commercial media outlets proved less visible as private threats to redirect government advertising and to use a 2013 Media Bill encouraged substantial self-censorship by individual journalists, editors and media houses. The year was also marked by a series of popular *demonstrations* against corruption, 'big man' politics and insecurity, and by a protest march that followed a series of incidents in which women were stripped in public for wearing mini-skirts and for allegedly being 'indecently dressed'.

Little progress was made on *transitional justice*. The National Assembly failed to discuss the Truth, Justice and Reconciliation Commission report, which had been submitted in May 2013, while the public *vetting of police*, which had begun in December 2013, stalled in early 2014, after the National Police Service Commission declared that the Treasury had failed to transfer the necessary funds. By the end of the year, plans for a special division of the High Court, which activists had insisted should deal with international crimes including mid- to high-level perpetrators of the 2007/8 post-election violence, had morphed into plans for an International Organised Crimes Division, which would be geared towards international cases, such as terrorism, drug trafficking and cybercrime, rather than international crimes as defined by the ICC's Rome Statute. Indeed, the most significant steps towards transitional justice were taken by non-state actors. This included the unveiling of a *memorial* to the 1984 Wagalla massacre in February, which was built by the Kenya National Commission of Human Rights, a German development agency and local organisations.

Foreign Affairs

On 5 December, the *ICC*'s Office of the Prosecutor (OTP) *withdrew charges against President Kenyatta* for his alleged role as an indirect co-perpetrator of crimes against humanity committed during the post-election violence of 2007/8. The fact that this development followed a series of postponements by the Court ensured that the decision was widely expected and prompted little protest. However, while Kenyatta lauded the development as proof of his innocence, the OTP insisted that charges were only dropped because it was impossible to fully investigate and prosecute the crimes. The chief prosecutor cited the death, bribery and intimidation of key witnesses and the non-compliance of the Kenyan government in handing over requested records as insurmountable hurdles to a successful prosecution.

This left only Ruto and Sang to face charges of crimes against humanity of murder, forcible transfer and persecution as indirect co-perpetrator and contributor to the commission of crimes, respectively. These crimes were allegedly committed by 'Kalenjin warriors' against government supporters in parts of the Rift Valley between December 2007 and February 2008 as part of a plan by ODM politicians to gain power, and to punish and drive out government supporters, who predominantly hailed from the Kikuyu and Kisii communities. Ruto and Sang's trial had begun in September 2013, and 2014 saw the duo travel regularly to and from *The Hague* to hear prosecution witnesses. The Kenyan government continued to insist it was complying with the ICC, but Kenyatta simultaneously displayed his support for his deputy and Sang when, after the withdrawal of charges against him, he announced: "As they say, one case down, two more to go."

In practice, the government's *anti-ICC strategy* was multi-stranded. First, Kenya continued to employ 'shuttle diplomacy' by sending emissaries around the world to lobby for support and strengthen bilateral relations. At the same time, the government worked through regional bodies such as the *AU* to build pressure on the ICC as a neo-imperial institution. Finally, the government sought to *counter-shame* the Court by depicting the OTP's charges as baseless and biased, and as detrimental to regional peace and development on the basis that charges targeted democratically elected leaders of a regional powerhouse in an area wracked by terrorism.

Counter-shaming was achieved, in large part, through the organisation of public displays of support for the president and his deputy by foreign governments, the AU and Kenyan citizens. For example, in October, Kenyatta made history as the first sitting head of state to appear before the ICC in The Hague. However, formal *judicial proceedings* were overshadowed by *parallel theatrics*, as media coverage focused on the address that Kenyatta made to a joint session of Parliament prior to travelling, the temporary appointment of Deputy President William Ruto as acting president, Kenyatta's departure and arrival at Nairobi airport, demonstrations in The Hague, and Kenyatta's public statements. Images portrayed the president's relaxed demeanour, the deputy president's support for his colleague, demonstrations held on the steps of the ICC building led by the always colourful Senator Mike Sonko, and the warm reception the president received on his departure from and arrival in Nairobi and The Hague. Through such efforts, Kenyan elites proved particularly adept at counter-shaming the ICC and at questioning its neutrality, interpretation of events and potential impact.

These strategies were effective at mobilising public and regional support against the ICC, but they also *strained relations* with *traditional donors* – most notably the UK and the USA, which ICC critics presented as key 'neo-imperial' supporters of the Court. Diplomatic relations were further troubled by the government's altercations with leading civil society activists and associated claims that they were mere mouthpieces of foreign donors. Relations reached a nadir in February, when the National Security Advisory Committee publicly accused USAID of funding mass protests with the aim of toppling the Kenyan government. However, after this point, relations generally improved, as Western donors largely avoided public criticism of the Jubilee administration.

The exception was the question of security and *travel advisories*. In May, al-Shabaab declared that their struggle had turned fully to Kenya, in response to the Kenyan military's invasion of Somalia in 2011 and the subsequent integration of Kenya's armed forces into the AU Mission in Somalia (*AMISOM*). This was followed by an increase in terrorist attacks on Kenyan soil, which – together with intelligence of planned attacks on foreign nationals and the seeming incapacity of Kenya's security services to prevent or adequately respond to attacks – prompted the USA, Australia, Britain, Canada, France and New Zealand to introduce, and then extend, travel advisories for parts of northern Kenya and the Coast. Jubilee politicians and supporters denounced the advisories as 'economic sabotage', which further troubled Kenya's relations with Western diplomats.

In this context, the Jubilee government increasingly reached out to neighbouring countries in the *EAC*, and to other potential diplomatic allies and trading partners. In the EAC, Kenya retained close relations with the so-called 'coalition of the willing' – namely President Museveni and the Ugandan government and President Kagame and the Rwandan government – and, in March, the three governments introduced a common tourist visa. However, the fact that this agreement omitted Tanzania reflected the extent to which Kenya's southern neighbour feared Kenyan dominance, which, as in the 1970s, continued to present a significant obstacle to substantive regional integration.

The importance of bilateral relations with EAC countries was further underlined during the protracted negotiations over a controversial *EPA* with the *EU*. Following prolonged negotiations, the region missed the EU deadline for a new agreement by 1 October, due to the EAC's insistence that countries be allowed to impose export taxes in some instances so as to promote local processing. An agreement was reached soon thereafter. However, by choosing to stand with other members of the EAC, Kenya prioritised regional relations over short-term economic interests. While Burundi, Rwanda, Tanzania and Uganda would have continued to enjoy duty-free access to the EU under the 'anything-but-arms' agreement that applies to least-developed countries, Kenya would have faced tariffs of between 4% and 24% on a range of exports to the EU. Progress also continued on the Northern Corridor Integration Projects, with Ethiopia, Rwanda, South Sudan and Uganda committed to 14 projects that included infrastructure, energy, transport, information and communications technology and trade.

Kenya also continued to forge deeper economic relations with *China*. Thus, in the wake of Kenyatta's state visit to China in 2013, the Chinese premier visited Kenya in May, when a number of deals were signed including a $ 3.3 bn loan on mixed concessional and commercial terms to finance the new standard-gauge railway. Kenya also sought to strengthen diplomatic relations in newer markets. These included *Ethiopia*, where Kenyatta carried out a state visit in March, when high-level talks led to agreements on bilateral trade and investment. Principals also used the visit to restate their commitment to the Lamu Port Southern Sudan-Ethiopia Transport Corridor (LAPSSET), which included plans for a new road, railway and pipeline across the three countries, a port and oil refinery in Lamu, and an airport in Isiolo. Then, in April, Kenyatta went on a state visit to *Qatar*, where he signed four trade-related agreements. In May, he travelled to Nigeria for a World Economic Forum on Africa and, in October, he made the first visit by a Kenyan president to *Turkey* where – in addition to signing various trade agreements – he opened the first Kenyan embassy in Ankara and vowed to strengthen Kenya-Turkey cooperation at both the bilateral and multilateral levels.

Socioeconomic Developments

The government's development plans continued to be articulated through *Vision 2030*, which had been initiated under President Kibaki and included a series of ambitious and high-profile *infrastructure projects*, such as a new standard-gauge railway and LAPSSET. These projects were marred by delays and allegations of *corruption*. Thus, the building of a standard-gauge railway from Mombasa to Nairobi, Kampala, Kigali and Juba was delayed by a legal dispute in Uganda between two Chinese companies and several government agencies over the award of contracts. The Kenyan part of the line also proved controversial due to the high costs of a contract awarded to a Chinese company and lack of competitive tendering. Moreover, suspicions of large-scale corruption survived lengthy investigations by, and approval of, the transport and investment parliamentary committees. This was indicative of a more general expectation of corruption, which was reflected in TI's global Corruption Perceptions Index, which saw Kenya fall from 136th to 145th place.

In August, the Kenya Ports Authority signed a contract with a Chinese construction company to build the first three berths of a new port in Lamu as part of *LAPSSET*. However, little progress was made with other aspects of this project due to economic and political uncertainties. LAPSSET was predicated on South Sudan's participation in the *oil pipeline* project, but the renewal of conflict in South Sudan, together with an agreement between Juba and Khartoum on the use of the existing pipeline running from South to North Sudan, threw doubt on the willingness of foreign investors to finance a southern route. The issue of foreign finance also proved more general, since none of the countries were able to underwrite any of the planned infrastructure projects. During the year, a slightly different configuration of LAPSSET, which was not dependent on Juba's involvement, and which would involve a pipeline from northern Uganda, through Kenya, carrying crude oil for export from a limited port development at Lamu, became increasingly likely. However, even this was put in doubt by the fall in global oil prices towards the end of the year.

Offshore *oil and gas* was found during the year, which increased excitement about Kenya's potential as a hydrocarbons exporter in future years, following earlier oil finds in Turkana County. However, as the year progressed it became increasingly clear that public expectations were unrealistically high. First, oil was unlikely to flow before 2018 and still required heavy investment in the needed infrastructure and new legislation. Second, Tullow Oil plc, the main company involved in the exploration and development of oil fields in northern Kenya, reported dismal profit margins for the financial year, raising concerns about its capacity and willingness to continue activities in the region. Third, a history of inter-ethnic tension and violence in northern Kenya, and paucity of security provision, raised concerns that oil could exacerbate local conflicts and become a new site of struggle. Finally, the USA's increased reliance on domestic oil through the exploitation of shale deposits, and reports that China could soon follow in the use of this new fracking technology, led to a fall in the global price of oil. Together, these ensured that the exploitation of oil reserves continued to be a highly political issue, which many foreign investors proved reticent to support.

Concern grew during the year regarding the size of Kenya's *public sector wage bill*, which rose to over 55% of government revenue, or about 13% of GDP. This was due, in part, to the large number of 'ghost workers', who were estimated to be paid at least $ 1 m per month, as well as the large number of politicians and government advisors who enjoyed extremely high salaries. However, it was also exacerbated by *devolution*, which prompted the hiring of staff across the 47 new counties. This included unnecessary duplication in many areas, as county governments hired staff with similar skills to those seconded by the national government. Indeed, the costs of devolution – and the fact that many county governments imposed new or higher levies at the local level, but seemed to spend most of their budget on salaries, 'sitting allowances', foreign trips, offices and cars – was the main source of public dissatisfaction with this new tier of government. Public perceptions reflected realities. Thus, a World Bank report titled 'Decision Time: Spend More or Spend Smart?' estimated that only ten counties spent more than 30% of their budget on development during the 2013/14 financial year, and that, on average, counties spent 46% on wages and salaries, 30% on administrative recurrent expenses, and 21% on development projects. The report warned that high wage bills could 'crowd out' growth initiatives.

The disbursement of new resources to county governments, competition between local leaders, use by MCAs of powers to impeach governors and to remove county executives to leverage for contracts, and the weakness of county-level auditing processes and oversight, also meant devolution increased the ability of politicians and state officials to allocate jobs, procurement and other resources as *patronage*. In turn, devolution was widely associated with the localisation of endemic *corruption* at the national level down to new county governments.

The *Anglo-Leasing* affair, the largest corruption scandal during President Kibaki's presidency, re-entered the news when the finance minister secured approval to pay KSh 1.4 bn of outstanding payments to two foreign companies. The minister argued that Kenya's refusal to comply would damage the country's reputation and that interest penalties continued to mount. However, the idea that Kenya would continue to pay billions of shillings to mysterious companies for services that were never provided prompted significant public outcry.

The economy was also troubled by a slump in *tourism*, which was reflected in a significant contraction of the hotel and restaurant industry. This was largely a result of insecurity and media reports of terrorist attacks in areas such as Lamu County, which is also home to Lamu Island – one of the country's most famous tourist havens – and the imposition, and then extension, of travel advisories. This followed closely on the heels of other negative news stories; most notably a decision by several UK-based tour operators to evacuate customers from coastal resorts in May, and a series of bomb blasts in Nairobi and Mombasa in the same month, which left scores dead and many more injured. Analysts also suggested that, while the Ebola epidemic remained geographically limited to West Africa, simplistic international media portrayals of this 'African disease' and popular stereotypes had a negative impact on tourist and business numbers across the continent. The collapse of the tourist industry had a disproportionately negative impact on the historically marginalised coastal area, as reflected in a decrease in arrivals at Mombasa airport and reports of near-empty hotels, the introduction of new rotational shifts for staff, and unusually low numbers of future bookings.

Wildlife poaching also saw a resurgence, with elephants, rhinos and lions the main targets. The subsequent fall in animal numbers raised further concerns about the future of Kenya's tourist industry, which is largely reliant on visitors to the country's game parks and coastal beaches. Conservationists highlighted that the northern white rhino came one step closer to extinction after the natural death of a male rhino in Ol Pejeta Conservancy, which left only six of the subspecies in the world, and only one male.

Kenya was also adversely affected by a global slump in the price of *tea*, the country's largest export commodity, which fell to a six-year low. The failure to negotiate a new EPA by the EU's October deadline also led to fears that some Kenyan exports would have to face high tariffs. This would have had a particularly negative impact on Kenya's *horticulture* exports, especially cut flowers, which temporarily faced tariffs of around 8%. However, exports regained duty-free access to the EU before the end of the year after an EPA was signed in mid-October and key EU institutions fast-tracked Kenya's re-entry into the system of trade preferences. At the same time, *remittances* – the country's largest source of foreign exchange – continued to gradually increase, while the global price of *coffee* remained stable.

Poor rains in the first half of the year highlighted the impact and dangers of *climate change*, and the need to invest in *reforestation*. At the same time, a World Bank Inspection Panel report, which criticised a World Bank-supported National Resources Management Project that operated from 2008 to 2013, underlined the practical tensions between the protection of the country's forests and the rights of recognised indigenous forest-dwelling peoples.

Below average rains during the main March-May wet season contributed to rising food prices, which – together with high energy and transport costs – led to *inflation* reaching 8.4% in August. However, inflationary pressures decreased during the second part of the year with inflation falling to 6% by the end of the year. This was due to a fall in global oil prices and a reduction in electricity tariffs after the country became increasingly reliant on cheaper geothermal power. This proved critical, as cheaper energy and fuel prices helped to offset the inflationary pressure of a gradual *depreciation* of the Kenyan shilling, which resulted from low inflows of foreign exchange from tea and tourism, and the strengthening of the US dollar.

The success of Kenya's *debut Eurobond* issue in June, which raised $ 2 bn, together with the negotiation of Chinese loans to finance a new railway, and the signing of a new country partnership strategy with the World Bank in June (for the disbursement of loans and financial guarantees worth $ 4 bn over five years), underlined the country's ongoing ability to attract *external funding*. This was despite growing concerns regarding insecurity, and was generally attributed to Kenya's diversified economy and status as East Africa's regional hub – with East Africa predicted to have the strongest growth of all of SSA's four sub-regions – and the burgeoning attraction of emerging or frontier markets to international investors.

Kenya revised the measurement of the *economy* by shifting the base year from 2001 to 2009 to incorporate structural economic changes and the emergence of new sectors, such as mobile phone banking, that had taken place in the meantime. The National Bureau of Statistics started the *rebasing* process in April and results released in September suggested that Kenya's nominal GDP in 2013 was about 25% larger than previously thought. Indeed, despite insecurity and a fall in tourist numbers, real *GDP growth* was buoyant at 5.1% in the first half of 2014, as growth rates fluctuated from 4.4% in the first quarter and 5.8% in the second, to 5.5% in the third. The overall 2014 growth rate was forecast to attain 5.2%. Growth was particularly driven by investment in infrastructure and construction, financial services and communications. It was also pushed by rapid urbanisation, a burgeoning middle-class and the growth of shopping malls and supermarkets, which ensured the relatively rapid growth of the country's wholesale and retail trade markets. Absolute poverty levels continued on a trajectory of gradual decline. Nevertheless, many complained of the high costs associated with devolution, endemic corruption and high levels of inequality, and questioned the benefits brought by economic growth in and of itself.

Rwanda

Susan Thomson

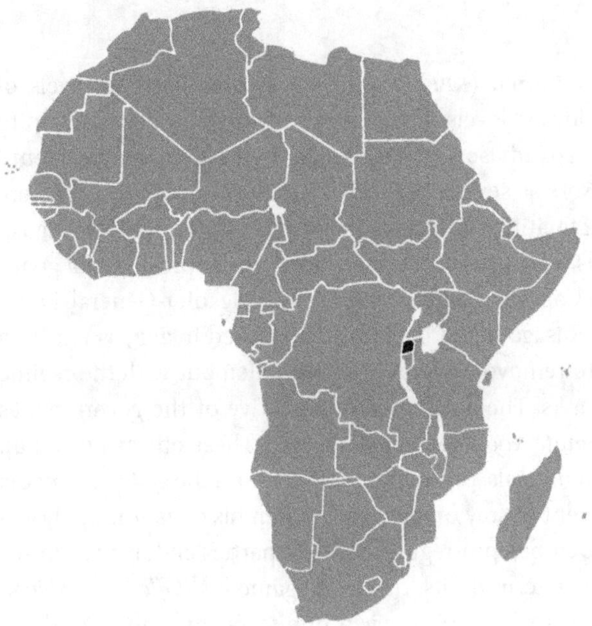

The ruling RPF continued to maintain strict controls on political and public life, and the regime, led by President Kagame, faced little internal political opposition. Progress continued in the fields of public service delivery and the economy. The government marked the 20th anniversary of the 1994 genocide in April with a series of memorial and commemoration activities. The RPF gained some standing with its international donors, many of which restored aid following Kigali's November 2013 dismantling of the M23 rebel group, a proxy militia operating in the neighbouring DRC. Foreign aid disbursements had declined in 2012–13, following the release of a UN report accusing the government of supporting military rebellion in eastern DRC. By the end of 2014, foreign aid accounted for 35% of Rwanda's budget, marking the return of aid dollars, albeit at levels below those allocated before the release of the 2012 UN report. Relations with donors remained tense, notably because they continued to chastise the government for its ongoing political repression. Bilateral relations with the DRC were strained, with Kigali accusing Kinshasa of not doing enough to contain the conflict in the Kivu regions. Regional and UN-led peace talks failed to resolve the conflict in eastern DRC, despite Rwanda's wish to cooperate with the Congolese army to contain it. The economy proved to be quite resilient:

 | DOI 10.1163/9789004305052_037

despite some foreign aid cuts, the effects of continued global recession and lower domestic public spending, economic growth accelerated to a relatively healthy projected rate of 6.5%.

Domestic Politics

The ruling *Rwandan Patriotic Front* (*RPF*) continued to dominate all levels of sociopolitical life, from the lowest levels of the administrative bureaucracy up to *President Paul Kagame*'s cabal of advisors. There was an upheaval in the president's inner circle of *military advisors* as several recently retired or former officers were imprisoned on allegations of inciting violence or insulting the president. In August, three senior military officials were arrested: former head of the presidential guard Colonel Tom Byabagamba, Captain David Kabuye and Brigadier-General Frank Rusagara. Both Kabuye and Rusagara had been forcibly retired in 2013 as part of a broader government effort to remove soldiers who had fallen out with the regime and to end dissent in the ranks. The arrests were indicative of the government's continued *campaign to eliminate Kagame's political rivals*. These efforts heated up in 2014, as senior government officials, pro-regime activists and the state-run media formally called on the president to stay on past 2017, when his constitutional two-term limit would expire. In October, pro-regime political parties endorsed a constitutional referendum to remove term limits. In July, Kagame *reshuffled his cabinet*, appointing a new prime minister, dropping seven ministers, and moving others. The post of *prime minister* was given to *Anastase Murekezi*, a long-time ally of the president, who had held numerous ministerial positions in the last decade. His appointment instigated a shift across the government, as the entire cabinet was constitutionally required to resign and be sworn in again upon the appointment of a new prime minister. The most important portfolios – interior, finance, foreign affairs and defence – remained in the same hands, prompting analysts to note that the reshuffle was probably employed as a tool to discipline those who deigned to challenge the president's authority, while also hinting at strategic power alliances within the government in the run-up to the 2017 elections.

These *military* and *government shake-ups* sustained a broader mood of *domestic disillusionment* with the RPF. Members of the RPF's core constituency – the urban, educated and English-speaking Tutsi – felt that Kagame had lost his vision for ethnic unity and economic prosperity for all Rwandans. There was in addition an ongoing government tendency to scapegoat the political opposition and an increasing tolerance of nepotism and bribery among members of the ruling clique. In December, *TI* acknowledged this trend in its Corruption Perceptions Index, noting that Rwandans regularly paid bribes for basic service delivery. It was notable that dissatisfied ethnic Tutsi were not clamouring for increased democracy or a more economically inclusive Rwanda. Rather, dissatisfaction with the regime was expressed in complaints of their lack of access to credit and other economic benefits of RPF rule. As a result, there was no organised or viable opposition to Kagame's political rule. The president still commanded the loyalty of much of the Rwandan Patriotic Army, so a coup was unlikely. Political opponents of the regime, ethnic Hutu, Tutsi and Twa alike, continued regularly to accuse Kagame of *increasing authoritarianism* and of trampling on civic and political rights and freedoms, which had intensified since 2010.

International and domestic human rights organisations regularly accused the RPF government of *harassment and intimidation* of its *political opponents and journalists*. The RPF continued to acknowledge its control of the political sphere, citing state security and economic growth as taking priority over political freedoms. On the same grounds, RPF members and allies justified their call for a constitutional revision to allow Kagame to run for a third term in 2017. *Opposition parties* remained constrained in their activities. Victoire Ingabire, president of the *FDU-Inkingi* party, remained in prison for endangering state security and promoting ethnic divisionism; the Supreme Court had increased her sentence from eight to 15 years in December 2013. Other FDU leaders, including Sylvain Sibomana, were also still in prison, effectively leaving the party leaderless. In October, *HRW* released a statement alleging flaws in the legal process that had led to Sibomana's conviction. In April, the *Democratic Rwanda Green Party* (*DRGP*), whose leader Frank Habineza had once regularly critiqued government policy, joined the *National Consultative Forum of Political Organizations*, a coalition of political parties that operated in alliance with the ruling RPF. Analysts contended that this marked the cooption of the DRGP, effectively eliminating it as an independent voice to hold government to account or to offer an alternative vision for Rwanda.

In April, opposition parties based outside Rwanda formed the *Coalition of Political Parties for Change* (*CPPC*) with the purpose of uniting the opposition and forcing the government to engage in political dialogue. It was founded in Belgium by the leaders of seven opposition parties: United Democratic Forces (FDU-Inkingi); '*Forces Démocratiques de Libération du Rwanda*' (FDLR); Democratic People's Front (PDP-Imanzi); Party for Democracy in Rwanda (PDR-Ihumure); Social Party (PS-Imberakuri); Rwandan Dream Initiative (RDI-Rwiza Rwanda); and Rwandan Democratic Union. The CPPC spokesperson and figurehead was *Faustin Twagiramungu*, who had been Rwandan prime minister in 1994–95 and a presidential candidate in the 2003 election. The inclusion of the FDLR weakened any potential impact the Coalition might have on Rwandan politics, as the RPF refused to engage in negotiations with it. The RPF continued to maintain that the FDLR was a destabilising presence for Rwandan peace and security, as its primary goal was to finish the Tutsi genocide of 1994. By year's end, Kagame had yet to acknowledge the existence of the CPPC, muting any effect it might have on opening up the Rwandan political sphere. In addition, the primary external opposition party, the *Rwandan National Congress* (*RNC*), did not join the Coalition, further minimising any impact it might make. The RNC was made up of former senior RPF officials, and its absence from the CPPC demonstrated the extent to which the opposition was fractured and lacked leadership. In addition, international and domestic political analysts believed the RNC posed no serious political or military threat, noting that the party had been unable to raise significant financial or moral support from Rwandans living in the diaspora, thus limiting its influence abroad and at home.

Key RNC members were murdered or injured in 2014 in what analysts understood to be a series of RPF-led revenge attacks on former allies. In January, *Patrick Karegeya*, former head of Rwanda's external intelligence services and a prominent government opponent exiled in South Africa, was found murdered in a hotel room in Johannesburg. Other RNC members were also attacked and threatened outside Rwanda, including a March attempt on the life of former army chief of staff, General *Kayumba Nyamwasa*. The attempt on Nyamwasa's life marked the third such attempt in South Africa, where many key members of the RNC lived in exile. The government denied any involvement in these attacks, but Kagame came close to publicly condoning Karegeya's murder later in January, when he said, among other things, "Whoever betrays the country will pay the price." The *USA*, in rare public criticism of the government, publicly condemned Karegeya's murder. In March, the South African government threatened to sever diplomatic ties with Rwanda over attacks on its soil.

The *media* remained tightly controlled, and thus dominated by pro-government views. Journalists were unable or unwilling to engage in reporting on politically sensitive issues. In April, *Reporters Without Borders* reported on the deteriorating climate for journalism in Rwanda. Two independent journalists fled into exile in April. *Stanley Gatera*, editor of the independent news website '*Umusingi*', fled after he was charged with attempted extortion following his interview on Rwanda's restrictive media environment with the '*Al-Jazeera*' *programme* 'People and Power'. Eric Udahemuka of the Kinyarwanda-language newspaper '*Isimbi*' also fled the country in April, just a week before the official launch of the commemoration events for the 20th anniversary of the genocide. In February, Reporters Without Borders released its *World Press Freedom 2014 Index*. Rwanda was ranked 162nd out 180 countries, largely as a result of the government's continued intimidation and harassment of journalists. 'Good Morning Rwanda', the popular phone-in programme broadcast by Flash FM, was banned in June. Also in June, following international condemnation of the crackdown on critical journalism, Agnès Uwimana of the Kinyarwanda-language newspaper '*Umurabyo*' was released from prison, after serving four years for endangering national security and defamation.

The reprieve was short-lived as the government suspended the licence of the *BBC*'s Kinyarwanda-language service in October following the transmission of the documentary '*Rwanda: The Untold Story*', which covered the role of the RPF in the 1994 genocide, and the revenge killings its soldiers perpetrated before, during and after the genocide. The government accused the BBC of falsifying history. The media self-regulatory body, the *Rwanda Media Commission* (*RMC*) objected to the suspension of the BBC, and its president, Fred Muvunyi, challenged the *Rwandan Utilities Regulatory Authority* (*RURA*) for suspending the BBC service without consulting the RMC. Muvunyi then became the target of a systematic smear campaign on social media, when journalists close to the government argued against the need for the RMC. It had been created in September 2013 in response to international criticism of the lack of press freedoms in Rwanda, with a limited mandate to issue press accreditations and regulate media content on the basis of a code of professional ethics. Since its inception, RURA had undermined the credibility of the RMC, including most recently creating a commission of inquiry in November to investigate the validity of the claims made in 'The Untold Story'.

Civil society remained cowed in 2014 as state intimidation, harassment and infiltration continued unabated. The sole independent human rights group, the '*Ligue Rwandaise pour la Promotion et la Défense des Droits de l'Homme*' (LIPRODHOR), had taken legal action against the government in 2013 in protest at a takeover of its leadership by members of the ruling RPF. The Rwanda Governance Board, the state body with oversight of national NGOs, had recognised the new leadership. After numerous adjournments, a court in Kigali ruled in August on procedural grounds that the case was unfounded. The ousted LIPRODHOR leaders filed an appeal in September, which was ongoing at the end of the year. In September, two police officers were arrested in connection with the *murder of anti-corruption activist* Gustave Makonene. After initially denying the murder charges, both suspects pleaded guilty in pre-trial hearings in October and the trial was ongoing at the end of the year. Makonene, coordinator of *TI Rwanda*'s Advice and Legal Advice Centre in Rubavu, had been found dead in July 2013. In June, the pro-government 'New Times' newspaper published an 'assessment' of *HRW*'s work in Rwanda by the Ministry of Justice, which grossly misrepresented the organisation's work. Among other allegations, it accused HRW of supporting the FDLR.

The *UN special rapporteur on freedom of association and assembly*, Maina Kiai, visited Rwanda in January, expressing concern about restrictions on civil society and political parties. In his report to the *UN Human Rights Council* in June, Kiai raised additional concerns, including the prevailing opposition to vigorous debate and free expression of opinion by public and private citizens, the government's hostility toward peaceful initiatives by its critics and the existence of a legal framework that silenced dissent through laws that made it illegal to question the authority of the government. Kiai's report noted that individuals and organisations that broached the *sensitive subject of RPF crimes* before, during and after the 1994 genocide were regarded as enemies. Talking about those crimes, and effectively departing from the official version of Rwanda's recent history, could result in serious consequences, such as charges of *genocide denial, genocide ideology* or *divisionism* (inciting ethnic division). Since 2000, Rwanda had passed a number of laws that may originally have been intended to prevent and punish hate speech of the kind that had led to the 1994 genocide, but in practice since 2008 had restricted free speech and imposed strict limits on how the genocide and other events of 1994 could be referred to. The government rejected several of Kiai's findings, challenging the UN for meddling in domestic affairs.

In November, the *International Criminal Tribunal for Rwanda* (*ICTR*) announced that its work would continue through 2015. It also released for the first time the judgments and indictments of the court in Kinyarwanda, marking a rare moment of collaboration between the Court and the government. Nine suspects wanted by the ICTR continued to evade justice. The ICTR and the *UN mechanism for international criminal tribunals* launched a new initiative in July to track down and arrest these remaining fugitives. Domestic courts in several foreign countries tried Rwandans for genocide crimes under the principle of *universal jurisdiction*, and further cases were pending. In the first such prosecution in France, conducted by a newly-established war crimes unit, a court in Paris tried former intelligence chief Pascal Simbikangwa and sentenced him in March to 25 years in prison for genocide and complicity in crimes against humanity. In February, a court in Germany sentenced former Rwandan mayor Onesphore Rwabukombe to 14 years in prison for aiding and abetting genocide.

At home, Rwandan courts continued to try individuals alleged to have threatened state security or made ethnic divisionist claims in public. Internationally acclaimed singer *Kizito Mihigo*, journalist Cassien Ntamuhanga, and co-defendants Agnès Niyibizi and Jean-Paul Dukuzumuremyi were arrested in April and charged with offences against the state and complicity in terrorist acts for allegedly collaborating with the RNC and FDLR. In November, Mihigo confessed to all the charges. Ntamuhanga and Dukuzumuremyi pleaded not guilty and Niyibizi had yet to enter a plea. The trial was ongoing at the end of the year. In January, the trial of *Joel Mutabazi*, a former presidential bodyguard forcibly returned from Uganda to Rwanda in October 2013, and 15 co-accused, began before a military court in Kigali. The defendants were charged with terrorism, murder, forming an armed group, and other offences linked to alleged collaboration with the RNC and the FDLR. Mutabazi and several co-defendants stated in court that they had been tortured and forced to sign statements. In October, Mutabazi was found guilty of all charges and sentenced to life in prison. Thirteen defendants received sentences ranging from three months to 25 years. Two were acquitted.

Foreign Affairs

As in previous years, foreign affairs were dominated by Rwanda's presence (critics would say interference) in *eastern DRC*. In February, *Rwanda's envoy* to the *UN* asked the UNSC to reject the conclusions of the *Group of Experts* (GoE) report on rebel activity in the DRC. Released in January, the report documented Rwanda's support for the recently disbanded Congolese *M23* rebel group. Rwanda's inability to effectively deny its involvement in the M23 further highlighted its tenuous relations with its international donors, as many had suspended aid based on the 2012 UN GoE report that first detailed Rwanda's support for the rebel group. In addition, the episode demonstrated the continued lack of constructive dialogue between senior representatives of the DRC and Rwanda. The Rwandan government, led by Kagame and *Foreign Minister Louise Mushikiwabo*, did not deny the allegations as they had with the release of earlier GoE reports. Instead, they highlighted in speeches to international audiences *Rwanda's role in peacekeeping* in African locations, while simultaneously reminding them of the failures of the international community to intervene to stop the 1994 genocide. This tactic was often employed by Kigali when its international standing was at risk. The government probably did not want the GoE report to hang over the *commemoration of the 20th anniversary of the genocide*, held in April. International delegations from across the globe descended on Kigali to mark the occasion. Kagame used his anniversary speech to remind international audiences of their collective failure to help Rwandans in 1994, and since, with its various suspensions of aid. Rwanda's position on its activities in the DRC was under increased scrutiny following the *FDLR's announcement of its disarmament* in February, and the April commemorations marked a good time to focus the attention of the international community.

Martin Kobler, head of the UN peacekeeping force in the DRC (MONUSCO), urged cautious scepticism of the FDLR's stated intention to disarm, which played into Rwanda's long-term strategy of refusing to enter into peace talks with the rebel group. Also in February, the Congolese army announced a new campaign against the FDLR, which Rwanda had long pushed for. In June, *Rwandan and Congolese armies* exchanged gunfire near the border town of Goma, breaking the fragile peace that had held in the region since November 2013, when the M23 laid down its arms. The clash illustrated the fragility of regional efforts to address the disarmament of the FDLR, as both countries' armies had just committed to redouble their efforts in March. Addressing the clash in a press conference in Kigali in June, Foreign Minister Mushikiwabo reminded the USA and the UN of Rwanda's continued concerns about the instability and insecurity brought about by the presence of the FDLR. Her press conference was in partial response to January talks between the FDLR and the RNC, hosted by *Tanzania's President Jakaya Kikwete*. The talks followed on from Kikwete's May 2013 suggestions that Kigali engage directly in peace talks with the FDLR. Rwanda's position on talks with the FDLR was firmly against, and Kigali considered Kikwete's hosting of two opposition political parties to be a diplomatic insult. In August, regional and international efforts to disarm the FDLR intensified. The *ICGLR* and *SADC* both issued a six-month ultimatum to the leaders of the FDLR, which had had little effect by the end of the year.

Kikwete continued to be diplomatically isolated in the broader Great Lakes Region, as Rwanda made its displeasure at his 'meddling' in national security issues clear to regional and international partners alike. In May, regional integration within the *EAC* gathered steam, with *Kenya, Uganda* and *Rwanda* pushing ahead to deepen regional ties. Tanzania and Burundi remained largely on the sidelines of new developments, which included the February launch of a single tourist visa, and the pilot introduction of a Single Customs Territory scheme in April. Rwanda's ties with Kenya deepened over the course of the year as diplomatic and economic relations improved following the failure of the *ICC* to indict Kenyan President Uhuru Kenyatta for crimes against humanity that he allegedly ordered in 2007. Diplomatic ties with Uganda continued apace. Presidents Museveni and Kagame met three times on matters of mutual interest, including containing the FDLR, regional peace and security, and trade and investment. Ties with *Burundi* remained frosty and showed little sign of thawing at year's end. In July, Burundian fishermen found dead bodies floating in Lake Rweru, on the border between the two countries. Rwanda publicly identified them as Burundians, while Burundi called on Rwanda not to export its problems. By the end of the year, no investigation had been launched by either government. Rwanda's military was also active in various *AU* peace-keeping missions, as the sixth largest contributor. Over 4,000 RDF troops were deployed as peacekeepers in the CAR, Sudan (Darfur), Liberia and South Sudan, and in other non-African locations. The *UN Department of Peacekeeping* censured Rwanda in December concerning General Jean Bosco Kazura over allegations that he had supervised death squads during the 1994 genocide.

In March, *South Africa* – a primary contributor to UN peacekeeping forces in the DRC – expelled three Rwandan diplomats for alleged ties to the attempted murder of political dissident *Nyamwasa* in Johannesburg. This second attempt on Nyamwasa's life on South African soil followed the assassination of RNC co-founder Patrick Karegeya in Johannesburg in January. Early in June, the Belgian authorities began providing former prime minister *Faustin Twagiramungu* with police protection in his country of exile. In September, diplomatic relations between South Africa and Rwanda reached a low point when a South African court sentenced two Rwandans for the attempt on Nyamwasa's life.

Relations with many of Rwanda's bi- and multilateral *aid donors* – including the USA, the UK, Germany, Sweden, the Netherlands, Belgium, and the EU – stabilised in the course of 2014, as suspended or delayed aid disbursements were restored. *Aid flows* remained lower overall, weighing in at some 35% of the overall budget, down by 10% from aid flows in 2013. The reductions also ushered in a change in the way foreign relations were managed, with donors providing payments to specific projects rather than general budget support. Following the 1994 genocide, the government had generally only accepted budget support to allow it to provide the necessary funds to rebuild Rwanda in the aftermath of the genocide. This general support had ended in 2012, and the resumption of reduced and conditional aid flows in 2014 signalled an international community that no longer engaged Kigali solely on its own terms. In April, just before the official launch of genocide commemoration events, the *US House Foreign Affairs Committee* recommended a reduction in US military assistance to Rwanda, but the House eventually voted not to cut military aid following the August *US-Africa Leaders Summit*. Presidents Kagame and Obama met on the sidelines of this summit, with Obama assuring Kagame of the USA's continued military, political and humanitarian support. In October, *Belgium* agreed a $ 17 m grant to improve decentralised governance and health care service delivery at the local government level. In September, the *EU* committed to a € 460 m programme to support the security sector, health and agriculture up to 2020. In October, the *World Bank* committed to a $ 400 m package to support the privatisation of the agricultural sector. The return of aid monies suggested that donors were reluctant to confront the authorities about the repressive political climate at home and abroad.

The government also continued to consolidate its diplomatic and economic relations with *China*. In December, the Chinese ambassador to Rwanda delivered a message to parliament, committing to continued economic cooperation and technical partnerships. This commitment to deepening relations followed China's $ 10 m trade investment in textile manufacturing in Kigali in July. Relations with *France* continued to be frosty. In April, during a speech marking the launch of the commemoration of the 20th anniversary of the genocide, Kagame accused France of direct involvement in planning the killings. France immediately cancelled the planned participation of its envoy in the commemoration. Kagame also accused *Belgium* of complicity in the genocide. The Belgian envoy, Foreign Minister Didier Reynders, chose not to cancel his trip, pointing out that his government was paying homage to Rwandan lives lost, not to the RPF government. Throughout 2014, *European countries*, including France, Norway, Sweden, Germany and the Netherlands, refused to honour Rwanda's extradition requests, instead bringing domestic proceedings against Rwandan genocide suspects in their national courts.

For the first time, Rwanda received *awards for its development policies*, marking a change from the kudos it had received for its *post-conflict reconstruction and reconciliation* policies. In May, Kagame received the World Telecommunications Society award for his government's commitment to broadband connectivity. Also in May, he received the African Banker Award in recognition of Rwanda's impressive economic growth. In June, Kagame highlighted his government's commitment to economic development by announcing the opening of five new trade missions, including in Abu Dhabi, Angola and Israel.

Socioeconomic Developments

The year was dominated by events and activities related to the *commemoration of the 20th anniversary of the 1994 genocide*, with the government showcasing its social reconciliation and economic development policies. The government highlighted its ambitious development plans, including improved institutional governance and technocratic competence, a zero-tolerance policy on corruption, and continued economic growth. The government intensified its public commitment to economic growth and private-sector development, despite feeling the pinch of shortfalls in donor revenue. In May, the *International Financial Corporation*, the World Bank's private sector investment wing, launched its first *Rwandan franc-denominated bond*, which raised $ 22 m. In a speech announcing the bond, and again in August, Kagame noted his government's intention to attract up to $ 1 bn through a second *Eurobond issue*. The government had issued a $ 400 m bond in 2013, which was oversubscribed by $ 3 bn. Analysts urged caution as borrowing against an ambitious development plan without sustained local revenue was considered risky in the long term. Kagame addressed these critics at his monthly press conference in September, saying that Rwanda's business environment was attractive to both domestic and international investors. As noted in the World Bank's notes on the occasion of signing the *Second Economic Development and Poverty Reduction Strategy* (EDPRS 2) in 2013, low levels of corruption and technical competence should encourage donors to support Rwanda's economic development plans. The World Bank's endorsement of economic policies fell on deaf ears, however, as donors did not increase their aid commitments, and *FDI flows* fell by 12% to $ 390 m. To offset the tepid international aid environment, the government redoubled its efforts to deepen Rwanda's integration into the *EAC*, including joining the East Africa Payment System (EAPS) in December. EAPS is a network designed to reduce bank fees and transaction costs. Other efforts to modernise the financial sector included upgrades to the Kigali *Stock Exchange* to better accommodate foreign currencies, and the approval of a deposit guarantee fund by parliament, both in May. In September, the Bank of Kigali reported a 29% increase in income, indicating a healthy well-capitalised sector.

Increasing domestic revenue through *taxation* was another government priority, and was tied to poverty reduction policies and programmes. In September, in a speech before local government officials at the 7th annual '*imihigo*' (*performance contracts*) *conference*, Kagame chided officials for putting personal economic gain ahead of national development goals. When government officials, most of whom were appointed and paid by the RPF, did not meet the goals set out in their performance contract, they were relieved of their duties by a council of their peers, citing either corruption or incompetence. At the meeting, Kagame relieved dozens of officials from all levels of government of their posts, reminding them that their commitment had to be geared to community development and poverty reduction. Kagame further stated that tax collection should be fair and equitable; local officials who did not tax the population fairly were a threat to national development. The representatives of donor governments present at the speech acknowledged the discipline and meritocracy that the imihigo performance contracts provided, but did not increase aid commitments. The comments preceded news of the government's efforts to increase the number of individuals paying taxes. In October, *Finance Minister Claver Gatete* announced in parliament that the government had increased domestic tax revenue by 7% to a total of 16% of GDP. Data on how the increase was accomplished and who was paying were not provided. In April, the World Bank released a report stating that lower than average *rainfall* would continue throughout 2014, and that consumers should brace themselves to pay higher prices for staple foods. The government took the news seriously, rolling out an *emergency irrigation plan* in May, and releasing food from its strategic reserves to reduce price pressures.

In September, the World Bank's *Doing Business Index* reported that Rwanda had further improved its ranking to 32nd out of 189 countries by cutting red tape, getting construction permits and streamlining administrative procedures. In June, the World Bank's 2013 *Country Policy and Institutional Assessment* report was published, with Rwanda receiving the highest ranking in Africa. This made it eligible for an increased funding allocation of $ 726 m for 2014–17. The primary challenge for the government to continue its robust economic growth was *infrastructure deficiencies*. In August, progress on the planned railway to link Rwanda with the port of Mombasa (Kenya) stalled, owing to a dispute between the Ugandan government and the Chinese firm contracted to build the line. In September, Tanzania announced that it had finalised a deal with the World Bank and other donors to expand its port; Kigali played down the news with Kagame saying at his October press conference that he did not trust the Tanzanian government to live up to its commitments to regional integration. In December, Rwanda signed a five-year contract to *import electricity* from Kenya, bringing in 30 MW through a high-voltage line via Uganda. Also in December, private and donor monies joined to contribute another 40 MW to the national grid. The Nyabarongo I hydropower plant (28 MW) was brought on line as well as the Gigawatt Solar Project. In November, a 4G broadband network was launched in Kigali, the result of an initiative between the government and Korea Telecom to provide cheaper and quicker access to the Internet.

Throughout 2014, the government continued the implementation of the third phase of its *National Land Use and Development Master Plan*, first introduced as part of the Roadmap 2017 programme in January 2010. The plan had three phases: first, the merger of the local land usage policies devised in 1998 with the Master Plan; second, the creation of an urban development plan; and third, the implementation of the Master plan, once the peasantry had been taught how to use their land efficiently. In the second phase, representatives of the *Rwanda National Resources Authority* joined the small (less than 0.5 ha) plots of rural peasants into larger, more economically viable plots that could then be used for cash crops. As in 2013, the government *displaced countless subsistence farmers*, entrusting control of land use to local government officials. The Master Plan augmented the government's 2010 mono-cropping policy and shaped the food insecurity and poverty levels of rural households. The policy made it illegal for subsistence farmers to grow crops for their own families. Instead, they were told by the local authorities to grow coffee, tea and other export crops that earned foreign currency. In March, DFID published a report which stated that the land tenure system and the land use master plan were progressing well, and would improve food security in rural Rwanda. The findings of this report contradicted those of a Swedish report published in 2013, for which the government expelled the authors from the country.

In October, UNDP released an assessment of country progress towards the *MDGs*. Rwanda was one of a handful of low-income countries that was on track to meet its goals with respect to gender equality in primary and secondary education, primary school enrolment rates, reductions in HIV/AIDS and malaria prevalence, maternal mortality, and climatic shocks, and improving access to the financial sector for low-income earners. In July, the World Bank reported that Rwanda's *GDP per capita* had risen to $ 639, up from 2013 but still short of the roadmap 2017 target of $ 1,000 per person per annum.

Finance Minister John Rwangombwa presented an *expansionary budget* in May. Despite donor cuts, the budget focused on both capital expenditure and improving infrastructure and boosted government spending by 4.5%. The target remained improving infrastructure and reducing poverty. Despite poor weather, diminished commodity prices for tea, and weak tourism receipts, the 2014 *GDP growth rate* was projected to have speeded up considerably to probably around 6.5% (compared with 4.7% in 2013), while the year's average *inflation* fell to just 1.8% (down from 4.2% in 2013).

Seychelles

Rolf Hofmeier

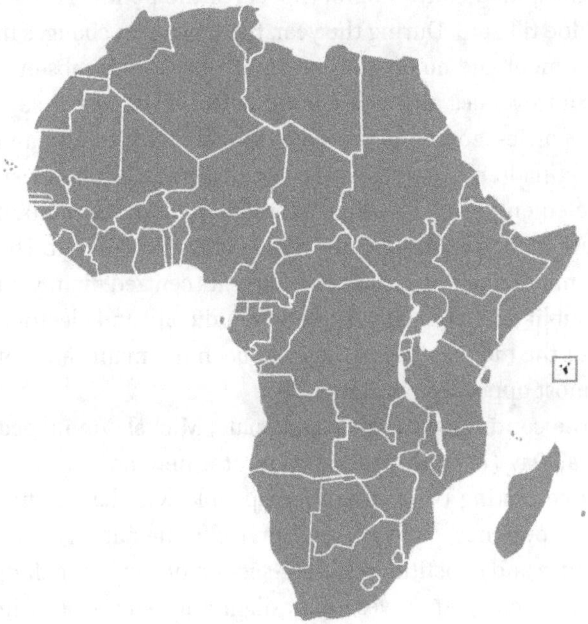

Politically, 2014 was another unspectacular and quiet year, with no outstanding changes or events. President Michel and his long-ruling Parti Lepep continued in undisputed control of all political affairs. The opposition parties remained weak and showed signs of being resigned to the sustained popularity of the president and the government. Michel went to great lengths to promote a sense of national unity and reconciliation after the earlier climate of divisive politics. On the international stage, Michel continued with his efforts to enhance the recognition of his tiny state and specifically to be seen as a champion of the interests of small island developing states. Economic performance was again quite satisfactory, with somewhat slower growth, stabilised figures for the tourism industry, further moves to liberalise the economy and maintenance of the remarkable level of social well-being of the population. Six years after the initiation of drastic economic reform measures, Seychelles continued to be praised by international organisations as a role model for successful reform-oriented policies. The earlier threat of Somali pirate activities came to an end.

 | DOI 10.1163/9789004305052_038

Domestic Politics

On the back of resounding victories in the 2011 presidential and parliamentary elections, *President James Michel* and his long-ruling *Parti Lepep* (PL, People's Party) continued to be in practically undisputed control of all aspects of the political scene. The next elections were not due till 2016. During the year, there were no changes in the composition of the government and no by-elections took place. In the absence of any significant political controversies and as a consequence of the rather subdued activities of opposition parties, 2014 thus turned out to be another calm and uneventful year. The year 2013 had ended with continued disagreement between the PL and key opposition elements over the long-standing contentious issue of electoral reform and the creation of an enabling fully democratic environment. The controversies between government and opposition had for years centred mainly on demands for un-politicised public services, an independent judiciary and electoral body, and the liberalisation of the media; these issues had been the main cause of the 2011 election boycott by most opposition parties.

In an effort to overcome the continuing political stalemate, Michel announced in his speech on the National Day (18 June) the creation of a new non-partisan *National Consultative Forum* consisting of 14 prominent people who had distinguished themselves by their "experience, goodwill and service to the nation". They were approached by State House and constituted a cross-section of society, including the Catholic bishop, business representatives, other dignitaries and, strictly in their private capacity, even members of the main opposition *Seychelles National Party* (SNP). Chaired personally by the president and also including Vice President Danny Faure, the Forum first assembled on 31 July and had held five meetings by December. The deliberations covered a wide range of national issues, including political subjects such as pending electoral legislation, political party registration and measures to de-politicise state functions. It remained to be seen, however, to what extent the discussions of the Forum would really lead to substantial legal and administrative changes and might thus usher in a new, more conciliatory political climate. Some amendments to the electoral legislation were introduced in December.

The composition of the National Assembly, with just a single opposition MP from the *Popular Democratic Movement* (PDM), tended to give the impression of a *de facto* reversion to the former era of a one-party regime. Michel and the PL leadership were, however, quite keen to avoid this impression and to maintain a conciliatory climate with regard to other political parties and general civil society interests. PDM chairman David Pierre was acknowledged as official opposition leader in the National Assembly. Pierre continued to hold regular monthly meetings with Michel in a cordial atmosphere, without much public attention, to exchange views on all current issues; he generally refrained from any aggressive confrontation with the government and stressed his understanding of constructive opposition.

PL conventions on 1 March and 31 May celebrated the party's golden jubilee (it had been founded by Michel's predecessor France Albert René as the Seychelles People's United Party), but also conspicuously emphasised strengthening national unity and removing the symbols of the one-party-state era. A statue commemorating René's deposition of the country's first president, James Mancham, (in 1977) was removed from the city centre and taken to the PL headquarters. The National Day was celebrated for the last time on 18 June, commemorating the new 1993 constitution that ended the one-party era. In future, the National Day would be 29 June, to celebrate Seychelles' independence in 1976. Mancham, after a long period in exile, had for some time assumed the role of a non-partisan elder statesman, representing Seychelles in various international forums and supporting Michel's conciliatory approach. Members of the business community also expressed sympathy for the PL's course, with only minor continuing resistance from the old guard of the former socialist era.

As a consequence of their 2011 election boycott, the traditionally strongest opposition party, the *SNP*, and its veteran leader, Wavel Ramkalawan, remained largely relegated to the role of political bystanders, with no means of exercising any substantial influence on public affairs. In comparison with former years, the SNP was thus restricted to a much lower level of activity. A disappointingly small protest march at the end of December against rising prices and newly introduced taxes proved its clear loss of mobilisation power. Despite a succession of electoral defeats, Ramkalawan was re-elected in July as SNP leader for another three-year mandate; in response to the electoral law amendments, he expressed the intention to end the boycott and participate in the 2016 elections.

In April, veteran opposition politician Ralph Volcère resigned as interim leader of the small *Seselwa United Party* (*SUP*), which had only been created in 2013 as an indirect successor to Mancham's earlier Democratic Party. Volcère disagreed strongly with Mancham's conciliatory attitude towards Michel and the PL, felt constrained to pursue a sharper opposition and was exhausted after 30 years in politics (partly in exile). Robert Ernesta took over as the new SUP leader.

Volcère also resigned as editor of the island's oldest publication "Seychelles Weekly". *Media* restrictions had in the past long been a major bone of contention between René's regime and the opposition, although a gradual liberalisation of the situation had in recent years been tolerated by the authorities. A report by a Paris-based media consultant, released in March, found the media to be generally free, but experiencing difficulties in obtaining access to official information. In June, Reporters without Borders assessed the media situation to be polarised and partisan and ranked Seychelles relatively low at 103rd (out of 180 countries). A new Seychelles News Agency was launched in April.

Foreign Affairs

The government continued to pursue active public diplomacy to raise the visibility of its mini-state on the international stage. Since 2014 had been declared by the UN as the year of *Small Island Developing States* (SIDS), Seychelles used the opportunity to portray itself as a champion and natural leader of the SIDS group at the global level and specifically to raise concern about the inherent dangers of climate change for these countries. Michel attended the 3rd UN SIDS conference in early September in Samoa and played an active part in attempts to strengthen the 39-member Alliance of Small Island States (*AOSIS*). In mid-November, Seychelles hosted a ministerial AOSIS meeting in preparation for the UN climate conference in Lima (Peru) in December. Seychelles was expected to assume the AOSIS presidency in 2017, while the government, with AOSIS and AU support, also continued its campaign for Seychelles to be a candidate for a non-permanent seat on the UNSC in 2017. On 23 August, Michel attended the 4th *IOC* heads of state summit in Moroni (Comoros), and in November Seychelles hosted a tourism ministers meeting from the *IORA*. All these activities served to enhance Seychelles' international profile. In December, the country was at last admitted to the *WTO* after almost two decades of strenuous negotiations.

The most important *visitors* during the year were President Jorge Carlos Fonseca from *Cape Verde*, who was guest of honour during the National Day celebrations in mid-June, and President Mahinda Rajapaksa from *Sri Lanka* in late June (his second visit within a year). In both cases, cooperation agreements on the basis of shared interests as island states and tourism destinations were signed. The government announced its intention to open its tenth embassy, in Sri Lanka, in the near future, thereby underlining its interest in intensifying cooperation within the Indian Ocean neighbourhood. President *Michel* participated in the high-profile US-Africa summit in early August in Washington DC, visited New Zealand ahead of the AOSIS conference in Samoa, attended the UN climate change summit in September in New York and was in France in early December on a working visit, mainly to promote tourism and other economic interests.

The previous years' threat from *Somali pirate activities* in the Indian Ocean practically came to an end after already showing a significant decline in 2013. No further piracy incursions were recorded in the Seychelles' vicinity, but some piracy suspects were still handed over to the Seychellois authorities by the international navies that continued to operate their anti-piracy patrols. Seychelles again served as an important support base for these international endeavours and was in May elected as co-chair of the UN contact group on piracy off the coast of Somalia. By October, 41 alleged pirates were still incarcerated in Seychellois prisons (of whom 25 had been sentenced), while 111 Somali pirates had by then already been repatriated to Somaliland or Puntland. Some concern also centred on a new phenomenon of increases in drug seizures.

Socioeconomic Developments

The Seychellois economy again demonstrated remarkable resilience in the face of prolonged global uncertainties. The general *macroeconomic performance* continued to be quite satisfactory, with a marked deceleration in the growth rate and a further reduction in inflation. The government proudly celebrated six years of its successful programme of reform, which had been introduced in late 2008 as a kind of shock treatment to ward off the near-collapse of the unsustainably indebted and heavily welfare-oriented economy. This significant change of policy orientation towards a liberal market outlook and an investor-friendly climate had effectively stabilised the situation, while safeguards for the social sectors continued to be maintained. In the 2014 *HDI*, Seychelles was ranked 71th in the 'high' human development category (no longer in the 'very high' category due to a somewhat modified methodology), ranking second of all SSA countries. The World Bank listed Seychelles as an upper middle-income country. In the World Economic Forum's Global Competitiveness Index 2014/15, Seychelles was ranked 92nd (out of 144) and seventh in SSA. The World Bank's Doing Business Report 2015 showed the country in 85th position (out of 189) and sixth in SSA. With an annual per capita income of about $ 25,000 (PPP), it was clearly in a different league from most of the rest of Africa. All MDGs were largely achieved; health and education services were of excellent quality.

Due to somewhat weaker demand for Seychelles' two main exports (tourism and canned tuna), the projected *GDP growth rate* for 2014 was revised down (by the IMF) to 2.8% (compared with impressive growth rates, based on revised national statistics, of 7.9%, 6.0% and 6.6% for the years 2011, 2012 and 2013, respectively). Consumer price *inflation* was brought down further to an annual average of 1.4%, compared with 7.1% in 2012 and 4.3% in 2013. Strong growth in personal earnings and private sector credit contributed to a surge in imports and to putting further pressure on the balance of payments. As a result, the exchange rate of the Seychelles rupee (SR) fell by 11% in nominal effective terms from early August to late October, although the SR had slightly appreciated in the two previous years. The flexible exchange rate regime served as a safety valve in helping to manage the pressures and restore external equilibrium. Foreign exchange reserves continued to grow considerably and reached $ 480 m by mid-year, equivalent to a comfortable five months' import coverage (compared with just two weeks' at the height of the 2008 crisis). The structural deficit of the tiny import-dependent island's *balance of trade* remained unchanged, with imports amounting to about double the value of exports; about half the latter was accounted for by tuna fish and most of the rest by oil product re-exports. The *current-account deficit* was provisionally projected to have risen from a revised 15% of GDP in 2013 to about 22% and was expected to remain at that level in the medium term. The key *tourism sector* had a rather difficult year with a marked fall in visitor numbers from Europe during the first half of the year. Final 2014 visitor statistics eventually showed a total of 232,667 visitor arrivals, just 1% higher than in 2013. Estimated tourism earnings fell, however, by about 8% to around $ 315 m, reflecting reduced spending abilities from traditional tourism markets (France, Italy). Germany for the first time topped the list of visitors, while new markets (Russia, UAE, China) continued to grow remarkably. FDI inflows (mainly for new tourism projects) remained substantial and were an important factor in closing the current-account deficit. In mid-May, a new quota system for recruitment of foreign workers came into force as part of the government's strategy to safeguard jobs for Seychellois: 24% of the 55,000 *labour force* was made up of foreigners (predominantly from India and Bangladesh). The perceived competition in the local labour market from growing numbers of Asian workers (mainly in the construction and tourism sectors) led to occasional expressions of xenophobic sentiment, which were also fuelled by the many land and luxury real estate purchases by affluent Arab investors.

The government consistently continued a policy of *strict fiscal discipline* in pursuance of its goal to gradually redress the huge public debt that had been accumulated during the earlier welfare-oriented socialist era. It was well on track to achieve the set target of bringing *public debt* down to below 50% of GDP by 2018. External debt was already down to 37% of GDP, a remarkable decline from 90% in 2008. For the seventh consecutive year, an overall *budget surplus* was achieved (projected at 2% of GDP).

On 4 June, the *IMF* approved a new $ 17.6 m Extended Fund Facility (EFF) arrangement in support of the government's socioeconomic reform programme to follow on from the earlier successfully concluded EFF, which had expired in December 2013. A first review of the new EFF was conducted in September and formally approved in December, bringing disbursements to $ 4.8 m. Programme implementation and economic fundamentals were assessed to be strong and all performance criteria under the EFF had been met, although the Seychelles' external position had somewhat weakened in mid-2014. The agreed structural agenda had remained broadly on track, despite some technical delays.

The national airline, *Air Seychelles*, took delivery of its third large aircraft in late November and started new regional connections to India, Madagascar and Tanzania. To support the tourism industry, efforts were also made by the government to commit other airlines to offer more flight connections. The *offshore financial sector* showed further strong expansion with over 10,000 new company registrations during the year; total registrations had reached an estimated 140,000, compared with 650 in 1996. Weaknesses were exposed in respect of offshore banking services, however. In November, the Central Bank was forced to take control of the Bank of Muscat International, since it had run into problems with its international correspondent banks. The government rejected repeated accusations that it tacitly facilitated money-laundering scams and in October formally agreed to respect new OECD fiscal transparency regulations. Although not blacklisted, Seychelles nevertheless remained under suspicious scrutiny.

No tangible progress was made with regard to the possibility of *oil* or *gas* finds in the Seychelles' extensive maritime zone. Further seismic data were gathered, but no firm agreements with interested international companies to start exploratory drilling were as yet in sight. The Public Utilities Corporation began the installation of wind turbines and also planned to make use of solar energy. The government continued to actively promote its concept of the specific values of a '*blue economy*', centred on the abundant maritime resources of the country's large exclusive economic zone. Among the initiatives taken in that endeavour, Michel opened a blue economy summit conference in Abu Dhabi in January and hosted a first national forum on the blue economy in Victoria in December.

Somalia

Stig Jarle Hansen

The general situation in Somalia continued to improve somewhat. The forces of the AU, and their fledgling Somali allies, advanced throughout 2014, and the Islamist al-Shabaab were forced to abandon several cities. Conditions in the capital, Mogadishu, were improving and construction activities were rampant, although some districts remained dangerous. In the north of the country, conditions were stable, although serious challenges continued to be evident. Somalia was, however, still struggling with several long-term problems. First, al-Shabaab still controlled the middle Juba territory and large parts of Mudug, in addition to several smaller cities. Although not able to defeat the forces of the AU in open combat, al-Shabaab showed itself able to survive all over southern Somalia, and implemented large-scale terror attacks throughout 2014 in both Somalia and Kenya, with several indications of increasingly significant sympathetic support in Tanzania and Burundi. Second, several other conflicts that did not involve al-Shabaab grew in importance throughout the year. Tensions emerged between clan-based government forces and the Benadiri in lower Shabelle region, between government forces and local groups in Duhsamareb and Jowhar, and in the north between local militias, mostly hailing from the Sool and Sanaag provinces and Puntland/Somaliland. Significant and often clan-based tensions also emerged between various regional entities and

 | DOI 10.1163/9789004305052_039

between several of these and the central government. Underlying were serious disagreements over the degree of centralisation of powers in the central government. Third, state-building processes were lacking, and important governmental services, such as the police, received infrequent pay, and rampant corruption and ill-discipline plagued the whole government sector, including the Somali armed forces.

Domestic Politics

Somalia had experienced a troubled political history since the emergence in the early 2000s of new forms of Somali central governments. The current governance structure was based around a process whereby a technical selection committee had screened candidates nominated by clan leaders using the so-called 4,5 formula; this gave each large clan family (Dir, Hawiye, Darod, Digil-Mirifle) a 2/9 share of the representatives, while minority clans together got a 1/9 share, and had led to the formation of a parliament in 2012. This parliament had subsequently elected a president, Hassan Sheikh Mohamud, from the Hawiye/Abgal/Wa'eysle clan lineage, who had a solid background in the aid and research sectors of Mogadishu. Under this system, the president appoints a prime minister, who in turn forms a cabinet, which must then be approved by the parliament.

President Hassan Sheikh Mohamud had been relatively successful in addressing some of the problems of the previous administration by, for example, improving the salary system for civil servants, and enabling the army and the police to be paid more regularly. However, the president also frequently changed prime ministers: 2014 saw the *removal* of his second *prime minister, Abdiweli Sheikh Ahmed* (Darod/Marehan, Ugas Shermarke) in early December, after Mohamud initiated a motion of no-confidence against him in parliament. Abdiweli's removal was partly a result of his challenging the president by attempting to reshuffle his cabinet. The prime minister attempted to weaken one of the president's most loyal allies, Farah Sheikh Abduqadir (Reer Aw Hassan, Sheikal, Hawiye), by demoting him to minister of husbandry and livestock, and he also changed other post-holders. The reshuffle highlighted tensions that had begun when the prime minister fired the head of security, Abdullahi Mohamed Ali 'Sanbalolshe' (Hawiye, hawadle), a move that the president felt stepped on his prerogatives.

An underlying tension contributing to the personnel changes was the major issue surrounding *federalism* and the existence of *regional states*. After new regional states were declared, the borders with older states had to be demarcated. Abdiweli's approval of Puntland's claim to Northern Mudug created animosities in Mogadishu, alienating the president's clan allies in central Somalia. However, the president's appointment of *Omar Abdirashid Ali Sharmarke as new prime minister* on 17 December was still in a sense considered 'Puntland-friendly'. The new prime minister, who had served as prime minister once before in 2009–10, hailed from the Puntland region and was the son of Abdirashid Ali Sharmarke, who had served as Somalia's second president in the 1960s. Sharmarke began to assemble a cabinet that included many of the ministers who had been removed, but faced opposition in parliament. The vote approving the suggested new cabinet list did not take place till the end of the year, however, so the first test of strength for the new prime minister was left till January 2015. The cabinet was likely to again be dominated by personalities from the Somali diaspora, like Sharmarke himself, with his Canadian-Somali background.

Somalia consisted of *three major regional states* that in theory accepted the central government in Mogadishu. *Juba State* was controlled by its president, Ahmed Mohamed Islam (Darod/Ogadeen, Mohamed Subeir), a former al-Shabaab leader who very often acted, non-violently, in opposition to President Mohamud. Then there was the so-called *Southwestern State*, led by its president, Sharif Hassan Sheikh Adan (Digil/Mireifel, Ranhanwhein, Siyed), who had been the speaker in the transitional parliament and was a close ally of Mohamud. Adan had issues with Ahmed Mohamed Islam over the demarcation of the borders between the two regional states, but this appeared to have been solved when a Memorandum of Understanding between the two was signed in Kismaayo on 30 December. The semi-autonomous state of *Puntland* was led by Somalia's former prime minister, Abdiweli Muhamed Ali Gaas (Darood/Harti, Omar Mahmoud), who had taken the post upon winning a tightly-contested election in the clan-selected Puntland parliament on 8 January, defeating Puntland's incumbent president, Abdirahman Mohamed Farole.

In the *central areas*, attempts were also made to establish wider regional states, but local administrations (as in the cases of Galmudug State, Himaan and Heeb State and Hiraan) prevailed, accepting in theory the authority of the central state, but not conforming to the constitutional requirements for a regional state. The autonomies enjoyed by the regional states and the other local entities were widespread, and it could be argued that, outside Mogadishu, regional leaders were the de facto leaders. However, the tension around the federal issue in Somalia remained; there was no precise description of the federal system in the constitution, and these tensions were expected to hamper the democratic elections scheduled for 2016.

Somaliland, an entity based around the borders of the former British colony of Somaliland in north-west Somalia, had its relatively independent political dynamics and further consolidated its democratic system based around a three-party system, in which the parties were nominated through local elections. During 2014, Somaliland was faced by three major political crises. The first was a showdown over the leadership of the ruling *Kulmiye party*, led by the veteran *President Ahmed Mohamed Muhamoud 'Silanyo'* (Isaq, Haber Jalo), born in 1936 and a pre-civil-war minister in Siad Barre's Somali government. As Silanyo was growing older, two other party veterans, Muse Bihi Abdi (Isaq, Habar Awal, Saad Mussa) and Abdelazzis Samale (Isaq, Habar Awal, Saad Mussa), attempted to situate themselves to take over the party and possibly to stand in the 2015 presidential election. Samale was closer to Silanyo, but was in the end defeated by Bihi, and was demoted from the position of minister of finance, leaving the position open to Somaliland's (and Somalia's) first female minister of finance, Zamzam Abdi Adan. Samale was not removed from the cabinet, but took the education portfolio. Musa Bihi agreed not to challenge Silanyo in the 2015 presidential race. Kulmiye remained united ahead of the elections, and Musa Bihi as party chairman seemed to be the first in line for succession to the leadership, although Silanyo confirmed his intention to stand in the election and remain as president for five more years.

Kulmiye attempted to remove the leader of the *opposition Wadani party* (one of the two permitted opposition parties in Somaliland), Abdirahman Mohammed Abdullahi 'Irro' (Haber Younis, Isaq), speaker of the lower house of parliament, who faced impeachment after he allegedly acted unconstitutionally over procedures. However, the attempt ended in failure, and Irro remained the speaker after mediation by the elders in the upper house led by Saleban Mohamoud Aden and Haji Abdi Waraabe. Irro was re-instated, although he had publicly to accept some of the blame for the crisis. The last major challenge facing Somaliland was the rebellion of a *Gadabursi tribal leader*, Suldan Abubakar Cilmi Wabar (Dir, Gadabursi, Jibril Yunis), who declared that the Gadabursi region of Awdal was, from 5 December, no longer part of Somaliland. The Gadabursi had normally remained loyal to Somaliland, but a small group initiated low-level attacks against Somaliland forces. The group was still small, and the majority of the Gadabursi remained loyal to Somaliland.

In the *border areas* between *Puntland* and *Somaliland*, i.e. the provinces of Sool, Sanaag and Cayn, local groups continued to oppose Somaliland, and to a lesser extent Puntland. Some of the resistance was organised around the so-called Kathumo State, established in 2012. However, defections to Puntland and Somaliland military victories put Kathumo State on the defensive. Further north, Warsangeli subclans waged a small-scale insurgency against the Puntland authorities. The Galgalla insurgency was influenced by militias loyal to al-Shabaab, under the leadership of Yasin Osman Khalid (Kilwa, Darod, Warsangeli, Dubayas). Al-Shabaab intensified hostilities in these areas, and attacked a Puntland police station in Bosasso on 13 January. Al-Shabaab were able to recruit amongst other local clans, but were not in a position to challenge Puntland for territorial control. They were also weakened symbolically by the defection of Said Atom, a veteran commander in the area.

Further south, al-Shabaab faced a situation where they were losing ground, and where US drone strikes were having an impact on their leadership. They were also facing a cleavage in the wider global jihadi movement (between al-Qaida and the so-called Islamic State [IS]) and rumours of clan tensions. Al-Shabaab dominance was now restricted to the middle Juba province and parts of Mudug, where cities such as Jilib were under their control. Al-Shabaab was also able to control villages in Bay-Bakool and Hiraan in a semi-permanent form, as long as the AU forces and their Somali allies did not send out determined patrols. In Middle and Lower Benadir, al-

Shabaab were still able to wage a guerilla war but in Mogadishu they were less able to carry out guerilla actions, although their terrorist attacks continued.

The increasing number of battlefield withdrawals was affecting al-Shabaab's reputation, as did a series of US drone attacks. In January, one such attack killed al-Shabaab commander Sahal Iskudhuq, but the biggest US victory was the killing of the important al-Shabaab leader Ahmed 'Godane' (Isaq (Diir), Arab) on 1 September. Al-Shabaab managed to minimise the damage, however, as he had left a political will in which he appointed his relative Ahmed Diryeh 'Abu Ubaidah', from the Diir clan, as his successor. Diryeh was related to Godane's mother's family and was loosely connected to him clan-wise.

Diryeh's appointment was contested by veteran al-Shabaab commander Mahad Mohamed Ali 'Karate' (Ayr, Haber Gedir, Hawiye) and a group around him. They resisted what was perceived as the northern dominance of al-Shabaab and inclined somewhat to IS, but intensive negotiations eventually eased the tensions. Al-Shabaab was in general on the decline, but was still formidable. It was not likely that it would be dislodged from the Somali countryside, although the provinces it controlled were under threat. Security forces were inadequate to keep villages permanently free of al-Shabaab's presence; the Somali army was too clan-based and ill organised, and the AU forces too few. It therefore appeared that al-Shabaab would be able to survive in the countryside for years to come. They were also seemingly able to expand regionally, and there were reports of al-Shabaab-affiliated activities in both Burundi and Tanzania, although it was hard to say how close groups that initiated such actions really were to the al-Shabaab leadership. Al-Shabaab activities in Kenya were also on the rise, with two massive attacks close to Mandera, and a major possible al-Shabaab attack in Mpeketoni (near Lamu).

There were several other parallel conflicts in southern Somalia. In Lower Benadir, the clan composition of the Somali army, which was in general recruited from the Ayr clan or the Haber Gedir of the Hawiye, had created specific tensions. In the 1990s, these clans occupied the area and local groups, especially from the Biyemal clan, were poorly treated and abused as slaves. There were strong indications that this practice was continuing, and several Biyemal militias organised themselves in order to attack the government, a conflict that al-Shabaab were potentially able to turn to their advantage. In Hiraan, there were smaller conflicts, and in Galmudug, local Ahlu Sunna Wal Jamaa militias also fought the government.

Foreign Affairs

The security of Southern Somalia and the containment of al-Shabaab continued to depend on the forces of the *AU Mission in Somalia* (AMISOM), a military force initially created in 2007, but drastically expanded when Kenya intervened in Somalia in 2011 and was included into *AMISOM* in 2012, as was the case with Ethiopia which re-engaged in 2012. Djiboutian and Sierra Leonean contingents were added to the Ugandan, Burundian, Kenyan and Ethiopian forces (plus Nigerian and Ghanaian police), making a total of 22,126 men and women, of which some 550 were police and the rest soldiers. In late 2014, the Sierra Leonean contingent was withdrawn when a routine replacement was considered inappropriate due to the Ebola outbreak in that country.

Several of the suppliers of troops to AMISOM had their own strategic allies inside Somalia. *Kenya*, which hosted some 425,000 Somali refugees and had signed agreements with the Somali government for their return, had its closest allies in the south-western Juba State, and Kenyan forces remained in Kismayo despite earlier promises that they would withdraw from the city. *Ethiopia*'s influence in Juba State was growing, however, and was also clear both in Somaliland, which was allowed to train its officers at the Ethiopian Harrar military academy, and amongst the Marehan militias in upper Juba. *Djibouti* and its forces in the Hiraan valley were logistically dependent on Ethiopian forces, and Djibouti's role in Somalia had to be seen in the light of Djibouti's increasing closeness to Ethiopia. Ethiopia and Kenya, despite some serious differences, were generally able to cooperate quite regularly on the basis of their 1963–64 pact, Africa's oldest military pact, whose exact wording remained secret. Regional struggles between the various actors for power and regional leadership were quite apparent. This was reflected, for example, when Uganda, the largest supplier of troops, manoeuvred for the leadership of the AMISOM forces, but Uganda had no strong local Somali allies.

During the year, in strong contrast to earlier periods, Mogadishu saw visits by many foreign ministers and high-level UN and World Bank leaders. Somalia was seen as a project for Turkey's "new ottoman" policies; *Turkey* was active in Mogadishu and had taken the initiative in supporting Somaliland-Somalia negotiations, which had begun in Istanbul in 2013, although they had broken down on several occasions as Turkey was regarded by the Somalilanders as being somewhat pro-Mogadishu. Turkey was symbolically important as one of the first countries to re-open an embassy in Mogadishu and President Recep Erdoğan, who in 2011 had been one of the first heads of state to visit Somalia, planned another visit for January 2015.

Qatar also opened an embassy. It had several close allies in the Somali cabinet and occasionally intervened to provide political support on the Somali domestic political scene, as well as being very active in the charity sector. *Yemen* was another important player, and Yemen's private arms markets were the major suppliers of small arms. Yemen was a major recipient of Somali economic refugees trying to make their way to Saudi Arabia and the Gulf states; 236,000 Somali refugees were registered in Yemen, although the popularity of Yemen as a destination was dwindling. Yemen was also fishing extensively in Somali waters, and had agreements regulating fishing activities with Puntland and Somaliland.

Somalia saw the installation of an American military mission; the *USA* also designated an ambassador to Somalia, Katherine S. Dhanani, operating out of Nairobi. The year also saw the notable opening of a Chinese embassy in Mogadishu on 13 October. By year's end, 11 countries had *embassies* in Mogadishu: China, Djibouti, Ethiopia, Iran, Italy, Qatar, Sudan, Turkey, Uganda, the UK and Yemen.

Outsiders such as the Interpeace group also played a significant role in Somali and Somaliland politics. The Somalian president had been in close partnership with Interpeace before assuming the presidency and was close to several of the researchers affiliated with them. Indeed, the foreign NGO sector remained a potent route to power in Somalia.

Socioeconomic Developments

The Somali economy remained hard to assess and estimates of the GNP and other measures of growth were difficult because of the lack of reliable statistics. The IMF nevertheless produced some estimates, calculating the nominal *GDP* at $ 9,857 m in 2014, with a *growth rate* of 6%. Somalia's 10.5 m inhabitants were still in a fragile situation, dependent on foreign support and remittances sent home from the large Somali diaspora. The total value of *remittances*, estimated at about $ 1.3 b in 2012, accounted for an equivalent of about 35% of Somalia's total GDP and thus was of major importance for the Somali economy. Somali workers in the diaspora were often in the West and in the Gulf states. The flow of remittances came under threat of being severely curtailed when Western banks came under political pressure to close their cooperation with Somali remittance companies during 2014.

The expected drop in remittances was also expected to have an influence on *budget* calculations, but this had not yet been incorporated into the calculations for the new budgets of the central state and the various regional entities. The Somali national budget for 2015 foresaw expenditure of $ 216 m, a slight drop compared with the $ 218 m budgeted in 2014. The Somaliland government had a larger budget than the central Somali government, and approved a $ 251 m budget for 2015, the largest in Somaliland's history, perhaps influenced by the extra cost of the upcoming 2015 election. The central Somaliland government would have some $ 180 m to spend. Both Somali states and their regional administrations had major problems with collecting taxes, and were in reality dependent on fees from markets, ports and airports, which were easy to collect, although corruption was rampant everywhere.

The Somali private sector was dominated by the *livestock industry*; it provided income for an estimated 60% of the population, contributing 40% of the total GNP and 50% of export earnings. Livestock exports went through the ports of Berbera and Bosasso in the north, mostly to the Gulf states. In the south, the main livestock outlet was the border town of Garissa (Kenya). The main export was live animals, which made the sector less efficient as more storage space was needed and the production chain ended outside Somalia. Exports had long been relatively insecure because the main importer, Saudi Arabia, banned or restricted imports on the grounds of inadequate disease controls on the Somali side. Somalia also exported agricultural products, mainly maize and bananas from the Shabelle and Juba valleys.

The Somali *fishing industry* had significant potential, as the Somalia coastline is the longest in East Africa. Marine resources had been mainly exploited by foreign fishermen, as Somalia had in the past failed to declare a 200 nm economic zone, originally declaring these areas as territorial waters but failing to have the claim accepted. In a proclamation dated 30 June, the economic zone of Somalia was properly declared, and data were submitted to the UN Convention on the Law of the Sea. In Puntland, probably Somalia's most important fishing region, biometric registration took place through 2014, enabling the Puntlanders to better control their fishing industry. However, Somalia and its regional states will have no viable navy in the near future, thus severely restricting any efforts to stop illegal fishing.

Another potentially profitable sector, *oil and gas*, suffered from similar problems to those of the fishing industry. Several companies had invested and announced exploratory drilling in the border areas of Puntland and Somaliland, the most prominent perhaps being DNO, a Norwegian company, and the Somali government was in contact with several larger oil companies. However, the authorities in Puntland, Somaliland and Mogadishu were all issuing their own licences, and disputes over which entity had a legitimate claim led to local conflicts, causing several of the oil investors in turn to freeze their operations through 2013 and 2014. In the far south, Kenya and Somalia had a contested border, making oil and gas exploration more difficult. The issue was brought to the International Court of Justice by Somalia. In Somaliland, TGS Nopec had carried out seismic surveys as early as 2009 and, in the south, Soma Oil & Gas conducted extensive seismic surveys in exchange for Production Sharing Agreements for an area of up to 60,000 sq km, finishing in December 2014. The seismic surveys were promising, but foreign investors were reluctant to invest, perhaps in view of the problems described above. Another cause of this reluctance had clearly been the notorious problem of Somali *piracy activities*, which had caught global attention for years, but piracy had already been declining drastically since 2012.

The Somali *telecommunications sector*, consisting of around 20 major companies, continued to do well, and was investing outside Somalia. The sector had benefitted from the lack of regulation, but the lack of standardisation between the various telecom providers hurt consumers. New legislation was passed to start the standardisation process, and several companies coordinated their activities on a voluntary basis; three signed an agreement on 22 July. The Somali *financial sector* also suffered from lack of regulation, as well as from the threatened ban on remittances from the West, since the largest financial companies, such as Dahabshil, were dependent on the handling of remittances. Other, more regular finance institutions opened throughout 2014, including the International Bank of Somalia and Premier Bank. Another small milestone was the opening of the first ATM in Mogadishu, owned by Salaam Somali Bank. The nucleus of a Somalia Stock Exchange was also starting to emerge, opening offices in Mogadishu and Kismayo. The institution, initially tied to the Kenyan stock exchange, was scheduled to open fully in 2015.

International financial institutions also returned to the city during the year. The *World Bank* set up a Multi-Partner Fund for Somalia, a facility to finance items of emergency expenditure in Somalia's budget. Somalia remained heavily dependent on foreign aid. The 2015 Humanitarian Response Plan consisted of requests for $ 863 m to meet humanitarian needs. Somalia still had 1.1 m IDPs, and 731,000 Somalis were defined by the UN as in urgent need of humanitarian assistance, although the rainfall had generally been quite good. A continuing major humanitarian problem was the lack of access to the areas controlled by al-Shabaab. Somalia's high illiteracy rate, with only 37.8% of adult Somalis able to read, also hampered productive investment and the development of democratic institutions.

South Sudan

Peter Woodward

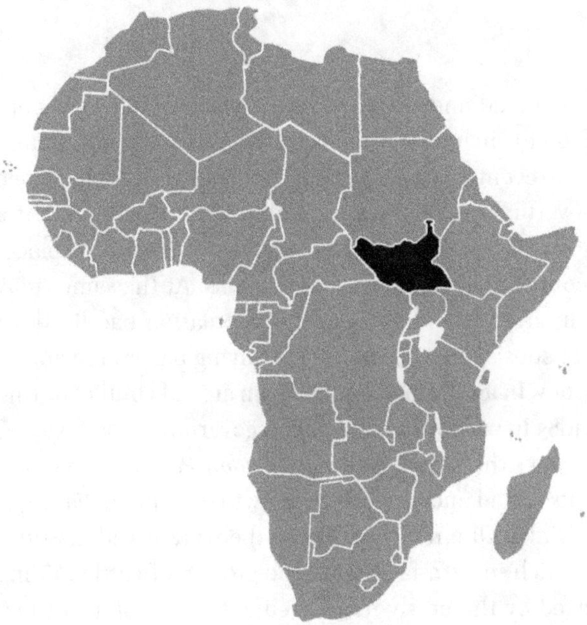

The year started in the worst possible circumstances following an eruption of violence in Juba on 15 December 2013 within the presidential guard that appeared to reflect ethnic tensions between Dinka and Nuer soldiers: fighting spread rapidly across the country, especially along the length of the Nile valley from Juba in the south to Malakal in the north. It was to leave a trail of devastation during the course of the year that laid waste to the main towns and saw inter-tribal fighting in many areas. As well as thousands of dead, the widespread fighting left hundreds of IDPs and many refugees fleeing into Sudan to the north and Ethiopia to the east. The spark that produced the devastation was caused by the crisis in national politics, which had worsened steadily in 2013. It had centred on the growing rift between President Salva Kiir, a Dinka, and Vice President Riek Machar, a Nuer (the Dinka and the Nuer being the two largest tribal groups), which had led to Kiir sacking Machar, to which the latter had responded by announcing his intention to challenge Kiir in the presidential election scheduled for 2015. The international community, horrified by the apparent collapse of the world's newest state, then only two years old, responded with humanitarian relief led by the UN Mission in South Sudan and military engagement in the form of Uganda's controversial intervention

 | DOI 10.1163/9789004305052_040

in support of Kiir. In addition, there were repeated efforts, led by the regional IGAD, to bring about talks between the political leaders, but although a number of ceasefires were announced, they were repeatedly broken.

Domestic Politics

The speed with which *conflict* spread and the scale of the *violence* reflected both the ethnic diversity of South Sudan, including traditional rivalries and tensions, and the socioeconomic changes of recent years, especially the emergence since 2000 of the oil sector, on which government revenues were almost entirely based. At a local level in the areas of the oil wells, mainly in the north, there was some displacement of population, which contributed to inter-tribal tensions. At the same time, a monetised economy grew in areas where most of the population had lived for centuries by complex forms of subsistence, frequently involving pastoral reciprocity, with little if any use of money. In addition, it had been an area of conflict during and after the civil wars from 1983 to 2005, when the Sudan government had backed local, often tribal, militias against the largely southern *Sudan People's Liberation Army* (SPLA), while the SPLA itself had encouraged the growth of *local militias* loyal to it, especially amongst the Dinka. One result had been the widespread distribution of automatic weapons, which in turn facilitated the growth of cattle raiding and counter-raiding encouraged by the newly monetised economy. Efforts at disarmament after the Comprehensive Peace Agreement (CPA) of 2005 were of limited effectiveness, while local militias continued to have significant importance on the ground. Following South Sudan's independence in 2011, *President Salva Kiir* had won over some of the major militias to the SPLA – now the national army – which in consequence grew rapidly. At the time, he was widely applauded since this was seen as a peace move, and one that would deny future militia allies to Sudan in the event of continuing differences between the two governments. From an estimated 40,000 SPLA soldiers at the time of the CPA, the army had expanded to 240,000 by 2011, with a further 90,000 police and other paramilitary personnel. This absorbed a major slice of government expenditure and was dependent on continuing funding from oil, which brought in 98% of government revenue. It was becoming commonplace to hear South Sudan described not as a state with an army, but an army with a state.

The *crisis in 2013* grew from South Sudan's dispute with Sudan over oil revenues and the decision by the former to close the pipeline in early 2012, apparently believing that this would force Sudan to agree a new deal. However, it brought financial crisis in both countries, and made the South Sudan government unable to pay all the local militias now on the SPLA payroll, which brought rapid discontent. At the same time, splits in the government were widening, with Kiir trying to become more controlling and others seeking to introduce more accountability into the *Sudan People's Liberation Movement* (SPLM), the dominant ruling party. *Riek Machar*, who had been *sacked as vice president* in June 2013, was one of the leading figures calling for reform, and it was when an SPLM congress was about to discuss reform steps in Juba in December 2013 that the fighting started and spread like wildfire the length of the country.

By the beginning of 2014, there had already been heavy fighting in Juba itself. Dinka elements in the SPLA were seeking out and killing the local Nuer population: many of the latter fled while 20,000 sought refuge in UN camps around the city. Fighting was also severe in Bor, about 100 km to the north, where a largely Nuer militia led by Peter Gadet Yaka took control. Gadet's force had been absorbed into the SPLA shortly after independence but now showed its support for Machar, who proclaimed himself head of the *SPLA-In Opposition* (SPLA-IO) in the confrontation with Kiir. For a while, there were fears that Gadet's force would be in a position to threaten Juba. However, that danger was averted with the help of Ugandan forces, and in subsequent fighting Bor changed hands repeatedly, leading to widespread devastation of the town. As in Juba, many sought sanctuary in UN camps, which offered some measure of security, even though the conditions were very poor.

Further north, the towns of Bentiu and Malakal were similarly devastated as they also changed hands several times. *Gadet* was named as the overall *commander of the opposition forces* and had the apparent aim of taking control of what was called Greater Upper Nile, comprising three of the ten states of South Sudan: Unity, Upper Nile and Jonglei. This was the main oil fields area and the strategy appeared to be to wrest control of them from the government, thus cutting almost all of Juba's revenues and bringing about Kiir's downfall. There was much speculation as to where the rebels were acquiring weapons, including the possibility that Sudan was supplying at least some of them and using the rebels to take back the oil fields it had lost with South Sudan's secession in 2011.

While many of the *rebel forces* – perhaps as many as 50,000 – were defectors from the SPLA and the police, other rebel militias were composed of youth from local communities, especially amongst the Nuer. They became known generally as various sections of the 'White Army', as many of the fighters were pastoralists who were accustomed to rubbing themselves with ash before fighting. In a number of incidents, people who sought sanctuary in churches and mosques, hitherto seen as places of safety, were attacked and killed. The extent of Machar's influence on these young White Army militias was thought to be limited, creating a further problem for peace-making. Overall, the level of fighting fluctuated during the year: in the rainy season in the middle of the year it died down somewhat, but it was never entirely halted and was still on-going at year's end.

The UN estimated that *over one million people* had been *displaced* in the fighting, some to UN camps, which bulged with over 100,000 people, while a comparable figure had fled north into Sudan and 200,000 east to Ethiopia. The camps were not equipped for such an influx and delivery of relief was very difficult. In addition, the fighting severely disrupted normal annual agricultural production, while livestock raiding intensified in many areas, exacerbated by the tribal mobilisation of the conflict. With a real threat of famine requiring food aid for up to two million people out of a total population of less than 12 million, the UN made desperate calls for money, but, with other simultaneous crises on the international agenda, pledges of aid amounted to less than half of the $ 1.8 bn sought.

The scale of the fighting that had broken out in December 2013 brought rapid international attempts to encourage peace. Both the UN Secretary General Ban Ki-moon and IGAD leaders led by Ethiopia urged *reconciliation talks*, and in January representatives of Kiir and Machar met in Addis Ababa (Ethiopia). However, the talks were indecisive and were followed by a sequence of others throughout the year, though to little effect. Under international pressure, led by IGAD, the parties to the conflict would meet and even agree to ceasefires, but they failed to materialise on the ground, leading to speculation over whether they were serious, or indeed whether in the event of a serious agreement political leaders actually had the power to enforce a ceasefire.

As pressure mounted on the two main leaders, they finally held a *direct meeting in Addis Ababa in May*, with Machar pressing the case for a more *devolved federal government* ('federal' was widely seen as a euphemism for opposition to Dinka domination). There was even talk of a new interim government, but it came to nothing and SPLA-IO pulled out of the talks. In August, however, the two sides were back in Addis Ababa, where IGAD tried to take a more pro-active role. Various proposals were put forward, including that Kiir remain as president while Machar would return to government as prime minister or come back as vice president, with both men standing down at the 2015 elections. The two men rejected both these proposals and a modified plan that would see a transitional period of 30 months to a delayed election. SPLA-IO also accused IGAD of being pro-Kiir, since he would effectively remain in place, and thus talks again ended without agreement. It was not until the very end of the year that new hopes appeared for negotiation, with pressure mounting on the government, especially with the falling international price of oil. Machar put forward a new 10-point plan for peace in December, while IGAD expressed its frustration at the lack of progress and spoke of the damaging regional implications. New talks were proposed in the quieter venue of Arusha (Tanzania) in early 2015.

While the fighting focused attention on Kiir and Machar, its was also clear during the year that Kiir had other critics among the country's political elite. Indeed, it was not only Machar but also a wider group that set up the *diverse political movement* of the *SPLA-IO*. It included a few who had been National Congress Party figures in southern Sudan before independence and, more importantly, leading reformers in the SPLM, who had become alarmed both by what they saw as the increasingly autocratic rule of Kiir and by increased restrictions on the press and other media. These figures included some members of the family of John Garang, the SPLA's original leader, who was killed in a helicopter crash in 2005, as well as senior figures in the SPLM and government, including Pagan Amum, Deng Alor, John Luk and Peter Nyaba. Shortly after the fighting broke out in December 2013, 11 high-ranking politicians were detained, though seven were released and at IGAD's insistence flown to the first round of peace talks in Addis Ababa. Four of them were eventually charged, but the trial soon collapsed in disarray. In an effort at reform, Kiir did make some sackings, including in the military, and sought to reform the security system, but this did little to restore his political reputation or assuage the growing numbers in the opposition. It was also announced that the 2015 elections would be postponed, officially to help reconciliation efforts.

Foreign Affairs

South Sudan's foreign relations saw a shift in emphasis as a result of the conflict. *Uganda* had long been a base of the SPLA during the decades of civil war and some SPLA leaders had invested there, including in buying family homes. In addition, many southern refugees had fled there and not all had moved back when the fighting ended. After the peace in the south, oil wealth began to accumulate in Juba in particular and very quickly scores of Ugandan businessmen set up in the city, soon clogging the road from Nimule on the border with lorries bearing container loads of imports. South Sudan had become one of Uganda's largest regional trading partners, worth over $ 600 m by 2013, and Uganda had developed a vested interest in supporting Kiir's government. As early as January 2014, Ugandan troops, with air support, were arriving in Juba. It was claimed that in the early stages of the fighting these forces were vital in preventing the fall of Juba when Gadet's troops attacked from Bor. It was also revealed that South Sudan was paying for these troops, though Uganda responded by saying that it would pay. In spite of international protests, Uganda's forces were still there by the end of the year, having been engaged in a number of different areas. It seemed that a combination of commercial self-interest and Uganda's President Museveni's determination to play an active role as the longest standing regional leader had remained firm.

While growing ever closer to Uganda, South Sudan's relations with *Sudan* appeared ambiguous. Officially, Sudan supported Kiir; the oil was flowing once more, though at a reduced level, and the two countries had agreed to establish a demilitarised zone along their common border. However, behind the scenes there were fears amongst some in South Sudan that its northern neighbour was supplying weapons to SPLM-IO, or at least allowing the passage of arms from elsewhere, possibly Eritrea. In response, Sudan continued to warn South Sudan against its alleged support for rebels in Sudan. In addition, troops were not pulled back from the border, whilst trade between the two countries was severely disrupted.

Kenya was also involved. As the country that had hosted the CPA talks between Sudan and the SPLA on behalf of IGAD, it felt a responsibility to be actively involved in peace talks in 2014 and was in close touch with both Kiir and Machar. It also had significant business interests in South Sudan, including in banking, communications and the retail sector. *Ethiopia* had been less affected, but found itself hosting 200,000 refugees from South Sudan and required international support to cope. Early in the year, it called for the withdrawal of Ugandan forces, believing that they had led to an increase in the level of fighting. The East African neighbours were also involved in IGAD mediation efforts. *IGAD* had been the official body behind the CPA of 2005 and remained responsible for the talks in 2014, but there were differences within it, especially over Uganda's military involvement in South Sudan. During the course of negotiations, Uganda was criticised for being biased in favour of Kiir, thus encouraging the rebels and risking the possible fragmentation of South Sudan. The IGAD region already had one failed state – Somalia – and there was no wish to see another breakup.

IGAD's concern was shared by *China*, which, having invested heavily in the oil sector as well as in infrastructure and other construction projects, was the country with the largest economic stake in South Sudan. In spite of its repeated claims that it was not active in politics in Africa, it found itself involved. At one point, it announced that it would not be sending arms to the government, only for an arms deal worth $ 38 m to be reported in July. In September, Machar and other SPLM-IO leaders were invited to Beijing for talks. China announced shortly afterwards that it would be sending 700 troops to serve with the UN – the first time it had ever committed troops to UN peacekeeping operations anywhere in the world.

The *USA* was particularly concerned about the violence that had sprung up so suddenly. Longstanding US sanctions against Sudan meant that it had few economic interests in South Sudan, but some in Washington felt that, as the effective leader of the Troika (USA, Britain and Norway) that had promoted the whole peace process, it had played a major role in bringing South Sudan into existence. President George W. Bush had been actively concerned and there had been a Christian and humanitarian lobby that encouraged separation following the CPA. In January, with Juba under threat, the US embassy was hastily evacuated, while the US joined Ethiopia in calling in vain for Uganda's forces to be withdrawn. As the situation worsened, the US Fund for Peace, which had been working in South Sudan, reported that it was now the most fragile country in the world, even weaker than Somalia. Secretary of State John Kerry made a brief visit to Juba, and Kiir reciprocated with a trip to Washington, where Kerry said that, in the view of the US, it was Machar who was most responsible for the failure of successive peace talks. Kerry even alluded to the threat of genocide if strong action was not taken, as reporters made comparisons with the Ethiopian famine of 1984 and the Rwandan genocide of 1994. There were also hints of US sanctions against certain military figures it held particularly responsible for the atrocities on the ground.

The *UN* also took an active role. The UN Mission in South Sudan (UNMISS), one of its largest missions, with some 12,000 troops and police, was severely stretched by the crisis. Around 100,000 civilians took shelter around the various camps, while the UN warned repeatedly of the danger of food shortages. UNMISS tried to bring in extra troops, but it proved slow and equipment was in short supply for the mainly African troops, not of all whom were adequately trained. UNMISS also suffered losses, including the shooting down of a helicopter by Gadet's forces. UN Secretary General Ban Ki-moon visited Juba and was aware of the scale of the crisis and the obstacles to its resolution. Soon afterwards the UNSC described the situation as presenting the worst famine threat in the world. The *EU* also maintained its engagement, sending monitoring teams to some of the most troubled areas and issuing travel bans and freezing assets of the two military commanders, Gadet for the rebels and Santino Deng of the SPLA. It was also involved in humanitarian relief.

Less involved were the countries of the Middle East. With conflicts taking place across the region, little attention was given to South Sudan, though it was noted that it sent its first ambassador to Israel in September. The one Arab exception was *Egypt*, which remained concerned about South Sudan's position regarding the Nile waters. In particular, it did not want South Sudan to sign the Entebbe agreement of upper Nile riparian states, which it regarded as anti-Egyptian in relation to the outstanding water issues. As a sweetener, in March the two countries signed a bilateral trade agreement.

Socioeconomic Developments

The *impact of the fighting* in 2014 was *devastating*. The wide-ranging conflict was estimated to have caused between 50,000 and 100,000 deaths, while many more people had been displaced and were in need of relief. Prospects for the IDPs and refugees seeking to return home remained bleak, even if a peace deal was agreed and implemented. Many had lost their possessions, lands and livestock and would need support in the future. In addition, the general informal sector on which three-quarters of the population depended, and which was estimated to produce 70% of GDP, had been left severely damaged. Many of those who lived by subsistence farming and informal trading had not been able to plant crops and prepare for the coming year. The disruption to subsistence farming caused by the fighting was likely to mean the continuation of shortages, even in the event of peace.

With so many displaced, and millions in need of *food relief*, the pressure on international agencies, especially the UN, was almost overwhelming. Longstanding issues regarding aid were exacerbated by the crisis. With the security services thought to be the first priority in the government budget, little was available for social services in a country where half the population were already living below the poverty line, and only a quarter were literate. In May, Oslo (Norway) hosted a *debt relief meeting* at which $ 600 m was pledged, but aid agencies were known to feel that the government expected them to step in not only to feed the hungry, but also to provide various basic services. The Netherlands, hitherto a significant donor, announced in September that it was cutting aid.

The *formal economy* was also hard hit. Oil was absolutely central to government revenues but production was disrupted by the fighting and was estimated to have fallen to 140,000 b/d in 2014 from 250,000 b/d in the previous year. Production in Unity State was halted after SPLA-IO forces seized a number of wells, though it was less affected in the other oil-producing state, Upper Nile, where Chinese-funded local militias maintained government control. It was hoped that peace would bring a return to higher output, though the potential for government revenue to rise was offset by the sharp decline in world oil prices. Fighting also severely damaged the infrastructure. Major towns along the Nile in particular were virtually destroyed, greatly disrupting trade. The country's limited communications were damaged, with the few all-weather roads, as well as local airports, seriously damaged. Trade with neighbouring states, especially in East Africa, was also down, affecting livelihoods in what had been a vibrant sector in recent years. At the end of the year, South Sudan was left hoping for better, but fearing the situation could still get even worse.

Sudan

Peter Woodward

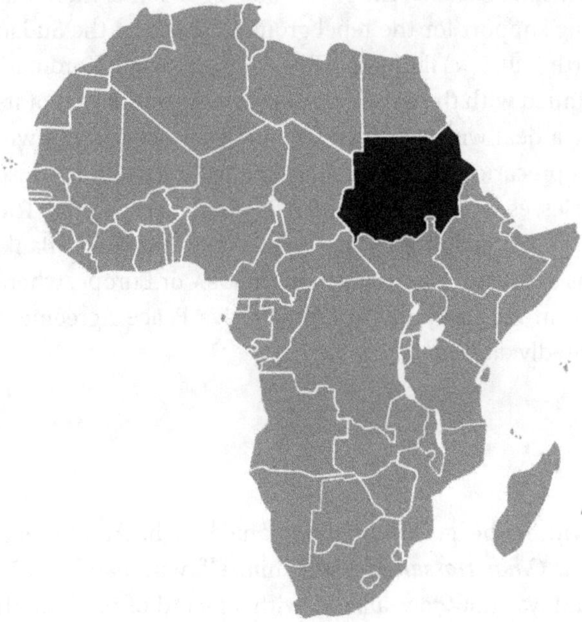

The year turned out to bring an inconclusive continuation of the numerous problems long present in the country, but worsened by the economic crisis resulting from the dispute over revenues from the South Sudanese oil fields in 2012. The long-term problems included Sudan's political leadership, the attitudes of political parties and the continuation of armed conflict in a number of outlying areas, most notably Blue Nile, South Kordofan and Darfur. The significance of these problems, especially as they affected the central regions of the Nile Valley, had been managed in large part by the rapid oil-backed growth of the economy in the early 2000s. However this was curtailed first, to a limited extent, by the global financial crisis of 2008, and then, more directly, by the dispute over oil revenues with South Sudan shortly after the latter seceded from Sudan, which had resulted in the stoppage of oil flows for over a year. The government's response had been to impose large-scale anti-austerity measures in 2013, which produced wide-scale demonstrations. The government had then put down the protests by force, and in 2014 the security crackdown continued, though with less visible resistance following the repression and resulting deaths of over 200 people in 2013. Politically, it sought to press

 | DOI 10.1163/9789004305052_041

ahead towards the elections due in April 2015, while trying to take opposition parties with it in a process labelled 'National Dialogue'. For the opposition parties, the major issue was how far they would engage with the government before the elections (they had boycotted the 2010 elections at the last moment) and how far they could cooperate amongst themselves against the government. For some, there was also the possibility of showing support for the rebel groups, especially the Sudan People's Liberation Army-North (SPLA-N) fighting in Blue Nile and South Kordofan. Economically, austerity continued with the government regaining only a part of its earlier oil revenues following a deal with South Sudan, while also seeking to win international assistance in its precarious position. This entailed maintaining close relations with the Gulf countries, especially Qatar, and Asia, particularly China. The government also sought more understanding with the IMF and the World Bank, although there were few signs of greater sympathy from the USA or Europe, where the hopes of democratic reform raised by the Comprehensive Peace Agreement (CPA) of 2005 had been repeatedly dashed.

Domestic Politics

During the year, tensions within the government remained high. At the centre was the future of *President Omar Hassan al-Bashir* himself, who had been in power since the 1989 coup and was now 70 years old, with a record of past health problems. Some in the ruling circles thought that there should be a new presidential candidate at the forthcoming elections and speculation was rife for much of the year. However, in the end al-Bashir asserted his intention to stand again. He claimed that he was still the best leader for the country, though his critics said he was primarily concerned for his own position should he stand down, especially as he was still facing ICC charges of war crimes and crimes against humanity in Darfur. In the leadership group around al-Bashir, it became clearer that the security chiefs were emerging as dominant over the civilian figures. Ever since 1989 there had been *tension between military-security leaders and the Islamist-minded civilians* who had masterminded the coup. That tension had come to a head in 1999 with the split between al-Bashir and the Islamist eminence grise, Hasan al-Turabi. Though al-Turabi was defeated, a number of civilian politicians belonging to the ruling National Congress Party (NCP) continued to have leading roles in the regime. However, as the situation had deteriorated in recent years, with a rise in popular disturbances and armed conflicts in three regions, the influence of the civilians had waned, and al-Bashir, himself a military man, had increasingly looked to like-minded colleagues in the regime such as the recently appointed First Vice President General Bakri Hasan Salih and security chief Nafie Ali Nafie. This trend was illustrated by the leaked minutes of a meeting of senior military and security personnel held in August, in which they discussed with NCP leaders how they might put down the ongoing conflicts, how to handle the forthcoming elections in ways that would give a modicum of respectability to an NCP victory, and how to improve the security services' grip on the general population. The leak circulated widely and its authenticity was broadly accepted, both inside and outside the country.

On the face of it, the government was pursuing a constitutional path towards the upcoming elections, but in reality its strategy was to play cat and mouse with the opposition political parties, which meant manoeuvring around the issue of *National Dialogue* that had been on the table since the secession of South Sudan. At the start of the year, some in NCP circles were even talking about the possibility of a government of national unity, but that idea was soon quashed and National Dialogue returned to its central position in government strategy. In April, in an apparent attempt to help the process, al-Bashir released some political prisoners, eased press controls and announced his readiness to enter into a roundtable dialogue with opposition parties. There were even claims that al-Bashir had agreed to a two-year 'transitional government', though this was swiftly denied. However, as the dialogue proved hard to develop, there was a return to more coercive measures, including the brief imprisonment of Sadiq al-Mahdi, the former democratically elected prime minister, for criticising the levels of violence used by the army in Darfur. Through all these manoeuvres, al-Bashir maintained his determination to hold the elections on schedule, and as the year ended it was announced that 17 political parties had committed themselves to take part in April 2015.

Sadiq al-Mahdi remained the leader of the *Umma Party*, one of the two oldest Sudanese parties, which during the course of the year increasingly distanced itself from the government's efforts to develop the National Dialogue process under its direction if not control. By the end of the year, al-Mahdi was asserting that his party would not be contesting the upcoming elections under the existing arrangements. Other political figures were more equivocal. As the year came to an end, *Mohamed Osman al-Mirghani*, the leader of the *Democratic Unionist Party*, the other main traditional party, had still not made clear his position on dialogue or participation in the 2015 elections. He had always shown an inclination to lead from the rear, while his party had long been less than united. However, the historical record of the Khatmiyya leaders over many decades had been to avoid opposing the existing government. A final decision by al-Mirghani to participate in the elections was expected to cause divisions in the opposition camp to the advantage of the government. Meanwhile, some of the Islamist parties edged closer to the government. Following his apparent downfall in 1999, *al-Turabi* had set up his own *Popular Congress Party* and become more supportive of the government, partly in an attempt to shore up the endangered Islamist movement generally, and partly seeking to rehabilitate himself. In apparent contrast, another formerly influential Islamist, Ghazi Salah al-Atabani, had left the NCP to form his own Reform Now Movement and called for the postponement of the 2015 elections. He briefly returned to dialogue and in September represented the government in Addis Ababa in the signing of a declaration of principles between it, the Sudan Revolutionary Front (SRF) and the Umma Party, although this seemed to be more about going along with the AU and its support for the National Dialogue than indicating any serious meeting of minds: Ghazi soon drifted off once more to the gathering opposition movement.

With Islamist groups generally rallying around the government's intention to push ahead with elections in April 2015, more *secularist parties* were coalescing by the year's end into a firmer confrontation with the government. The Umma Party had appeared more equivocal, but in the autumn leaders were saying that the country was heading for collapse and they turned more towards the rejectionist groups, including those in armed rebellion. In September, Sadiq al-Mahdi signed the Paris Declaration with Minni Minnawi, the veteran Darfuri heading the SRF. Al-Bashir claimed that the CIA and Mossad were behind the Paris Agreement. Leaders of the coalition of groups known as the National Consensus Forces (NCF) met in Addis Ababa in December to announce their *Sudan Call*, whose declared aim was "To dismantle the one-party state regime and replace it with a state founded on equal citizenship through popular struggle, including popular uprising, to secure a solid foundation to secure the rights of Sudanese people to be liberated from totalitarianism, violence and enforced poverty, and to enjoy well-rooted democracy, just peace and balanced development." The main signatories were the well-known human rights lawyer Amin Mekki Medani, Farouk Abu Eissa, leader of the umbrella NCF, Sadiq al-Mahdi and Minni Minnawi. On their return to Khartoum, the first two were immediately detained, while the others remained outside the country.

While domestic politics focused on developments in the capital, armed conflicts continued in the outlying regions of Darfur, southern Blue Nile and South Kordofan. The *conflict in Darfur* retained many of its old characteristics, though with some intensification during 2014. In local terms, many issues had long related to land, and particularly the accusation that relations between nomadic and semi-nomadic 'Arab' tribes and more settled farming communities had seen the collapse of traditional patterns of conflict resolution, with the result that there were hundreds of thousands of IDPs in UN camps. The hybrid UN-AU Mission in Darfur (UNAMID) maintained a peacekeeping force of almost 16,000 in the region, but it was handicapped by logistical and other problems and had limited influence overall. The government claimed that some IDPs had returned to their homes but, with local security very weak, many remained in and around the camps. There was particular controversy in September with a claim from a UN official that soldiers of the Sudan Armed Forces had raped 200 women and girls in one village, though the government said that an inquiry had rejected this. In northern Darfur, the search for gold continued to provoke conflict. The government, desperate for foreign exchange, was keen to encourage these exploration activities.

Meanwhile, efforts to reach an agreement between the government and the main opposition movements in Darfur continued without success. The Qatar-backed Doha Document for Peace in Darfur failed to gain support beyond the Liberty and Justice Movement set up by the former Darfur governor, Tijani Sissi, in 2011. Indeed, Sissi himself admitted at a press conference in Khartoum in December that there had been little implementation of the Darfur Agreement. In Addis Ababa, the AU continued trying to bring other factions, including the Justice and Equality Movement and the Sudan Liberation Movement/Army, into the peace process but without success.

Fighting also intensified in the Nuba Mountains of *South Kordofan*. During the years of civil war between north and south in Sudan, the southern Sudan People's Liberation Army (SPLA) became firmly established amongst the Nuba people, and when South Sudan seceded in 2011 the SPLA-N remained and continued the fight against the Khartoum government. The latter stepped up its rhetoric against the SPLA-N, claiming that it would suppress it by the end of 2014. With the regular army making little progress, the government brought in irregular elements of the Janjaweed, who had fomented so much of the fighting in Darfur and were now re-branded as the Rapid Support Force. Fighting intensified, especially around Kadugli, but the SPLA-N continued to hold its own and even claimed significant victories.

The SPLA-N also sought to maintain its position in *southern Blue Nile*, but fighting here was less intense than in South Kordofan. The SPLA-N forces under the respected former governor, Malik Agar, were pushed back towards the border with South Sudan, partly because the combination of air control and accessible terrain was more favourable to government forces there than in the Nuba Mountains. The AU had hoped to broker talks between the government and the SPLA-N, but the former was not prepared to make sufficient concessions and, when talks in Addis Ababa failed in April, fighting intensified on the ground.

The theme of situations being unresolved also continued in *Abyei*. There was less conflict than in 2013 in this disputed border area between Sudan and South Sudan, in part due to the UN's successful deployment of an Ethiopian peacekeeping force, but little progress was made concerning its future – whether it would remain wholly or partially part of Sudan or join South Sudan. The Ngok Dinka, who wished to join their fellow Dinka in South Sudan, had held a referendum of their own in 2013, which showed overwhelming support for joining the southern neighbour, but the result had not received significant support domestically or internationally. Meanwhile, in 2014 the nomadic Messeriyya Arabs, who wished to remain in Sudan, launched a large-scale migration of their cattle onto the disputed land. The positions of the governments of Sudan and South Sudan also remained largely unchanged on the issue. In principle, a de-militarised zone on both sides of the border was supposed to have been established, but in reality both governments still maintained significant forces up to the border. The situation was complicated by the failure to complete the delineation of the border itself. This should have been finished in 2013, but progress by 2014 was still slow. The complicated situation on the border limited the free movement of trade between the two countries in the Abyei area that had been intended when South Sudan separated in 2011.

Foreign Affairs

Relations with *South Sudan* were once more at the centre of Sudan's external relations. While disputes about the sharing of revenues from the oil pipelines had dominated relations in 2012–13, the central issue in 2014 was the effect on Sudan of the conflict that erupted within South Sudan at the end of 2013 and continued throughout 2014. Officially, Sudan supported President Salva Kiir in his efforts to oppose the rebellion by former vice president Riek Machar and his SPLA-in-Opposition. However, some critics suggested that Khartoum might tacitly be giving aid to Machar's side. Machar had a history with Sudan, which had supported him in his split from the mainstream SPLA under John Garang in 1991, and he was later made a vice president by al-Bashir, though he soon left to return to the SPLA. It was suggested that Sudan might see Machar's latest revolt as a way to fragment South Sudan and to capture its main oil fields, which lie towards the Sudan border in territory where the revolt was centred. It was also said that this represented a quid pro quo for Sudan's concern that, despite past agreements to the contrary, the Juba government was helping the SPLA-N in South Kordofan and southern Blue Nile. It was reported that South Sudan maintained contact with SPLA-N and that SPLA-N members helped Kiir in the fighting against Riek Machar. With South Sudan consumed by conflict, it was perhaps unsurprising that progress was slow on a number of outstanding issues, some dating back as far as the CPA of 2005: as noted above, the border demarcation remained uncompleted, while final agreement on the sharing of the pre-2011 national debt and details of citizenship also remained unfinished.

The situation in South Sudan also influenced Sudan's relations with *Uganda*. Uganda sent forces to support Kiir's government in the conflict with Machar's rebels and Sudan was concerned that a precedent might be set for African armies being used elsewhere to intervene in conflicts in other countries. To underline the point, in May al-Bashir accused Uganda's President Museveni of supporting rebel groups in Sudan. Relations with *Ethiopia* always needed careful management. Economic ties between the two countries had continued to expand, with Sudan supplying oil to Ethiopia and flows of hydro-electric power in the opposite direction projected to grow. In addition, at the end of the year landlocked Ethiopia announced its intention to make use of Port Sudan as an alternative route for its imports. On the other hand, Sudan had to tread carefully in relation to the on-going construction of Ethiopia's Grand Renaissance Dam on the Blue Nile close to Sudan's border. *Egypt* had been very concerned about the project from the outset, given the possibility that it would impact negatively on the volume of water flowing down to Egypt, where the water supply has long been under pressure. Sudan thus found itself between two much larger countries and their potentially competing water policies, as well as needing to maintain its own supplies for irrigated agriculture, which it wanted to expand. Historically, Sudan had sided with Egypt on Nile water affairs and in August, doubtless with that in mind, Egypt wanted Sudan to mediate. Sudan was wary of taking sides, though in the same month it entered into a new border defence agreement with Ethiopia, which was concerned about possible attacks on the new dam. Sudan also had to maintain working relations with *Eritrea.* While many refugees from the repressive Asmara regime crossed into Sudan, Eritrea's cooperation was significant in preventing a new outbreak of conflict in eastern Sudan, one of the poorest areas of the country.

In the *Middle East,* Sudan had been closest for some years to Iran and Qatar. The connection to *Iran* started in the 1990s, since both countries saw themselves as radical Islamist regimes, even though Sudan is Sunni while Iran is Shi'a. The relationship was particularly significant for Sudan's security services, which received extensive training from Iran, and there was also a developing arms trade between the two countries. *Qatar* also sought to differentiate itself from other Gulf states by embracing the regime in Sudan and cooperated with regard to Darfur in particular, as well as providing much needed financial support. However, these relations caused concern in other parts of the Arab world. *Saudi Arabia* had long perceived Iran as a threat, while the new regime under al-Sisi in Egypt was concerned about Qatari support for Islamists such as the Muslim Brotherhood. Saudi Arabia was joined by the UAE in announcing in April that financial sanctions would be imposed on Sudan, a powerful lever given the latter's weak economic situation. Saudi Arabia also continued to severely restrict the number of Sudanese working there. Under pressure, Sudan first announced that it had rejected an Iranian offer to build air defence facilities at Port Sudan (some suggested that this was a possible threat to Saudi Arabia) and then in September announced that it would close Iranian cultural centres in the country. Al-Bashir went on the hajj to Saudi Arabia, and also held talks with the government there. Relations with *Egypt* also remained somewhat cool, given the connections between Sudan's Islamists and the ousted Muslim Brotherhood in Egypt. During a visit by al-Bashir to Cairo after his hajj, Egypt reasserted its intention to retain control of the disputed border region of Halayab: this was always a temperature gauge of relations between the two countries. In *Libya,* Sudan and Qatar were both associated with the Islamist groups holding de facto power in Tripoli, which led the 'official' government, located in Tobruk, to expel the Sudanese ambassador in response to Sudan's alleged supply of arms to Tripoli. Explosions at a military arms depot at Geili, just north of Khartoum, in July prompted speculation that *Israel* might be involved. It was well known that Israel monitored the movement of arms from Sudan to Hamas in Gaza and had launched attacks in the past. *Turkey* also remained active in Sudan, especially in commercial affairs, though the weakening of Sudan's economy reduced the levels of activity.

Relations with the *West* remained difficult. In the *USA*, Sudan continued to attract critical attention, which was highlighted by the case of Meriam Yahya Ibrahim, who was married to an American national. She was sentenced to death for apostasy (according to the judge, she was originally a Muslim but had converted to Christianity), though she was pregnant and so her execution would be delayed until the baby was two years old. Meriam refused to renounce her religion to save her life and her case caused international outrage, with widespread appeals for clemency. An appeal court eventually overturned her sentence after she had given birth in prison and she was able to make her way to America. With publicity of that kind, there was little chance that President Obama would weaken the longstanding US sanctions on Sudan, which had a significant financial impact on the country. *Europe* was hardly more understanding, even though Sudan had earlier hoped for its support in seeking to end US sanctions. The EU, however, did make an agreement with Sudan to counter people trafficking.

In *Asia*, China remained Sudan's most active partner, though it was increasingly aware of the political difficulties its involvement in the country brought. Nevertheless, it remained particularly involved in a range of infrastructure projects, which helped towards a slight economic recovery during the year.

Relations with *international organisations* remained difficult. The *UN* still maintained a strong presence in Darfur through UNAMID, a peacekeeping force of 16,000 in a region where the government still had its own forces and where the Doha peace process had failed to bring some of the major rebel groups on board. Tensions rose throughout the year, with the government seeking to put pressure on the UN: as the year was ending, UNDP country director Yvonne Halle and UN resident coordinator Ali al-Za'artori were expelled from the country. With UNAMID's agreement with the government due to be renewed in June 2015, al-Bashir made it clear that he wanted to see an exit strategy for the hybrid force as it was becoming a burden on the country. The government also crowed in December when the *ICC* admitted that its investigation of the charges against al-Bashir over Darfur had been frozen, though the court insisted that this did not mean that they had been dropped. Meanwhile in Addis Ababa, the AU High-Level Implementation Panel, led by former South African president Thabo Mbeki, endeavoured to pursue peace in the areas of conflict, though with little success.

Socioeconomic Developments

During the year, Sudan was seeking to recover from the situation experienced since 2012 as a result of landlocked South Sudan's decision to close the pipelines from its oil fields through Sudan to the Red Sea. While a number of factors exacerbated relations between the two countries, at the heart of South Sudan's decision had lain its belief that Sudan was in effect robbing it of some of the revenues that, under existing arrangements, should belong to South Sudan. The impact of the closure of the pipelines on Sudan had produced a crisis. With the dramatic loss of revenues, Sudan was plunged into a growing *financial crisis* that soon impacted on the population at large as a tough austerity package cut subsidies on basic products, causing shortages and inflation. The upshot was *popular demonstrations* against the government in September – the largest yet seen: the response was repression, with hundreds killed in the country's main cities. However there were signs of some *recovery*, at least according to the IMF: in contrast to the 2.2% contraction in GDP in 2012, it estimated that *macroeconomic growth* had recovered, with GDP up by 3.3% in 2013 and 3.1% in 2014.

The situation nevertheless remained fragile, with continuing difficulties, as the finance minister readily acknowledged. *Inflation* grew for much of the year, reaching nearly 50% by July and, though it had fallen to under 30% by the end of the year, it was still far higher than any rise in income experienced by most of the population. Over 50% of the population were estimated to be living below the poverty line, especially in rural areas. At the same time, the *Sudan pound* (SDG) remained under pressure. The official exchange rate, which had been SDG 5.9:$ 1, was lowered by 3% by the Central Bank of Sudan, but the black market rate was much higher, reaching nearly SDG 10:$ 1, which created pressure to lower the official rate again.

In the face of this pressure, *fiscal policy* became even tighter – despite widespread hostility to the effects of austerity. The spending cuts since 2012 were maintained, and it was intended that oil subsidies would be cut further in the future. In an attempt to offset the consequences, there were professed intentions to expand social and welfare provision, with health and education services in 2014 stretched to breaking point in many areas. At the same time, spending on the security services and the armed forces was undisclosed, though known to be by far the largest budget item, estimated to be in the order of 40% of government expenditure. Corruption was also reported as widespread in the public and private sectors, with no serious government attempts to address it.

Agreement on *oil pipeline rents* with South Sudan in mid-2013 meant that some revenues from the passage of oil came in, totalling $ 884m for 2014. However, this was based on a set rent of $ 10 per barrel and, with global oil prices falling, South Sudan was aiming for a more flexible figure in future. The resumption of oil income helped to stabilise foreign exchange reserves, albeit at a low level. Reserves at the end of the year were in the order of $ 1.7 bn, still barely enough to cover two months' worth of imports.

At the same time, Sudan's *external debt* remained high at approximately $ 45 bn, most of it arrears dating back many years. The government had repeatedly tried to persuade creditors to enter into debt-forgiveness agreements, and France and the

Netherlands indicated some preparedness to help, while appeals were also made to the IMF and the World Bank for understanding. Sudan received some help from the Arab world: the Arab Monetary Fund made a loan of $ 380 m, while Qatar made $ 1.2 bn available for credit guarantees. The AfDB also granted $ 168 m for various projects.

Sudan's financial situation was adversely affected by the continuing *US sanctions* that resulted from it remaining on the list of countries supporting international terrorism. One consequence was that the government tried to use the euro or the Saudi riyal for transactions as far as possible. The effect of sanctions was shown very dramatically in 2014, when the US fined the French bank BNP Paribas $ 8.9 bn for violations in transactions with Sudan, Iran and Cuba in 2002–9. In January, some Saudi banks also suspended their business activities in Sudan, under pressure, some believed, from the US.

These difficulties restrained the expansion of Sudan's performance in a number of areas. Ever since Sudan's *oil production* took off in the late 1990s, there had been hopes that the sector would continue to expand. The secession of South Sudan, where most of the oil was produced, was a major setback and hopes for growth in Sudan were limited in 2014. Officials had predicted a production output of 170,000 b/d in 2014 but in the end the figure remained at 120,000. While there was a small increase in production in the western Kordofan region, exploration produced little elsewhere, and the dramatic fall in the global oil price made future efforts unlikely for some time. Much of Sudan's current production was used locally, with some going to Ethiopia.

With the fall in oil production and revenue since 2011, Sudan had placed much hope on *gold*. In ancient times it had been a significant gold producer, while in modern times there had been new efforts at gold production in both the state and private sectors. These hopes continued in 2014 with the aim of raising output to 70 tonnes, though it was generally thought that this was an optimistic estimate. In the informal sector, Sudan's 'gold rush' had produced some inter-communal tension – it was seen as a factor in the violence in north Darfur. Nevertheless, gold made a significant contribution to Sudan's export earnings.

Many, including the World Bank and the IMF, argued that, in the longer term, Sudan had to turn seriously to its *agricultural sector*. Historically, this had particularly involved cotton, as well gum arabic and sesame, and these continued to play some part in exports. More recently, sugar production had also expanded and cereal production grew quite sharply too, from 2.9 m tonnes in 2013 to some 5 m tonnes in 2014. This was an important development in view of Sudan's reliance hitherto on imported wheat in particular. The production of *livestock*, much of it for export to Saudi Arabia and the Gulf, also increased in 2014. However, some disruption to agriculture was caused by heavy rains, which led to flooding along the Nile for the second year running. In addition, a number of foreign concession areas, mainly granted to investors from the Gulf, did not lead to the amount of activity in the sector that had been hoped.

One more optimistic note for the economy was the continuation of *China*'s support for *infrastructure*. Ever since its first involvement with Sudan in the 1990s, China had been involved in the expansion of the road network, including a number of strategic bridges. In western Sudan, it had supported the extension of the first paved road linking the Kordofan and Darfur regions to the central areas of the country, and this was completed as far as El Fasher in 2014. The government hoped that this would contribute to economic growth in outlying areas and simultaneously to a more peaceful political environment. Sudan's long-neglected rail network was also improved with Chinese help. The vital line from Khartoum to Port Sudan via the rail hub at Atbara was rebuilt, while China also supplied new modern passenger trains in the hope of attracting passengers back from the roads. Work also continued on a network of dam developments. China first erected a major dam at Merowe on the main Nile, and was building a new one downstream at Kajbar. On the Atbara River, the eastern tributary of the main Nile, China was also involved with two more dams: one, at Setit, began to store water during 2014, and the other, the Roseires Dam on the Blue Nile, across the border from Ethiopia's Grand Renaissance Dam. Dam building was controversial, both because of its impact on local peasant farmers in the areas involved, and in the view of critics who questioned its sustainability in the light of potential silting (as with the Aswan High Dam in Egypt) and the possible effects of climate change. In December, China offered a $ 700 m loan for the building of the long-discussed new international airport for Khartoum. It was to be situated 40 km from the city centre on the west bank of the Nile and also involved the building of a new bridge across the Nile 20 km south of Khartoum. Critics pointed out that most of these new projects were in central areas of the country and might add to the long observable trend towards focusing resources there, thus further exacerbating the sense of neglect and marginalisation in poor outlying areas, including those already experiencing conflict.

Tanzania

Kurt Hirschler and Rolf Hofmeier

Throughout the year, most political attention was again absorbed by discussions over the progress of the constitutional review process that had been initiated in 2012. In February, a Constituent Assembly began lengthy deliberations about the detailed formulation of the text of a new constitution that was to be submitted to a general referendum for final approval. The most contentious issue proved to be the delicate question of the future structure of the Union between Zanzibar and the Mainland. While the long-ruling Revolutionary Party (CCM) favoured the continuation of the current system, the suggested draft text of the constitution that had been prepared in 2013 had surprisingly proposed a new three-tier set-up. Fundamental disagreements over the way forward led in April to the exodus of most opposition members from the Constituent Assembly. In October, the CCM majority eventually passed the text of a new constitution and announced a final referendum for April 2015. The acrimony over the constitution strengthened cooperation among the political opposition, while internal power struggles between various CCM factions continued as the party tried to regain some of its lost credibility and was already gearing up towards the next elections in October 2015. A major financial scandal and accusations of high-level corruption severely damaged the government's reputation by the end of the year.

 | DOI 10.1163/9789004305052_042

The somewhat strained relations between Tanzania and its EAC partners recovered markedly with improved cooperation on ambitious plans for major infrastructural projects. Bilateral relations with Rwanda, however, continued to be unfriendly and fraught with reciprocal accusations over the handling of Rwandan opposition groups based in the DRC, where a Tanzanian military battalion was engaged with a peacekeeping mandate. Macroeconomic performance remained quite satisfactory and continued to be generally commended by international donors, who were, however, increasingly vocal in their criticism of the lack of government action on the corruption scandal. Substantial parts of promised budget support funds were temporarily withheld, thus seriously complicating the government's fiscal situation. Expectations centred on prospects for Tanzania becoming a major gas producer remained high, but the reaping of tangible benefits was still several years away.

Domestic Politics

The wrangling over the *constitution review process* was strongly aggravated by conflicts between the *long-ruling Revolutionary Party* ('Chama cha Mapinduzi', CCM) and a coalition led by the main opposition parties. The first and second drafts for a new constitution, which had been prepared in 2013 by the *Constitutional Review Commission* (CRC) after an intensive process of public hearings and gathering popular opinion, met long-standing demands from opposition parties and civil society organisations alike, but were strongly rejected by the CCM. The dominant party, however, managed to regain control over the process by using its clear majority in the decisive *Constituent Assembly* (CA), which was mandated to debate and improve the CRC's second revised draft and come up with a final proposal that would be put to all eligible Tanzanians in a referendum.

The *628-member* CA was composed of 346 members of the National Assembly, 81 members of the Zanzibar House of Representatives and 201 delegates from various groups of society; 386 of them were men and 242 women, and 416 came from the Mainland and 212 from Zanzibar. According to the government, about 570 societal groups had proposed more than 5,500 people as suitable candidates for CA membership; it was the prerogative of the president to finally select and appoint the 201 delegates from the names submitted. The list of those chosen was announced on 7 February and was received with mixed feelings. Civil society organisations and the media criticised the fact that several politicians were among those appointed, including many who were affiliated with the CCM. The government, however, explained that it had selected a balanced representation of Tanzanian society with regard to age, gender, religion, regional origin and political affiliation.

The CA was convened on 18 February and in principle given 70 days to complete its task, but the Constitutional Review Bill authorised the president to extend the deadline by 20 days if necessary. The first month of CA sittings was overshadowed by quarrelling about agreements on standing orders and procedures, elections of officials and demands by CA members for an increase in their daily allowances, without any substantial aspects of the draft text being debated. Some NGO and media observers criticised this behaviour as disgraceful and were already calling for the CA to be disbanded as a waste of resources. Minister of East African Cooperation *Samuel Sitta* was elected *CA chairman* on 12 March with an overwhelming majority, after the former attorney- general, Andrew Chenge, had withdrawn his candidacy. As former parliament speaker (until 2010) Sitta had earned some respect from the opposition for his independent stance – which in contrast had made him unpopular among some of CCM's internal factions. It soon became apparent that the CCM was not willing to allow the CA to follow any line that was not in accordance with the party's interests: all but two of the 14 CA committees were chaired by CCM politicians. Furthermore, in his inaugural CA address on 21 March *President Jakaya Kikwete* dropped his previous apparent support for the CRC's draft texts and backed the CCM position on the contested envisaged structure of the Union between Zanzibar and the Mainland. Three days earlier, the *CRC chairman, Joseph Warioba,* had presented the gist of the CRC's draft to the CA and stressed that it represented the opinion of the majority of the population as expressed during the public hearings, but he failed to make an impact on the CCM members of the CA, who enthusiastically applauded Kikwete's speech.

Although the CRC's draft had proposed several important and controversial constitutional changes, such as reduced powers for the president and increased accountability of MPs to an empowered electorate, the debate centred primarily on the recommendations for the *future structure of the Union.* Whereas opposition parties and most delegates from civil society organisations and from Zanzibar favoured the three-tier structure proposed in the CRC's draft (implying the creation of a new government structure for Tanzania Mainland in addition to the already existing Zanzibar government and a drastically reshaped Union government), the CCM strongly rejected this fundamental change in the country's polity, arguing that the operation of three governments would be far too expensive and could also break up the Union. The president's surprisingly open support for his party's position during the crucial CA inauguration was seen by many as a go-ahead for CCM hard-liners, and was therefore strongly criticised by the opposition as a breach of neutrality – and as undermining the CRC's strenuous work.

Apart from antagonism over contentious standing orders and procedures (including a controversy over open or secret voting), even the *basic mandate of the CA* was disputed. Whereas opposition parties and many civil society members were of the opinion that the CA was only tasked to improve and streamline the CRC's draft, the CCM saw the CA as authorised to completely overhaul the draft and reject any of its clauses. These different interpretations of the CA's role, the antagonism about the Union structure, and early position-taking in view of the general elections due in

2015, laid the CA's discussions open to robust party politics and distrust. This quickly led to the formation of *two rival factions* before the end of March. CA members from the main opposition parties, Chama cha Demokrasia na Maendeleo (CHADEMA; Party of Democracy and Progress), the Civic United Front (CUF) and the National Convention for Construction and Reform – Change; NCCR-Mageuzi), and some from the group of 201 civil society representatives, formed the Coalition of the Defenders of the People's Constitution (known by its Swahili acronym *UKAWA*) to join forces and increase pressure for the adoption of the CRC's draft and the three-tier government structure. With almost 200 members, UKAWA represented around one third of the CA membership. In response, CCM members and some of their allies formed a group called 'Tanzania Kwanza' (Tanzania First).

The confrontation between the two camps escalated when the draft text's most controversial chapters concerning the Union were debated. On 16 April, *UKAWA announced its boycott of the CA*, accusing the CCM of using its majority to protect its party interests. Only ten days later, having reached the original 70-day deadline, the *CA was adjourned* to allow time (and space) for parliament to convene for the regular budget session. With an amendment to the Constitution Review Bill, the CA was given an additional 60 days and reconvened on 5 August. Several fruitless attempts were made by civil society organisations, religious leaders, CA chairman Sitta and even the UNDP to persuade the UKAWA leadership to return to the CA.

UKAWA tried to win support from the general population through public rallies and intensified the *cooperation among its member parties*. On 9 May, Freeman Mbowe (CHADEMA), the official opposition leader in parliament, reshuffled his shadow cabinet and included members of the CUF and NCCR-Mageuzi. CHADEMA's previous claim that it was the only relevant opposition party in parliament had hitherto alienated the other parties. On 26 October, the three parties plus the politically insignificant National League for Democracy signed a *Memorandum of Understanding* for further cooperation after a public rally in Dar es Salaam. The parties agreed to jointly campaign for a 'No' vote in the referendum on the new draft constitution scheduled for 30 April 2015 and to field and support joint candidates in all the 2015 elections, including the presidential election.

On 9 September, UKAWA leaders met Kikwete and seemed to have agreed to *postpone the constitution review process until after the 2015 elections*, and to make some amendments to the electoral laws in order to level the playing field for the elections. Kikwete, however, made it clear that he had no legal mandate to suspend the CA and, since CA chairman Sitta rejected any deviation from the legally prescribed path, the remaining *CA members resumed their work on 5 August* and continued to deliberate the details of the new constitution. There was, however, some anxiety about whether the remaining CA members would meet the *required separate two-thirds majority* from both parts of the Union to approve the final document. After a three-day process of voting chapter by chapter, Sitta announced on 7 October that the text of a new *draft constitution* had been *approved* by the *required quorum* from both parts of the Union. However, there were serious allegations that the quorum had only been met by dint of irregularities in the process. Absent CA members were allowed to vote via SMS, at least one CA member from the Mainland was counted as a Zanzibari (to narrowly meet the separate Zanzibar quorum) and an opposition MP from Zanzibar who had boycotted the CA found his name among those who had approved the proposed constitution. Although including more than two-thirds of the CRC draft's ('Warioba draft') articles, the new draft ('Sitta draft') *differed significantly with respect to most contentious issues*. It retained the current two-tier government structure, rejected clauses that aimed to limit the president's powers and proposed the right for voters to recall their MPs, and excluded the limitation of MPs' terms in office. Nevertheless, the final draft did include provisions that improved the rights of women and children, provided for an independent National Electoral Commission, and allowed independent unaffiliated candidates to compete in elections.

On 19 January, Kikwete *reshuffled his cabinet* for the second time during his second term. This had become necessary after the death of Finance Minister William Mgimwa in January and the dismissal of four ministers in December 2013, following massive human rights violations during the anti-poaching operation 'tokomeza ujangili' (wipe-out poaching). The deputy finance minister, Saada Mkuya Salum (from Zanzibar), was appointed finance minister, while former UN deputy secretary-general Asha-Rose Migiro was appointed minister of justice and constitutional affairs, an important portfolio in view of the ongoing critical constitutional review. In late June, Kikwete established a commission under the chairmanship of retired principal judge and former ambassador Hamisi Msumi to *investigate the anti-poaching operation* of 2013. It was also to investigate allegations that the operation had been sabotaged by high-ranking politicians and business people who were allegedly involved in ivory smuggling, which had increased dramatically.

A financial scandal (Independent Power Tanzania Ltd (*IPTL*) or *escrow account scandal*) gained significant political prominence in November, although initial revelations had already emerged in March and the underlying case had a history that went back more than a decade. In late November, overcoming legal injunctions to block a public debate, the Parliamentary Accounts Committee (PAC) tabled the findings of a report by the Controller and Auditor General (CAG) about a previous dubious deal in the energy sector and the suspicious transfer of large sums from an escrow account at the Central Bank to private overseas accounts of politicians, civil servants and business people. Subsequent to press reports in March, PAC chairman Zitto Kabwe had pressed for the CAG to investigate the case. In May, Prime Minister Mizengo Pinda announced that the government had also ordered investigations to be undertaken by the CAG and the Preventing and Combating of Corruption Bureau (PCCB). The escrow account had been established at the Central Bank in 2002 in a long-running dispute between the state-owned electricity supplier Tanesco and the privately-owned power company IPTL about charges Tanesco had to pay to IPTL for its services. Tanesco had deposited funds in the escrow account pending the resolution of the dispute. In late 2013, the Kenyan company Pan Africa Power Solutions (PAP) had bought IPTL, which was in provisional liquidation, and the energy ministry had authorised the release of about $ 122 m from the escrow account to PAP. Some of the money had been transferred to a Tanzanian businessman, who in turn distributed it to several senior officials. After the PAC reported its findings to the National Assembly, the *parliament* (inclusive of the ruling CCM) *passed a resolution* on 28 November that called on Kikwete to dismiss Prime Minister Pinda, Energy Minister Sospeter Muhongo, Attorney-General Frederick Werema and other officials for authorising the transfer from the escrow account to PAP. Although declaring that he had not done anything wrong and that his advice had been misunderstood, Werema resigned on 17 December. On 23 December, Kikwete dismissed Minister of Lands Anna Tibaijuka for allegedly accepting a $ 1 m 'bribe' from the aforementioned businessman. Tibaijuka, hitherto regarded as a prominent CCM personality, categorically denied any wrong-doing and explained that she had taken the money in good faith as a donation for a school where she served as a fundraiser. Pinda and Muhongo remained in post, but Kikwete ordered further investigations into the case to be undertaken by the PCCB.

Although the revelation of several scandals had tarnished the ruling party's image in previous years, the *CCM performed well in elections* during the year. In February, the CCM won 23 of 27 wards in municipality by-elections. On 16 March, the son of the deceased finance minister easily won the seat that had been held by his father in by-elections in Kalenga (Iringa Region). Kikwete's eldest son, Ridhiwani, secured an 85% landslide victory on 6 April in by-elections in his father's former constituency, Chalinze (Coast Region). Regular *local government elections* on 14 December – immediately after the 'escrow scandal' had clearly raised the political temperature – also brought a clear 75% victory for the CCM. However, opposition parties improved their results significantly compared with the last local elections in 2009, when the CCM won almost 94% of the seats. As in 2009, the 2014 elections saw numerous shortcomings, such as missing voter lists, incorrect candidates' and voters' names, and a shortage of voting materials, which left numerous voters unable to cast their votes and led to chaotic situations and violent clashes in some polling centres. The problems were due to local authorities' failure to complete preparations in time and more generally to the Ministry of Regional Administration and Local Government's incompetence in handling elections. Calls were therefore made that local government elections should in future be administered by the National Electoral Commission.

The *next general elections in 2015* were already casting their shadow. The CCM appeared somewhat apprehensive, fearing that in-fighting between rival factions could potentially split the party. However, such fears had been expressed in the run-up to all previous elections, but the party had always managed to prevent itself from falling apart. After two terms in office, Kikwete was constitutionally barred from running for the presidency again, so the *selection of his successor* – scheduled for April or May 2015 – was expected to be a very sensitive and contentious issue. In 2008, the forced resignation of the then prime minister, Edward Lowassa, in connection with serious corruption allegations (the 'Richmond saga') had left the party split ever since into an anti-Lowassa and a pro-Lowassa camp. Before his resignation, Lowassa had been seen as a quasi-natural successor to Kikwete, his close ally. Despite his ouster, he remained an important and influential, but highly controversial figure in the CCM. The closer the nomination process drew, the more anxiously were his movements watched by other rival factions. In February, the CCM ethics committee issued a serious but inconsequential warning to Lowassa and five other prominent party members for having started campaigning prematurely for the presidential nomination. No clear pattern of likely candidatures had emerged by year's end, but rumours about a growing number of possible candidates abounded. An opinion poll released by the local NGO 'Twaweza' in November showed a continuing strong, but declining popularity of the ruling party: 51% expressed allegiance to the CCM and 23% to CHADEMA.

Internal rifts in CHADEMA, the main opposition party, continued to weaken its standing. On 2 January, Zitto Kabwe, one of its most articulate and popular politicians, who had been surprisingly stripped of all his party positions in late 2013 for an alleged putsch against the elected leadership, had successfully filed an injunction in the High Court to restrain the party from deliberating, discussing or determining the issue of his membership until his appeal to the party's governing body against his removal had been decided. In view of the unresolved conflict between CHADEMA's leadership and Kabwe, the registration of a *new political party*, the Alliance for Change and Transparency (*ACT*), in May was noted with interest. Several CHADEMA members defected to ACT, accusing the CHADEMA leadership of having illegally amended the party's constitution and misused party funds for personal interests. These developments led to speculation that Kabwe might also join the ACT if he were expelled from CHADEMA. No final decision was taken before the end of the year, and Kabwe continued to play an influential role in parliament. Mbowe was re-elected as CHADEMA's chairman for a third term during the party's congress in mid-September and its secretary-general, Wilbroad Slaa, was also confirmed in office.

In a worrying continuation from 2013, further *bomb blasts* in Tanzania's most important tourist hubs, Zanzibar and Arusha, caused injuries and death. In *Zanzibar*, two bombs exploded in February, fortunately without causing any casualties: one in front of the Anglican Cathedral in Zanzibar's historical centre and the other in a popular tourist restaurant. On 13 July, another bomb attack in front of a mosque killed one person and injured several others. In *Arusha*, one person was killed and 15 were injured when a bomb exploded in a popular bar on 13 April. On 3 July, two Muslim clerics were injured by a bomb thrown through the window of their house. A week later, eight people were severely injured by a bomb attack on an Indian restaurant. An employee was injured on 5 May by a bomb hidden in a donations box in a Lutheran church hostel in Mwanza. Although the police arrested several people, it remained unclear whether the attacks were linked and who was behind them. Speculation about the perpetrators ranged from linking them to criminal networks to connecting them with the Somali terror group al-Shabaab.

In a ruling on 20 June, the East African Court of Justice banned the Tanzanian government from constructing a paved *road across the northern Serengeti*. The case had been filed in December 2010 by the Kenyan NGO, African Network for Animal Welfare. The government appealed against the ruling, however, and announced that it would instead upgrade the existing dirt track to an all-weather gravel road. The *Maasai land rights* issue attracted international attention in November, when newspapers reported that the government was again pursuing its plans to evict about 40,000 Maasai pastoralists from their traditional land and to sell some 1,500 km² of land in Loliondo district, north-east of the Serengeti, to a UAE safari hunting company. After international protests, the government had announced in 2013 that it would stop the project and now confirmed this through separate public statements by Minister for Natural Resources and Tourism Lazaro Nyalandu and President Kikwete.

Reacting to continuing *attacks against people with albinism*, the government launched a new campaign to prevent ritual killings and to persuade communities in the most affected regions to fight against the crime and abandon occult beliefs that threaten the lives of people with albinism.

Foreign Affairs

Generally good relations with the *donor community* were somewhat overshadowed by increasing impatience with corruption and the continuing misuse of donor funds. The fading readiness to tolerate high-level graft was illustrated in October by a decision by the group of main donors (Canada, Denmark, the European Commission, Finland, Germany, Ireland, Japan, Sweden, the UK, the World Bank and the AfDB) to suspend the release of almost $ 500 m in pledged general budget support funds to the 2014/15 budget in response to the escrow account scandal; the suspension was to last until a satisfactory investigation and course of action was undertaken by the government. On 11 December, the US government similarly announced that it would postpone approval of up to $ 700 m under the Millennium Challenge Corporation while awaiting plausible government action. Despite these irritations and increasing pressure to curb corruption, relations with the main donors remained generally good and development cooperation activities and good diplomatic relations remained as amicable as they had been for years.

The traditionally good relations with *China* were strengthened further. The 50th anniversary of the establishment of diplomatic relations between the two countries was celebrated on various occasions throughout the year. China had become Tanzania's largest trading partner and the second largest investor after the UK, with huge investments mainly in infrastructure, the energy sector, the extractive industries and IT-technologies. Tanzanian-Chinese relations also included cultural, academic and medical cooperation activities and a rapidly growing tourism sector. The celebrations were highlighted by Vice-President Li Yuanchao's visit to Tanzania (21–26 June) and Kikwete's six-day state visit to China in October. Nevertheless, several complaints tarnished China's image in Tanzania. Chinese businesspeople were found to be heavily involved in smuggling ivory, rhino horn and tropical hard woods such as ebony, and were found guilty of bribing Tanzanian officials. Counterfeit and poor-quality Chinese products flooded the Tanzanian market and electrical appliances and medical drugs in particular caused serious harm to consumers. Chinese contractors were accused of carrying out cheap but sub-standard work on infrastructure projects. In a newspaper interview, the Chinese ambassador to Tanzania regretted that such "bad Chinese habits" were damaging Chinese-Tanzanian relations.

In a continuation of the antagonism that had arisen in mid-2013, relations with *Rwanda* remained tense. Although any direct contact with Rwandan President Paul Kagame was avoided, Kikwete sent Minister of State Mark Mwandosya for a week-long visit to Kigali in February to improve diplomatic ties. Remarks by Foreign Minister Bernard Membe, however, extended the war of words when he called the 'Forces Démocratiques de Libération du Rwanda' (FDLR) rebels "freedom fighters" and repeated the accusation that Rwanda had backed the M23 rebels in the DRC and was destabilising the region. Kigali repeatedly accused Tanzania of backing the FDLR, regarded by the Rwandan government as its arch enemies. Despite these political tensions, pragmatic cooperation on joint infrastructure projects in preparation for the central corridor transport system was not interrupted. A Tanzanian *army battalion* continued to be engaged in the eastern *DRC* as a vital part of the UN's Force Intervention Brigade (FIB) that was mandated to pro-actively contain the threats emanating from the existence of a number of so-called 'negative forces' (rebel groups and militias). Rwanda insisted that the FIB should actively engage against the remaining FDLR rebels, but no such action was undertaken and only a January 2015 ultimatum was set for the FDLR to finally surrender. A new conflict with *Kenya* arose in December, when the Kenyan authorities banned Tanzanian tour operators from picking up tourists from Nairobi airport, allegedly in retaliation for Kenyan tourist vehicles being banned from Tanzanian national parks.

The efforts of the SADC Forum of Former Heads of State and Government mediation team, comprising former presidents Joaquim Chissano, Thabo Mbeki and Festus Mogae, to solve the long-standing *Lake Nyasa border dispute* between *Malawi* and Tanzania again proved futile as both sides maintained their positions. The new Malawi President Peter Mutharika insisted that Malawi's ownership of the entire northern part of the lake was not negotiable. However, he (as well as Kikwete) ruled out all military options and affirmed that an amicable and peaceful resolution of the issue needed to be found through the efforts of the SADC mediation team.

As in previous years, Tanzania played an important role in successfully mediating in a regional conflict. In April, a Tanzanian battalion joined the UN peacekeeping mission in South Sudan and, since the IGAD-led peace process in Addis Ababa had clearly failed to find a mutually acceptable solution to the *civil war* in *South Sudan*, Kikwete offered to conduct complementary talks in Tanzania to mend the conflict between the three warring Sudan People's Liberation Army (SPLA) factions. The talks, organised, facilitated and supervised by the CCM, began with an initial dialogue, held near Arusha in mid-October. The three SPLA groups recognised divisions in the SPLA as the underlying cause of the conflict, as well as their collective responsibility for the war, and finally signed a roadmap agreement to re-unite the party. The process was supported by several other international actors, such as the South African ANC and former Finnish President Martti Ahtisaari's Crisis Management Initiative.

The strains that had in 2013 temporarily threatened to pull the member countries of the *EAC* apart and to seriously undermine the *integration process* were by and large overcome, but not entirely eliminated. An understanding was reached that member countries were free to pursue joint infrastructural or other development programmes outside of the formal framework of the EAC. This particularly referred to the development of the axes of the so-called 'Northern Corridor' (hinterland of the port of Mombasa) and 'Central Corridor' (hinterland of Dar es Salaam). Tanzania no longer felt excluded, as had been the case in 2013, from the Northern Corridor infrastructure summits and participated as an observer, while pushing its own agenda for a faster development of the Central Corridor. A certain underlying competition between the two concepts was nevertheless inevitable. During a regular EAC summit in November in Nairobi (Kenya), Kikwete was expected to assume the annually rotating EAC chairmanship from Kenya's President Uhuru Kenyatta, but the summit was cancelled at the last minute because Kikwete was still recuperating from an operation he had undergone in the USA and was unable to attend.

Socioeconomic Developments

The overall *macroeconomic performance* continued to be quite robust and in line with the strong continuous growth trend that had persisted since the early 2000s.

Tanzania remained in the group of the fastest-growing and most consistently performing economies in Africa, although it was still characterised by a very low level of material wealth for the majority of the population. In the 2014 *HDI* (data for 2013), Tanzania was ranked 159th (out of 187 countries), in the 'low development' category. A new set of national accounts data nevertheless showed that Tanzania's GDP was significantly higher than had until then been assumed. As in several other African countries, the national accounts base year had been updated from 2001 to 2007 to better capture important changes in the relative weight of different economic activities. The upward revision for the base year 2007 showed *GDP* to have been *27.8% higher* than previously calculated. On the basis of the new data, average *per capita income* was now estimated to have reached $ 948 in 2013 and about $ 985 in 2014 – fairly close to the government's declared goal of soon reaching the status of 'middle-income country' (defined by the threshold of a $ 1,045 per capita income).

In the face of continuing global economic and financial uncertainties, Tanzania's economy again proved to be remarkably resilient. This was also partly due, however, to the fact that the level of monetisation of the economy and the degree of trade openness with the rest of the world were still considerably lower than the average for SSA, thus shielding the country from negative repercussions. The *GDP growth rate* for 2014 was estimated at 7.1%, very similar to 2013 and quite consistent with the growth trend of most preceding years. Climatically, it was a fairly good year, which allowed the agricultural sector to grow by close to 5%. A bumper harvest of about 2.5 m tonnes of maize led to consideration of possibly exporting up to 1 m tonnes to China in 2015. Since 2011, Tanzania had managed to be more than self-sufficient in basic staple foods. Both the industrial and service sectors grew by about 8%. Expectations of a faster and more fundamental transformation of the economy were increasingly linked with prospects for a significant natural gas production, although full commercial exploitation was still a number of years away. Tanzania's ranking was practically unchanged at 121st (out of 144 countries) in the World Economic Forum's Global Competiveness Index 2014–15, and at 131st (out of 187 countries) in the World Bank's Doing Business 2015 report.

While high *inflation* rates (16% in 2012) had been a major cause of growing popular discontent, inflation was successfully contained in 2014 at an annual average of 6.1% and a low of 4.7% in December. This was largely due to stable food prices as a consequence of favourable weather conditions and to lower domestic fuel prices, resulting from the fall in global oil prices. This also contributed to the relative stabilisation of the *exchange rate*, with only minor fluctuations during the year: the rate in December was TSh 1,735 : $ 1, just 10% lower than in January due to the dollar's global appreciation, while the exchange rate with the euro remained stable. The *structural trade deficit* was brought down by about 5% to $ 5,470 m, principally as a result of a slightly (by 1%) reduced import bill of $ 10,918 m, due to cheaper oil prices. Export earnings grew moderately by 3.6% to $ 5,448 m. On balance, just about half of Tanzania's import needs were covered by its own export earnings. The (preliminary) *current-account deficit* was thus estimated to have been somewhat reduced to about 13% of GDP. Gross *foreign reserves* were slightly down at $ 4.4 bn (compared with $ 4.6 bn in 2013) by the year's end, sufficient for a comfortable import coverage of almost five months. While the *external debt* had previously been substantially reduced to a low of $ 4.2 bn in 2006 as a result of concerted debt cancellations under the HIPC initiative, it had lately been increasing again rather fast, reaching $ 14.2 bn at year's end (compared with $ 11.6 bn at end-2012). *FDI* inflows remained very substantial, while *tourism earnings* (over $ 1.5 bn spent by more than 1 m visitors) were once again Tanzania's most important foreign exchange earner, even topping gold. The idea of raising funds with a Eurobond issue on the international financial markets had been under discussion since 2011, but again did not materalise and was postponed into 2015.

IMF missions visited Tanzania in February and October to review the performance of its current programmes. On 25 April, the IMF simultaneously concluded the regular Article IV discussions and the third and final review of an arrangement under the *Standby Credit Facility* (*SCF*) that had been approved in July 2012 as a precautionary measure against the potential downside risks of a global slowdown. In February 2013, the government had drawn $ 114 m under the SCF to support the currency, but no further withdrawals were made before the expiry of the SCF on 30 April 2014. The IMF commended the Tanzanian authorities for the broadly satisfactory implementation of their economic programme, underlining that preserving macroeconomic stability was essential for continued strong growth; some concern was expressed about the need to contain public spending within the limits of the budget provisions and about the current-account deficit (about 14% of GDP) remaining among the largest in the region. Tanzania was judged at low risk of debt distress. On 16 July, the IMF approved a new three-year *Policy Support Instrument* (*PSI*), an unfunded IMF instrument designed for countries that do not need balance of payments financial support, but were helped to implement effective economic programmes. A previous PSI had been operative from 2010 to 2013. A first review under the PSI was undertaken by the IMF's October mission and scheduled to be formally approved in January 2015. Macroeconomic performance was judged to have been satisfactory until mid-year 2014, but to have deteriorated thereafter, with rising risks stemming from delays in disbursements of donor assistance (see above: escrow account scandal) and external non-concessional borrowing, as well as shortfalls in domestic revenues. The PSI programme was broadly on track through the end of 2014, with good progress on the agreed structural reforms, but the targets on domestic revenue were missed. Of particular concern was the accumulation of substantial payment arrears in the public sector.

On 12 June, Finance Minister Saada Mkuya submitted her 2014–15 *budget* to parliament. A review of the previous financial year's outturn showed that the overall *fiscal deficit* for *2013–14* had been considerably brought down to an officially reported 3.4% of GDP (compared with 5% in 2012–13), but analysts considered this somewhat misleading as a rapid accumulation of arrears owed to the private sector and pension funds (roughly estimated as equivalent to about 1% of GDP) had already started to occur, thus bringing the actual deficit closer to about 4.5% of GDP. It was evident that the budget revenue targets had been set over-optimistically and that the government's revenue collection efforts were deficient. This situation led to a general under-execution of the initial 2013–14 budget, ending up with only 84% of the planned financial volume. Particularly hard hit were all development expenditure items, including priority sectors identified under the 'Big Results Now' initiative, of which only 65% were executed. This had a clear delaying effect on the progress of Tanzania's ambitious development goals.

The *2014–15 budget* was again based on rather optimistic assumptions. Total expenditure was budgeted at TSh 19,850 bn (about $ 12 bn), an increase of 8.1% over the 2013–14 budget figures. Again, 68% was foreseen for recurrent expenditure and 32% for development programmes. In the budget speech, an intention to reduce the traditional heavy dependence on external aid funds and to increase domestic revenue generation capacity was emphasised, but the short-term chances of success remained uncertain. The execution of the budget during the first two quarters of the financial year (until December) proved to be exceptionally challenging. Domestic revenue collection still remained slightly below target, while most of the planned general budget support funds (about $ 600 m) were withheld by the group of development partners; only about one-tenth of the total had reached the Treasury by the end of October with no new developments before the end of the year. To simply maintain its regular operations, the government turned to a big increase in domestic borrowing, incurred a further accumulation of arrears and had to slow down the implementation of planned projects. Domestic debt grew by 24% to the equivalent of $ 4.7 bn.

Optimistic expectations of a substantial economic upturn in the near future centred on increasingly promising prospects for the exploitation of Tanzania's substantial *natural gas* resources, although full commercial benefits were only expected to build up from the 2020s onwards. With more ongoing exploration activities, proven gas reserves were updated to 55 trillion ft^3, but more seemed quite probable. The fourth gas and oil licensing round for new offshore blocks and the Lake Tanganyika area came to an end in May. New model production-sharing agreements had been introduced in October 2013, which increased the role of the parastatal Tanzania Petroleum Development Company in the gas sector. Four major international oil companies were involved in planning the future commercial exploitation; no firm decisions were as yet made on the possibility of a liquefied natural gas plant. The significant drop in global oil prices raised fears that developments in Tanzania might take much more time than had been forecast. The political opposition repeatedly complained about the lack of transparency of plans relating to the gas sector. The on-going construction of a Chinese-financed gas pipeline from Mtwara to Dar es Salaam was poised to be completed in mid-2015. This would mean a significant increase in *electricity* generation and hopefully end the long-endured problems of recurring *power failures*. Despite a shock electricity tariff increase of 40% in January, the heavily loss-making power utility TANESCO continued to be a major financial burden on the government.

The improvement of the country's physical *infrastructure* continued to be a major focus of the government's development strategy, although the implementation of announced projects often remained rather uncertain. In September, the World Bank committed $ 565 m for an expansion of the port of Dar es Salaam. The construction of a large entirely new port near Bagamoyo, to be financed and constructed by China, was not yet begun. Various plans for either the rehabilitation of the central railway line or the construction of a new standard-gauge railway were discussed, but remained without any concrete confirmation. Chinese investors began work on an ambitious $ 3 bn project for the exploitation of coal reserves and iron-ore deposits in the south-west, including the construction of a new railway link. *Gold* production continued to contribute significantly to overall growth and exports, although declining in importance because of a slump in global prices. New *mining* ventures were about to start production of nickel and uranium and were faced with protests from environmentalists.

Uganda

Volker Weyel

With the 2016 elections drawing closer, Uganda saw a dazzling blend of drama, tragedy and farce. Drama could be seen in the progressive wrecking of the position and ambition of the prime minister throughout the year. Tragedy unfolded in the 'Mountains of the Moon', where clashes involving neighbouring ethnic groups resulted in a heavy death toll. And farce played out when a general who had absconded to London in May 2013, when he was coordinator of intelligence services, returned home unmolested at year's end. The problems in adjacent countries continued to beleaguer Uganda, but it was largely able to safeguard its national interests. On the international stage, a Ugandan was elected president of the 69th session of the UN General Assembly. The economic situation improved further, thanks to a prudent fiscal and monetary policy. The pervasiveness of corruption, however, persistently plagued the country and made relations with donors uneasy. The start of the envisaged oil production was still in its preparatory stages.

Domestic Politics

Almost immediately after the February 2011 elections, Ugandans had started guessing whether *President Yoweri Kaguta Museveni*, in power since 1986, would once

 | DOI 10.1163/9789004305052_043

again seek re-election five years later. Whilst he constantly referred to the members of the ruling National Resistance Movement (NRM) as the ones who should decide, the general public consensus was that he would. In some quarters of the party, *Prime Minister Amama Mbabazi* was also seen as a serious contender, but during the year he became the most prominent political casualty on the path to the 2016 presidential and parliamentary elections.

Mbabazi, a long-standing loyal supporter of Museveni, believed that he would be the first in the often cited 'queue' for the succession once Museveni left office, but he did not declare any plans to stand against Museveni nor did the latter show any intention of giving up his position. In September 2010, with Museveni's support, Mbabazi, then minister of security, had been re-elected secretary-general of the *NRM* by the delegates of the party's National Conference, whilst keeping his cabinet post. In 2011, he had been appointed prime minister, but did not relinquish his party position as expected, which put him in a position to build what might be perceived as an alternative power base. His background in intelligence, his experience in the day-to-day running of government business and his thorough knowledge of the party and its personnel were complemented by the expectations of those who, for various reasons, wanted the incumbent to retire. Most vocal was a group of disgruntled young party members calling itself the NRM Poor Youth Forum, reflecting the concern over the high rate of youth unemployment. Museveni's camp took early precautions against a potentially emerging challenge. On 9 February, seemingly on the initiative of some MPs from the east and north of the country (not from the west, home to both Museveni and Mbabazi), the NRM legislators resolved, during a retreat at the National Leadership Institute in Kyankwanzi, to call on Museveni "to offer himself" as the party's presidential candidate in the 2016 elections. They acted on the proposal of NRM caucus spokesperson Evelyn Anite, the Northern Youth MP hailing from Arua. Subsequently, NRM MPs were given the equivalent of $ 1,600 per sub-county of their constituency to consult their voters on the Kyankwanzi resolution; each rally participant expected to receive $ 2–$ 4, which generated scuffles in some places.

With the formal NRM convention decision still pending and the prime minister himself publicly keeping quiet, his outspoken wife Jacqueline Mbabazi, head of the NRM Women's League, deplored "fascist tendencies" in the party. Mbabazi's deposition proceeded: on 18 September, Museveni replaced him as prime minister with the widely respected Health Minister *Ruhakana Rugunda* (a veteran politician who belonged, like Mbabazi, to the Bakiga ethnic group). Otherwise, the cabinet saw no change except that Betty Bigombe, who had formerly negotiated with Lord's Resistance Army (LRA) leader Joseph Kony, gave up her seat in parliament, resigned her barely significant post as state minister for water and returned to the World Bank, as had been announced in June.

A month after his unceremonious sacking as prime minister, Mbabazi, having lost ground in the NRM leadership, was forced to take 'leave' as the party's secretary-general. On 15 December, 10,000 delegates met in Kampala at an *NRM National*

Conference and swiftly amended the party constitution, making the appointment of the secretary-general subject to the proposal of the party chairman to the Central Executive Committee instead of by election by the party delegates as before. On 22 December, Chairman Museveni nominated Justine Kasule Lumumba, a woman MP from the east and government chief whip, as the new NRM secretary-general.

Museveni, being comfortably in control of the armed forces, the NRM and the government, had nothing to fear from other parties. At the end of January, the main *opposition* force, the Forum for Democratic Change (FDC), appointed Philip Wafula Oguttu, a former journalist, as leader of the parliamentary opposition in place of Nathan Nandala-Mafabi. This strengthened the hold on the party of the FDC president, Major Gen. (ret.) Mugisha Muntu, who had in 2012 fought a bitter battle over the FDC leadership with Nandala-Mafabi. 'Iron Lady' Cecilia Ogwal, once the acting secretary-general of the Uganda People's Congress (UPC), and now a member of the FDC, became the opposition's chief whip. UPC president Olara Otunnu still faced a host of internal opponents. The Democratic Party celebrated its 60th anniversary, which made it the country's oldest party.

Ahead of the 2016 elections, the confidence of opposition parties and civil society in the electoral process waned. The existing Electoral Commission was widely seen as a government tool, and demands for the appointment of a credible Commission before the elections were articulated. Some exchange over *electoral reforms* between the NRM and the opposition parties that were represented in parliament took place through a neutral platform, the 'Inter Party Organisation for Dialogue', but no practical results materialised during the year.

The issue of the '*rebel MPs*' – four independent-minded NRM legislators critical of corruption who had been expelled from the parliamentary party in 2013 – resurfaced when the Constitutional Court ruled on 21 February that they must vacate their seats since they had lost their party allegiance. Speaker of Parliament Rebecca Kadaga, who had safeguarded the rights of these MPs despite pressure from the government, was now ordered to refuse to allow them to take their seats. On 6 March, however, the Supreme Court decided that the implementation of this ruling be delayed until the MPs' appeal had been heard and the case was still pending at year's end.

A controversial decision of the Parliament Appointments Committee, which had in 2013 accepted the president's proposal to extend by two years the term of Chief Justice Benjamin Odoki, despite his having reached the mandatory retirement age, suffered a rebuff. The Constitutional Court ruled on 4 August that Odoki's re-appointment was "inconsistent with and/or in contravention of" a number of articles of the Constitution. Another controversy dating back to NRM MP Cerinah Nebanda's demise at the end of 2012 rumbled on. According to a government-commissioned autopsy, her death had been related to alcohol and drug abuse, but this had been put in doubt by some MPs who suspected poisoning with state involvement. Nebanda's boyfriend, who early in the year had been sentenced to four years in prison for causing her death, was acquitted in July following an appeal.

A parliamentary inquiry, started in 2013, cleared the government of neglect in connection with the 2000 Kanungu massacre, when about 1,000 followers of a doomsday cult had been killed by its leadership after the millennium apocalypse did not materialise. The cult had been registered, initially as an NGO, but it was judged that it was not up to the authorities to assess its religious import.

The *Anti-Pornography Bill*, 2011, passed by parliament on 19 December 2013, received presidential assent on 6 February. The new law provided for a Pornography Control Committee, charged "to take all necessary measures to ensure the early detection and prohibition of pornography" and "to educate and sensitise the public". It foresaw that various stakeholders would be represented on the nine-member body, including media companies, the arts and entertainment industry and religious leaders. A popular misunderstanding that the law banned miniskirts led to molestations of women, followed by consideration that the act be reviewed.

The controversial *Anti-Homosexuality Bill*, 2009, passed on 20 December 2013, was at first treated with utmost caution by Museveni. A panel of scientists was appointed to advise him as to whether there was "a scientific/genetic basis for homosexuality" and whether homosexuality could "be learned and unlearned". In a statement dated 10 February, the experts concluded that homosexuality, which in their view "can be influenced by environmental factors" such as culture or peer pressure, was "not a disease" and "not an abnormality". During the Kyankwanzi retreat, NRM caucus spokesperson Anite interpreted this as meaning "homosexuality is not a disease but merely an abnormal behaviour which may be learned though experiences in life". Despite international pressure, including US President Obama's rebuke that "enacting this legislation will complicate our valued relationship with Uganda", Museveni signed the bill into law on 24 February, thus satisfying NRM expectations and public opinion at home whilst demonstrating a courageous posture towards the West. The ensuing legal challenge to the act by some individuals and NGOs, however, served his interests no less, given his awareness of donor opinion and resulting cuts in aid. On 1 August, the Constitutional Court annulled the new act because the bill had not been adopted in parliament with the required quorum (as had already been pointed out by the prime minister in December 2013); the judges did not delve into the merits of the case. The attorney-general desisted from appealing against the court order, and Museveni soon told NRM legislators that a re-enactment of the law was not a priority.

The *HIV and AIDS Prevention and Control Bill*, 2010, was approved on 13 May and received presidential assent on 31 July. It stipulated that "reasonable care" must "be taken to avoid transmission of HIV", dealt with protection, counselling, testing, the care of affected persons and the "rights and obligations of persons living with and affected by HIV and AIDS", and established a Trust Fund. Criticism by human rights organisations revolved around the provision that a "person who wilfully and intentionally transmits HIV to another person" would be liable to imprisonment of "not more than ten years", and the expected "routine HIV test" of pregnant women and their partners.

The Public Private Partnership Bill, 2012, passed on 17 July, was sent back to parliament by the president, who opposed the provision to make all agreements of this type subject to parliamentary approval. The Public Finance Management Bill "to provide for fiscal and macroeconomic management" and also for the establishment of the Petroleum Fund was adopted by parliament at the end of November but awaited presidential assent.

The farce connected with General David *Sejusa aka Tinyefuza* involved a number of actors. In May 2013, after alleging that Museveni had a hidden plan to assassinate senior government and army leaders in order to pave the way for his son Muhoozi Kainerugaba to succeed him as president, Sejusa had made off to London and launched an anti-Museveni manifesto. However, after informal contacts with government representatives, Sejusa unexpectedly returned to Uganda in mid-December (to coincide with the NRM party conference), and was received by the head of the Internal Security Organization. He was still considered a serving army officer, but no charge of desertion was brought against him.

Brigadier Muhoozi Kainerugaba remained in charge of the elite Special Forces Command (SFC) of the *Uganda People's Defence Forces* (*UPDF*). In May, Museveni ordered cabinet to dissolve the inefficient National Agricultural Advisory Services programme and used this to further extend the role of the army by deciding "to deploy UPDF officers to spearhead the drive against poverty". In every constituency, an army officer would be posted in order "to ensure food security and commercial farming". The military's focus on agriculture even included the UPDF take-over of the 'Miss Uganda' contest which made news internationally: in Bukalasa Agriculture College, the competing beauties had to spend a week getting acquainted with pig-rearing and other farm work. The Samora Machel SFC Training School in Nakaseke was commissioned by the president on 11 November.

Allegations levelled over the years by politicians from the *north*, such as Otunnu, that the present government's army had perpetrated crimes against the Acholi in the course of action against the LRA had long been ignored. In January, Museveni publicly acknowledged that excesses had been committed by "rogue elements" of his army.

Public protest was not widespread, but when it did occur, the state frequently reacted with unabashed repression, leading to the Inspector General of *Police*, General Kale Kayihura, being dubbed 'Afande Teargas' in March by the wife of Prime Minister Mbabazi, and the Ugandan political order being labelled 'rule by law' (replacing 'rule of law') by AI in October. This aspect of police work was barely reflected in the 'Annual Crime and Traffic/Road Safety Report' for 2013, released in

April, which stated that the crime rate had shown a slight downward trend, "consistent with the crime trend since 2006". It also pointed to cases of human sacrifice, the number of known cases of ritual murder reported in 2013 being 12 (almost all involving children as victims), one more than in 2012. On 16 April, at the Police Training School in Kabalye, Masindi district, Museveni passed out part of the first regiment of the elite Police Field Force, the new riot police, who had been trained by North Koreans. The police force, which numbered about 45,000, celebrated its centenary (officially due in 2006) in October. A recruitment drive was announced, citing the need to bolster the force ahead of the elections. Candidates were required to bring recommendations from local area chairpersons, district internal security officers and resident district commissioners.

The issuing of electronic National *Identity Cards* was launched by the president on 2 December.

An unexpected *outbreak of violence* occurred in the '*Mountains of the Moon*', the Rwenzori range in western Uganda. The clashes involved neighbouring ethnic groups that had joined forces during the 1960s Rwenzururu rebellion. Attempts by the Rwenzururu kingdom (which had disputable historical credentials) of the Bakonzo in Kasese district to add even unwilling 'subjects' to its fold – namely the Basongora and Banyabindi in Kasese as well as the Baamba, Babwisi and Vonoma/ Babutuku in Bundibugyo district – had met with resistance, manifested in the July 2012 clashes in Bundibugyo. There, the installation of a cultural leader of their own gained some popularity, and a monarchy had been crafted by local elders for a historically acephalous society. On 30 May, a retired army officer, Martin Ayongi Kamya, was crowned the Omudhingiya wa Bwamba in the presence of President Museveni. On 5 July, orchestrated attacks were carried out in the districts of Kasese, Bundibugyo and Ntoroko, targeting police posts, a bank, army barracks and the residence of the Omudhingiya. The attackers, Bakonzo activists, had spears, pangas, sticks and some guns and were mainly after guns and money. Three days later, the government estimated the number of people killed at 92, almost three-quarters of them attackers. Defence Minister Crispus Kiyonga, himself a member of the Bakonzo ethnic group, named the issue of cultural institutions, which had started with the controversial Rwenzururu kingship, as one of the underlying causes. In Kasese, poor economic conditions and conflicts over land were also a factor, and the Basongora and Banyabindi in the district, as well as Bakonzo living in Bundibugyo district, complained of marginalisation. In parliament, Kiyonga admitted "intelligence failure", which would be "rectified". He drew a resigned conclusion: "To have a situation in the country where people still think that witchcraft can protect them from bullets and therefore daringly attack an army barracks, is a clear indication of the long road we still have to travel to achieve socio-economic transformation." The attacks were repelled by the security forces, but the following few days saw mob justice and reprisal killings, bringing the possible total death toll to much more than 100 people. Initially, over 170 suspected participants in the original attack were tried in military courts, while many others were quickly given amnesty.

Nineteen persons were arrested in Kampala on 13 September for allegedly preparing a *terrorist* attack related to the Somali al-Shabaab. At the end of December, two prominent Muslim clerics were murdered and speculation linked this to the Allied Democratic Forces, an Islamist group operating in the east of the DRC but perceived as a terrorist threat to Uganda.

Kampala Lord Mayor Erias Lukwago, who had been impeached by city councillors in 2013 but had subsequently won an appeal in the High Court, was nevertheless prevented from returning to his office after a Court of Appeal ruling. The government re-appointed his adversary, Jennifer Semakula Musisi, as executive director of the Kampala Capital City Authority for another three-year term running to April 2017. Her energetic measures to improve the quality of life in the city yielded visible results, although the high-handed, sometimes violent actions taken against people like petty street vendors drew public criticism.

At an event to mark International Anti-Corruption Day, 9 December, Prime Minister Rugunda launched another National *Anti-Corruption Strategy* for the next five years. A donor representative at the event pointed out that corruption was "theft", deploring the use of euphemisms such as "unaccounted for funds", "financial mismanagement" and "public losses". Earlier in the year, the Inspectorate of Government expressed suspicion that a large road project "was awarded in a dubious manner and that the costs were unrealistic", referring to the 74 km Mukono-Katosi road in Mukono district. In July, the former permanent secretary in the Ministry of Local Government was sentenced to a ten-year prison term by the Anti-Corruption Court over loss caused to government in connection with the procurement of 70,000 bicycles that were never delivered; in November, after appealing, he was released on bail. More than 1 tonne of ivory, partly recovered from poachers, vanished from the stockpile of the Uganda Wildlife Authority; its executive director and some staff members were suspended in November. The Chinese-funded standard-gauge railway project to connect Mombasa with South Sudan and Rwanda via Uganda saw heavy competition between two Chinese constructors, with high-ranking Ugandan government officials involved in shady deals.

In May, Museveni attended in Rakai the celebration for the tenth anniversary of the coronation of Kamuswaga Apollo Sansa Kabumbuli II of Kooki, once a tributary dominion within *Buganda*. A dispute arose over land whose titles had been returned to the Buganda kingdom by Museveni in April in fulfilment of the August 2013 memorandum of understanding, but which was alleged to belong to Kooki. In August, six years after the death of the last Kyabazinga of *Busoga*, and after much infighting and pressure by Speaker of Parliament Kadaga (hailing from Busoga), a successor was chosen by ten of the 11 heads of the hereditary traditional chiefdoms. William Nadiope Gabula IV was crowned in Museveni's presence by Bunyoro King Solomon Gafabusa on 13 September in Bugembe, Jinja district.

On 26 November, UNESCO added the male-child cleansing ceremony of the *Langi* ethnic group, "a healing ritual for a male child believed to have lost his manhood", to the List of Intangible Cultural Heritage in Need of Urgent Safeguarding. *West Nile* celebrated the 100th anniversary of its incorporation into the then Uganda Protectorate.

Foreign Affairs

On 11 June, Foreign Minister Sam Kutesa, endorsed by the African Regional Group of the *UN General Assembly*, was elected by acclamation as president of the 69th session (2014/15) of this principal organ of the UN. This enabled President Museveni to deliver his address to the General Assembly when its general debate opened on 24 September, directly after the presidents of Brazil (by tradition the first) and the US as host country. Among the objectives of his tenure, Kutesa named the promotion of the reform of the UNSC, the UN Alliance of Civilizations initiative and gender equality. On 10 December, Human Rights Day, Kutesa launched the 'International Decade for People of African Descent' (2015–24) with the theme "recognition, justice and development".

Among major *international events* attended by Museveni were the 2–3 April 4th EU-Africa Summit held in Brussels and the 4–6 August US-Africa Leaders' Summit in Washington, called by President Obama. Within a brief span, he managed to be granted a papal audience at the Vatican (27 October) and receive the North Korean titular head of state and the US Africa Command (AFRICOM) commander in Entebbe on the same day (30 October).

Museveni handed over the chairmanship of the *ICGLR* to Angolan President Eduardo dos Santos on 15 January in Luanda and of *COMESA* to DRC President Joseph Kabila on 26 February in Kinshasa. In the *ICC* case against Kenyan President Uhuru Kenyatta, Museveni was at the forefront of the opposition to the ICC, asking African countries to consider withdrawing their membership (although Uganda itself had referred the LRA issue to the ICC in December 2003).

Kenya, Rwanda and Uganda officially launched a joint tourist visa on 20 February. Their presidents met in Kampala for the 4th Tripartite Infrastructure Summit, with the aim of speeding up the *EAC* integration process and initiated the northern corridor integration project. This 'Coalition of the Willing' (which also included EAC aspirant South Sudan), after much acrimony in 2013, mended fences with the other two EAC member countries. Four more high-level meetings, now named Northern Corridor Integration Projects Summits, were held during the year, with Burundi and Tanzania participating as observers. Three Tanzanian citizens, who had seen this initiative as excluding Burundi and Tanzania in contravention of the EAC treaty, had taken the case to the East African Court of Justice, but they withdrew the file on 2 September. Ugandan Margaret Nantongo Zziwa (NRM), who had been elected speaker of the East African Legislative Assembly for a five-year term in 2012, was impeached on 17 December by an overwhelming majority, mainly for alleged organisational "misconduct". Two days later, Daniel Fred Kidega (NRM) was elected unopposed as her successor.

The agreement between the *DRC* government and the M-23 mutineers, which had been achieved in 2013 through the 'Kampala Dialogue', proved fragile. In mid-December, over 800 former M-23 fighters temporarily escaped from Bihanga camp in Kamwenge district, where they were cantoned, having refused repatriation to the DRC.

The internal strife that had broken out in *South Sudan* in mid-December 2013 led to the active involvement of the UPDF, initially to secure the return of Ugandan nationals to their home country. This was in fact the start of a thinly-veiled and subsequently officially declared military intervention, with the UPDF taking part in operations against opponents of South Sudanese President Salva Kiir and his faction. By year's end, the influx of South Sudanese *refugees* numbered 159,303 people registered by the UNHCR, and there were even more refugees from the DRC: 187,838 Congolese constituted 44.5% of the total 422,435 refugee population.

In *Somalia,* the Ugandan contingent (which had included SFC troops since 2011) still provided the bulk of the AU Mission (AMISOM) forces, which made notable military advances. The UPDF pointed out that the intelligence it had collected had enabled the US to kill al-Shabaab leaders in an air strike. These successes were overshadowed by reports of sexual abuse by peacekeepers. Some soldiers were suspended after an internal investigation for taking bribes from colleagues who wanted to be deployed in AMISOM. On 15 May, the UN Guard Unit, consisting of 410 UPDF troops, took up its responsibilities for protecting UN personnel and installations.

In the frame of the AU Regional Task Force, UPDF action against the remnants of the *LRA* in the CAR, though still hampered by the civil war there, continued with enhanced US assistance, including Air Force Special Operations forces. Financial support came from the EU. There were some defections from the LRA and its numbers apparently dwindled further, but none of the senior commanders was apprehended. The bulk of the LRA again moved into the DRC. On 23 May, the AU extended the mandate of the AU Regional Cooperation Initiative against the LRA for a further 12 months. On 10 December, the UNSC called upon the affected countries (Presidential Statement 2014/25) "to ensure that the LRA does not find safe haven".

Though a planned military aviation exercise was cancelled as part of US sanctions in response to the homosexuality legislation, close links with *AFRICOM* continued. Exercises included a joint training exercise for US marines and sailors with UPDF soldiers in the Singo Peace Support Training Centre from October to December, to improve "interoperability between the US and UPDF militaries". Emphasis was on 'Military Operations in Urban Terrain' and counter-measures against improvised explosive devices. Chief of Defence Forces General Edward Katumba Wamala was inducted into the 'International Fellows Hall of Fame' of the US Army War College on 18 September in Carlisle barracks in Pennsylvania, from where he had graduated in 2000.

International campaigning, usually echoing the views of LGBT organisations, and media attention were focused on the *homosexuality* legislation. The cause of Ugandan homosexuals was financially supported from abroad, including € 30,500 raised at the 2014 Nuremberg Peace Banquet for the activities of Kasha Jacqueline Nabagesera, one of the petitioners against the new law in the Constitutional Court, who in 2013 had received the Nuremberg Human Rights Award.

Socioeconomic Developments

Economic recovery continued to be recognisable, but the governor of the Bank of Uganda, Emmanuel Tumusiime-Mutebile, gave an indication in November that its continuation could not be taken for granted in the run-up to the 2016 elections. He recalled the pressure put upon the Bank in early 2011 to finance a supplementary budget of about $ 260 m, which had in fact been "used for electioneering" and eventually plunged "the economy into chaos", and promised not to allow this to happen again.

The third review under the current Policy Support Instrument (PSI), a mechanism under which economic programmes were designed in collaboration with the *IMF* (who also did the monitoring), was completed on 10 December. The IMF Executive Board saw the macroeconomic outlook, supported "by sound policy implementation", as generally favourable. Although regional instability had its consequences and the implementation of major public investment projects moved slowly at times, the performance under the PSI was judged "satisfactory", including the cap on net domestic financing by government and the reduction of government arrears. But the "indicative target on tax revenue was missed", partly due to weaknesses in tax compliance. The "recent elimination of many tax exemptions" was welcomed, "if accompanied by strict enforcement".

In her 19 November letter of intent to the IMF, Finance Minister Maria Kiwanuka called the "implementation of the revenue enhancing package" a key priority. She stated that recently "economic growth was slightly lower than projected" but was confident "that growth is rebounding".

Real *GDP growth* in the financial year 2013/14 (running from July to June) was estimated at 5.2%. For 2014/15, the government projected that growth would reach 6.1%, with the stated aim of restoring an annual growth rate of 7% in the medium range. At the end of November, the Uganda Bureau of Statistics announced a GDP *rebasing*, including new sectors of the economy such as ICT and the entertainment industry, and changing the base year from 2002 to 2009/10. This resulted in a GDP increase of 13% and made the debt-to-GDP ratio appear much more comfortable.

The financial environment improved considerably, with a return to low *inflation* and with strong currency reserves. Annual core inflation stood at 2.7% in December, whereas headline inflation (including food crops, fuel and electricity) reached 1.8%. This was partly attributable to a good harvest and to the effects of a decline in the global crude oil price, which lowered transport costs. The 2014 calendar year saw the average annual inflation rate fall to 4.3% from 5.5% in 2013. The medium-term goal of keeping annual core inflation at 5% was maintained. The development of the *exchange rate* of the national currency against the dollar was less comforting. The Uganda shilling (UGX) depreciated markedly by 9.7% during the calendar year, due to the global strengthening of the dollar, decreasing export receipts and growing importer (and also private citizens') demand mainly during the second half of the year.

Finance Minister Kiwanuka announced the *2014/15 budget* entitled "Maintaining the Momentum: Infrastructure Investment for Growth and Social Economic Transformation" on 12 June. It planned expenditure of UGX 15,054 bn (approximately $ 5.9 bn), representing an increase of around 14% over the projected 2013/14 budget. Domestic sources were to contribute 81.8% (UGX 12,321 bn), consisting of taxes (UGX 9,577 bn), non-tax revenues (UGX 206 bn), government securities issue (UGX 1,437 bn) and drawdown from government savings (UGX 1,102 bn). Donor support for part of the budget continued, though to a lesser degree than before (18.2% in 2014/15 compared with 20% in 2013/14) and to some extent reflecting donor misgivings about rampant corruption and legislation on homosexuality. The donor contribution of UGX 2,733 bn to the total budget resources consisted almost completely of project aid (UGX 2,664 bn, a slight increase compared with 2013/14), whereas direct budget support amounted to a mere UGX 69 bn. The priority set by the minister was "infrastructure development in transport and energy", namely "enhancing the availability of electricity". She underlined the significance of the "maintenance of national security and defence", and allocated 7.1% of the total budget for "professionalization and equipping the security agencies". Proposed measures to generate state income included, apart from the scrapping of various tax exemptions, a 10% excise duty on fees charged for mobile money transfer withdrawals and an increase in excise duty on sugar, petrol and diesel – classic mass consumer goods. Most controversial was the planned re-instatement of duty on paraffin, which had been halted the year before. Its reintroduction was initially rejected by parliament but MPs voted in favour on 8 October, after the president's intervention.

A Parliamentary Forum on *Social Protection* was launched in February. Its background was a pilot transfer programme (Social Assistance Grants for Empowerment, SAGE), started in 2011 in 14 districts, under which small cash grants were given to the elderly and other particularly vulnerable groups. There was lobbying for rolling out SAGE Senior Citizens Grants to the whole country.

The previously postponed national *census* was conducted; 27 August was the census night. Provisional results were announced in November and indicated a total population of 34,856,813 and an annual growth rate (2002–14) of 3.03%. If this rate continued, the population would reach 46.7 m in 2025.

Having seen *Ebola* outbreaks before, Uganda used its experience and sent health workers to affected countries in West Africa. Two Ugandan doctors died (one having lived in Liberia for years), and another was saved after being treated in Germany.

Crude *oil reserves* were estimated at 6.5 bn barrels (plus 500 bn cubic feet of non-associated gas), but commercial oil production was not expected to begin before 2018. In a legal wrangle over the capital gains tax owed by the Tullow Oil company, the Tax Appeals Tribunal ruled on 16 June that Tullow's liability amounted to $ 407 m (of which $ 142 m had already been paid). The company referred to an exemption it had been given, stating it was "extremely disappointed" because of the ruling "that the then Minister of Energy did not have the legal authority to grant such an exemption", and vowed to challenge it.

According to the 2014 TI *Corruption Perceptions Index* published in early December, all EAC member states did worse than in the year before. Uganda ranked 142nd of 175 countries (compared with 140th in 2013, 130th in 2012, and 143rd in 2011). Rwanda and Tanzania were ahead of Uganda, while Kenya and Burundi lagged behind.

PART 6

Southern Africa

Henning Melber

As in previous years, the general stability of the sub-region was in stark positive contrast to most other parts of the continent. Tensions eased further in Zimbabwe as ZANU-PF renewed its political control, and the uncertainty over legitimate governance in Madagascar was resolved with inauguration of the president elect in December 2013. An attempt to overthrow the government in Lesotho failed, mainly due to the immediate response by South Africa, without significant damage. As in previous years, however, a peace dividend was hardly visible in terms of the overall socio-economic situation of the majority of the sub-region's population. Progress in regional cooperation and improvements in living standards for the ordinary population remained modest.

Elections, Democracy and Human Rights

During the year, an unprecedented number of *elections* took place in the sub-region. Within seven months, voters in South Africa (7 May), Malawi (20 May), Mozambique (15 October), Botswana (24 October), Namibia (28 November) and Mauritius (10 December) went to the polls. While the dominant parties in South Africa, Mozambique, Botswana and Namibia, all in political power since the first democratic elections in their respective countries, remained in government, elections in Malawi and Mauritius resulted in political transitions.

Celebrating 20 years of democracy, *South Africa* held its fifth general elections for the national parliament and provincial governments on 7 May. The results brought no sensational surprises in the subsequent distribution of the 400 national assembly seats among 13 out of 29 competing parties. The balance of power showed only gradual shifts, but later events in the new parliament gave evidence of some significant new changes in atmosphere. The African National Congress (ANC) remained the dominant party with minor losses, the Democratic Alliance (DA) was strengthened as the official opposition and the Economic Freedom Fighters (EFF) as the new kid on the block became a viable third force. The Inkatha Freedom Party had to share votes with its breakaway National Freedom Party. The support base of the Congress of the People (COPE) – a break-away party after the ousting of Thabo Mbeki as state president – had seemingly returned to the ANC, which compensated for some of the losses to the EFF and the DA. Mamphela Ramphele's newly created Agang SA did not have to bother about the future: with just two seats in parliament, her party turned out to be a non-starter. Ramphele, a former vice chancellor of the University of Cape Town and a deputy director at the World Bank in Washington,

 | DOI 10.1163/9789004305052_044

even opted out of accepting a parliamentary seat, which ended her political career before it had started in earnest. In contrast, Bantu Holomisa expressed relief that his United Democratic Movement (UDM) survived. The worse results five years before had suggested that they should be written off. Eight of the 13 parties in parliament received together fewer votes than the number of spoilt ballot papers. They were the Freedom Front Plus, the UDM, the African Christian Democratic Party, COPE, the African Independent Congress, Agang SA, the Pan Africanist Congress and the African People's Convention. Despite some significant losses in Gauteng, the ANC retained a majority in all of the provinces except the Western Cape, which remained under the control of the DA. While the ANC maintained its dominance, a closer look at the results showed that they did not contain much good news for the party. This election was far from being a rubber-stamping exercise; there were signs of the ground shifting. While the ANC appeared confident to have survived the range of scandals and in-fighting unharmed, it had no reason for complacency. Dissenting voices from the grassroots were louder and more radical than ever before.

Presidential, parliamentary and local elections in *Malawi* took place on 20 May. The presidential election turned out to be a highly contested and close affair with tensions mounting over the results. President Joyce Banda of the People's Party (PP), trailing in third place with 20.2% of the votes, originally claimed that the outcome was rigged. For days, Malawi's political stability was under threat. The election observers sent by the AU and SADC, headed by Namibia's former president and the Namibian foreign minister, straightaway declared the election and its outcome to have been free and fair. Banda, after initial legal battles, finally conceded defeat more than a week later and thereby avoided the escalation of lingering tensions into violence. The leader of the Democratic Progressive Party (DPP) and brother of the late former president Bingu wa Mutharika, Arthur Peter Mutharika, who received 36.4% of the vote, was officially declared the winner and next head of state. He was sworn in on 2 June in the absence of his predecessor, who boycotted the ceremony. Lazarus Chakwera of the Malawi Congress Party (MCP) came second with 27.8% of the vote, and Atuele Muluzi of the United Democratic Front (UDF) came fourth with 13.7%. The DPP won 51 seats in the National Assembly, closely followed by the MCP (48), and then by the PP (26) and the UDF (14).

In *Mozambique* the electorate went to the polls on 15 October after a fragile agreement had been secured that Renamo would once again challenge the Frelimo government, which had been in power since independence. After some legal disputes the Constitutional Council confirmed the results on 29 December. Frelimo's presidential candidate, Filipe Nyusi, was elected with 57% of the votes and replaced Armando Guebueza, who had served the permitted two terms in office. Renamo's Afonso Dhlakama came second with 37% and Daviz Simango of the Mozambique Democratic Movement (MDM) – who had been with Renamo until 2008 – came third with 6%. In the national parliament, Frelimo secured 141 seats, Renamo 89 and the MDM 17. Five provincial assemblies had a Frelimo majority, three a Renamo majority, and in the absence of an absolute majority MDM had a deciding vote in the remaining two. Local and international observer groups criticised the elections for the lack of a level playing field, but recognised the outcome nonetheless.

In contrast, elections in *Botswana* took place on 24 October without any major objections to the results, though one might argue that the position of the political establishment, in government since independence, gave it an advantage over its rivals. As usual, however, the electoral process was conducted peacefully, with the governing Botswana Democratic Party (BDP) competing for votes with the main opposition parties, the Botswana Congress Party (BCP), and the Umbrella for Democratic Change (UDC). Out of the 57 directly elected seats, the BDP took 37 with 47% of the popular vote, the UDC 17 (30%) and the BCP 3 (20%). The distribution showed that the first past the post system benefitted the governing BDP.

The most comfortable result in the sub-region was in *Namibia*, where the people voted on 28 November. The South West African People's Organisation (SWAPO), which like the ANC had turned from a liberation movement into a political party, increased its dominance, winning over 80% of the vote and 77 out of the 96 seats in the National Assembly. The remaining 19 seats were shared between nine of the 15 opposition parties that ran in the election. Many of these had hardly been active on the campaign trail. Somewhat unexpectedly, the Democratic Turnhalle Alliance (DTA) achieved a political comeback and emerged with 4.8% of the votes and five seats as the new official opposition, while the Rally for Democracy and Progress (RDP), the former official opposition, had to accept defeat with 3.5% of the vote and three seats. Four other parties obtained two seats each, and three more parties one seat each. The opposition was more divided than ever before. SWAPO's presidential candidate Hage Geingob was elected with a whopping 86.7% of the vote, while the president of the DTA, McHenry Venaani, and the president of the RDP, Hidipo Hamutenya, trailed with 5% and 3.4% respectively.

Voters in *Mauritius* went to the polls on 10 December. As in Malawi, the outcome brought about a political change by popular vote, in which the former government was replaced. A total of 62 seats in the National Assembly were up for grabs (plus an additional seven so-called top-up seats, which were allocated on the basis of ethnic representation of minorities). The Alliance Lepep obtained 49.8% of the vote and 47 (plus four) seats, the 'Parti Travailliste'-'Mouvement Militant Mauricien' alliance came second with 38.5% of the votes and 13 seats (plus three), with the Rodrigues People's Organisation snatching the last two seats reserved for the electorate in the island of Rodrigues with 1.1%. Navin Rangoolam conceded defeat, while the 84-year-old Anerood Jugnauth (the country's president between 2003 and 2012) became prime minister for the third time.

The newly elected head of state in *Madagascar* resumed office and political control at the beginning of the year and relative political stability returned to the island state, which benefitted from the fact that its government enjoyed international recognition. Its long-term political isolation and the resulting socio-economic setbacks were still hardly overcome, however, showing once again the consequences of politics matter for economic performance.

Battles for political power disturbed the relative peace in the mountain kingdom of *Lesotho*, where months of simmering tensions between the head of state (backed by the police) and the army escalated in late August into efforts by those parts of the military loyal to their dismissed general to remove prime minister Tom Thabane from office. The coup attempt failed after Thabane managed to escape to South Africa. Thanks to a SADC-backed intervention (largely driven by South Africa), political order was restored within weeks but remained fragile. General elections were scheduled for early 2015.

There was uncertainty over *Zambia*'s political future, too, caused by the death in office of the ailing president Michael Sata at the end of October. This led to an immediate contest over who would be his successor. Vice President Guy Scott proved to be a controversial interim president and acting party president. From the beginning, he faced many challenges from other influential members of the governing party. The fierce in-fighting over the nomination of the next presidential candidate absorbed most of the party's energy for the rest of the year.

Meanwhile, ZANU/PF in *Zimbabwe* re-established political control over the country. Severe in-fighting within the opposition MDC-T led to the depolarisation of the political landscape. The main focus shifted to the succession debate and the meteoric promotion of President Mugabe's wife, Grace, who was obviously being groomed by her husband to succeed him. Factional disputes within the party went on without any democratic process, but neither did they lead to the degree of violence witnessed in previous periods.

The firm political control exercised by the dos Santos family clan in *Angola*, who also had a commanding grip on the economy, continued to foster clientelist relations, large-scale corruption and embezzlement. At the same time media freedom continued to deteriorate, youth protests were met with violent repression by the state authorities and the country's human rights record worsened even further. Similarly in *Swaziland*, the autocratic ruler King Mswati III and his security apparatus ensured that no meaningful organised opposition could emerge. Indeed, their firm grip on any political activity by civil society or the trade unions actually increased. Media freedom was curbed further, trade union activism was prohibited and labour organisations were banned. A so-called Suppression of Terrorism Act served as a tool to eliminate all oppositional challenges. The incarceration of political opponents, particularly trade union activists, continued unabated, despite international protest, as did the lavish spending of the royal family, who remained unimpressed by widespread poverty. Civil society groups in *Mozambique* were also put under stricter control. Intimidation and prosecutions to suppress divergent views, especially criticism of the government, led to restricted freedom of expression, not least as a result of increased self-censorship. In contrast, the situation for human rights activists in *Zimbabwe* did not deteriorate; with the renewed strength of ZANU/PF, the country seemed to have left behind the worst forms of state terror, though the situation remained far from acceptable. In *Botswana*, the ongoing government policy of restrictions on the Basarwa, and the reluctance to allow gays, lesbians and bisexuals to register their association, damaged the reputation of those in political power further.

As in previous years, the annual *Mo Ibrahim Index* of African governance (assessing progress under four distinct categories: safety and rule of law; participation and human rights; sustainable economic opportunity; and human development) was released in early October. As usual, it placed the regional aggregate of Southern Africa ahead of all other sub-regions on the continent. Top scorers remained, as in previous years, Mauritius (rank 1/overall score 81.7 out of 100) and Botswana (3/76.2), followed by South Africa (4/73.3) and Namibia (6/70.3). Despite its political turmoil, Lesotho ranked 10th with a score of 62.3, followed by Zambia (13/59.4), Mozambique (22/52.2) and – as in the year before surprisingly high – Swaziland (24/51.5). It remained a mystery that a country with an autocratic royal family that does not consider representation of the people by political parties to be necessary, should receive such a relatively good score, with a place in the upper half of the list. Madagascar ranked 33rd (48.2), followed by Angola (44/40.9). Zimbabwe (46/38.0) remained among the lowest ranked nations in the index (which includes 52 countries). Given the situation in some of the countries ranked highest, the reliability of such overviews and the extent to which they are able accurately to measure the situation on the ground, were once again called into question. The ranking by the annual *Freedom House* report was in most cases similar, although the ordering on political rights and civil liberties (with 1 being the best score and 7 the worst) varied slightly: Mauritius (1 for political rights/2 for civil liberties), Namibia (2/2), South Africa (2/2), Botswana (3/2), and Lesotho (2/3) were classified as 'free', Zambia (3/4), Mozambique (4/3) and Madagascar (5/4) as 'partly free', and Zimbabwe (5/6), Angola (6/5) and Swaziland (7/5) as 'not free'. It recorded an improvement for Zimbabwe but downgraded Zambia. Notably, in marked variance from the Mo Ibrahim Index, Swaziland ranked as the worst performer in the sub-region. According to the TI *Corruption Perception Index* for 2014, Botswana, ranked 31 and Mauritius 47, out of a total of 174 countries, were the least corrupt, followed by Lesotho and Namibia (both at 55), South Africa (67), Swaziland (69) Zambia (85), Malawi (110), Mozambique (119), Madagascar (133), Zimbabwe (156) and Angola (161).

With the 2015 SADC Gender Protocol (SGP) deadline fast approaching, a Southern Africa Gender Protocol Alliance initiated a campaign that reviewed the regional gender equality framework. A regional summit was held in Johannesburg in May. On 25 July, the Alliance released its 2014 Barometer. A *Gender and Development Index* (SGDI) measured progress against 23 indicators in six sectors (education, political participation, the economy, health, HIV and AIDS, and the media). It remained largely stagnant with a minor increase from 66% to 67%. The SGDI for

Angola, Botswana, Madagascar, Mozambique and (notably) Swaziland rose, but fell for Lesotho, Malawi, South Africa and Zambia, while Mauritius and Zimbabwe registered no change. With regard to the six sectors, the SGDI dropped on average by 1% in governance (as a result of the decline in women's political representation in Swaziland, Malawi and South Africa). HIV and AIDS saw a 2% drop, while economy and health each improved by 2%. Major achievements included the adoption of a quota for women in parliament in Zimbabwe and the implementation of an electoral list by SWAPO in Namibia based on gender equity, which meant that every second candidate had to be female.

Socioeconomic Developments

The oil price shock towards the end of the year started to have negative effects on the Angolan oil industry, while consumers in other countries benefitted from lower petrol prices, which reduced the low inflation rates even further. A major economic bottleneck emerged with an *energy crisis*, which was largely the result of the limited capacity of the South African utility giant Eskom – which produced an estimated 45% of the continent's electricity and 95% of South African energy – to generate more power. In the absence of any meaningful investment since the end of Apartheid and the dependency of other countries (particularly Namibia) on energy supply from South Africa, companies as well as individual users suffered from the delivery impasse in South Africa, which had started to introduce load shedding. Eskom implemented temporary power cuts to residents and businesses and limited its energy supply to several hours each day, although in reality Eskom failed to provide electricity even during those hours. This led to economic losses for businesses and greatly affected public institutions and private households. Plans were announced to overcome the shortage by building three coal-fired power stations that would generate 17,000 MW, thus increasing the current capacity of 40,000 MW.

In February, South Africa's President Zuma announced that the government expected nuclear power and shale gas to provide considerable *new sources of energy*, though without providing details of how this would be achieved. By the end of the year, the announced investments had not brought about the planned expansion of energy production. Economists claimed that the energy shortage was a major cause of sluggish economic growth and decline in foreign investment. The year recorded a total of 15 days of rolling blackouts in urban areas, which had a negative effect on the electricity-intense mining and natural resource processing sectors. The business community claimed that, without the energy crisis, some 500,000 jobs could have been created. In November, the World Bank approved a $ 20 m grant to generate investment in a regional large-scale sustainable energy project under the Southern African Power Pool. The project coordinates the power systems of 12 SADC countries, of which nine were so-called operating members. South Africa occupies a crucial position as the continent's energy giant. in terms of both production and consumption.

Economists expressed growing concern that the energy crisis might affect not only domestic production but also *foreign investment*. According to a survey by Ernst & Young, Southern Africa remained the leading region in terms of absolute numbers of FDI projects, with South Africa the largest destination. The survey also noted a substantial increase in investment in Mozambique and Zambia. The African Economic Outlook 2014 confirmed that once again the Southern African region also enjoyed the greatest share of intra-African value added in its exports and presented new evidence that South Africa was playing the role of a 'headquarter economy' in the region.

The report of a seminar held in March and published by the Global Initiative Against Transnational Organized Crime analysed the way in which foreign actors had engaged with domestic criminal groups, both on the upper echelons of the state, and through alliances with local communities. The group of 20 experts identified ways in which foreign criminal networks had impacted local crime groups. It concluded that globalisation and technological advances contributed to the proliferation of traditional forms of *organised crime* whilst also promoting a shift towards sophistication in financial crimes that required professional services. In combination with the increased complicity of states in criminal activity, this created challenges for the traditional set of responses focused on the nation state, national legal frameworks and enforcement tools. Participants concluded that organised crime is increasingly a challenge that is crossing borders and perpetuating insecurity across the sub-region.

With regard to *food security*, the sub-region compared favourably with the rest of SSA. According to a report of the Economist Intelligence Unit, South Africa and Botswana ranked highest, while Mozambique and Zambia were considered to be among the countries with the highest proportions of undernourished people. Maize prices remained high or increased owing to tight supplies, strong demand, currency depreciations and concerns about future harvests. Over previous years, Madagascar had recorded the greatest deterioration in overall food security in the sub-region owing to political insecurity, but with the new political stability conditions improved during the year.

Ahead of the SADC annual summit, the Southern African People's Solidarity Network held the *SADC People's Summit* on 15–16 August in Bulawayo. Some 2,500 participants from a wide variety of civil society agencies adopted the Bulawayo Communiqué 'Reclaiming SADC for SADC People's Development – SADC Resources for SADC People's Development'. The wide ranging catalogue of concerns included the mismanagement and looting of resources by foreign investors and transnational corporations in active collaboration with governments and the latter's failure to enhance access to adequate food and essential social services. The plethora of demands included the formulation and implementation of a SADC-wide basic income grant policy "in the wake of hunger and poverty becoming a daily experience for the majority of citizens in the region". As USAID confirmed at the end of the year: "While Southern Africa has seen significant economic growth achievements, the overall number of people living in poverty has grown over the past two decades. Botswana, Lesotho, Namibia, and South Africa have some of the highest levels of income inequality in the world."

Sub-regional Organisations

All 12 countries in the sub-region were members of SADC (15 members in total). Madagascar's membership, suspended since the coup in 2009, was reinstated following the formation of a legitimate government based on democratic elections. Zimbabwe hosted the 34th *annual SADC Summit* of Heads of State and Government at Victoria Falls (Zimbabwe) on 17–18 August under the theme 'Economic Transformation and Leveraging Resources for Sustainable Economic and Social Development Through Beneficiation and Value Addition'. Following the planned sequence, President Mugabe was elected SADC Chairperson for 2014–15. President Khama of Botswana became the deputy chairperson and was designated his successor for the following year.

Lesotho had originally been scheduled to take over the leadership of the SADC *Organ on Politics, Defence and Security Cooperation* (OPDSC) from Namibia in August. This was deferred to 2015 because of Lesotho's political impasse and the shaky security situation. Instead, President Zuma was elected as the chairperson and Prime Minister Thabane as his deputy. It was speculated that South Africa's initiative to stand in for Lesotho was the result of Zuma's visit to Lesotho on 29 July, when the proposal was made.

The summit called upon all member states to fully support Mauritius's demand for the restoration of its sovereignty over the *Chagos Archipelago*, without which, according to the Summit's final communiqué, the decolonisation of Africa was not complete. Among the four protocols adopted was a new arrangement for the *SADC Tribunal* (not signed by Botswana), which reduced its mandate. Under the new protocol the Tribunal would deal only with inter-state disputes and no longer with cases brought by individuals. The protocol maintained that it was mandated by the "review of the role, responsibilities and terms of reference of the SADC tribunal [that] led to recommendations that require a new protocol". But the commissioned review had earlier explicitly recommended the retention of jurisdiction over disputes between natural and legal persons and SADC member states. Nowhere had it recommended that the old Tribunal be dissolved and a new protocol adopted. The

SADC leaders, however, had ignored the recommendations of the independent legal experts they had commissioned and turned instead to their ministers of justice and attorneys general, who had made the proposal to reduce the Tribunal's authority to inter-state mediation. As the director of the Southern African Litigation Centre commented in the weekly 'Mail & Guardian' of 29 August, this marked "the quiet death of an important SADC institution" and was a major setback to the protection and promotion of human rights for citizens and residents in the sub-region.

The *SADC Council of Ministers* (COM) met on 14–15 August at Victoria Falls in preparation of the annual summit. It reports to the Summit to advise on policy issues and the efficient functioning of the SADC Secretariat, the implementation and administrative organ of SADC. The COM also develops and elaborates on the SADC 'common agenda' and strategic priorities for the year, and approves and oversees the implementation of SADC policies, strategies and programmes, in particular the Regional Indicative Strategic Development Plan (RISDP) and the Strategic Indicative Plan. The SADC Secretariat, based in Gaborone (Botswana) and headed by Dr Stergomena Tax from Tanzania as SADC executive secretary, has limited operational autonomy and reports to the COM.

The *RIDSP*, originally conceptualised and successively implemented as from 2003, was scrutinised and adjusted by a Task Force, established by and comprised of members of all SADC states. A desk assessment of the RISDP initiated during 2011 led to an updated Draft RISDP 2015–20 and its Draft Implementation Framework, which were submitted to the 34th SADC Summit in August. The Summit directed the SADC Secretariat to finalise the document. It stressed the prioritisation of industrialisation and its implementation strategy for consideration by the COM at a later stage. The Revised RISDP (2015–20) identified four main priority areas: a) promoting industrial development and market integration through, among other policy interventions, the strengthening of productive competitiveness and supply side capacity of member states and, additionally, accelerating the movement of goods, and facilitating financial market integration and closer monetary integration; b) providing and improving infrastructure support for regional integration, chiefly through the SADC Regional Infrastructure Development Master Plan, approved at the Summit of Heads of State and Government in Maputo in August 2012; c) promoting peace and security; d) promoting special regional programmes such as education and human resources development; health, HIV and AIDS and other communicable diseases; food security and trans-boundary natural resource exploitation; environment; statistics; gender equality in terms of the 50–50 SGP directive; science, technology and innovation, and research and development.

As from April, *SACU* (which included Botswana, Lesotho, Namibia, South Africa and Swaziland) had with Paulina Elago its first Namibian national as Executive Secretary. Elago was appointed for a five-year period. The world's oldest customs union held the first Regional Trade Forum on 24 July in Johannesburg. Intra-SACU imports had grown from R 58,649 m in 2002/3 to R 111,887 m in 2013/14, a growth rate of over 90% since the initial implementation of the agreement in 2004. The revenue sharing formula among the member states remained contested: South Africa continued to express reservations regarding the preferential treatment of the smaller economies, but they depended to a larger extent on income from SACU as revenue for their annual budgets.

The SADC *EPA* Group (Botswana, Lesotho, Mozambique, Namibia, South Africa and Swaziland, with Angola as an option to join the agreement in future) concluded negotiations on an EPA on 15 July. This pre-empted almost at the last minute the 1 October deadline imposed by the EU, after which Botswana, Namibia and Swaziland would have lost preferential access to the EU market for their exports of beef, fish, sugar and other goods. The other members of the sub-region negotiated EPAs as part of other regional groups, namely Central Africa (DRC) and Eastern and Southern Africa (Malawi, Mauritius, Zambia and Zimbabwe). The signing followed lengthy and protracted negotiations with the EU as the largest trading partner of the SADC EPA group. In its statement of 5 September, the EU stressed that the EPA allowed for "meaningful new market access" into SACU mainly with regard to the export of agricultural and fishery products. What the EU praised as "a pioneering move" and "a new period of cooperation and partnership in agricultural products" was the result of lengthy horse-trading. South Africa's Minister of Trade and Industry Rob Davies, in an article published late in the year, expressed satisfaction at these results. They were an improvement for South Africa compared with the earlier Trade, Development and Cooperation Agreement with the EU, but it remained to be seen how far all parties would benefit from the agreement.

Angola

Jon Schubert

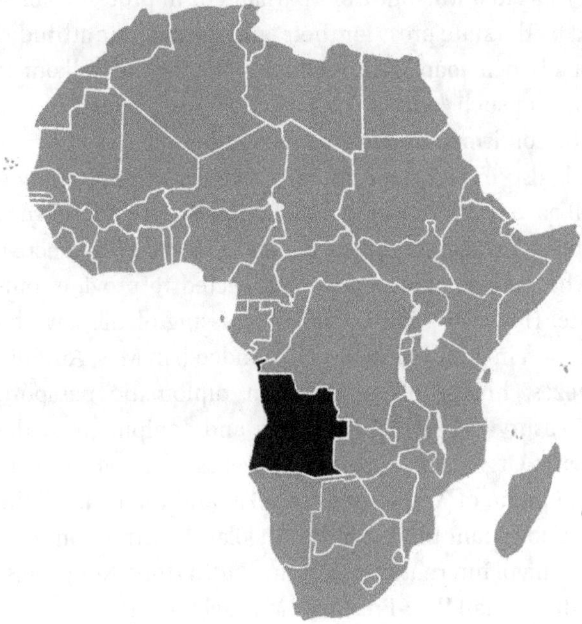

The political year was again marked by dominant-party politics, increasing repression of dissent, and the coming to light of several spectacular cases of grand corruption and mismanagement. Nonetheless, Angola successfully established itself as a regional power-broker and attracted unabated interest from foreign investors. However, the economy, still dominated by the oil industry, stagnated and was seriously affected towards the end of the year by an oil price shock. Accordingly, commodity prices rose even further, and social expenditure remained far under the actual needs of the population.

Domestic Politics

Domestic politics were still strongly dominated by long-standing President José Eduardo dos Santos and the ruling 'Movimento Popular de Libertação de Angola' (MPLA). *Opposition parties* felt even more 'asphyxiated' in the National Assembly than in the previous two years of the current legislative period, and complained that all their initiatives to hold the Executive accountable were voted down by the MPLA's absolute majority, or quashed by the courts. Demands that parliamentary debates

 | DOI 10.1163/9789004305052_045

be broadcast on television in their entirety, as stipulated by the 2010 Constitution, were also blocked. In June, opposition parties 'União Nacional pela Independência Total de Angola' (UNITA), 'Convergência Ampla de Salvação de Angola – Coligação Eleitoral' (CASA-CE), 'Partido de Renovação Social' (PRS), and 'Frente Nacional de Libertação de Angola' (FNLA) staged a walkout from parliament in protest against this, and were duly lambasted by the state press for their "anti-democratic attitude". The vice president of the MPLA bench, João Melo, while recognising the walkout as a form of democratic protest, said such "empty chair politics" were bound to fail, and that it would eventually be confirmed that the MPLA was right.

In September, UNITA tried, also in vain, to oppose a revision of the *nationality law*, claiming the draft bill gave President dos Santos unconstitutional powers. The bill stipulated that the president could grant Angolan nationality by decree, for example, to foreigners who had rendered or were expected to provide "outstanding services" to the state. However, even before the passing of the law, the government had ample discretion in granting nationality. Indeed, in May, António Famtosonghiu Sampo Menezes, holder of an Angolan diplomatic passport, was blacklisted by the US Treasury for providing money and equipment to the Zimbabwean Central Intelligence Organisation. Sampo Menezes, as it was revealed, was a Chinese national by the name of Xu Jinghua 'Sam Pa', and the head of the Chinese International Fund, a dominant player in the Angolan construction market, and president of China Sonangol International Holding Ltd, a Hong-Kong registered company associated with Angolan Vice-President Manuel Vicente.

Thus, dos Santos' dominance over all branches of government continued. In May, he nominated João Lourenço as *new defence minister*. Lourenço, an old-time party member and military general, had been secretary-general of the MPLA from 1999 but fell from grace in 2006. His 'rehabilitation' was commented on in Angola as being a means to put pressure on Vice President Vicente by re-opening the question of the succession to dos Santos, and to quell discontent within the army about the lack of leadership exercised by the previous defence minister, Cândido Pereira Van-Dúnem. Alternative interpretations said building up Lourenço as future vice president under Vicente that would meet the MPLA's approval was a means for dos Santos to secure the position of Vicente, who was still unpopular with the party, as his appointed successor. Generally, dos Santos was seen as trying to neutralise critical voices from the MPLA's 'Old Guard' by nominating them as provincial governors, and replacing them in the party leadership with his allies.

In September, dos Santos also dismissed the *governor of Luanda*, Bento Sebastião Bento, replacing him with Graciano Francisco Domingos. However, Angolan commentators said this change of personnel was unlikely to resolve the capital's challenges, and that the root cause of these problems was the mode of governance, which was characterised by strong and recurring interference from the central government.

In October, the *MPLA youth wing*, JMPLA, held its congress, at the margins of which its secretary-general Sérgio Luther Rescova claimed that "substituting the MPLA in its leadership of the country would mean substituting the people", further underlining the sense of entitlement prevalent in the ruling party. Rescova also denied that the JMPLA gave out free alcohol to encourage people to attend its rallies, or that people joined the party for opportunities for personal, financial betterment.

Finally, the *MPLA's 5th Extraordinary Congress* took place in Luanda on 4–6 December. Dos Santos had previously announced that no party leadership mandates would be renewed at the congress, thereby quelling potential discussions about his succession. Thus the congress was mainly self-congratulatory in tone, with MPLA luminaries lauding the path of progress and international recognition the country had embarked upon under dos Santos' wise leadership. However, such sentiments of supremacy were interlaced with some *paranoia*, exacerbated by the poor performance of the national economy during the year. In the run-up to the congress, the MPLA's provincial first secretary, Bento Bento, said on 15 November that UNITA was preparing "violent demonstrations" against the party and its leader and asked MPLA militants to "close ranks" around dos Santos. On 17 November, Minister of Interior Ângelo Veiga Tavares recommended "firmness and redoubled vigilance" against "repeated veiled" attempts to overthrow the democratic and constitutional order, including the "deliberate negative usage" of the Constitution and the law. And MPLA Secretary for Peripheral and Rural Mobilisation Bento 'Kangamba' dos Santos (President dos Santos' nephew by marriage) also appealed for civic and democratic order, and for taking a stand against citizens of other political formations, as well as for "insults and confusion" to be ignored, as "patriotism, unity among Angolans [...] and mutual respect" stood above all.

Corruption remained a dominant issue: in January, Minister of Interior Ângelo Tavares Veiga dismissed the entire directorate of the Immigration Office ('Serviço de Migração e Estrangeiros', SME) for corruption. Investigations revealed that the SME directorate had issued over 14,000 work visas at a charge of between $ 5,000 and $ 15,000 over the period of a year, netting revenues of $ 90 m, which remained unaccounted for. This was only one of the examples that emerged during the year, with high-level corruption cases coming to the fore – most spectacularly in late April, when dos Santos authorised a sovereign guarantee of $ 5.7 bn to Angola's second-largest commercial bank, Banco Espírito Santo Angola (BESA), to cover the bank's loans portfolio, after investigations revealed that 70% of the $ 5.9 bn loans on its books were irrecoverable 'bad loans'. Subsequent inquiries revealed that BESA's former CEO, Álvaro Sobrinho, had very liberally given generous *loans to the MPLA elite*, without any securities, including allegedly $ 800 m to the president's sister, Marta dos Santos. When dos Santos tried to exert some pressure on the debtors to repay the loans, MPLA Vice President Roberto de Almeida was quoted on Angolan news site 'Club-K' as having thought the $ 10 m loan he had received for property development was a gift, which he had no intention of repaying. However, UNITA queried the legality of the sovereign guarantee, pointing out that the amount exceeded the $ 2.4 m cap enshrined in the law. Ultimately, the crisis was prevented from spreading when the government first put BESA under administration by the National Bank, then allowed Angolan investors including state oil company Sonangol to buy out the bank, thus ultimately nationalising the bank through the backdoor, and safeguarding the investment interests of the ruling elite. Even after the takeover by Sonangol, politically connected companies, such as Grupo Geni, owned by general 'Dino' and Isabel dos Santos, as well as Portmill, general Kopelipa's investment holding, remained major shareholders.

In an unrelated case in April, Dutch oil company SBM Offshore revealed it had paid $ 22.7 m in 'commissions' to Angolan officials between 2007 and 2011 in exchange for *oil concessions*. Less publicly, in May, Oil Minister José Maria Botelho de Vasconcelos also authorised Sonangol to sell 10% of its 50% share in an oil block to an Angolan private company called Prodoil. As investigative news site 'Maka Angola' revealed, Prodoil was owned by a holding owned again by Marta dos Santos and two of her sons. In August, 'Global Witness' also revealed that multinational oil companies had since 2012 donated $ 175 m from their corporate social responsibility accounts to Sonangol's 'Research and Technology Centre', with commitments to disburse an equal amount again by 2016, though the Centre was nowhere near to being in existence at the time of the report.

Opposition MPs deplored the fact that prisons were overflowing with "chicken thieves", while those who stole "millions from the treasury" remained unpunished, and condemned a *culture of impunity* and corruption in the judiciary and police force. A judge who sentenced several police officers in February for earlier extralegal killings was transferred to the eastern Lunda Sul province with his salary payments suspended for three months.

The year saw a worsening climate for human rights and *freedom of speech*. In February, Queirós Anastácio Chiluvia, the adjunct director of 'Rádio Despertar', a broadcaster affiliated with opposition party UNITA, was detained in Cacuaco while trying to report on the beating up of detainees inside the municipal police headquarters. Following three days in detention, Chiluvia faced a summary judgment and was sentenced to six months' conditional detention for "disrespect, libel, and defamation" and "illegal practice of the profession" of journalist. This was indicative of the pressure put on 'Despertar', which together with the Catholic Church's 'Rádio Ecclésia' remained one of the few independent *media* outlets. Most radio and television stations, as well as newspapers, remained either state-owned, or under the control of regime-affiliated private investors. This climate of censorship was not limited to criticism of the government, however: in March, a 'Despertar' journalist said he had been prohibited from inviting two guests to discuss the internal failings of UNITA.

Overall, it was mainly government critics and opponents who faced severe and swift repression. In June, 19 school teachers in Huíla province were detained for three days following a demonstration calling for better pay and training. The strike was ended after two months, as teachers wanted to avoid the cancellation of the entire academic year, though the teachers' union said not many of their demands had been heard. Slum clearances with *forced evictions* and housing demolitions continued in central Luanda, as well as in the provincial capitals of Benguela and Lubango. In April, for example, residents of the Cacuaco municipality of Luanda barricaded the main thoroughfares in protest against the lack of notice and excessive violence of the authorities in demolishing their houses. In the countryside, locals also denounced the illegal expropriation of plots of land by MPLA leaders. The persecution of female street vendors, or 'zungueiras', continued, with numerous reports of arbitrary detentions and demands for 'fines' in exchange for their release. When youth protesters called for a demonstration in support of the 'zungueiras' in March, the governor of Luanda promised to meet with the street vendors, and said President dos Santos had suspended the police officers responsible with immediate effect, after which the demonstration was called off.

Subsequent *youth protests* throughout the year, however, were swiftly repressed by the police, who routinely rounded up from a few dozen to over 150 protestors at a time, detained them in police vans, beat them up, and then released them some 150–200 km outside the city limits. On 22 and 23 November, a rally calling for dos Santos' resignation was violently broken up in Luanda. Student activist Laurinda Gouveia was detained by the police and beaten for two hours with iron bars, cudgels, electric cables and, in one instance, a mobile phone charger. Other activists were also thrashed with steel cables and truncheons, and released outside the city limits with their phones and money 'confiscated'. Similar violent repression also took place in other provinces, including Huíla and Cabinda. In apparently unrelated news, in June, the migration authorities expelled the coordinator of the EU's Support Programme for Non-State Actors, though local observers remarked that the non-renewal of her visa was probably linked to meetings with the abovementioned 'youth revolutionaries'. In a positive development, the youth activist Manuel Nito Alves – detained in 2013 for insulting the president – was acquitted by the tribunal for lack of evidence.

In October, an association of 15 NGOs active in monitoring *human rights* said the situation had worsened "considerably". Secretary of State for Human Rights António Bento Bembe accused the NGOs of bad faith, saying they did not want to see the "visible progress" made by the Executive on human rights. Similarly, Angola's passing of the Universal Periodic Review of Human Rights at the UN in Geneva in October was hailed in state-owned news media as a great success and further proof of these advances, while more independent sources reported that the Angolan delegation had been "grilled" over the restrictions on free speech and public protest.

Even the *Catholic Church*, which had generally adopted a rather muted, conciliatory position since the end of the war, took a more vocal stance. In March, the president of the Bishops Conference (Conferência Episcopal de Angola e São-Tomé, CEAST), Dom Gabriel Mbilingui, said democracy and pluralism in Angola left much to be desired, and throughout the year some church leaders spoke out against human rights abuses and poor socio-economic conditions. At its second plenary session in October, CEAST also criticised the 'dubious quality' of public infrastructure works, which often remained uncompleted, and questioned the huge expenses incurred while the gap between poor and rich was growing. The plenary also criticised Canon Apolónio Graciano for his constant, enthusiastic public endorsement of the MPLA, saying this had caused the church some embarrassment.

The government's counter-insurgency campaign continued against the low-level separatist guerrillas of the 'Frente para a Libertação da Enclave de Cabinda' (FLEC) in the oil-rich *Cabinda province*. CASA-CE deputy José Lelo said in February that the province was still experiencing a climate of war, citing armed confrontations between army units and FLEC in Buco Zau municipality, as well as the regular disappearance of citizens. UNITA also denounced an increase in serious human rights violations in the province, and claimed that, despite Defence Minister Lourenço's announcement in October that the conflict had ended, political assassinations, arbitrary detentions, and restrictions on public demonstrations were on the rise.

Human rights violations at the hands of public and private security forces also continued in the diamond-producing areas of the *Lunda Norte and Lunda Sul provinces*. In March, local police killed seven artisanal miners, while various others 'disappeared' following a police operation in Saurimo. In September, an anonymous source within the state security services claimed a plan had been approved to assassinate José Mateus Zecamutchima, the president of the autonomist and regularly repressed 'Movimento do Protectorado Lunda Tchokwe', by staging a car accident or a burglary, though Zecamutchima himself said these plans were old. In December, a video was published on the internet, allegedly showing employees of the private security company K&P torturing two 'illegal' DRC artisanal miners. One positive related development was that in May the MPLA submitted a bill to parliament limiting the type of firearms that agents of private security companies were allowed to carry to small- and medium-calibre weapons, and requesting the carrying of licences issued by the police.

In October, the Institute of National Languages recommended the adoption of the Bantu spelling of place names with 'k' in preference to the Portuguese orthography with 'c', thereby taking a first step towards mitigating the confusion over the spelling of Angolan place names such as Kwanza-Sul (Cuanza Sul) and Kuando Kubango (Cuando Cubango).

Foreign Affairs

Overall, Western interest in investment opportunities increased, while Angolan diplomacy placed growing importance on South-South ties. Moreover, Angola successfully pursued its strategy to become a regional power broker. Angola's election in October as non-permanent member of the *UNSC* for the period of 2015–16 was clearly a fruit of these efforts, as was the higher visibility that Angola gained as chair of the ICGLR. Taking over the *ICGLR chairmanship* from Uganda in January, Angola publicly took a lead in the question of the disarmament by military force of armed rebel groups in eastern DRC and said it would consider committing some of its own troops to regional peacekeeping operations there – though no decision had been made by the end of the year. Angola did, however, commit troops to the UN military mission in the *CAR* in September, after granting $ 10 bn in support of Interim President Catherina Samba-Panza's transitional government when she visited Luanda in March. The money, earmarked for the payment of public sector salaries, was then partially embezzled in the CAR, prompting much outrage there. By comparison, Angola's commitment to *SADC* remained more ambivalent. In January, Minister of Commerce Rosa Pacavira said Angola's accession to the SADC free exchange zone remained on the government's agenda, though not before 2017, to give the country time to build up its own industrial capacity.

In bilateral terms, political and economic ties with *Portugal* continued to be among the most important, with Angolan investors strengthening their positions in the media, banking and construction sectors. With about 100,000 Portuguese economic migrants in Angola, bilateral ties were important, though strained by Portuguese investigations into the assets of Bento 'Kangamba' dos Santos.

Kangamba also remained under investigation in *Brazil* for procurement of prostitutes, though the arrest warrant issued in the previous year was suspended on payment of bail. Generally, however, relations remained strong, and fuelled by strong Brazilian commercial interests in the Angolan construction sector: following a state visit by dos Santos to Brazil, Angola's other main Lusophone partner granted a $ 2 bn oil-backed credit line for the construction and energy sectors, which equalled the bilateral trade volume of the previous year. The other *African Lusophone countries* also remained priority partners, though not necessarily in economic terms. In July, Filipe Nyusi, presidential candidate of Mozambique's ruling Frelimo party, visited Angola, to "drink from" the MPLA's experience. Angola also opened a $ 180 m credit line to nearby São Tomé e Príncipe, was "studying" investment opportunities in Cape Verde, and renewed ties with Guinea-Bissau following the election of a new government in June; relations had been strained following the 2012 coup there.

China remained one of Angola's key foreign partners, with a bilateral trade volume of $ 37 bn, and Angola was China's second-largest oil supplier after Saudi Arabia. In March, the Chinese Chamber of Commerce also created a legal and logistics assistance centre for the estimated 100,000 Chinese expatriates living in Angola. This was followed by a state visit in May by Chinese Prime Minister Li Keqiang, who donated 180 m Chinese yuan ($ 28 m) in support of economic diversification and signed a string of cooperation agreements, including on a geological survey of the country's mineral resources. However, a report in July blamed complicity by Angolan officials in making Angola the second-largest exporter of illegal ivory, 95% of which was sold to Chinese clients. Foreign observers, as well as a few domestic activists, also noted with some concern the involvement of Angolan regime figures in Chinese private companies, which made their gains in commercial ventures funded by oil-backed credits to Angola.

In April, Angola overtook Nigeria as the US's main Sub-Saharan supplier of oil, and in May, *US* Secretary of State John Kerry visited Angola as part of his Africa tour; he stressed that the US was not just there for business opportunities but wanted to establish a real partnership with Angola. In September, US General David Rodriguez, the commander of AFRICOM, also visited Angola with a view to reinforcing regional and maritime security cooperation.

In April, dos Santos made a two-day state visit to *France*, a clear signal that relations, strained by the 'Angolagate' scandal of the late 1990s, were on the mend, and indicative of heightened French interest in investment opportunities in Angola, which totalled € 10 bn. France was also the sixth-largest source of imports. Other *European interests* manifested elsewhere. In March, the Swedish Finance Minister recommended Angola to pension funds managers in his country as one of the most lucrative countries for investments. In November, Germany announced the signing of a defence cooperation agreement.

Regarding *South-South cooperation*, dos Santos visited Cuba in June, following his trip to Brazil, signing new agreements on cooperation in the health sectors and the training of cadres. A state visit to Angola by Chilean President Michelle Bachelet in August resulted in the creation of a bilateral economic cooperation commission.

Socioeconomic Developments

Oil production remained the main driver of economic growth, accounting for 70% of government revenue. However, despite public declarations that production would pick up again and be boosted to 2 m b/d in 2015, production levels fell in April to 1.54 m b/d. The government reacted by easing some local content restrictions, allowing, for example, French oil major Total to finalise its investment decision for a new offshore block in March. This, however, ran counter of union demands for increasing 'Angolanisation' of the workforce in the oil sector, and led to several shorter strikes. In May, production at the Angola liquefied natural gas project in Soyo had to be halted due to "a succession of technical faults". It was announced that the plant would not start operating again before mid-2015, thereby further denting revenue projections from the sector.

As from June, world oil prices started falling, from around $ 100 per barrel to $ 78 in November, and then hitting $ 57.33 per barrel of Brent crude at year's end. For the Angolan government, which in November had passed an expansionist budget for the coming year with revenue estimates based on a price of $ 81 per barrel, these developments came as a shock and forced the government to work on a *revised 2015 budget* at the end of the year. Already in March and April, foreign and domestic observers thus warned of the end of Angola's 'strong' economic growth of the previous year, revising their forecasts down from the official target of 7.9% GDP growth to a more realistic 3.9%; in October, the government itself revised its growth forecast to 3.1.%.

In September, the government also reduced subsidies on *fuel prices* for the first time since 2010, thereby raising pump prices from 60 Angolan kwanza (AOA) to AOA 75 ($ 0.75) per litre of petrol, and from AOA 50 to AOA 60 ($ 0.60) per litre of diesel. Although fuel remained heavily subsidised until the end of the year, when the government announced further reductions in fuel subsidies, these price hikes de facto acted as a regressive income tax on lower-income Angolans, for whom transport costs made up a significant part of household budgets. Higher transport costs then also had a direct impact on the prices of food items, as significant parts of the population depended on the informal market for their supplies and their earnings, which in turn depended on shared taxis.

In addition to these downward pressures on the economy, *social policies* remained out of step with the population's most pressing needs, which remained largely unaddressed. Even the OECD said in its May African Economic Outlook that Angola's economic growth had not reached the population. The imposition in March of new *import tariffs* as high as 50% on non-essential goods was a further measure of this. Although allegedly intended to stimulate the replacement of imports by locally produced food and goods and thus to help diversify the national economy, the measure drove up consumer prices, thereby hitting the poorest parts of the population hardest. Local observers noted that these protectionist measures, rather than serving their stated purpose, would only end up benefiting entrenched economic interests that controlled the import of foodstuffs. Similarly, a ban on the import of cement was decreed, as the government judged domestic production sufficient for national demand, although "internal supply constraints" made the negotiation of exemptions necessary until mid-year.

Accordingly, in July, business consultants Mercer designated Luanda the *world's most expensive capital* for expatriates for the second consecutive year. Angolan observers, however, noted that life was even more expensive and difficult for the local population, blaming the situation on political and economic power-holders who did not themselves feel the effects of these developments. In August, 'Jornal de

Angola' reported a rise in *armed crime* in Luanda, with attackers targeting cars that were stuck in the ubiquitous traffic jams in the morning and evening rush hours.

The *construction sector* contributed about 9% of GDP, and was mainly driven by public investments in the construction of roads and public infrastructure projects. In August, a new bulk iron ore terminal was completed at the southern port of Lobito, coinciding with the completion of the rehabilitation of the *Benguela railway line*, (Caminho de Ferro de Benguela, CFB) connecting the ports and coastal cities of Lobito and Benguela with Luau, in Lunda Sul, 1,344 km east on the border with the DRC. The upgrade to a wider Chinese gauge and heavy-duty rails linked the Angolan seaports to Katanga in the DRC and the Zambian Copperbelt, thereby potentially reducing export distances for these minerals from the current 8,000 km, via South Africa, to under 2,000 km. However, as the connecting lines on the DRC and Zambian side had not yet been completed, exports did not start until the end of the year. Moreover, although the rehabilitation of the line had been funded by public funds, three close confidantes of dos Santos – Vice President Vicente, and generals 'Kopelipa' and 'Dino' – expressed interest in acquiring the CFB as part of a planned privatisation of the lines. Minister of Transport Augusto da Silva Tomás reportedly opposed the plans, pushing for a fusion of the three railway lines as a national company, and the situation was still deadlocked at the end of the year.

The *diamond industry* also remained an important source of revenue, if not in terms of contributions to total GDP, then certainly in terms of enriching members of the ruling elite. In June, the government authorised the Israeli-Russian construction magnate Lev Leviev to sell Angolan diamonds directly abroad, thus raising potential revenues for Ascorp, a joint venture between Leviev and the state diamond mining company Endiama. Production levels stood at about 10 m carats, though the opening up of the Lulo concession in Lunda Norte and the Mundundo concession in Malange to prospecting was set to increase production levels further.

The banking sector was also expanding strongly, despite the failure of BESA (see above), though the overexposure of the entire sector to both public debt and the booming housing sector led several ratings agencies to downgrade their *sovereign ratings* for Angola, pointing out the risk of the housing bubble bursting and further banks going bust. By the end of the year, however, no further non-performing loans had been uncovered in other banks. In December, the Angolan *Sovereign Wealth Fund*, headed by the president's son José Filomeno 'Zénú' de Sousa dos Santos, announced its first investment plans – two years after its creation with a starting capital of $ 5 bn and following international evaluations judging it "lacking in transparency". $ 1.1 bn would be deposited in a fund that invested in energy, transport and industry in Subsaharan Africa, while $ 500 m would be invested in the hotel sector. Thus, any hopes that the Fund would contribute to job creation or help buffer the Angolan economy against oil price dependency were, for the moment, dashed.

The government finally managed to hold a *national census*, the country's first since independence from Portugal in 1975 (the last census was carried out in 1970). According to the head of the National Institute of Statistics, the census covered 99% of the population, recording a total population of 24.3 m, of which the largest part (6.5 m) lived in the capital, Luanda. Nationwide, 62.3% of the population lived in urban environments, and there were slightly more women (52%) than men (48%). Nonetheless, local elections, as required by the Constitution were delayed again, at least until 2017.

Despite a $ 70 m agreement with the World Bank passed in January to strengthen primary education, substantial challenges were still facing the *education* sector. A radio debate in January was indicative: following the publication of an international university ranking, two Angolan university lecturers expressed their "indignation" at the fact that no Angolan university had made it into the top 100 African universities, especially as the Mozambican Universidade Eduardo Mondlane, "which in practical terms belongs to a country with less wealth than ours", figured in the ranking. The third discussant, however, replied that this was exactly the problem of Angolan higher education, and that as long as study places and diplomas could be bought, theses were copied, and professors were unqualified to teach their subjects, the country could hardly achieve excellence. Primary and secondary education fared no better, with the national teachers' union declaring the government's 2002 education reform a failure and criticising the government's investment in buildings rather than in human resources. In the province of Uíge, a July report by 'Voice of America' revealed that 398 non-existent 'phantom' teachers were on the payroll of the provincial directorate of education, 'earning' AOA 240 m ($ 2.4 m) in 2013. And a report in July noted that children in Luanda's peripheral neighbourhoods were excluded from the formal education system for lack of birth certificates.

An Oxfam report ranked Angola among the world's worst three countries in terms of *food security*, mainly because of the high cost of food and extreme price volatility. This was again due to entrenched economic interests that benefited from high import prices, as well as poor transport and trading infrastructures for domestic produce. Even the state-owned 'Jornal de Angola', not usually known for its critical perspective, reported that 80% of the agricultural produce of Soyo province was spoiled every year because of the lack of a viable market. In February, Tyikenga Heipute, the traditional chief of the Muhimba in Tômbwa, Namibe province, said his people were on the brink of death because of the shortage of water and food. FAO nevertheless announced in February that Angola was on its way to attaining the MDG of halving hunger by 2015. Local NGOs active in the area of community development, however, criticised the government for superficial and unsustainable measures to combat hunger.

In March, the newspaper 'Agora' reported that the unemployment and old-age benefits the MPLA had promised to introduce in its 2012 electoral campaign had failed to materialise, and that no one was willing to speak openly about the issue, while in July Foreign Minister Chicoty restated the government's intention to create 1 m new *jobs* by 2017, a 2012 electoral promise that so far had failed to materialise. Most people thus continued to combine formal and informal employment to make ends meet, working for example as salaried teachers or public functionaries, but importing clothes or consumer goods for resale from neighbouring Namibia or the DRC, Europe, or China. Many also earned an income from the resale of water, given that over 50% of the population did not have regular access to clean water.

Also in March, Minister of Health José Van-Dúnem admitted that there were only 3,541 medical doctors in Angola, manifestly too few to provide the population with adequate services; many municipalities had only two doctors at their disposal. In the province of Huambo, for example, this translated into one physician for 16,000 inhabitants. Accordingly, malaria remained a major *public health* issue, and in March, WHO expressed concern that TB rates in Angola would continue to rise until 2017, given the government's lack of success in fighting the spread of the disease and official admissions that 2013 had seen an 11% increase in cases. Infant mortality remained the highest among all Portuguese-speaking countries, at 167 per 1,000 births. Official sources also said 200,000 people were living with HIV/AIDS, though statistics remained unreliable, with officials giving a higher number of 300,000 for the previous year. Finally, in a bid to prevent the potential spread of Ebola (although no cases were registered) the Ministry of Health posted notices in public hospitals requesting that family members bring their own gloves and masks when collecting the bodies of their deceased relatives. This received the dry comment: 'Our leaders only have Chanel gloves, and won't give them', perhaps fittingly as the 2014 budget only allocated 4.3% of spending to the health sector, a net decrease from the previous year.

Botswana

David Sebudubudu and Keratilwe Bodilenyane

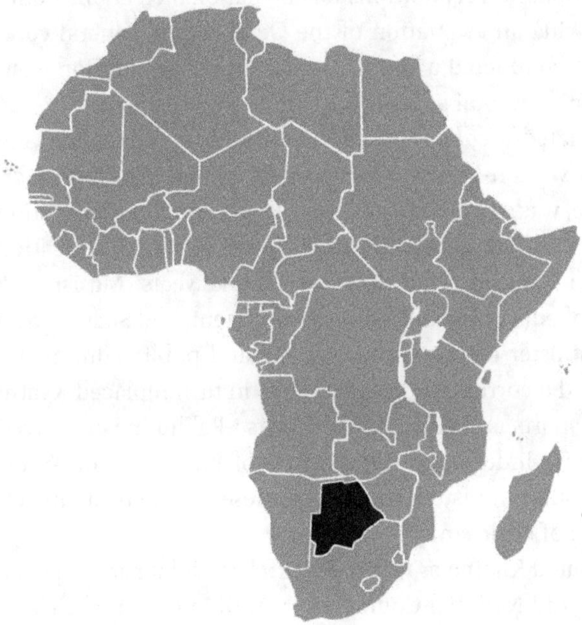

The year was dominated by the general elections in October. As expected, the Botswana Democratic Party (BDP) maintained its dominance – albeit with a reduced popular vote. However, the two opposition parties, the Botswana Congress Party (BCP) and the Umbrella for Democratic Change (UDC) – a coalition of the Botswana National Front (BNF), the Botswana Movement for Democracy (BMD) and the Botswana Peoples Party (BPP) – also mounted colourful campaigns. In addition, the Independent Electoral Commission (IEC) registered the highest number ever of independent candidates – suggesting that the political party primary elections were not straightforward. The economic performance continued to show signs of recovery and stability. The country maintained its foreign policy, and there were no noticeable changes in socio-economic developments and disparities.

Domestic Politics

A *by-election* in the constituency of Francistown West was held on 25 January and won by Habaudi Hubona of the BCP, the first elected female opposition MP. This

 | DOI 10.1163/9789004305052_046

secured the BCP leader Dumelang Saleshando the position of leader of the parliamentary opposition. BDP candidate Ignatius Moswaane was barred by a court order from submitting his name to the IEC after Whyte Marobela, who had lost the party primary election, challenged its outcome. Marobela approached the court after the BDP failed to address his complaint. Preparations for the national elections dominated during the year. Following an evaluation of the October 2013 general voter registration exercise, the IEC conducted a supplementary voter registration exercise from 21 February to 2 March. A total of 824,073 voters were registered.

President Ian Khama initiated a *cabinet reshuffle.* Minister of Education and Skills Development Pelonomi Venson-Moitoi, who had been criticised in some quarters for her poor performance, was granted special leave from 1 April, under Section 126 (2) of the Constitution, to coordinate and develop the Ministry's Education and Training Strategic Sector Plan on a full-time basis. Mokgweetsi Masisi took her place as acting minister of education and skills development, and Shaw Kgathi replaced Masisi as acting minister of presidential affairs and public administration. Vincent Seretse, who had a corruption case pending, in turn replaced Kgathi as acting minister of youth, sports and culture, and Keletso Rakhudu was moved from the Ministry of Trade and Industry to the Ministry of Education and Skills Development as another assistant minister. Appointing these ministers on an acting basis brought Khama a lot of criticism.

The *BDP* elected and validated Khama as its presidential candidate at its special congress on 4 April, and its 52nd National Council on 5 April in Gaborone. These were followed by the unveiling of the party's manifesto and parliamentary candidates on 6 April. Some senior members of the BDP who had lost in the party's primary elections in 2013 resigned from the party, citing irregularities in the conduct of the elections. MP Moeng Pheto left the BDP on 10 April following his suspension from the party, and stood as an independent candidate for Lentsweletau-Mmopane constituency. MP and former deputy speaker of the National Assembly Pono Moatlhodi resigned from the BDP on 14 April, ending his 39-year membership of the party. He later joined the BNF but contested the elections under the UDC banner. Moatlhodi retained the position of deputy speaker until the election.

On 17 March, the *BCP* revealed its 25-member shadow cabinet, the first in the party's history, and on 26 April released its election manifesto and launched Dumelang Saleshando as its presidential candidate and Gaborone Central constituency candidate. The BCP held its conference on 19–22 July in Gaborone, where it quashed prospects of joining the opposition coalition. Instead, it encouraged its members to vote for the opposition UDC in constituencies where it had no representation, a suggestion that was rebuffed by the UDC. Earlier, a delegation from the Communist Party of China had met the leadership of the BCP in January.

The *UDC* unveiled its election manifesto on 6 June and presented Duma Boko, the party's president, as its presidential candidate. The UDC coalition of the BNF, the BMD and the BPP agreed to use one symbol for the elections but to retain their individual party identities. The constituent members held the UDC conference in Serowe on 19–22 July. Interestingly, the Botswana Federation of Public Sector Unions (BOFEPUSU) declared its support for the UDC, a move meant to spite the opposition BCP, which had opted out of the coalition, and the ruling BDP, which had had an uneasy relationship with public sector unions since the public sector strike of 2011, when the BDP government refused to increase public worker's salaries by 16%, citing the economic downturn. However, the UDC suffered a setback with the *death of Gomolemo Motswaledi*, its secretary general and president of the BMD, in what some believed was a 'mysterious' car accident on 30 July. Botswana Police Service investigations found no 'foul play'. Motswaledi's party instituted its own parallel investigation, and its full report remained to be made public. However, according to Boko, "preliminary reports by experts engaged by the party suggest Motswaledi was murdered". Motswaledi's car accident took place amid unconfirmed accusations that Khama's government had a 'hit list' of opposition leaders, including Boko, who were allegedly targeted for elimination by the Directorate of Intelligence Services (DIS). Khama dismissed these reports, but they were repeated throughout the election campaign. A report by Business Monitor International suggested that the UDC posed a serious challenge to the BDP's hold on power, as it exploited the country's developmental challenges, including the tension between the unions and government.

On 6 August, Khama announced that Botswana's tenth parliament would be dissolved on 29 August, and set 24 October as the day for holding the eleventh general elections. Vice President Ponatshego Kedikilwe retired following the elections. The elections, which were free and peaceful, were contested by the BCP, BDP and UDC. In the *election results*, the BDP won 37 of the 57 directly elected seats (with 47% of the vote), the UDC 17 (with 30% of the vote) and the BCP three (with 20% of the vote). A number of senior BDP MPs lost their seats to the opposition. They included two ministers, four assistant ministers and the BDP's longest serving MP, Daniel Kwelagobe, who had been in parliament since 1969. The leader of the BCP, Dumelang Saleshando, also lost his seat. Saleshando was the only opposition candidate whose name appeared amongst ruling party politicians whom the BOFEPUSU specifically campaigned against, because he had failed to ensure that his party joined the UDC coalition. Of the 57 directly elected MPs, 33 were elected for the first time (18 BDP, 13 UDC and two BCP). Of the 824,073 registered voters, 698,409 cast their votes; 690,242 ballots were considered valid while 8,167 were spoiled. The number of women elected as MPs remained low.

After a legal dispute confirming the parliamentary standing orders, parliament endorsed Mokgweetsi Masisi as vice president by secret ballot, following his appointment by the president. Gladys Kokorwe and Kagiso Molatlhegi were elected speaker and deputy speaker of the *National Assembly*, respectively, following their nomination by the BDP caucus. Kokorwe defeated the former speaker, Margaret Nasha, by 41 votes to 21. Nasha was perceived to be aligned with the opposition after she published a book on 20 March that disparaged Khama. In April, she was refused permission to act as an observer in South Africa's 7 May election.

Parliament elected four *specially elected members* in line with Section 58 (2)(d) of the Constitution. Two of them had lost their seats in the general elections, one was a former permanent secretary to the president and the other was a former minister of finance and development planning, who was reappointed to the same ministry. All four were appointed ministers. In addition, a number of former BDP MPs, ministers and assistant ministers who had lost their seats at either the party primary elections in 2013 or the general election found their way back into public service as diplomats, civil servants or councillors. Of the 119 councillors nominated by the minister of local government and rural development, 115 were BDP and four UDC. This demonstrated the extent to which the BDP continued to use patronage to reward its members, including those who had been rejected by the electorate.

Allegations of *corruption and misappropriation* continued to make headlines. The most publicised allegations of public concern involved DIS Director General Isaac Kgosi, one of Khama's closest associates. Kgosi was ostensibly investigated by the Directorate on Corruption and Economic Crime (DCEC) for living beyond his means, which is a crime under the DCEC Act. Media reports suggested that Kgosi, amongst others, received around BP (pula) 900,000 from the former managing director of Debswana, Louis Nchindo, at a time when the latter was being prosecuted for corruption. The allegations were widely covered by the private sector media while state media remained silent. On 3 April, Khama confirmed that Kgosi was being investigated by the DCEC. On 27 June, the DCEC failed to secure a court order to prevent the 'Sunday Standard' from circulating information regarding a DCEC interview with Kgosi and investigation into his affairs. The newspaper was only prevented from "reproducing verbatim the extracts from the interviews conducted by the DCEC with persons whose names shall be made available to the publication for inspection, on condition that these names shall not be disclosed to third parties". As a result, there was pressure on Khama to dismiss Kgosi and have him prosecuted. Nevertheless, no charges of corruption were brought against him and, in September, he rebuffed the allegations and continued in post. Meanwhile, the case of Vincent Seretse, who had been appointed minister of trade and industry after the elections, was yet to be concluded by the courts. The DCEC finished a draft national anti-corruption policy, which remained to be approved by the cabinet and Parliament.

The tension between the *government and the BOFEPUSU* continued. On 23 April, the Court of Appeal affirmed a High Court judgement that the government's decision to expand the list of essential service workers using a statutory instrument was illegal. In May, the High Court reversed a government decision to 'de-register' BOFEPUSU. These cases demonstrated the government's intolerance of organisations that posed a threat to its power base. In August, during the dissolution of the tenth parliament, MP Daniel Kwelagobe (see above) called for "political tolerance to trade unions". Surprisingly, Festus Mogae, president of Botswana from 1998 to 2008, criticised the government for "failing to respect the rule of law", thus further strengthening concerns that Khama was intolerant of dissenting views.

Issues affecting *minority groups* also emerged. Matters concerning the Basarwa/San, including access to water, continued to attract criticism and negative publicity. Survival International called for a 'boycott' of the tourism sector – a major revenue earner for Botswana. In return, Khama barred Survival International, and they joined a number of individuals who were "unwelcome in the country". In June, there were media reports that a "former UN advisor on water, Maude Barlow, … condemned the government of Botswana for failing to protect Basarwa living in the Central Kalahari Game Reserve (CKGR) against international companies that are practising fracking in their ancestral land". A Basarwa rights activist, Jumanda Gakelebone, was elected as UDC councillor for New Xade on 24 October. On other issues affecting minorities, on 14 November a High Court judge nullified the government's decision not to allow the Lesbians, Gays and Bisexuals of Botswana (LEGABIBO) to register its association. The government indicated its intention to appeal against this ruling.

Foreign Policy

The *minister of foreign affairs* and international cooperation headed a delegation to the 22nd AU Ordinary Session of the Assembly of Heads of State and Government in Addis Ababa (Ethiopia) on 30–31 January, to the 4th Africa-EU Summit on 2–3 April in Brussels (Belgium) and to the US-Africa Leaders' Summit in Washington DC on 4–6 August. He made an official visit to Argentina on 16–19 September and led a delegation to the 69th Session of the UN General Assembly from 20 September to 2 October.

In contrast, *President Ian Khama* was less interested in such gatherings and kept trips abroad to a minimum. He attended the inauguration of Malawi's President Peter Mutharika on 2 June, and the SADC Summit on 17–18 August in Victoria Falls (Zambia), where he was elected vice chairman of SADC. On 11 November, former president Festus Mogae attended the funeral of Zambian President Michael Sata on Khama's behalf. From 17 to 20 November, President Jacob Zuma attended the 2nd Botswana-South Africa Bi-Annual Commission, at Khama's invitation.

Botswana maintained a *strong commitment to international relations*. On 19 February, it cut ties with North Korea following a UN Commission of Inquiry report that recorded "systematic, widespread and grave human rights violations" in that country. Botswana had suspended relations with North Korea in 2013. Azerbaijan's minister of foreign affairs visited Botswana on 25 February. On 21 March, Botswana contributed 16 tonnes of roofing and blankets to Burundi. On 12–14 May, King Letsie III of Lesotho visited. On 22 May, Botswana expressed concern at the increased political instability in Ukraine, and urged the involvement of non-aligned organisations such as the UN in restoring political stability in that country. On 3 June, Botswana criticised Sudan for condemning a woman to death for her Christian faith, and urged other countries to express their disapproval of Sudan's decision as it violated the woman's liberties. On 8 August, Botswana offered financial support for combating the Ebola epidemic in Guinea, Liberia and Sierra Leone. Botswana also extended financial aid to Palestine in response to the UN appeal geared towards easing "the plight of internally and externally displaced Palestinians".

Botswana and the *USA* had a diplomatic spat in September following the USA's disapproval of the arrest of the editor of the 'Sunday Standard' newspaper, Outsa Mokone. Mokone was arrested and charged with sedition after his paper carried a story that "detailed the president's involvement in a car accident". The charge came against the backdrop of the Kgosi affair (see above). In a press statement, Botswana disparaged the USA, reminding it to concern itself with "allegations of abuse in their own country, such as the recent alleged assault and detention without charge by law enforcement personnel of the Washington Post reporter, Wesley Lowery, while he was attempting to cover the unrest in Ferguson Missouri, subsequent to the fatal police shooting of 18 year old Michael Brown". The government's action attracted a lot of criticism. Media reports suggested that Botswana had 'apologised' to the USA. Mokone's arrest also attracted a lot of criticism, even from within the country. The decision to charge him was viewed in some quarters, including by Freedom House, as an attempt by Khama's government to muzzle the press, particularly the private sector press, which had been so critical of government. In its 'Freedom of the World', Freedom House categorised Botswana as 'partly free in Freedom of the Press'.

In September, the government of Botswana denied *Julius Malema* a visa to visit Botswana, a decision that did not surprise many. He had been expected to address a meeting to launch BNF Youth League Secretary, Arafat Khan as UDC council candidate for Borakalalo ward. Malema had previously called for a change of government in Botswana, and had also criticised Khama's government for its proximity to the USA. Malema's party, the Economic Freedom Fighters, called for Botswana's isolation.

A high-profile meeting was held in Gaborone on 24–26 November when the 23rd session of the Council of Member States of the International Institute for Democracy and Electoral Assistance, and the *Annual Democracy Forum* took place under the title 'fostering democracy and development through sound management of natural resources', a highly relevant theme for a country like Botswana that is heavily dependent on the exploitation of natural resources. The meeting was jointly organised by the Ministry of Foreign Affairs and International Cooperation, and the International Institute for Democracy and Electoral Assistance (International IDEA). Botswana held the International IDEA council chairmanship in 2014. In September, Botswana failed in its bid to secure the presidency of the ICC as its candidate, Athaliah Molokomme, was not endorsed by African countries.

Botswana had suspended its participation in SADC *election observer missions* following the 2013 Zimbabwe elections, citing non-compliance with the SADC Principles and Guidelines Governing Democratic Elections. However, it later revised its decision and sent observers to the Malawi 20 May elections following a response from the SADC Secretariat regarding its concerns on 24 April.

Socioeconomic Developments

The GDP growth rate was projected at 5.2%, slightly lower than the 5.8% recorded in 2013, while the IMF put GDP growth at 4.4%. The country's *budget surplus* continued. The 2014/2015 budget estimated revenues at BP 50.183 bn, and expenditure at BP 48.857 bn, thus projecting an initial surplus of BP 1.326 bn, which was reduced to BP 280.83 m, after supplementary funding. Customs and excise contributed 31.8% to the budget (plus non-mineral revenues at 31.2% and mineral revenues 30.4%). Foreign reserves were estimated at BP 79.0 bn in December. Inflation was maintained within the Bank of Botswana's medium range of 3%-6%, recorded at 4.6% in August and 3.8% in December.

The *stable economic environment* was affirmed by outside agencies. Moody's Investors Service awarded a credit rating of A2. Although, the IMF Article IV consultation found Botswana's economic performance outstanding, it nevertheless called for a reduction in the wage bill and for the tax base to be widened. The performance of the country's state owned enterprises (SOEs) underscored by the IMF Article IV consultation, remained 'uneven', with some realising satisfactory performance and others recording a loss. Efforts were in motion to rationalise and privatise some of the SOEs, as well as to improve their governance. Botswana ranked 74th out of 144 countries in the 2014–15 Global Competitiveness Report of the World Economic Forum, which identified the continued reliance on minerals as a major challenge. The Report also cited the quality of education as an issue of concern.

There were no major shifts in the *challenges* presented by inequality, poverty, unemployment and HIV/AIDS. According to the 2014 African Economic Outlook Report, Botswana recorded a Gini coefficient of 0.61, suggesting a comparatively uneven distribution of wealth. The national unemployment and poverty rates remained unchanged at 17.8% and 20.7%, respectively, suggesting that the economy had failed to generate more jobs. The government sustained its social safety programmes, meant to cushion poor, underprivileged and vulnerable groups. For instance, the government was in November supporting 35,236 orphans and vulnerable children, 34,845 destitute persons, more than 99,000 old-age pensioners, and 1,161 home-based patients. The various *social programmes* cost BP 1.8 bn, according to government figures. A further 66,757 people were employed monthly in labour intensive works at a cost of BP 581 m over the financial year. In line with efforts to eradicate poverty, 20,636 beneficiaries had been identified in November to be supported through alternative packages. Meanwhile, the development of a Botswana Poverty Eradication Strategy was under way.

Efforts to combat and mitigate the scourge of *HIV/AIDS* were maintained. The fourth Aids Impact Survey (BIAS IV) of 2013 put the number of people who had been tested at 70% in 2013, up from 56% in 2008. The same survey recorded a national prevalence of infection of 18.5%, which was a slight increase from 17.6% in 2008. The incidence rate registered a decline of 1.4% in 2013, from 1.5% in 2008. According to government data, 115,000 males had undergone safe circumcision in November, out of a projected target of 385,000. The mother-to-child transmission programme had also been effective, with transmission put at 2% or below, and with a target of less than 1% in 2015. HIV/AIDS has negatively affected the country's HDI.

Lesotho

Roger Southall

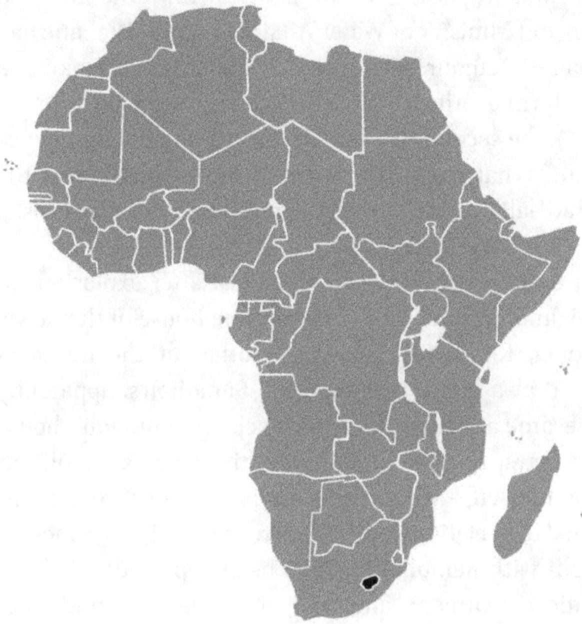

Disputes within the coalition government led by Prime Minister Tom Thabane of the All Basotho Congress (ABC) culminated in a no-confidence motion. Political uncertainty had already been amplified by an apparent attempt to assassinate the prime minister in January, and was laid bare by an open rift between the Lesotho Defence Force (LDF) and the Lesotho Mounted Police. Political deadlock led to attempted mediation by SADC and later by President Jacob Zuma of South Africa. However, after the prime minister announced the dismissal of the commander of the LDF in late August, the military attacked the police headquarters and surrounded Thabane's official residence, from where he had already escaped to South Africa. Within days, South Africa brokered an agreement that provided both for Thabane to return to Lesotho and for parliament to be re-opened in late September. Yet despite continuing SADC involvement, this deadline was not met, and parliament only resumed in late October. By this time, SADC had secured a deal whereby parliament would meet to complete pressing business, and then be dissolved in December pending new elections to be held early in 2015. Due to the political turmoil, both foreign affairs (apart from efforts by third parties to mediate in the domestic conflict) and socioeconomic developments offered little to report.

 | DOI 10.1163/9789004305052_047

Domestic Politics

By the end of 2013, Tom Thabane's ABC-led *coalition* with the Lesotho Congress of Democracy (LCD), led by Deputy Prime Minister Mothetjoa Metsing, and the Basotho National Party (BNP) was in peril. Powerful figures within the LCD had been charged with corruption and Minister of Water Affairs Timothy Thahane had been dismissed from the cabinet. Rumours were rife that the LCD was looking to forge an agreement with the former prime minister, Pakalitha Mosisili, who led the Democratic Congress (DC), the second largest party in parliament, and hence unseat the sitting government. What made the situation more volatile was the apparent alignment of General Tlali Kamoli, commander of the LDF, with Mosisili, while a new police leadership was backing Thabane.

Tensions between the army and the police became manifest after explosions in the capital, Maseru, on the night of 27 January. One was at the house of the newly appointed police commissioner, Khothatso Tsooana, another at the house of Liabiloe Ramoholi, and a third at a house neighbouring Ramoholi's, apparently bombed in error. It rapidly became apparent that the attack on Ramoholi's house had targeted Thabane, for the newspapers were soon reporting that Ramaholi was Thabane's lover, and Thabane himself – who was in the process of divorcing his estranged wife – freely admitted to a relationship of some ten years. As it happened, rather than spending the night with Ramoholi (as had been expected), Thabane was in South Africa for medical treatment, and escaped unscathed, unlike her 11-year-old son and two young relatives, who were injured. He offered to resign as prime minister if the revelation of his affair impacted negatively upon his government, but just four days later he was re-elected unopposed as leader of the ABC at the party's five-yearly national convention.

The *fall-out from the bombing* was dramatic. Tsooana, the new commissioner of police, propelled into his position by Thabane ahead of other more senior officers, had called in South African assistance to help with the investigation. As part of this, he issued a letter on 14 April requesting that eight LDF soldiers appear before the police. When the soldiers failed to appear and ignored an arrest warrant, the matter was elevated to the Security Committee, chaired by the deputy prime minister. Although both Kamoli for the LDF and Tsooana for the police appeared before the Committee, there was no progress, and an appeal was made for *SADC intervention*. A SADC delegation from the Organ on Politics, Defence and Security subsequently arrived on 21 May, only to disappear almost as rapidly to deal with the concurrent political crisis in Malawi. It only reappeared on 12 June, this time led by President Hifikepunye Pohamba of Namibia, chair of the Organ. In the meantime, Kamoli had called for an 'independent' investigation, objecting to the police conducting an enquiry into an attack in which the police commissioner had been a victim. Neither the Pohamba visit, nor a subsequent meeting between the prime minister, Kamoli and the police commissioner and his deputy at State House (Thabane's official residence) made any progress.

Political tensions had meanwhile continued to mount. On 18 March, the deputy speaker of parliament, who was in the chair, had refused a motion of no confidence in the government proposed by an opposition MP, which named Mosisili as an alternative prime minister. This led to the suspension of 14 MPs who had proceeded to disrupt the National Assembly's proceedings. Subsequently, Thabane had begun to strengthen his control of the state machinery. He had fired his political and economic adviser (who had chosen to form his own two-person political party) and replaced him with Lehlohonolo Tsehlana, a staunch ABC loyalist. Over the next three months, he also fired the government secretary (the most senior member of the civil service), replaced five principal secretaries (who presided over various government departments), and suspended the head of the Lesotho National Development Corporation and the head of the Correctional Service. These changes received the open condemnation of the deputy prime minister, who claimed at a Workers' Day rally on 1 May that senior civil servants who had been members of the DC had been replaced by members of the other ruling parties.

Continuing rumours of a realignment of the LDC with the opposition DC had then been given substance by an ABC constituency MP crossing the floor to the DC when parliament met on 12 May after an Easter adjournment of six weeks. Another ABC MP, a former minister recently dismissed from the cabinet, also resigned, and declared he would sit in parliament as an independent. Thabane's coalition had taken office holding the barest of majorities (61 seats in a 120 seat parliament), so these two departures signified its new status as a *minority government*, although the fluidity of the political situation was underlined by manifest disagreement within the LCD about Metsing's developing rapprochement with the DC. However, Thabane was loathe to risk a no confidence debate and, on 10 June, notice was given that parliament would be prorogued until 27 February 2015.

An unusual initiative to resolve the political deadlock was taken by the New Zealand government acting in association with the Commonwealth Secretariat. New Zealand has a Mixed Member Proportional (MMP) electoral system similar to Lesotho's, and from 30 June to 4 July hosted a visit by 25 Lesotho MPs, who were accompanied by senior civil servants and representatives of civil society. The delegation included Deputy Prime Minister Metsing but, significantly, Thabane was missing. Subsequently, Commonwealth expert adviser, Dr Rajen Prasad, who was also a New Zealand MP and who had accompanied the delegation, prepared a report that suggested how Lesotho's political parties could improve their working relationships. When published, the report made recommendations about how Lesotho's civil service might be depoliticised, how parliament might be reformed to adjust to an MMP environment, how parties might adjust to coalition politics and what procedures should be followed in the formation of governments after an election. However, the *Prasad report* was overtaken by events. After a visit to Maseru by President Jacob Zuma on 29 July, when he met with leaders of the parties separately, the coalition leaders flew to Windhoek (Namibia) the next day to meet with Pohamba. There, on 31 July, Thabane agreed to lift the prorogation of parliament within 14 days, and in return, Metsing agreed to cancel a recently signed agreement with the DC. He then proceeded to renounce the LCD's alliance with the DC on 14 August. Even so, the political dust was allowed no opportunity to settle.

On 29 August, Thabane announced the dismissal of Kamoli and his replacement as commander of the LDF by Brigadier Maaparankoe Mahoe. The following day, he was warned that his residence was likely to be attacked, and he fled across the border to Ladybrand. At 3 am on 31 August, soldiers from the LDF surrounded his official residence. The move by the army was widely viewed as a *coup*, with Radio Lesotho reporting that the police headquarters had also been surrounded, the police disarmed (one officer being killed and nine seriously injured), and Tsooana and other senior officers had also fled to South Africa. However, in an interview with the BBC, Thabane – who it emerged had written to Zuma asking for military support on 27 August – reported that he would be returning to Lesotho shortly.

Disturbed by developments, Zuma immediately summoned the coalition leaders and others to Pretoria, where they signed a joint declaration under a SADC letterhead committing them to restoring normalcy and to a reopening of parliament on 19 September. Subsequently, *Thabane returned* on 3 September, accompanied by a well-armed contingent of the South African Police Service (SAPS), who rapidly overcame the LDF soldiers guarding State House. SADC also despatched delegates to monitor the situation (although Thabane had wanted rather more). Meanwhile, Mahao (now Lieutenant General), who had also fled to South Africa, returned to the country under SAPS protection. He was backed up by army chiefs from Namibia, South Africa and Zimbabwe, whose mission was to urge Kamoli to hand over command. However, Kamoli refused to appear before them to accept his dismissal, and rumours spread that he had decamped to the mountains with an armed force (although other stories suggested that he was seeking medical assistance for a diabetic condition). What was clear was that Mahao lacked the support of the officer corps, and that Kamoli enjoyed the backing of Special Forces, Military Intelligence and the army hierarchy.

The military uncertainty prompted the ABC and BNP leaders to write to Zuma to say that they had no intention of opening parliament until certain security conditions were met. This prompted South Africa's Deputy President Cyril Ramaphosa to cancel a visit on 12 September for the announcement of the date of re-opening. Three days later, on 15 September, a *SADC* summit in Pretoria, chaired by President Mugabe of Zimbabwe as chairman of the regional bloc, discussed developments with Thabane and Metsing. SADC reportedly recommended that the corruption charges against Metsing be dropped, that parliament be re-opened and that

Metsing agree not to press forward with the vote of no-confidence. Instead, parliament should agree to early elections, while it was also apparently agreed that SADC military chiefs should visit Maseru to persuade Kamoli to resign. A subsequent communiqué indicated that the leaders of the coalition government had agreed to early elections, and mandated Ramaphosa to act as facilitator of a return to political and security stability. Ramaphosa followed up with visits to Maseru on 18 and 23 September, opened a SADC Observer Mission Secretariat, and recommended that all parties to the dispute, including Generals Kamoli and Mahao and Police Commissioner Tsooana, be re-assigned to further duties. Nonetheless, the impasse continued, and parliament remained prorogued.

Eventually, Ramaphosa pressured the leaders of the nine main political parties to sign a *Maseru Facilitation Declaration*, which committed them to a re-opening of parliament on 17 October and its dissolution in December pending elections to be held by the end of February 2015. When parliament did meet on the appointed date, political leaders received an unaccustomed tongue-lashing from King Letsie III, who berated them for their selfishness. Although the proceedings of the parliamentary sitting were not untroubled, parliament was dissolved on 5 December, with the early election being set for 28 February 2015. However, the sensible recommendations of the Prasad report had been ignored.

Foreign Affairs

Lesotho's foreign affairs were almost completely subsumed under the political crisis, which merely underlined that, while in theory the country enjoyed political sovereignty, in practice its independence was circumscribed by its dependence upon South Africa and the supervision of its affairs by SADC. Consequently, the only diplomatic development of note was the closing of the *Irish Embassy*, and its replacement by a consulate. The embassy had only been open since 2006, by which time the large majority of countries had withdrawn their representation to Pretoria. Ireland had become, for Lesotho, a major aid donor, but now the outgoing ambassador indicated that the embassy had fallen victim to Ireland's own economic troubles as a result of the global recession.

Socioeconomic Developments

The *budget* was presented in parliament by Minister of Finance Dr Leketekete Victor Ketso on 27 February. It made the usual noises about the promotion of development, employment generation, and infrastructural expansion and so on, but in essence was business as usual, although the minister did mention the need to mobilise additional financial resources as far as possible in order to reduce dependence on SACU, given South African moves to renegotiate the terms of the SACU treaty. The overall budget was proposed as M (maluti) 15.5 bn (compared with M 14.6 bn in 2013/14), made up of M 10.5 bn recurrent expenditure and M 5.0 bn capital expenditure. A *National Strategic Development Plan* for 2012/13–2016/17 was published in September, setting out a long-term vision. However, its suggestion that Lesotho would become a stable and prosperous democracy by 2020 was clearly at odds with the on-going political turmoil.

Madagascar

Richard R. Marcus

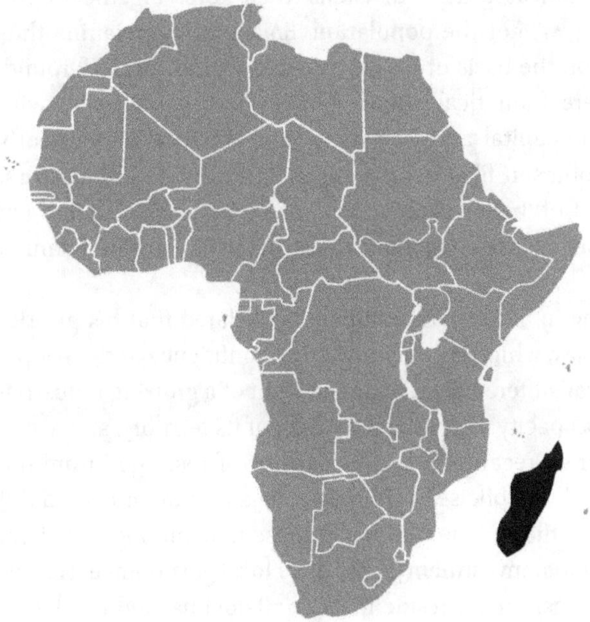

On 25 January, Hery Martial Rajaonarimampianina was sworn in as Madagascar's new president. This followed the first election since the overthrow of President Marc Ravalomanana in March 2009 and was a landmark towards normalisation after the country's isolation from the international community. The private sector had also suffered from a lack of diversified foreign investment. Domestically, established political parties were on the wane and civil society faced near-exclusion from the body politic. Poverty had soared by an estimated 8%, making the country the fourth-poorest in the world according to UN estimates. The election was broadly viewed at home and abroad as a 'trigger' and a return to constitutionality. The international community returned in force, foreign aid was ramped up, new domestic political space expanded, and the private sector showed signs of growth. Yet the return to electoral legitimacy did not prove to be a panacea. The political fragmentation and associated networks of influence that created the 2009–13 crisis were not resolved and the country remained at risk of a new crisis.

 | DOI 10.1163/9789004305052_048

Domestic Politics

Hery Rajaonarimampianina came second in the October 2013 first round of *presidential elections* with 16% of the vote. With Jean-Louis Robinson's 21.2%, the run-off election of December 2013 indicated deep divisions, their votes together representing the support of only 37.1% of the population. Rajaonarimampianina thus could not claim a mandate on the basis of his 53.5% victory in the second round. Moreover, the candidates were dramatically divided by region, with Robinson winning the districts around the capital and Rajaonarimampianina winning nearly all of the coastal regions. Robinson filed nearly 300 challenges with the electoral court, accusing his opponent of 'ballot stuffing' and claiming 'massive fraud'. On 17 January, the court dismissed all the challenges, declaring Rajaonarimampianina the undisputed winner.

On the eve of his swearing-in, Rajaonarimampianina declared that his priority was "to establish the rule of law, which is going to restore confidence in the people and their leaders". Madagascar suffered from poor oversight of a growing industrial mining sector, a diminished capacity to govern the whole of its territory, and a very internationally-recognised crisis regarding the illicit felling of rosewood from the country's fragile and universally publicised rainforests. Rajaonarimampianina did not commit to prosecuting traffickers, he did not propose new mining oversight, and he did not seek new regional investment to enhance local governance. He was supported by the outgoing transitional president, Andry Rajoelina, and needed to show that he was not a puppet of the former regime, staking new ground, while not destabilising his already *fragile political coalition*.

Political parties were inherently weak. Hery Rajaonarimampianina formed his own political party 'Hery Vaovao' during his presidential candidacy. It was not formed in time for the concurrent *legislative elections*, so it won no seats. 'Miaraka amin'ny Prézidà Rajoelina' (MAPAR), the party of the outgoing president, dominated those elections, taking 51 of 147 seats with the 'Mouvance Ravalomanana' of previous president (2002–9) Marc Ravalomanana taking 18 seats. Thirty-four seats (23%) were won by 'independents'. This meant that, in a semi-presidential system where the president appoints the prime minister, it was possible to appoint neither a prime minister from the president's party nor a prime minister who could play a reconciling role through cohabitation. There was no institutional way for Rajaonarimampianina to consolidate power in the executive.

A *lack of institutional consolidation* was the norm in Malagasy politics. What was not the norm was that Rajaonarimampianina came in without a personal political network on which he could rely. The Constitution ascribed an unusually large amount of power to the executive and Malagasy presidents routinely exerted more power than the Constitution afforded. The inability of the president to control the executive meant inherent *instability*. Rajaonarimampianina appointed

Prime Minister Roger Kolo on 16 April. This was met with extreme disapproval by former president Rajoelina, who openly accused the president of failing to appreciate his support and not-so-secretly hoped to be appointed prime minister himself in what many feared might become a power-shift in the executive akin to Vladamir Putin's accession to power in Russia. Other would-be prime ministers had equally negative reactions. In a further distancing move, days after taking power, Rajaonarimampianina dissolved Rajoelina's Special Intervention Force (FIS), which acted outside of the military chain of command and was accused of atrocities. However, its dissolution, with the firing of its leader, Colonel Lylson Rene Roland, was a sign that Rajaonarimampianina sought to be his own man. The choice of Kolo reflected the president's determination to appoint someone weaker than himself. Like Rajaonarimampianina, Kolo was largely a technocrat but, while the president was an economist and accountant and had served as minister of finance in the previous administration, Kolo had no previous political experience.

By the time Rajaonarimampianina appointed his 31-member *cabinet*, it was clear that he was aiming neither to share power nor to inherit the political network of another leader. His prime minister and many of his cabinet members were almost immediately on the outside looking in. He began forming his own *political network* from existing confidants in one of five places: 1) Air Madagascar, where he had once served as chairman, 2) the team he had worked with as minister of finance, 3) the Rotary Club, where he had served in various capacities alongside Madagascar's private sector elite, 4) Auditeurs Associés – CGA, the accountancy firm he had helped form in 1995, and 5) alumni of the Centre d'Études Diplomatiques et Stratégiques (CEDS) in Paris. Rivo Rakotovao, who had been his technical advisor when he was minister of finance, was made minister of state in charge of infrastructure and development. He was also an executive of the influential company, Silac, which amongst other things had become a pivotal force in the distribution of rice, the food staple, under Rajoelina. James Andrianalisoa, from Rajaonarimampianina's Air Madagascar days, was made head of Civil Aviation of Madagascar (ACM). One of Rajaonarimampianina's confidants, Solofo Rasoarahona, was a highly influential CEDS graduate and former partner in Auditeurs Associés. He was central in the appointment of CEDS alumni. The extreme blending of private sector and civil society networks to build a political coterie in Madagascar was the political invention of former president Ravalomanana. Rajoelina had succeeded him, using the same strategy and within the first months of the Rajaonarimampianina presidency it became apparent he would attempt the same.

By mid-year, it became clear that Rajaonarimampianina was having difficulty in creating his own political network. Those closest to him began fighting each other. Prime Minister Kolo tried to act forcefully only to find himself relegated to the margins of power, frequently not even invited to key policy discussions. Key parastatals struggling to gain post-conflict prestige and footing found themselves further in arrears with creditors. In September, Rajaonarimampianina asked Kolo for a *cabinet reshuffle*. The heart of the issue was less the competition from a weak cabinet than that the weak cabinet could not successfully fulfil its task of demonstrating economic and social progress at a time when the Malagasy people had set the clock ticking for results from the president. If the population were to give up, there would the threat not of new elections but of yet another charismatic leader taking to the streets and using segments of the military to overthrow the president.

Things went from bad to worse for the president with the *return of Ravalomanana*, who had been elected president in 2002 and 2006. His overthrow in March 2009 had been met with significant indignation by the international community and a strong but minority segment of the Malagasy population. The ousted president had fled to South Africa and it was from there that he had participated in the peace talks. While in self-imposed exile, Ravalomanana had been convicted in abstentia for the shooting of unarmed civilians by the presidential guard on 7 February 2009. The SADC-led Roadmap that had led to new elections provided for Ravalomanana's right to return but was vague on whether that meant an amnesty. He had attempted to return several times during the conflict, creating fears of instability. When he did finally did return on 13 October, he did so without the involvement or support of the sitting government. He appeared in his home neighbourhood of Antananarivo, Faravohitra, and immediately made a speech declaring that, despite the election result, he did not accept Rajaonarimampianina as president. This put the latter in a quandary. He could risk allowing a de facto amnesty and Ravalomanana gathering a following of rejectionists, or he could arrest him and risk making him a martyr. He chose instead to detain him indefinitely, declaring that he was in protective custody, safe from potential threats. At year's end Ravalomanana was still under house arrest, with all the comforts of his regal Antananarivo home and limited rights to receive visitors.

The National Assembly had begun to realign. Though MPs were barred from switching parties, many already had and, combined with independents, it looked as if 'Hery Vaovao' would soon dominate the legislature, despite not having put forward any candidates in the election. The prime minister's days were clearly numbered and the *highly fractured cabinet* was likely to be dissolved. Rajaonarimampianina had lost control of the national reconciliation movement and instead a coalition of unlikely opposition leaders had united in a provocative stance. Private sector forces rallied behind the opposition leaders and even civil society forces hitherto supportive of the president, such as the Catholic Church, looked luke-warm. Throughout December, there were rumours that foreign funds were circulating to certain constituencies of the highly fractured *military* to buy support should the opportunity to unseat the president arise. While the president's ouster was not imminent, a countdown was clearly under way on Rajaonarimampianina's ability to successfully form a support base that included the public, private, and civil society sectors.

Foreign Affairs

The *international community* was rapid and universal in accepting the presidential elections. There was an almost audible sigh of collective relief when the electoral court accepted the results on 17 January. This was significant because Rajaonarimampianina had not been universally supported or trusted during the election cycle. He had been perceived as too close to Transitional President Rajoelina and, as such, potentially influenced by him or other members of the illegitimate regime. The USA in particular was transparent in its support for Jean-Luis Robinson over Rajaonarimampianina. In the end, the desire to see a return to electoral democracy and to grasp a handle for re-engagement trumped such concerns. Given the role of the international community in supporting the roadmap to elections, and the elections themselves, any sign of rejection by even factions of the international community could well have triggered a new crisis.

A procession of international representatives began new conversations with the Malagasy government. The head of the SADC-led Election Observer Mission, Foreign Minister Netumbo Nandi-Ndaitwah of Namibia, announced that the voting process was "peaceful and in accordance with the provisions of the Electoral Act". On the diplomatic front, on 17 January French Foreign Minister Laurent Fabius was one of the first to announce his support for Rajaonarimampianina's government. The *SADC* leadership was equally enthusiastic, understandably indulging in some self-congratulation for leading Madagascar out of its morass. In January, Namibia dispatched Ambassador Tuliameni Kalomoh to head the SADC liaison office in Antananarivo. South Africa sent Deputy Minister of International Relations and Cooperation Marius Fransman to attend Rajaonarimampianina's inauguration and begin a new dialogue – this despite South Africa's role in hosting exiled former president Ravalomanana and long-term support for his return. On 5 February, SADC officially lifted Madagascar's suspension. Rajaonarimampianina attended his first official SADC meeting as head of state on 18 August in Harare (Zimbabwe), where he sought reconciliation with the African community. The *AU* and key African countries, including Tanzania and Zimbabwe, expressed support for the new government.

The *USA* was quick to recognise the elections and Rajaonarimampianina's victory but slower than its counterparts in finding a path towards engagement. Its position was tenuous, given its close relationship to the ousted Ravalomanana, the stronger position it had taken against the transitional government, and its vocal questioning of Rajaonarimampianina during the electoral process. In August, it sent a new chargé d'affaires and approved a new ambassador, Robert Yamate, set to arrive in January 2015. USAID spent much of the year planning its approach and mechanism for re-engagement.

France was the only foreign donor that had continued regular operations through the transition period. The rest of the donor community rapidly sought re-engagement. The largest donors, the *World Bank* and the *EU*, committed themselves in January to fully restoring aid programmes. They warned, however, that ramping up funding would take more than a year. The World Bank saw an operational change with the removal of Madagascar as a directorial hub for the region and the installation of Country Manager Coralie Gevers in February. Despite this lowering of mission leadership status, World Bank Vice President for the Africa Region Makhtar Diop visited Madagascar and met with Rajaonarimampianina in May. This was the first visit to Madagascar by a World Bank vice president and was widely viewed as a strong endorsement for new programming.

China continued to show interest in Madagascar but it was predominantly confined to extractive resources – mining and timber. The engagement of the two large, high-profile mining companies, Canadian Sherritt and British Rio Tinto, was significantly different from Chinese operations. In contrast, the Chinese were predominantly prospecting and for the time being had started small-scale operations. The hope by many in the international community, particularly the World Bank, EU and USA, was that the new legitimacy of the government would translate into new transparency in the extractive industries.

Socioeconomic Developments

Madagascar is one of the world's poorest countries and, after years of crisis, both the economy and the population remained highly vulnerable to endogenous and exogenous shocks. From 2013 to 2014, the country slipped in UNDP rankings from 151st to 155th out of 186 countries. The World Bank's World Data Indicator on *poverty* found that 87.7% of the population were living on $ 1.25 per day and 95% were on under $ 2 per day. There was a marked slide during the 2009–13 period, disproportionately impacting the majority rural population. As of 2014, UNDP ranked Madagascar the fourth-poorest country in the world. Life expectancy at birth was 64 years and rising, but this masked a relatively high under-five mortality rate. With a Gross National Income of $ 1,333, Madagascar had one of the lowest fiscal yields in the world. UNICEF reported that moderate to severe stunting took place in 49% of the population and that 37% of the population were underweight. Only 35% of the rural population had access to drinking water, compared with 78% of the urban population. Only 14% of the total population had access to sanitation. While HIV/AIDS rates were low (0.4%), malaria rates were high and Madagascar saw an uptick in the number of cases of Bubonic Plague.

Macroeconomic performance was mixed. GDP growth surged to (a provisional) 3.7%. The tourism sector continued to be slow, despite the potentially stabilising effect of there being a newly elected government, and the agricultural sector struggled in the face of shifting global market prices and natural disasters including cyclones and locusts. Madagascar ended the year with a 5.8% inflation rate, but certain key goods, including the food staple rice, continued to see marked increases in price. While most of the world saw the price of petrol drop, in Madagascar it rose owing to a greater domestic float. Thus, while aggregate inflation was in check, the average citizen felt the impact of increased food and transport costs. At the heart of economic development woes had been the ongoing disjuncture between a highly entrepreneurial society with a strong low-level *private sector* and a narrow production sector with high foreign product dependency and an export sector confined to low-yield unprocessed goods. Madagascar qualified again for *AGOA* preferential trade status as from 26 June, opening the potential reinstatement of up to 150,000 direct and indirect jobs. The country slid further down the World Bank Ease of Doing Business rankings to 163rd, compared with 142nd of 185 countries in 2012. The greatest declines came in starting a business, protecting minority investors, paying taxes, and construction permits. This reflected poorly on the expansion of private sector investment, particularly the diversification of foreign investment.

Agriculture continued to be the largest sector, but *mining* was growing rapidly. Artisanal mining, long established, made up less than 2% of GDP but accounted for as many as 100,000 formal jobs and a significantly higher number of informal ones. The industrial mining sector was new. There were two large operators, QIT (majority owned by the UK-based Rio Tinto) and Ambatovy (majority owned by the Canada-based Sherritt). QIT production of ilmenite had begun in 2009, with production covering about 2,000 ha in 2014; it would soon ramp up to 750,000 tons. Investment in the southern Anosy region was over $ 940 m. Forty-one mine workers died in operations during the year, with fingers pointed strongly towards company negligence with regard to workplace security. The Ambatovy site began production of nickel and cobalt in January and in September the company announced that proven and probable reserves exceeded 190 m tonnes.

The rise in industrial mining, an oil sands project by Total, new investment from Exxon, and other *extractive industries* had great potential to raise GDP, but was already a nascent destabilising force, both politically and economically. There was significant consternation in the sector about both the mining law and the oil law and, with considerable input from Exxon and the World Bank, the oil law was opened up for renegotiation during the year with a new law expected soon. The mining law was also likely to see changes. The law provided for royalties at the point of extraction, which led to unequal development at very localised levels. New interpretations of the law incorporated a larger share for those of the 22 regions that had extractive industries and more sharing of proceeds between communes (local government) close to points of extraction. On 5 June, the Extractive Industries Transparency Initiative, the leading international organisation monitoring mining governance, reinstated Madagascar after a five-year suspension. The new government nonetheless struggled to govern a sector that offered such apparent and multitudinous opportunities for extracting hard-to-trace funds. This was part of a larger struggle confronting Madagascar in the face of diminished governing capacity. Other sectors such as the illicit extraction of rosewood and, increasingly, the political economy of the beef industry presented similar challenges. Even social sectors such as health and education were not immune.

New *donor commitments* post-election were significant. The World Bank invested $ 173 m. In 2007, the EU had committed a € 577 m ($ 646 m) portfolio, only to see development projects frozen under Article 96 of the Cotonou Agreement in 2010. On 19 May, the EU lifted its ban, signing an 11th EDF, with new funds expected to flow in 2015. For their parts, France continued aid to Madagascar throughout the crisis and the USA committed to a new opening with a nearly $ 64 m USAID budget. The new flow of foreign aid was significant in a country in which 70% of the national budget had been derived from aid in 2008 and then abruptly cut. It was considered critical to Rajaonarimampianina's political survival to secure new opportunities for investment in the ailing infrastructure, an opening for improved governance mechanisms, and new investment opportunities leading to economic gains and jobs that could benefit communities. The aid was structured differently from before the political crisis, with a significantly higher focus not just on the structural issues of supply-side governance but also on the local and human challenges of demand-side governance. The fundamental belief was that improved livelihoods in Madagascar could not emerge without improved human engagement in social, political and economic decision-making at the local level. It was a country with new opportunities but struggling on a precipice, so each level needed to forge new horizontal and vertical bonds for the advancement – and the very survival – of the country.

Malawi

Tiyesere Mercy Chikapa-Jamali and Lewis B. Dzimbiri

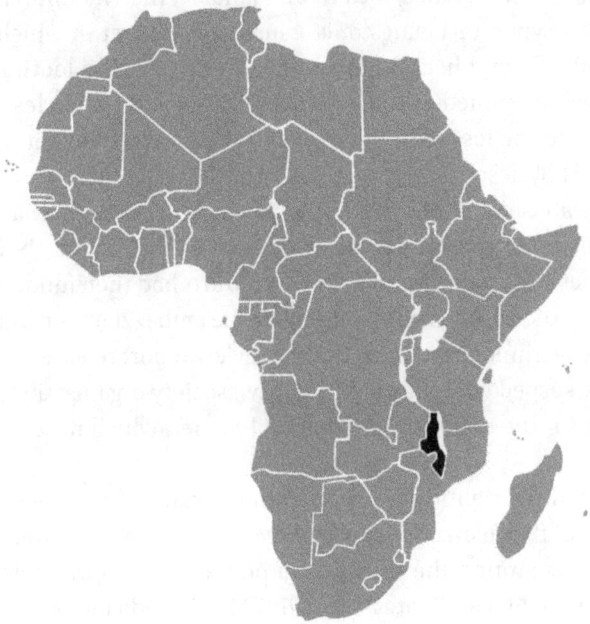

Malawi's tripartite election was the first of its kind in the country's history. The incumbent president, Mrs Joyce Banda, lost to Peter Mutharika, the Democratic Progressive Party (DPP) presidential candidate and brother of the late former president Bingu wa Mutharika. The suspension of aid and loans by donors continued in response to massive looting of public funds popularly known as Cashgate. This forced the government to adopt a zero-aid budget, which was to be largely financed by locally generated revenue with limited reliance on donor funds. The Malawi kwacha (MK) fell drastically in value during the second part of the year after it was floated on the market, resulting in a rise in commodity prices and the cost of living, while salaries remained static. This triggered various kinds of industrial action in the public and private sectors and by NGOs, pressuring employers, including the government, to raise salaries.

 | DOI 10.1163/9789004305052_049

Domestic Politics

Massive *plundering of public funds* within government, which was exposed in 2013, continued to be a major local concern, attracting criticism from various players both locally and internationally. For instance, locally, on 1 January, the The Church of Central Africa Presbyterian Synod of Livingstonia issued a statement in which it criticised President Joyce Banda and her administration for the massive looting of public money. It strongly condemned the government's failure to come clean on the circumstances leading to the loss of billions in taxpayers' money at central government offices, 'Capital Hill', describing it as an outrage to the country. Since the revelation of the massive abuse of public funds, the Banda administration had pledged to expose the names of all those involved, regardless of their status, but government had failed to meet this pledge in time. The UK's DFID had then funded a *forensic audit* by Baker Tilly, a UK-based firm, to investigate the embezzlement and mismanagement of Malawi government finances, but the review report released in February did not name those suspected of involvement. Civil society organisations criticised the forensic report for the deliberate omission of names, which raised a lot of suspicions.

Internal conflicts dominated the political arena in both the ruling and opposition parties. At the beginning of the year, *conflicts within the People's Party* (*PP*) were noted, especially since this was around the time of the primary elections. There were disagreements between the PP candidates, Cornelius Mwalwanda and Frank Mwenefumbo in Karonga Central constituency over election fraud and they prepared for another contest as the party announced a re-run of the primaries in the area. The dispute started when Mwenefumbo described the first primary elections, held on 21 December 2013, in their constituency, which were won by Mwalwanda, as unfair, citing a number of flaws ranging from allegations that Mwalwanda had flouted the party code of conduct to using chiefs to intimidate his supporters. Intense political campaigns were already underway in the constituency and, furthermore, some political heavyweights resigned from the PP in mid-January: PP vice president for the South Sidik Mia, PP vice president for the Central Region Dr Cassim Chilumpha, First Deputy Speaker of Parliament Jones Chingola, and Deputy Transport Minister Sam Ganda. Reasons cited included disputes over primary elections and undemocratic tendencies, but the resignations were viewed by ruling officials, including Banda, as the result of frustrations at being sidelined or not being given certain positions in the party. During February, Banda dropped the *State Vice President* Khumbo Kachali as her running mate and opted instead for a youthful minister, Sosten Gwengwe, arguing that the electorate preferred a young candidate and that Kachali's time had run out as she had planned to serve Malawi with him for only two years. The result was that the ruling party's first vice president had been conspicuously absent from major PP events, including the official launch of the party's campaign in April in the run up to the May elections.

On 16 January, Peter Mutharika's nomination as the *presidential candidate* of the opposition Democratic Progressive Party (DPP) was challenged on the grounds that he held a US Green Card. The constitution of Malawi bars the nomination of anyone who has allegiance to another country from participating in elections. Various commentators, legal experts and academics put forward their arguments and Mutharika was forced to give up his Green Card. Incidentally, the Malawi Electoral Commission, after consulting the attorney general, a senior Counsel with 20 years' experience and the Commission lawyers, announced that the holder of a Green Card, such as Mutharika, could not and should not thereby be barred from running. On 22 January, the Electoral Commission announced that at least 15 political parties (out of the 54 registered) had so far collected nomination forms to contest for presidency in the 20 May elections, more than in the 2009 general elections, when there were seven candidates. Of these, 12 parties eventually fielded a candidate.

On 21 February, the Malawi Human Rights Commission condemned Banda's administration for lack of transparency over the *sale of the presidential jet*, and other pressing national issues. The question of the whereabouts of the funds raised from the sale of the jet came barely days after 'The Nation' reported the disappearance of funds from government coffers. The opposition DPP followed suit in March by demanding an immediate explanation from the government on the sale of the jet, following revelations that it was actually exchanged for some second-hand military-class boats.

The conduct of *presidential, parliamentary and local elections* on 20 May, popularly known as 'tripartite elections', was the first of its kind: Malawians voted for their local government representatives, members of Parliament and the president at a single election. The electoral campaign started officially on 20 March, peacefully and unrestricted, as evidenced by the opposition parties' ability to hold their rallies freely. The Malawi Electoral Commission launched the election campaign period in Blantyre, calling on political parties and candidates to run a clean campaign. The Commission's chairperson, Maxon Mbendera, called on the parties to put forward to Malawians their capabilities for leading the country. The *presidential election* was the closest in Malawi's history. Of the total 5,285,278 votes cast, Mutharika received 1,904,399 (36.4%). Another opposition candidate, Lazarus Chakwera of the Malawi Congress Party (MCP), received 1,455,880 votes (27.8%), while Banda trailed in third place with 1,056,236 (20.2%). Atupele Muluzi of the United Democratic Front came fourth with 717,224 votes (13.7%) and the other presidential candidates shared the remaining less than 2% of votes. Despite efforts by the Gender Coordination Network to increase the number of women in Parliament, women won only 30 (16%) of the parliamentary seats, a significant decline from the 2009 elections which saw 22%

of seats taken by women. After close to ten days of difficulties faced by the Malawi Electoral Commission in tallying votes, various court injunctions and related stay orders and counter injunctions, and even an attempt by Banda to nullify the elections as fraudulent, opposition candidate Professor Arthur Peter Mutharika of the DPP was eventually declared the winner. Although there were numerous minor instances of disorder, missing polling materials and even violence in individual constituencies, election day itself was by and large peaceful and procedures were adhered to. In a few polling stations, voting had to be postponed to a later date either because ballot papers were missing or because candidates' names were misspelled, among other reasons. Delayed result announcements and somewhat chaotic vote-recounting procedures led to confusion in a number of constituencies, with allegations of manipulation, and protests that in some areas turned violent and resulted in deaths and injuries. Banda quickly accepted the outcome, although she continued to describe the election as fraudulent. Mutharika was sworn in as President of Malawi on 31 May, but Banda boycotted his inauguration ceremony on 2 June. During the inauguration, Mutharika talked tough on graft and vowed to crack down on corruption in government affairs.

In June, representatives of civil society organisations expressed mixed reactions to Mutharika's piecemeal assembly of ministers. He had appointed a *lean cabinet* of 18 ministries and deputies in order to improve efficiency and effectiveness in the civil service. As a result, over 40 principal secretaries faced dismissal in June. Much attention focused on the election of the *speaker of the National Assembly* on 16 June. Parliament elected MCP vice president Richard Msowoya as the seventh speaker of the Malawi Parliament in the multi-party era. Former first deputy speaker Mcheka Chilenje took up unopposed the position of first deputy speaker and Clement Chiwaya was elected second deputy speaker. MCP MP for Dedza North West, Alekeni Menyani, proposed on 26 June that Parliament should discuss the possibility of having a federal system of government in Malawi, but this was received with mixed reactions.

Huge attention was also given to *Mutharika's marriage* to his long-term sweetheart Gertrude Maseko on 21 June. The wedding took place at Casa Blanca at Ndata farm in Thyolo where, despite the chilly weather, thousands of people celebrated with the first couple.

Malawi celebrated 50 years of independence on 6 July. During the celebrations, among other things, Mutharika urged Malawians to remain united and work hard towards developing the nation. On 22 July, government rejected a proposal by the Malawi Electoral Commission that the cabinet should not be involved in the country's *electoral law reforms*. Electoral Commission chairperson Maxon Mbendera suggested that proposals for amendments to electoral laws should instead be dealt with directly by Parliament rather than undergoing a process of vetting by cabinet.

The year also saw some dramatic *diplomatic shake-ups*. Mutharika appointed nine new ambassadors on 26 October, replacing some of the ambassadors appointed under the previous government. The appointments included vocal human rights activist and former chairperson of the Council for Non-Governmental Organizations in Malawi, Voice Mhone, DPP party vice president Yunus Mussa and Ted Kalebe.

Foreign Affairs

The country's domestic affairs, especially the massive looting of public funds, impacted negatively on international *economic relations*. In January, the former British prime minister Tony Blair and his Africa Governance Initiative team pulled out as official consultants/advisors to President Banda on how to run the country. Although Blair insisted that the decision had nothing to do with the corruption scandal that engulfed the country, the withdrawal was nevertheless linked to it by various commentators. In a related development, on 20 January, US Ambassador Jeanine Jackson called on Malawians to hold government accountable for investigating and prosecuting people alleged to have taken part in embezzling taxpayers' money. In addition, on 25 March, Malawi's major donors under the Common Approach to Budget Support deplored the embezzlement of resources in front-line ministries, which they said had negatively affected social spending. Neither did the donors commit to resuming budget support for the 2013/14 national budget and they withheld about $ 50 m. In mid-January, the IMF decided to unlock $ 20 m through the ECF, but this decision was reversed towards the beginning of April, when the IMF announced that it would hold on to funding until after the results of the 20 May elections were declared. In August, the Global Fund to Fight Aids, Tuberculosis and Malaria asked Minister of Finance Goodall Gondwe for repayment of $ 937,905 (about MK 394 m) following abuse of funds in 2010.

On 12 June, the *IMF* advised Mutharika's newly elected government to ensure that fiscal plans were based on realistic estimates and that proposed expenditure should be within available resources so as to avoid accumulation of arrears or excessive amounts of domestic debt, if Malawi was to achieve macroeconomic stability. The IMF also urged the Mutharika administration to maintain some unpopular reforms started by former president Banda. In a related development, on 14 June, donors warned the DPP government that the mess of the Cashgate scandal had to be cleared up if aid was to resume. In July, the IMF also urged the government to tread carefully with regard to future borrowing as the national budget had very little room for further debt. On 16 July, the *World Bank* approved a project worth MK 1.8 bn that was intended to equip the country's young people with skills needed for jobs in high priority sectors. On 2 September, after Vice President Saulos Chilima had inspected *Israel*'s Mekorot National Carrier plants in Galilee, he invited water experts from Israel to visit Malawi to appreciate investment opportunities in water and irrigation ventures.

Malawi was one of the seven countries that have recently come under the scrutiny of the *UN Human Rights Committee* (UNHRC). For the first time since Malawi became party to the International Covenant on Civil and Political Rights in 1993, it presented a human rights report to the committee for examination. The UN human rights experts faulted Malawi on various human rights related issues, arguing that it was failing to protect civil and political rights. Examples included the failure to bring to book the murderers of Robert Chasowa, and incidences of extra-judicial killings, concerning which the experts argued that the response by the judiciary to the use of lethal force by the police was limited and needed to be enhanced. The UNHRC also referred to child abuse and recommended that laws be amended in order to deal with the problem effectively. In addition, the Committee was critical of Malawi's stance on homosexuality and also questioned, among other issues, the independence of constitutional bodies and poor record-keeping by state organs.

The *border dispute* with Tanzania *over Lake Malawi* continued during the year. On 25 March, Malawi and Tanzania rebuffed a proposal by the Forum of Former African Heads of State that resources from Lake Malawi should be shared as a first step towards resolving the dispute. The rigid positions adopted by both countries meant that the mediation talks ended in deadlock. The mediation team was headed by former president of Mozambique Joaquim Chissano. The month of June, saw the *deportation* of over 200 Malawians from South Africa in two days because they lacked the official documents that would render their stay legal.

Mutharika delegated former president Bakili Muluzi to represent him in Lusaka at *Zambia*'s celebrations for the 50th anniversary of its independence on 24 October. On 11 November, Vice President Saulos Chilima represented Mutharika at the funeral of Zambian President Michael Sata.

Socioeconomic Developments

The cost of *public utilities and services* continued to rise during the year. Monthly expenditure on basic needs in the cities of Lilongwe, Blantyre, Zomba and Mzuzu increased by 2.6% to MK 208,112 for a six-person household. On 5 February, the Malawi Energy Regulatory Authority raised the price of petrol by 10.3% from MK 760 per litre to K 839, diesel from MK 770 to MK 853.40 (10.8%) and paraffin from MK 638.90 to MK 719.90. The increase in fuel prices at the pump was bemoaned by both motorists and minibus commuters in an economy where the disposable income for an average Malawian was very low. In February, the Agricultural

Development and Marketing Corporation (ADMARC) lowered the prices of the country's staple food, maize, so that it was then selling at MK 5,000 per 50-kg bag, even before the start of the new harvest season. The low price was attributed to the plentiful supply of maize in ADMARC depots and many markets within the country. The year saw *shortages of hospital drugs*. From as early as January, most major district hospitals in Malawi ran out of essential drugs. This shortage was a direct result of the irregular to zero funding levels for health services and district hospitals due to the withdrawal of funding by major donors.

The rise in the prices of commodities and utilities in face of the kwacha's low purchasing power led to numerous *labour disputes*. In March, the Civil Servants Trade Union submitted a fresh petition to the office of the president and the cabinet demanding that the government immediately address some outstanding issues, including static salaries and the reduction of funding to ministries and departments. *Strikes* over the lack of salary increases and working conditions were the order of the day during the year and affected various sectors, including the judiciary, the health service and the university, apart from the main-stream civil service. In May, staff at Kamuzu Central Hospital (KCH) in Lilongwe staged a strike in protest over the allocation of accommodation intended for KCH staff to employees of the Ministry of Health headquarters. In November, judiciary employees in the three major cities went on strike calling for wage increases, and improvements in housing allowances and working conditions. The strike, which lasted nearly two months and affected the Supreme Court of Appeal, the High Court of Malawi, the High Court Commercial Divisions and the Industrial Relations Court in Blantyre and Limbe, had repercussions on the justice delivery system. On 8 December, employees of the Anti-Corruption Bureau (ACB) also downed tools after the expiry of a seven-day ultimatum they had given the government to raise their salaries. The workers rejected a 10% government offer, describing it as an insult. The strike took a dramatic turn when the government ordered police to seal ACB offices in Lilongwe, Blantyre, Mzuzu and Zomba. Parastatals also had their share of the industrial actions. On 20 August, employees of the Blantyre Water Board went on strike to press management to relocate the board's chief executive, Andrew Thawe, arguing that they were not happy with his management. They returned to work two weeks later after the office of the Comptroller of Statutory Corporations sent Thawe on leave to pave the way for investigations. In November, university support staff also went on strike for salary increases, forcing some colleges of the University of Malawi to close for six weeks.

On 1 September, Mutharika announced that the 2014/15 budget, which was pegged at MK 743 bn, would be a *zero-aid budget*, meaning that government would finance its recurrent expenditure from locally generated resources. Mutharika disclosed that the idea of a zero-aid budget was arrived at in response to the withholding of budgetary support by donors, which would have been expected to cover about 40% of expenditure. The national budget was expected to rise to MK 743 bn, a 16% increase on the previous year's MK 640 bn. However, the government's intention to draw up the 2014/2015 financial plan on the assumption that the country would not receive donor support came under criticism from economic experts as the cuts imposed on some services meant that many vital public services were sidelined during the year.

Revenue from *cotton sales* rose. *Maize* imports doubled after May due to lower prices in bordering Mozambique and Malawi itself also had a surplus of maize in comparison with the previous growing season.

Low prices and frequent market closures affected Malawi's *tobacco industry.* Even though the tobacco trade generated revenue that exceeded the $ 300 m target, trade figures released by Auction Holding Ltd showed that average prices had fallen by 12%. Many farmers complained about poor prices for their leaf on the auction floors. Tobacco sales were disrupted for more than an hour at Limbe Auction Floors in March when growers protested at the prices offered, which ranged from $ 0.85 to $ 1.40 per kg. The farmers said it was surprising that prices were not rising, even though their leaf was of good quality and well graded.

It was announced on 22 October that the depreciation of the kwacha had reached its worst point at MK 525:$ 1. Although the country's *foreign reserves* in the first half of 2014 increased by 72.9% compared with the same period in 2013, such progress was considered not enough to cover the cost of three months of recommended imports. As at October, reserves stood at 2.5 months, with further estimates of much lower import cover due to the vulnerability of tobacco, Malawi's main export, to weather conditions.

Mauritius

Sheila Bunwaree

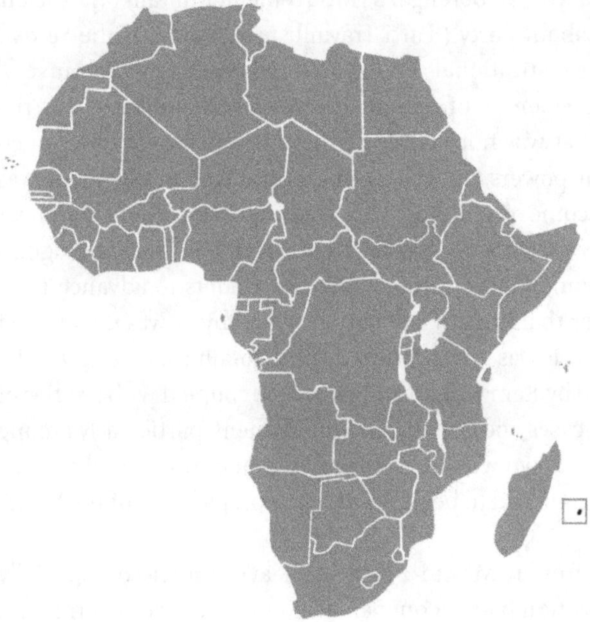

2014 will perhaps go down in the history of the island as the year that shook the Mauritian democratic picture perfect. The general elections brought defeat to former prime minister Ramgoolam as a precursor to his later arrest. While foreign policy largely involved Mauritius's traditional European partners, China and India took centre stage in international relations. Given its strategic location, Mauritius was also positioning itself as a gateway to Africa. Growing inequality and poverty presented the potential risk of social explosion. Despite efforts to alleviate poverty, the country experienced a rise in the number of poor households and a deteriorating Gini-coefficient.

Domestic Policy

Prime Minister Navin Chandra Ramgoolam called for *snap elections*, which took place on 10 December. In September, he and the leader of the opposition, Paul Berenger, concocted an alliance after several months of discussion, popularly called the 'coz coze' sessions. Their agreement was struck after the breakdown of a previous alliance, commonly dubbed the 'remake', between Berenger and Sir Aneerood

 | DOI 10.1163/9789004305052_050

Jugnauth of the 'Mouvement Socialiste Mauricien' (MSM), a former president of the republic. Berenger had lured him into leaving his presidential post to assist him in supposedly saving the country, but some months later Berenger broke the alliance to enter into a new deal with Ramgoolam.

Central to the alliance between Berenger's 'Mouvement Militant Mauricien' (MMM) and Ramgoolam's Labour Party ('Parti Travailliste' – PTR) was the *Second Republic Project* – a kind of constitutional arrangement wrapped in a discourse of greater power sharing and deepening of democracy. What was proposed was the setting up of a presidency that was not merely ceremonial but would have much greater and more significant powers, as well as immunity. The arrangement was that Ramgoolam would become president for a seven-year term and Berenger would be prime minster for five years. The population, which had expected significant electoral reform, saw some kind of ploy by the two leaders to advance their own personal interests rather than that of the nation. The Project was denounced by almost all opposition parties as the beginning of a totalitarian regime. The Second Republic as proposed by Ramgoolam and Berenger, coupled with a series of scandals, alleged corruption cases and growing unemployment, particularly among youth and women, did not go down well. Moreover, parliament was closed on May 12 on the grounds that extra time had to be devoted to the preparation of the White Paper on electoral reform.

The *closure of parliament* from 12 May to 4 July was heavily criticised, especially since the leader of the opposition had become an accomplice of the government. Parliament was dissolved on 2 October, prior to the snap elections on 10 December. The leader of the opposition was in negotiations with the prime minister. Large segments of the citizenry and opposition parties, apart from Berenger's, asked for the reopening of parliament, but to no avail. Citing Section 28 of the Constitution, which gives the presidency the responsibility to "uphold and defend the constitution and ensure that the institutions of democracy are protected", some civil society groups asked the president to remove the leader of the opposition but this was quietly ignored. Berenger resigned as opposition leader on 15 September and was replaced by Pravind Jugnauth. The population also took exception to the fact that the *audit report* for the year was not made public. For many years, the audit report had pointed to the excessive waste that was taking place in several public sector organisations, but for some reason the audit report was not available. The 'politics of opacity' was heavily punished by the population in the elections.

The *coalition* that was voted into power was the 'Alliance Lepep', composed of three parties: the MSM led by 84-year-old Aneerood Jugnauth, the 'Parti Mauricien Social Democrate' of Xavier Duval, and the 'Muvman Liberater' – a new splinter party of the MMM, formed in response to its alliance with the PTR. 'Alliance Lepep', under the leadership of Aneerood Jugnauth, won 47 of the elected seats, while the PTR-MMM alliance under Ramgoolam only took 13, and Ramgoolam himself lost his seat.

Another major political landmark was the mini *constitutional amendment* that came into force on 11 July, allowing Mauritians to stand as candidates without having to declare their ethnicity. Certain groups had long been asking for the removal of the 'Best Loser' system, a system designed to protect minority representation in parliament. Using a formula unique to the Mauritian electoral system, it selects eight unelected candidates on the basis of their ethnicity – seen by some as a wonderful mechanism to ensure the representation of the rainbow nation, but by others as the institutionalisation of communalism. Its opponents wanted it removed from the Constitution and they also called for the abolition of the obligation to declare one's ethnicity in order to participate in the elections. A left-leaning political party, known as 'Rezistans ek Alternativ', led by Ashok Subron, who had been denied the right to participate in the general elections in 2005 because they had refused to declare their ethnicity, had filed a complaint in the Supreme Court. The legal battle had proceeded to the Queen's Privy Council because the application had been rejected by the Supreme Court. On 20 December 2011, the law lords had concluded that the Privy Council had no jurisdiction to hear the plaintiff's request. Left with no choice, 'Rezistans ek Alternativ' had turned to the UN Human Rights Commission, which had ruled in their favour. Being a UN member state and a signatory to the UN Declaration of Human Rights, the government of Mauritius was bound to comply with the ruling. As the government had promised to produce a White Paper on electoral reform, the question of the declaration of ethnicity could no longer be pushed under the carpet, and so a mini amendment to the Constitution was introduced, removing the obligation for electoral candidates to declare their ethnicity.

While this amendment to the Constitution was seen as an important means of promoting nationhood and contributing to the de-ethnicisation of Mauritian politics, the Best Loser system remained in force and no real electoral reform took place. Although ethnicity as a category received a lot of attention, the *gender* question remained largely unattended to and gender equality declined in the elections. Of the 15 SADC countries, only Mauritius had fallen in its ranking for the percentage of women in parliament. From lying 10th with 19% of parliamentarians being women in the previous parliament, it had dropped to 12th position with a mere 12%.

Foreign Policy

Treaties of 'non double imposition' being central to Mauritius's efforts to grow as a *financial hub*, the country had been entering into such treaties with a large number of countries. Its Africa strategy led to the signing and ratification of a fiscal treaty with the Republic of Congo on 4 August and another with Malta on 15 October. A memorandum of understanding (MoU) was signed between the Board of Investment and the China-Africa Development Fund at an official ceremony on

24 September. The principal objective of the MoU was to promote economic growth and business prospects in Africa, as well as diversifying the production base.

Relations with *India* had been marked by a certain degree of upheaval, particularly around the non double taxation treaty, but with Narendra Modi's arrival on the scene as India's new prime minister in May, and the realisation that India had important maritime interests in the region, efforts were made on both sides to reinvigorate the relationship. This was reflected in the special invitation extended to Mauritius – the only non-South Asian Association for Regional Cooperation country – to attend Modi's swearing in ceremony on 26 May. Prime Minister Ramgoolam attended, and he and Modi discussed and explored avenues of further collaboration. Ramgoolam informed the Indian prime minister that a road map had been finalised focusing on seabed exploration for hydrocarbons and minerals, fishing, marine services and marine renewable energies, and invited India to enter into a partnership in the sector to pursue mutual interests. India's Foreign Minister Sushma Swaraj visited Mauritius on 1–3 November. While Mauritius struggled to raise funds for its infrastructural development, Sushma Swaraj confirmed a loan of Rs 19.5 bn to the government, part of which was to finance the 'metro leger' (light rail system), which was a subject of great contention locally. Many Mauritians had denounced the 'metro leger' project, arguing that it would be best to focus on water as the country's development priority. Water shortages led people to take to the streets in certain localities and the issue acquired such proportions that the opposition leader, Pravind Jugnauth (MSM), arranged a special meeting with Sushma Swaraj to explain to her that the 'metro leger' was not a priority for the country. During its electoral campaign, the MSM, with its allies, denounced the 'metro leger' project, arguing that they would not proceed with it if they came to power and, after the victory of the 'Alliance Lepep', the project was indeed set aside.

China had in recent years become an important market within the tourism diversification strategy. A high-level meeting between the Mauritius Tourism Promotion Authority and the China National Tourism Administration took place on 12 May and it was announced that China Southern Airlines was looking to operate a direct flight between Shenzhen and Mauritius.

Chagos and the Chagossians' plight remain an important question on Mauritius's foreign policy agenda. The UK government commissioned KPMG to carry out a feasibility study on the resettlement of the Chagossians early in the year. The study noted that no fundamental legal obstacles would prevent resettlement. The legal and constitutional framework, however, would need significant amendment in order to facilitate a resettlement. This would require a comprehensive consultative process with the Chagossians and other interested parties. Mauritius made it clear to all concerned that the Chagossian question was not only a matter of resettlement but also an issue of state sovereignty.

Socioeconomic Developments

The 2014 World Bank 'Doing Business Report' ranked Mauritius 20th out of 189 economies and first among African economies. It recognised notable improvements to coverage, scope and accessibility of credit information, which were helping the country to improve. While Mauritius did well on the business indicators and also managed to achieve a growth rate of some 3%, some other *macro economic indicators* were not so positive. The rate of investment to GDP at market prices was 19.4%, lower than the 21.2% of 2013. The share of the private sector in total investment fell to 74.4% from 76.4% in 2013, while that of the public sector rose to 25.6% from 23.6%. Gross domestic savings as a percentage of GDP at market prices were 11.6%. Mauritius remained a net importer, with imports representing 66.5% of GDP, while exports were at 52.8% of GDP. Public sector debt stood at 59.1% of GDP, causing people in certain quarters to worry that it might not be on track to meet the target of 50% of GDP by 2018. The budget deficit was 3.2% while inflation fell from 3.5% in 2013 to 3.3%. What worried the nation most was *unemployment*, which stood at 7.8%. Statistics for the third quarter demonstrated that around 46% of the unemployed were aged below 25 years, corresponding to an unemployment rate of more than 25% in that age group; the overall unemployment rate for women reached 11.4% with the indicator standing at 33.1% for those aged 16–24. Overall, the female participation rate in the labour market stood at 44.1% and was significantly below that of men at 75.5%.

Income *inequality* had increased since 2006/7 with the Gini coefficient rising from 0.388 in 2007 to 0.413. The share of total income going to the 20% of households at the lower end of the income range had fallen from 6.4% in 2001/2 to 6.1% in 2006/7 and fell again to 5.4% in 2013/14. In contrast, the share of income of the top 20% of households rose from 45.6% in 2001/2 to 47.4% in 2012, indicating growing inequalities. This widening gap was rather unlikely to diminish in the near future. Some people argued that the absence of a national minimum wage exacerbated the inequality problem. When he was minister of labour, Shakeel Mohamed (who was by the end of the year in the opposition), sought the help of the ILO in investigating the possibility of setting up a national *minimum wage*. A report on this was produced in the last quarter of the year but no further related work or action was undertaken. The introduction of a national minimum wage also featured in the manifesto of the 'Alliance Lepep', but only time would tell whether it would become a reality.

While increasing attention was paid to the growing inequality, very little was said about the precarious nature of work and the unacceptable conditions faced by many *foreign workers*. A few trade unions, including the Confederation of Private Sector Workers, called for the reformation of the Employment Rights Act and the

Employment Relations Act, which were perceived as anti-worker employment legislation. Mauritius remained the only country where workers can be sacked without compensation. High unemployment levels in the midst of growing poverty and inequality did not stop the government from bringing in foreign workers. There were some 40,000 foreign workers on the island while some 17,000 Mauritians were without jobs.

Mauritius remained trapped in a middle-income status with a GDP per capita of some $ 9,000. It aspired to become a high-income economy but lack of institutional reforms and *structural bottlenecks* continued to hamper development. The persistent mismatch between the training/education system and the labour market, the erosion of preferential arrangements on the international market, the multiplicity of crises – the food crisis, the eurozone crisis, the climate change crisis, the financial crisis, had important implications for small, isolated, resource-poor Mauritius.

Given the challenges, every effort was made towards *economic diversification*. Having transited from a monocrop sugar economy to become a textile and garment manufacturer, a tourism destination and an off-shore financial services centre, Mauritius was now looking at new areas, such as the ocean economy, the knowledge economy, and the strengthening of the IT and financial sector. A major threat to the knowledge economy/hub was the number of *educational scandals* that marred the tertiary sector. In the absence of a 'higher education bill', education became increasingly commodified and several offshore campuses/universities had entered the country through the Business Facilitation Act. Some of these institutions were delivering qualifications that were not recognized. A number of academic scams involved important political figures and their close associates and some of the universities involved were shut down. The official regulator, the Tertiary Education Commission, was also accused of being party to the establishment of some of these obscure post-secondary institutions.

While efforts were deployed to enhance traditional economic resources and boost new ones, such as the ocean and green economy, the country was accused of encouraging *tax evasion*. The European Network on Debt and Development published a report entitled 'Going Offshore', which described Mauritius as a fiscal paradise. It noted that $ 1.8 bn passed through Mauritius in 2013 and drew attention to the fact that such fiscal paradises could encourage further fiscal evasion as well as money laundering, both detrimental to development. Several Ponzi schemes were also uncovered, tarnishing the country's image further.

Europe's economic woes, with the euro slumping to a decade-low level of $ 1.16 in the last quarter of the year, were not good news. The relative weakness of the euro impaired Mauritian competitiveness, particularly with regard to the export of garments and textiles to the European market. Despite these challenges, the *tourism* sector experienced a rebound. Growth of 13% was registered from January to September, with 81,761 tourists, compared with 72,043 for the same period in 2013.

Mozambique

Joseph Hanlon

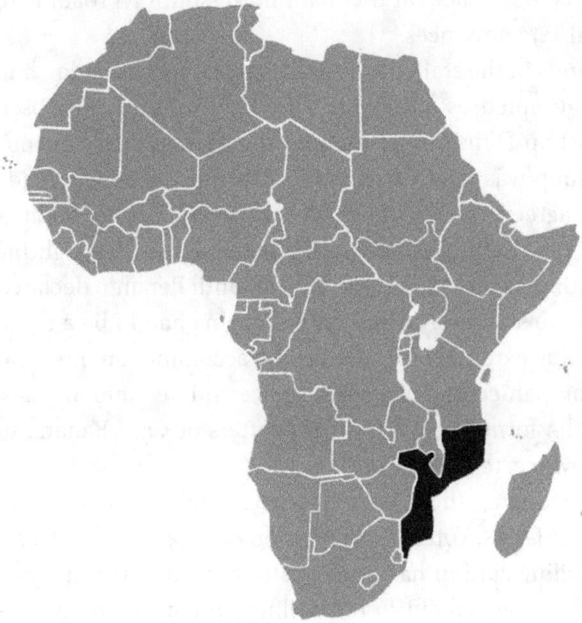

The ruling Frelimo party was re-elected in national elections on 15 October. The constitutional limit to two terms for a president in office forced Armando Guebuza to step down, although he remained head of the Frelimo party. Renamo agreed to a cease-fire in exchange for changes to the election law, but retained its militia. Renamo head Afonso Dhlakama gained 37% of the vote in the presidential elections, but claimed he had won and threatened a return to violence. Donor relations dominated foreign policy and the aid partners and agencies remained critically engaged in their relations with government. The run by international companies on stakes in the resource boom continued, mainly to secure access to the gas reservoirs.

Domestic Politics

An on-going small war and national elections dominated the political scene, with the *Renamo* (Resistência Nacional Moçambicana) opposition playing a key role in both. In January, it expanded its actions, and 70 to 100 Renamo fighters occupied a former base in Homoine district, Inhambane province. This was particularly

© KONINKLIJKE BRILL NV, LEIDEN, 2015 | DOI 10.1163/9789004305052_051 provocative, because Homoine was the site of the worst Renamo massacre of the previous war when on 18 July 1987 a large Renamo force swept through the town, killing 424 people, including patients lying in hospital beds. The return of Renamo created panic, and hundreds of people fled. There was also heavy fighting around Gorongosa and further attacks took place on the main north-south N1 road, with small attacks in Nampula and Tete provinces.

Renamo demanded *mediators* in the stalled talks taking place each Monday, and the government eventually accepted as 'observers' two Mozambicans proposed by Renamo: the Anglican Bishop Dinis Sengulane and the prominent academic, Lourenco do Rosario. The group was later extended to five, and seemingly made a difference: on 19 February, agreement was reached to change the election laws and Renamo agreed to participate in the elections. Despite this agreement, fighting escalated, with attacks on both the N1 road and the railway, until Renamo declared a *cease-fire* on 8 May. In order to stand for president, Dhlakama had to be a registered voter, and registration was extended for ten days to accommodate him. On 8 May, election officials, accompanied by journalists, police and Renamo officials, went into dense bush near the former Renamo headquarters at Casa Banana in Gorongosa district, Sofala province, to register him.

In multiparty elections since 1994, there have been electoral commissions at national, provincial and district levels. Voters must register; each register book lists up to 800 voters and each polling station has one register book and is usually in a school classroom. The count is carried out in the polling station as soon as voting ended, and the result is posted on the classroom door, which allows parallel counts. There had always been some fraud, in the form of stuffing ballot boxes, spoiling ballot papers for the opposition, and changing results. In the most extreme case, the Constitutional Council had found high-level fraud in which the provincial and district electoral commissions in the *local elections* in Gurué, Zambézia, on 20 November 2013 had changed the results to give the victory to Frelimo. It ordered the election to be rerun on 8 February. The second opposition party, Mozambique Democratic Movement, Movimento Democrático de Moçambique (MDM), won, and its candidate for mayor gained 55% of the vote.

Renamo alleged massive fraud in all the elections, and had always argued that the system should be politicised to allow Renamo people to observe more closely. In effect, the government agreed to accept any changes to the *electoral system* that Renamo proposed to parliament, and the law was passed largely as presented. The *electoral reform* was agreed by parliament in February. For the first time in a Mozambican election, polling stations had party-nominated staff. Previous elections had had five staff in each polling station, recruited from public applications. The revised law called for four recruited staff and three party nominees, one each from Frelimo, Renamo and MDM. Renamo had boycotted the electoral process and had not taken up its seats on electoral commissions. The previous National Electoral Commission (CNE) had five Frelimo, two Renamo (not taken up), one

MDM, three civil society, and two legal members. The changed CNE had five Frelimo, four Renamo, one MDM and seven civil society representatives. As part of an informal deal, the Muslim cleric Shaykh Abdul Carimo remained president (chair) and the additional civil society members were named by Renamo. There were similar changes at provincial and district levels. The elections were actually run by the Electoral Administration Technical Secretariat and there were 26 additional political appointments as deputy-directors general and department directors at national level, with similar changes at provincial and district level. In all, an additional 53,000 people were appointed by the three parties.

Despite the agreement and Dhlakama's registration, fighting resumed in June, with both government and Renamo military action, including daily Renamo attacks on the N1 road. Fighting suddenly stopped on 1 July. A *peace accord* was agreed in early August, and parliament approved a retrospective amnesty back-dated to March 2012 (to cover a shoot-out between police and Renamo in Nampula). It also covered three specific incidents in Sofala province in 2002, 2004 and 2011. A formal cease-fire was signed on 24 August, and on 27 August the army stopped providing military convoys on the N1. Dhlakama was escorted out of the bush at Gorongosa by five ambassadors and flown on 4 September to Maputo, where he met President Armando Guebuza the next day to confirm the cease-fire. Two weeks later, he launched his presidential election campaign.

Throughout the year, Renamo-government negotiations took place on the *demobilisation* of Renamo fighters and their integration into the Mozambican army, secret service and police. On 31 March, the government agreed to Renamo demands for an international group to oversee demobilisation and integration, with 70 Mozambican observers (half chosen by the government and half by Renamo) and 23 foreign observers (from Zimbabwe, South Africa, Botswana, Cape Verde, Kenya, Portugal, Italy, the UK and the USA). This was formalised in the peace accord as the Military Team of International Observers of the Cessation of Military Hostilities (EMOCHM – Equipa Militar de Observadores Internacionais da Cessação das Hostilidades Militares) and observers arrived at the end of September. However, Renamo had said on 14 April that it would demobilise only if there was a complete reorganisation and politicisation of the police and military, as in the electoral process, so that there were equal numbers of Renamo and Frelimo commanders. The government refused to accept this, and the talks remained deadlocked for the rest of the year; there was no demobilisation and Renamo retained its armed force. The EMOCHM military observers had nothing to do.

Meanwhile, *Frelimo* went through an unexpectedly fraught process to choose its *presidential candidate*. The Mozambican Constitution restricts presidents to two terms, and the party was not amenable to suggestions to amend the Constitution, so Armando Guebuza could not stand again. The Political Commission is the party's main decision-making body, but the larger Central Committee chooses the candidate. In December 2013, the Political Commission had selected three possible candidates, all close to Guebuza: Prime Minister Alberto Vaquina, Agriculture Minister Jose Pacheco and Defence Minister Filipe Nyusi. Party Secretary-General Filipe Paunde, a Guebuza loyalist, argued that only these three could be considered by the Central Committee, but this was opposed by the party old guard, led by Graça Machel and former president Joaquim Chissano, and backed by some opposed to Guebuza's increasingly autocratic tendencies. They forced two former prime ministers onto the list, Luisa Diogo and Aires Ali. At the 1 March Central Committee meeting, in the second round, Nyusi won with 135 votes but Diogo gained an unexpectedly high 61 votes.

Filipe Nyusi, a Maconde born in 1959 in Mueda, Cabo Delgado, was the only one of the candidates with a link to the war of liberation, having as a child attended the Frelimo school in Tunduru, Tanzania before Mozambican independence. He had completed his Mechanical Engineering degree in Czechoslovakia in 1990 and joined the northern railways (Caminhos de Ferro de Moçambique, CFM) in 1992 as assistant head of maintenance, moving up to be its executive director from 1995 to 2007. He had been a surprise appointment as defence minister in 2008.

The 15 October *national elections* were for president, national parliament, and ten provincial assemblies (Maputo city, the 11th province, already had a municipal assembly). During the electoral registration period – in 2013 for municipal elections and then 15 February to 14 May – 10,874,828 people registered, an estimated 89% of those who would be over the age of 18 years on polling day. Only three presidential candidates were able to provide the notarised signatures of 10,000 voters that qualified them to stand. Thirty parties put forward at least some candidates, but only the three main parties won seats. The 31 August to 12 October *electoral campaign* was more peaceful and witnessed fewer law violations than in the past, although there was some violence and harassment of the opposition in Gaza, Tete and Nampula provinces. Polling was well organised and peaceful, although Renamo attacked a few polling stations in Tete and Nampula.

The final *election results* were confirmed by the Constitutional Council on 29 December. They gave the presidential victory to Nyusi with 57% of the valid vote, followed by Dhlakama with 37%. The third candidate, Daviz Simango, mayor of Beira and leader of the MDM, obtained 6%. Simango had been expelled from Renamo in 2008 and had set up the MDM. Seats won in the national parliament (with seats in the 2010–2014 parliament in brackets) were distributed as follows: Frelimo 141 (191), Renamo 89 (51), and MDM 17 (8). Frelimo won majorities in five provincial assemblies and Renamo won majorities in three (Sofala, Tete and Zambézia), while in the remaining two (Manica and Nampula) the result was very close, with MDM holding the deciding vote.

National and international *observers* were highly critical of some parts of the process. The EU Observer Mission tempered its criticism by noting that "the parallel vote tabulation carried out by civil society organizations, considered serious and authentic, show results compatible" with those announced by the CNE and the Constitutional Council. In diplomatic language, the EU accepted that, whatever its complaints, Frelimo and Nyusi had won the election. But it also said that there had been an "uneven playing field". On the one hand, Renamo still had an armed force. On the other, Frelimo had vastly more money and used state resources in the campaign; the state-owned television station 'TVM' and daily newspaper 'Notícias' were biased in favour of Frelimo (in violation of the electoral law), while, according to the EU, the state-owned 'Radio Moçambique' was balanced.

On polling day and in the initial count at the polling stations, the Mozambique Political Process Bulletin used statistical tests to suggest that ballot box stuffing had taken place in 4% of polling stations, and that some votes for the opposition had been wrongly invalidated in 4.5% of polling stations. The EU was highly critical of tabulation processes at district, provincial and national levels. Although the revised election law meant that there were Renamo people at all levels in the electoral process, they failed to notice misconduct and in some cases added their signatures to manifestly false reports. Renamo and MDM both rejected the results, despite their presence throughout the process and the broad confirmation by the parallel count. By the end of the year, Dhlakama was threatening a return to war unless he was given power in the five provinces he claimed to have won.

Frelimo *pressure on outspoken civil society groups* increased during the year. The two most important groups, the Public Integrity Centre (CIP, Centro de Integridade Pública) and the Social and Economic Studies Institute (IESE, Instituto de Estudos Sociais e Económicos) were both forced to move when their leases were cancelled. IESE was only given two weeks' notice by the state property agency, APIE. In May the attorney-general's office questioned the founder and first director of IESE, Carlos Nuno Castel-Branco, under the State Security Law, accusing him of insulting the head of state in a Facebook post.

Mozambique finally *revised legislation* fixed in the Portuguese Penal Code of 1886, which had remained in force since independence in 1975. By contrast, Portuguese legislators, after the fall of fascism in Lisbon, had removed many inappropriate articles from the Portuguese code, but they had remained in place in Mozambique, even though they were never enforced. The drafting was carried out largely in secret, and on 20 March, after the revisions were published, there was a protest march by 13 civil society organisations claiming that the revised law still violated the rights of women, children and other groups. The draft was then revised again and most of the clauses objected to were revised or removed.

Justice Minister Benvinda Levi said on 19 March that 44 *kidnappings* had been reported for 2013 (31 in Maputo, nine in Matola, three in Beira and one in Nampula). More than 30 kidnappings took place in 2014. On 8 May, Dinis Francisco Silica Nhavotso, the presiding judge of the criminal instruction section of the Maputo criminal court, was assassinated; he had been in charge of the investigating kidnappings in Maputo over the previous two years and had just confirmed the detention of a businessman accused of leading one of the kidnapping rings.

Two men convicted of killing investigative journalist Carlos Cardoso on 22 November 2000 were themselves victims of *assassinations*. Vincente Ramaya had been the brain behind the largest banking fraud in Mozambican history when $ 14 m had been syphoned out of the Mozambique Commercial Bank on the eve of its privatisation. Cardoso had been investigating the fraud and Ramaya had been convicted of planning both crimes. He had been released from prison in 2013, only to be gunned down on 21 February in Maputo close to where Cardoso had been killed. Ramaya had moved the money into accounts of the Abdul Satar family. Ayoob Satar, who had also been convicted of killing Cardoso and released in 2013, was gunned-down in front of a bank in Karachi (Pakistan) on 2 July.

The president of the parliamentary ethics commission, Ana Rita Sithole, said in March that all MPs had left their other jobs and were in conformity with the Public Probity Law, which bans MPs from earning another salary from the government or a public company. At the end of November, parliament unanimously passed a freedom of information law proposed by journalists, making public documents and archives open to anyone wishing to see them.

Foreign Affairs

The election year meant that the government's full attention was absorbed by domestic affairs. Hence bi- and multilateral relations were mainly confined to *interaction with donors*. The $ 850 m government guaranteed Eurobond agreed on 5 September 2013 for Ematum (National Tuna Company) continued to dominate donor relations. The bond issue was agreed in secret without parliamentary approval. Not all the investment was for fishing boats; some of the money was used for military patrol boats and there was no explanation for where other amounts went. In late 2013, several budget support donors had withheld $ 87 m, as the government revealed in its IMF 'Letter of intent', published on 29 May.

When donor grants were at their peak, 19 donors had given some aid directly as government *budget support*, but the number had now dropped to 13. The UK was the largest donor to end budget support. Pledges announced in early June were for only $ 325 m, compared with $ 400 m in 2013, with the World Bank, the EU and Sweden making the largest commitments. The chair of what was still called the G19, Italian Ambassador Roberto Vellano, said the fall in budget support was a direct result of the Ematum bond, and that donors were demanding an "action plan on fiscal transparency".

The IMF led the *donor attack* on the government over Ematum. In a 9 May statement, Naoyuki Shinohara, deputy managing director and acting chair of the IMF Executive Board, pointed to the need for "public financial management reforms and the identification of fiscal risks" and stressed that Mozambique "requires a transparent project analysis, prioritization and selection process, and should be informed by the implications for the debt sustainability. Furthermore, strict monitoring of project implementation is essential to ensure value-for-money in the use of public resources." Budget support was meant to be a joint project, and targets were set for both donors and the government. On 16 May, it was announced that in 2013 budget support donors had met only four of their 33 targets, compared with 20 out of 33 met by the government, although this included only two of six agreed targets under 'good governance'. The full report on 2012 state spending was only presented to parliament on 2 April. It showed that *aid* had funded less than 30% of the state budget, compared with 60% two decades earlier. This was partly because donors had only given two-thirds of the $ 2.1 bn promised. Of this, $ 890 m had been in grants and $ 510 m in loans. To meet the shortfall, government had collected an extra $ 160 m in domestic revenue, and cut capital expenditure by 20%, with reduced spending on water, roads and agriculture.

Socioeconomic Developments

Inflation stood at 1.93%, down from 3.54% in 2013. GDP growth was estimated at 7.5%. Tax collection was $ 4.87 bn, 4% above the target.

Gas developments continued, despite the falling prices of oil and gas. An IMF Working Paper 'Natural Gas, Public Investment and Debt Sustainability in Mozambique' said that the country had the largest proven natural gas reserves in Africa, and the eighth largest in the world. The gas fields, largely offshore in the northern Rovuma basin, contained at least 180 trillion cubic feet of gas, far more than anyone had expected. The World Bank's 'Generating Sustainable Wealth from Mozambique's Natural Resource Boom' predicted government hydrocarbon revenue of $ 9 bn per year by 2032, of which 90% would be from gas and 10% from coal. Two companies controlled the two major gas fields, ENI of Italy and Anadarko of the USA, and they planned to produce liquefied natural gas (LNG). The government wanted them to share an LNG plant, but the companies refused. On 25 November, the Council of Ministers approved separate LNG plants, a floating offshore plant for ENI and an onshore plant for Anadarko, costing an estimated $ 15 bn each. ENI was expected to start producing LNG in 2020 and Anadarko in 2021. In order to raise these amounts, the companies were required to have contracts to sell the gas, and in March Anadarko announced that two-thirds of its LNG had been pre-sold, mainly to Asian countries that wanted an assured supply. When exploration companies found large reserves of oil, gas or coal, they expected to make their profit by selling those reserves on to production companies, and with falling prices they also wanted to reduce their risk. Both companies sold parts of their areas during the year. ENI, the operator in Area 4, retained a 50% share. Its partners were the Chinese company CNPC (20%), and Kogas, Galp Energia and Mozambique's National Hydrocarbon Company ENH (each with 10%). Anadarko, the operator in Area 1, had a reduced

26.5% stake. Its co-owners were Mitsui of Japan (20%), ENH (15%), PTT of Thailand (8.5%), and three Indian companies ONGC Videsh (16%), Oil India (4%), and BPRL Ventures (10%). Mozambique imposed a 32% capital gains tax on these sales. Rosário Fernandes, president of the Tax Authority (Autoridade Tributária), said in March that $ 1.3 bn in capital gains tax had been collected from five transactions over the previous two years. During the rest of 2014, taxation on seven more transactions was expected to produce over $ 1 bn.

Port logistics for the gas industry in Cabo Delgado was to be handled by a Mozambican state company in partnership with a Nigerian-Italian logistics company. A new port was to be constructed in Palma, where Anadarko's gas liquification plant was to be built, and a second port in Pemba, adjoining the small one currently run by the state ports and railways company Portos e Caminhos de Ferro de Moçambique (CFM). Construction needed to start in 2015 so that work on the gas plant could begin that year. There was a complex chain of companies. In January, Ports of Cabo Delgado, Portos de Cabo Delgado (PCD), a state company owned half by CFM and half by the state oil and gas company Empresa Nacional de Hidrocarbonetos (ENH), was given the lease to run port and logistics terminals in Pemba and Palma. On 23 April, without going out to public tender, PCD granted the concession to ENHILS, which in turn was 51% owned by ENH Logistics (owned by ENH) and 49% by Orlean Invest, whose majority shareholder was the Italian billionaire Gabriele Volpi; a minority shareholder was Atiku Abubakar, the former vice president of Nigeria. He was publicly accused by the US Senate Permanent Sub-Committee on Investigations of using Orlean for money laundering.

Coal prices fell to one-third of their 2011 peak, making coal mining in Tete unprofitable because of the 600–1000 km distance by rail to the nearest port. Rio Tinto, which had bought the Benga mine from Riversdale for $ 3.8 bn in 2012, sold it to the Indian state company International Coal Ventures (ICVL) for just $ 50 m on 8 October. ICVL owned 65% of the mine and wanted coal for Indian state-owned steel and power companies. The remaining 35% was owned by the private Indian company Tata Steel. The Brazilian multinational Vale owned a coal mine at Moatize and 80% of the railway to Nacala and the new coal port there, which began operations at the end of 2014. On 8 December, Mitsui of Japan paid Vale $ 763 m for 15% of the mine and railway.

Fraudulent invoicing of trade by big foreign companies was causing an average of $ 187 m per year in *revenue losses*, according to a study funded by the Danish government. Two studies by CIP showed that political parties, including Frelimo, were misusing their tax exempt status on a grand scale. CIP reported that Frelimo had carried out large-scale duty-free imports for private companies, including 2,291 Chinese motorcycles and 7,009 Chinese freezers in two years. CIP also found that three small parties with no representatives in a local or national assembly or any visible political presence had imported 427 cars in just one year.

Campaigns by peasant organisations including the National Peasants Union (União Nacional de Camponeses) delayed the huge *ProSavana programme* in the Nacala corridor in Nampula and Niassa provinces. The joint Japanese-Brazilian programme had originally been set up to encourage large-scale Brazilian investment, but lack of land and peasant protests had forced a rethink. Only one project had gone ahead, Agromoz (Agribusiness de Moçambique), owned by Grupo Américo Amorim (one of the richest men in Portugal and the largest shareholder in Banco Único de Moçambique), Intelec Holdings (where ex-president Armando Guebuza was a major shareholder), and Pinesso (one of the big Brazilian soya companies), which was actually running the plantation. In November, there were complaints that more than 1,000 small farmers had lost their land and houses and had received compensation of less than $ 200 each. Some only produced their own food, but others had become small commercial farmers already producing soya for the market. There were also protests against the only large Chinese agricultural investment, a rice farm near Xai-Xai, Gaza.

In competing reports early in the year, the *World Bank* said Mozambique should spend more on education while the *IMF* said it should spend less. In its report 'Generating Sustainable Wealth from Mozambique's Natural Resource Boom', the World Bank said that anticipated gas and coal revenues should be used to "frontload public investments" and that Mozambique should increase spending on education, public health and infrastructure. But the IMF disagreed, and stressed that priority should be given to "containing the public wage bill". It accepted that "the lion share of the wage bill goes to education" and that there should be a reduction in salary increases and recruitment. The government effectively rejected this. In his 'Letter of Intent' to the IMF, Finance Minister Manuel Chang only committed to lowering the *wage bill* in the medium term. He retained a commitment to salary increases and to a resettlement subsidy for staff moving to rural areas. He said the government wage bill for the year would be 11% of GDP, which for the IMF was too high. In a 14 March statement, the head of an IMF mission to Mozambique, Doris Ross, repeated the call for "moderation in new hiring" and reducing the wage bill – effectively hiring fewer teachers and nurses. The use of the public sector wage bill as an indicator had a neo-liberal, *pro-privatisation* bias, because the more education and health care was provided by the private sector, the lower the public sector wage bill would be. Thus the IMF was not objecting to more education, just to more state education.

In two other reports published in May, the IMF pointed to the continued downward trend in *agricultural productivity* of cereals and vegetables, and concluded "that the main challenges facing Mozambique still relate to increasing production and productivity in the agriculture and fishery sectors". The Fund also pointed to the failure to create jobs and warned that "making growth more inclusive by generating more employment is clearly a major challenge". Naoyuki Shinohara underlined this in his 9 May statement, pointing to Mozambique's "2013 shortfall on priority spending" and noting that "making growth more inclusive will require generating more employment".

After negotiations in April, *minimum wages* were increased substantially, and for the first time most of the 15 minimum wages were near to, or more than, $ 100 per month. In an election year, the rural minimum wage was raised 26% to $ 105 per month. For the first time, the rural minimum wage was higher than the civil service minimum, now $ 99 and only increased by 10%. In US dollar terms, minimum wages had doubled since 2007, when they had been $ 43 for agriculture and $ 64 for non-agriculture. The minimum wage had been only $ 24 in 1996.

Mozambique ranked 25th of 45 countries in a Hunger and Nutrition Commitment Index published in June. It was said to have a low commitment to tackling *hunger and malnutrition*. Neighbouring Malawi ranked 3rd and Tanzania 7th, and both were said to have high commitment. Mozambique was criticised for low spending on health and agriculture, limited access to water and sanitation, and low registration of children. The index was created by the Institute of Development Studies, backed by British and Irish aid. In August, Deputy Minister for Women's Affairs and Social Welfare Virgilio Mateus admitted that 43% of Mozambican children were chronically malnourished. Child mortality remained high, but was falling. In 2003, 153 out of every 1,000 children born died before their fifth birthday; by 2011, this mortality rate had fallen to 97 per 1,000 live births.

Namibia

Henning Melber

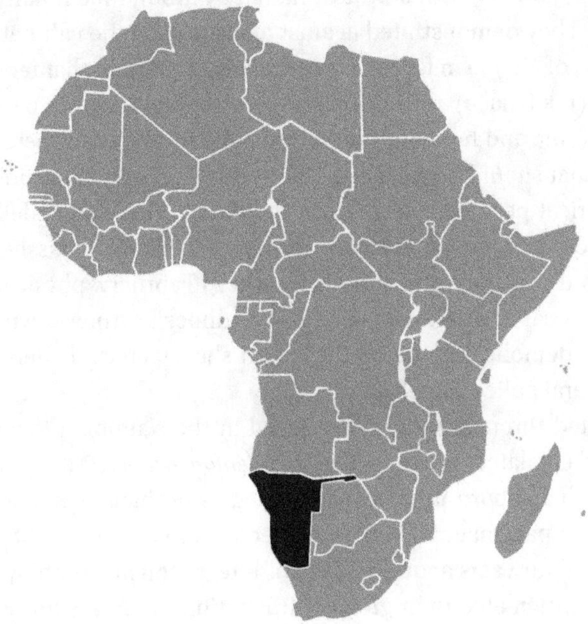

The second half of the year was dominated by preparations and campaigning for the national and presidential elections at the end of November. The dominant South West African People's Organisation (SWAPO), the former liberation movement, in political power since Independence, retained its political hegemony as expected and even extended its control in the legislature. The SWAPO parliamentary majority adopted far-reaching constitutional amendments in August, including increasing the number of seats in the National Assembly and the National Council as from the next five-year term, and adding to the executive powers of Hage Geingob as the next elected head of state. Foreign policy continued with a 'looking East' orientation, while the controversial EPA was finally signed. Macroeconomic data suggested little change in terms of both socio-economic trends and the stark inequalities in the distribution of wealth. Social protest against government policy was on the increase, with mounting confrontations, though the general climate remained one of relative stability.

 | DOI 10.1163/9789004305052_052

Domestic Politics

The *growing frustration* over government expenditure on infrastructure, which was considered unnecessary and as only serving the symbolic architecture of those in political power, erupted on 13 January with a protest march by around 100 mainly young people in Windhoek. They demonstrated against allocation by the cabinet, reported in local print media, of N$ 700 m for the construction of a new parliament building. The 'Tintenpalast' (ink palace), the administrative building complex dating back to German colonial rule and home of the National Assembly, was considered an anachronistic relic that should be replaced. The youth demonstrators, not visibly affiliated to any political party, handed over a petition, which demanded that the money should be spent on more important priorities in the light of massive youth unemployment and a deteriorating health sector. On 19 February, physical violence erupted in a squatter camp on the outskirts of Windhoek's former township, Katutura, when police demolished one of the illegal shacks erected there; stone throwers damaged several police vehicles.

Social protest also mounted through a group organised in the Namibian Exile Kids Association (NEKA) and escalated into the *killing of a demonstrator*. NEKA had been formed by young Namibians born in exile, who (often as orphans) came to independent Namibia without patronage or family connections to the new political elite. They had complained for years about the lack of integration and employment opportunities and had articulated their growing frustration in various forms of peaceful protest. On 27 August, NEKA activists once again demonstrated outside SWAPO headquarters. Police dispersed the crowd with tear gas and opened fire. A fleeing young mother was shot in the back and died on the spot.

Activists of the *Swapo Party Youth League* (SPYL) condemned this repressive act and the SPYL leadership, in open defiance of party solidarity, attended the funeral of the victim in her northern Namibia home village instead of the launch of the party manifesto in Windhoek. From within the ranks of SPYL officials also emerged the most spectacular forms of protest seen thus far. Its Secretary of Information Job Amupanda together with two other leading activists symbolically occupied an urban plot in an up-market Windhoek suburb on 9 November. Later dubbed an *'affirmative repositioning'*, this initiative expressed frustration over speculative land deals in Windhoek by members of the political municipal administration. Such property transactions were profitable only to a few selected cronies, while ordinary citizens could not afford to purchase plots. The SWAPO leadership (president, secretary general and their deputies) immediately suspended the SPYL activists. After being informed that the authority to suspend them rested solely with the members of the party's much larger Politbureau, they declared that this was a matter of urgency that required immediate intervention. Despite such new dissent, the elections shortly afterwards remained peaceful and without any spectacular events or surprises.

On 27 August, the National Assembly adopted a new *Electoral Bill*, which introduced, among other things, the use of electronic voting machines. The law stipulated that a paper trail was required to visibly confirm to the voter the choice made. But then the Indian company that had delivered the equipment announced that it was impossible to comply with the law without testing the technology. The elections held end of November therefore violated the legal provision that had been adopted.

The SWAPO parliamentary majority also voted for far-reaching *constitutional amendments*, tabled on 31 July without prior consultation and amidst subsequent strong objections by other parties and a broad civil society alliance; these concerns were raised in a public statement on 21 August. The more than 40 amendments increased the number of seats by one-third from 72 to 96 in the next National Assembly to be elected. The same expansion by one-third was set for the National Council, based on the now 14 (originally 13) regions of the country. The appointment of regional governors by the head of state was also introduced as a constitutional clause. President Hifikepunye Lucas Pohamba had already been making such appointments, guided by an earlier law. This law and its implementation violated the original constitutional clause, which foresaw the election of governors by the other elected members of the regional councils. The amendments also consolidated *presidential control over state affairs* and added further power to an already strong executive president. The president now had the sole discretion to appoint or dismiss all heads of the state's security organs and was hence in exclusive control of all security agencies. Namibia's de facto one-party democracy thereby moved as from the next legislative period even closer to a one-person democracy, depending upon the degree to which the office holder was willing to use – or abuse – the presidential powers.

SWAPO's *electoral college* took place on 30–31 August. Delegates voted for the party list for the elections on the basis of the 'zebra style regulation' adopted by an extraordinary party congress in 2013. It had decided that every second candidate on the list (after the seated party leadership, ranking highest by virtue of their offices) had to be female. This was also considered to have been the ultimate reason for the earlier decision to increase the number of seats in the National Assembly – to avoid too many of the old male comrades falling by the wayside. Despite this cautious initiative, the election result came as a total surprise and was dubbed a 'tsunami' by some media. Among those who did not make it onto the total list of 96 candidates were four ministers, five deputy ministers and the speaker, as well as some other MPs. Accusations of 'de-campaigning', which accused party internal factions of having mobilised against certain candidates, thereby violating party rules, caused unrest and tensions. While the party's secretary-general announced an investigation into the allegations, it was also confirmed that the list remained valid. According to the constitutional amendments adopted, the next state president would be entitled to nominate in total eight additional MPs without voting rights; they would also be entitled to cabinet appointments. As a result, speculation continued for the rest of the year as to who would be offered access to political office by the new elected president before the swearing in of the next parliament. On 28 November, close to 900,000 Namibians (72% of a registered electorate of more than 1.2 m, out of a total estimated population of 2.3 m) voted in the country's fifth *parliamentary and presidential elections* since Independence. The use of electronic voting machines resulted in an embarrassing logistical and technological disaster. Thousands of voters were reportedly unable to participate in the elections due to various hiccups, despite often queuing for most of Election Day, if not longer (some polling stations remained open until the next morning while voters waited through the night). Even with extended opening, an undisclosed number of Namibians were denied their fundamental right to make a choice. While this had no serious impact on the results, it threw a shadow on their democratic integrity.

The result was predictable, though the extent of *SWAPO's overwhelming dominance* surprised most observers. While the former liberation movement had secured well above a two-thirds majority in every election since 1994, the party this time crossed the 80% mark and took 77 seats in direct competition with 15 other parties. Nine opposition parties won a total of 19 of the 96 seats in the National Assembly for the next five-year legislative period, starting with Independence Day on 21 March 2015. The opposition was more divided than ever before, underlining the lack of meaningful political alternatives. Presidential candidate Hage Geingob topped the presidential vote with a whopping 86% against eight other contenders, scoring even higher than his predecessors Sam Nujoma and Hifikepunye Pohamba.

The signs of *democratic authoritarianism* suggested that, while the country fulfilled all the formal criteria for a democracy (multi-party state, regular elections, democratic constitutional principles, civil liberties and a fairly independent judiciary, combined with independent media and freedom of speech), there was not a level playing field. While observers testified to free and fair elections, the term 'fair' seemed to be relative. SWAPO was the only party that had the machinery and financial means (not least through massive donations from a private sector that benefitted from government and state business) to mobilise countrywide. Evidence of the unfair practices possible in such an environment included SWAPO's purchase of considerable time from the state owned Namibian Broadcasting Company (NBC) for the live televising of its final political star rally.

Notwithstanding these limitations and despite a new degree of social protest in both words and deeds, no meaningful credible social and political alternatives to SWAPO were in sight. On the contrary, the ruling party's approval ratings remained unchallenged. Findings of an *Afrobarometer* survey presented in March concluded that the "political system seems to deliver more democracy than the population seems to demand", while a participatory political culture had not yet been developed. While democratic consolidation might be a feature in the institutional domain, "democratic values, behaviours and expectations are yet to catch up".

This did not prevent a comparatively good ranking in the Bertelsmann Stiftung's Transformation Index released early in the year, which placed Namibia in the overall status index at 30th out of 129 countries, and 25th in political transformation.

Foreign Affairs

A series of bilateral interactions with *African states* took place during the year. Nigerian President Goodluck Jonathan attended the Independence Day celebrations as part of a state visit on 20–21 March. President Pohamba attended Senegal's Independence Day ceremonies on 4 April as the guest of honour. Namibia announced that it would open an embassy there. Pohamba visited Swaziland on 14–17 May reciprocating a state visit by King Mswati III in 2013. Former head of state Sam Nujoma, as head of the AU observer mission, and Foreign Minister Netumbo Nandi-Ndaitwah, as head of the SADC Electoral Observer Mission, declared the *elections in Malawi* of 30 May "generally credible" and "peaceful, free, transparent and credible, reflecting the will of the people", respectively. During October, *South Africa* finally lived up to a promise made during a state visit by President Zuma in November 2013 to donate N$ 100 m in support of the drought relief programme in Namibia.

The *look East* policy continued. While on a state visit to *China*, Prime Minister Geingob met President Xi Jinping on 8 April. He confirmed the will to create a favourable environment for closer collaboration with Chinese investors. Chinese business interests in Namibia remained high and the number of Chinese locally resident remained a constant matter of speculation and provoked strong feelings among ordinary people. In December, a local newspaper claimed to have information that China had negotiated with the government to use the deep-sea port of Walvis Bay as a naval base. A delegation from *North Korea* headed by the deputy minister for trade made a visit on 15–17 May and explored further intensification of trade relations. The North Korean state construction company Mansudae Overseas Project Group of Companies, a subsidiary or alias of Korea Mining Development Trade Corporation (KOMID), had in the past 15 years won several major tenders for prominent public works, especially for national monuments and government offices. During the year, it was building an ammunition factory at the Luiperdsvalley military base outside Windhoek. KOMID was among the companies on the boycott list attached to the UNSC Resolution 1718 (2006). All business transactions with the listed companies were in violation of the resolution.

The long controversy around the EU-initiated *EPA* was finally brought to an end during negotiations in July, when the SADC group, in which Namibia was the most vocal advocate, reached a compromise on some of the most contentious issues (such as the elimination of subsidies on all products exported to Namibia, the right to export duties on some products, an infant industry protection strategy and non-compliance with the Most Favoured Nations clause). But while ratifying the adjusted agreement, Namibia continued to look for additional options to expand trade relations. After two years of negotiations, a trade cooperation treaty was signed with *Turkey* on 5 November.

UN Secretary-General (UNSG) *Ban Ki-moon* visited on 24–25 June for the official opening of the UN offices (already operational for seven years). He applauded the country for its democratic policy and the media freedom, as well as for its human rights record. President Pohamba complained that Namibia's classification as an upper-middle-income country would not reflect the huge income discrepancies inherited from colonialism and would negatively impact on efforts to reduce poverty. He also urged the UNSG to address UNSC reform, in order to make the UNSC more democratic and representative and to provide a permanent seat for an African nation. Pohamba's renewal of blame of Apartheid for the current skewed income provoked critical comments from the public. The minister of health and social services declared on behalf of Pohamba in a statement on 8 December that a decline in *donor health funding* had negatively impacted on Namibia's ability to deliver high-quality, effective and accessible health services.

Socioeconomic Developments

In February, the *IMF* published the 2013 Article IV Consultation, which applauded Namibia for "impressive strides in economic development" since Independence. But it also concluded that this had not resulted in sufficient job creation and lower inequality. A matter of special concern was the high cost of state-owned enterprises (SOEs) and the need "to put them on a financially viable footing".

Minister of Finance Saara Kuugongelwa-Amadhila tabled the *annual budget* for the fiscal year 2014/15 on 19 February. With an estimated expenditure of N$ 60.3 bn it represented a 26.7% increase of N$ 12.7 bn on the previous year and thereby the second largest growth in expenditure since Independence. This could be seen as a sign of investments in line with the election year. Staff costs rose from N$ 17.5 bn to N$ 22 bn (mainly for salaries in education and the military), representing 37% of total expenditure. Projected revenue increased by 25% to N$ 52.5 bn, of which SACU revenue was estimated at N$ 18.1 bn or 34.7% of total revenue. The minister in her budget speech admitted to "a significant risk" with regard to the "uncertainty regarding future SACU revenues due to on-going reforms". The budget deficit was projected at N$ 7.6 bn or 5.4% of GDP, to be covered mainly from domestic market borrowing. Total debt increased to about N$ 38.5 bn or 27.2% of GDP.

In terms of *sectoral allocations*, education again received the largest share with N$ 13.1 bn (22.7%). Defence was the second largest, with N$ 6.6 bn. Another N$ 6.1 bn was allocated to the health sector and N$ 6 bn to the Finance Ministry.

The last included transfers of N$ 2.5 bn each to SOEs and foreign and domestic interest rate payments to cover growing debt services. The fiscal policy was nevertheless widely considered as relatively sound both by local economists and by international financial institutions and rating agencies. Once again, the budget that was presented, as well as the subsequent analyses and debates in the public sphere through local media, financial experts and think tanks, testified to a high degree of transparency and accountability in comparison with most other practices on the continent.

The election year left its mark with another N$ 8.3 bn put aside for regional and local government, housing and rural development, with a continued emphasis on the provision of low-cost *housing* throughout the country, for which a special mass housing scheme had been launched in 2013. Its implementation, however, left much room for improvement. Many cases were reported of tenders being awarded to newly created companies in Namibian ownership that had no specific competence except good connections to SWAPO's inner circle. After tenders were awarded, these local 'tenderpreneurs' often sub-contracted foreign companies and pocketed considerable portions of the money as brokers. Many of the projects were delayed, remained incomplete or were sub-standard, and criticism mounted. As a result, the government decided towards the end of May to put the N$ 2.9 bn mass housing project introduced in 2013 on hold. Similarly, the Targeted Intervention Programme for Employment and Economic Growth (*TIPEEG*) announced with much fanfare in 2012 and allocated a total of N$ 14.5 bn for the three-year period, had created by the time of the budget presentation over 15,000 permanent and over 67,000 temporary jobs – many fewer than originally promised. Critics bemoaned the fact that large amounts of the money under TIPEEG were wasted on intermediaries rather than being invested effectively in lasting employment creation, and that no coherent strategic plan existed for efficient investment.

Despite the continued high budget allocations to *education*, efficiency remained low. In January, the examination results for the school year that ended in December were released. Of about 42,000 higher secondary school leavers, only some 10,800 met the minimum admission criteria for university studies. According to the 'Global Information Technology Report 2014' released by the World Economic Forum in April, mathematics and science education in Namibian schools was deteriorating and it ranked Namibia 128th out of 148 countires. The overall quality of the education system was ranked 118th, while the 95% adult literacy rate compared favourably with many other countries on the continent. *Unemployment* remained at an estimated high 30% (widely considered a conservative figure), and much higher in the age group to 30 years, with more than half in that age group without employment. Similarly, *poverty*-related features affected more than half of the population and remained a challenge in a country ranked as a higher-middle-income country with an annual average per-capita income of some $ 6,000, while at the same time, according to the UNDP Human Development Report, having the highest Gini-coefficient (which measures the unequal distribution of wealth) of all countries.

Mining remained the backbone of the *economy*, with diamonds (off- and on-shore), zinc and lead mainly exploited in the southern regions, gold and copper concentrated in the central and northern parts and uranium in the Namib desert along the Atlantic coast. Many international mining companies ran the operations, with a growing Chinese ownership mainly in the uranium sector. Fisheries and agriculture added to the central relevance of the primary sector, while tourism was another source of income. Manufacturing remained low but its share in GDP gradually increased.

Energy supply remained a bottleneck. Dependency on power supplied by South Africa's utility company Eskom came under threat due to shortages of power in South Africa itself. This required further plans to secure future access to new sources. In April, the national power utility NamPower announced plans to set up a N$ 3 bn solar hybrid power plant and a waste oil recycling plant at the mining town of Arandis some 50 km from the Atlantic coast. A further N$ 7 bn was announced to be invested in transmission expansion to ensure reliable delivery of electricity to all parts of the country over the next few years. Finally, the establishment of a N$ 3 bn 250 MW long-term generation facility was planned for the Erongo region.

The Namibia *2011 Census Mortality Report* was released by the National Statistics Agency on 29 July. It recorded 44 deaths for every 1,000 live births and 604 maternal deaths per 100,000 live births. Fertility rates remained at an average of 3.9 children – among the lowest in SSA. Death by accidents (1,613), suicide (673) and murder (472) contributed to the overall recorded causes of mortality amounting to around 22,668 registered deaths, mainly due to illness. Life expectancy stood at 53 years for men and 60 years for women. Suicide rates were markedly higher than the world average and ranked among the highest in the world in the northern region, while traffic-related deaths were proportionally the highest worldwide. *HIV prevalence* had gradually declined in recent years but remained high. A 2014 Surveillance Report presented at the end of December showed a fall in the percentage of pregnant women who were HIV-positive from 18.2% in 2012 to 16.9%. But as the minister of health and social services concluded, the overall sustained high prevalence implied a need for continued expansion of antiretroviral treatment services. A long legal battle over the forced *sterilisation of HIV-positive women* in public hospitals was brought to an end by a final verdict of the Supreme Court on 3 November, when it ruled that the rights of three claimants had been violated by forced sterilisation, a practice documented since 2007. Despite a slight decline in mainly AIDS-related *tuberculosis* cases to just below 10,000 during the year, Namibia ranked according to WHO figures as the fourth-worst TB affected country in the world.

An *Afrobarometer* survey published in March pointed to a "strong perception among Namibians that inequality and unemployment are the key problems that

Namibian democracy needs to address". In a subsequent survey, summarised on 18 November, 78% of the respondents favoured the adoption of a Basic Income Grant; more than 80% wanted a reform of the tender system to "eliminate nepotism and favouritism"; 86% criticised the emphasis on party loyalty and its reward system by means of 'jobs for the boys'; and 87% objected to further salary increases for political office bearers and executives in SOEs.

At the end of the year, many international media ranked Namibia among the world's most attractive tourist destinations. This accentuated the contrasts between rich and poor in this 'land of wide open spaces', where much room for improvement remained.

South Africa

Sanusha Naidu

A highlight of the year was the celebrations for the twentieth anniversary of South Africa's political transition to a democratic dispensation in 1994, when the African National Congress (ANC) became the ruling party. This was a significant milestone for reviewing the country's political and socioeconomic achievements and challenges, as well as the status of its democratic future. The other main focus was the fifth national and provincial democratic election.

Domestic Affairs

For the first time, the generation born after Nelson Mandela took office (commonly called 'born frees') was able to vote in the national and provincial parliamentary *elections* on 7 May without the political baggage of the past. Much of the attention focused on what would influence and shape the voting attitudes of this cross-section of the population, often referred to as Mandela's generation. The second and more poignant factor that emerged for this election was that it marked the first real test of President Zuma's five years in power amid the controversies related to corruption scandals, irregular procurement of state resources and four cabinet

 | DOI 10.1163/9789004305052_053

reshuffles, which had characterised his administration. The third issue, linked to the last, was closely related to Mandela's legacy, which the ruling ANC sought to invoke in what some commentators interpreted as an attempt to win a sympathy or loyalty vote following the passing away of this global iconic figure in December 2013. Fourth was the pragmatic question of whether *opposition* parties would be able to consolidate their electoral footprint. The Democratic Alliance (DA), as the official opposition, had pulled out all the stops to garner significant support, mainly among African voters. For smaller opposition parties, the critical issue was whether they could sustain their political relevance by improving their electoral support at the polls. This was definitely aligned to the final issue: the emergence of two *new political parties*, namely Agang SA and the Economic Freedom Fighters (EFF).

While the phenomenon of new parties emerging on the eve of elections was not new, the circumstances that led to the rise of these two parties made the electoral landscape more intriguing. Formed eight months prior to the election, the *EFF* was led by the former ANC youth league leader, Julius Malema. Ousted from the ANC for bringing the party into disrepute, he played on the sentiments of the disaffected voters who felt economically vulnerable and excluded from state benefits. The EFF effectively translated such feelings into populist support for itself. Unfortunately for *Agang SA*, which had been formed in early 2012 by Mamphele Ramphele, a former political activist and manager at the World Bank, the razzmatazz of its presence soon dissolved into a spiral of poor timing, internal strife and a botched merger with the DA.

The Independent Electoral Commission (IEC) had three voter registration periods that saw a total of 25,381,293 South Africans being registered for participation in this election. They cast 18,402,492 valid votes, constituting a voter turnout of 73.4%. IEC officials noted that they were caught by surprise by the *higher voter turnout* than in previous years. There was never any doubt that the ANC would remain in power for another five years. The more strategic question was what would be the final percentage that would see the ruling party over the finish line. Speculation was rife that the ANC might even dip below the 60% mark. In the months leading to the election, the ruling party had lost appeal in certain sections of the electorate, especially among the youth and in some lower-working-class groups. There were attempts to consolidate the party's footprint in Gauteng, which became a hotly contested province, with the DA spending R (rand) 100 m trying to secure a victory in South Africa's economic heartland. The ANC's own internal polling indicated that the party could expect to get 62%-64% of the vote, which reflected levels it had obtained in 1994.

Twenty-nine political parties contested the national election, of which thirteen managed to attract enough votes to win seats in the National Parliament. The challenge for the smaller political parties was to establish their relevance and identity amongst a discerning electorate, especially in view of the upcoming local government elections due in 2016. The official results were announced by the IEC on 10 May. The

ANC scored 62.2% and interpreted this as a vindication of its electoral campaign slogan 'A Good Story to Tell' and a sign that the electorate still had confidence in its ability to govern. But the result demonstrated a fall in support for the party from the 2009 election, when it had received 65.9% of the vote. Though a relative decline of 3.7% might be construed as a negligible drop in support, it represented in absolute numbers hundreds of thousands of lost votes.

The DA broke the 4 m mark in voter support, increasing its level of support to 22.2% from 16.7% in 2009, and appeared satisfied with its performance, although it missed its declared goal of 30% by some way. The DA remained in control of the Western Cape, where it managed to improve its performance to 59.4% from 51% in 2009. The ANC, on the other hand, which sought to recapture control of the Western Cape, only managed to improve its performance by 1.4% from 2009 (31.5%) to 32.9%. The DA made substantial gains in Gauteng, registering a 9% increase in its electoral footprint to 30.8% (up from 21.8% in 2009).

Unfortunately for the ANC, *Gauteng* recorded the largest loss in voter support for the party of over 10% from 64% in 2009 to 53.6%. Not only did this rattle the party in terms of its identity among voters in the province, but it also raised significant issues as to whether the party had suffered the consequences of the policies it had endorsed such as the controversial e-tolls, not to mention social service delivery protests and the issues related to Zuma's use of state funds to upgrade his homestead in Nkandla, which were seen as undermining the party's electoral impact in the province.

The biggest winner was the EFF. Despite its often unrealistic election promises, the party did significantly well in securing 6.4% of the vote. Most analysts had predicted 4%–6%, so the newly-formed party with its signature red beret exceeded expectations. In Gauteng, where the EFF took 10.3% of the vote, the ANC was the casualty. In two provinces, Limpopo and North West, the EFF unseated the Congress of the People (COPE) and the DA, respectively, to become the official opposition. Overall, the EFF secured third place on the national results list, as well as in the majority of the provinces, except in Kwazulu Natal, where it was fourth, given that Kwazulu Natal is an ANC stronghold. The support for the EFF could be interpreted as a 'protest vote' against the ANC, especially on the part of lower-working-class constituents, who wanted to demonstrate their frustrations with the ruling party's inertia and disregard for their interests.

The other significant trend to emerge from this election was the contraction of smaller political opposition parties. COPE, which had emerged as a splinter party from the ANC in 2008 following the resignation of the then-president Thabo Mbeki, was the main sufferer from voter dissatisfaction. COPE only managed to win 0.7% of the vote compared with 7.4% in 2009. At the provincial level, COPE had lost the confidence of its supporters, especially in the Northern Cape and the Eastern Cape, where the party's proportion of the votes fell from 16.7% and 13.7%, respectively, in

2009 to 3.6% and 1.2%. This loss was indicative of the party's implosion as a result of leadership struggles. It would appear that the DA and EFF gained as a result of COPE's poor showing. Another telling feature of the election was the emergence of the National Freedom Party (NFP), which had broken away from the Inkatha Freedom Party before the 2011 municipal elections. The party demonstrated its resolve both nationally and provincially by gaining 1.6% in the national ballot and 7.3% within KwaZulu Natal. The NFP's support base appeared to be constituencies in rural areas and women.

Observers noted a *realignment of power structures*, both party internal as well as in the way the electorate responded to what had previously been perceived as traditional voting constituencies. For all political parties, the lessons learnt from this election were to not under-estimate the sophistication of the electorate and, more importantly, that voters use their vote to demonstrate their frustrations with inefficiencies, poor governance, unfilled promises and lack of service delivery. Critics were quick to point out that the outcomes of the election did not reflect any significant shifts in voting behaviour because the ANC still remained the major winner and South Africa continued to have a system dominated by one party. As Collette Schulz-Herzenberg pointed out, however, this view had to be contextualised within the broader electoral landscape, where the ANC's majority status was slowly being eroded. According to her, "the proportion of eligible voters voting for the ANC decreased steadily since its peak at 54% in 1994 to 35% by the end of the second democratic decade. Despite its continued electoral dominance ... the party has suffered significant losses over twenty years of democracy." This seemed to indicate voter apathy in the ANC's electoral base.

The election was not free of incidents: some polling stations opened late; there was a shortage of voting materials at some stations and long queues due to the ill-preparedness of electoral officials. In other instances, opposition parties such as Agang, the DA and EFF lodged complaints about irregularities ranging from dumped ballot papers outside of Pretoria the day after the votes were counted and ballot papers found stored at an ANC party agent's house on the East Rand, to accusations of collusion between IEC officials and ANC personnel and claims of vote rigging by the EFF. The IEC dealt with the issues by opening investigations and in some of the cases taking punitive action against its own officials. This did not have drastic implications for the integrity of the elections. Rather, it was the *integrity of the IEC* that was brought into question. In April, the IEC was caught in another controversy related to a leasing agreement involving several IEC personnel, including former chairperson Pansy Tlakula, who had already been investigated by the public protector in 2013. According to the public protector's report then and a report compiled by the National Treasury in March, there were irregularities in the procurement process of the leasing agreement. In dealing with the legal battles, the IEC's chief electoral officer, Mosotho Moepya, took a decision to allow the IEC to cover Tlakula's legal fees. The IEC deputy chairman, Terry Tselane, responded to the issue by noting that Moepya had made this decision without authorisation and that the IEC had called for a report on the matter. Not only did this plunge the IEC into another scandal on the eve of the elections, but it also cast a shadow on its impartiality and raised questions of public trust in the institution; several opposition parties instituted court actions against Tlakula, claiming that her integrity had been compromised. In September, Tlakula resigned as IEC chairperson after a protracted year-long battle to clear her name, when the Electoral Court recommended in June that the National Assembly (NA) should remove her.

On 24 May, Zuma was inaugurated to serve a second presidential term. His *cabinet* saw some significant changes. Cyril Ramaphosa was sworn in as deputy president with Deputy Finance Minister Nhlanhla Nene promoted to minister of finance. Nene became the first black minister to be appointed to hold this portfolio since the democratic elections in 1994. The newly constituted cabinet consisted of 35 ministers with 14 members from the previous administration returning to serve in the fifth administration in democratic South Africa. Critics immediately pointed out that the bloated cabinet was expensive and unwieldy. The second Zuma government also saw the creation of three new ministries: the Ministry for Telecommunications and Postal Services, Ministry of Water and Sanitation, and Ministry for Small Business Development. The composition of the cabinet also gave significant insight into Zuma's brand of politics. Of the 14 returning cabinet members, the following kept their portfolios: Angie Motshekga (basic education), Maite Nkoana-Mashabane (international relations and cooperation), Ebrahim Patel (Economic Development), Blade Nzimande (higher education), Fikile Mbalula (sport and recreation), Rob Davies (trade and industry); and Aaron Motsoaledi (health). Others were moved: Jeff Radebe was moved from minister of justice to minister in the Presidency while the former minister of police, Nathi Mthetwa, was appointed minister of arts and culture; Collins Chabane, who had served as minister in the Presidency for performance, monitoring and evaluation, became minister of public administration. In a more dramatic shift, Zuma announced the merging of the National Planning Commission and the Performance Monitoring and Evaluation Ministry into the Presidency to harmonise planning and monitoring functions. The merged ministry was also responsible for youth development. Other cabinet choices signalled the entry of unknown ministers, especially in the state security cluster. For analysts, the appointments in the security cabinet sector indicated a growing sense of *insulation around the executive*. In particular, Nathi Mwetha's selection as arts and culture minister was seen as a demotion in response to his handling of the public protector's investigation of the 'Nkandlagate' scandal.

Following the inauguration, the fifth parliament was instituted. In delivering the *State of the Nation Address* (SONA) on 17 June, Zuma highlighted economic growth and job creation as key drivers for the National Development Plan (NDP). Again it was the same old mantra, but this time with added emphasis that the government's plans over the next five years were to advance policies that would reduce poverty, inequality and unemployment. This followed closely the 13 February SONA, in which Zuma had stressed the need to revitalise the growth of the economy to meet the NDP targets. In both instances, the SONA speeches seemed to be a repetition of issues identified in the Zuma administration's previous term, without adding how this was to be achieved or setting out a pragmatic plan of action.

While the elections and post electoral trends dominated headlines for the first half of the year, more critical issues emerged relating to internal politics in the ANC's tripartite alliance partner, Cosatu (Congress of South African Trade Unions), as well as in respect of the separation of powers between the executive and independent institutions that served to strengthen the country's democratic governance processes. Amid deep divisions in the federation, *Cosatu* held its central executive committee meeting on 22 February to discuss, among other things, the sensitive issue of whether the second largest affiliate in its ranks, the National Union of Mineworkers of South Africa (Numsa) should remain part of the labour organisation. In December 2013, Numsa had passed a resolution at its special congress, which included calling for Cosatu to withdraw from the tripartite alliance and retract electoral support for the ANC. The Cosatu-Numsa friction reflected a growing factionalism in the federation, which some analysts had seen as emerging even before the Marikana crisis in 2012. This unravelling of the labour movement was seen to be linked to the capture of the movement by a pro-Zuma camp and the rise of an anti-Zuma faction in response. Other analysts believed that the breakdown of relations between Cosatu's executive and Numsa was a symptom of deeper structural issues that undermined the federation. In their opinion it was argued that Numsa's expulsion from the organisation in November was not only because of the affiliate's intransigence regarding its anti-ANC position but also because the federation's structures had been weakened by internal corruption issues.

Numsa's expulsion set into motion speculation about the formation of a new workers' party by the union. In response, Numsa's president, Irvin Jim, announced that the union would be launching a new social movement called the United Front (UF). The launch was scheduled for December but was delayed. The UF's imminent launch brought into focus the possibility of Numsa contesting the 2016 local government elections, raising profound questions over the impact this would have on Cosatu's electoral support for the ANC and whether it would split the affiliates within the federation as well as the working-class vote. The expulsion of Numsa certainly caused serious divisions in Cosatu, with some affiliates throwing their weight behind the union, but it also tested the resolve of the tripartite alliance with regard to its own future.

On the eve of Christmas, Anwar Dramat, the head of the Directorate for Priority Crime Investigation, also known as the *Hawks*, which targets organised crime, economic crime, corruption and other serious crime issues, was suspended by the minister of police because of a pending investigation into his alleged involvement in facilitating the illegal rendition of Zimbabweans in November 2010. Media reports noted that the suspension was politically motivated. There was speculation that Dramat could have been initiating an investigation into 'Nkandlagate'. At the same time, the legal question was raised of whether it was constitutional for the police minister to take such a decision. Central to the legality of the suspension was a Constitutional Court ruling on 27 November, which set aside provisions in the South African Police Service Amendment Act and gave the minister sole discretion as to whether or not to suspend the head of the Hawks. The Constitutional Court ruling also stated that the Hawks should be given 'adequate' independence but pushed for parliamentary oversight to be amplified: under the relevant section of the Act, the minister was required to notify parliament, and a committee of the NA was required to consider the pending suspension before it could be legally implemented. The Dramat issue raised concern over the separation of powers in relation to the three spheres of government and was expected to put confidence in the country's governance under observation.

The Farlam Commission of Inquiry into the shooting of the *Marikana* miners continued to hear testimony, including from Deputy President Cyril Ramaphosa. The Commission experienced extended delays in its hearings due to the loss of vital documents (including video evidence), the death of witnesses and a legal battle over state funding for lawyers representing the families of the miners killed, injured and arrested. In September, the president extended the term of the Commission to March 2015.

Xenophobia continued to plague South Africa. In May, three foreign-owned shops in Alexandra were looted. In June, local youths attacked Somali shopkeepers in Mamelodi East, Pretoria. The latter incident resulted in two Somalis being killed and around 100 men, women and children fled their shops and homes. In August, the Department of Home Affairs announced the creation of the 2014 Zimbabwean Special Dispensation Permit (ZSP), to replace the 2009 Dispensation of Zimbabweans Project. The allowed holders of permits received under the previous dispensation to live, work, conduct business and study in South Africa for the duration of the permit, valid until 31 December 2017. The introduction of the ZSP was a welcome move in view of more stringent visa requirements that were announced early in the year and gazetted in May. But there was also uncertainty as to whether border post officials would understand the new visa rules, especially regarding returning visa holders coming back into the country.

The new *visa regime* also saw major changes to six fundamental areas related to short- and long-stay applications. In particular, rules related to business visas and critical skills were tightened. Quota and exceptional skills work permits were replaced by a critical skills permit, while the business visa was required to be accompanied by a recommendation letter from the Ministry of Trade and Industry. The challenge under the critical skills visa was for employers to show why such skills could not be sourced domestically, in line with the publication of a critical skills list. In addition, critics saw the inclusion of the Ministry of Trade and Industry in the consultative procedure for both business and critical skills visa applications as delaying the process even further.

During the second half of the year, there were intense parliamentary debates regarding the public protector's report on the financing of Zuma's private residence, *Nkandla*, in KwaZulu Natal. The joint committee set up by parliament to review the report was viewed as biased by opposition parties. In a united front, opposition parties claimed that ANC MPs on the committee had engaged in a process aimed at shielding Zuma. In September, opposition parties walked out of the committee, arguing that they would not legitimise a flawed process that would undermine the Constitution. Part of the opposition's frustrations sprang from the refusal by ANC MPs to agree to answer questions and to enforce Public Protector Thuli Madonsela's directive that Zuma repay a portion of the funds spent on the R 246 m refurbishment of his home. Despite the walkout, the committee continued its deliberation as the ANC presence on the committee constituted a quorum. In November, the committee released its findings, which stated that it would be premature to conclude that Zuma had benefited unfairly from the security upgrades to Nkandla, as the public protector's report had alleged. Rebecca Davies commented in the 'Daily Maverick' that the report exonerated Zuma "almost entirely, while seeking to place blame on officials portrayed as having run riot on the project". The committee also resolved that Zuma did not need to pay back the money since there was no rational basis for suggesting that he had benefitted unduly from the security upgrades.

'*Pay back the money*' became a haunting slogan that engulfed the NA on 21 August when the house descended into chaos during a question and answer session with Zuma. EFF MPs insisted that he respond to the question of when he would repay the money related to Nkandla, to which he replied that he had done so a week before. Not satisfied with the response, EFF MPs persisted with the chant, which led to the sitting of the NA being suspended by the speaker, Baleke Mbete, who called in security personnel to remove the EFF MPs when they refused to leave. Fighting erupted between MPs and security staff, and the event was widely commented upon in the media as a disgraceful act of intolerance and weak handling of the matter by the ANC parliamentary group.

Foreign Affairs

South Africa's international engagements were defined by the celebration to mark the *twentieth anniversary* of the advent of democracy. Most embassies and foreign missions held events to commemorate this historic moment in post-apartheid history, including contributions made by the international community in the anti-apartheid struggle. The country's foreign policy did not undergo any fundamental shifts and represented a continuity with the Zuma administration's first term. Africa remained a pivot in South Africa's international engagements, especially in relation to the BRICS countries, the UN General Assembly, and the G20. In the run up to the 6th *BRICS Summit* hosted by Brazil on 14–16 July, South Africa was considered as joint frontrunner with India to host the headquarters of the BRICS Development Bank. China's last-minute coup to secure the headquarters of the Bank, which was renamed the New Development Bank, saw Pretoria concurrently setting up its African Regional Office, which was expected to be located in Johannesburg.

In maintaining South Africa's role as broker and negotiator of peace and stability, Deputy President *Cyril Ramaphosa was appointed special envoy* to South Sudan as well as for Sri Lanka and Lesotho. Ramaphosa was tasked to provide assistance in bringing about peace and reconciliation in these countries, which were emerging from internal conflicts. In the cases of South Sudan and Sri Lanka, Zuma's initiative was in response to a call for assistance by the two governments. Ramaphosa's position was tested following a political impasse in *Lesotho*. Appointed as mediator on behalf of South Africa and SADC on 15 September, his efforts aimed at stabilising the country's political environment ahead of elections in February 2015 (two years ahead of schedule) by continuing consultations with key political stakeholders around the Maseru security accord that was signed on 23 October. But sentiments in Lesotho regarding Ramaphosa's mediation were not always positive. Critics said that, in pushing for the implementation of the Maseru accord, he was only serving the interests of the party that would be declared the winner of the upcoming election. Observers who argued that Ramaphosa's job was made difficult by the unwillingness of stakeholders to comply and work together rejected these claims. In other peace and stability efforts, South Africa was appointed to replace Lesotho as chair of the *SADC Organ on Politics, Defence and Security*, seen as a crucial role for maintaining stability in the region. Subsequently, South Africa led electoral observer missions to Mozambique and Mauritius.

South Africa's foreign policy ambiguities were highlighted in September when the *Dalai Lama*'s application for a visa to attend the World Summit of Nobel Peace Prize Laureates, to be hosted in Cape Town in October, was refused, for the fourth time in five years. The Summit was moved to Rome in protest. Reactions included calls for Zuma to intervene and resolve the issue by granting the spiritual leader the visa. Archbishop Desmond Tutu described the ANC as being "worse than the apartheid government". The Dalai Lama visa fiasco raised further concerns about South Africa's commitment to the Mandela legacy of human rights values – in the year when Pretoria was celebrating the twentieth anniversary of its return to the international fold and its embrace of multilateralism for a just, reformed and international order based on the rule of law.

A report by *HRW* underlined the contradictions in South Africa's role, which was described by the minister of the Department of International Relations and Cooperation (DIRCO) as "a progressive agent for positive change". The report concluded that the country's voting record on country specific situations and some rights issues at the UN had been considerably disappointing. Examples included the March session, when South Africa, jointly with Russia, Ethiopia, Saudi Arabia, Egypt and China, sought to weaken a resolution on the right to peacefully protest. The report highlighted the inconsistency in South Africa's stance on the question of crimes against humanity. In June, South Africa had supported an amendment to a protocol in the African Court of Justice and Human Rights that provided for immunity from prosecution for serving heads of state and senior government officials, including with regard to war crimes, crimes against humanity and genocide. This was seen as a direct contravention of the country's overall support for international justice and clashed with what was described by scholars Chris Alden and Maxi Schoeman as South Africa's global and continental role of "mediator-integrator, bridge, anti-imperialist agent, developer, and regional leader and protector". This was tested during a meeting of the AU in Addis Ababa (Ethiopia) in early October, when it was deliberated whether African states should remain part of the ICC, which they saw as unfairly targeting continental leaders. Botswana and Nigeria explicitly stressed their continued support for the Court, while Pretoria seemed more tepid in its response. The predicament for Pretoria was to navigate multiple roles and their corresponding identities, all the while balancing official policy stances with realities.

Despite South Africa's sometimes peculiar stance on its international obligations, a landmark ruling by the Constitutional Court created a precedent in upholding the country's role in *international criminal justice*. The Southern African Litigation Centre and the Zimbabwean Exiles Forum lodged an application to compel South Africa to abide by its domestic and international legal obligations to investigate and prosecute high-level Zimbabwean officials accused of crimes against humanity. In its ground breaking judgment, the Constitutional Court unanimously ruled that the South African Police Service should investigate crimes against humanity perpetrated in Zimbabwe in 2007. The ruling also put into focus the way in which South Africa's international commitments to justice could serve as a platform to further the rule of law in view of a weakened SADC Tribunal.

South Africa expelled three Rwandan diplomats linked to an attack on an exiled Rwandan general's home in Johannesburg on 6 March. This was after the murder in mysterious circumstances of Rwanda's former spy chief Patrick Karegeya on 1 January in an upmarket hotel in Johannesburg. *Rwanda* retaliated by expelling six South African officials. Tensions between the two countries intensified and complicated joint peace efforts in the eastern DRC. While Rwandan President Kagame maintained that the government was not responsible for the attacks, South Africa's granting of asylum to the former army chief after a failed coup attempt against Kagame strained relations further. On 10 September, the four accused in the attempted murder of former General Faustin Kayumba Nyamwasa, who had been shot in the stomach in June 2010, were sentenced to eight years' imprisonment by a South African court.

South Africa's new visa regime also caused tensions with *Kenya*. The diplomatic standoff with Nairobi included almost double visa fees for Kenyans applying to stay longer than 30 days in South Africa, as well as a charge for a visa for up to 30 days, which had previously been free. The new regulations incensed Kenyan officials, who warned that they would reciprocate.

In November, the bodies of 74 of the 81 people killed in the collapse of a Nigerian church guesthouse were flown back to South Africa. The incident increased tensions with *Nigeria*. Pretoria accused Abuja of not doing enough to investigate the incident and said the Nigerian authorities had not reacted quickly enough to rescue those trapped under the rubble. It also complained that Nigeria took too long to release the bodies. Nigerian church leader T.B. Joshua also came under fire, with the DA calling for the DIRCO minister to institute a class action against him as well as to investigate "the assistance of the South African government and the cooperation of the Nigerian government in as far as the tragedy is concerned". The ANC youth league were more militant in their response, demanding that Joshua be barred from entering the country until an investigation into the disaster was completed.

Socioeconomic Developments

The focus of the country's socio-economic developments was built around the twentieth anniversary. The ANC's election motto, 'A Good Story to Tell', based on the release of the *twenty-year review*, informed the first half of the year's programme prior to the May elections. The review noted that the country had embarked on an ambitious project of democratic nation-building and socio-economic transformation. South Africa was a markedly different place from the one it had been in 1994, in almost every respect. The report concluded that the country had made remarkable progress and had "emerged from its deeply divided and violent past into a peaceful, robust and vibrant democracy that has made major strides in improving the lives of its citizens" and asserted that South Africa had achieved or was on track to meet many of the MDGs by 2015. It also indicated that poverty had been reduced and the quality of service delivery had improved, but that corruption in both the public and private sectors was "impeding service delivery, undermining public confidence in the state and the economy, and reducing economic growth, competitiveness and investment." The report emphasised that the NDP would inform and serve as the government's roadmap.

The overall *socio-economic performance* for the year, however, yielded less than satisfactory results, and was also affected by drops in global trade demand and high unemployment. In the first quarter, GDP showed a negative growth rate of –1.6%, while improving to 0.5% in the second quarter before regaining some momentum in the following six months. In August, the 'Mail and Guardian' reported that the country had narrowly missed spiralling into a technical recession following data released by the state statistics agency, Stats SA, which showed negative growth in the first and second quarters of the year. Stats SA also reported that the economy grew by 2.1% in the third quarter and 4.5% in the fourth quarter. Notwithstanding the recovery in the last two quarters, the economy only grew by 1.5% over the year, which was significantly lower than the 2.2% recorded in 2013, despite the World Bank revising the country's economic forecast to 2% in June. The Washington based International Financial Institution highlighted "tight monetary policy combined with labour strikes and deficient electricity supply" as reasons that "will keep growth subdued in South Africa". Analysts also noted that GDP data was well below the 5% growth needed to stimulate job creation for more than 7 m active young people seeking jobs.

Strike action by workers in the mining and manufacturing sectors in the first half of the year cut into productivity at a time when global demand for commodities was easing. A five-month strike in the platinum industry, which ended in June, took its toll on the economy by severely denting foreign exchange earnings. Production losses as a result of the strike by the 70,000 miners were estimated at almost $ 2.2 bn, according to the mining companies involved. Towards the end of November, the end of a protracted postal strike was in sight. At the centre of the dispute were calls for a 7% wage increase and permanent employment for more than 7,000 casual workers. The disruption caused by the strike led to a high level of frustration among customers unable to access essential services.

The South African economy's weaker performance suffered further when Standard & Poor's downgraded the country's sovereign *rating* to one level above junk status and Moody's decided in August to lower the ratings of South African banks; Fitch maintained South Africa's credit rating at BBB in a note issued in December, but revised its outlook to negative, citing concerns over growing current account and budget deficits. Further revisions, which could be made if the economy failed to regain momentum, would probably result in higher borrowing costs in 2015.

To contain rising *inflation and weak economic growth*, the Monetary Policy Committee of the Reserve Bank (South Africa's central bank) increased interest rates twice during the year, by 50 basis points each time. The beginning of the year saw two petrol price rises, with economists cautioning that this would place an onerous burden on household budgets, transport costs and the indirect impact on food prices for consumers. The volatility of the rand was cited as the main reason for the increase. Towards the end of the year, as the price of Brent crude dipped to below $ 60 a barrel, there was talk of consumers enjoying some relief at the pumps in early 2015. Inflation eased to 5.3% in December, the lowest in more than a year, after peaking at 6.6% in June. Lower oil prices also helped to contain inflation, even as the rand depreciated by 10% against the US dollar during the year.

The year also saw the appointment of a new *central bank governor*. In September, Gill Marcus announced that she would be stepping down as governor of the Reserve Bank when her five-year term came to an end in November. The announcement met with mixed reactions in the markets. The rand weakened amid speculation as to who would succeed her. The appointment eventually went to the Bank's deputy governor, Lesetja Kganyago, and was viewed favourably by the markets as a continuation of the Bank's credible monetary policy.

Finance Minister Nhlanhla Nene delivered his maiden *medium term budget* speech to Parliament in October and warned that South Africa was facing a new age of 'pain' in its economy. He stated that the country had reached an economic crossroads where the government's previous counter cyclical approach to stimulate spending was no longer viable. He went on to say that "over the last five years, expansionary policies cushioned South Africa from the effect of the global crisis", but "public debt is now approaching the limits of sustainability. Debt-service payments consume a growing share of the national budget, narrowing the space to expand public services and investment." As part of the government's response, the minister acknowledged that fiscal consolidation could no longer be postponed. He outlined a threefold proposal for change, which would affect almost all South Africans and which entailed that, over the coming two years, the government would lower its consumption expenditure by R 25 bn; the overall government spending ceiling would be lowered; and tax revenue would be increased by at least R 27 bn. The new fiscal proposals signalled, in Nene's words, "a call to action to all of us to take the pain". This move was seen as an unavoidable measure to narrow the budget deficit, stabilise debt and begin to rebuild fiscal space and also aimed to appease international credit rating agencies.

The *energy crisis* escalated. March saw the country experience load shedding for the first time since 2008. The resumption of the rolling blackouts emerged as a result of Eskom, South Africa's electricity supply company, not being able to increase generation capacity and it was noted that it would need to secure more substantial funding to meet electricity demand. While both the outgoing CEO Brian Dames and the former minister of public enterprise, Malusi Gigaba, apologised to the nation, Eskom board chairman Zola Tsotsi warned South Africans that the country was facing prospects of more steep load shedding "for some time, even when new capacity comes online" because it would take time to build confidence in the new capacity's reliability. In November, the load shedding rollouts intensified due to the collapse of a coal storage silo at the Majuba power plant, which provided approximately 10% of South Africa's electricity. An article published by the 'Financial Times' in December predicted that, after years of poor planning and under-investment, supply would remain severely constrained into 2015 and beyond. Economists also warned that the load shedding would impact on the country's FDI attractiveness and credit ranking. The electricity outages affected the two major sectors of the economy, mining and manufacturing, which not only added to the country's economic woes but also caused alarm among small businesses, concerned about how this would affect consumer spending during the festive season. The troubles of *Eskom* as the public utility provider continued when it emerged that performance bonuses amounting to R 24.4 m had been paid to its top three executives, with other top brass receiving bonuses of R 62.8 m. With the South African public having to pay increased electricity tariffs and experience higher levels of blackouts, there was a public outcry against these exorbitant payments while Eskom was in a financial and operational crisis. The DA called for Eskom to be privatised, while the ANC countered that this was not likely to happen. In addition, Eskom also toyed with the idea of asking staff to consider voluntary redundancy packages as a means to address the utility's capital crisis.

Financial problems continued to undermine *South African Airways* (SAA). Following the portfolio committee on public enterprises oversight visit to the SAA offices in November, it emerged that the state-owned enterprise needed a capital injection in order to be able to operate to capacity; it would otherwise face liquidation. To address the crisis, the airline was given 90 days to develop a viable financial plan that would return the airline to solvency; stem operational losses; sort out regulatory compliance; and ensure proper governance and accountability mechanisms. The last was seen as the most critical issue facing the airline when Public Enterprise Minister Lynne Brown replaced most of the board and sent the board chair on 'special leave'. The appointment of acting CEO Nico Bezuidenhout following the board ructions also came under scrutiny, with questions being asked about his qualifications.

The state-owned *South African Broadcasting Company* (SABC) also came under fire regarding the qualifications of its chief operating officer, Hlaudi Motsoeneng, and chairperson, Ellen Tshabalala. An investigation, which dragged on for more that six months, caused considerable tension regarding parliament's oversight role. The parliamentary portfolio committee asserted that it had sought to question Communications Minister Faith Mutambi and the SABC board regarding the appointment of the two executives. In October, Tshabalala successfully obtained an interim stay from the Western Cape High Court halting the committee's inquiry into whether she had lied about her academic qualifications.

Corruption continued to blight the country's socio-economic landscape. The NGO Corruption Watch noted, in its response to TI's 2014 Corruption Perception Index report, that the South African authorities should not take comfort from the fact that the country's ranking of 67th with a score of 44 out of 100 had not slipped further in the index. The 'Mail and Guardian' reported that, despite that the ANC-led government having in the past few elections listed fighting corruption as one of its top priorities, little progress had been made in convincing the population that the war would soon be won. The newspaper went on to say that "the implication of the politically connected in corruption has also added to the loss of faith in government's will to stop dishonesty and theft of public funds." Critics pointed out that the endemic corruption in public sector departments also meant stress on service delivery outputs.

Swaziland

Marisha Ramdeen and Senzwesihle Ngubane

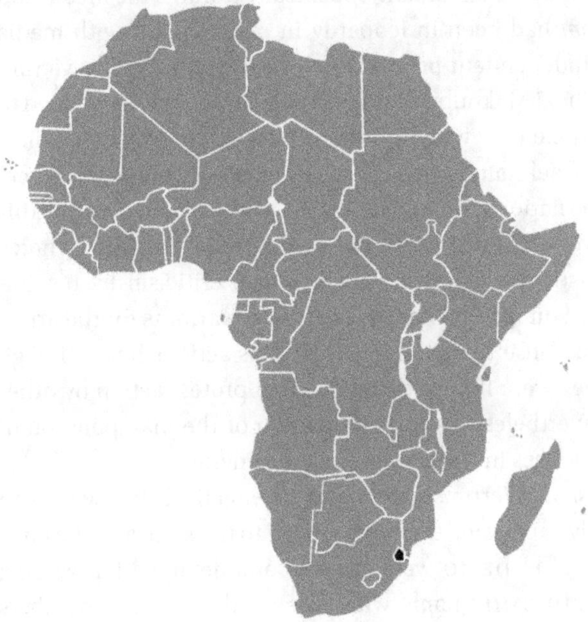

Political intimidation and existing media censorship, coupled with what appeared to be a flawed justice system, dominated Swaziland's political landscape during the year. International criticism mounted and the suspension of AGOA by the USA resulted in the downsizing of textile firms and a further negative effect on the declining economy. Excessive spending by the royal family, coupled with the king's controversial vanity project, Sikhuphe Airport, in the face of debilitating poverty and disease, continued to cause resentment among ordinary citizens. Actions and organised voices of protest on the part of various political actors calling for political reforms, no matter how constrained they were internally, continued, despite high risks.

Domestic Politics

While King Mswati III hailed the 2013 national elections as successful, the full election results and the figures for voters participating were never released. There was therefore no clear way of determining voter turnouts or what the trends were.

 | DOI 10.1163/9789004305052_054

The country is described as a monarchical democracy but all political parties are banned from taking part in elections. Pro-democracy groups such as the People's United Democratic Movement (PUDEMO), which is also the state's main opposition formation, continued to pursue democratic reforms. The government, however, engaged in a severe clampdown on dissent, specifically towards the media and labour unions. *Media freedom* had been in jeopardy in recent years, with media controlled by the state and independent print and televised media groups victimised. On 25 July, journalists Bheki Makhubu and Thulani Maseko were sentenced to two years in prison for an article they wrote questioning a case involving a police officer and Chief Justice Michael Ramodibedi. The sentence was met with outcry from both the local and international communities. In acknowledgement of this situation, Bheki Makhubu won the Press Freedom Award at the CNN/Multichoice journalism awards. Chief Justice Ramodibedi did not take criticism by his colleagues lightly. It was reported on 19 May that he had issued warrants for the arrest of three High Court judges because they disagreed with his actions but, although the warrants were issued, they were not executed due to a protest action by other judicial officers. This was nevertheless a strong indication of the manipulation of judges and the existing weaknesses in the legal system in general.

Furthermore, the *Suppression of Terrorism Act* was used effectively by the state to arrest Swazi people for merely expressing their opposition to the state and the king. On 23 April, seven members of PUDEMO were arrested and detained for wearing T-shirts and berets bearing PUDEMO's name when they gathered with members of the public in support of the arrested journalists. Despite the state's threatening stance towards pro-democracy activities, protest actions, such as the May Day event and the Global Week of Action for Democracy in September, continued. Following the May Day event, Swazi activists Mario Masuku and Maxwell Dlamini were arrested for terrorism after making speeches before approximately 7,000 people at the gathering.

On 8 October, the Swazi minister of labour and social security announced a *ban on labour unions*, which is in violation of the ILO Convention 87 prescribing protection of freedom of association and the right to organise. Workers' rights were already seriously compromised and the ban could be expected to lead to further infringements. A serious case in point was an incident in which approximately 500 textile employees of the Taiwanese-owned company Texray required medical treatment after inhaling poisonous fumes. According to a statement by the Trade Union Congress of Swaziland (TUCOSWA), "doors at the factory were locked making it difficult for workers to escape fumes.... close to 500 workers collapsed and had to be treated in various medical institutions." Following this incident, workers were forced to return to work, and work overtime to make up for losses in production. On 30 October, however, the government expressed its full support for the ILO gender-based violence convention set to be considered in Geneva in 2016, providing a basis for hope that this would change and improve rights for women, not only in the labour force, but in the social environment, too.

Swaziland's *human rights* record could be described as dismal; human rights violations continued to take place, mainly at the hands of the police, in addition to violence against women and children. The police seemed to have adopted a shoot-to-kill policy, which had been increasingly evident in recent years. Since December 2013, six suspects were shot and killed by police in various incidents. On 4 March, students were assaulted by police when they staged a school boycott after being denied the opportunity to take part in sporting activities. On 21 September, it was reported that more than 30 girls were caned for failing to participate in the annual Reed Dance ceremony. Some were beaten so badly that they needed medical treatment.

Foreign Policy

In response to the human rights abuses taking place, many international organisations expressed their condemnation. The Congress of South African Trade Unions showed continued support for unions and pro-democracy groups by joining TUCOSWA in calling for intense actions during the Global Week of Action for Democracy and also expressed its condemnation of the arrest of Mario Masuku. However, the *South African government* revoked the political asylum permits of three Swazi political activists who had sought asylum there since 2005 and who were high-ranking members of the Communist Party of Swaziland. The activists were reportedly told by South Africa that "Swaziland was a democracy and they faced no threat if they returned to the Kingdom".

While relations between the *EU* and Swaziland were cordial, the former criticised developments in domestic politics. Formal statements were issued by an EU spokesperson, outlining concerns regarding the severe punishment of Bheki Makhubu and Thulani Maseko. The EU statement, released on 1 April, reminded Swaziland that, under the Cotonou Agreement as the framework for Swaziland's cooperation with the EU, it had committed to a policy to respect democracy, the rule of law and human rights principles, which included freedom of expression and freedom of the media.

Denmark also voiced its concerns regarding political freedoms in the country. During a meeting with King Mswati on 5 June, the Danish ambassador urged Swaziland to comply with the demands of the ongoing AGOA negotiations, which would include changes to the notorious Suppression of Terrorism Act, which AI had called inherently repressive. Apart from the government, organisations based in Denmark, such as African Contact and the Red-Green Alliance, campaigned for the release of the journalists. In addition, on 26 June, the *USA* officially suspended

AGOA, citing the country's weak record of human rights and its failure to amend laws relating to civil, political and workers' rights.

International support for political reforms also came from the British Trades Union Congress (TUC). In a statement released on 10 October, the TUC urged the British government to step up and do more towards campaigning and calling for reforms and respect for human rights in the Kingdom of Swaziland. The statement also specifically expressed its support for the release of the political activists. The American Federation of Labour and Congress of Industrial Organisations (AFL-CIO), an umbrella body of trade unions in the USA, also joined those that were already condemning Swazi government actions that continued to impinge on fundamental freedoms. The AFL-CIO statement in particular came in the wake of the prime minister's statement threatening civil society activists who attended civil society events on the margins of the US-Africa Leaders' Summit on 4–6 August.

Socioeconomic Developments

The Swazi government continued to rely heavily on customs duties from SACU, from which it derived a significant portion of its revenue. The manufacturing, agricultural and textile sectors dominated the market, but external factors determined its successes and failures. Since the closing of the wood pulp industry in January 2010, the economy had relied heavily on the sugar industry. There was more focus on the *agricultural sector*. In a joint effort by the government, the EU and FAO, approximately 20,000 smallholder farmers were helped to produce more and higher quality food and connect with new markets. As drought and disease had a severe impact on the agricultural sector, this attempt sought to revitalise the farming sector and increase exports. The country had benefitted from trade under AGOA, so its suspension had severe repercussions on the economy, and on the *textile industry* in particular. Texray announced that approximately 1,450 workers would lose their jobs, as the company had previously sold all its merchandise to the USA.

Food security became a dire problem. Low rainfalls together with a mismanaged economy resulted in increased hunger. A majority of the population lived on less than $ 2 a day and, with an inflation rate of 5%-6% over the year, people could not afford to buy food. Furthermore, the kingdom was too dependent on food imports. According to a Global Hunger Index Report, more than 3 in 10 people in Swaziland were undernourished. Approximately 40% of the population suffered from stunted growth due to malnutrition and life expectancy was 49 years. On a positive note, harvests improved and were higher than in 2013. Maize output was up 22% and, according to the Vulnerability Assessment Committee, food insecurity decreased by 23%, indicating the improvement in cereal production. However, high levels of unemployment and the impact of HIV/AIDS continued to negatively affect food security.

Mismanagement of public assets was also largely to blame for this situation. *Sikhuphe Airport,* named King Mswati Airport, which had been under construction for ten years, was officially opened on 7 March. The airport, whose opening ceremony alone cost $ 600,000, had been dubbed the king's vanity project, though he declared it would elevate the country to first-world status. The airport had not yet been granted an operating licence by the International Air Transport Authority, however, was not equipped with hangars or office space, and was situated about 80 km from Mbabane. It was constructed at an estimated cost of $ 300 m, but no commercial airlines apart from Swaziland Airlink had yet made use of it, and neither did the king use it when travelling in his private jet.

King Mswati, who presented his fourteenth wife at the annual Reed Dance that took place from 31 August to 2 September, is Africa's third-wealthiest monarch, with an estimated personal fortune of $ 100 m. In spite of his wealth, his annual household budget rose by more than 10% to $ 61 m, over and above the 13% increase allocated to him in 2013. The king also generated income from other sources. He received dividends from locally operating multi-national companies such as cell phone giant MTN, sugar conglomerates Illovo and Remgro, Sun International hotels and beverages firm SAB Miller. The South African-based newspaper 'Sunday Times' reported that the king also earned income from Tibiyo Taka Ngwane, a trust held by the king to benefit the nation, although the money was channelled directly to the royal family. The wealth exhibited by the King is in vast contrast to the majority of *poverty*-stricken Swazi people. This paradox of wealth on the one hand, and debilitating poverty on the other, and the perceived failure of the state to deal effectively with the latter was once more reflected in August, when a severe diarrhoea outbreak took the lives of at least 36 children, while more than 500 more were hospitalised after the government said it did not have money to pay for available vaccines, although it was reported two months later that the government had spent $ 1.7 m on a top range of BMW cars.

Such developments, with high levels of poverty affecting the majority of the population side-by-side with opulence among very few elites, informed the view that the *calls for change* were not about to end. Calls for political reform were made not only in hope of seeing the opening up of political space so that genuine and free political activity could thrive, but also with the intention of expanding the possibility of the development of a state system responsive to the needs of ordinary citizens.

Zambia

Edalina Rodrigues Sanches

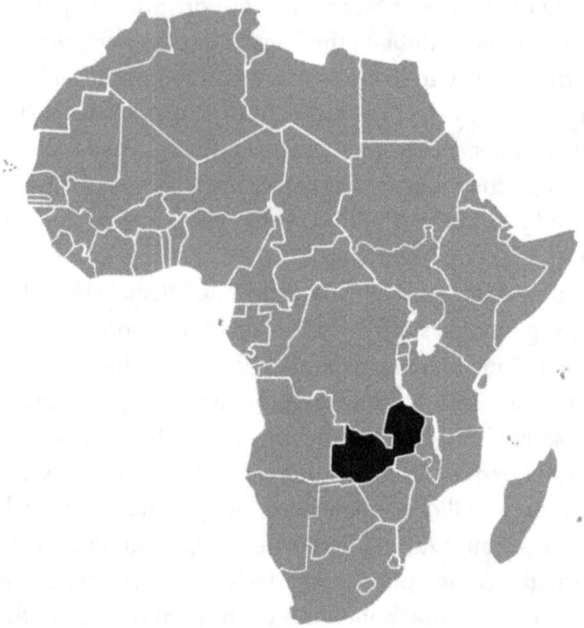

Zambia celebrated its golden jubilee on 24 October. Incumbent President Michael Sata, who did not attend the celebrations, died shortly afterwards after a period of failing health. Infighting escalated in the ruling Patriotic Front (PF) over leadership issues. Secretary General Edgar Lungu was chosen as the PF candidate for the 2015 presidential election at a highly contested and petitioned General Conference. The PF was the major winner in the parliamentary by-elections. The government released the long due draft constitution. There were landmark steps on freedom of speech and NGO registration. Economic diplomacy set the tone of the 'new foreign policy'. China continued to be the most important trading partner. Economic growth remained above 6%. Maize production reached record levels. The kwacha dropped to its lowest level ever, and copper prices fell to their lowest since 2009. Fuel prices were reduced twice following a global drop in oil prices. Public debt increased.

 | DOI 10.1163/9789004305052_055

Domestic Politics

On 28 October, *President Michael Sata died* in London at the age of 77, just four days after the celebrations of Zambia's golden jubilee – 50 years of independence – thus becoming the second president of Zambia to die in office, the first being Levy Mwanawasa in 2008. Sata's health had been a source of speculation almost from the start of his presidential mandate in 2011. During the year, he had been increasingly absent from public events, particularly in the second semester. His death intensified an already existing conflict between the party's main cadres over leadership issues. The *succession deadlock*, which could have been avoided if Sata had openly designated a successor, had important consequences for the stability and cohesiveness of the PF. In particular, it led to several episodes of factionalism and polarisation and eventually to the dismissal of prominent party cadres and cabinet ministers.

The political year started with *major ministerial reshuffles*. As early as March, Sata nominated eight new ministers for the portfolios of foreign affairs (Harry Kalaba replaced Wylbur Simuusa), information and broadcasting (Joseph Katema replaced Mwansa Kapeya), lands, natural resources and environmental protection (Mwansa Kapeya replaced Harry Kalaba), agriculture and livestock (Wylbur Simuusa replaced Robert Sichinga), commerce, trade and industry (Robert Sichinga replaced Emmanuel Chenda), community development, mother and child health (Emerine Kabansh replaced Joseph Katema), local government and housing (Emmanuel Chenda replaced Emerine Kabanshi) and tourism and arts (Jean Kapata replaced Sylvia Masebo). These portfolios had changed hands most since the start of Sata's mandate (particularly foreign affairs and information and broadcasting, which had each been the responsibility of five different ministers).

The ruling PF faced huge internal tests that threatened the unity of the party. Sata's ill health and unwillingness to choose a successor triggered infighting and the dismissal of important party cadres. In fact, *PF factionalism* was on the rise. Two camps had already formed in 2013, one backing Defence Minister Geoffrey Bwalya Mwamba and the other PF Secretary General and Justice Minister Wynter Kabimba as presidential candidates. Mwamba was eventually to be dismissed from the party and only the High Court stopped the PF from actually expelling him, so the dispute over the Sata succession turned into a different contest between Kabimba and Finance Minister Alexander Chikwanda. Kabimba was able to garner most support, including importantly Sata's, for whom he had been a legal advisor in earlier years (1986–88). In August, however, Kabimba launched suspicions that Chikwanda was protecting the interests of the mines and his own business interests, and the intense debate that followed led Sata to fire Kabimba, both as justice minister and as secretary general of the party. Although Kabimba argued that he was merely trying to expose corruption in government, many saw this as an attempt to get rid of Chikawanda. Sata chose Edgar Lungu to replace Kabimba.

Sata's death refuelled the succession battles, with the *presidential election* set for 2015. Vice President Guy Scott, who was constitutionally barred from standing for the PF at the election because of his Scottish parentage, gained influence over proceedings as acting president, but his appointment was questioned from the outset by some party members, especially Lungu. In November, after less than a week as acting president, Scott unexpectedly suspended Lungu as secretary general and warned PF members against indiscipline and infighting over the succession. The dismissal drew criticism from within the PF and led to rioting by some of Lungu's supporters in Lusaka. Scott eventually stepped back and reinstated Lungu one day after dismissing him. The method for selecting the party's candidate was one of the issues that set Lungu and Scott against each other and once again divided the party into two factions. Supporters of Lungu maintained that the party's Central Committee should pick the presidential candidate (who would be Lungu), while supporters of Scott insisted that the party constitution should be followed and that the PF should thus hold a General Conference for that purpose. Lungu's faction tried various strategies to avoid a conference, including threatening to resign and block the 2015 national budget and suspending their financial contributions to the party. Their most extreme action, however, took place on 21 November, when about 25 members of the party's Central Committee suspended Scott as the party's acting president for 60 days. Scott retaliated and suspended 16 members of the Central Committee on 22 November. The two factions eventually agreed to hold a General Conference to pick the presidential candidate, in which nine, out of the ten PF members who had filled out their nomination papers, competed. However, the 'real contest' set Lungu against Miles Sampa, who was supported by the Scott-led faction. Lungu was elected to be the candidate, but Scott considered his election null because the accreditation process was not followed. The results were taken to the courts, with both candidates claiming to be the party's legitimate presidential candidate. The party remained in deadlock for a few weeks and only united behind Lungu days before the official nomination of presidential candidates on 20 December.

Opposition parties also had their internal challenges. In the Movement for Multi-party Democracy (MMD), most members of the party's National Executive Committee (NEC) expressed public dissatisfaction with Nevers Mumba's leadership and wanted fresh elections within the party. Mumba had been the party leader since 2012, after being unseated by the PF, but faced opposition from within the party from the outset. Many important cadres did not see him as the party presidential candidate for the 2015 election and wanted to bring back former leader Rupiah Banda. In November, the NEC decided to suspend Mumba, alleging gross misconduct, but after the case was brought before the High and Supreme Courts, the latter ordered the MMD to restore Mumba as party president and ruled that the party should not implement the resolution to adopt Banda as the party's candidate.

Mumba filed his nomination papers by 20 December. In the United National Independence Party (UNIP), opposition to its president, Tilyenji Kaunda, for overstaying his period in office had steadily increased over the previous two years and eventually split the party in two. UNIP Active was launched to gather together all the factions and members of the party, address the leadership crisis in the party, and to lead the party to a National Congress. This group also wanted to bring legality to the party's structures (its Central Committee, Provincial Committees and District Committees), which lacked proper implementation and functioning, but it was considered by UNIP leaders to be illegal and representing an act of indiscipline. On a different note, the United Party for National Development (UPND), the Forum for Democracy and Development and the National Restoration Party (NAREP) showed a higher level of consensus about who their presidential candidates would be – namely Hakainde Hichilema, Edith Nawakwi and Elias Chipimo, respectively. Good *transparency* practices were followed by NAREP. In April, it made public its financial statement for 2013, which revealed that the party had a total income of ZK 1.603 m in 2013, including from programme support (ZK 903.466), donations (ZK 614.000) and membership contributions (ZK 83.600). The party spent ZK 1.597 m, including on elections (ZK 386.000), wages (ZK 339.705), provincial tours (ZK 266.100), training and workshops (ZK 280.372) and other expenditure.

New parties and alliances were set to contest the 2016 general elections. Former PF cadre and minister, Wynter Kabimba, formed the Rainbow Party, with the slogan 'United We Can'. An alliance brought together the former ruling MMD party, Frank Bwalya's Alliance for a Better Zambia, the People's Party and the Zambia Empowerment Democracy.

The PF was the biggest winner in the 2014 *by-elections*, with new MPs elected in Mkushi South (Davies Chisopa), New Vubwi (Margaret Miti) and Zambezi West (Christabel Ng'imbu). The MMD was the biggest loser since it had held a majority of seats in parliament before the by-elections but managed to keep only one (Kasenengwa: Victoria Kalima). The UPND retained its seat in Solwezi Central (Dawson Kafwaya) as well as in Katuba (Jonas Shakafuswa). After 13 rounds of parliamentary by-elections since 2011, the PF finally managed to secure a majority in parliament by September.

In October, just days before commemoration of Zambia's 50 years of independence, the government finally released the *draft constitution*. The document, had been leaked at the end of 2013 by anti-government media, and had been under examination by the PF cabinet and the Technical Committee from the start of 2014. It was eventually released after persistent pressure on the government from opposition parties, stakeholders and civil society organisations, including the Southern African Centre for the Constructive Resolution of Disputes.

A report of the international Committee to Protect Journalists put Zambia on a list of risk countries where *press freedom* had declined most in 2013. Nevertheless,

2014 saw a landmark change in freedom of expression regulation. The High Court ruled that publication of false news with intent to cause fear and alarm to the public was unconstitutional, as it contravened the protection of freedom of expression. This was important as the PF government had resorted to this ploy to silence its critics, ranging from opposition parties to civil society organisations.

NGOs and TI Zambia won an important battle against the government. Throughout the year, prominent civil society organisations refused to follow the government's directive to register under the NGO Act of 2009, which was seen to severely inhibit their independence and freedom. After extending several deadlines for registration, the government stepped back from imposing the *NGO Act of 2009* upon the NGOs, while the latter agreed to review this controversial proposal. In particular, the government suspended punitive measures set up to pressure NGOs to register under the new Act, while eight NGOs – including TI, ActionAid and the Forum for Democratic Process – withdrew their lawsuit against government over the Act. Zambia's score on the *corruption perception index* remained the same as in 2013 at 38 out of a possible 100.

Foreign Policy

In February, Foreign Affairs Minister Wylbur Simuusa stated that *economic diplomacy* would be the main component of Zambia's new foreign policy. Particular attention would be paid to economic cooperation by facilitating trade and attracting foreign investment in strategic national fields (e.g. mining, agriculture and tourism). These goals remained central to the government throughout the year and were pursued by the next minister to take over foreign affairs, Harry Kalaba. The enhancement of bilateral relations with *China* continued to be a priority. In fact, China's special status in the government's foreign relations was strongly emphasised by Kalaba in the presence of the Chinese Vice President Li Yuanchao, who visited Zambia in June for the inauguration of the photographic exhibition of 50 years of Zambia-China cooperation at the Lusaka Museum. President Sata and First Republican President Kenneth Kaunda also stressed the relevance of this partnership for the country's development, mainly for the implementation of several infrastructure projects.

In March, Zambia assumed the two-year rotational chairmanship of the UN's Group of Landlocked Countries (LLDCs). Ambassador Dr Mwaba Kasese-Bota was elected to the chairmanship. Relations with the *Arab oil emirates* featured prominently. In September, Mines, Energy and Water Development Minister Chris Yaluma stated that an agreement had been reached with his Saudi Arabian counterpart in which the latter promised to supply Zambia with "significant quantities" of petroleum on a long-term basis. He also declared the government's intention to pursue deals with Oman and the UAE to ultimately lower fuel prices in Zambia.

An earlier agreement with Kuwait, in the form of its Kuwait Fund for Arab Economic Development, foresaw the construction of a teacher training college in Northwestern Province, specialising in science, mathematics and technology.

In October, the governments of Zambia and *Angola* agreed on the withdrawal of visa requirements between the two countries, and on the need to link their business communities by roads and railway lines. In November, Harry Kalaba declared that the government would set aside ZK 2 m to open up new embassies, including in Australia and the UAE, to assist in repositioning Zambia within the global economy.

Despite speculation about his health, President Sata still managed to attend some *international summits*. In February, he attended the 22nd AU Summit, which focused on agriculture and food security and the 17th Common Market for Eastern and Southern Africa held in Kinshasa (DRC), and in April the 4th Africa-EU Summit in Brussels, where he also held bilateral meetings with the president of the European Commission, Jose Manuel Barroso, and Polish Prime Minister Donald Tuska.

However, Sata was hardly seen in public from mid-year. In August, he did not attend the 34th SADC Summit of Heads of State and Government held in Victoria Falls, and in September he delegated his ministers to represent him at high-level meetings at the 69th UN General Assembly, including the General Debate, the Climate Summit, the International Conference on Population and Development and the LLDCs. Henry Kalaba was delegated to deliver Zambia's statement to the UN General Assembly.

Socioeconomic Developments

The Zambia Demographic and Health Survey for 2007–14 revealed dramatic *improvements in some MDGs*: infant mortality fell from 70 deaths per 1,000 live births to 45 (against a 2015 MDG target of 36); under-five mortality fell from 119 deaths per 1,000 live births to 75 (against a 2015 MDG target of 64); and maternal mortality fell from 591 deaths per 100,000 live births to 398 (against a 2015 MDG target of 162). Zambia was ranked the 44th most peaceful country in the world, according to the 2014 Global Peace Index compiled by the Institute for Economics and Peace, being surpassed in Africa only by Mauritius and Botswana. The government recorded the largest ever maize harvest of 3,350,671 tonnes for the 2013/14 season. Nonetheless, this was also the year in which Zambia was considered the *most undernourished country* in Africa, and the second-most globally, with 48.3% of the population being undernourished, according to the State of Food Insecurity in the World report (annually produced by FAO, WFP and IFAD).

Economic growth remained above 6%, driven largely by copper infrastructure investment and supported by domestic demand. But the country's small size and relatively undiversified economy was affected by the fall in copper prices, economic slowdown in China, which accounts for the majority of copper exports, the global decline in fuel prices, and rising debt due to major public investments on infrastructure projects. In fact, the copper price fell to its lowest levels since 2009, particularly as a result of dramatic drops in oil prices, which fell by over 50% from mid-June. On the back of this, the Energy Regulation Board announced two reductions in fuel prices, in November and in December.

Another factor affecting economic performance was the way the PF government handled *pubic investment* priorities. Although the government carried out important projects to address the country's infrastructure deficiencies – connectivity, electricity, agriculture and mining infrastructures – these set Zambia's debt on a strong upward path. Projects included the Link Zambia 8000 Project (whose first phase envisaged the construction of 2,300 km of roads) and the Luangwa Bridge-Feira Road. As result of growing infrastructure investment, Zambia's *external debt* increased markedly to 17% of GDP by year's end, from 11% of GDP in 2010. The government eventually ran out of money and several projects had to be stopped and postponed, including the new international airport in Lusaka. Responding to this difficult economic year, the *national currency*, the kwacha, set a new record low. At the end of March, the Bank of Zambia had to inject $ 70 m into the financial sector to stabilise the kwacha, whose depreciation was accelerating (trading above ZK 6.40:$ 1).

Fitch nevertheless maintained Zambia's sovereign rating B (stable outlook) because of the country's *stable macroeconomic performance*, visible in continued GDP growth and low inflation rates. Similar assessments led Moody Investors Service to support Zambia's stable credit profile (B1) towards the end of the year. However, Doing Business 2015, an index for regulatory ease of doing business for local firms compiled by the International Finance Corporation of the World Bank (with rankings benchmarked to June 2014), reported that Zambia had fallen to 111th out of 189 countries. This was a significant decline as the country had ranked 83rd and 90th in Doing Business 2014 and Doing Business 2013, respectively.

Social unrest escalated in response to the government's policy of freezing wages. In 2013, Finance Minister Alexander Chikwanda had proposed a two-year wage freeze on public sector salaries and deferred new recruitment to 2015. This was meant to create fiscal space for the provision of basic social services and reduce money spent on the public sector wage bill. In May, ten unions representing public sector workers declared a dispute with government over its wage freeze policy, while Labour Minister Fackson Shamenda claimed that the wage freeze was aimed at harmonising the public sector wage structure.

Scrutiny of the *mining sector* intensified. The auditor general's report for July, on the management of wildlife, stated that nine mines were carrying out activities without licences in various national parks in the country; namely Fwaya-fwaya, Kapili-Nkesa, Jeff, Shell, Chipembele, Mwase Phiri, Kamusizya and Lupita in Lukusuzi national park and Easi Fuels mine in Kafue national park. In a highly publicised case, the Zambia Environmental Management Agency (ZEMA) stopped

China Jiangsu from mining illegally in Chongwe's Shantumbu area as the licence had originally been given to Vikram Investment Ltd. The Community-Based Natural Resources Management Forum also secured a win, when they were granted an injunction that temporarily stopped the development of the Kangaluwi Kangaluwi Copper Project in the Lower Zambezi National Park. News released in January indicated that Lands, Natural Resources and Environmental Protection Minister Larry Kalaba had overturned ZEMA's decision to block this project.

Regarding *bilateral economic trade agreements*, in May the government in collaboration with the COMESA put in place a committee to look at ways and means of increasing exports to the AGOA market in the USA. In July, Zambia and other African countries declined to sign the EPA with the EU, considering the export duties to be unfavourable to their countries' aspirations. The EU, as one regional block, offered full duty-free and quota-free market access to countries signing the EPA, who committed to opening at least 75% of their markets to the EU. The signing of this agreement was a condition for accession to the 'Everything but Arms' programme, which gave LLDCs full duty-free and quota-free access to the EU for all their exports, with the exception of arms and armaments. However, most African countries, and particularly Zambia's Minister of Commerce, Trade and Industry Emmanuel Chenda, contended that duty on exports compromised existing bilateral accords within the continent and would undermine the countries' ability to promote value-addition on raw materials, and thus to trigger the process of industrialisation and development.

Zimbabwe

Amin Y. Kamete

During the year, factional fights in both major parties were played out in the open. While the succession war in the Zimbabwe African National Union-Patriotic Front (ZANU-PF) seemed to have produced a victor – at least for the time being – the conflicts in the fractured and weakened opposition Movement for Democratic Change-Tsvangirai (MDC-T) raised more questions than answers. There was no substantive shift on the foreign affairs scene, the only movement being the lifting of targeted sanctions on some individuals and companies. The economy did not perform well, with critics and commentators indicating that the country was rapidly sliding back to the harrowing meltdown of 2008. 'Illegal' Western sanctions continued to be government's favourite scapegoat for the economic woes.

Domestic Politics

Relations between the major political parties remained strained as acrimonious exchanges, name-calling, accusations and counteraccusations persisted. The MDC-T continued to insist that the 2013 elections were rigged, with Morgan Tsvangirai characteristically refusing to recognise Robert Mugabe as the legitimate president.

 | DOI 10.1163/9789004305052_056

The bad blood came to the fore early in the year when the parties clashed over the passing of the Electoral Amendment Bill. The Bill was gazetted on 3 January. It aimed at aligning the Electoral Act with the new constitution. The Bill was fast tracked through parliament and was passed by the ZANU-PF-dominated house on 4 January. The MDC-T raised concerns that the amendments did not go far enough to guarantee free and fair elections and this view was echoed by other critics of the regime. They accused ZANU-PF of seeking to re-introduce postal voting, bar Zimbabweans in the diaspora from voting, legalise the use of voter registration slips and deny automatic access to the voters' roll. These issues had already been at the heart of the acrimony in the poisoned electoral landscape in 2013.

The *MDC-T* was rocked by internal disagreements and a *struggle for supremacy*, which apparently started when deputy treasurer general and former energy minister Elton Mangoma, in a letter to Tsvangirai, called for leadership renewal. Mangoma urged Tsvangirai to "consider leaving the office of the president of the movement", under a plan to restore hope and confidence in the party. The letter was reproduced in the state mouthpiece, 'The Herald', on 27 January and tore the opposition party apart. While ZANU-PF and the state-controlled media hailed Mangoma's letter, its reception in the MDC-T was decidedly hostile. Mangoma claimed he was a victim of violence within the party. On 31 January, the MDC-T National Executive formally censured Mangoma and passed a resolution branding him "MDC in name only". Tensions continued to rise in the MDC-T as Tsvangirai loyalists called for Mangoma to be punished. On 15 February, Mangoma was reportedly assaulted at the MDC-T headquarters in the presence of Tsvangirai. On 7 March, the MDC-T National Council suspended Mangoma as deputy treasurer general pending his appearance before an Independent Disciplinary Tribunal in accordance with the party constitution. On the same day, party secretary-general Tendai Biti, believed to be among the sponsors of the anti-Tsvangirai movement, quickly dismissed the controversial decision as null and void, arguing that due process had not been followed in line with the party constitution. On 16 February, MDC-T bigwigs boycotted a Tsvangirai rally in Harare. They included Biti, Mangoma, youth assembly chairperson Solomon Madzore, youth secretary-general Promise Mkwananzi, and Harare provincial chairman Paul Madzore. On 26 April, the Biti faction, now calling itself the *Renewal Team*, announced Tsvangirai's suspension from the party by the MDC-T National Council, accusing him of a "remarkable failure of leadership" and of transforming the party "into a fiefdom of the leader". In turn, on 29 April, Tsvangirai announced the expulsion of Biti, along with eight other members. Tsvangirai accused Biti of being an 'opportunist' who was being manipulated by ZANU-PF.

The *power struggle in the MDC-T* dragged the courts into its wrangles. On 27 June, in response to a case brought by the Tsvangirai faction, the High Court barred the Renewal Team from passing any resolutions on the party's behalf before the courts had sat to resolve the power struggle. In defiance of the court ruling, on 29 June, Biti and his Renewal Team announced the expulsion of Tsvangirai for alleged misconduct. The wrangles continued throughout the year with each faction claiming they were the genuine MDC. The Tsvangirai faction had control of most of the party's assets, including the party headquarters and the majority of the legislators elected on the MDC-T ticket, although a number of the parliamentarians backed Biti's faction. Tsvangirai also had the grassroots support in urban areas.

The two MDC breakaway formations took steps to unite. On 26 November, Biti's Renewal Team and Welshman Ncube's MDC-N officially signed a unity pact, coming together under a new movement dubbed the *Democratic Union*. Biti announced that the two formations had carried out the first part of the reunification exercise. There was widespread scepticism about the new party's chances of success. Biti's group did not appear to have grassroots support, while Ncube's party had performed dismally in the 2013 election, in which it had failed to win even a single seat and had gained a presence in parliament only through proportional representation.

Although they celebrated the power wrangles in the opposition, *ZANU-PF infighting* almost tore that party apart too. The two factions, led by Vice President Joice Mujuru and Justice Minister Emmerson Mnangagwa, continued to jostle for supremacy, battling relentlessly to succeed President Robert Mugabe. For most of the year, Mujuru appeared to have the upper hand; her faction had trounced Mnangagwa's in the party's provincial elections at the end of 2013, with figures loyal to Mujuru winning control of nine out of ZANU-PF's ten provinces. This was a significant victory for her. According to the then party constitution, provincial chairpersons and their executives played a central role in electing the party's national chairperson, two vice-presidents, and future presidential nominee.

In what looked like a boost to the Mujuru faction and the *downfall of Information Minister Jonathan Moyo*, on 6 June Mugabe described Moyo as "the devil incarnate", accusing him of appointing people who were sympathetic to the opposition as editors of state-owned newspapers. This was interpreted as an attack on the Mnangagwa faction, as Moyo was a known Mnangagwa ally. On 7 June, at the funeral of party stalwart Nathan Shamuyarira, Mugabe accused Moyo of fomenting divisions within the party. In a clear reference to Moyo, he described divisive elements in ZANU-PF as "weevils in our midst". Mujuru appeared on course to win the succession battle. Buoyed by the attack, ZANU-PF Secretary for Administration, Didymus Mutasa, a staunch Mujuru ally and Mugabe confidante, indicated that the party would "treat weevils by spraying Gamatox [a powerful pesticide] and they will all die".

Mujuru's attack on the media following *revelations of corruption* – which implicated a number of people aligned or sympathetic to her faction – did not help her. Early in the year, in what was seen as an extension of ZANU-PF's factional wars, the media exposed massive salary scandals in public institutions, including the national broadcaster. The state-controlled media played a significant part in this exposure. As acting president, Mujuru told a meeting on 8 February that detractors were behind the exposure. She said the corruption scandals should not be discussed in the media but should be handled by the Office of the President. Observers interpreted this as an attempt to gag the media and the intervention was widely condemned, with the MDC-T calling for Mujuru to resign for condoning corruption. This might have signalled the beginning of the dramatic weakening of the Mujuru faction. In defiance of Mujuru, on 20 February, Moyo urged both private and public media to intensify efforts to expose corruption, indicating that corruption was "the biggest vice that threatens national interest".

The Mujuru faction's fortunes took a further dive during the chaotic *elective conference of the ZANU-PF youth league*, held in August. Revelations on 8 August that delegates had gone to bed hungry prompted Mugabe's family to intervene by providing food. The fact that the person charged with fundraising for the event was the Mujuru loyalist Mutasa, did not augur well for the Mujuru faction. In his conference speech on the same day, Mugabe accused Mutasa of destroying the party, claiming that he had failed to mobilise resources as he concentrated on manoeuvring to secure power at the forthcoming ZANU-PF elective congress at the expense of the party. Mugabe revealed that his party was broke, saying thousands of party supporters attending the conference were facing transportation and accommodation challenges, while also going for the whole day on empty stomachs. The conference descended into chaos when voting took place, with accusations of irregularities and outright vote rigging and kidnappings. Rival factions squabbled over the choice of leaders, which resulted in a secret ballot. The accusations of impropriety were repeated by Mugabe on 14 August. He said he was embarrassed by the way senior officials had interfered with the operations of the youth league to the extent of coercing them to choose a leader they had never liked. The Mujuru faction, which emerged as the winner in the chaotic voting, was the target of the accusations. Unsurprisingly, there were claims that Mutasa was biased against the Mnangagwa faction.

The second half of the year witnessed the *political rise of Mrs Mugabe*, which culminated in the decapitation of the Mujuru faction. Oppah Muchinguri, the then women's affairs secretary, played a pivotal role. In July, it was announced that she was to relinquish her post in favour of Grace Mugabe, the president's wife. Speaking to a provincial paper on 1 August, Muchinguri launched a thinly veiled attack on Mujuru, suggesting she was impatient for President Mugabe to step down. On 5 August, at the youth conference, Muchinguri claimed the party was succumbing to factionalism, urging the youth to desist from divisive tendencies and rally behind Mugabe and his wife. Following the announcement that Muchinguri was to make way for her in the Women's League, Mrs Mugabe embarked on a series of 'Meet the People' rallies and 'Thank You' rallies, which took her to all provinces of the country. It was at these rallies that she unleashed vicious attacks on Mujuru and her allies, accusing her, among other things, of corruption and plotting to unseat Mugabe.

She called on Mujuru to resign. At one of the rallies, Mrs Mugabe revealed that she had ordered her husband to "baby dump" his deputy. On 15 August, as expected, the *Women's League conference* in Harare endorsed the nomination of Mrs Mugabe as the sole candidate for the position of Women's League national secretary. This heralded her entry into active politics, adding what commentators indicated would be another dimension to the ZANU-PF succession battles. Observers saw Mrs Mugabe's elevation as a ploy by the Mnangagwa faction to neutralise Mujuru. On 9 October, Muchinguri confirmed this observation when she revealed that Mrs Mugabe's ascendency was a well-thought-out and calculated plot to stop political rivals from gaining ground in the ZANU-PF succession struggles. She pointed out that the plan was designed to scuttle Mujuru's bid for the presidency. In September, Mrs Mugabe controversially graduated from the *University of Zimbabwe* with a PhD in sociology, fuelling speculation that the award was meant to strengthen her credentials for political office. The doctorate torched a controversy. There were protests and speculation, with critics insisting that the doctorate had not been earned, but was a political conferment by a university where her husband is the chancellor. Rumours circulated that this was a 'super-speedy' PhD, completed in two months. Joining the chorus of condemnation – with some urging the return of the degree – the Zimbabwe National Students Union (ZNSU) announced that they would take President Mugabe to court over the awarding of the controversial doctorate to his wife. Unsurprisingly, ZANU-PF and the state media strongly defended the award. Instead of referring to Mrs Mugabe as 'Amai' (Mother), they began referring to her as 'Doctor Amai'.

Mrs Mugabe's elevation was confirmed at the party's elective congress in December. Contrary to widely held perceptions that she was a tool of the Mnangagwa faction, it later emerged that she might have presidential ambitions of her own. On 3 October, she said she had "so much ambition", a statement that was widely interpreted as signalling her presidential aspirations. Mrs Mugabe's attacks on Mujuru acted as a catalyst for the *decimation of the Mujuru faction*. By the time the congress was held, many of the Mujuru-aligned party chairpersons had been suspended or paralysed. They included Ray Kaukonde, the hitherto powerful chairperson of Mashonaland East province. He was accused of being the main funder of the Mujuru faction and was removed on 10 November, bringing to six the number of provincial chairpersons suspended in the run-up to the congress. The culling of Mujuru loyalists was extended to other party stalwarts. On 13 November, ZANU-PF expelled war veterans' leader Jabulani Sibanda and suspended party spokesperson Rugare Gumbo, who was finally expelled by the party's central committee on 3 December. On the same day, in a move seen as designed to further weaken the Mujuru faction, the central committee endorsed amendments to the party's constitution and nominees to the central committee. The amendment allowed Mugabe to directly appoint his deputies, giving him sole power to anoint his successor. As the congress approached, Mujuru faction bigwigs continued to fall. On 24 November, Mutasa lost his seat on the central committee following defeat in the party elections. On 25 November, Mujuru lost her bid to secure a central committee post after her district of origin, Mount Darwin, rejected her application. In other elections, a number of other senior party members linked to her faction failed to make it. Among the politburo members who suffered the same fate were cabinet ministers Dzikamai Mavhaire, Francis Nhema, Flora Buka, Tendai Savanhu and Simbarashe Mumbengegwi. By the time the ZANU-PF Sixth National People's Congress began on 2 December, the Mujuru faction had been effectively neutralised.

The *ZANU-PF elective congress* (Harare, 2–7 December) confirmed the fall of the Mujuru camp and the rise and triumph of the Mnangagwa faction. Mujuru and her senior loyalists, notably Mutasa and Gumbo, did not attend. Mnangagwa was appointed as vice president of the party and Mrs Mugabe was confirmed as the Women's League boss, which automatically propelled her onto the party's politburo. Mugabe criticised Mujuru in his closing remarks on 7 December. Reflecting the complexity of the balancing game in ZANU-PF, he closed the congress without announcing who his deputies would be. Indicating that he would not be rushed, he promised to announce the politburo and presidium the following week. This delay was a violation of the party's constitution, which requires him to appoint politburo members and members of the presidium during the sitting of congress.

On 10 December, Mugabe finally announced the *politburo and presidium*. As expected, Mujuru and her loyalists were sidelined. The positions of vice president and second secretary of the party were handed to Emmerson Mnangagwa and the little-known diplomat Phekezela Mphoko. In contrast to the previous arrangement, in which the president, his two deputies, secretary for administration and national chairperson constituted the presidium, the presidium now comprised only the president and his two deputies. A *cabinet reshuffle* was announced on 11 December, when Mugabe replaced Mujuru, seven ministers and a deputy minister who had been fired earlier. Mnangagwa and Mphoko were, as expected, appointed as the two vice presidents. The former would continue as minister of justice, legal and parliamentary affairs, while the latter took over the national healing, peace and reconciliation portfolio.

There were no significant changes in *human rights, democracy and the rule of law*. The police continued to be criticised as a partial force serving ZANU-PF. On 29 January, police arrested five NGO activists for participating in a demonstration in Chitungwiza. They were released without charge. On 27 February, police arrested 12 leaders of the ZNSU during a demonstration against poor education standards at Harare Polytechnic. They were reportedly beaten in police custody. On 13 February, police violently broke up a march by Women of Zimbabwe members who intended to petition parliament over the deteriorating national economic situation. In Victoria Falls, on June 28, four members of the Bulawayo Agenda were arrested and detained on charges of contravening the Public Order and Security Act (POSA). When the case went to court, they were acquitted. On 14 July, the little known Transform Zimbabwe political party leader Jacob Ngarivhume and 13 party supporters were arrested and detained at the Gweru Central Police Station on charges of breaching POSA. Ngarivhume was acquitted in court.

Foreign Affairs

As in previous years, relations with most African and Asian countries and organisations remained largely friendly. There was some movement in the strained relations with the OECD countries, but little real change. ZANU-PF continued blaming the country's woes on 'illegal' Western sanctions.

SADC as a block remained steadfast in its support of Mugabe. After the 2013 elections, SADC's mediation role in Zimbabwe ended and so Zimbabwe was no longer a constant item on the agenda for SADC meetings. However, Tsvangirai still approached SADC with grievances. On 18 August, he wrote to SADC indicating that Zimbabwe needed an urgent return to legitimacy and calling for fresh polls. SADC ignored him. On 19 November, he expressed disgust at the conduct of South Africa following the release of a damning report on the 2002 presidential elections in Zimbabwe. He accused South Africa and SADC of turning a blind eye to atrocities in Zimbabwe. Like SADC, the *AU* continued to stand by Mugabe. On 1 February, the AU summit took the position that African leaders would not attend the EU-Africa Summit scheduled for April in Belgium if the EU did not invite Mugabe. When his wife was denied a visa, Mugabe boycotted the summit. Zimbabwe remained active in continental ventures. In August, Zimbabwe was a party to the Algiers Declaration on the establishment of the African Mechanism for Police Cooperation (*AFRIPOL*).

Mugabe's stature in Africa seemed to rise. On 30 January, the AU summit officially opened in Addis Ababa (Ethiopia) and Mugabe was elected first vice chair of the AU Bureau, a supreme organ of the AU tasked with steering the organisation's agenda with the assistance of the AU Commission. Mugabe represented Southern Africa in his new post. In August, he took over as chair of SADC at the two-day SADC Heads of State and Government Summit in Victoria Falls, which began on 17 August.

Good relations with *China* continued, but there were signs that China was not going to give Zimbabwe a blank cheque. In August, Mugabe went to China on a week-long state visit. The two countries signed several deals, mostly in the area of infrastructure development, but details remained sketchy. It later emerged that China had made no commitment to providing budgetary support and Finance Minister Patrick Chinamasa asserted that Zimbabwe was not seeking any. On 25 August, Chinamasa signed a 'securitisation framework' with the China Export and Credit Insurance Corporation (Sinosure) for various projects for which

Zimbabwe was seeking funding. In a sign that Beijing was tightening its lending terms and expected debtors to be more accountable, Chinamasa reported on 10 September that Zimbabwe had to pay $ 180 m in Chinese loan repayments or face losing its credit line.

Zimbabwe's relations with its traditional ally *Russia* remained good. Russian investors stepped up their presence in Zimbabwe, competing with China for a share of the country's rich resources, including platinum, diamonds, commodities and a bank. On 5 June a Russian daily reported that a Russian consortium of Russian Vi Holding, Rostec and Vnesheconombank had announced that they planned a $ 3 bn investment to build Zimbabwe's largest platinum mine.

Zimbabwe continued to cooperate with *Iran*. In September, Minister of Small and Medium Enterprises Sithembiso Nyoni underlined Iran's progress in various industrial spheres. She said Zimbabwe would import quality medicines and medical equipment from Iran. Nyoni held a meeting with Iranian Minister of Cooperatives, Labour and Social Welfare Ali Rabiyee and they discussed the expansion of cooperation.

Relations with the EU thawed a little. In what it said were measures to encourage reform, the EU suspended targeted sanctions against eight Zimbabwean government officials on 17 February, but maintained the restrictive measures against Mugabe and his wife. However, Zimbabwe's head of delegation to the African-Caribbean-Pacific and EU Joint Parliamentary Assembly said any claims made by the EU that it would lift standing travel bans were incorrect because of the need for economic reform. On 30 October, the EU announced the lifting of its 12-year suspension of direct financial aid to the government of Zimbabwe. This was seen as a major step towards the normalisation of the frosty EU-Zimbabwe relations. The EU also announced that from 2015 it would start a € 234 m five-year funding programme to support health, agriculture and governance initiatives.

There was little improvement in *relations with the USA*. On 5–6 August, US President Barack Obama hosted the US-Africa Leaders Summit in an effort to strengthen American ties with the continent. Mugabe was excluded because he was still a Specially Designated National and was not on the list of invited heads of state released on 23 January. Mugabe's spokesperson, George Charamba, dismissed Obama's decision to snub Mugabe as an indication that the summit was not about the USA and Africa, but about the USA and certain African countries. The USA maintained targeted sanctions on 113 Zimbabwean individuals and 70 entities – mostly farms and legal entities owned by the targeted individuals. During the year, two US citizens were prosecuted in the Federal District Court in Chicago for engaging in "public relations, political consulting and lobbying" US officials to lift sanctions against Mugabe and Zimbabweans on the targeted sanctions list in exchange for payment.

Relations with *multilateral organisations* changed little. On 10 January, the IMF announced that its management had approved a request for a six-month extension of the Staff Monitored Program to allow time for Zimbabwe to strengthen its policies and deliver on outstanding commitments under the programme. On 27 March, it said it would shortly be resuming its resident representative office in Harare. The IMF had not had a resident representative in Zimbabwe for almost a decade. On 18 June, the IMF Executive Board concluded the Article IV consultation. Significantly, the report noted that Zimbabwe's economic rebound experienced since 2009 had ended. On 27 September, the IMF said it would not lend more money to Zimbabwe, because the country was in arrears with repayments of previous loans. The World Bank's lending programme also remained inactive due to arrears. The Bank's role was limited to technical assistance and analytical work. At the beginning of the year, Zimbabwe owed the IMF and the World Bank $ 124 m and $ 1 bn, respectively. In its outlook for 2013–15, the AfDB reported that its operations in Zimbabwe had been limited by the country's arrears situation. Nevertheless, the bank remained engaged through policy dialogue, technical assistance and capacity building, and knowledge and advisory services through the Fragile States Facility. It also supported infrastructure development in the water and energy sectors through the African Water Facility and management of the Zimbabwe Multi-Donor Trust Fund (Zim-Fund), as well as providing some support to the private sector.

Socioeconomic Developments

The IMF confirmed that the economic recovery enjoyed during the Government of National Unity years had ended, although *economic indicators* did not plunge. In many cases, this was rather a slow-down or slow decline. Reserve Bank of Zimbabwe figures showed that the December consumer price index stood at 99.5%, and the year-on-year price increase at – 0.8%. According to Economist Intelligence Unit (EIU) estimates, real GDP growth was 3.0%. The EIU put the nominal GDP at $ 2.5 bn. The current account balance, excluding transfers, was – $ 1.045 bn, while total international reserves dropped to $ 448 m from $ 475 m in 2013. In the budget statement, the finance minister forecast that the public and publicly guaranteed debt burden would be $ 8.4 bn by December, comprising an external debt of $ 7.2 bn and a domestic debt of $ 1.2 bn. The minister admitted that the country was in debt distress, characterised by large external payment arrears against a background of limited fiscal space and rising domestic debt. Zimbabwe's ability to mobilise resources to finance its economic strategy (ZIMASSET) was therefore compromised, "undermining the process of socio-economic development and poverty reduction". Zimbabwe performed poorly in a number of world *league tables*. It was ranked 171st out of 189 economies in Doing Business 2015 and the World Economic Forum's Global Competitiveness Report 2013–14 ranked Zimbabwe 131st out of

148 countries. The Human Development Index for 2013 was 0.492, which placed Zimbabwe 156th out of 187 countries – an improvement on 160th in 2012.

On the *humanitarian* front, the country faced a number of challenges. In late January and early February, heavy rains in parts of the country resulted in deaths and displacement of people, coupled with destruction of property. The worst affected areas were Chivi and Masvingo districts in Masvingo province and Tsholotsho district in Matabeleland North province. On 11 February, the government launched an international appeal for $ 20 m to help some 20,000 people displaced by the floods. According to ReliefWeb, by the end of February, an estimated 2,194 households had been moved to the Chingwizi resettlement camp. By May, the more than 15,625 people evacuated remained in dire living conditions. In February, the Ministry of Health and Child Care reported that at least 38 people had died as a result of *waterborne and related epidemics*, including diarrhoea and dysentery. There were 16 suspected new typhoid cases. At the end of February, a typhoid outbreak was reported in Harare's high-density suburb of Mabvuku, with at least nine cases confirmed. The suburb had gone for four months without water supplies. In July, a typhoid fever scare hit parts of Harare; 18 new suspected cases were recorded in one week.

In terms of *food security*, according to WFP estimates released in July, the country would have a cereal harvest surplus of 253,174 tonnes from a total cereal harvest of 1,680,293 tonnes. The proportion of households with an acceptable food consumption score increased to 68%. The number of people estimated to be food insecure for the 2014/15 consumption year was estimated to be 565,000, representing 6% of the rural population. This was a decrease from 2013 figures. Projections by the Commercial Farmers Union put total agricultural production at 2.5 m tonnes up from 1.6 m tonnes in 2008 at the height of the economic problems. However, according to EIU figures, the production of wheat, sugar and soya beans showed a marked decline compared with 2000, before the controversial land reform programme was launched. Tea was the only crop that saw an increase. Production of the staple crop, maize, was still less than half the output in 2000.

On *demographic indicators*, according to 2014 estimates, the death rate stood at 10.6 deaths per 1,000 people. The net migration rate was estimated at 21.8 migrants per 1,000 people. The flow of Zimbabweans into South Africa and Botswana in search of better economic opportunities did not show signs of abating. Average life expectancy for the total population was 55.7 years, while the infant mortality rate was estimated at 26.6 deaths per 1,000 live births. Rankings published by the 'African Economist' magazine in June showed Zimbabwe leading the literacy rate in Africa, coming in at 91%, despite a decade-long economic crisis that had impacted negatively on the quality of education.

Progress was reported in the country's response to the *HIV/AIDS* scourge. According to the Zimbabwe AIDS Response Progress Report 2014 (for 2013), about

46,000 deaths had been averted by antiretroviral therapy (ART), with infections averted by prevention of mother-to-child transmission (PMTCT) totalling 15,000. A combined total of 324,000 life years were gained by ART and PMTCT. The HIV incidence rate was 0.98, compared with 1.25 the previous year. There were 61,476 HIV-related deaths during the year, down from 87,335 in 2012. HIV prevalence among pregnant women aged 15–24 was 9.9% compared with 11.6% in 2012.

The education and health delivery systems continued to experience problems of staffing, equipment and funding, and health and educational personnel contributed significantly to the brain drain. Industrial actions and threats of industrial action arising out of salary disputes were a constant feature throughout the year, further compromising these sectors. At the beginning of the year, the Progressive Teachers' Union of Zimbabwe (PTUZ) said its members would go on strike when schools opened the following week if the much-awaited salary negotiations with the government failed to yield positive results. There were still problems by the end of the year. On 23 December, the PTUZ was again threatening to strike following the government's failure to pay annual bonuses. In October, about 300 junior doctors went on strike when the government failed to meet their ultimatum to address their demands for a pay rise from $ 283 to $ 1,200 a month. In addition to industrial unrest, *workforce redundancies* hit the economy. They were a major issue that exacerbated Zimbabwe's already high unemployment rate. According to the Retrenchment Board, some 1,300 people were made redundant in the first quarter alone. Significantly, manufacturing laid off 550 workers and services 200. Company closures, low levels of FDI and liquidity problems were major contributory factors. The loss of jobs fuelled the informalisation of the economy and migration, mostly to other southern African countries, particularly South Africa and Botswana.

There appeared to be some movement in the controversial *indigenisation policy*, with reports of a major government climb-down in the state-owned 'Sunday Mail'. On 25 May, in an interview with Jonathan Moyo, the newspaper reported that the Indigenisation Act would be amended and investors would be allowed to recover costs. In addition, a production-sharing model would be proposed. The paper interpreted this as a victory for former Reserve Bank governor, Gideon Gono, and moderates in the government. There was no let-up in the dismal performance of *parastatals and local authorities*. In addition to the massive corruption over salaries unearthed at state enterprises, parastatals such as Ziscosteel, National Railways of Zimbabwe, ZBC and Air Zimbabwe continued to perform badly, as did all local authorities. According to the 'Zimbabwe Independent' newspaper, the situation was attributable to, among other things, the sustained and systematic militarisation of parastatals, public enterprises and local authorities. This had contributed to breeding a culture of patronage, corruption and looting as these institutions were staffed mainly by people who did not have the requisite qualifications, experience or competence to run them efficiently and profitably.

On 27 November, Finance Minister Patrick Chinamasa presented the *2015 national budget* with the theme "Towards an Empowered Society and Inclusive Economic Growth". Chinamasa proposed a $ 4.1 bn budget. Like all previous budgets, its most notable feature was the dominance of civil servants' salaries. Of this budget, $ 3.3 bn, representing 81% of total expenditure, would go towards employment costs, leaving a balance of $ 798 m for operations, debt service and capital development programmes. The proposed allocation for the capital budget was $ 341 m, while that for operations and maintenance was $ 384 m. Chinamasa projected a GDP growth rate at market prices of 3.2% for 2015, admitting that such levels of growth remained inadequate for the country "to begin making a dent at the prevailing levels of capacity utilisation in the economy and high unemployment". Positive growth was projected in all sectors. Notably, manufacturing which had a growth rate of -4.9% was projected to grow by 1.7%. In contrast, the projected growth for agriculture, hunting and fishing was 3.4% down from 23.4%.

www.ingramcontent.com/pod-product-compliance
Lightning Source LLC
LaVergne TN
LVHW080115011026
849160LV00013B/1108
* 9 7 8 9 0 0 4 2 9 1 5 3 9 *